Food Price Policy in an Era of Market Instability

United Nations University—World Institute for Development Economics Research (UNU-WIDER) was established by the United Nations University as its first research and training centre and started work in Helsinki, Finland, in 1985. The purpose of the institute is to undertake applied research and policy analysis on structural changes affecting developing and transitional economies, to provide a forum for the advocacy of policies leading to robust, equitable, and environmentally sustainable growth, and to promote capacity strengthening and training in the field of economic and social policy-making. Its work is carried out by staff researchers and visiting scholars in Helsinki and via networks of collaborating scholars and institutions around the world.

United Nations University World Institute for Development Economics Research (UNU-WIDER)

Katajanokanlaituri 6 B, 00160 Helsinki, Finland

www.wider.unu.edu

Food Price Policy in an Era of Market Instability

A Political Economy Analysis

Edited by

Per Pinstrup-Andersen

A study prepared by the United Nations University—World Institute for Development Economics Research (UNU-WIDER)

OXFORD
UNIVERSITY PRESS

OXFORD
UNIVERSITY PRESS

Great Clarendon Street, Oxford, OX2 6DP,
United Kingdom

Oxford University Press is a department of the University of Oxford. It furthers the University's objective of excellence in research, scholarship, and education by publishing worldwide. Oxford is a registered trade mark of Oxford University Press in the UK and in certain other countries

First Edition published in 2015

Impression: 1

Published in the United States of America by Oxford University Press
198 Madison Avenue, New York, NY 10016, United States of America

British Library Cataloguing in Publication Data
Data available

Library of Congress Control Number: 2014940452

ISBN 978–0–19–871857–4

Printed and bound by
CPI Group (UK) Ltd, Croydon, CR0 4YY

Foreword

Food price volatility is a major challenge facing the global agricultural system today, most vividly illustrated during the global food crisis of 2007–9 when prices spiked for key staple commodities such as wheat, rice, maize, and soybeans. Given the variety of reactions by countries experiencing food price shocks, the crisis offered an excellent natural experiment for generating knowledge on responses to price volatility in particular, and on the political economy of agricultural policy-making more generally.

In 2010, United Nations University World Institute for Development Economics Research (UNU-WIDER) along with collaborating partners—Cornell University and the University of Copenhagen—enthusiastically welcomed Per Pinstrup-Andersen's proposal to direct a broad-ranging research project on fourteen low- and middle-income countries to uncover which political economy factors, ranging from the constellation of different interest groups to the nature of political institutions, explain variations in policy responses across countries.

The in-depth academic research is valuable for at least three target audiences. First, it informs international organizations and donors about which types of policy interventions can mitigate price volatility and whether this is feasible given a country's political economy context. Second, it helps policy makers to better understand the trade-offs of certain policy interventions. Third, it generates knowledge about the agricultural policy-making process in developing countries, which remains incredibly scarce despite the importance of agriculture to these countries' economies.

This book is the distilled essence of the large, multi-disciplined academic project condensed into a compact form for the reader to enjoy and absorb the policy implications.

I hereby express my sincere appreciation and admiration of the academic skills of Per Pinstrup-Andersen, along with his three senior advisors, Philip Abbott, William Lyakurwa, and Robert Paarlberg, and fellow coordinator Danielle Resnick, formerly of UNU-WIDER, for directing the project, building a top-notch research team, upholding highest-quality academic standards on all fronts, and finally gathering the research to a rich harvest.

UNU-WIDER gratefully acknowledges the financial contributions to its research programme from the governments of Denmark, Finland, Sweden, and the United Kingdom. This publication is supported by an agreement with Cornell University Division of Nutritional Sciences under Subagreement No. 60891-9461.

Finn Tarp

Helsinki, February 2014

Preface

In 2007–8, international market prices for rice, wheat, and corn all spiked sharply upward. By April 2008, the price of maize (corn) available for export had doubled compared to two years earlier; rice prices had tripled in just three months; and wheat reached its highest price in 28 years. Riots broke out in a number of developing countries, and it seemed that hunger was certain to increase as well. The *New York Times*, in a lead editorial, declared these surprising changes to be a 'World Food Crisis'. Robert Zoellick, President of the World Bank, warned that high food prices were particularly dangerous for the poor, who must spend half to three-quarters of their income on food. 'There is no margin for survival', he said.

A global financial crisis in late 2008 to early 2009 caused international food prices to fall briefly, but then in 2010 wheat prices increased sharply once more, and just as this second food price spike seemed to be passing a severe summer drought in the USA in 2012 sent international corn prices spiking upward yet again.

This unusual series of international food price spikes between 2007 and 2012 reset global expectations and debates over food. The spikes were not just disruptive on their own terms, they called into question what had been a comforting assumption among most economists that over the long term agricultural commodity prices would fall rather than rise, and that international food markets would be a reliable source of supply.

Controversies persist over both the causes of these commodity price spikes and their impacts on poverty and malnutrition worldwide. In their recent *State of Food Insecurity in the World* (2012), the Food and Agriculture Organization (FAO) reduced their estimates of the incidence of malnutrition due to the 2007–8 food crisis, noting that 'Some large countries were able to insulate themselves from the crisis through restrictive trade policies and functioning safety nets, but trade restrictions increased prices and volatility on international markets'. Moreover, some import-dependent small countries, especially in Africa, were exceptionally hard hit. A key distinguishing feature was the success of food security policy implementation to mitigate the effects of world markets on domestic outcomes.

Most countries pursued a wide range of policies to stabilize their food prices at home. Import tariffs were reduced; exports were taxed or banned; parastatals imported grain; buffer stocks were released; domestic prices and production were subsidized; and safety nets were expanded. Policies typically utilized existing institutional mechanisms, designed more often to address production shortfalls rather than world price spikes, with few innovations in policy regime noted. It was also easier to expand existing safety nets than to institute new programmes. Political decision-making at times hampered the need to change or expand the scope of those institutions. As a consequence, a wide variety of outcomes was observed, due as much to problems of implementing existing policies as to picking the right mechanisms.

Contemporary scholarship on this dangerous new market dynamic has long been hampered by a poor understanding of how national governments make policy decisions when caught in a suddenly destabilized international food price environment. Why do most cut tariffs, some subsidize imports, and a few ban exports? Why do some have domestic buffer stocks they can release, while others do not? When they release such stocks to keep domestic prices low, do they target the poor and vulnerable, or only the urban middle class and their own power base? Why do some try to keep domestic prices low for consumers under circumstances of shortage, when a price increase might be necessary to encourage more domestic farm production? Why can some governments quickly adjust policy settings to adapt to changing international circumstances, while others face problematic delays? Why do some countries focus on stabilization, helping consumers broadly, while others utilize safety nets to protect the poor? Reliable answers to these political economy questions are elusive because they require carefully structured comparisons of policy actions taken within dozens of separate political systems, something that can be accomplished only by a large and well-led international team of scholars, each with a different country specialty, but all asking the same questions under a common research template, applied over a common time period.

When the original price spikes of 2007–10 took place, it was Professor Per Pinstrup-Andersen, previously Director General of the International Food Policy Research Institute (IFPRI), who saw the research opportunity, assembled the necessary international team of scholars, and hammered out the common political economy template. The results of this careful effort are available to all in this newly published book. As advisors to this ambitious project, we knew it would be a one of a kind achievement that political economy scholars would be able to use for years as a valuable resource. We witnessed the diligence and commitment of the research team both in polishing the separate country chapters and then in assembling and comparing the findings of these chapters to derive the larger generalizations that finally emerged. We commend the research team and its leader, and thank them for this important book.

Philip Abbott, William Lyakurwa, and Robert Paarlberg

Acknowledgements

First and foremost I want to thank the United Nations University—World Institute for Development Economics Research (UNU-WIDER) Director, Finn Tarp for unwavering professional, moral, and financial support from the initial project idea to the completion of this book. I am very grateful to Danielle Resnick for her constructive and timely intellectual (political science in a network of economists) and logistic contributions to all aspects of the project; to Henrik Hansen for his intellectual insights and contributions to the preparation of the analytical framework; to Derrill Watson for his intellectual contributions to the development of the framework for the political economy analyses and the outstanding synthesis; to the three project advisors—Philip Abbott, William Lyakurwa, and Robert Paarlberg—for their intellectual leadership; to Suresh Babu, Kenneth Baltzer, and Shane Bryan for outstanding syntheses; to Lisa Winkler for her editorial and administrative support; to Mary-Catherine French for administrative and secretarial support; to Lorraine Telfer-Taivainen for her advice and support of the preparation of the book and for facilitating collaboration with Oxford University Press; to Adam Swallow for guidance in the preparation of the book manuscript; and to the Bill and Melinda Gates Foundation, the UNU-WIDER, and Cornell University for financial support of the project that led to this book. My colleagues at the Bill and Melinda Gates Foundation, Prabhu Pingali, Ellen McCullough, and Tuu-Van Nguyen, provided valuable intellectual input to the project. Last, but by no means least, I want to thank all the network members for a most stimulating interaction and collaboration, and for enhancing my conceptual and empirical understanding of the political economy of food policy.

Per Pinstrup-Andersen
Cornell University
August 2014

Contents

Part VII. The Political Economy of Food Price Policy in High-income Countries

Part VIII. Conclusions and Recommendations

List of Figures

List of Tables

List of Abbreviations

ADB	Asian Development Bank
ADF	Augmented Dickey-Fuller unit root test
ADMARC	Agricultural Development and Marketing Corporation
AFAN	All Farmers Association of Nigeria
AFC	Agricultural Finance Corporation
AfDB	African Development Bank
AFF	agriculture, forestry, and fishery
AGRA	Alliance for a Green Revolution in Africa
AGRICOM	Agriculture Competences
AL	Awami League
AMIS	Agricultural Market Information System
AMR	Assistance au Monde Rural
ANC	African National Congress
APRU	Agricultural Policy Research Unit
ASCOSEN	Association of Senegalese Consumers
ATM	automated teller machines
BB	Bangladesh Bank
BDR	Bangladesh Rifles
BIDS	Bangladesh Institute of Development Studies
BNDES	Banco Nacional do Desenvolvimento
BRICS	Brazil, Russia, India, China, and South Africa
bu	bushel
CAADP	Comprehensive Africa Agriculture Development Programme
CAB	Consumers' Association of Bangladesh
CACP	Commission for Agricultural Costs and Prices
CAMA	Consumers Association of Malawi
CET	Common External Tariff
CFA	Communauté Financière Africaine

CIEM	Central Institute for Economic Management
CIF	cost, insurance, and freight
CII	Confederation of Indian Industry
CNCR	National Council of Rural Consultation and Cooperation
CNES	National Confederation of Senegalese Employers
COFCO	China National Cereals, Oil and Foodstuffs Import and Export Corporation
COMTRADE	Commodity Trade Statistics Database (UN)
COSATU	Confederation of South African Trade Unions
CPC	Communist Party of China
CPD	Centre for Policy Dialogue
CPI	consumer price index
CPU	Central Planning Unit
CPV	Communist Party of Vietnam
CRR	cash reserve requirement
CSA	Central Statistical Agency
CSO	Central Statistical Office
CSC	Centre for Social Concern
CSI	Center for Social Innovation
CSOs	civil society organizations
DFID	Department for International Development (UK)
DO	demand order
ECM	error correction model
ECX	Ethiopian Commodity Exchange
EDRI	Ethiopian Development Research Institute
EEA	Ethiopian Economic Association
EGTE	Ethiopian Grain Trade Enterprise
EP	European Parliament
EPA	Environmental Protection Agency
EPRDF	Ethiopian People's Revolutionary Democratic Front
ESA	Eastern and Southern Africa
ESF	exogenous shocks facility
EU	European Union
FAO	Food and Agriculture Organization
FAOSTAT	Food and Agriculture Organization Statistics Division
FBCCI	Federation of Bangladesh Chambers of Commerce and Industry

FCI	Food Corporation of India
FDI	foreign direct investment
FEC	Federal Executive Council
FEWS	NET Famine Early Warning Systems Network
FIRJAN	Federação da Indústria do Rio de Janeiro
FISP	Farm Input Subsidy Programme
FMARD	Federal Ministry of Agriculture and Rural Development
FMAWR	Federal Ministry of Agriculture and Water Resources
FOB	freight on board
FPMC	Food Pricing Monitoring Committee
FRA	Food Reserve Agency
FSTG	Food Security Thematic Group
FUM	Farmers Union of Malawi
FY	fiscal year
G8	Group of 8
G20	Group of 20
GASC	General Agency for the Supply of Commodities
GATT	General Agreement on Tariffs and Trade
GDP	gross domestic product
GIEWS	Global Information and Early Warning System
GMP	guaranteed minimum price
GOANA	Grand Agricultural Offensive for Food and Abundance
GOE	government of Egypt
GTAM	Grain Traders Association of Malawi
GTAZ	Grain Traders Association of Zambia
IAPRI	Indaba Agricultural Policy Research Institute
ICM	Institute of Cereals of Mozambique
IDSC	Information and Decision Support Centre
IFAD	International Fund for Agricultural Development
IFPRI	International Food Policy Research Institute
IFSS	integrated food security strategy
IMF	International Monetary Fund
INR	Indian rupees
IPSARD	Institute of Policy and Strategy for Agriculture and Rural Development
JCTR	Jesuits Centre for Theological Reflection
KIHBS	Kenya Integrated Household Budget Survey

KIPPRA	Kenya Institute for Public Policy Research and Analysis
KKV	Kazi Kwa Vijana (cash-for-work programme)
KNBS	Kenya National Bureau of Statistics
KRDS	Kenya Rural Development Strategy
KTDA	Kenya Tea Development Authority
LAB	Land Agricultural Bank
L/C	letter of credit
LG-FE	Leading Group—Finance and Economy
LG-RW	Leading Group—Rural Works
LOASP	Agricultural, Forestry, and Livestock Act
LOP	law of one price
MAL	Ministry of Agriculture and Livestock
MARD	Ministry of Agriculture and Rural Development
MAZ	Millers Association of Zambia
MCCI	Metropolitan Chamber of Commerce and Industry
MCP	Malawi Congress Party
MDGs	Millenium Development Goals
MGNREGS	Mahatma Gandhi national rural employment guarantee scheme
MiFID	Markets in Financial Instruments Directive
MMD	Movement for Multi-party Democracy
MoA	Ministry of Agriculture
MoAFS	Ministry of Agricultural and Food Security
MoC	Ministry of Commerce
MoFDM	Ministry of Food and Disaster Management
MoFED	Ministry of Finance and Economic Development
MoFNP	Ministry of Finance and National Planning
MOIT	Ministry of Industry and Trade
MOST	Ministry of Science and Technology
MOU	memorandum of understanding
MPS	Monetary Policy Statement
MSPs	minimum support prices
MT	metric tonne
MTBE	methyl tertiary-butyl ether
NA	National Assembly
NAAIAP	National Accelerated Agricultural Input Access Programme
NADP	National Agricultural Development Programme

NAMBOARD	National Agricultural Marketing Board
NAMC	National Agricultural Marketing Council
NASFAM	National Association of Smallholder Farmers of Malawi
NBE	National Bank of Ethiopia
NBER	National Bureau of Economic Research
NBR	National Board of Revenue
NCAP	National Centre for Agricultural Economics and Policy Research
NCPB	National Cereals Produce Board
NDP	National Democratic Party
NDRC	National Development and Reform Commission
NEC	National Economic Council
NFCRP	National Food Crisis Response Programme
NFRA	National Food Reserve Agency
NFSA	National Food Security Act
NFSM	National Food Security Mission
NGO	non-governmental organization
NIB	National Irrigation Board
NISER	Nigerian Institute of Social and Economic Research
NPC	National People's Congress
NRA	nominal rates of assistance
NSPS	National Social Protection Strategy
ODI	Overseas Development Institute
OECD	Organisation for Economic Co-operation and Development
OMS	open market sale
OPC	Office of the President and Cabinet
OTS	one-time settlement scheme
PAPA	Plan for Action for Food Production
PASA	Structural Adjustment Programme for the Agricultural Sector
PBDAC	Principal Bank for Development of Agricultural Credit
PDS	Parti Démocratique Sénégalais
PMC	Price Monitoring Cell
PPP	purchasing power parity
PRSP	Poverty Reduction Strategy Papers
PS	Parti Socialist du Sénégal
PSE	Producer Support Estimate
PSNP	Productive Safety Net Programme

R&D	research and development
RDP	Reconstruction and Development Programme
REVA	Return to Agriculture programme
RFS	Renewable Fuel Standard
RIFAN	Rice Farmers Association of Nigeria
RKVY	Rashtriya Krishi Vikas Yojana
SACP	South African Communist Party
SADC	Southern African Development Community
SAFEX	South African Futures Exchange
SAPs	structural adjustment programmes
SFP	single farm payment
SGA	State Grain Administration
SGR	Strategic Grain Reserves
SOE	state-owned enterprise
SPIDS	Union of Professionals of Industries and Mines
SRA	Strategy for Revitalization of Agriculture
SSA	sub-Saharan Africa
STATS	SA Statistics South Africa
TCB	Trading Corporation of Bangladesh
TRAINS	Trade Analysis and Information System
UEMOA	West African Economic and Monetary Union
UNACOIS	National Union of Traders and Industrialists of Senegal
UNCTAD	United Nations Conference on Trade and Development
UNDP	United Nations Development Programme
UNFPA	United Nations Population Fund
UNU-WIDER	United Nations University—World Institute for Development Economics Research
URAA	Uraguay Round Agreement on Agriculture
USAID	United States Agency for International Development
USDA	United States Department of Agriculture
VAT	value added tax
VFA	Vietnam Food Association
WFP	World Food Programme
WITS	World Integrated Trade Solution
WTO	World Trade Organisation
ZACA	Zambia Consumer Association
ZNFU	Zambia National Farmers Union

Notes on Contributors

Assefa Admassie is the Director of the Ethiopian Economic Policy Research Institute which is an affiliate of the Ethiopian Economics Association. In addition, he is an adjunct associate professor at the Department of Economics at the Addis Ababa University in Ethiopia. His research area is in the field of development economics and includes agricultural finance, food policies, child labour, poverty analysis, impact evaluation, and information and communications technology.

Suresh Chandra Babu is a senior research fellow and a programme leader for capacity strengthening at the International Food Policy Research Institute. His research interest focuses on translating policy research into impact on reduction in poverty, hunger, and malnutrition, and he currently conducts research on strengthening organizational capacity and policy processes for effective implementation of intervention programmes and policies in developing countries.

Kenneth Baltzer is an associate professor at the Department of Food and Resource Economics (IFRO) at the University of Copenhagen, Denmark. He teaches International Economics and Development Economics and his research interests include the study of agricultural commodity markets and the political economy of international trade.

Shane Bryan is a research analyst specializing in food systems and poverty reduction. He is currently working as a consultant for the International Potato Center (CIP) in Lima, Peru.

Antony Chapoto is a research fellow at the International Food Policy Research Institute. His research interests focus on agricultural productivity, smallholder farm commercialization, food markets and policy in Africa.

Blessings Chinsinga is an associate professor at the Department of Political and Administrative Studies (PAS) and Deputy Director of the Centre for Social Research (CSR), Chancellor College, University of Malawi. His main research interests include political economy of development, public policy analysis, institutions and development, poverty reduction and rural livelihoods, and local level politics.

Ephraim W. Chirwa is Professor of Economics at Chancellor College, University of Malawi. He holds an MPhil from the University of Cambridge and a PhD from the University of East Anglia. His research interests include microeconomics, industrial economics, farming households and agricultural systems, small scale enterprise development, microfinance and rural financial institutions, and food security.

Kavery Ganguly is Deputy Director at the Food and Agriculture Centre of Excellence (FACE), Confederation of Indian Industry (CII). Her research interests include the socioeconomic impact of agriculture and food policies in India and other South Asian countries. Her work primarily involves studying various agricultural values and the role of different stakeholders in unlocking the potential.

Ahmed Farouk Ghoneim is a professor of economics at Cairo University. He is a research fellow at the Economic Research Forum (ERF) and the Center for Social and Economic Research (CASE). He works as a consultant to several international organizations including the World Bank, WTO, UNCTAD, UNDP, and WFP. His research interests include trade policy, competition, and food policy.

Harry de Gorter is a professor in the Charles H. Dyson School of Applied Economics and Management, Cornell University. His research focus is on agricultural trade policy and much of his recent work has been on biofuels and agricultural trade reform and the Doha development agenda, especially the impact of subsidies and protection on developing countries.

Ashok Gulati is Chairman of the Commission for Agricultural Costs and Prices (CACP) since 2011. Prior to this, he was Director at the International Food Policy Research Institute (IFPRI) for more than ten years. He was a member of the Prime Minister's Economic Advisory Council and has held distinguished positions in state government offices. He has been deeply involved in agri-policy analysis and advice in India. A prolific writer, he has authored several books and articles on Asian agriculture with a focus on India.

Jikun Huang is the Founder and Director of the Center for Chinese Agricultural Policy of the Chinese Academy of Sciences and Professor at the Institute of Geographical Sciences and Natural Resources Research. His research focuses on agricultural policy and rural development. He has published about 400 journal papers with 200 papers published in international journals.

Johann F. Kirsten is a professor and Head of the Department of Agricultural Economics, Extension and Rural Development at the University of Pretoria in South Africa. His research interests focus on agricultural policy, land reform, and the commercialization of smallholder farmers. Recently his research interests also shifted to the economics of origin foods.

Louise Knops is Researcher at the Centre for European Policy Studies (CEPS), Brussels. Her research interests include agricultural and food policy, political economy, and European politics and institutions. She currently focuses on the 2013 reform of the EU's Common Agricultural Policy (CAP).

Nguyen Manh Hai is the Director of the Research Department for Public Service Policies at the Central Institute for Economic Management (CIEM) in Vietnam. His research interests focus on food and agricultural policies, labour market and land market reforms, environmental, climate change, and green growth impacts, and on policies addressing public service reform.

Claudio Massingarela is a lecturer of data analysis at the University of Science and Technology in Mozambique. His research interests focus on poverty and the socioeconomic analysis of rural development in Mozambique.

Bernardo Mueller is a professor at the University of Brasília in Brazil. His research and publications have been in the area of political economy, new institutional economics, and in complex adaptive systems applied to the economy.

Charles Mueller has recently retired as a full professor at the Department of Economics, Universidade de Brasília, where he started in 1972, except for a three-year interval (1986–9) as Director and President of IBGE, Brazil's statistical office; he remains at the university as a senior associate researcher. He completed his undergraduate studies at the Universidade de São Paulo, and his Master's and PhD at Vanderbilt University (1974). His main areas of interest are agricultural, environmental, and development economics—areas in which he has published extensively.

Virgulino Nhate holds a Master's degree in economics and is a provincial director of planning and finance at Manica Province, Mozambique. Previously he was Head of the Department of Populations Studies at the National Directorate of Studies and Policy Analysis of the Ministry of Planning and Development. His research interests focus on poverty analysis, income redistribution, and social protection.

Jonathan Makau Nzuma holds a PhD in agricultural economics and business from the University of Guelph, Canada. He is a lecturer at the Department of Agricultural Economics, University of Nairobi, where he specializes in agricultural policy, international trade, microeconomics, production economics, development economics, livelihood assessment, and research methods.

Aderibigbe S. Olomola is a research professor at NISER, Ibadan. Since 2012 he has been Senior Economist/Consultant at the International Food Policy Research Institute (IFPRI) Abuja, Nigeria. His research interests focus on agricultural finance and development policies, microfinance, agricultural commodity value chains, poverty reduction, performance of agricultural research institutions, public expenditure, and public service delivery.

Per Pinstrup-Andersen retired in 2013 from positions as the H. E. Babcock Professor of Food, Nutrition and Public Policy, the J. Thomas Clark Professor of Entrepreneurship, and Professor of Applied Economics at Cornell University; he is now Professor Emeritus and Graduate School Professor at Cornell University, as well as Adjunct Professor at Copenhagen University. He served ten years as the International Food Policy Research Institute's Director-General and Chair of the High-Level Panel of Experts for Food Security (HLPE) and seven years as Department Head; seven years as an economist at the International Center for Tropical Agriculture, Colombia; and six years as a distinguished professor at Wageningen University. He is the 2001 World Food Prize Laureate and the recipient of several awards for his research and communication of research results. His publications include more than 400 other books, refereed journal articles, papers and book chapters, including recent books on *Seeds of Contention, Ethics, Hunger and Globalization, Agricultural Trade Liberalization and the Least Developed Countries, Case Studies in Food Policy for Developing Countries, Food Policy for Developing Countries*, and *The African Food System and its Interaction with Human Health and Nutrition*.

Selim Raihan is Professor of Economics at the University of Dhaka in Bangladesh, and Executive Director of the South Asian Network on Economic Modeling (SANEM). His research interests focus on international trade including the issues related to the WTO and regional trading agreements, analysis of food price policies and poverty, labour market dynamics, economic growth, and political economy of taxation.

Gordon C. Rausser is the Robert Gordon Sproul Distinguished Professor at the University of California, Berkeley, and is currently on leave at Oxford University. Professor Rausser has published more than 250 articles and books, written over 100 commissioned papers and governmental reports, and has won 16 national awards for teaching and research. His current research focuses on industrial organization, commodity and food markets, complex financial contracts, public/private partnerships, and theoretical and empirical analysis of political economy.

Danielle Resnick is a research fellow in the Development Strategies and Governance Division at the International Food Policy Research Institute and formerly a research fellow at United Nations University—World Institute for Development Economics Research (UNU-WIDER). Her research focuses on the political economy of development, democratization, decentralization, and agricultural policy processes, with a regional concentration on sub-Saharan Africa.

Scott Rozelle is a professor and the Director of the Rural Education Action Project (REAP), Freeman Spogli Institute, Stanford University. His research interests focus on food, agricultural and rural development policies in China.

Vincenzo Salvucci is a postdoc at the Development Economics Research Group (DERG), University of Copenhagen, Denmark. He is currently working as Resident Adviser at the National Directorate of Studies and Policy Analysis (DNEAP) of the Ministry of Planning and Development in Maputo, Mozambique. His research interests focus on poverty analysis in developing countries.

Johan Swinnen is Professor of Economics and Director of the LICOS-Centre for Institutions and Economic Performance at the Catholic University of Leuven, Belgium. He is also a senior research fellow at the Centre for European Policy Studies (CEPS), Brussels, where he directs the programme on food security and development policy. He was previously Lead Economist at the World Bank and Economic Advisor at the European Commission. He is President of the International Association of Agricultural Economists.

Theodore Talbot is an economist with the Development Economics Research Group (DERG) at the University of Copenhagen and an external research associate of the Institute for International Integration Studies at Trinity College, Dublin. His research interests include rural economic development, survey-based welfare metrics, and industrial development.

Kristine van Herck is a PhD student at the Centre for Institutions and Economic Performance (LICOS) of the Catholic University of Leuven, Belgium. Her research interests include agricultural labour and land markets, food prices, the EU's Common Agricultural Policy (CAP), and agricultural markets in Central and Eastern European countries.

Derrill D. Watson II is an assistant professor and Chair of the Department of Economics at the American University of Nigeria. He and Per Pinstrup-Andersen have written a textbook on *Food Policy for Developing Countries*. His research examines food policy, economic growth, and ethics.

Jun Yang is an associate professor at the Center for Chinese Agricultural Policy (CCAP), Chinese Academy of Sciences. His research interests focus on international trade, agricultural policies, and sustainable development, as well as the theory and application of the general equilibrium model.

Part I
An Overview

1

The Political Economy of Food Price Policy

An Overview

Per Pinstrup-Andersen

1.1 Introduction

How do governments respond to abrupt food price changes and why do they respond as they do? Answers to these two questions are important to help us understand policy-making, to predict how policy makers are likely to respond to future food price volatility and to support policy makers as they confront such volatility. This book, which is based on a three-year research project, provides such answers for fourteen developing countries, the European Union, and the USA. Syntheses across country studies draw lessons expected to be useful among and beyond the study-countries. The project was undertaken by a network of researchers, including the chapter authors, supported by three senior advisors (Philip Abbott, William Lyakurwa, and Robert Paarlberg) and coordinated by Per Pinstrup-Andersen, Cornell University, and Project Director with United Nations University World Institute for Development Economics Research (UNU-WIDER); Derrill Watson, Cornell University; Finn Tarp, UNU-WIDER; Danielle Resnick, previously UNU-WIDER, now International Food Policy Research Institute (IFPRI); and Henrik Hansen, University of Copenhagen. The network researchers, advisors, and collaborators met at three workshops and interacted frequently through reviews and revisions of draft versions of the working papers posted on the UNU-WIDER website. The chapters of this book are based on revised and shortened versions of these working papers.

Food price volatility since 2007 provides a natural experiment for the research. While much has been written about the nature, content, and causes of these food price fluctuations (e.g., Trostle 2008; Abbott, Hurt, and Tyner

2009; Abbott 2009; Dawe and Slayton 2010; Headey and Fan 2010; Abbott and Borot de Battisti 2011; FAO et al. 2011; Wright 2011; Martin 2012; de Gorter, Drabik, and Just 2013), little is known about the political processes that led to the policy responses and the relative power, behaviour, and influence of the participating stakeholder groups. Understanding how and why governments responded as they did will help enhance existing knowledge of the political economy of food price policy and assist governments in their policy-making as they confront future food price fluctuations.

Although price fluctuations in the world market may influence expectations and related action at the national level, the response by national governments to world market food price fluctuations will depend largely on the extent to which the prices are transmitted or expected to be transmitted to national markets. Thus, an analysis of the degree of price transmission is an important first step towards understanding the political economy issues at the national level. Such an analysis is undertaken in each country study (Chapters 6–21) and synthesized by Baltzer in Chapter 2. In addition to price changes transmitted from the world market, domestic food prices are influenced by domestic factors and domestic policies will respond to both. The policy responses are synthesized by Bryan in Chapter 3. The policy process will influence the choice of policy interventions and the interventions will influence the processes. The processes are presented in each country study and synthesized by Babu in Chapter 4. Political economy aspects, the focus of this book, are analysed in each country study and synthesized by Watson in Chapter 5. An overview of the content of the book is presented in this chapter and the last chapter (Chapter 22) draws the main generalizable lessons from the research and suggests policy recommendations in preparation for future food price increases and food price volatility.

1.2 The Global Food Market

The global food market entered an era of instability in 2007. Large and abrupt fluctuations in the world market prices of wheat, rice, and maize combined with an increasing food price trend, raised concerns about future food supplies, prices, and household food security. Except for a small upward blip in the middle of the 1990s, real food prices in the world market decreased very significantly from the middle of the 1970s to the end of the 1990s. Beginning in 2000, a very slow real food price increase continued until the middle of 2007, when the world market prices of wheat, rice, and maize began a very rapid increase. The increase lasted for 8–12 months, depending on the cereal, after which they experienced an abrupt fall. Since then, two more price spikes have occurred (2010–11 and 2012). The tripling of rice prices between

October 2007 and April 2008 is particularly interesting because it was 'not caused by adverse shocks to rice production or low rice stocks' (Dawe and Slayton 2010: 17). This is an illustration of the powerful effects of national trade policies and irrational or poorly informed expectations and resulting behaviour by the public and private sector or as stated by Dawe and Slayton (2010: 25) in the case of rice: 'government policy decisions were decisive in sparking and fuelling the crisis'. Estimates by Headey (2011) and Martin and Anderson (2012) found that 45–50 per cent of the rice price increase during 2007–8 was due to export restrictions.

Several developments contributed to both fluctuations and the increasing price trend.[1] As prices continued to fall during the period 1975–2000, agricultural development was all but ignored by governments, international development banks, and bilateral donors. Public investment in developing countries' agriculture, rural infrastructure, and agricultural research fell and the falling prices made private investment less interesting and feasible. Relatively little new land was brought under cultivation, primarily because the necessary infrastructure investments were not made. A large share of smallholders chose off-farm labour over investments in improved farm productivity and many became net buyers of food. The rate of yield growth for wheat, rice, and maize slowed while population and income growth and the diet transition continued to increase the demand for food and feed. Expansion of the production of biofuel from sugar, maize, oil palm, rapeseed, soybeans, and jatropha competed with food production for land and water, and excess demand reduced cereal stocks. Extreme weather events, which caused drought, floods, and increased production fluctuations in several countries, reduced supplies. Fluctuations in oil prices and the dollar exchange rate further contributed to food price fluctuations. Thus, excess demand, which was covered by stock drawdown, was amplified by decreasing and fluctuating supply during the beginning of the 2000s.

Food prices are very sensitive to changes in the supply–demand balance (both supply and demand are very price inelastic in the short run). Therefore, even small changes in supply and demand, caused by, for example, extreme weather events and expanded biofuel production, respectively, may cause large price changes, particularly if stock levels are low. As international cereal prices began to increase, some of the news media painted various degrees of doomsday scenarios[2] and investors became more interested in the futures

[1] The importance of differentiating between food price increase and price volatility for the choice of policy interventions is discussed in Chapter 22.

[2] While the news media can be extremely useful in promoting transparency in the action by both the public and the private sector, a large share of the media reporting during the food price increases in the world market from the middle of 2007 to the middle of 2008, and again in the subsequent food price spikes, exaggerated the expected consequences by failing to differentiate between a price spike and a long-term price increase. When prices fell during the second half of

market for cereals, particularly wheat and maize. Irrational expectations by investors who interpreted upward prices as a long-term trend rather than a spike, added to price volatility. Export bans and other restrictions by cereal exporters, reduced import tariffs by importing countries, and removal of VAT on food in several countries placed additional pressures on the supply–demand situation in the world market.

While as mentioned above, much has been written about the causes of the food price volatility and the increasing food prices since 2007, there is no consensus in the literature about the relative importance of each of the factors mentioned above. Attempts to apportion cause to each of the relevant factors are hampered by the interaction among them. However, there seems to be widespread agreement that export restrictions were very important. Sharma (2011) found that one-third of the 105 countries he surveyed used export restrictions for cereals during the period 2007–11. As mentioned above, Headey (2011) and Martin and Anderson (2012) found that 45–50 per cent of the increase in the world market price for rice during 2007–8 was caused by export restrictions. Bouët and Laborde Debucquet (2010) estimated that 30 per cent of the increase in the international price for wheat was caused by export restrictions. Expanded biofuel producton is estimated by Rosegrant et al. (2008) and Abbott, Hurt, and Tynes (2011) to account for 30–40 per cent of the cereal price increase during 2007–8. De Gorter and Just (2007), de Gorter (2008), and Collins (2008) concluded that biofuel policies were the principal cause of the cereal price increases.

Sanders et al. (2008), Wright (2009), and Martin (2012) reason that speculation on the futures market was not a significant contributor to cereal price fluctuations while Ghosh (2010: 72) concludes that 'The dramatic rise and fall of world food prices in 2007–8 was largely a result of speculative activity in global commodity markets'. Timmer and Dawe (2010: 7) conclude that 'the sudden spike in wheat and corn prices was due to financial speculation'. They further argue that increasing futures prices affect storage and hoarding behaviour by farmers and traders, which itself would affect supply and prices. Using data from the Chicago Board of Trade, Torero (2011: 4) reports that the volume of commodity index funds traded increased 'by 157 per cent, 200 per cent, and 169 per cent for maize, soybeans, and soft wheat during the period 2006–11 and that only 2 per cent of these futures contracts has resulted in the delivery of real goods'. He further states that the

2008, the media was very quiet. Predictions of continued rapid food price increases leading to a situation of absolute global food scarcity and an implicit assumption of perfect price transmission of international cereal prices to low-income people in low-income countries lead much of the media and unfortunately also some international organizations to conclude that global food price fluctuations resulted in widespread increases in poverty, food insecurity, and malnutrition, developments that, in fact, did not happen.

volume of maize futures traded worldwide 'is more than three times greater than the global production of maize'. Such statistics lends credibility to the argument that speculation had a major influence on the prices of three commodities.

Trostle (2008) and Wright (2011) conclude that imbalance between supply and demand resulting in stock drawdown to very low levels followed by supply expansions and stock build-up is the key explanation for the recent food price fluctuations. A large share of recent analyses supports the conclusion that market fundamentals, i.e., the supply–demand situation, are the primary cause of the recent food price volatility. However, in a world with poorly integrated food markets, the global supply–demand situation may say little about the situation in particular national and local markets. Enhanced export restrictions and reduced import restrictions reduce supplies and increase demand in the world market with resulting increasing prices, with the opposite effect in the participating countries. Variability in production and policies in a few major cereal exporters may result in large supply changes and associated price volatility in the world market, irrespective of what happens in the rest of the world.[3] As illustrated in the chapters to follow, the above mentioned factors are integrated with action by governments and the private sector based on lack of information, poor predictable ability, and irrational expectations. Conflicting goals and relative power among stakeholder groups have played an important role. An understanding of these and related political economy factors are essential to understand the behaviour of both the public and private sector.

Whether resulting from world market price changes or national factors, national governments and the private sector responded to the actual and expected food price changes in the world market in different ways. In some cases policy interventions, particularly trade interventions by large exporters and importers, and private sector action contributed to further price volatility in the world market while in others the effect was to dampen the volatility. Similarly, poorly implemented policy interventions and private sector action increased domestic price volatility in some cases, while they improved price stability in most. An understanding of the constellation, goals, and relative power of stakeholder groups—the political economy issues—and how they vary among countries is important to explain the observed differences in the response to food price volatility by the public and private sector. That is the focus of the rest of the book.

[3] According to Food and Agriculture Organization Statistics Division (FAOSTAT) (accessed 24 June 2013) the USA accounted for 50 per cent of worldwide maize export in 2010; the USA and Canada accounted for one-third of all wheat export; and Thailand and Vietnam accounted for about 50 per cent of all rice export (on a milled equivalent basis).

In Chapter 2, Baltzer provides a synthesis of the estimates of price transmission in the fourteen study-countries. He concludes that several of the countries are poorly integrated into world cereal markets and domestic food price volatility tends to result primarily from domestic supply shocks caused by extreme weather events, political turmoil, inappropriate macro policy, and mistrust and miscommunication between governments and the private sector. The price transmission from the world market to domestic markets in these countries tended to be low and in some countries the domestic price volatility exceeded the volatility in the world market. Low price transmission was also found in large middle-income countries such as China and India because of trade restrictions to maintain domestic price stability, while other large middle-income countries such as Brazil and South Africa allowed a high degree of pass-through of international prices of some cereals, notably rice and wheat, to the domestic markets. On the basis of an analysis of food price volatility in the world market and in 15 African countries during 2007–10, Minot (2012: p. v) found increased food price volatility in the world market but no evidence that 'food price volatility has increased in the region'. While high food price volatility in the world market may draw more attention by the news media and decision makers, country-specific factors such as extreme weather events and adverse policy interventions, may have much more serious implications for domestic food prices and household food security.

Most of the study-countries experienced large food price fluctuations during the period 2007–12, whether transmitted from the world market or caused by national factors. As synthesized by Bryan in Chapter 3, their policy responses varied widely. Bryan concludes that the responses were often uncoordinated, sometimes contradictory, poorly targeted, and sometimes mismanaged. The policy outcomes varied among countries but were frequently disappointing. Attempts to manage the supply of cereals on the domestic markets through procurement and release from storage and trade policy were unsuccessful in some countries but successful in others, notably China and India. Export bans and removal of import tariffs were effective in reducing price fluctuations in some countries but contributed to price increases in the world market by reducing supplies and increasing demand. Food and fertilizer subsidies implemented in several countries were difficult to manage and the fiscal costs were high. Where targeting was attempted, leakage was large. Expansions of existing social safety net programmes successfully helped to compensate low-income people for higher food prices in some countries, notably Brazil and South Africa. Bryan draws four lessons from the synthesis: First, consider costs before deciding on policy action; second, consider trade-offs between short-term emergency measures and measures with longer term effects; third, base the crisis responses on evidence from experience from past policies; and fourth, spend the time between food price crises to generate the evidence needed to make evidence-based policy decisions.

In Chapter 4, Babu discusses various frameworks for analysing policy processes and concludes that a combination of such frameworks is required to describe the processes and how the various stakeholder groups participate in them. The policy response to the food price fluctuations in a particular country depends on the existing policy process as well as the resources available, experience from past policies, and the policies currently in place. The policy process followed was influenced by the nature and degree of decentralization as well as the size of the country, the existing institutions and the degree of participation in policy-making. On the basis of the country studies, Babu concludes that democratically elected governments are more likely to select policies that benefit or at least do not antagonize powerful stakeholder groups over first-best policies from an efficiency point of view. The news media, the private sector, and non-governmental organizations (NGOs) played an important role in the choice of policies. As might be expected, authoritarian regimes tended to take action to maintain political stability and promote economic growth, taking into account the wishes of non-government stakeholder groups only as needed to achieve those two goals. The policy process tends to be different in a period of crisis than between crises. The capacity by governments and other stakeholder groups to engage in the design and implement interventions to deal with future food price crises should be strengthened. In particular, there is a need for more action-oriented research to enhance the evidence base for future policy interventions.

In Chapter 5, Watson combines the diverse policy responses and processes reported in Chapters 6–21, and synthesized in Chapters 3 and 4, with political economy theories in order to address the key question of this book: Why did governments take the action they took? Three models of government behaviour underlie the country-level analyses. The first, which Watson calls the 'naive model', is based on the assumption that the government is a unitary, benevolent entity that aims to maximize social welfare in the most efficient way. While a large share of economic analysis of government decision-making is based on that assumption, it is rarely found. The second model, which represents the behaviour reported in several of the country studies, deviates from the first by including fragmented government, self-interested government actors, and path dependence. The third model, which is reflected in the behaviour of some of the governments studied, is what is normally referred to as the rent-seeking model. It aims to maximize a weighted social welfare function in which the weights reflect the relative power and goals of the various stakeholder groups. Fragmented government decision-making resulting in contradictory policy interventions; uncertainty and incorrect estimates and forecasts; rent-seeking by policy makers and private sector groups; and mutual mistrust between governments and the private sector, contributed to policy failure to varying degrees in most of the countries. Path dependence, i.e., modifying existing policies and institutions rather than designing and implementing new ones, was characteristic of the policy responses to the food price volatility in virtually all the countries. Similarly, even when the evidence showed that the rural poor suffered more than the urban poor from the food price volatility, existing urban bias in policy-making was enhanced. Protection of government legitimacy trumped poverty alleviation. Contrary to the heavy-handed dictates by the international community forcing national governments to take specific action during the period of widespread economic adjustment, policy responses by national governments to the food crisis were rarely dictated, but rather supported, by donors and international organizations.

While the above mentioned syntheses attempt to draw generalizable lessons from the country studies, a more complete understanding of the political economy of food price policy is obtained from in-depth country-specific analyses reported in Chapters 6–21. The country studies are presented according to the degree to which each country is expected to be integrated with world food markets. Low-income landlocked countries (Chapters 6–8) are followed by other low-income countries with limited dependence on food import (Chapters 9–10). Then follow low and middle-income countries heavily dependent on food imports (Chapters 11–14). Major food exporters, including Vietnam and four of the five BRICS (Brazil, Russia, India, China, and South Africa) countries are presented in Chapters 15–19 and selected political economy issues in the USA and the European Union (EU) expected to affect developing countries are discussed in Chapters 20 and 21.

As reported by Admassie for Ethiopia (Chapter 6), Chinsinga and Chirwa for Malawi (Chapter 7), and Chapoto for Zambia (Chapter 8), the government food policy of these landlocked African countries focused on maize. This is so because of the importance of maize in the diet of people in these countries and because maize availability and prices are key factors in maintaining government legitimacy. The price transmission from the world market was low and weather-related production fluctuations and policy interventions were the primary causes of domestic food price fluctuations. Malawi and Zambia were successful in expanding maize production and storage facilities were stretched to the limit and beyond. However, maize prices did not fall. Malawi introduced price controls, domestic trade restrictions and export bans which all failed because of lack of implementation capacity by the parastatals and opposition by private traders. In Zambia, large farmers and millers benefitted from direct access to high-level policy makers. Chapoto reports that Zambia's response to increasing maize prices was a clear illustration of path dependence void of policy innovation. Policy implementations were delayed and in some cases ineffective because of mutual mistrust between the government and the private sector, adverse behaviour by traders and millers, and opposing self-interests among key stakeholder groups. Rent-seeking behaviour was common.

Admassie (Chapter 6) found that increasing aggregate food demand in excess of supply expansions placed upward pressures on domestic food prices in Ethiopia and made the market more susceptible to abrupt fluctuations caused by adverse weather and policies. Admassie found that the executive branch of the Ethiopian government was all powerful. Neither the opposition parties nor other stakeholder groups, such as the private sector, NGOs, and the news media, appear to have had significant impact on the design and implementation of the policy responses.

Many of the political economy issues found in the two countries characterized as low-income countries with limited dependence on food import (Kenya and Mozambique) are similar to those found in the three landlocked countries discussed above. Although they imported significant amounts of cereals, they experienced low levels of price transmission from the world markets to domestic markets. Both of them experienced large food price fluctuations caused primarily by weather events and policy interventions. Ethiopia and Kenya (Nzuma, Chapter 9) followed a similar set of policy responses, which included export bans and reduced import tariffs for cereals, release of cereal stocks, subsidies for agricultural inputs, and social safety nets for urban consumers in Kenya and the rural poor in Ethiopia. Avoiding social unrest and maintaining legitimacy appear to have been important goals. According to Nzuma, the policy responses in Kenya suffered from several policy reversals, ineffective export restrictions and post-election political turmoil. Kenya experienced massive production shortfalls due to drought and political turmoil. Uneven distribution of power with the Kenyan government and a weak policy-making process contributed to the reversals and inefficiencies. Both countries pursued policy interventions to increase agricultural productivity, with emphasis on subsidies for fertilizers and other inputs. While, as mentioned above, such policies resulted in large production increases in Malawi and Zambia, the impact is less clear in Ethiopia and Kenya and, according to Nhate, Massingarela, and Salvucci, they failed to increase productivity in Mozambique (Chapter 10).

Four of the study-countries (Bangladesh, Egypt, Nigeria, and Senegal) depend heavily on rice and wheat import. The food price transmission from the world market to domestic markets would be expected to be high but, as discussed by Baltzer in Chapter 2, the degree of transmission varied among the countries due to differences in foreign trade policy. While self-sufficiency in rice has long been a national objective in Bangladesh, domestic production has fluctuated widely because of weather-related calamities and policy interventions causing large fluctuations in import demand (Raihan, Chapter 11). During the period 2007–8, the country was run by an unelected caretaker government backed by the military and the role of other stakeholder groups, including the private sector and NGOs, was very limited. Similar to the case of Kenya, the distribution of power in the Bangladeshi government was very uneven, with the Ministry of Finance having overall decision-making power over food and agricultural policy initiatives. This, together with extortions and unofficial payments in the supply chain caused delays and inefficiencies. The government undertook several initiatives to promote agricultural development such as fertilizer and fuel subsidies as well as expanded funding of agricultural research and agricultural credit. The impact of these measures is yet to be measured.

Ghoneim (Chapter 12) estimates that 30–40 per cent of the price fluctuations in the world market were transmitted to Egypt's food market. This is less than what might be expected in view of the country's heavy dependence on food imports and is a result of the Egyptian government's heavy intervention in the food sector along with fragmented markets, anti-competitive behaviour, and inefficiencies in the subsidy system. Declining real wages, increasing poverty, inefficiencies in the social safety net, and increasing media attention, together with increasing and fluctuating food prices have placed pressures on the government to focus on food policy. By reducing import tariffs on various food commodities and banning rice exports while maintaining large fuel and food subsidies without effective targeting, the action by the Egyptian government illustrates the path dependence discussed by Watson in Chapter 5. Although the fiscal costs of these policies are very high and possibly unsustainable in the longer run, Ghoneim concludes that the current political leadership favours the status quo to avoid negative social and political repercussions from any reform, particularly because of the political uncertainties following the recent revolution.

In Chapter 13, Olomola reports that, contrary to Ethiopia, Vietnam, China, and other countries with a highly centralized policy-making arrangement, Nigeria's policy response was heavily influenced by several stakeholder groups including the federal government, politicians, the news media, and producer associations. Because of the conflicting stakeholder goals and desires, the development of a policy agenda was slow and difficult, although the output from a meeting of the state governors and the president resulted in a set of policy interventions (release of cereals from reserves, import of half a million tons of rice for distribution at subsidized prices, and suspension of import tariffs on rice) that were approved and implemented within a short period of time. Producer associations, the news media, and millers played important roles in the design and implementation of the policy responses. Although the influence by consumers is unclear, they benefitted from the policy interventions, such as expanded rice import and the import tariff waiver, because they were successful in reversing food price increases. A guaranteed minimum price aimed to compensate farmers for the potential income loss from that reversal.

Resnick (Chapter 14) reports that Senegal was particularly vulnerable to food price increase in the world market because of its heavy dependence on imports coupled with two seasons of poor cereal production. The price transmission from the world market to the Senegalese market was particularly high for rice but also significant for other food commodities such as wheat and dairy products. A lack of an agricultural strategy to expand domestic food production and the urban population's preference for imported food added to the severity of the impact of the global food price fluctuations. In response to demands and pressures from various stakeholder groups including consumer groups, trade unions, the news media, and five major street demonstrations, the government introduced an array of policy interventions such as consumer subsidies, social protection schemes, and suspension of import duties and value added taxes at very high fiscal costs. The government also launched a high-profile agricultural initiative which, according to Resnick, was too focused on achieving short-term goals rather than long-term structural changes to the agricultural sector needed to achieve the stated goal of food self-sufficiency. In an attempt to satisfy the broad range of well-organized stakeholder groups that advocated for specific interventions, Resnick concludes that the government failed to properly target and implement the many policy interventions and forfeited the opportunity to devise a financially viable, social protection programme and a long-term agricultural strategy.

The policy response to the global food price volatility differed among the five major food exporting developing countries included in this book (Vietnam and the four BRICS countries). Three of the countries (China, India, and Vietnam) protected domestic food markets from the price fluctuations in the world market through trade policies (primarily export restrictions) that reduced price transmission. By keeping domestic food prices lower than they would have been with full pass-through, consumers gained while producers lost. In all three countries, rapidly increasing prices of the main staples (particularly rice and wheat) might lead to political instability and the main goal of the policies to reduce price transmission was undoubtedly related to political legitimacy, dressed formally as a food security goal. The other two major exporters (Brazil and South Africa) continued exports and permitted international prices to reach domestic markets, thus benefitting farmers while expanding existing subsidy schemes and other social safety nets to compensate low-income consumers. Both Brazil and South Africa have strong farmer associations with direct access to the policy-making process. Brazilian consumers were partially protected by a strong currency appreciation.

Although the political power in Vietnam is relatively centralized, Nguyen and Talbot (Chapter 15) report that there is political space for other stakeholder groups, including civil society, international organizations, research institutes, and the news media. Although the central government sets quantity goals for rice export, several government entities are involved in policy implementation and Nguyen and Talbot found a mismatch between policy instruments implemented by two distinct sets of actors with two distinct objectives: to insulate consumers from increasing rice prices and to ensure profits for rice farmers. Such mismatch may result from the government's attempt to balance the competing interests of consumers and producers. Lack of information and deficient forecasting for rice production led to policy reversals.

India's export bans for wheat, common rice and large stocks of cereals basically de-linked world market prices and domestic prices for rice and wheat during 2007–8 (Ganguly and Gulati, Chapter 16) and added significantly to price volatility in the world market. Domestic prices remained stable until mid-2009 when severe droughts caused production shortfalls and rapidly increasing prices. Ganguly and Gulati conclude that the Indian government's heavy emphasis on policy interventions, such as food subsidies and rural employment guarantee programmes, expected to have short-run impact, diverts public funds away from investments in agriculture and rural infrastructure, which would have a much greater impact on poverty alleviation and economic growth in the longer term.

In response to the rapidly increasing world market prices for cereals, the Chinese government decided to stabilize domestic food prices and did so very successfully (Huang, Yang, and Rozelle, Chapter 17). A set of policy interventions consisting of the release of government cereal stocks, long-term futures contracts with exporting countries, increasing agricultural subsidies, support of farmers' risk management, higher food subsidies and enhancement of the social safety net for urban consumers, the suspension of any expansion of biofuel production which competed with food production and increased investment in agricultural technology, and water availability, served both the rural and urban populations well while strengthening the government's legitimacy. The highly centralized governance system, amply supported by relevant evidence of expected impact of alternative policy interventions, was able to respond rapidly and effectively to the emerging food crisis. Together with the Indian trade policies mentioned above, the Chinese policy interventions amplified the food price increase and volatility in the world market. To avoid such beggar-thy-neighbour policies Huang, Yang, and Rozelle suggest that a new global governance system is needed to coordinate actions among major food importers and exporters.

According to Mueller and Mueller (Chapter 18), past inequalities and hyperinflation have guided the Brazilian government to prioritize fiscally sound social inclusion. The international food price increases in 2007–8 might therefore be expected to cause concern because they might undermine both social inclusion and price stability. Yet, the policy response and the reaction by society were very limited. Domestic cereal prices did increase during 2007–8, but much less than the increase in the world market. Rather than restricting cereal exports to control domestic prices, as done in China, India, and Vietnam, exports were continued at the higher world market prices. Farm incomes increased and increasing wages of the rural labour force largely compensated for the higher food prices. The existing extensive system of social protection targeting transfers to low-income people was expanded to compensate for higher food prices and no new policies or programmes were designed. According to Mueller and Mueller, the global food price volatility caused very limited disagreements among the various stakeholder groups.

Similar to Brazil, South Africa (Kirsten, Chapter 19) did not implement any major policy change in response to the international food price volatility beginning in 2007. Existing trade policy for food and agricultural commodities (basically undistorted) were not changed. The comprehensive social welfare programme that had been in place since 1998 was expanded to compensate for the negative effects of price increases, but no new policies were designed. Lobbying by farmers may have been instrumental in maintaining an unfettered trade regime for agricultural commodities and lobbying by trade unions and consumer groups probably contributed to the expansion of the transfer programmes. Although the news media was actively engaged in the debate about the food price volatility, Kirsten concludes that it had very little or no policy impact.

As in the case of Brazil and South Africa, the USA's direct response to the international food price increase and volatility was very limited, but the impact of US policies, particularly the biofuel policies, on international food prices, was very significant (Rausser and de Gorter, Chapter 20). Although the direct effect was on maize and soybean prices, spill-overs to wheat and rice were large. Several stakeholder groups within the USA including growers' associations, fuel transporters, biofuel producers, and some environmentalists, and the energy security community supported the promotion of biofuel while others, including livestock producers and food processors, opposed. Rausser and de Gorter suggest that US macroeconomic policies as well as energy and sugar policies also contributed to global food price volatility.

The common agricultural policy of the EU had little or no impact on food price volatility in the world market since 2007 and the potential for influencing the world market prices is very limited. Food prices in the EU followed the changes in world market prices, but the scale of change was much smaller (Swinnen, Knops, and van Herck, Chapter 21). Average prices for EU producers increased by less than 20 per cent in real terms during the first price spike and less during the second spike. Real consumer prices for food increased by only 5 per cent during 2005–12, with very little volatility. Food price changes triggered several policy initiatives within the EU, including increased social spending to protect poor consumers and revisions of the EU biofuel policies to reduce the use of food crops for biofuel. Instead of expanding food aid to developing countries, the EU established a €1 billion food facility and supported initiatives by G20 to reduce price volatility and improve market information.

In Chapter 22, Pinstrup-Andersen presents a brief summary of the major policy lessons from the work reported in the book. The objective is to complement rather than repeat the many lessons reported in the synthesis chapters by Baltzer, Bryan, Babu, and Watson. Recommendations about specific policy interventions and their political feasibility are likely to be most successful if made within the specific political economy context. However, on the basis of the findings reported in this book, some policy recommendations are likely to be relevant for many countries. Eight such recommendations are presented in Chapter 22. They are: the strengthening of the policy-relevant evidence base; the appropriate use of trade policy and limiting the interference in price signals; the reduction in fiscal costs of short-term interventions; investments to increase the food supply elasticity; facilitating effective risk management tools; improving the management of public sector grain stocks; making the demand for raw materials for biofuel price-related; and improving the collaboration between the public and private sectors.

References

Abbott, P. C. (2009). 'Development Dimensions of High Food Prices'. OECD Food, Agriculture and Fisheries Working Paper No. 18. Paris: OECD Publishing.

Abbott, P., and A. Borot de Battisti (2011). 'Recent Global Food price Shocks: Causes, Consequences and Lessons for African Governments and Donors'. *Journal of African Economies* 20 (AERC Supplement 1): i12–i62.

Abbott, P. C., C. Hurt, and W. Tyner (2009). 'What's Driving Food Prices?' Farm Foundation Issue Report. Minneapolis, MN: University of Minnesota.

Bouët, A., and D. Laborde Debucquet (2010). 'Economics of Export Taxation in a Context of Food Crisis: A Theoretical and CGE Approach Contribution'. IFPRI Discussion Paper No. 00994. Washington, DC: IFPRI.

Collins, K. J. (2008). 'The role of biofuels and other factors in increasing farm and food prices: a review of recent developments with a focus on feed grain markets and market prospects'. Supporting material for a review conducted by Kraft Foods Global, Inc.

Dawe, D., and T. Slayton (2010). 'The World Rice Market Crisis of 2007–08'. In D. Dawe (ed.), *The Rice Crisis: Markets, Policies and Food Security*. London: FAO and Earthscan.

de Gorter, H. (2008). 'Explaining Agricultural Commodity Price Increases: The Role of Biofuel Policies'. Paper presented at the Rising Food and Energy Prices: US Food Policy at a Crossroads conference, Oregon State University, Corvallis. 2 October. Available at <http://arec.oregonstate.edu/sites/default/files/faculty/perry/degorter.pdf>. Accessed 1 March 2013.

de Gorter, H., and D. R. Just (2007). '"Water" in the US Ethanol Tax Credit and Mandate: Implications for Rectangular Deadweight Costs and the Corn–Oil Price Relationship'. Paper prepared for the Allied Social Science Association annual meeting, New Orleans, 4–6 January 2008. Available at <http://papers.ssrn.com/sol3/papers.cfm?abstract>. Accessed 1 March 2013.

FAO, IFAD, IMF, OECD, UNCTAD, WFP, the World Bank, the WTO, IFPRI, and the UN HLTF (2011). 'Price Volatility in Food and Agricultural Markets: Policy Responses'. Policy Report prepared for the G20 summit meeting in November 2010.

FAOSTAT (2013). Accessed 24 June 2013. Available at: <http://faostat.fao.org/>.

Ghosh, J. (2010). 'The Unnatural Coupling: Food and Global Finance'. *Journal of Agrarian Change* 10(1): 72–86.

Headey, D. (2011). 'Rethinking the Global Food Crisis: The Role of Trade Shocks'. *Food Policy* 36: 136–46.

Headey, D., and S. Fan (2010). 'Reflections on the Global Food Crisis: How did it Happen? How has it Hurt? And How can we Prevent the Next One?' Research Monograph 165. International Food Policy Research Institute. Washington, DC: IFPRI.

Martin, W. (2012). 'Managing High and Volatile Food Prices'. Trade Policy Issues Paper, IATRC TPI #2012-6. St. Paul, MN: International Agricultural Trade Research Consortium.

Martin, W., and K. Anderson (2012). 'Export Restrictions and Price Insulation during Commodity Price Booms'. *American Journal of Agricultural Economics* 94(2): 422–7.

Minot, N. (2012). 'Food Price Volatility in Africa: Has it Really Increased?' IFPRI Discussion Paper No. 01239. Washington, DC: International Food Policy Research Institute.

Rosegrant, M. W., T. Zhu, S. Msangi, and T. Sulser (2008). *The Impact of Biofuel Production on World Cereal Prices*. Washington, DC: International Food Policy Research Institute.

Sanders, D. R., S. H. Irwin, and R. P. Merrin (2008). 'The Adequacy of Speculation in Agricultural Futures Markets: Too Much of a Good Thing?' Marketing and Outlook Research Reports. Urbana-Champaign, IL: University of Illinois at Urbana-Champaign, Department of Agricultural and Consumer Economics.

Sharma, R. (2011). 'Food Export Restrictions: Review of the 2007–10 Experience and Considerations for Disciplining Restrictive Measures'. FAO Commodity and Trade Policy Research Working Paper No. 32. Rome: FAO.

Timmer, D., and D. Dawe (2010). 'Food Crises Past, Present (and Future?): Will We Ever Learn?' In D. Dawe (ed.), *The Rice Crisis: Markets, Policies and Food Security*. London: FAO and Earthscan.

Torero, M. (2011). 'Food Prices: Riding the Rollercoaster'. 2011 Global Food Policy Report. Washington, DC: IFPRI.

Trostle, R. (2008). 'Global Agricultural Supply and Demand: Factors Contributing to the Recent Increase in Food Commodity Prices'. Economic Research Service, Outlook Report WRS-0801 (2008). Washington, DC: USDA.

Wright, B. D. (2009). *Speculators, Storage, and the Price of Rice*. Berkeley, CA: University of California, Giannini Foundation of Agricultural Economics.

Wright, B. D. (2011). 'The Economics of Grain Price Volatility'. *Applied Economic Perspectives and Policy* 33(1): 32–58.

Part II

Synthesis of Findings from Country Studies

2

International to Domestic Price Transmission in Fourteen Developing Countries during the 2007–8 Food Crisis

*Kenneth Baltzer**

2.1 Introduction

This chapter synthesizes the evidence of price transmission from international markets to domestic markets during the 2007–8 food crisis experienced by the fourteen countries studied in this volume. It covers the markets for three grain commodities: maize, wheat, and rice.

The degree of price transmission from international to domestic markets during the 2007–8 food crisis varied significantly across countries. The country studies reviewed in this chapter discuss a wide range of factors that may serve to explain this variation, notably active stabilization policies and poor market integration due to high transportation costs and market imperfections. In several countries, domestic prices are largely unrelated to international prices and therefore reflect purely local shocks, such as harvest failures and political turmoil, which are independent from, but coincide with, the global crisis.

The empirical literature on price transmission that has emerged since the crisis generally comes to similar conclusions. Abbott and Borot de Battisti (2011) investigate price transmission patterns for a number of African countries (including a few others, such as China and Brazil, for comparison) by

* The author would like to thank all the authors of the fourteen case studies, upon which this synthesis is based, for their useful comments and quality control of an earlier version of this study. Also, the study has benefitted greatly from constructive input by Shane Bryan, Derrill Watson II, Per Pinstrup-Andersen, and an anonymous reviewer. Finally, a special thanks to Per Pinstrup-Andersen for his encouragements and great patience throughout the process.

plotting international and local commodity price indices and estimating price transmission elasticities. They find great variation in price transmission from almost none in China to virtually complete in Brazil. In Africa, countries like Nigeria and Ethiopia appear to be closely linked to the world markets, whereas most of the other countries show limited and/or lagged responses, suggesting that world market pressures are resisted by domestic market institutions. Abbott and Borot de Battisti also identify certain patterns, such as much greater price transmission for highly traded commodities (for instance rice) compared to non-tradable ones (millet and sorghum), and higher price transmission rates for import-dependent countries, including rice in Senegal, Mali, Burkina Faso, Niger, Malawi, and Uganda; maize in Malawi and Uganda; and wheat in Ethiopia.

Such findings are supported by other studies on countries in Africa (Benson, Mugarura, and Wanda 2008; Cudjoe, Breisinger, and Diao 2010; Minot 2011), Asia (Dawe 2008; Robles 2011), and Latin America (de Janvry and Sadoulet 2010; Robles 2011).

Most African countries experienced commodity price increases which were lower than the international prices, but in a few countries, notably Ethiopia and Malawi, food prices grew more rapidly than on the world market (Minot 2011). This suggests that other shocks than the world market prices were at play. Similarly, Benson et al. (2008) argue that the increasing food prices in Uganda could be better explained by domestic or regional factors (for instance, spill-overs from harvest shortfalls in neighbouring Kenya) rather than by the global food crisis.

Transmission of rice prices in Asia was limited in most cases, notably India, the Philippines, and Vietnam (Dawe 2008). Interestingly, Dawe finds a relatively high degree of pass-through (64 per cent) in China, which is in stark contrast to the almost flat local prices shown by Abbott and Borot de Battisti (2011). However, Dawe's paper was one of the first analyses on the global food crisis, and the prices of rice were only available up to late 2007, i.e. before the international rice prices accelerated. Based on more recent data covering the international spike in rice prices, Robles (2011) finds that the pass-through of rice prices was actually lower in Bangladesh (34 per cent), a rice importer, than in Pakistan and Vietnam (around 51 per cent), two rice exporters.

De Janvry and Sadoulet (2010) and Robles (2011) report quite low price transmission elasticities in a number of Latin American countries (Costa Rica, Ecuador, El Salvador, Guatemala, Honduras, Mexico, Nicaragua, Panama, Peru, and the Dominican Republic). Indeed, in Nicaragua (maize), Honduras (maize), and the Dominican Republic (rice), the pass-through may even have been negative. In general, price transmission elasticities are estimated to be below 20 per cent, with notable exception being rice markets in Mexico (almost 50 per cent) and wheat-to-bread price transmission in Ecuador (just over 40 per cent).

Through a synthesis of the fourteen country studies and with the support of food price data from Food and Agriculture Organization (FAO)'s Global Information and Early Warning System (GIEWS), this study provides an overview of the price transmission patterns experienced by the countries during the food crisis period. The data is summarized graphically by plotting monthly series of local maize, rice, and wheat prices against international benchmark prices. Additionally, the wealth of information offered by the country-study authors is reviewed in an attempt to gather some broad insights into how food price policies, domestic institutions, and other factors affected price transmission.

2.2 Conceptual Framework

2.2.1 *What is Price Transmission?*

The fundamental theoretical basis for price transmission is the law of one price (LOP) (Fackler and Goodwin 2001). The LOP can be written as

$$|p_w - p_d| \leq t \quad (1)$$

where p_w and p_d are the prices of a commodity on the world market and the domestic market respectively and t represents the transaction costs associated with importing or exporting the commodity.[1] Equation (1) states that the gap between the international and the domestic prices of a commodity should never be larger than the transaction costs.

The positive transaction costs effectively create a price band between import parity, $p_w + t$, and export parity, $p_w - t$. If domestic supply and demand conditions are such that the domestic price lies within the price band, no international trade is profitable. In contrast, if domestic supply is sufficiently large relative to demand to press domestic prices below export parity, incentives for international arbitrage should ensure that domestic prices do not stay too far below export parity for too long. Similarly, relatively tight domestic supplies, which push domestic prices close to or above the import parity, should invite importers to satisfy the excess demand at import parity. In effect, if the domestic price is within the parity bounds and the commodity is non-traded, we would expect the domestic price to be determined by domestic supply and demand condition and be unrelated to international

[1] Transaction cost is a general concept used to capture a variety of pecuniary and non-pecuniary costs associated with trading, such as transportation costs, import tariffs, waste, spoilage, and opportunity costs due to delays, profit margins, etc.

prices. Instead, if the commodity is traded, the LOP predicts a close relationship between the international and domestic prices.

In reality, the distinction between isolation from the international markets and world market integration is not as clear-cut as the theoretical discussion above would suggest. For instance, Mozambique and Kenya are both import-dependent in cereals, yet some studies (e.g. Minot 2011) have found that these countries are poorly integrated with the world markets. In contrast, even isolated markets, like the maize market in Ethiopia, appear to display some long-term relationship with the international markets (Loening, Durevall, and Birru 2009). In general, we are likely to find that domestic prices in all countries are determined by a mix of domestic factors as well as transmission from international prices. The relative strength of domestic versus international factors varies greatly from country to country depending on how well countries are integrated with the world market. The rest of this section discusses briefly a number of factors which may influence market integration.

2.2.2 *Imperfect Market Integration*

Transaction costs cover costs of transportation due to poor infrastructure (particularly if countries are landlocked), imperfectly competitive markets, regulatory costs, and tariffs as well as taxes. The higher the transaction costs are, the more likely it is that domestic prices fall within the parity bounds and commodities are non-traded. This is often the case with some of the basic staples in sub-Saharan Africa (SSA), such as millet, sorghum, cassava, and teff, but it also sometimes happens with internationally traded commodities. In such cases, the LOP no longer applies and we should not expect significant price transmission across borders. Yet, sometimes it still takes place. Demand substitution may link non-traded with traded commodities. As the price of the traded commodity increases following an international price shock, demand may shift towards non-traded commodities resulting in higher prices on these as well. Such cross-commodity price transmission may be weak, as Resnick (Chapter 14) indicates in the case of Senegal; or relatively strong, as appeared to have been the case in Ethiopia (Rashid 2011).

The trade status of an individual country tends to persist over time. Countries are often consistently net importers, net exporters, or separated from international markets. There are, however, exceptions. For instance, due to improvements in agricultural productivity, Malawi has shifted from import dependence to becoming largely self-sufficient in maize (Chirwa and Chinsinga, Chapter 7). South Africa, which is a regional trade hub for many commodities, varies between being net importer and net exporter of maize. Such trade regime shifts complicate price transmission analysis. Moving from trading to non-trading status may disrupt the price transmission mechanism. Shifting from exporter to importer (or vice versa) may cause sharp changes in domestic prices independently from international price movements as the domestic price changes from export parity to import parity. Needless to say, considering the trade status and particularly changes in trade status is important for evaluating price transmission.

Many of the country studies in the sample, notably for Egypt, South Africa, Bangladesh, Senegal, and Zambia (Chapoto, Chapter 8; Ghoneim, Chapter 12; Kirsten, Chapter 19; Raihan, Chapter 11; Resnick, Chapter 14), suggest that the domestic food supply chains are characterized by high concentration and non-competitive behaviour. Imperfect competition in the supply chain adds additional margins to the transaction costs and thus influences the degree of price transmission. A large literature on supply chain price transmission argues that imperfect competition may be an important explanation for asymmetric price transmission, i.e. the observation that increasing prices are transmitted relatively strongly down the value chain, whereas lower prices are transmitted incompletely and/or with significant lag. Such asymmetries also complicate price transmission analyses.

Public policies may heavily influence the degree of price transmission. All countries in the sample use fiscal regulatory instruments such as tariffs, subsidies, and value added tax (VAT), which directly add to or subtract from the transaction costs. Non-fiscal government market interventions, such as non-tariff trade barriers, parastatal grain traders (China, India, Vietnam, Ethiopia, Malawi, Zambia, and Egypt), and price controls (notably Senegal), disrupt the price transmission mechanisms in ways that are harder to generalize. Most countries responded to the global food crisis by expanding existing policies or introducing new regulations. The next section investigates in more detail these policy responses' likely impact on price transmission.

2.3 Political Intervention

During and after the global food crisis period, most governments in developing countries pursued a range of policies in attempts to reduce the transmission of the higher international prices to the domestic markets or to limit their adverse consequences (e.g., see Demeke, Pangrazio, and Maetz 2011 for a review). The fourteen country studies in the present sample describe similar policy responses (see Bryan, Chapter 3, for a comprehensive synthesis). The discussion of the possible impacts of policy interventions on price transmission is organized under three types of policies: trade policies, domestic policies, and macroeconomic policies. I end this section by briefly discussing issues surrounding design and implementation of policies.

2.3.1 *Trade Policies*

Border policies were pursued by many of the countries in the form of export restrictions and reductions of import tariffs (see Bryan, Chapter 3). Export restrictions are discussed first and import tariff waivers second.

By restricting exports, governments sought to reduce or completely disrupt the link between the international and the domestic prices. Obviously, the policy is likely to have the greatest effect when the export restriction is binding, i.e., if the country is already exporting the commodity or would have done so in the absence of the restriction. This is not to say that export restrictions are necessarily ineffective for an importer. If a cereal importer's price stabilization policies are effective or the country experiences a bumper harvest, domestic prices may drop below export parity, thus creating incentives for exporting to neighbouring countries that are stabilizing local prices less aggressively. Still, a consistent food importer may face additional obstacles to changing trade status in the short term as prospective exporters need to establish new export channels, demonstrate compliance with quality standards, etc. (Dawe 2010).

Export restrictions were implemented by China, Egypt, Ethiopia, India, Kenya, Malawi, Vietnam, and Zambia (Bryan, Chapter 3). They were, however, not likely to be equally binding everywhere. China, India, Vietnam, and Egypt appear to have had both the capacity (indicated by exports in the recent years) and the incentive (the international prices being higher than the domestic equivalents) to export rice, and in India's case, wheat. In contrast, it is doubtful that the export bans in Ethiopia and Kenya had much of an impact on price transmission. Although these countries have exported small quantities of maize in the recent past, the local prices have been much higher than the international prices. Malawi and Zambia are borderline cases: both have been exporting a small maize surplus to neighbouring countries recently. The domestic prices were roughly at par with international prices during the summer of 2008, whereas the prices in neighbouring countries, such as Mozambique and Kenya, were considerably higher. It is therefore quite possible that exports could have continued had the ban not been in effect (Chirwa and Chinsinga, Chapter 7, and Chapoto, Chapter 8, both report that some informal trade did take place in spite of the bans).

Suspending import tariffs may briefly halt or reverse the increase on domestic prices, but it will not sever the link to international prices. On the contrary, eliminating tariffs reduces transaction costs which may strengthen rather than weaken the market integration. Several countries suspended import tariffs on grains to partially compensate for the increasing international prices (Demeke et al. 2011). However, in many cases the tariffs were very low to begin with and hence the tariff waivers might only have had a marginal effect on price transmission.

Bangladesh, Egypt, and Senegal temporarily removed tariffs on rice and wheat, but they were already relatively low, between 2 and 10 per cent, so the impact must have been modest (United Nations Conference on Trade and Development (UNCTAD) TRAINS (Trade Analysis and Information System) database). Tariffs were much higher in Kenya and Nigeria and the tariff waivers have likely softened the impact of the higher international prices. It is noteworthy that these two countries experienced significant domestic price shocks in spite of the policy responses (see the discussion on price transmission in Kenya and Nigeria in sections 2.4.3 and 2.4.4 below).

2.3.2 *Domestic Policies*

Domestic policies cover interventions that are designed to adjust domestic prices directly (e.g., food subsidies, suspension of VAT, or direct price controls), policies implemented to increase domestic food supply (e.g., release of grains from strategic grain reserves and long-term improvements in agricultural production), and social protection policies. Investments in agriculture and other efforts to improve agricultural productivity are long-term measures which are unlikely to have a major effect on price transmission patterns within the food crisis period. Also, social protection policies (such as income transfers and food for work programmes) should not affect price transmission directly, although they may contribute to maintaining food demand (Demeke et al. 2011). These policies are therefore not the focus of this synthesis.

Food subsidies and elimination of domestic duties work largely the same way as tariff waivers, except that they affect domestically produced commodities and not just imported food. The impact of higher international prices on domestic retail prices is reduced, but market integration should, if anything, be strengthened by the lower transaction costs. Such price support policies were attempted in Bangladesh, China, Egypt, Ethiopia, Kenya, Mozambique, Senegal, Vietnam, and Zambia (Bryan, Chapter 3), but it is not possible to get a complete overview of their likely impact. We have little information on the size of the subsidies and VATs, and we know generally little about the extent to which subsidies were applied (universally or specifically targeted).

Price controls may completely disrupt the price transmission mechanism if they are successfully enforced. Among the fourteen study-countries, only Ethiopia, Malawi, and Senegal attempted to control prices directly. The experiences of Malawi and Senegal demonstrate the difficulties associated with fixing prices when enforcement mechanisms are lacking. In Malawi, a price band was supposed to be maintained through open market grain procurement and sales by ADMARC, a parastatal trader, but the agency lacked the necessary funds for its operation (Chirwa and Chinsinga, Chapter 7). In Senegal, the government promised to subsidize rice distributors in return for observing the price ceiling, but the policy backfired when the government was unable to disburse the funds on time (Resnick, Chapter 14).

Releasing grain from public stocks should not by itself directly affect price transmission if domestic markets are perfectly integrated with the world market. Any excess supply at prevailing world market prices would simply be exported. However, if markets are imperfectly integrated, possibly as a result of export restrictions, expansion of domestic supply should help depress domestic prices.

Among the fourteen study-countries, Bangladesh, China, Ethiopia, India, and Nigeria attempted to expand domestic supply by releasing stocks (Bryan, Chapter 3). It is difficult to evaluate the likely impact of such policies. Most of the country studies do not specify exactly how much grain was released, and the ones on Bangladesh, Egypt, Malawi, Senegal, and Zambia report that private traders responded to their governments' attempts at stabilizing prices by hoarding grain. If such behaviour is widespread, private stockpiling of grain could render public efforts at stabilizing prices largely ineffective.

2.3.3 *Macroeconomic Policies*

Macroeconomic policies, such as fiscal and monetary policies, tend to be blunt instruments for achieving food price stabilizing objectives. However, the food crisis and the food price policies discussed above have macroeconomic repercussions, so it is instructive to briefly review the role played by macroeconomic policies during the food crisis period.

Consider first fiscal policies. Attempting to stabilize food prices or alleviating the impacts of higher food prices is very expensive. Most of the food price policies pursued by the fourteen countries either reduce government revenue (suspension of import tariffs and VAT) or increase outlays (food subsidies, social transfers, and agricultural investments). They are not likely to be sustainable if needed for an extended period of time (Abbott and Borot de Battisti 2011). As a result, food price policies may temporarily reduce price transmission, but once fiscal constraints force governments to roll back the policies, the link between the international and the domestic prices is re-established, possibly with a lag. Several countries in the sample approached the fiscal limits during the crisis, partly due to aggressive grain market regulation. For instance, Egypt managed to expand relatively generous food subsidies by cutting other government expenses (such as fuel subsidies) (Ghoneim, Chapter 12), while price policies in Malawi and Senegal were rendered ineffective by lack of funds (Chirwa and Chinsinga, Chapter 7; Resnick, Chapter 14).

Several of the country studies view the food crisis from a monetary perspective. Admassie (Chapter 6) suggests that relatively accommodating monetary policies in the years prior to the food crisis were responsible for a significant portion of the observed Ethiopian food price inflation. In addition, the food crisis also coincided with rising general inflation in India and Bangladesh (Raihan, Chapter 11; Ganguly and Gulati, Chapter 16). One of the key responses to the crisis in these countries was tightening monetary policy. In contrast, Brazil found room for loosening monetary policies slightly by extending public credit, despite a strong focus on anti-inflationary policies (Mueller and Mueller, Chapter 18).

In a theoretical fully flexible economy, monetary policies should not influence the price transmission mechanism. Demand-driven inflation would increase domestic cereal prices denominated in local currency, but the exchange rate would depreciate by the same rate thus cancelling the effect of inflation on prices measured in foreign currency (US$). Economies are, however, not fully flexible and it is unlikely that exchange rate movements completely negate inflationary pressures, particularly in the short run. For instance, Ethiopia pursued a strongly inflationary monetary policy up to and during the food crisis period while placing strict controls on foreign exchange. As a result, the currency depreciated only marginally and the general inflationary pressures drove US$-denominated cereal prices higher (Minot 2011).

Exchange rate movements also greatly affect how US$-denominated price increases are transmitted to local-currency prices (Dawe 2008; Abbott and Borot de Battisti 2011). In this study, all price transmission evidence presented is measured in US$ prices in order to fully concentrate on the price transmission mechanism. Still, it is worthwhile briefly considering how exchange rate variations impacted on how domestic consumers experienced the food crisis. Consider for instance Brazil, where the price of maize rose by 122 per cent in US$ terms between June 2006 and June 2008. However, as the Brazilian real appreciated relative to the US$ over the same period, local currency denominated prices increased only by around 60 per cent. Most countries in the sample saw currency appreciation relative to the US$ (although not to the extent that Brazil did), but there are also exceptions. Due to the inflationary monetary policies in Ethiopia, the birr depreciated during the food crisis period and the price of maize rose by 189 per cent in US$ terms and 220 per cent when measured in local currency units.[2]

2.3.4 *Policy Implementation*

Policy interventions only work as intended if they are designed and implemented properly. Many of the country studies provide examples of

[2] The numbers are own calculations based on price data obtained from the FAO GIEWS food price database and exchange rates from International Monetary Fund (IMF) financial statistics.

interventions that have gone awry due to lack of information, poor government capacity, and political concerns, or corrupt practices.

Policy makers do not operate in an environment of perfect information, particularly when dramatic events, such as the global food crisis, call for swift action. Many of the studies indicate that government interventions based on poor information have been less effective or have even exacerbated the situation. For instance, incorrect harvest forecasts led the government of Vietnam to reduce the number of export licenses in a situation where Vietnam could have benefited from improved terms of trade (Nguyen and Talbot, Chapter 15). In contrast, the government of Malawi apparently overestimated the maize harvest and entered an export contract with Zimbabwe that could not be filled (Chirwa and Chinsinga, Chapter 7). One of the key lessons learned by the South African government from an earlier local food crisis in 2002–3, was the importance of accurate and timely information which led the government to establish a network for monitoring food prices more closely (Kirsten, Chapter 19).

Whether or not appropriate policies are designed, many governments, particularly in SSA, have limited capacity to implement the policies properly. Several of the country studies report that policies could not be enforced. For instance, substantial informal cross-border trade took place in Kenya, Malawi, and Zambia in violation of export bans (Chirwa and Chinsinga, Chapter 7; Chapoto, Chapter 8; Nzuma, Chapter 9). Malawi and Senegal imposed price controls, but they were largely ignored (Chirwa and Chinsinga, Chapter 7; Resnick, Chapter 14). Also, many of the policies pursued by the governments, such as food and input subsidies, import and VAT waivers, and social safety nets, put severe strain on the countries' fiscal resources.

An important constraint on policy implementation is the political economy of food price policy generating rent-seeking behaviour. The political environment shapes the choice, specific design, and implementation of food price policies, and policy implementation is also often influenced by politics and corruption. For a more in-depth analysis of the political economy of food price policy, see Watson (Chapter 5).

2.4 Price Transmission Patterns

The local grain markets in each of the fourteen countries in the country-study sample responded to the rising international grain prices in a variety of ways. Although no two stories are exactly the same, I attempt to identify some common patterns by classifying the fourteen countries into four categories: 'free traders', 'exporting stabilizers', 'importers', and 'the isolated'. This classification is based on an assessment of the local markets' exposure to international price shocks, largely determined by the countries' trade status and the strength and effectiveness of the food price policies pursued by the countries as detailed in the country studies. I chose the classification scheme to provide a rough guide to what kind of price transmission patterns we should expect to find. The classification is as follows:

1. Free traders: Brazil and South Africa are well-integrated into the global cereal markets as net importers, net exporters, or both (depending on harvests). They responded to the food crisis with few and relatively weak food price policies and we would therefore expect them to display a high degree of price transmission. As we will see, this is also largely what we find, although the picture is distorted a bit by trade regime shifts.
2. Exporting stabilizers: China, India, and Vietnam are all net exporters of rice, and they reacted forcefully to the rising international prices with strong food price policies. We would expect to see relatively weak price transmission in these countries as they have a powerful instrument, export restrictions, at their disposal. We find that in China and India these policies effectively stabilized local prices during the period, but the Vietnamese policies appeared to have had a limited impact.
3. Importers: Bangladesh, Egypt, Kenya, Mozambique, and Senegal are consistently dependent on imports of their main staples. They are exposed to international price volatility and in contrast to exporters they have very few means available for stabilizing local prices. Thus, we would expect price transmission to be relatively high. As we will see, the picture is rather mixed due to local factors and distorting policies.
4. The isolated: Ethiopia, Malawi, Nigeria, and Zambia are poorly integrated into global cereal markets and are largely self-sufficient in their main staple. In these cases, we would expect that domestic prices are primarily determined by local supply and demand factors and largely unrelated to global prices. Interestingly, we find that in spite of the countries' relatively isolated status, they all experienced sharply increasing food prices during the crisis period.

In the following, I summarize the price transmission patterns observed in the countries in these four groups, and discuss some of the main factors influencing the patterns. Ideally, this summary would present estimates of price transmission elasticities. There are, however, technical and conceptual problems involved with such methods, when applied to the food crisis period, primarily that the standard methods may not be strictly valid.[3]

[3] Technically, the price series are likely to be strongly non-stationary during the food crisis period, even in first-difference form, and standard inference methods may therefore not be valid.

Although these issues may be solvable, such attempts are beyond the scope of this synthesis. Instead, to give as clear and transparent picture of the price transmission patterns as possible, I provide a graphical representation of the international and domestic prices, and discuss in a bit more detail the main factors influencing the patterns.

2.4.1 *Free Traders*

The first group of countries consists of Brazil and South Africa. I call the group the free traders as both countries appear to be closely integrated into the world grain markets. In addition, they were pursuing fairly liberal food price policies during the crisis (as detailed in Mueller and Mueller, Chapter 18; and Kirsten, Chapter 19). This is also reflected in the relatively close co-movement of local maize, rice, and wheat prices with their international equivalents as illustrated in Figures 2.1, 2.2, and 2.3.

In most markets, the prices move close together. There are, however, a few exceptions. In South Africa, the price of maize seems to be a lot more volatile

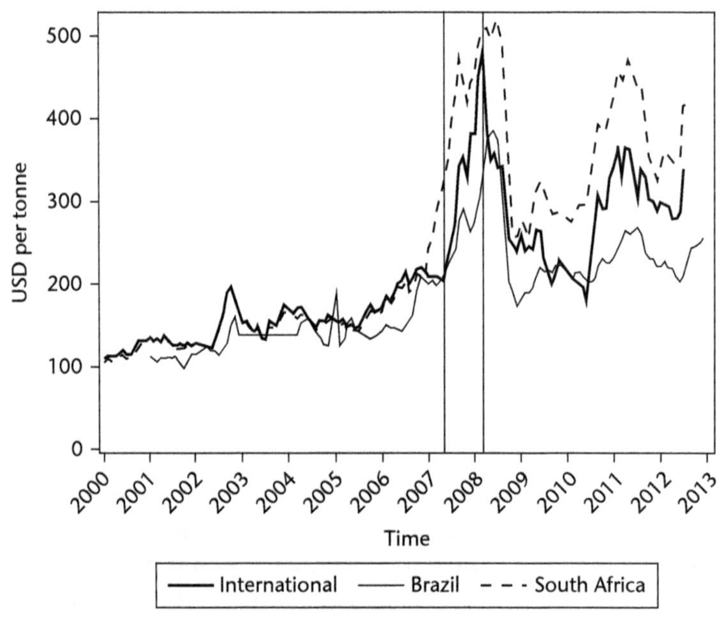

Figure 2.1 Maize prices in Brazil and South Africa

Note: International: US Gulf, no. 2', yellow maize. Brazil: national average, yellow maize, wholesale. South Africa: Randfontain, white maize, wholesale. US Gulf, no. 2 refers to the specific maize variety used to designate the international maize price. This is the most commonly used benchmark for an international maize price.

Source: FAO GIEWS food price database.

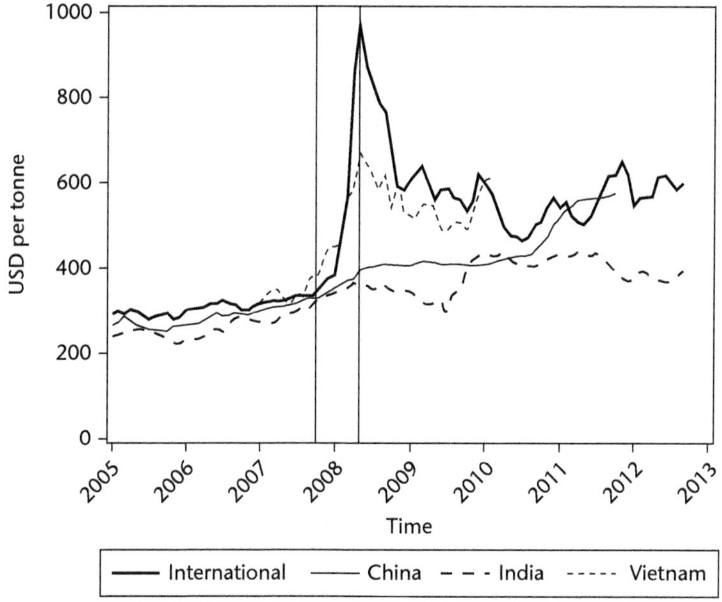

Figure 2.2 Rice prices in Brazil

Note: International: Bangkok, 'Thai 100% B'. Brazil: national average, wholesale. Thai 100% B refers to the specific rice variety used to designate the international rice price. This is the most commonly used benchmark for an international rice price.

Source: FAO GIEWS food price database.

than the international prices. There are relatively large gaps between the South African and the international maize price in 2002, 2004, 2006, and the second half of 2007, but the gaps seem to disappear briefly in 2003, 2005, and 2008. The South African maize market is characterized by substantial variation in production around what is needed to satisfy demand (FAOSTAT 2013a). As a result, South Africa shifts continuously between being a net importer and a net exporter of maize. When South Africa is a net importer, as in 2002, 2004, 2006, and 2007 (according to data from FAOSTAT 2013b), the domestic price approaches import parity, whereas periods of net exports (2003, 2005, and 2008) drive prices towards export parity (NAMC 2007, 2009). Kirsten (Chapter 19) finds that when such trade regime shifts are accounted for, the evidence suggests that South African grain markets are highly integrated into the world markets.

The only other market in this group which experienced regime shift during the crisis period is the Brazilian market for rice. Brazil is traditionally a rice net importer, but at the peak of the crisis in 2008, the country exported around 81,000 tons more than it imported, compared to a net import of 500,000 tons in 2007 (FAOSTAT 2013b). A shift in trade status could account

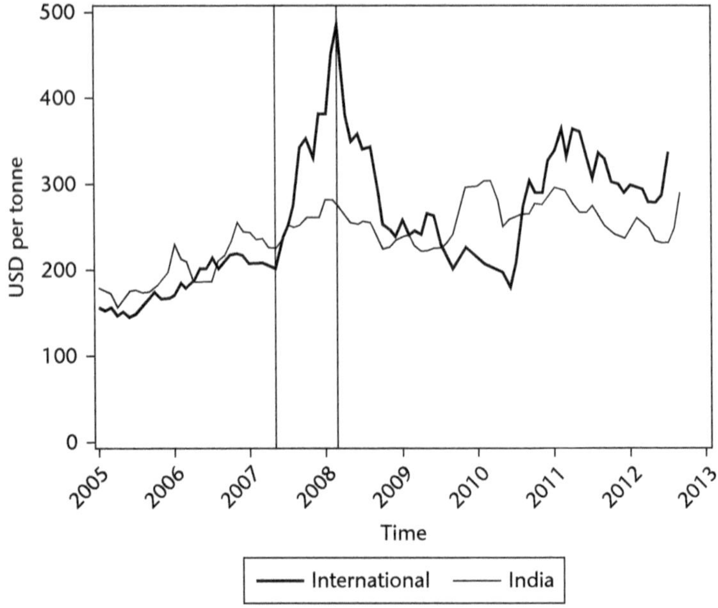

Figure 2.3 Wheat prices in Brazil and South Africa

Note: International: US Gulf, no. 2, hard winter red. Brazil: national average, wholesale. South Africa: Randfontain, wholesale. US Gulf, no. 2, hard winter red refers to the specific wheat variety used to designate the international wheat price. This is the most commonly used benchmark for an international wheat price.

Source: FAO GIEWS food price database.

for the relatively modest transmission of the international price peak as the domestic price declines (relative to international prices) from import parity towards export parity.

Both Brazil and South Africa are consistent net importers of wheat (FAOSTAT 2013b), so the domestic wheat prices tend to move closely with international prices (NAMC 2009). In Figure 2.3, discrepancies are evident during and after the global food crisis period, but the overall impression of substantial market integration remains.

2.4.2 *Exporting Stabilizers*

China and India successfully managed to stabilize local rice prices, primarily by banning exports. Vietnam also introduced export restrictions, but the stabilization policies were less effective. Common features of these three countries are that they are all net exporters of rice (India and Vietnam being two of the largest rice exporters in the world), and that grain trade tends to be heavily regulated. It therefore appears to have been relatively easy for these countries to control domestic grain supply, and stabilize prices. Evidence of this is illustrated in Figures 2.4 and 2.5.

Whereas the rice prices in China and India as well as wheat prices in India were virtually flat during the food crisis period, the price of rice in Vietnam did show a partially muted response to the surging international prices. One explanation may be that the Vietnamese prices are retail prices (wholesale prices were not available) which include additional marketing and profit margins. Another possibility is provided by Nguyen and Talbot (Chapter 15): the Vietnamese government sets rice export limits (by advice of the Ministry of Agriculture and Rural Development (MARD)) based on projected rice surplus and not rice prices per se. In the spring of 2008, MARD forecast a lean rice crop which prompted the government to reduce the maximum export quota by one million tons to 3.5–4 million tons for 2008, and impose a temporary three-month moratorium on signing new export contracts. In any event, the projection turned out to be faulty and rice farmers produced a bumper crop. The Vietnamese policies took the tip off the price spike but were not sufficient in isolating the domestic market completely.

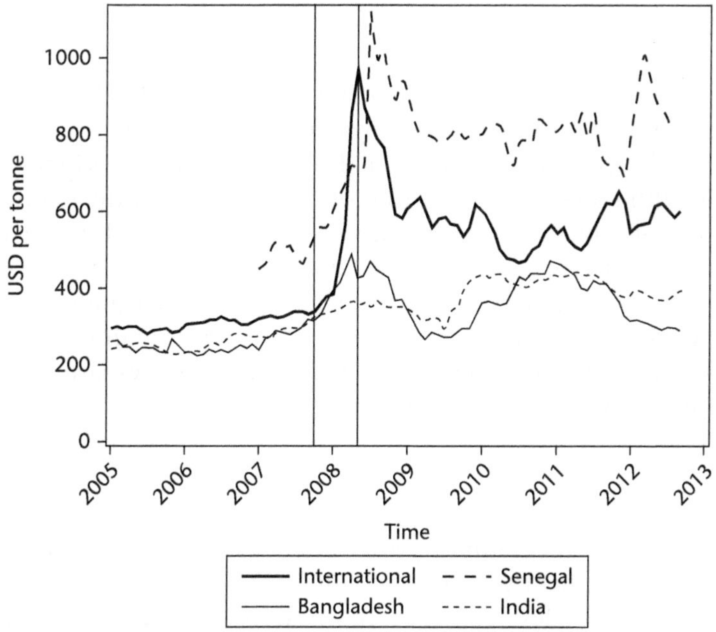

Figure 2.4 Rice prices in China, India, and Vietnam

Note: International: Bangkok, Thai 100% B. China: Hunan province, first quality, wholesale. India: Delhi, wholesale. Vietnam: Hanoi, retail.

Source: FAO GIEWS food price database.

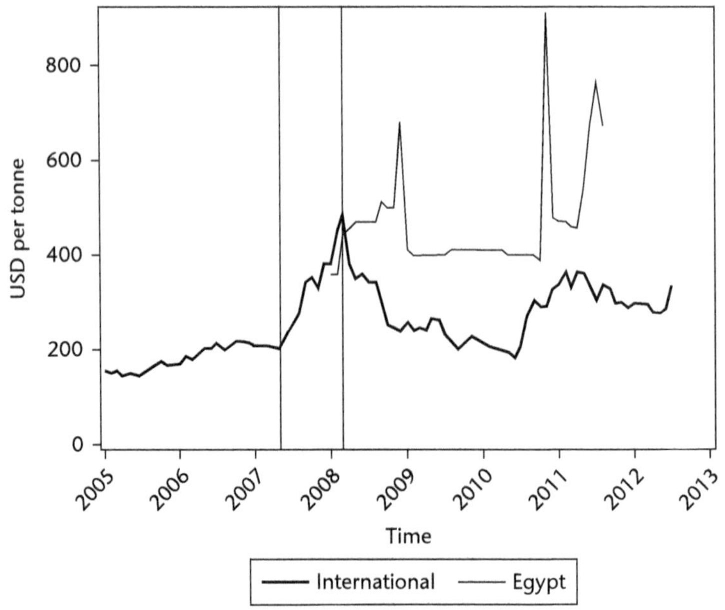

Figure 2.5 Wheat prices in India

Source: FAO GIEWS food price database. International: US Gulf, no. 2, hard winter red. India: Delhi, wholesale.

The Indian wheat and rice prices show an upward trend in the second half of 2009 (Figures 2.4 and 2.5). Ganguly and Gulati (Chapter 16) refer to this as a form of delayed price transmission. However, the increases in prices have less to do with (belated) transmission of price changes in the international market, but may be better explained by specific factors within India. India experienced relatively poor harvests in 2009, and following the food crisis of 2007–8, the government started to buy larger quantities of grain in an effort to expand the strategic grain reserves. Also, the MSPs for grains were adjusted upwards in the wake of the crisis, and the resulting higher farm gate prices were transmitted down through the value chain.

2.4.3 *Importers*

Five countries in the sample, Bangladesh, Egypt, Kenya, Senegal, and Mozambique consistently depend on imports for the supply of their main staple, rice in Bangladesh and Senegal, wheat in Egypt, and maize in Kenya and Mozambique.

Figure 2.6 shows the rice prices in Bangladesh and Senegal plotted against the international prices. I have also included the Indian rice price as India is the main supplier of Bangladeshi rice imports (Hossain and

Deb 2010). In fact, judging from Figure 2.6, the Bangladeshi rice price appears to be more closely related to the Indian price than the international (Thai export) price. Although both Senegal and Bangladesh were exposed to the international price volatility, they experienced the global crisis rather differently. In Bangladesh, the price shock is visible but quite modest. In Senegal, the rice price rose sharply and has stayed at a relatively high level ever since.

Rather than explaining why the rice prices increased in Bangladesh in the early 2008, a more interesting question is why they did not rise further. Raihan (Chapter 11) reports that the government in Bangladesh did seek to stabilize the rice prices but they had limited tools at their disposal. The most effective short-term policy response was the suspension of a 5 per cent import tariff on grains, which had at best a marginal effect. More importantly, Bangladesh managed to secure a supply of around half a million tons of rice from India in February 2008, just before the international price skyrocketed. However, it took a long time for the two governments to agree on a price and the first delivery arrived in April, just as the domestic rice harvest was about to hit the market (Hossain and Deb 2010). The 2008 season turned out to produce a bumper

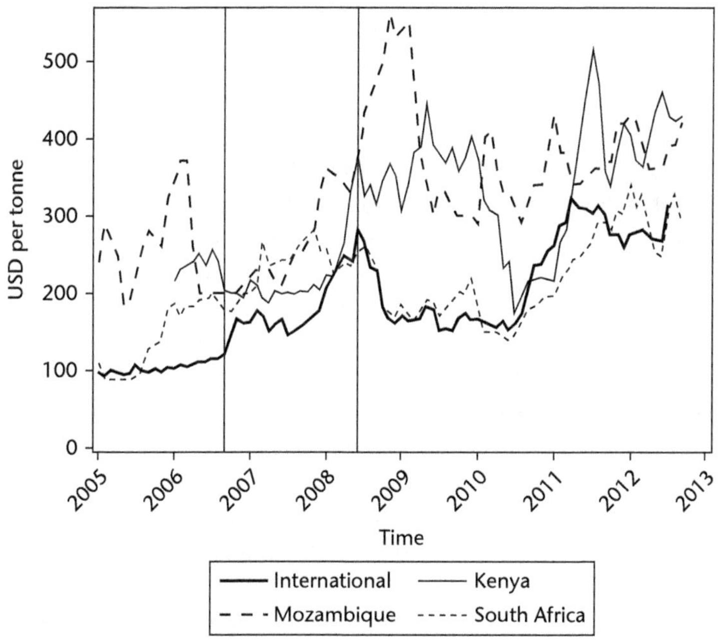

Figure 2.6 Rice prices in Bangladesh and Senegal

Note: International: Bangkok, Thai 100% B. India: Delhi, wholesale. Bangladesh: Dhaka, wholesale. Senegal: Dakar, imported, retail.

Source: FAO GIEWS food price database.

harvest, partly due to a massive supply response. In fact, for the first time in almost a decade, Bangladesh produced more than it used (FAOSTAT 2013a).

However, the question remains why private traders did not utilize the arbitrage opportunities and export rice from Bangladesh. The government did impose a ban on exports, but Dawe (2010) suggests that it had little effect in practice. As a traditional rice importer, Bangladesh lacks the capacity (in terms of quality assurance mechanisms and reputation) to export large quantities of rice in the short term.

Like Bangladesh, Senegal had few options available for reducing the impact of higher international rice prices. Import tariffs were already very low, and their suspension must have had little impact. To make matters worse, Senegal suffered two consecutive seasons of poor harvests in 2006–7 and 2007–8 due to shortages in agricultural inputs and irregular rainfall patterns (Resnick, Chapter 14). According to data from FAOSTAT (2013a), production in 2006 and 2007 was down almost 19 per cent compared to the average of the preceding three years. In response, the Senegalese government attempted to regulate rice prices directly. Senegal has had a long tradition of fixing bread prices, but as such price ceilings were extended to rice and other commodities, they could not be enforced and were therefore largely ignored. In response, the government struck an agreement with rice distributors by offering subsidies in return for lower retail prices. However, the subsidies turned out to be unsustainable and might actually have exacerbated the crisis. As the government was unable to pay out the subsidies on time, rice distributors started to stockpile rice in anticipation of future subsidy payments. As a result, rice prices continued to rise (Resnick, Chapter 14).

In the case of Egypt, it is difficult to assess the extent to which international prices were transmitted to domestic markets due to the lack of data: wholesale prices and retail prices are only available from January 2008 onwards. The evidence, shown in Figure 2.7, indicates a relatively stable retail price, but the apparent price stability was broken by short-lived spikes in late 2008, 2010, and 2011. The 2008 spike may represent a delayed response to the global food crisis; international wheat prices were also climbing in 2010 and 2011. Even so, any close relationship between international and Egyptian prices is not obvious. This rather mixed picture is consistent with the literature. Despite substantial wheat imports, Baffes and Gardner (2003) find that Egyptian wheat markets were very poorly integrated with global markets. However, Conforti (2004) and Rapsomanikis, Hallam, and Conforti (2006), show a long-term relationship between the Egyptian wholesale wheat prices and the international wheat prices after (but not before) 1989, despite strong regulation of Egyptian wheat markets.

An elaborate social protection infrastructure already existed in Egypt prior to the crisis. Large quantities of locally produced and imported wheat are

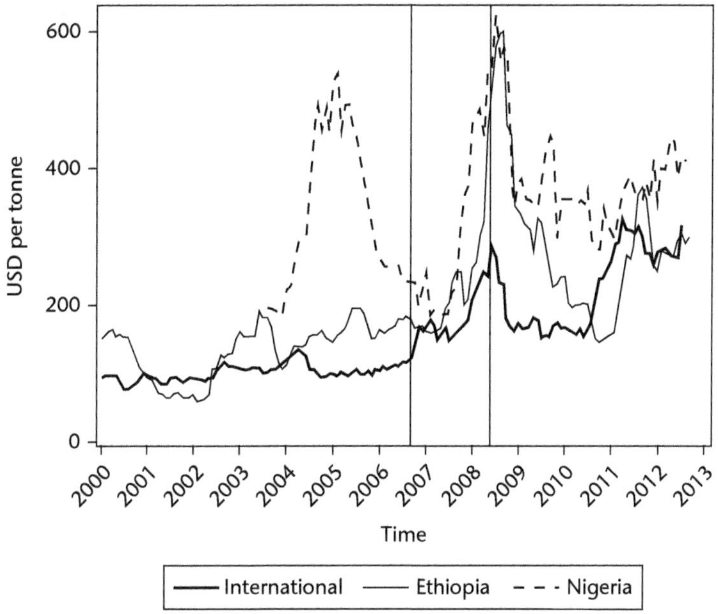

Figure 2.7 Wheat prices in Egypt

Note: International: US Gulf, no. 2, hard winter red. Egypt: Lower Egypt, retail.

Source: FAO GIEWS food price database.

procured by the General Agency for the Supply of Commodities (GASC, a government agency), milled in public mills, and processed in public bakeries into baladi bread which is sold in public shops at subsidized prices. In addition, a range of subsidized basic commodities (such as sugar, oil, and rice) are distributed to a large part of the population on the basis of ration cards. Although the social safety net is hugely expensive, inefficient, and mired by corruption and massive leakage, it does appear to have shielded the poor beneficiaries from the worst impact of the global food crisis (Ghoneim, Chapter 12).

Figure 2.8 shows the wholesale price of maize in Kenya and Mozambique, together with the international price and the maize wholesale price in South Africa, the main supplier of the two countries. The maize prices in Kenya and Mozambique rose substantially during the food crisis period but as the international and South African prices collapsed in the second half of 2008, domestic prices stayed at a high level. In the case of Mozambique, maize prices peaked half a year after the global crisis.

Closer inspection of the two countries suggests that domestic factors played a major role in the domestic maize price formation. Although Kenya and Mozambique are both consistent maize importers, Minot (2011) cannot find significant long-term relationship between the international (or South

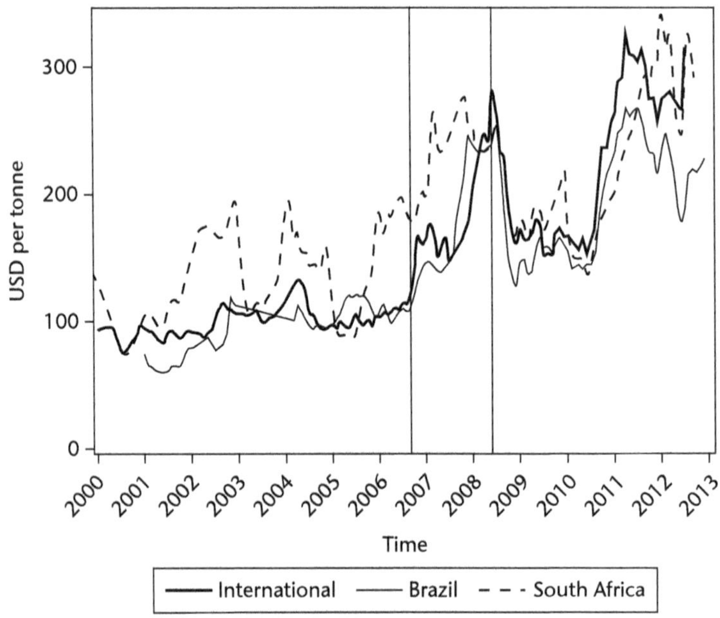

Figure 2.8 Maize prices in Kenya and Mozambique

Source: FAO GIEWS food price database. International: US Gulf, no. 2, yellow maize. Kenya: Nairobi, wholesale. South Africa: Randfontain, white maize, wholesale.

African) and domestic prices (however, he does find evidence of rice market integration in Mozambique).

In Kenya, several years of drought-induced poor harvests generated a need for large imports of maize in 2008 (Benson et al. 2008; Nzuma, Chapter 9). According to FAOSTAT (2013a), production in both 2008 and 2009 was down by 20 per cent compared to the average of the previous three years. As the developing global food crisis prompted neighbours, such as Tanzania and Malawi, to restrict their exports, the Kenyan government struggled to fill import orders throughout 2008. When the import needs were finally satisfied during 2009 (another drought-ridden year), imports of maize jumped from around 114,000 tons in 2007 and 244,000 tons in 2008 to 1.5 million tons in 2009 (FAOSTAT 2013b). Insofar as the massive increase in imports represents a buildup of an acute supply shortage, it is not surprising that the maize prices increased in 2008 and persisted throughout the year. What is, perhaps, surprising is that Kenya was unable to satisfy its import needs for such a long time in the aftermath of the global food crisis. Although the regional export bans stayed in effect throughout 2008, Kenya's main import supplier of maize was not Malawi or Tanzania but South Africa, which did not restrict maize exports. In fact, according to the data from the UN Commodity Trade Statistics Database

(COMTRADE), South Africa ended up supplying two-thirds of Kenya's maize imports in 2009.

The picture is not quite as clear in the case of Mozambique. FEWS NET (2009) reports that the country was hit by floods, rainfall deficits, and wild-fires in different areas which affected harvests adversely. It is, however, not clear if these events were particularly severe compared to the earlier years. Maize harvests in 2007 and 2008 were around the same size as the average of the previous three years (FAOSTAT 2013a). Arndt et al. (2008) suggest that part of the domestic price shock was due to the unusually high international prices as the government did little to prevent price transmission (see also Nhate, Massingarela, and Salvucci, Chapter 10). Also, part of the price volatility in Figure 2.8 seems to be seasonal. Prices tend to increase towards the 'hunger season' from October to January (FEWS NET 2009), as output from the second harvest is no longer available to cushion the prices (Arndt et al. 2008). The large price spike following the global price peak coincides with this period.

2.4.4 *The Isolated*

Among the fourteen countries included in the sample, Ethiopia, Malawi, Nigeria, and Zambia are relatively isolated from the international cereal markets. Ethiopia experiences substantial variations in maize production over time (FAOSTAT 2013a), but domestic storage serves to close the gaps between production and use with little reliance on international trade (Tadesse and Guttormsen 2011). Demand for maize in Nigeria tends to follow domestic supply quite closely (FAOSTAT 2013a), although Nigeria is dependent upon imports of rice (Olomola, Chapter 13). Malawi and Zambia have traditionally depended on maize imports from neighbouring countries, but both countries recently managed to become largely self-sufficient in maize and even produced a small surplus for exports (Chirwa and Chinsinga, Chapter 7; Chapoto, Chapter 8; FAOSTAT 2013a, 2013b).

Figure 2.9 shows the maize prices in Ethiopia and Nigeria together with the international reference price. Both countries experience sharply increasing prices during the global food crisis period, but the domestic price spikes are substantially larger than the international price shock. It also takes longer for the domestic prices to come down again—especially in Nigeria.

There is some debate over the extent to which the Ethiopian food prices were driven by domestic factors or the international crisis. The isolated (and landlocked) nature of Ethiopia together with its very limited international food trade would suggest that the domestic market should be fairly unrelated to international markets. However, the evidence appears to be mixed. In their empirical studies, Ulimwengu, Workneh, and Paulos (2009) and Minot

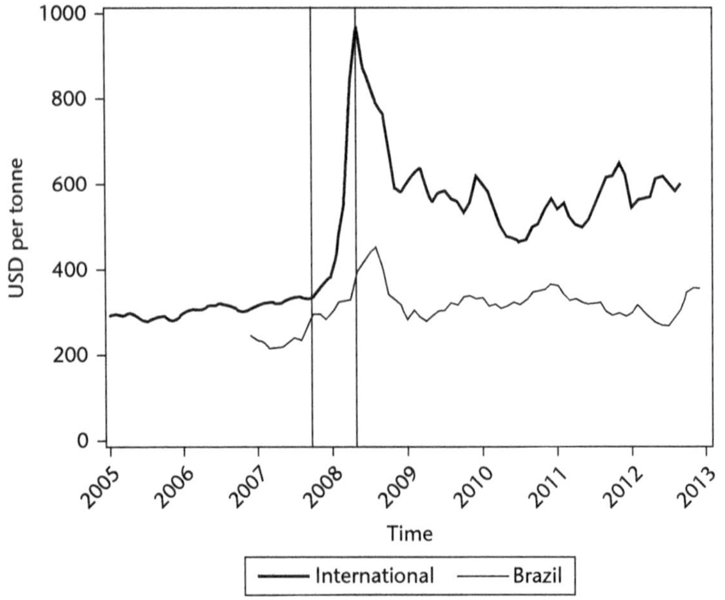

Figure 2.9 Maize prices in Ethiopia and Nigeria

Source: FAO GIEWS food price database. International: US Gulf, no. 2, yellow maize. Ethiopia: Addis Ababa, wholesale. Nigeria: Kano, wholesale.

(2011) find no long-run relationship between Ethiopian maize, sorghum, or wheat markets. In contrast, Conforti (2004) and Loening et al. (2009) do find long-run co-integration between the Ethiopian and international grain prices.

Admassie (Chapter 6) argues that the Ethiopian crisis was primarily caused by long-running domestic factors, such as increasing grain demand due to economic growth and more well-developed social safety nets, stagnating grain supply, and inflationary monetary policy. The trigger came in 2008, when the surging global energy prices led to a shortage of foreign exchange reserves which prompted the government to ration the foreign exchange available for other purposes such as imports of food.

The inflationary monetary policy explanation for the observed food price inflation has gained a lot of traction, particularly among economists at the World Bank and the IMF (Haji and Gelaw 2012). Foreign exchange controls prevented the currency from depreciating and rapidly rising prices denominated in domestic currency translated directly into high food inflation measured in US$ (Minot 2011).

There is little doubt that Ethiopia experienced high and growing general inflation in 2007 and 2008. It is less clear, however, that food inflation was necessarily driven by demand fueled by expansionary monetary policies.

Food inflation, particularly in cereal prices, was substantially higher than non-food inflation during the food crisis period (FAO/WFP 2009). While demand-driven inflation does not necessarily entail that all prices grow by the same rate, it is still remarkable that Ethiopia had the largest food inflation rate relative to non-food inflation in the developing world (3.5 per cent per month) in 2008, and negative relative food inflation in both 2009 and 2010 (Headey et al. 2012).

In the light of this discussion, it is unlikely that Ethiopian food prices were determined by solely domestic or international factors. In support of this assertion, Haji and Gelaw (2012) decompose food price inflation into different components and find that a number of factors affected domestic food prices, including domestic price level, world grain prices, domestic fuel prices, and non-food prices. Unfortunately, it is not straightforward to assess the relative weight of the different factors in forming domestic prices.

Admassie (Chapter 6) presents another piece of interesting evidence, reproduced here using data from FAO. Figure 2.10 shows a relatively close relationship between different Ethiopian cereal prices—indeed the maize and wheat prices appear to be much more closely related to each other than their respective international counterparts. This is consistent with the explanation of food prices being driven by inflationary monetary policy. But it could also

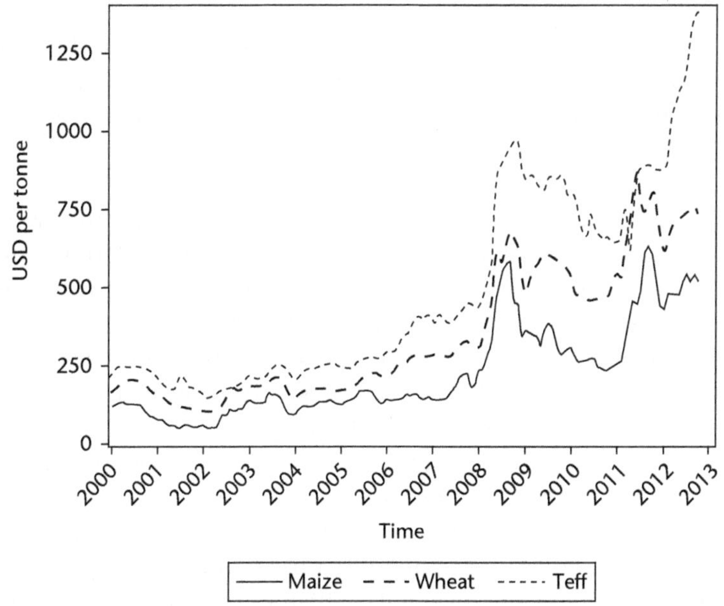

Figure 2.10 Maize, wheat, and teff prices in Ethiopia
Source: FAO GIEWS food price database.

indicate an additional (and sometimes forgotten) channel of price transmission. Price increases in one grain commodity are likely to spill-over to other related commodities as demand shifts from more expensive to cheaper staples.

In Ethiopia, this mechanism appears to be quite strong. Rashid (2011) finds a close relationship between the wheat and maize prices, but the correlation between these and the teff price is limited. Furthermore, his analysis suggests that transmission from maize to wheat is stronger than vice versa. It is possible that whatever influence the global cereal markets have on the Ethiopian prices, it works through a single commodity rather than through multiple commodities simultaneously.

Nigeria has not been studied as closely as Ethiopia and less data is available. However, there appear to be many similarities with the Ethiopian case. Nigeria is self-sufficient in maize, yet maize prices spiked along with (and greatly surpassing) the international price during the 2008 food price crisis (see Figure 2.9). However, unlike Ethiopia, Nigeria also experienced a surge in maize prices in 2005 that was almost as large in nominal terms as the one in 2008. This earlier price spike occurred at a time where international prices were relatively stable which suggests that the Nigerian maize prices are predominantly driven by domestic factors. There was no obvious shortfall in production in 2005, but there was a small surplus in 2006—equivalent to 10 per cent of production (FAOSTAT 2013a). It is possible that a part of the price spikes in 2005 and 2008 reflects unusually low prices in 2006 and 2007, following an increase in production in 2006.

Nigeria imports a substantial part of its rice consumption, but unfortunately no data on the Nigerian rice prices were available on a monthly basis. Yearly averages presented by Olomola (Chapter 13) show that rice prices also rose in 2008, but more detailed price transmission patterns cannot be established for rice.

The maize prices in Malawi and Zambia are depicted in Figure 2.11 along with the international price and the regional reference price in South Africa. Both the domestic price series show an upward trend during the food crisis period, but generally the prices display a relatively high volatility and do not show any obvious relationship with any of the reference prices. Minot (2011) finds weak (insignificant) long-run links between the international prices and a few of the local Malawian markets close to the border, but no evidence of any long-run relationship between the Zambian and international prices. Both countries face very high international trade costs and international trade in maize is strictly under the control of the government (Chirwa and Chinsinga, Chapter 7; Chapoto, Chapter 8). They both have a history of relatively frequent food crises during which local maize prices increase rapidly relative to international prices, latest in 2005–6. All this suggests that prices are mainly

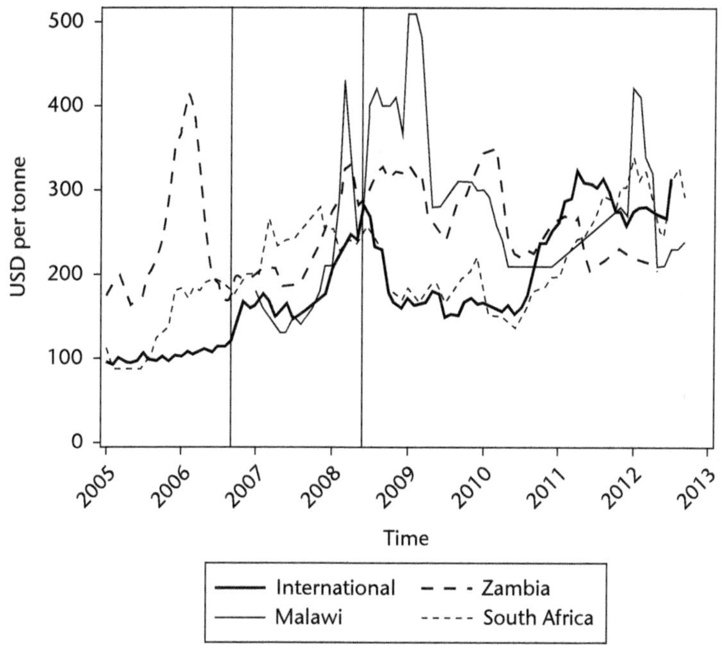

Figure 2.11 Maize prices in Malawi and Zambia

Source: FAO GIEWS food price database. International: US Gulf, no. 2, yellow maize. Malawi: Lilongwe, retail. Zambia: national average, white maize, retail. South Africa: Randfontain, white maize, wholesale.

determined by domestic factors and that international prices should play a very limited role.

Malawi experienced good weather and a bountiful harvest in 2007 (the surplus was smaller, but still positive in 2008). Zambia faced flooding in parts of the country and output declined slightly in both 2007 and 2008, compared to 2006. However, 2006 was a good year, and harvests in 2007 and 2008 were still in line with a long-term upward trend (FAOSTAT 2013a). Chirwa and Chinsinga (Chapter 7) and Chapoto (Chapter 8) suggest that the local crisis was largely precipitated by government mismanagement combined with private hoarding behaviour. In Malawi, very poor quality of information about the domestic maize supply led the private sector to believe that there was a shortage of maize, inducing speculative hoarding of maize in anticipation of higher prices in the future. In response to the initial price increases, the government banned exports (and cancelled a partially filled export agreement with Zimbabwe) and tried to restrict private domestic trading in an effort to control prices. These initiatives merely reinforced the signals of supply shortages and led to more intensive hoarding of maize. In Zambia, reports of flooding initiated the increase in maize prices, and as the government responded by banning exports, speculative forces similar to those in Malawi added to the price pressure.

Although there appears to be little direct relationship between the global food crisis and the local crises experienced in Malawi and Zambia, it is possible that the high global prices acted as catalysts for the local market tensions. Chirwa and Chinsinga (Chapter 7) and Chapoto (Chapter 8) suggest that the local maize prices were largely driven by hoarding, driven by expectations of higher prices. It is possible that these expectations were also influenced by the global food outlook, just as the global food crisis could have inspired greater unease among the government officials and prompted them to misjudge the appropriate policy response.

2.5 Conclusion

Drawing a few general conclusions from fourteen very different stories on how the global food crisis was experienced and managed is not an easy task. Yet, it is possible to identify certain patterns shared by several of the countries. Here are the most important ones: the synthesis categorized the fourteen countries according to their trade status to generate predictions regarding the price transmission patterns. The four categories are:

1. Free traders: as well-integrated and open agricultural economies, Brazil and South Africa were expected to exhibit a relatively large degree of price transmission. The evidence presented here is consistent with this prediction, although the close relationship between the South African and international maize price is sometimes masked by changes in trade status (between exporter and importer), which cause the domestic price to shift between export and import parity.
2. Exporting stabilizers: China, India, and Vietnam are exporters of rice, and they all have effective state-control over exports. Although the countries' strong exporter status should generate a close relationship between domestic and international prices, effective price stabilization policies (primarily in the form of export restrictions) were expected to reduce price transmission substantially in the time of crisis. This prediction is strongly supported in the cases of China and India, but the Vietnamese retail rice prices showed a surprisingly strong pass-through of international prices, despite export restrictions.
3. Importers: of the fourteen countries in the sample, Bangladesh, Egypt, Kenya, Mozambique, and Senegal are consistently dependent upon imports of their main staple. Unlike exporters, the import-dependent countries have few stabilizing policies available, and price transmission

was therefore expected to be substantial. However, the evidence painted a rather mixed picture. While Bangladesh managed to contain domestic rice prices at relatively low levels (indeed, price pass-through was smaller than in Vietnam), domestic prices in Kenya, Mozambique, and Senegal rose rapidly during the crisis and stayed high long after the international crisis had subsided. Egypt appears to have been greatly affected by the food crisis as well, but the evidence is more difficult to evaluate due to data limitations.

4. The isolated: Ethiopia, Nigeria, Malawi, and Zambia are poorly integrated with the international cereal markets and are largely self-sufficient in their main staple. Due to these countries' relatively isolated status, we should expect domestic prices to be independent from the international prices. It is therefore striking to observe that they all faced rapidly increasing domestic prices during the food crisis period. In Ethiopia and Nigeria, the maize price spike surpassed the international prices by several orders of magnitude, and Malawi and Zambia experienced persistently high prices.

The synthesis discusses two overall reasons for why we observed unexpected price transmission patterns: issues related to the implementation of policies and various domestic factors. Although food price policies aimed at controlling local prices were implemented in most countries, they were not equally effective everywhere. Export bans were not always binding (e.g. Ethiopia and Kenya), and in Vietnam export restrictions were reportedly designed to counter a perceived domestic shortfall rather than the international crisis. Suspended import tariffs were often already low, particularly in import-dependent countries (e.g., Bangladesh, Egypt, Mozambique, and Senegal). Many of the policies, particularly food subsidies and tax exemptions, represented a heavy drain on government finances and were unsustainable in the long term (as acutely felt in Egypt, Malawi, and Senegal). Also, many of the country studies suggest that government mismanagement rendered policies less effective or even exacerbated the crisis (Nigeria, Malawi, Senegal, and Zambia).

It is difficult to evaluate to what extent the local price shocks reflected domestic factors or were driven by the global crisis. On the one hand, it is remarkable that almost all of the countries experienced domestic price shocks that coincided with the global price spike (sometimes with a short time lag), even those (such as Ethiopia, Nigeria, Kenya, and Mozambique) that empirical research suggests are poorly integrated with the world markets. On the other hand, correlation is not the same as causation and certain signs indicate that domestic factors must have played a primary role in many countries. In Ethiopia, Kenya, Nigeria, and Mozambique, local shocks were much greater than the global shock, and it is hard to explain how price transmission alone could have generated such a major local price response. In Egypt, Malawi, and Zambia, the domestic prices spiked during the food crisis period, but apart from that, local prices show very little obvious relationship to international prices. Also, several of these countries, including Nigeria, Mozambique, and Zambia have earlier experienced episodes of great price volatility that were clearly not related to international prices. It is also possible to identify local supply constraints that can explain a substantial part of the local price shocks: harvest failures in Kenya and Senegal, flooding in parts of Mozambique and Zambia, generally tight markets combined with inflationary policies in Ethiopia, and poorly designed and implemented food policies in Malawi, Senegal, and Zambia. On a more positive note, a domestic supply response may also explain why the food crisis in Bangladesh was relatively benign: a bumper harvest was beginning to hit the markets just as international rice prices spiked.

References

Abbott, P., and A. Borot de Battisti (2011). 'Recent Global Food Price Shocks: Causes, Consequences and Lessons for African Governments and Donors'. *Journal of African Economies*, 20 (suppl. 1): i12–i62.

Arndt, C., R. Benfica, N. Maximiano, A. M. D. Nucifora, and J. T. Thurlow (2008). 'Higher Fuel and Food Prices: Impacts and Responses for Mozambique'. *Agricultural Economics*, 39: 497–511.

Baffes, J., and B. Gardner (2003). 'The Transmission of World Commodity Prices to Domestic Markets Under Policy Reforms in Developing Countries'. *The Journal of Policy Reform*, 6(3): 159–80.

Benson, T., S. Mugarura, and K. Wanda (2008). 'Impacts in Uganda of Rising Global Food Prices: The Role of Diversified Staples and Limited Price Transmission'. *Agricultural Economics*, 39: 513–24.

Conforti, P. (2004). 'Price Transmission in Selected Agricultural Markets'. Commodity and Trade Policy Research Working Paper 7. Rome: Food and Agriculture Organization (FAO).

Cudjoe, G., C. Breisinger, and X. Diao (2010). 'Local Impacts of a Global Crisis: Food Price Transmission, Consumer Welfare and Poverty in Ghana'. *Food Policy*, 35(4): 294–302.

Dawe, D. (2008). 'Have Recent Increases in International Cereal Prices Been Transmitted to Domestic Economies? The Experience in Seven Large Asian Countries'. ESA Working Paper 3. Rome: Food and Agriculture Organization (FAO).

Dawe, D. (2010). 'Can the Next Rice Crisis Be Prevented?'. In D. Dawe (ed.), *The Rice Crisis: Markets, Policies and Food Security*. London and Washington, DC: Food and Agriculture Organization (FAO) and Earthscan.

de Janvry, A., and E. Sadoulet (2010). 'The Global Food Crisis and Guatemala: What Crisis and for Whom?'. *World Development*, 38(9): 1328–39.

Demeke, M., G. Pangrazio, and M. Maetz (2011). 'Country Responses to Turmoil in Global Food Markets: The Nature and Preliminary Implications of the Policies Pursued in the 2006–08 Episode'. In A. Prakash (ed.), *Safeguarding Food Security in Volatile Global Markets*. Rome: Food and Agriculture Organization (FAO).

Fackler, P. L., and B. K. Goodwin (2001). 'Spatial Price Analysis'. In B. L. Gardner and G. C. Rausser (eds), *Handbook of Agricultural Economics*, vol. 1, Part 2. Amsterdam: Elsevier.

FAO GIEWS (2013). 'Global Information and Early Warning System: Food Price Data and Analysis Tool'. Rome: Food and Agriculture Organization (FAO).

FAO (Food and Agriculture Organization)/WFP (World Food Programme) (2009). 'Special Report: Crop and Food Security Assessment Mission to Ethiopia'. Rome: FAO/WFP.

FAOSTAT (Food and Agriculture Organization Statistics Division) (2013a). 'Food Balance Sheets'. Rome: FAO.

FAOSTAT (Food and Agriculture Organization Statistics Division) (2013b). 'Trade Database, Crops and Livestock Products'. Rome: FAO.

FEWS NET (Famine Early Warning Systems Network) (2009). 'Mozambique Food Security Outlook'. FEWS NET and USAID (United States Agency for Interntional Development).

Haji, J., and F. Gelaw (2012). 'Determinants of the Recent Soaring Food Inflation in Ethiopia'. *Universal Journal of Education and General Studies*, 1(8): 225–33.

Headey, D., F. B. Nisrane, I. Worku, M. Dereje, and A. S. Taffesse (2012). 'Urban Wage Behaviour and Food Price Inflation: The Case of Ethiopia'. Ethiopia Strategy Support Programme II Working Paper 41. Addis Ababa: IFPRI (International Food Policy Research Institute) and EDRI (Ethiopian Development Research Institute).

Hossain, M., and U. Deb (2010). 'Volatility in Rice Prices and Policy Responses in Bangladesh'. In D. Dawe (ed.), *The Rice Crisis: Markets, Policies and Food Security*. London and Washington, DC: FAO (Food and Agriculture Organization) and Earthscan.

Loening, J. L., D. Durevall, and J. A. Birru (2009). 'Inflation Dynamics and Food Prices in an Agricultural Economy: The Case of Ethiopia'. Policy Research Working Paper 347. Washington, DC: World Bank.

Minot, N. (2011). 'Transmission of World Food Price Changes to Markets in Sub-Saharan Africa'. IFPRI (International Food Policy Research Institute) Discussion Paper 1059. Washington, DC: IFPRI.

NAMC (National Agriculural Marketing Council) (2007). 'The South African Food Cost Review 2007'. Pretoria: NAMC.

NAMC (National Agriculural Marketing Council) (2009). 'The South African Food Cost Review 2009'. Pretoria: NAMC and the Department of Agriculture, Forestry and Fisheries.

Rapsomanikis, G., D. Hallam, and P. Conforti (2006). 'Market Integration and Price Transmission in Selected Food and Cash Crop Markets in Sub-Saharan Africa'. In A. Sarris and D. Hallam (eds.), *Agricultural Commodity Markets and Trade*.

New Approaches to Analyzing Market Structure and Instability. Cheltenham and Northampton, MA: Edward Elgar and FAO (Food and Agriculture Organization).

Rashid, S. (2011). 'Intercommodity Price Transmission and Food Price Policies: An Analysis of Ethiopian Cereal Markets'. IFPRI (International Food Policy Research Institute) Discussion Paper 1079. Washington, DC: IFPRI.

Robles, M. (2011). 'Price Transmission from International Agricultural Commodity Markets to Domestic Food Prices: Case Studies in Asia and Latin America'. Washington, DC: IFPRI (International Food Policy Research Institute).

Tadesse, G., and A. G. Guttormsen (2011). 'The Behavior of Commodity Prices in Ethiopia'. *Agricultural Economics*, 42(1): 87–97.

Ulimwengu, J. M., S. Workneh, and Z. Paulos (2009). 'Impact of Soaring Food Price in Ethiopia'. IFPRI (International Food Policy Research Institute) Discussion Paper 846. Washington, DC: IFPRI.

UN COMTRADE (United Nations Commodity Trade Statistics Database) (2013). 'United Nations Commodity Trade Statistics Database'. Accessed through World Integrated Trade Solution (WITS). New York: United Nations Statistics Division.

UNCTAD (United Nations Conference on Trade and Development) TRAINS (Trade Analysis and Information System) (2013). 'Trade Analysis and Information Systems'. Accessed through World Integrated Trade Solution (WITS). Geneva: UNCTAD.

3

A Cacophony of Policy Responses

Evidence from Fourteen Countries during the 2007–8 Food Price Crisis

*Shane Bryan**

3.1 Introduction

This study is a synthesis of all policy responses reported in fourteen country studies. Drawing from the rich accounts supplied by country-study authors, it provides an overview of each country's crisis response including details as to the magnitude, timing, and other policy particulars. Although this study is primarily intended as a synthesis, it also examines differences in policy responses across countries and, where available in the country studies, presents evidence concerning the factors which mitigated or enhanced policy effectiveness.

The remainder of the study proceeds as follows. Section 3.2 lays out the framework used to classify policies and countries. Section 3.3, which covers policy responses, is divided into three sub-sections according to policy type—price policies, output policies, and safety nets. Each sub-section in Section 3.3 is further divided according to country type. In this way the study reviews price policies for each of the three country types—interveners,

* This study would not have been possible without the hard work of the country-study authors and the author extends his first thanks to them. Earlier versions of this study benefited from the constructive comments of a number of reviewers including Robert Paarlberg, Lynn Brown, Kenneth Baltzer, and Derrill Watson II to whom the author owes hearty thanks for their sharp insights and corrective guidance. Finally, the author would like to thank Per Pinstrup-Andersen for his comments and guidance during the entire process. The author takes sole responsibility for all remaining errors and omissions.

observers, and dabblers—then output policies, and lastly safety nets. Finally, Section 3.4 provides concluding observations.

3.2 Analytical Framework

In order to facilitate comparison between different countries and the policies each pursued, this study has been structured around policy type—increasing production, reducing or stabilizing prices, or protecting vulnerable groups—and country category. The three policy types loosely follow Wiggins et al. (2010), but with at least one notable exception. Wiggins et al. only consider short-term policy responses. To provide as much detail as possible regarding crisis responses, this study includes all policies. More than just comprehensiveness, this approach is justified in that policy is not made in a vacuum and implementing one policy may influence a government's will or ability to implement others. A final point regarding short-term versus medium-term and long-term responses is that some policies defy such classification. Short-term production subsidies may have long-term impacts; furthermore, without the benefit of hindsight it is difficult to determine whether a policy intended to be temporary actually was.

Countries have been organized into three broad categories according to the degree to which they responded to the crisis. The first and largest category, consisting of Egypt, Ethiopia, Kenya, Malawi, Senegal, Zambia, China, and India, will be referred to as the interveners. This designation represents the willingness of each of these eight countries to go to extraordinary lengths to manage food prices. The second category of countries, consisting of only South Africa and Brazil, will be referred to as the observers; authorities in both countries took note of developments in food markets, contemplated taking action, but, believing existing social safety nets sufficient, ultimately decided to do little more than continue monitoring developments. The third category of countries defies categorization as either interveners or observers and will be referred to as dabblers. Bangladesh,[1] Mozambique, Nigeria, and Vietnam responded to the crisis, but are distinct from interveners in that these countries' responses were more restrained. It is an open question why these countries demonstrated more restraint than their intervening counterparts, though it may be due to political economy concerns (Watson, Chapter 5) or underlying structural factors (Baltzer, Chapter 2).

[1] As will be demonstrated later in the study, Bangladesh is somewhat of a borderline case and responded in many ways more like an intervener. It was ultimately included among dabblers because it failed to implement broad untargeted subsidies or price controls and because its export ban was mostly symbolic. All other interveners put into place binding export restrictions, price controls, untargeted subsidies, or some combination of the three.

3.3 Policy Responses

3.3.1 *Price Policies*

Following Wiggins et al. (2010) price policies refer to measures intended to reduce or stabilize food prices. Price policies can be implemented at the border (e.g., export bans and tariff adjustments) or within the domestic market (e.g., price controls and untargeted subsidies). This is a departure from typical policy classifications and is intended to capture the economic rationale behind these policies during the crisis period. To present all of the policies as concisely as possible, this study has divided price policies into four sub-categories: supply management measures; export bans; tariff and VAT adjustments; and price controls, broad subsidies, and monetary policy (see Table 3.1).

INTERVENERS

Each of the eight countries in this category responded with price policies, and nearly all of them responded with at least one price policy from each of the four price policy categories making price policy the most common response among interveners. Despite these interventions, prices almost invariably spiralled out of control—China and India being the two exceptions. Underlying structural factors and domestic market conditions account for much of the price behaviour experienced in the present sample (Baltzer, Chapter 2). Lack of market integration, for example, mitigated transmission and poor harvests reduced the ability of many interveners to effectively manage prices. As discussed by Baltzer (Chapter 2), these factors were possibly compounded by grain substitution and the resulting spill-over of price hikes from one grain market to another. In addition, many of the intervener country studies implicate the strategic behaviour of market participants as exacerbating price movements and reducing policy effectiveness. This behaviour, especially hoarding, has also been recognized in the broader literature (Timmer 2009; Jayne and Tschirley 2010). A final factor discussed by country-study authors as to why policies succeeded or failed to control prices is the actual effectiveness of the policy itself. Many authors fault poorly formulated policies, lack of funding, flawed implementation, or poor timing or coordination for the lack of anticipated results. Where evidence is available in the country studies that such factors were at play, it is woven into the discussion which follows.

All of the interveners in our sample engaged in activities to manage grain supply (see Table 3.1). Many authors report both release of reserves into the market and increased procurement. In most cases it is unclear if these actions were undertaken simultaneously so that increased procurement

Table 3.1 Intervener price policies

Country	Supply Management	Export Bans	Import/Export Tariffs & VAT	Price Controls, Broad Subsidies & Monetary Policy
Egypt	Wheat procurement increased from 1.8 million tons in 2006/7 to 2.5 million tons in 2007/8	Export ban on rice (Apr. 2008)	Export tariff on rice (late 2006), increased in 2007 and 2008; suspension of rice import tariffs (Apr. 2008)	Food subsidies doubled between 2006/7 and 2008/9, mostly for baladi bread; 15–22 million people added to ration card system (Jan. 2008)
Ethiopia	Informal suspension of WFP local procurement; increased imports	Export ban on teff, wheat, maize, and sorghum (Dec. 2006); later expanded to all cereals (Jun. 2008)	VAT and turnover tax suspended for all major food items and cereals (Mar. 2008)	Price ceiling on certain foods; enforced by task force with mandate to close shops and arrest non-compliant traders Release of at least 5,000 Mt of emergency wheat reserves to mills; sales to urban mills at subsidized prices Loose monetary policy leading up to crisis; tighter during crisis with reserve requirements increased from 5% to 10% in 2007 then 15% in 2008; liquidity requirements for commercial banks increased to 25% (Apr. 2008)
Kenya	Increased efforts to build stocks through aggressive importation	Export ban on food crops (Oct. 2008)	Wheat import tariff reduced from 35% to 10% (Jun. 2008); maize import tariff suspended VAT on wheat and maize flour suspended	Maize sold to millers at Ksh 1,750 per 90 kg bag, Ksh 200 below the gvt's producer price

Malawi	National Food Reserve Administration increased procurement efforts	Maize exports banned (Apr. 2008) and no export licenses issued in 2007/8 season		Maize ceiling increased (2007/8); to maintain the ceiling, large private traders temporarily banned from domestic market (Aug. 2008) Macro policy dampened inflation, contributed to relatively stable exchange rates
Senegal	Five-year contract with Indian gvt to procure 600,000 Mt. of rice annually (Mar. 2008)		Import tariff on wheat (5%) and rice (10%) suspended (Jul./Aug. 2007) 18% VAT for all levels of bread production chain lifted Jul./Aug. 2007)	Price ceiling for wheat & baguettes (Nov. 2006); price ceiling for scented broken rice (Jul. 2007); rice subsidy given to distributors to maintain the ceiling (Apr.–Jul. 2008)
Zambia	Gvt maize imports from South Africa	Maize exports banned (Jan. – Aug. 2008–9); wheat exports banned (Jun. 2009)		Large-scale maize millers subsidized at 50% (Dec. 2008), later reduced to 40% (Mar. 2009); total subsidized sales of app. 120,000 Mt
China	Release of wheat, rice, and maize reserves (late 2007); increased foreign procurement through futures contracts (late 2007)	Food and feed exports banned (late 2007)	Suspension of maize export subsidies (Nov. 2008); 5% export levy raised on food grains Suspension of VAT rebates for maize; VAT removed from rice & wheat	Loosening of monetary policy in late 2008, more as a result of the financial crisis
India	Wheat procurement doubled in 2008/9 to 22.7 million Mt. Large quantities of rice and wheat released from stocks	Wheat exports banned (Feb. 2007); exports of common rice banned (Oct. 2007), but no effect on existing contracts	Zero import duty on selected food items	Reserve ratios lowered and money supply increased at a rate of about 20% in 2006/7 and 2007/8

Source: country studies.

neutralized the downward price pressure exerted by releasing additional grain, or if release and procurement were sequentially coordinated. In many cases it is also unclear that the supply increase was of sufficient quantity to have more than a marginal price effect. Finally, although each intervener responded with some form of supply management, there is great variation in the instrument used. In fact, considerable diversity in the details of policy responses is apparent within and between all policy categories and sub-categories and is an overriding characteristic of crisis responses in the present samples.

Interveners such as Ethiopia, Kenya, Senegal, and Zambia report having attempted to procure grains from abroad. Kenya and Zambia looked to South Africa and Senegal signed a five-year contract to import Indian rice. Ethiopia's 2007 and 2008 wheat imports came from multiple sources, especially Romania, Bulgaria, Ukraine, the United States, and Italy (Admassie, Chapter 6). Nzuma (Chapter 9) reports that Kenya's imports suffered major delays, perhaps because the government suspended plans to import maize then later reversed its decision. Senegal's procurement appears to demonstrate long-term thinking in an environment of rising and volatile food prices. However, the Senegalese government entered into the agreement with India in March 2008 when international prices were near their peak and may have paid a high price for the precaution. In contrast to many other interveners, Huang, Yang, and Rozelle (Chapter 17) report that China's supply management response was well coordinated. The Chinese government first increased foreign procurement by entering into futures contracts in late 2007, and soon after put into place an export ban. By buying on the futures market before banning exports, China may have protected itself from the rise in international prices many have attributed to such trade restrictions. Huang et al. also report China released a significant amount of grain from reserves, though release apparently did not keep pace with procurement as stocks increased substantially over the crisis period (Baltzer, Chapter 2). Similarly, although Ganguly and Gulati (Chapter 16) report India released large quantities of rice and wheat, procurement must have outstripped release as stocks increased for both grains, especially for wheat which rose by an extraordinary 8.9 per cent (Baltzer, Chapter 2).

Admassie (Chapter 6) reports that Ethiopia released emergency wheat reserves directly to consumers through consumers' associations organized at local levels and to flour mills, although it is unlikely the quantity was sufficient to influence overall domestic price (though it is conceivable that such release significantly lowered local prices). Ethiopia also distributed significant quantities through other channels (Chapter 6). Egypt is somewhat of a special case in that the government is the largest buyer of domestically produced wheat during normal years and also a major distributor; still

Ghoneim (Chapter 12) reports that procurement rose significantly in 2007–8 to 2.5 million tons, up from 1.8 million in 2006–7. Finally, Malawi increased domestic procurement efforts through its National Food Reserve Agency (NFRA). Chirwa and Chinsinga (Chapter 7) implicate procurement efforts as *exacerbating* rather than ameliorating Malawian maize price increases.

In an effort to manage prices, seven out of the eight interveners banned exports (see Table 3.1). Only Senegal, which is not usually a grain exporter, failed to put a ban in place. Among the earliest interveners to apply bans are Ethiopia, India, and China. Ethiopia's ban came in late 2006, prior to the steep run-up in international prices. This is likely a reflection of domestic conditions, namely high general inflation rooted in loose monetary policy (Admassie, Chapter 6). The latest intervener to ban exports was Kenya which apparently did not ban exports until October of 2008, months after international prices had begun a precipitous decline. The timing of this response is perplexing, especially given Kenya's extremely high domestic prices and trade position (Baltzer, Chapter 2). Perhaps then the Kenyan ban was mostly symbolic in nature. Nonetheless, Nzuma (Chapter 9) implicates the ban as reducing producer and consumer welfare, a possibility which is echoed by other country-study authors regarding their own countries' bans.

Of the seven interveners which implemented bans, four (Egypt, Kenya, Malawi, and Zambia) note that such measures were problematic and suffered reduced effectiveness, especially due to informal cross-border trade or strategic behaviour by the private sector (e.g., storing grain until the ban is removed). The India, China, and Ethiopia study authors reported no difficulties implementing export bans. In the cases of India and China, border measure effectiveness was facilitated by state-controlled grain sectors, while in the case of Ethiopia the absence of problems may be due to domestic grain prices which were in some cases triple the international price, thus removing export incentives (Baltzer, Chapter 2).

Tariff adjustments and modifications to value added tax (VAT) likely played a minor role in protecting consumers from food price increases during the global crisis (Demeke et al. 2009; Baltzer, Chapter 2). Still, three-fourths of interveners used such measures in an attempt to insulate consumers, Malawi and Zambia being the two exceptions. Egypt and China imposed export tariffs on certain grains; in the case of Egyptian rice the tariff was put in place as early as late 2006. Ghoneim (Chapter 12) reports the tariff was increased in 2007 and 2008 before ultimately being abandoned in favour of a ban due to traders' ability to circumvent the tariff. The ban apparently suffered similar challenges (Ghoneim, Chapter 12). Four of the interveners included in our sample also reduced or eliminated import tariffs, though as discussed by Baltzer (Chapter 2) and elsewhere in the literature, tariffs were generally very low to begin with and it may be that more interveners failed to lower import tariffs because they were already at zero (Malawian maize) or because the country was self-sufficient (Zambian maize). Kenya is perhaps an exception, having considerably reduced wheat and suspended maize import tariffs from initially high levels. Kenya and Senegal combined import tariff adjustments with elimination of VAT and China combined elimination of VAT with its export levy and suspension of export incentives. While VAT reductions only covered a few specific food items in every other country, Ethiopia, the sole intervener not to combine changes in VAT with tariff adjustments, suspended VAT across the board for all major food items and cereals.

Interveners were much more likely than any other group to respond to the crisis with sweeping subsidies or price edicts (see Table 3.1). The two exceptions to this are India and China which both preferred the use of stocks to manage prices, perhaps because more than any other interveners they had stocks at their disposal. Among the remaining six interveners, Malawi responded with price controls, Kenya and Zambia with general subsidies, and Egypt,[2] Ethiopia, and Senegal with a combination of the two (although at least for Senegal the two approaches were sequential rather than combined—when price controls failed, general subsidies were implemented). With the exception of Ethiopia, which accompanied price controls with stringent enforcement measures (Admassie, Chapter 6), country-study authors report major difficulties administering price controls. Egypt's hybrid subsidy and rationing system reportedly suffers from massive leakage and poor targeting; Malawi's price ceiling was put into place at an inopportune time for traders, moreover, the implementing agency lacked the funds necessary to defend the ceiling; and, among other obstacles, Senegal's implementing agency was also underfunded (Chirwa and Chinsinga, Chapter 7; Ghoneim, Chapter 12; Resnick, Chapter 14).

A total of five interveners are reported to have employed broad subsidies to mitigate price increases, and all but Egypt did so through subsidized sales to millers (see Table 3.1). Kenya, Senegal, and Zambia are each reported to have experienced difficulties with subsidized sales, especially the problem of millers receiving subsidies but failing to pass benefits through to consumers. Ethiopia reports only minor difficulties administering miller subsidies, and these were largely overcome by the appointment of a monitoring task force and measures to ensure that wheat was milled and sent to bakeries, and that bakeries sold at prescribed prices (Admassie, Chapter 6). Beyond facing implementation difficulties, general subsidies raise concerns over fiscal sustainability. Fiscal concerns are especially salient in the case of Egypt which

[2] Egypt did not implement price controls per se. However, certain food items are subject to price controls under the ration card system. In this sense, and because heavy subsidies and the ration system were in place before the crisis, Egypt is a special case.

embarked on a massive increase in subsidies and added up to 22 million people to its ration card system (Ghoneim, Chapter 12). As discussed below, fiscal concerns are not limited to price policies.

Monetary policy is a blunt instrument and only four interveners are reported to have used it during the crisis—albeit each for different reasons. China and India were both responding more to the international financial crisis than the food price crisis and thus loosened monetary policy. This response aimed to keep interest rates low, credit markets primed, and to maintain an acceptable rate of overall growth. Admassie (Chapter 6) reports the remarkably high food prices seen in Ethiopia were partially a result of loose monetary policy, and Ethiopia eventually took measures to reduce money supply and reign in overall inflation, though not until 2009. Chirwa and Chinsinga (Chapter 7) note that Malawi's sound macroeconomic policy dampened inflation, maintained a high level of fiscal discipline and helped maintain relatively stable exchange rates.

OBSERVERS

The Brazilian and the South African government believed existing safety nets were adequate to mitigate the negative impacts of food price increases and that interventionist responses would result in more harm than good (see Table 3.2). In light of this, the Brazilian government's decision to suspend rice exports in early 2008 appears problematic. However, Mueller and Mueller (Chapter 18) report the ban only affected government stocks, which are equivalent to about 10 per cent of domestic consumption in recent years, and that a private sector ban was never considered. Given that the ban only affected a fraction of consumption needs, it seems likely the ban was at most precautionary and possibly only symbolic. The only other price policy reported for either country is a loosening of monetary policy in Brazil. Similar to India and China, this response had little to do with food prices and much to do with the international financial crisis. South Africa is not reported to

Table 3.2 Observer price policies

Country	Supply Mgt.	Export Bans	Import/Export Tariffs & VAT	Price Controls, Broad Subsidies & Monetary Policy
Brazil		Suspension of gvt rice exports (did not affect private trade)		Loose monetary policy with credit expansion and lowering of interest rates
South Africa				

Source: country studies.

have implemented any price policies and the government appeared particularly wary of such responses (Kristen, Chapter 19).

DABBLERS

All dabblers responded to the crisis with measures to reduce or stabilize prices, though to a much lesser extent than interveners (see Table 3.3). Only two dabblers banned exports, just one used broad subsidies, and not a single dabbler responded with price controls. In addition, relative to interveners, dabbler responses tended to come later, were of a reduced magnitude, and had limited impact.

Three of four dabblers used stocking policies to manage the crisis (see Table 3.3). Bangladesh and Nigeria are reported to have both released stocks and increased procurement efforts. Releases from Bangladesh were reportedly targeted and thus might be considered safety nets, however, the

Table 3.3 Dabbler price policies

Country	Supply Management	Export Bans	Import/Export Tariffs & VAT	Price Controls, Broad Subsidies & Monetary Policy
Bangladesh	Targeted release of stocks through public channels; failed attempt to increase wheat and rice procurement	Banned exports of common rice (May 2008)	5% import duty on rice and wheat suspended VAT suspended for commercial importers (2007/8)	Tight monetary policy to curb inflation; the Taka/Dollar exchange rate remained relatively stable
Mozambique			Import tariffs for wheat, rice & maize reduced from 25% to 2.5% (early 2008)	Food & fuel subsidies increased by 967% in 2009
Nigeria	Release of 65,000 Mt of grain crops and garri; foreign and domestic rice procured (110,000 Mt) and sold at subsidized prices (May–Oct. 2008)		50% rice import levies suspended (May–Oct. 2008)	
Vietnam	Businesses ordered to procure all paddy rice at above-market floor price set by gvt (2008 & 2009)	Lower rice export quota (Mar. 2008) followed by a 3-month ban on new contracts (Apr.–Jun. 2008)	VAT suspended for most age-related activities (Jun. 2008)	

Source: country studies.

quantity released was so massive that prices were probably affected (Raihan, Chapter 11). Although Nigeria's release was relatively small and suffered from implementation challenges including leakage to prominent figures and politicians, Olomola (Chapter 13) suggests it still may have helped to reduce prices. Nigeria and Bangladesh reportedly experienced difficulties in their release and procurement efforts. Baltzer (Chapter 2) shows that, at least in the case of procurement, the obstacles must have been overcome as wheat stocks increased in both countries and rice stocks increased in Bangladesh. Vietnam can also be considered to have engaged in procurement, though the mechanism differed from all other countries (Nguyen and Talbot, Chapter 15).

All dabblers with the exception of Vietnam, which is a net grain exporter, adjusted import tariffs in an attempt to mitigate price increases. Bangladesh had relatively low tariffs to begin with, but Nigeria suspended a considerable rice tariff and Mozambique reduced high tariffs for all of its major grains (Olomola, Chapter 13; Nhate, Massingarela, and Salvucci, Chapter 10). While the Vietnamese government did not adjust import tariffs, it did reduce and later ban rice exports and also suspended VAT for most agriculture-related activities (Nguyen and Talbot, Chapter 15). Bangladesh followed Vietnam in banning exports and suspending VAT; however, given that Bangladesh exports limited quantities of rice, Raihan (Chapter 11) reports the ban had no effect. Finally, although Vietnam banned exports, its ban was fundamentally different than intervener bans in that it only prohibited new contracts and was in place for a mere three months, after which the government actually encouraged exports (Nguyen and Talbot, Chapter 15).

In terms of price controls, monetary policy, and broad subsidies, there is little to report since dabblers predominately avoided such responses (see Table 3.3). Not a single dabbler implemented price controls, although Bangladesh is reported to have created committees to monitor prices (Raihan, Chapter 11), and only Bangladesh used monetary policy in an attempt to curb inflation. Mozambique is the sole dabbler which reported increased food subsidies. Unfortunately, it is only reported that food and fuel subsidies were increased and it is unclear whether these were targeted (and thus more of a safety net policy); it is also not clear how much of the subsidy increase was allocated to fuel and how much to food.

There is no single answer as to why dabbler price policy responses were more restrained than those of interveners. In terms of geography and crop importance, two of the dabblers in our sample are in Africa and two in Asia. Bangladesh and Vietnam are predominately rice economies while cassava dominates in both Nigeria and Mozambique (followed by maize in Mozambique and yam in Nigeria where maize, rice, and wheat play relatively minor but still important roles). In Bangladesh, the more measured response may have something to do with the country's history of recurring food crises which have caused it to gradually refine its response over many decades (Raihan, Chapter 11). In Vietnam, it may be more the result of a bumper crop and an economy consisting of many small rice producers which stood to gain[3] from price increases (Nguyen and Talbot, Chapter 15). Nigeria's responses may have been tempered by the fact that it is a large producer and households are reliant on mostly non-traded foods such as yam and cassava. In the case of Mozambique it is difficult to point to a specific structural factor, though perhaps the importance of cassava played a role. Finally, although it is impossible to attribute moderate price policy responses to any single factor, it is noteworthy that all dabblers responded with major (and in some cases novel) initiatives to expand agricultural output, often with an eye to the long term (see Table 3.4).

3.3.2 *Output Policies*

Output policies consist of measures taken to augment production. These include input subsidies, tax incentives, price supports, and transportation and market infrastructure among others. As with price policies, output policies have been organized into sub-categories. The three sub-categories are input subsidies and tax incentives, price supports and farm credit, and other output policies (see Table 3.5).

INTERVENERS

At the core of interveners' output responses were a combination of input subsidies and price supports. This is not surprising given that these programmes were mostly in place before the crisis and thus the main thrust of the response was consistent with historical precedent. Still, not all interveners' output responses were as readily predictable. In some instances the crisis engendered policies which are remarkable in that they represent discontinuity with past policies or include novel features. In the case of Senegal, for example, the crisis created an opening for a momentum shift in which policies that were already formulated were abruptly displaced by new and reportedly inferior ones. China, in contrast with Senegal's shift to inferior policies, achieved a retrenchment in expansionist biofuel policy. As is discussed in more detail toward the end of this section, Kenya, Ethiopia, and India are also among interveners which pursued policies with noteworthy features.

[3] Vu and Glewwe (2011) find mixed evidence regarding welfare impacts of price increases. Small increases may lower poverty while larger increases may cause poverty to increase slightly. On the whole, welfare impacts from price increases are positive since gains outweigh losses, but the positive welfare impact is not distributed evenly and most households suffer losses.

Table 3.4 Dabbler output policies

Country	Input Subsidies & Tax Incentives	Price Supports & Farm Credit	Other
Bangladesh	Fertilizer subsidies increased by 35%; 40% fuel subsidy rate; electricity rebates for agro-based industries Crude oil customs duty suspended; duty-free facility continued for farmers wishing to import fertilizers	MSP increased for wheat by 44%, paddy rice by 60%, and aman rice by 30% Expansion of ag. credit	Endowment Fund for Ag. R&D created (2007/8)
Mozambique			Plan for Action for Food Production introduced (PAPA 2008); aimed to increase production & promote commercialization & increased processing; doubling of the ag. budget as a share of GDP Plan to increase storage to capture PAPA surpluses (Jul. 2008) Promotion of alternative transportation
Nigeria		Minimum Support Prices introduced in 2009 Credit to increase rice processing capacity made available on favourable terms; farm credit expanded	UN helped develop a framework to deal with food prices; new National Food Security document (2008) went beyond expanding output; gvt created a special fund for ag. development Funds earmarked to complete 17 outstanding silo projects as well as 11 new silo projects
Vietnam	Favourable tax changes intended to promote ag. investment (Dec. 2010)	Expansion of ag. credit (Apr. 2010)	Investments to improve rural marketing (Jan. 2010); pilot ag. insurance projects (Mar. 2011); new storage & upgrades to existing (Sep. 2009) 3.8 million hectares set aside for rice, no urban or industrial encroachment through 2020 (Dec. 2009) New requirement to reimburse farmers for land taken for industry (Dec. 2009)

Source: country studies.

Table 3.5 Intervener output policies

Country	Input Subsidies & Tax Incentives	Price Supports & Farm Credit	Other
Egypt		72% increase in wheat procurement price (2007/8); changed to setting maize procurement price before planting (2010)	Greater enforcement of limits on rice production area to try and boost wheat production in 2007/8; increase in storage capacity (2010)
Ethiopia			Establishment of the Ag. Transformation Agency to boost productivity; creation of a commodity exchange
Kenya	Inputs procured by the gvt and sold at steep discounts (Mar. 2009); FAO and World Bank US$50 million input subsidy programme (May 2008)	Increased maize procurement price to Ksh 1,750 per 90 kg bag (2008) and later to 1,950 US$5 million AGRA and IFAD supported expansion of ag. credit (2008)	Renewed efforts to improve irrigation NAAIAP (see input subsidies and discussion below)
Malawi	Fertilizer subsidy rate increased to 90% in 2007/8 (from 67%), then decreased in 2008/9	125% increase in producer price (2007/8) to MK45 per Kg	
Senegal	FAO programme provided US$1.5 million to buy inputs for vulnerable small-holders		Grand Offensive for Food & Abundance (GOANA) launched to move toward self-sufficiency & raise ag. investment (May 2008)
Zambia	Fertilizer subsidy rate increased from 50% to 75%; subsidy programme expanded from 120,000 to 200,000 farmers (Feb. 2008) Ag. equipment VAT zero rated (2009); customs duty removed from commercial trucks; tariffs suspended for certain inputs & equipment	Maize MSP increased by 16% and then 35% in 2008; further increases in 2009	25% gypsum import tariff suspended to promote domestic fertilizer production (2009)
China	Input subsidy increase; levy on phosphate fertilizer exports (Feb. 2008); 100% levy on all fertilizer exports (May–Dec. 2008)		Retrenchment of expansionist bio-fuel policies & new restrictions on land competition between food & fuel
India	Fertilizer subsidies increased in 2007/8 and again in 2008/9	Wheat MSP increased 30% (2007/8); maize, rice, & pulses by 30–50% (2008/9) Rs 600 billion debt waiver for 30 million farmers (Feb. 2008); expanded to 43 million farmers in 2009	Nation Food Security Mission (NFSM) launched in 2007/8 to boost staple output Increased spending under the National Ag. Devt. Program, a portion of which aims to extend Green Revolution to East India

Source: country studies.

As evidence that interveners were keen to expand near-term grain supply, nearly all of those in our sample increased input subsidies; the two exceptions being Egypt and Ethiopia (see Table 3.5). In the case of Egypt, Ghoneim (Chapter 12) relays that the government is routinely involved in input markets, providing subsidies for fertilizers, irrigation, and fuel. However, there were no adjustments as a result of the crisis. The Ethiopian government proposed a fertilizer subsidy, but it was never implemented. The remaining six interveners are all reported to have responded by increasing subsidies under existing programmes or by creating new programmes. This is in sharp contrast to output-enhancing tax and tariff incentives, which were only reported by two countries—Zambia and China. Finally, input subsidy increases for three interveners, Kenya, Senegal, and India, were implemented as part of a larger programme to boost agricultural productivity. This is discussed further in the section on 'other' output policies.

Two additional approaches interveners used to boost output were increased price supports and expansion of farm credit (see Table 3.5). The latter was only implemented by two countries, India and Kenya, while five employed the former. Although India is not reported to have explicitly expanded credit, the government did waive a vast amount of outstanding agricultural loans and is thus still included in the credit category. Kenya's credit expansion was implemented in collaboration with multi-lateral partners and is noteworthy in that it included agricultural and business training. In terms of farm supports, there was a great deal of variation in the proportion of the increase. Unfortunately, interpreting such variation in proportional increases is complicated by differences in prevailing conditions across countries and grain markets, as well as by differences in initial support prices. In the end, what is clear is that price support increases were common among interveners and considerable in magnitude. On the one hand, Malawi more than doubled its (maize) producer price in the 2007–8 season and Egypt increased its wheat procurement price by approximately three-quarters. Zambia (maize) and India (wheat, maize, and rice), on the other hand, increased minimum support prices by only about a third. In the case of Zambia, Chapoto (Chapter 8) reports the initial increase in the 2008 season was only 16 per cent. However, due to competition from the private sector and the resulting inability of the government to meet its procurement targets, the price was later increased. Similar difficulties were experienced by other interveners including Malawi, Kenya, and Egypt.

As discussed above, many countries pursued policies which are difficult to classify. Although such policies were more common among dabblers than interveners, most interveners implemented at least one policy belonging to the category 'other' (see Table 3.5). These other policies can be further divided into two groups. On the one hand, many countries implemented relatively isolated policies aimed at a particular aspect of production. Examples include: Egypt's enforcement of rice area limits and increase in storage capacity, Kenya's revived irrigation efforts, Zambia's efforts to promote domestic fertilizer production, and perhaps China's biofuel retrenchment. The remainder of this section will focus on the second type of other policies—overarching policies consisting of multiple programmes intended to expand agricultural output.

Ethiopia, Senegal, Kenya, and India are all numbered among interveners which introduced wide-ranging programmes to enhance agricultural productivity (see Table 3.5). Ethiopia established the Agricultural Transformation Agency and Admassie (Chapter 6) reports this was accompanied by a whole host of initiatives intended to expand production—increased investment in research and development (R&D), extension services, and infrastructure development among others. Also among the country's crisis responses was the government's decision to provide incentives to foreign investors, particularly India and China. Admassie indicates this led to 3.5 million hectares changing hands with a similar amount planned to be exchanged in the near future. This is perhaps the most controversial response and a sizeable literature has developed debating the merits of so-called land grabs. Finally, Ethiopia's 2008 introduction of a commodity exchange is also noteworthy, although at inception trading remained limited (Chapter 6).

In Kenya, several of the responses reported by Nzuma (Chapter 9) fell under the country's larger National Accelerated Agricultural Input Access Programme (NAAIAP). A few of the features under what Sheahan et al. (2012) refer to as 'a comprehensive multi-million dollar fertilizer and improved seed subsidy and training programme' include: input subsidies, agricultural credit offered on favourable terms, and training on improved farming methods and business management. As is the case with numerous policy responses, it is unclear how much the NAAIAP was initiated in response to the crisis and how much it was a result of existing political momentum (Sheahan et al. 2012). This theme receives further attention in subsequent sections and is treated comprehensively by Watson (Chapter 5).

The Senegalese government responded to the crisis with the Grand Offensive for Food and Abundance (GOANA). In many ways GOANA represents continuity with past agricultural plans which also tend to emphasize output expansion and greater self-sufficiency (Resnick, Chapter 14). Although GOANA is included as a larger agricultural development strategy and reportedly realized some short-term success, it should be emphasized that the initiative received a tepid response from stakeholders and was deemed unsustainable by the national FAO director (Resnick, Chapter 14). Unfortunately, GOANA is also reported to have displaced what were considered by some as superior strategies which had been developed with stakeholder participation.

India is reported to have implemented a number of initiatives intended to increase productivity, food security and sustainability. These initiatives include the National Food Security Mission (NFSM), the National Agricultural Development Programme (NADP) and, somewhat later, the National Food Security Act (NFSA)—though these policies probably represent pre-crisis momentum more than crisis responsiveness. As discussed by Watson (Chapter 5), the government's response was in part conditioned by the right to food movement which preceded the onset of the crisis. This is particularly true of the NFSA. In the case of the NADP, Ganguly and Gulati (Chapter 16) applaud what appear to be novel efforts to expand the Green Revolution to East India and address sustainability issues. Nonetheless, the resources behind these efforts are apparently so inadequate that the whole affair is dubious (Ganguly and Gulati, Chapter 16).

OBSERVERS

As with price policy, observers' production response was trivial (see Table 3.6). Brazil reports expanding access to agricultural credit and South Africa investing in productivity-enhancing infrastructure. In the case of Brazil, credit expansion simply continues a trend begun in about 2000; the measures in South Africa were reportedly limited to areas of deep poverty and strategic political importance (Kirsten, Chapter 19). Beyond pre-existing safety-nets mentioned earlier in the study and discussed in more detail below, the trivial output response may be because neither country experienced an acute shortage and, as middle-income countries, both have populations which depend relatively less on unprocessed grain as a part of their food basket. Another possibility is that they were counting on a natural production response as farmers themselves reacted to price signals. Finally, it also may be because both countries were operating under more stringent fiscal constraints. No matter the cause, output policy responses among observers were at most negligible.

Table 3.6 Observer output policies

Country	Input Subsidies & Tax Incentives	Price Supports & Farm Credit	Other
Brazil		Expansion of ag. credit	
South Africa			Promotion of household & community production; investments in productivity enhancing infrastructure including irrigation and input packages

Source: country studies.

DABBLERS

Dabbler output policy responses were varied and identifying an overall strategy which defines the group is difficult (see Table 3.4). Bangladesh belongs more with interveners in that it too focused on expanding short-run production through a combination of subsidies and price supports. Besides Bangladesh, no dabblers are reported to have increased price supports (although Nigeria introduced minimum support prices in 2009). In addition, apart from comprehensive programmes which are discussed later, Bangladesh is the only dabbler reported to have increased input subsidies. Despite wide variation in dabbler output responses, one pattern is clearly discernible: dabblers responded to the crisis with far-reaching policies which appear to address long-term concerns.

As noted above, only one dabbler increased input subsidies while two made tax or tariff adjustments to facilitate output expansion (see Table 3.4). Bangladesh increased fertilizer subsidies considerably and also targeted fuel and energy, the latter by instituting electricity rebates for agro-based industries. The other dabbler to promote agriculture through tax policy adjustment was Vietnam which continued a legacy of favourable tax arrangements for farmers, agricultural investors, and agri-businesses by making fresh tax reductions during and in the aftermath of the crisis (Nguyen and Talbot, Chapter 15).

Price supports were used only by Bangladesh while various forms of credit expansion were reported by three of the four dabblers. Nigeria extended concessionary credit to increase rice processing capacity and took measures to expand the pool of financing available to commercial farmers. Bangladesh shared Nigeria's objective of expanding farm credit but took the additional step of easing restrictions and facilitating credit access for importers. The Vietnamese government made collateral-free loans available for agricultural activities.

All dabblers pursued policies categorized as 'other', and in most cases these policies appear to be significant in scope (see Table 3.4). The possible exception to this is Bangladesh's Endowment Fund for agricultural research and development—Raihan (Chapter 11) notes that R&D spending actually decreased between 2007 and 2009 despite the fund. In contrast to Bangladesh, the Nigerian government requested technical assistance from the United Nations (UN) Country Team which, together with a number of other multi-lateral organizations, apparently played a significant role in the country's crisis response—at least on paper (Olomola, Chapter 13). Mozambique is similar to Nigeria in that it also developed a major strategy to address not only the crisis, but broader agricultural and food security objectives. A key difference between the two is that the Mozambique government is reported to have developed the strategy internally while Nigeria apparently received considerable outside input. Vietnam's 'other' policies are distinct from those of the other dabblers in that they do not belong to one overarching programme, but are rather a collection of isolated policies which nonetheless demonstrate a certain degree of cohesion.

The crisis is reported to have led to a number of significant changes in Nigeria, not least of which is the 2008 National Food Security Programme (NFSP) document. Olomola (Chapter 13) deems this document 'a major paradigm shift' in that it goes beyond output expansion, and it was reportedly accompanied by a host of policies aimed at modernizing the rural sector and promoting agricultural research and development. The government is also reported to have collaborated with multi-lateral partners to develop a second major strategy document, the National Food Crisis Response Programme (NFCRP). Although this was also accompanied by a number of initiatives to promote food security, Olomola criticizes the document's omission of the more innovative features of the NFSP and notes that its implementation was marred by difficulties.

In Mozambique, the crisis led to the 2008 Plan for Action for Food Production (PAPA). Broadly directed at expanding output and promoting commercialization and agro-processing, Chapoto (Chapter 8) terms PAPA the 'operational tool' for the previously approved 'Green Revolution Strategy'. With regards to novel features, PAPA appears to be more conservative than Nigeria's approach, although it does include provisions to intervene in the value-chain, promote rural processing, and enhance the flow of goods. At the same time, Chapoto (Chapter 8) reports the adoption of PAPA entailed an ambitious doubling of the agricultural budget as a share of GDP (up to 8 per cent). The immediate cause of this impressive funding growth may have been the food price crisis, however, even with this increase Mozambique's agricultural budget remains below the 10 per cent commitment made under the Maputo Declaration.

Vietnam is not reported to have unveiled a grand agricultural strategy as a response to the crisis, but the country did enact a number of legislative measures which are of note. Among these measures were policies to promote rural marketing, enhance the efficiency of rice exports, assist farmers in mitigating risk through pilot insurance projects, and to reduce post-harvest losses through storage expansion and upgrades. In addition, the government took measures to prevent industrial encroachment on agricultural land. These included a major set-aside programme of 3.8 million hectares dedicated solely to rice production until 2020, and a new requirement to reimburse farmers for land appropriated for industrial purposes. The majority of these measures came during 2009 and 2010 in the aftermath of the initial crisis.

3.3.3 *Safety Nets*

Safety nets consist of cash or in-kind transfers which are targeted at specific vulnerable groups. These transfers may be conditional, such as programmes which require labour or school attendance, or unconditional. Safety net tables in this study have been sub-divided according to the conditionality of the transfer. For the purpose of presentation, school feeding and public sector wage increases have been included with conditional transfers even though they are not true conditional programmes.

INTERVENERS

The crisis elicited a dizzying array of safety net policies and five of the eight interveners are reported to have made adjustments in an effort to mitigate the harmful effects of food price increases (see Table 3.7). Of those who did make use of safety nets, Egypt's and Ethiopia's were the most extensive followed by China's. In Senegal, safety nets were mostly donor-initiated and on a small scale, in China, Egypt, and Kenya they were mainly governmental, and in Ethiopia safety nets were a hybrid of the two. Lastly, three of the five safety net users reported experiencing factors which reduced policy effectives (Egypt, Kenya, and Senegal), especially poor targeting.

Unconditional transfers were employed more widely than conditional transfers by all interveners, except perhaps Ethiopia which relied heavily on its Productive Safety Net Programme (PSNP) (see Table 3.7). In terms of the form of such transfers, Egypt's consisted of both cash transfers and subsidized sales through its ration card system. Ethiopia also used a ration card system, and like Kenya, sold grain at subsidized prices to poor consumers. Resnick (Chapter 14) reports that Senegal released grain reserves to the poor, and although these were given freely, the magnitude of the transfer was rather small and only in place for three months (see Table 3.7). China is the only intervener to rely solely on cash transfers and is also unique in that the increase in transfers was automatic based on the consumer price index (CPI). All other interveners employed transfers in a more ad hoc fashion, retaining greater discretion as to the ultimate magnitude.

Two interveners (Ethiopia and Kenya) channelled resources to consumers through conditional transfer programmes, two increased public sector salaries (Egypt and Ethiopia), and two made adjustments in school feeding programmes (Ethiopia and Senegal) (see Table 3.7). Unlike Kenya's cash for work programme which was not implemented until 2009, Ethiopia's PSNP existed before the crisis, during which it was expanded to support 8 million people from an initial plan of 5 million in 2008 (Admassie, Chapter 6). An additional difference between the two countries is that Ethiopia's programme is several orders of magnitude larger than that of Kenya. School feeding played

Table 3.7 Intervener safety net policies

Country	Unconditional Transfers	Conditional Transfers, School Feeding, Public Wage Increases
Egypt	Certain vulnerable groups added to the ration card system: widows, divorced women, women heading households, and chronically sick persons; prices and quantities for ration card items adjusted Social pension doubled from LE 80/mo. to LE 160/mo. and coverage increased from 650,000 persons to 1 million from 2005-7 Education grant increased from LE 20/mo. per child to LE 40 (2008)	30% increase in public sector salaries compared to the usual increase of 10% (May 2008)
Ethiopia	Procured 520,000 Mt of wheat, 515,000 Mt of maize from intl. mkt and distributed through the Urban Food Rationing Programme and subsidized sales to flour mills (2008); release of wheat and maize reserves to the poor at subsidized prices (190,000 Mt of wheat in 2007) WFP and other NGOs channelled about 200,000 Mt of food into Ethiopia during the crisis; WFP provided food assistance to 11 million people in 2008 rather than the 1 million it had planned	PNSP coverage in non-PNSP areas increased from 4.6 to 6.4 million people (2008); PNSP daily wage increased from ETB 6 to ETB 10/day Expansion of existing school feeding programmes Public salaries increased
Kenya	Subsidized maize meal distributed to poor districts (Dec. 2008); cost for 2 kg was Ksh 55 rather than the Ksh 72 market price	Ksh 15 billion Kazi Kwa Vijana cash for work programme launched to create 300,000 jobs within 6 months (Mar. 2009)
Malawi		
Senegal	Food vouchers for 17,400 households amounting to CFS 1.9 billion (2008, donor supported); 20,000 Mt. of rice distributed to vulnerable rural consumers through the AMR programme (May–Aug. 2008) Targeted cash transfers to mothers of children 0–5 yrs. through NETS programme (donor supported)	School feeding for 80,000 children in Dakar (2008, donor supported)
Zambia		
China	Semi-targeted food subsidies to urban consumers and students, vary at provincial level but considerable in size; automatic based on CPI	
India	No increases reported, though transfers are large and have increased over time	

Source: country studies.

a relatively minor role in Senegal where a donor supported programme, established in 2008, covered about 80,000 children. Ethiopia's much larger school feeding programme was expanded during the crisis and reportedly benefited 482,000 students in 2008 (Admassie, Chapter 6). It is also reported that the Ethiopian government made a modest increase in public sector salaries, though this was probably not enough to offset the rising food prices and may have increased inflationary pressure (Admassie, Chapter 6). In Egypt, on the other hand, the salary increase is reported to be substantial. None of the other four interveners, Malawi, Zambia, China, and India, is reported to have responded to the crisis with conditional transfers, school feeding or increases in public sector wages.

OBSERVERS

Both of the observers in our sample credit comprehensive and effective safety nets, which were in place before the crisis, as obviating the need for further responses (see Table 3.8). Brazil reportedly increased payments under Bolsa Familia in 2007 and 2008, though such increases were marginal. Mueller and Mueller (Chapter 18) argue that, due to other programmes and structural factors, marginal increases may have been all that were necessary. Bolsa Familia is also noteworthy in that it is reportedly well-designed, avoiding the leakage so often associated with such welfare programmes. Besides Bolsa Familia, Mueller and Mueller report that the Programme for Food Acquisition was in place prior to and during the crisis. While it is unclear if the programme was ramped up to meet additional needs, an impressive 13 million people reportedly received benefits in 2009. South Africa apparently considered its safety net programmes adequate and made no extraordinary adjustments as a result of the crisis besides limited distribution of food parcels (Kirsten, Chapter 19).

DABBLERS

The solitary dabbler to have responded to the crisis with significant changes to safety net programmes is Bangladesh, which used a combination of conditional and unconditional transfers as well as scaling up of school feeding (see Table 3.9). In terms of conditional transfers, in 2008–9 the government scaled up the Test Relief programme which provides in-kind transfers in exchange for work. Raihan (Chapter 11) also reports scaling up of targeted food distribution (an unconditional transfer programme). The only other

Table 3.8 Observer safety net policies

Country	Unconditional Transfers	Conditional Transfers, School Feeding, Public Wage Increases
Brazil	Bolsa Familia increased transfers	
South Africa	Comprehensive combination of safety net & welfare programmes in place before the crisis; no changes made as a response to the crisis	Targeted distribution of food parcels

Source: country studies.

Table 3.9 Dabbler safety net policies

Country	Unconditional Transfers	Conditional Transfers, School Feeding, Public Wage Increases
Bangladesh	Targeted food distribution more than doubled from 372,000 Mt in 2005/6 to 786,000 Mt by 2008/09	Significant scaling up in the 2008/9 crop year of the Test Relief programme to 360,000 Mt of wheat and rice School feeding scaled up
Mozambique		
Nigeria	Conditional Cash Transfers (CCT) programme launched to provide N5,000/child to extremely poor households to send their children to school and participate in free gvt health care programmes (Dec. 2008)	
Vietnam		

Source: country studies.

dabbler reported to have used targeted safety nets during the crisis is Nigeria, though this programme was aimed at education and healthcare rather than food security and was not a direct response to the crisis (Olomola, Chapter 13).

3.4 Conclusions

In terms of the types of policies pursued and the specifics of formulation, timing, and implementation, the fourteen countries in our sample displayed remarkable diversity in their crisis responses. The eight interveners in our sample share in common a vigorous attempt to control prices, but the primary measures used range from price controls, to supply management, to broadly administered consumer subsidies, to trade policy, especially export bans. Dabblers' efforts to control prices were more limited and the most common crisis response in this group of countries was output expansion. Even among dabblers the primary means used to expand output varied. Bangladesh used price supports and input subsidies, Mozambique and Nigeria developed new comprehensive plans, and Vietnam employed a suite of isolated but interrelated policies which share features with many crisis responses without resembling that of any single country.

Despite such heterogeneous responses, some general observations can be made. First, with the exception of Brazil and South Africa, crisis responses in all countries exacted a high fiscal cost. Tariff reductions, VAT suspensions, and export bans all entail lost revenue. Even as revenues were declining, crisis responders were creating new programmes, expanding membership in existing programmes and increasing benefit levels. Egypt, for example, planned to spend LE9.5 billion in 2007–8 on food subsidies but expanded programming for a final cost of LE16.4 billion. India's crisis response is reported to have contributed to a more than doubling of the fiscal deficit between 2007–8 and 2008–9 and the cost to Senegal is estimated at around US$748 million. Soaring food, fuel, and fertilizer prices compounded these budgetary burdens even when governments took no additional actions. In Zambia, for example, Chapoto (Chapter 8) reports the 2008 fertilizer budget was initially approved for US$42 million but two months later price increases caused the cost to be inflated by an additional US$68 million. To make matters worse, many programmes are reported to have suffered reduced effectiveness due to factors such as poor targeting and corruption. This was reported widely enough that is receives separate treatment below.

All dabblers and interveners in our sample, with the notable exception of China, reportedly experienced difficulties responding to the crisis. In the case of China, Huang, Yang, and Rozelle (Chapter 17) report that the crisis response was comprehensive, well coordinated, and the policies had the intended impact. Among countries which experienced difficulties, there were a range of reasons given for reduced policy effectiveness. Government procurement efforts met with difficulties given the scarcity of grain on the market in Bangladesh and Nigeria while Malawian and Zambian efforts reportedly contributed to price increases. India had no trouble *procuring* grain, but reportedly had inadequate storage facilities leading to considerable waste. Kenyan fertilizer subsidies may have ended up in the hands of Ugandan farmers due to smuggling while Zambian fertilizer subsidies are reported to suffer from poor targeting, corruption, leakage, poor delivery, and other factors which mitigate their effectiveness. The vast Indian debt waiver is reported to have disproportionately benefited wealthier farmers just as Egyptian subsidies and ration card benefits apparently accrue more to the wealthy than the poor. Ganguly and Gulati (Chapter 16) note that Indian safety nets have generally not been very effective; subsidized maize meal in Kenya was designed in such a way that the intended beneficiaries could not access it; and Senegal's attempt to distribute rice was poorly targeted and experienced funding problems besides. Kenya, Senegal, and Zambia tried subsidizing millers and distributors but the benefits reportedly never made it to consumers. Nigeria released grain from stocks but it was captured by powerful intermediaries. Malawi and Senegal attempted administrative price controls—both failed. Export bans were problematic and some traders simply stored grain in anticipation of the lifting of the ban (Egypt and Vietnam) while others circumvented the ban by exploiting porous borders (Zambia and Kenya).

In seeking an explanation for the myriad failings outlined above, it is appealing to blame ad hoc responses and to prescribe more preparedness.

Similarly, given that the only two countries in our sample (Brazil and South Africa) not to have intervened in food markets had well-functioning safety nets, it is tempting to conclude that if more countries had such measures in place the crisis would not have elicited such drastic responses. However, judging by the experiences of countries like China and Ethiopia, it would be a mistake to conclude that safety nets alone prevent more interventionist responses. Furthermore, Brazil and South Africa are both middle-income countries with relatively lower poverty rates; for lower income countries with exceedingly high poverty rates safety nets present additional obstacles. And while it is true that many countries' ad hoc policies were problematic, more preparedness may not prevent countries from abrupt reactions to crises. Political and structural factors influence the extent to which governments are willing to be involved in food markets, as does historical precedent. Another, less recognized reason why some governments may have intervened during the crisis is overestimation of the negative impacts. Initial food security impact assessments significantly overstated the problem and this sensationalism may have increased the pressure felt by governments to intervene. Further research is needed to parse out the relative weight of these various factors and to build a more complete understanding of why governments continue to meddle in food markets despite evidence that such interference is welfare-reducing. In that regard, the current political economy study makes a solid contribution.

References

Demeke, M., G. Pangrazio, and M. Maetz (2009). *Country Responses to the Food Security Crisis: Nature and Preliminary Implications of the Policies Pursued*. Rome: FAO Agricultural Policy Support Service.

Jayne, T. S., and D. Tschirley (2010). 'Food Price Spikes and Strategic Interactions between the Public and Private Sectors: Market Failures or Governance Failures'. *Commodity Market Review*, 121–38. Rome: FAO Commodities and Trade Division.

Sheahan, M., R. Black, and T. S. Jayne (2012). 'What is the Scope for Increased Fertilizer Use in Kenya?' International Development Working Paper 125. Lansing: Michigan State University.

Timmer, C. P. (2009). 'Causes of High Food Prices'. Economics Working Paper Series 128. Manila: Asian Development Bank.

Vu, L., and P. Glewwe (2011). 'Impacts of Rising Food Prices on Poverty and Welfare in Vietnam'. *Journal of Agricultural and Resource Economics*, 36(1): 14–27.

Wiggins, S., J. Compton, S. Keats, and M. Davies (2010). 'Country Responses to the Food Price Crisis 2007/08'. London: UKAID.

4

Policy Processes and Food Price Crises

A Framework for Analysis and Lessons from Country Studies

*Suresh Chandra Babu**

4.1 Introduction

The recent food price crisis brought forward a discussion on how countries design and implement food policies (FAO, WFP, and IFAD 2012; IFPRI 2012). Policy responses to the crises depended on several factors, including the rate and extent to which price fluctuations transfer from international markets to domestic markets; the vulnerability of the country to the vagaries of food prices; pressure to act from opposition parties, development partners, and producer and consumer groups; the capacity of the actors in the policy process; and the evidence generated by the research community on the potential and real effects of increasing food prices. Identifying and understanding how these factors contribute to the policy process is critical for preparing policy makers to better face food price crises in the future.[1]

* The author thanks Per Pinstrup-Andersen for his encouragement in writing this chapter, sharing the country case studies and for providing valuable comments on the first draft of this chapter. Thanks to Danielle Resnick for discussions on various models of the policy process and for several valuable suggestions that shaped the contents of the chapter. The author alone is responsible for its contents.

[1] In this chapter we use the theories of policy processes as an investigative tool to understand how various actors and players shape up and influence the policy decision-making (Sabatier 2007). There is a large volume of literature on the political economy of policy-making that looks at how policy makers balance sound economic policy-making with political realities (Meier 1991; also see Watson, Chapter 5). While studies of political economy of policy-making often use policy process theories (Birner et al. 2011), mainstream political economy analysis addresses issues such as the measures of protection, modelling political games among the actors, and the role of political institutions (Rausser and Swinnen 2011; Bates and Block 2010). This paper focuses on the factors contributing to the effectiveness of the policy process during the time of

The recent food price crisis and the responses of the policy makers in developing countries provide an unprecedented opportunity to analyse the policy processes in these countries, with particular regard to the individual and organizational capacity in the policy process and the political and socioeconomic context in which the policies are developed. Studying the political realities policy makers face in policy design and programme interventions can help place the policy outcomes in proper perspective. Further, understanding the institutional and governing environment in which polices are made can help to identify opportunities that enhance roles and contributions of various actors and players to the policy-making process. In addition, given the limited research on the policy-making process in developing countries in general, an analysis of the food policy-making processes in countries in various stages of development and operating under diverse political environments can add to the broader literature on policy processes.

A comparative study of policy processes in developing countries in the context of the food price crisis is important for several reasons. First, understanding the nature of policy-making and the roles that various actors play in the policy process can help in designing interventions to address future food crises. Second, food policy-making in developing countries during a crisis period provides an opportunity to study the similarities and differences in policy processes with respect to their responsiveness. Third, studying the food policy process aids in developing a framework to understand the policy process in developing countries in general. Fourth, insights from the knowledge gaps and the capacity gaps that developing countries face could help in designing interventions that strengthen the policy process to better respond to a food policy crisis. Finally, the lessons learned from the policy process in one country could be useful for another country with a similar political and socioeconomic environment to address food policy challenges.

The rest of the chapter is organized as follows. The following section reviews the policy process literature and its relevancy to developing countries and Section 4.3 introduces a framework to analyse the policy process in developing countries in the context of the food price crisis. Using this framework, Section 4.4 provides an analysis of the policy process in country studies in the context of policy-making during the food price crisis. Lessons from the analysis of the policy processes are presented in Section 4.5. Section 4.6 concludes.

food price crisis and complements two other synthesis papers by Bryan (Chapter 3) on the typology of policy responses and by Baltzer (Chapter 2) on the nature and magnitude of food price transmission from international to local markets.

4.2 Policy Process in the Context of Food Crisis: A Review of Literature

How does policy-making in times of crisis differ from policy-making in times of relative calm? Who are the players and actors in the policy process? What triggers the policy process? How is the policy process conducted and what roles do different players play in the policy process? These questions have been of interest to policy scientists for a long time and have garnered increased interest in developed countries in the last 30 years.

We briefly review some of the archetypical models of policy processes in the context of food policy-making in developing countries. Appendix Table 4.A1 (at the end of the chapter) presents an overview of selected policy process models and their characteristics, used under normal circumstances and under crisis situations. A key tenet explored in this chapter is that given a certain degree of political openness, does the policy process differ according to the context and time available for decision-making? For example, policy-making during a crisis may involve overnight decisions with little or no open consultation while the release of genetically modified crops may involve protracted debate and discussion over several years.[2] We look first to the linear model for answers, then to the interactive model and the multiple stream model, followed by the institutional development and rational choice model, policy learning and diffusion model, advocacy coalition framework, and lastly, the policy entrepreneurship model.

At its simplest, the policy process can be thought of as six stages that occur in a sequential fashion (Figure 4.1). This linear model suggests that the policy process commences with problem identification or the setting of a policy agenda, moving from stage to stage until the policy is either abandoned, effectively ending the policy process, or there is recognition that the policy must be revised, and the process repeats.

The linear model suggests that the policy process is a simple, sequential process (Nakamura 1987), but this is seldom the case in reality. In most situations only a partial adoption of this model (involving the four stages beginning with problem identification to policy implementation in Figure 4.1) is realized. Further due to lack of follow through in terms of monitoring, impact assessment, and policy learning renders the linear model invalid in reality. The linear model has also been criticized for its inability to trace causality, for being top-down, for the lack of attention to the iterative process of

[2] Political openness may vary within democracies and within authoritarian regimes. Broad grouping of the countries such as democracies and dictatorships will not be sufficient for a fuller understanding of the policy processes.

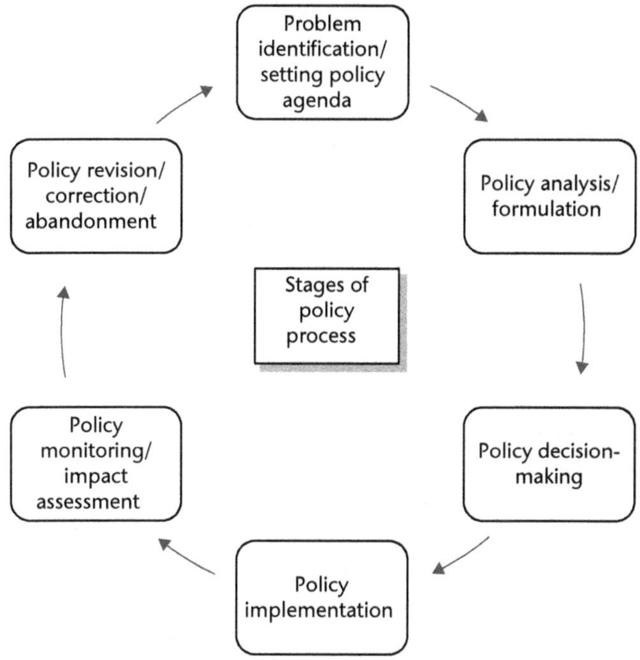

Figure 4.1 The stages of the policy process
Source: author's compilation.

policy-making, and for ignoring multiple levels of policy-making (Sabatier 2007). It also fails to account for political economy factors.

Even so, a partial adoption of the linear model may be seen in developing countries' policy-making when there is an urgent policy problem, for example when responding to a food price crisis, or when there is a clear need for a policy solution and any quick help from the government would result in at least a marginal change over the current situation acceptable to a majority of the stakeholder groups. For example, the recent food policy-making processes in countries such as Ethiopia and Nigeria seem to have followed the selected stages of linear models at least partially.[3]

In most cases, however, policy processes are more complex and non-linear than as shown in Figure 4.1. According to Sabatier (2007), they involve a plethora of stakeholders and interest groups who have differing understandings of the

[3] For example, recent efforts in establishing the Agricultural Transformation Agency in Ethiopia and the development of the Agricultural Transformation Agenda in Nigeria could be categorized only as a partial adoption of the linear model of policy process. They are partial in the sense that only the first four stages of the policy process are followed and that too with limited analysis and evidence. The later stages such as policy monitoring, impact assessment, and the policy learning and revisions are not taken seriously. For these reasons the linear model is not fully valid in reality.

problem and alternative approaches to solving it. The interactive policy process model is an improvement over the linear model in that it recognizes that there are multiple policy choices and that several actors and stakeholders interact to shape the debates and dialogues that result in multiple policy outcomes (Stone 2002; Omamo 2004). The advantage of this model is that it encourages broad participation and helps determine how policy debates affect the policy process.

The multiple stream approach to the policy process identifies three streams—problems, policies, and politics—which operate together (Kingdon 1984). In the first stream, problems are recognized and defined depending on the way policies are formulated and as political events unfold. The second stream identifies policy alternatives whether or not they are solutions to recognized problems or are affected by political considerations. In the third stream, political events move along their own trajectories, whether or not they are related to problems or policy proposals. In this model, entrepreneurial policy makers influence policy by making connections across the three streams. If the entrepreneurs are successful, policy solutions emerge. Under the multiple streams model of policy process, policy-making entails collective decision-making under conditions of ambiguity and uncertainty, which makes it an appealing policy process model (Zahariadis 2003). However, an application of this model to the developing country context could be limited by the lack of policy entrepreneurs in the countries who have the ability to bring the three streams of the policy process together.

Court and Young (2003) developed a similar framework with multiple dimensions, but looked at different aspects of the policy process: context (politics and institutions), evidence (credibility and communication), and links (influence and legitimacy). From a review of more than 50 case studies of research policy linkages, they found that context influenced the extent to which research results were used in policy-making, that generated evidence was used more frequently when it was accompanied with clearly communicated possible solutions, and that the links between researchers and policy makers were important, particularly informal links, but the extent and ways in which trust, legitimacy, openness, and formality affected the links remained unclear.

The institutional development and rational choice model expounded by Ostrom and her associates has an important place in the context of collective action in policy and programme design related to natural resource management (Ostrom 2011). Using self-governing institutions as its focal points, this approach identifies policy-making venues according to the policy actors involved, the policy action needed, the policy context, and the policy arena in which the policy process evolves. The research community and other stakeholders can develop effective strategies and understand the policy institutional framework within which they are operating, using this institutional development framework (Ostrom 1986).

Policy learning and diffusion models focus on how countries faced with similar policy challenges learn from each other. Volden et al. (2008) show how learning from the results of the political process in other countries can influence the beliefs of policy makers with regards to the implications of policies that are currently under discussion. The evidence generated by domestic think tanks and the results garnered from global, regional, and other national policy research organizations could play a key role in policy learning and the diffusion of specific lessons in their own countries. Such cross-country evidence can support the policy makers and determine the policy agenda.

Policy processes in developing countries, as in many advanced countries, are gradual processes in which policy changes occur incrementally (Baumgartner and Jones 1993). Slow policy processes are explored through the advocacy coalition framework (Birner et al. 2011), which recognizes the need for a timespan of at least a decade to see policy change occur. Developed initially by Sabatier and Jenkins-Smith (1993) this framework explains policy change through the development of coalitions of different policy actors with shared beliefs that are homogenous and stable over time. These beliefs could be the result of policy shocks and policy learning that initially occurred from a policy change. Major policy changes (or policy reforms) occur when several coalitions find common ground. Non-political stakeholders can play effective roles in this process by generating evidence and advocating for their cause to sway public opinion and hence the beliefs of the policy players.

In summary, the above review of literature indicates that while there may be no one model that fits squarely with the policy process of a developing country, a combination of models can help describe the nature of the policy process and how various actors and players position themselves to play meaningful roles in the realm of policy-making. In the context of the food price crisis, as will be seen in the following sections, several elements of these models are useful to describe the nature of the policy process. In order to help the analysis of key characteristics of the policy process, we develop a conceptual framework that brings together various elements discussed in the above review of literature.

4.3 A Framework for Studying Food Policy Processes in Developing Countries

Applications of the policy process models to study the policy phenomenon are limited in developing countries. Studies that use well-established models tend to identify the most applicable model to study a policy process when, in reality, policy processes may follow combinations of elements of several policy processes. Figure 4.2 presents a stylized framework by combining elements from the various policy process models reviewed in the previous section.

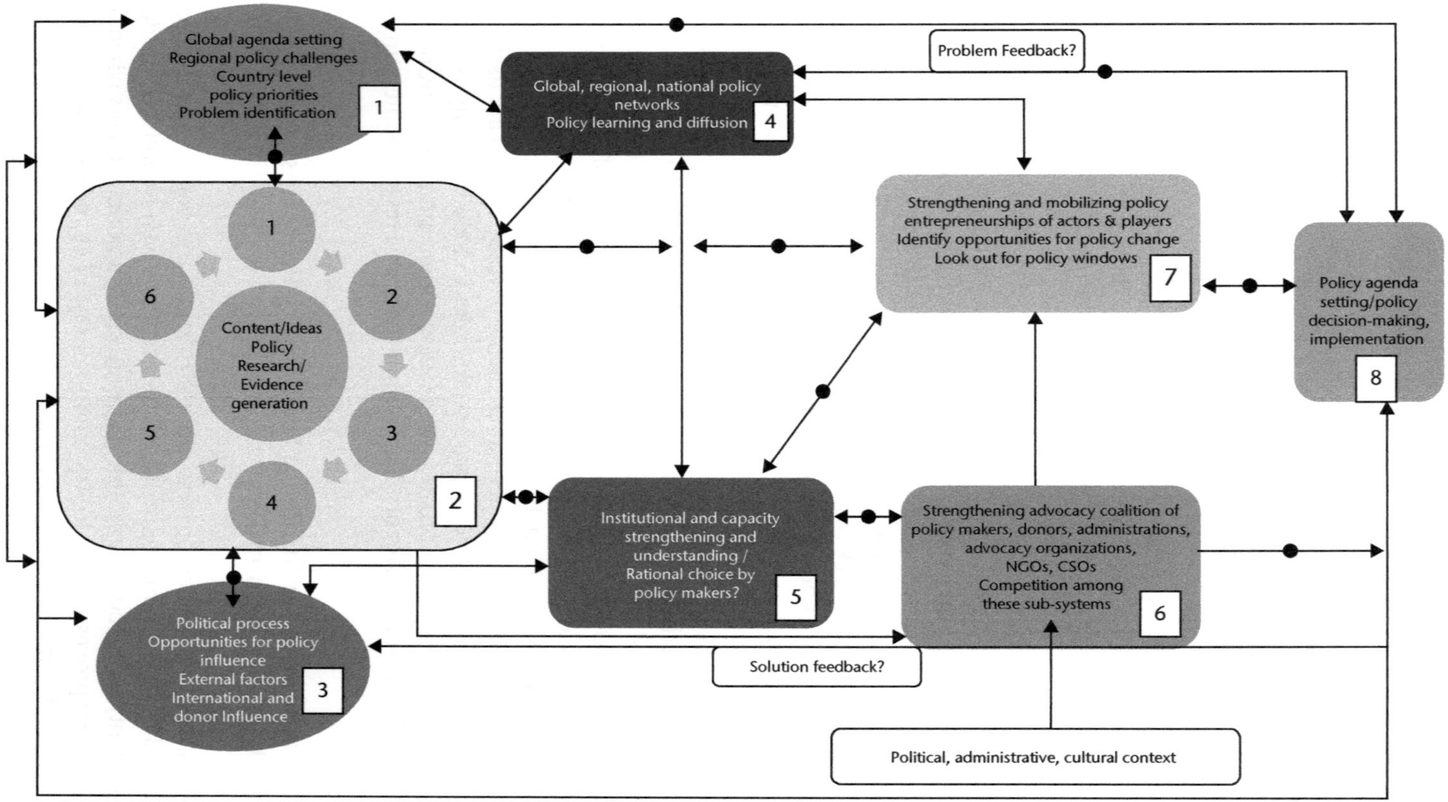

Global agenda setting
Regional policy challenges
Country level
policy priorities
Problem identification
1
Global, regional, national policy
networks
Policy learning and diffusion
4
Problem Feedback?
Content/Ideas
Policy
Research/
Evidence
generation
1
2
3
4
5
6
2
Strengthening and mobilizing policy
entrepreneurships of actors & players
Identify opportunities for policy change
Look out for policy windows
7
Policy agenda
setting/policy
decision-making,
implementation
8
Institutional and capacity
strengthening and
understanding /
Rational choice by
policy makers?
5
Strengthening advocacy coalition of
policy makers, donors, administrations,
advocacy organizations,
NGOs, CSOs
Competition among
these sub-systems
6
Political process
Opportunities for policy
influence
External factors
International and
donor Influence
3
Solution feedback?
Political, administrative, cultural context

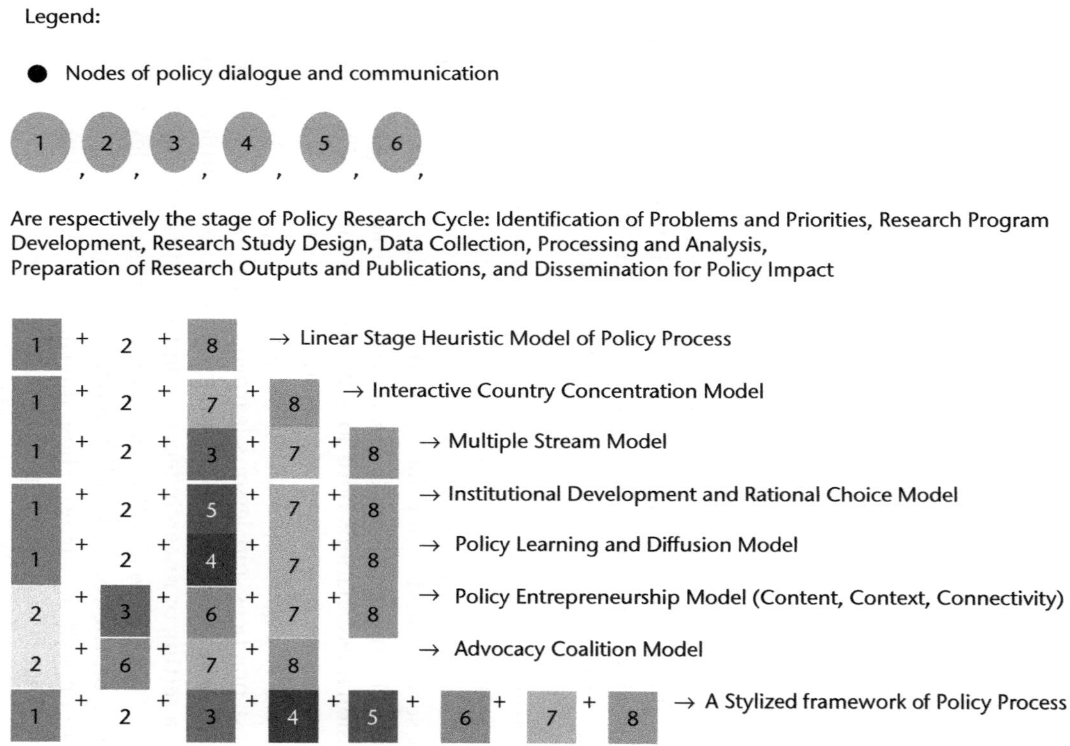

Figure 4.2 A stylized framework of policy process in developing countries
Source: author's compilation.

The process is initiated when policy issues are identified either from global, regional, or country-level food security goals (ellipse 1) or from research projects (square 2). Local problem identification and priority setting in terms of national agricultural and food security strategies and priorities based on the interplay of global agendas, national policy challenges, and country-level priorities is given in ellipse 1, in the top left corner of Figure 4.2.

All developing countries use research and analysis to some degree to design their national and sectoral strategies. Depending on the country's domestic capacity, external technical assistance may be used for research and analysis. In the last 20 years, however, the development of policy research organizations in several developing countries has resulted in local policy research capacity supporting the policy process.[4] The policy research and analysis cycle, which contributes context, ideas, and evidence to the policy process, is given in Box 2 in Figure 4.2. The link between the research and policy processes again varies depending on the nature of the political and administrative processes, the socioeconomic context and the culture of decision-making. These cross-cutting factors also influence the political process itself, which also depends on the level of involvement of various internal and external influences on the policy process as seen in Box 2 in Figure 4.2.

Policy learning and the diffusion of policy lessons from geographical regions and from international policy networks play increasingly important roles in the policy process. These lessons move through several pathways. Public servants and policy makers learn from the national and global debates in which they participate; researchers and analysts participate in their professional associations both locally and internationally; and civil society organizations (CSOs) are increasingly connected to international non-governmental organizations (NGOs) and aid agencies which communicate best practices and lessons learned on the issues and problems they deal with. The extent to which a policy problem is identified through global agenda setting or research depends on the political leadership at the country level. Policy issue identification also depends on the level of influence of donors on the country policy process and the amount of internal pressure from opposition parties. These internal and external pressures are crucial determinants of how the political and policy processes operate for a particular issue. These elements are depicted in ellipse 3 in Figure 4.2

[4] With the recognition that technical assistance by donors to policy development has not resulted in local capacity, the 1990s saw the establishment of policy think tanks in most of the African countries. Initiated with the support of UNDP and the World Bank, these policy think tanks became one of the sources of local capacity for policy analysis and research, although their capacity to produce high quality research going beyond consultancy reports still remains a challenge.

and are arguably the most important from a political economy perspective. Recognizing the linkages between policy learning and diffusion, and research and evidence generation is important for understanding how new ideas are formed, tested, and evaluated. This aspect of the policy process is depicted in Box 4 in Figure 4.2.

Translating evidence of policy alternatives and strategies into implementable programmes requires institutional capacity to formulate and monitor the rules and regulations that govern the public sector, private sector, and CSOs in a country. Institutional analysis thus becomes critical to explain why different levels of institutional development result in policy outcomes of differing quality. Similar to the institutional development framework, the rational choice policy process model focuses on understanding the linkages and relationships between bureaucratic figures and the legislature. National assemblies are becoming increasingly responsive to emerging problems and, with the provision of relevant information on policy choices, could be effective in driving policy outcomes (Babu and Ergeneman 2005; Ostrom 2011). The institutional analysis and development aspects of the policy process are given in Box 5 in Figure 4.2.

The advocacy coalition model of the policy process assumes actors with similar objectives and similar stakes in the policy process collude to strengthen their position in the policy debate. Actors and players form advocacy groups and engage in the policy process to advance their goals and objectives. They may interact with local institutions, borrow ideas from research, and learn from their own policy and political processes, as shown by Box 6 in Figure 4.2.

Strengthening institutional capacity to develop and alter rules and their interpretation can help in modifying policy outcomes (see Boxes 1, 2, 5, and 7 in Figure 4.2). Policy outcomes in developing countries are increasingly influenced by various internal players who collaborate with each other to promote specific policy pathways. A wide range of players, actors, and institutions with a common ideology and belief system can advocate for a specific set of policy options (Sabatier and Weibles 2007). However, sub-groups of these actors may compete for different policy outcomes and understanding their differences could explain the adoption of particular policies within a certain political environment (see Boxes 2, 6, 7, and 8 in Figure 4.2).

While the strength of advocacy coalitions depends on the policy problem at hand, complementing them, or at times replacing them, with policy entrepreneurs who can better mobilize their cause and identify policy windows, can aid in advancing their policy agenda. Policy entrepreneurs are also influenced by local institutional arrangements and policy lessons learned from other sectors and countries that face similar policy challenges, as shown by Box 7 in Figure 4.2.

The policy entrepreneurship model relies on the strengthening and mobilization of key policy leaders and supplying them with adequate information. Policy entrepreneurs often wait for policy windows to open (Maxwell 2006). The food price crisis opened such windows in many developing countries, although due to a lack of collective policy leadership within the food system in general as well as among policy makers in government ministries responsible for food security, it is unclear how effectively these opportunities were used to achieve food security (see Boxes 2, 3, 6, 7, and 8 in Figure 4.2). Specific policy options are chosen by policy makers based on how successful political leaders were previously. Learning from peers who operate under similar political systems characterizes the policy diffusion framework. In Figure 4.2, Boxes 1, 2, 4, 7, and 8 jointly illustrate the policy diffusion framework. Lessons from policy adoption and implementation suggest solutions to the actors and players in various stages of the policy process. Finally, the policy or set of policies agreed upon and implemented are seen in Box 8.

In summary, the stylized framework presented above attempts to capture various aspects of the policy process in developing countries, since no one individual framework or model could fully explain policy-making given the wide range of policy-making processes. It should be noted that, while the application of these frameworks is still new, even in developed countries, very little effort has been made to understand their implications in the context of development policy-making in developing countries. The applicability of this framework, partially or fully, to food policy-making will differ depending on the nature and extent of the crisis and on the country context.

In the next section we apply the framework to analyse the policy processes and their outcomes in the case-study countries. One way to apply the framework is to identify country archetypes and examine whether they followed similar policy process in responding to the food crisis. Alternatively, one can identify specific policy outcomes such as export bans vs. enhancing social safety nets and analyse whether they are generated by similar policy processes. In what follows we combine these two approaches to identify the most important factors that contribute to variations in policy-making processes to derive lessons for future policy-making.

4.4 Synthesis of the Policy Processes in Country Studies

The policy process theories reviewed above identify different pathways that countries take to develop and implement policies. They help to locate various sub-systems of interest to study the policy process and can be useful to identify areas that could be improved to facilitate food policy decision-making such as political openness, information access, and the negotiation skills of actors and players. How did the country studies fare with respect to these characteristics? To what extent was the policy process influenced by these characteristics? How can these characteristics be modified to improve the performance of the policy process to better respond to food crises in the future? Answers to these questions could be useful to enhance the efficiency of the policy process.

In order to understand the policy process during the food price crisis, we look at the triggers of policy responses, country responses, the key actors and players in the policy process, and their approaches toward policy-making.

4.4.1 *Policy Triggers*

Several domestic and external factors triggered policy responses to the food price crisis in the country studies. One of the major policy triggers was the widespread understanding that there was a rise of international food prices. Price transmission differed (Baltzer, Chapter 2). Food exporters such as India, China, and Vietnam with food security concerns reacted strongly and quickly to stop or slow their exports, mainly in response to actual or potential criticism they might have faced internally. Policy reactions to the international food price increase were also significant in countries that were not seriously affected by it. This was the case for African countries including Nigeria, Kenya, Zambia, and Malawi mainly due to pressure from civil society and consumer groups to act. The fear of these groups taking to the streets, which has implications for the stability of the governments, moved governments towards quick responses to the food price crisis. In Nigeria's National Assembly, food-related CSOs were more redoubtable than members of the opposition parties. Thus, at least in some of the countries, internal domestic factors influencing policy decision-making seem to be more influential on policy outcomes than external factors. Finally, countries such as Brazil and South Africa that traded more freely made little effort on the domestic front to respond to increasing international prices.

4.4.2 *Policy Responses*

Policy responses varied depending on the type of policy process, existing policies, and available resources at their disposal. Developing country governments chose responses that ranged from increasing incentives for production to market interventions, such as export bans and import tariffs

(Bryan, Chapter 3). On the supply side, countries provided incentives, usually through subsidies for the adoption of modern technologies, such as fertilizer and seeds. This was the case in Malawi, which strengthened a pre-existing fertilizer subsidy programme. Countries such as China, India, Kenya, Senegal, and Zambia used input subsidy programmes to help farmers increase their production levels. In order to maintain sufficient supply in domestic food markets, countries resorted to export bans, import tariffs, or both. To reduce the pressures of domestic price increases on consumers, some countries, including China, Ethiopia, and Nigeria, released stocks of food reserves in the market to stabilize prices. Countries that were chronically vulnerable to food deficits relied on food aid to meet the increased market demand for food. Policy learning and diffusion occurred among the countries. For example, Vietnam has been following and implementing similar policy measures as China; South Asian countries closely watched, and responded to policy actions of India; and South Africa's policy moves on food trade affected policy discussions in several southern African countries.

Protecting vulnerable populations through safety nets was a key intervention that was further strengthened during the food price crisis. Countries such as China, Brazil, Egypt, Ethiopia, India, Senegal, South Africa, and Zambia reinforced their public support for social programmes to protect their poor and food insecure populations. Targeted food distribution through food for work and cash transfer through guaranteed employment programmes helped to ease the burden of the high food prices on the poor in India and Bangladesh. Open market sales to poor consumers in selected localities seemed to be a quick response to reduce the pressure from opposition parties (for example, rice in Bangladesh and pulses in India).

Watson (Chapter 5) provides a complete treatment of policy responses announced by the governments and reported by the media. Each government faced a different set of domestic pressures that pushed them to act in a timely manner. In democratic countries, such as India and Bangladesh, the rise in domestic food prices following the global food price increase forced governments to act or respond in ways to avoid criticism from the opposition or from the media. Authoritarian regimes such as China and Vietnam acted proactively to avoid any political instability and addressed the concerns of various stakeholders even though they were not engaged in any formal consultations. In open democracies such as Nigeria and Zambia the food price increases were met by riots in the streets by consumers and other disenchanted groups. This resulted in further debate in some national assemblies on the food price increase and actions followed.

Policy processes differed depending on the nature and level of decentralization. In large countries such as India and China, policies made at the central level took time to permeate to decentralized levels, whereas in small countries such as Malawi and Senegal, policies were only made at one level. In India for example, the state governments allocated additional resources to protect their vulnerable population. Although politically motivated to a large extent states like Andhra Pradesh and Tamil Nadu provided rice for Rs. 1 per kg (US$0.02/kg). Policy processes also differed depending on the trade orientation of the countries. Openly trading countries like Brazil and South Africa did not have much to decide as the private sector may already be functioning sufficiently well to import food to take advantage of domestic price increases or export surplus food. Closed economies such as Bangladesh and India on the other hand, often needed to change policies to meet their development goals (Balzter, Chapter 2). Institutional development and capacity for facilitating policy debate and dialogue could accelerate or delay the policy-making process. The latter mostly applied to long-term policies. However, some policy changes had to be made so quickly, that in many countries, there was not much debate. Export bans, for example, were quickly agreed upon due to their populist nature. Countries with well-established social safety nets needed to make small changes to their policy course to protect their citizens. The cases of Brazil and South Africa in this volume illustrate this well.

4.4.3 *Key Actors and Players in the Policy Process*

Policy processes were influenced by the types of participants and their ability to raise issues openly. In countries like China, Vietnam, and Ethiopia, ruling parties, their committees, state councils, and government ministries were key players in designing intervention policies. In countries where political institutions permitted open discussion, such as Malawi, Zambia, Mozambique, India, and Bangladesh key actors and players in the policy process included members of national assemblies, policy advisors, the private sector, consumer groups, national and international NGOs, farmer associations, and development partners. In Bangladesh, opposition parties and their policy advisors were quick to point out weaknesses in the proposed food security and safety net programmes (Watson, Chapter 5).

The roles of the stakeholders in the policy process were influenced, for the most part, by the severity of the problem, the willingness of the government to listen to them, and their perceived influence on policy outcomes. Some actors in the policy process, particularly the media, private sector, and CSOs tended to raise their voices early on, depending on how they or their constituencies were affected by the price increases. How policy makers responded to these voices depended to a greater extent on the power and influence of these entities in the policy process. In Senegal, for example, the vocal complaints from the consumer and producer groups forced President Wade to act (Resnick, Chapter 14). Public data availability of international food prices and the corresponding local trends helped some country governments determine if the concerns raised by these entities were true. As a result, policy debates in countries like India and Bangladesh focused on the causes of the price increases.

4.4.4 *Political Institutions*

Political institutions provide a broad structural framework for understanding how countries respond to a food price crisis. Institutional arrangements and the functioning of political institutions may offer explanations of the structure of policy processes in some countries (Bates and Block 2010). The extent of a society's involvement in policy debates and the use of evidence in such debates may also explain the nature of the policy process. The media also helps to gauge the level of tolerance of government functionaries for open debate and dialogue on policy problems.

At the policy-making level, the nature of the political system has a profound influence on the choice of policy instruments and the speed of the policy process in responding to a food crisis. Democratic governments with strong opposition parties in their national assemblies tend to act on the food price crisis with a sense of accountability, even if they may not choose the first best policy that satisfies all the stakeholder groups (Watson, Chapter 5). For example, India reacted with an export ban mainly due to pressure from opposition parties who blamed the government for allowing cereal exports while the country's population faced higher food prices. The Vietnamese government, on the other hand, responded with a similar intervention, but it turned out not to be necessary. Vietnamese policy makers later apologized to the cabinet committee explaining that the decision for the export ban on rice was based on incorrect calculations (Ngan 2011). Due to the absence of a functional opposition, the government was not held accountable for its error.

4.4.5 *Formal Organizational Units with a Food Security Mandate*

The existence of formal institutional structures with food security mandates, such as food security units or food policy units within the government, helped to speed up the policy process because of their linkages to policy makers at different levels. For example, the food security units in the Office of the President in Kenya and in the Ministry of Economic Development took leadership to convene policy dialogues and brought information for policy-making. The quality of their human resources and the organizational effectiveness to contribute to information generation and to monitoring and evaluation, as well as their ties with the policy leaders, helped to hasten the debate and decision-making in the policy process.

In implementing policy responses, governance arrangements and administrative structures and procedures played crucial roles. Supervisory and regulatory mechanisms were important for providing feedback to the policy process on interventions. Without such feedback, policy implementation tends to operate in a veil of ignorance. For example, although the Malawi government imposed an export ban on maize following the food price increase, it had no way of knowing how much maize remained in the country due to this ban because of the weak administrative capacity to monitor the informal trade between traders in Malawi and neighbouring countries such as Mozambique, Zambia, Zimbabwe, and Tanzania. In contrast, when India imposed an export ban on rice, due to strict border control, the policy affected the flow of rice into Bangladesh's markets, which had significant implications on the deliberations and intervention strategies contemplated by policy makers in Bangladesh.

4.4.6 *The Role of the Private Sector and Civil Society Organizations*

An active presence of the private sector in the policy process makes a difference in a country's response to a food crisis. The confidence that the private sector has in government policy is critical for its effective involvement in the food and input markets. Further, in countries where the private sector is asked about its potential challenges and is supported by the government through short-term credit, the implementation of market interventions becomes more effective. In Bangladesh, for example, the private sector has become an effective partner of the government to import the food needed to supply the domestic market. In China, the private sector that exported fertilizer was affected by the restriction of fertilizer export. However, domestic support to farmers helped the private sector to gain from such interventions. Thus irrespective of whether a country is market economy or centrally planned, successful policy-making in the food sector needs to involve regular consultation with the private sector to enable them to function effectively and profitably.

In response to the food crisis, Nigeria implemented a massive support programme to increase fertilizer use. The implementation of this programme largely involved the private sector for the importation and transportation of the fertilizer. Regular consultations with the private sector has helped the government policy makers to gain a better understanding of the challenges the private sector faces and to address them through interventions as necessary, such as improving customs processes (personal communication with officials of the Fertilizer Department, Federal Ministry of Agriculture and Rural Development, Nigeria). CSOs also play a vital role in food policy debates when they are allowed to participate. For example, in Malawi, the federation of NGOs with a food security mandate raised common voice towards the food security of people in vulnerable areas. In Nigeria the network of food security NGOs meets with the Minister of Agriculture and Rural Development on a regular basis. In many developing countries, the emergence of food security CSOs during the development of the Poverty Reduction Strategy Papers has helped to cement their participation in food and agriculture policy processes.

In countries with strong CSOs, the CSO-contributed information on the causes and consequences of a food crisis has shaped the policy debates. For example, in India the CSOs engaged in the 'right to food' movement were highly critical of the government during the food price crisis and this further strengthened their position in the policy process. However, the capacity of CSOs to meaningfully contribute to the policy development process is still limited in many countries.

4.4.7 *Food Security Committees and Taskforces*

In addition to the food security units that operate within government ministries, governments in several countries such as Kenya and Malawi relied on the recommendations of special task forces or committees to guide their policy decisions. These taskforces are normally convened by the government food security units described above, but not always. For example, in Kenya, the National Food Security Committee in the President's Office played a key role in working with the Kenya Food Security Steering Group in the provision of information to the policy process. In addition, Kenya's Inter-ministerial Committee on Drought and Food Security convened regularly to discuss the food security situation in the country. A similar committee, the Vulnerability Assessment Committee, exists in Malawi within the Ministry of Economic Planning and Development. This committee regularly monitors the country's food security situation. The commitment of the country's government to its food security goals and the existence of food security strategies and policy statements provide a good point of departure for discussions during the policy process. The political commitment of leaders to address food security problems also contributed to focused deliberations in the policy process. The formation of special committees and taskforces also helped to quiet the opposition and to buy time, particularly when the committee was composed of respected food policy researchers and advisors.

4.4.8 *The Role of Academic Researchers and Think Tanks*

Academic researchers in universities and think tanks were a key source of evidence on policy alternatives in countries such as India, China, Vietnam, Bangladesh, Ethiopia, Malawi, Kenya, Nigeria, and Zambia. However, some countries used these research groups more effectively than others. Policy makers in some countries relied mostly on confidential discussions with researchers from think tanks to generate information that supported their policy options. For example, Indian policy makers regularly consulted the National Centre for Agricultural Economics and Policy Research (NCAP) for their inputs on policy issues. These reports, however, are not published but shared as policy notes to policy makers (personal communication with researchers of NCAP). Similarly, the Bangladesh Institute of Development Studies (BIDS) was often called upon by Bangladesh's Ministry of Commerce to guide its policy-making process (personal communication with researchers of BIDS).

In Vietnam, however, the Institute of Policy and Strategy for Agriculture and Rural Development (IPSARD) was heavily relied upon to support the policy direction preferred by the Ministry of Agriculture but the advice given by IPSARD was not fully based on independent analysis (personal communication with researchers of IPSARD). This experience generated serious discussion among IPSARD's researchers on how to make IPSARD independent of the Ministry of Agriculture in order to play a more effective role in providing evidence on policy alternatives, in the way that the Chinese Center for Agricultural Policy does in China. Think tanks in African countries seemed to have played limited roles in the policy process compared to their Asian counterparts. The Ethiopian Development Research Institute (EDRI), the Kenya Institute for Public Policy Research and Analysis (KIPPRA), the Agricultural Policy Research Unit (APRU) in Malawi, the Nigerian Institute of Social and Economic Research (NISER), and the Indaba Agricultural Policy Research Institute (IAPRI) in Zambia played some role in contributing to the policy process, directly or indirectly. However, gross capacity limitations, lack of funding, and a low level of trust of the government continues to limit the role of think tanks in food policy processes in much of Africa.

4.4.9 *Presence of Food Security Monitoring Systems*

Countries that have active food security and nutrition monitoring systems seem to have responded to food crisis more quickly than others. For example, the Famine Early Warning Systems Network (FEWS NET) in many southern African counties made food price data continuously available to policy makers through monthly newsletters. However, two major challenges in such externally-driven monitoring systems are the sharing of data with government institutions and departments and the low level of trust that policy makers have in the information generated by these monitoring systems. In cases where the vulnerability assessments are conducted jointly with government departments, as was the case in Kenya, the reports were more readily accepted in the policy process and were useful in identifying targeted areas for intervention. One major insight from this experience is that unless local systems for food security and nutrition monitoring are strengthened, information for designing interventions to protect the poor and the vulnerable may not be effectively used in the policy-making process.

4.5 Lessons from the Country Studies

Twelve lessons can be drawn from the analysis of the policy processes discussed above.

1. *Crisis vs. non-crisis policy process*: policy processes are, in general, different during a crisis period compared to a period of relative calm. Due to time limitations and pressure to act, policy makers tend to make decisions with minimal consultation during a crisis period relying mostly on policy advice from a close circle of advisors. In the long run, however, there is evidence of more inclusive decision-making, particularly in more open democracies.
2. *Political institutions and policy consultations*: the nature of the political institutions in a country determines the extent of consultation and stakeholder participation. Short-run policy outcomes could be similar even if the nature of the political system and the source of pressure to act vary. This is true even among some authoritarian regimes. Country-specific analysis is needed to explore the differences between the policy processes under similar political regimes.
3. *Gaining recognition and access to the policy process*: the advocacy coalition model was visible in some countries during the food price crisis. The crisis presented an opportunity for several organizations to become more active and vocal by working together to achieve food security goals. In some countries, food security-oriented CSOs gained importance and acceptance by policy makers when it was realized that their input was particularly constructive.
4. *The policy process as collective action*: policy processes can be seen as processes of collective action when actors and players take proactive roles

to find their niche within the system. Yet collective action does not necessarily improve the effectives of the policy process.[5] Participants who oppose policy solutions proposed by policy makers may make the process less effective. Thus, political incentives can encourage policy makers to actively engage specific policy actors in the policy process. This also reflects on the choice of members to the task forces and committees organized to address food price crises. Capacity for collective action is a challenge in countries when access to information and evidence varies among entities.

5. *Crisis as an opportunity for long-term strategy development*: the multiple-streams framework of the policy process was seen in several countries where the food price crisis brought a window of opportunity for various food and agricultural problems to be brought forward by different groups including adaptation to climate change, natural resource degradation, and opening up local food market chains for foreign investment. The crisis also pulled together various groups of policy proponents and raised differing views on potential solutions. However, it is not clear if countries used this opportunity effectively to develop long-term strategies to achieve food security.
6. *Formation of stronger coalitions*: in some countries the food price crisis provided an opportunity for the formation of advocacy coalitions. In Nigeria, for example, the agro-processors and millers came together to seek concessions for their operations even though they were competitors. Similarly, NGOs working toward food security came together to form a united network.
7. *Involvement in long-term policy dialogues with increased legitimacy*: continuous engagement of key actors that were involved in the policy process during the crisis period could aid in designing long-term interventions. In Nigeria, for example, a recent consultation with the food security CSOs showed that the CSOs that brought the increasing food prices to the attention of the government formed a coalition of food security NGOs and consulted at both the state and federal level (FMARD 2010). Thus the food crisis provided an opportunity for the CSOs to become

[5] Effectiveness of the policy process may be an important goal in itself for policy makers who seek to engage a wide range of actors and players to develop policy alternatives. It measures if the actual policy outcomes are in line with the desired or optimal policy outcome (from the perspective of the benevolent social planner). Better and more informed collective action by stakeholders by no means guarantees the desired outcome for all, as their expectations will differ. Nevertheless, coming together and working together on a policy problem makes future inclusiveness in policy-making more likely and enhances the quality of debate and dialogue in the present.

more prominent and reinforce their legitimacy and participation in future policy dialogues.

8. *Improved communication among stakeholders*: the interactive model of the policy process was observed in countries where policy consultations brought various stakeholder groups together. This was more evident in open and democratic countries than in authoritarian regimes where interactive processes of policy-making remain limited to the ruling parties and the councils appointed by them. The food price crisis mobilized key players to work together by increasing their communication and interactions. At the same time, the challenges that CSOs and private sector organizations faced in addressing the food crisis emerged during these discussions and, through increased interaction, they were forced to improved their communication skills, especially with other players in the policy process.
9. *Implementation challenges*: many of the discussions, policy dialogues, and consultations that took place during the food crisis period focused not only on the policy options that the government was considering, but also on the challenges that it will face in implementing the policies. These interactions highlighted capacity challenges at all levels—the system level, organizational level, and individual level.
10. *Role and independence of research organizations in the policy process*: while research and academic organizations were consulted in countries such as India, China, and Vietnam, these organizations belonged to, and were funded by, their respective governments. The level of independence in evidence generation differed between countries. In some more democratic countries, policy makers, researchers, and bureaucrats worked well together to achieve their goals and objectives; however, these discussions were mostly internal and resembled the institutional rational choice model in that the relationships between the government, think tanks, and political leaders were driven by a specific set of institutional rules.
11. *Strengthening the capacity of actors and players in the policy process*: in some of the countries, CSOs are allowed to play meaningful roles in the policy process, but are grossly constrained by a lack of capacity to do so. Strengthening the capacity of CSOs to identify the problem and to develop local solutions by analysing their data is a first step to increasing their effectiveness in the policy process. The media has played a significant role in several countries to highlight the problem of increasing food prices and their effects on poor households. However, the quality of reporting and information sources could be improved

by strengthening the capacity of the journalists and increasing their access to research-based evidence.

12. *Role of monitoring systems*: regular information on the status of food insecurity and the vulnerability of households in different geographical areas of a country is a crucial ingredient in policy-making. Yet even where there are functioning data collection systems, much of the collected data is not processed in time, only a portion of what is processed is analysed, and only a portion of what is analysed is used in the policy process. Improving the capacity of the taskforces and parliamentary committees to effectively demand information will improve the quality of the policy debate. Finally, enhancing implementation capacity to translate policy and programme interventions and to receive feedback on the impact of the implemented interventions is crucial for the policy process.

4.6 Concluding Remarks

In this chapter an attempt is made to understand the policy-making processes that were followed when developing responses to the recent food price crisis to draw lessons for improving and strengthening these processes to better face such crises in the future. After reviewing the broader literature on the frameworks, theories, and models of policy processes, we developed a combined framework that could be applied to food policy-making in developing countries. Following several rounds of cross-country discussions and analyses of country-level policy-making, we identified the nature of policy processes in selected countries. A key lesson learned is that by strengthening the role of various players and actors, and empowering them by increasing their capacity for research, analysis, communication, and advocacy, their participation in food policy-making processes can be enhanced. However, their participation is conditional on the nature of the political institutions in the country. A broader insight from the review of the policy processes is that not one theory alone can fully explain the food policy-making process. A combination of theories is at work in any particular country. Identifying the most important actors as well as their roles is crucial to improve policy-making processes. Policy processes are affected by various factors depending on the political, socioeconomic, and cultural contexts of the countries. Understanding the nature and magnitude of these factors will help in devising strategies that could help development partners and policy makers to guide the development of open, transparent, and effective policy processes that can result in better policy outcomes.

Appendix Table 4.A1 Models of policy process: a summary of their characteristics and use

Policy process models and principal authors	Disciplinary approach	Description of policy process	Major assumptions of the model	Use of models for food policy-making	
				Under normal circumstances	Under crisis situation
Classical linear model (Nakamura 1987)	Political science/ policy studies	Decision makers seek and use information generated by research/analysis in policy-making	Demand for evidence exists; information supplied is based on analysis; information is used in policy-making	To defend and support government's stand on various policy issues, particularly when existing policies are challenged by actors of the policy process	Quick policy decisions are made in close consultation with groups and institutions funded by or supported by the government
Interactive model of policy process (Stone 2002; Stone et al. 2001)	Policy science/policy entrepreneurship/ policy research-linkages	Several actors and stakeholders interact and debate policy options that could result in variety of policy outcomes	Government is open to debate and dialogue; actors and players are well informed about policy problems; allows better ownership by the stakeholders	Long-term and medium-term strategies such as poverty reduction strategies and agricultural development strategies often involve multiple stakeholders and organized interaction	Not preferred in situations requiring quick policy decisions; prolonged debates can increase cost and reduce benefits of policy interventions
Multiple stream approach (Kingdon 1984)	Political science	Three streams of problem, policies, and politics operate together to produce policy outcomes	Policy solution depends on presence of all three streams; policy entrepreneurs are assumed to play key role in connecting the problems to policies bringing political realities into consideration	Specific food policy interventions such as food subsidies and social safety nets/often depend on a group or groups of individuals bringing problem and policies together in the context of specific political conditions	Food price crisis provided opportunity to NGOs in some countries to highlight the problems of food security and enter policy arena. For example, 'Right to Food' advocacies used food price crisis to strengthen their case both in India and Nigeria

Institutional development and rational choice model (Ostrom 1986; Ostrom 2011)	Institutional development/ collective action	Policy and intervention programmes can be developed in response to a crisis situation at the local community level	Self-governing institutions exist and the players are capacitated to identify solutions after analysis of the problem	Food-based interventions in drought prone communities; management of irrigation systems, community forest resources, and land and water resources	During crisis period policy solutions often emerge at the macro level; village-level food reserves to protect the vulnerable group during lean seasons; local price volatility will involve policy responses at the community or district levels
Policy learning and diffusion model (Berry and Berry 1992); (Baumgartner and Jones 1993)	Political science	Policy makers learn from policy solutions developed by neighbouring districts, states, regions, or countries and adapt them to their situations	Policy makers have access to knowledge base on what worked in similar policy situations in other settings	Long-term policy development such as national agricultural investment plans and opposition to GMOs in selected African countries are some examples of use of policy learning and diffusion model	During the food crisis period, politically motivated decision by some countries to ban export of food grains gathered momentum with other countries following similar policy paths
Advocacy coalition framework (Sabatier and Jenkins-Smith 1993)	Policy science	People/groups of people with similar ideology could form coalitions to promote specific policy agenda	Policy makers can be persuaded through advocacy; policy process environment allows for coalition formation	Role of CSOs and NGOs that work towards poverty alleviation come together with one voice to develop poverty reduction strategies; federations of farmers' organizations have been effective in forming advocacy coalitions	Network of NGOs working food security areas come together to advocate for policies to reduce food prices. Some of them jointly took to streets to get the attention of policy makers

Source: Author's compilation.

References

Babu, S. C., and A. Ergeneman (2005). 'Food Policy Dialogue with Indian Parliamentarians'. *Journal of International Communication*, 11(1): 41–54.

Bates, R. H., and S. Block (2010). 'Political Institutions and Agricultural Trade Interventions in Africa'. *American Journal of Agricultural Economics*, 93(2): 317–23.

Baumgartner, F., and B. Jones (1993). *Agendas and Instability in American Politics*. Chicago: University of Chicago Press.

Berry, F. S., and W. Berry (1992). 'Tax Innovation in the States: Capitalizing on Political Opportunity'. *American Journal of Political Science*, 36 (August): 715–42.

Birner, R., S. Gupta, and N. Sharma (2011). 'The Political Economy of Agricultural Policy Reforms in India: Fertilizers and Electricity for Irrigation'. Washington, DC: International Food Policy Research Institute (IFPRI).

Court, J., and J. Young (2003). *Bridging Research and Policy: Insights from 50 Case Studies*. Overseas Development Institute (ODI) Working Paper 213. London: ODI.

FAO (Food and Agriculture Organization), WFP (World Food Programme), and IFAD (International Fund for Agricultural Development) (2012). 'State of Food Security'. Rome: FAO.

FMARD (Federal Ministry of Agriculture and Rural Development) (2010). 'National Agricultural Investment Plan, 2011–2014'. Abuja: FMARD.

IFPRI (International Food Policy Research Institute) (2012). 'Global Food Policy Report, 2012'. Washington, DC: IFPRI.

Kingdon, J. (1984). *Agendas, Alternatives, and Public Policies*. Boston: Little, Brown & Co.

Krebs, V. (2004). 'Power in Networks'. Available at: <www.orgnet.com/PowerInNetworks.pdf> (accessed 1 August 2009).

Maxwell, S. (2006) 'What's Next in International Development? Perspectives from the 20% Club and the 0.2% Club'. Working Paper No. 270. London: Overseas Development Institute (ODI).

Meier, G. (1991). *Politics and Policy Making in Developing Countries*. Washington, DC: Center for Social Innovation (CSI) Press.

Nakamura, R. (1987). 'The Textbook Process and Implementation Research'. *Policy Studies Review*, 1: 142–54.

Omamo, S. (2004). 'Bridging Research, Policy, and Practice in African Agriculture'. Development Strategy and Governance Division Discussion Paper 10. Washington, DC: International Food Policy Research Institute (IFPRI).

Ostrom, E. (1986). 'An Agenda for the Study of Institutions'. *Public Choice*, 48: 3–25.

Ostrom, E. (2011). 'Background on the Institutional Analysis and Development Framework'. *Policy Studies Journal*, 39(1): 7–27.

Rausser, G. C., and J. Swinnen (2011). 'Governance Structures, Political Economy and Public Policy'. *American Journal of Agricultural Economics*, 93(2): 310–16.

Sabatier, P. (2007). *Theories of the Policy Process*. 2nd edn. Boulder, CO: Westview Press.

Sabatier, P., and H. Jenking-Smith (1993). *Policy Change and Learning: An Advocacy Coalition Approach*. Boulder, CO: Westview Press.

Sabatier, P., and C. M. Weibles (2007). 'The Advocacy Coalition Framework: Innovations and Clarifications', in P. Sabarier (ed.), *Theories of the Policy Process*. 2nd edn. Boulder, CO: Westview Press.
Stone, D. (2002). 'The Dilemmas of "Bridging Research and Policy"'. *Compare*, 32(3): 285–96.
Stone, D., S. Maxwell, and M. Keating (2001). 'Bridging Research and Policy'. Working Paper. Coventry: Warwick University.
Volden, C., M. Ting, and D. P. Carpenter (2008). 'A Formal Model of Learning and Policy Diffusion'. *American Political Science Review*, 102: 319–32.
Zahariadis, N. (2003). *Ambiguity and Choice in Public Policy*. Washington, DC: Georgetown University Press.

5

A Political Economy Synthesis

The Food Policy Crisis

*Derrill D. Watson II**

5.1 Introduction

Food policy papers have generally sought to explain levels of chosen policies (e.g., size of a tariff or a fertilizer subsidy). Once the policy has been determined, the studies critique how well they are implemented and measure which policies are the most effective at accomplishing different goals in a given context. Some of the studies are summarized by De Gorter and Swinnen (2002) and Karp and Perloff (2002). Fewer papers attempt to understand why and when governments choose different types of policies, which would improve policy analysts' ability to encourage pro-poor policies which are more likely to be enacted, or to adapt policies which are more palatable to policy elites.

This chapter is a synthesis of political economic insights which can be gleaned from the fourteen country studies reported in Chapters 6–19. While Bryan (Chapter 3) describes which policies were chosen and Babu (Chapter 4) the processes by they were chosen, this chapter's main duty is to bring the diverse policy processes into a common framework in order to identify why different policy responses were chosen. The narratives provided in the country studies are combined with political economic theories, primarily to demonstrate how the studies fit into the political economic literature.

* This chapter has markedly benefited from comments by Rob Paarlberg, Phil Abbott, and participants at the Food Policy Network Workshop at Cornell University. I also appreciate the research assistance of Ochuware Imodagbe.

For many governments, the rapid rise in food prices represented not only a food price crisis, but a food policy crisis. Policy processes are described as being ad hoc, unprepared, confused, and contradictory. In some cases, the governments themselves are described as being in panic. Government actions and inactions sparked fierce debate and riots across the globe.

There are several reasons to study food price movements through a political economy lens. First, international price changes and the degree of price transmission from international to domestic prices are likely to be influenced by government policies as discussed by Baltzer (Chapter 2). Second, government policies determine how the effects of food price changes are distributed among the population, partly through policy impacts on price transmission. The World Bank (2010) further contends that the ad hoc, sudden changes in trade policy constitute policy failures, as did the well-intended but ill-conceived attempts to prevent hoarding and block futures markets. These policy failures added to speculative behaviour and excessive, panicked importing.

This chapter emphasizes three models of government behaviour that implicitly underlie the political economy discussions in the country studies. In the section on internal factors, governments are considered in isolation from their citizens and initially assumed to have pursued exogenous social welfare goals as efficiently as possible. Though I refer to this as the 'naive' model because it abstracts from political realities, a microfoundation justification is given. The assumptions in the naive model are relaxed in the following sub-sections to allow for fragmented government, self-interested government actors, and path dependence. In the following section on external factors, governments maximize a weighted social welfare function in which different stakeholders or lobby groups receive different weights. I refer to this as the rent-seeking model. Sub-sections discuss the private sector and protests.

5.2 Internal Political Economic Factors

5.2.1 *Government Goals: Unitary, Benevolent Government*

> Claim 1: much of the common policy response can be explained by a social welfare function maximizing government.

To understand why the governments chose the policies they did, we need to ask what the governments' primary goals were, temporarily abstracting from the politics which inform those goals. In the naive model, governments have exogenously given goals which they pursue in the most efficient manner possible, subject to the constraints they face.

There are two reasons for starting from there. The first is that this is the benchmark from which most other economic models of governmental decision-making depart. We can then ask how governments' behaviour deviates from that of a first-best or second-best optimization of those goals, to identify what is missing from this description of government behaviour. Second, five of the country-study authors indicate that their governments try to maximize a social welfare function that weights different interest groups approximately equally, with Brazil and India being the strongest supporters of the model. The naive model is not only interesting as a benchmark, but it provides useful predictions in its own right.

The casestudy authors were asked to rank order which of eight possible goals were the most important for their government as it responded to rising food prices (Table 5.1). The second column shows the average rank given by the study authors with a lower number representing a higher priority. For most governments, the stated first priority of their food policies was to reduce hunger and food insecurity. As Bryan (Chapter 3) observes, more than three-fourths of the countries intervened in multiple ways to reduce prices. As a practical matter, very little policy attention was given to the nutritional aspects of food security; ensuring access to available supplies of grains and staples was the primary target for most governments. Reducing poverty and increasing national food self-sufficiency were among the three most important goals in the majority of the governments. A significant number of cases

Table 5.1 Policy priorities of the country-study governments (n=13)

Goal	Average Response (Rank from 1 to 8)	Number Responding that the Goal was among the Top 3 Priorities	Number Responding that the Goal was not Important (Rank 8)
Address poor nutrition/ food insecurity	2.5	9	0
Reduce poverty	3.8	8	3
Increase national food self-sufficiency	4.0	8	3
Contain social/political unrest	4.7	5	4
Secure the government's power...or political or economic rents	5.1	5	4
Stabilize macroeconomy	5.8	4	7
Ensure a minimum farmer income	6.5	0	7
Maintain international relationships	8.0	0	13

Source: survey of the country study authors.

further indicate the importance of stability: achieving stable macroeconomic conditions, reducing social and political unrest, and keeping the current government in power.

Ensuring minimum farmer incomes and maintaining international relationships were primarily important to the developed countries' governments and ignored by the developing countries' governments. However, notice in the final column that roughly half of the governments made ensuring a minimal farming income at least somewhat of a priority while none considered their policies' impacts on other countries. In light of the potential for policy spill-overs seen in the food price crisis, this willful ignorance is alarming and should be addressed by the involved international organizations (Pinstrup-Andersen and Watson 2011; Baltzer, Chapter 2).

This section focuses on the first goal; reducing food insecurity. One reason for this is the complementarity between reducing poverty, increasing national food self-sufficiency, and reducing food insecurity. While these goals are not equivalent, it is difficult to identify a policy measure undertaken to increase self-sufficiency which at the same time might not reflect a desire to reduce food insecurity. However, it should be noted that any complaints that the policies selected were not very efficient at addressing hunger apply doubly for addressing the problems of poverty and national self-sufficiency. Another reason is that very few of the governments invested in long-term national self-sufficiency: the vast majority of policies intended to increase food production did so by introducing economically unsustainable fertilizer subsidies or by increasing grain stocks. Mozambique provides one important exception to this rule, where spending on agriculture nearly doubled. Their Food Production Action Plan invested in multiple agricultural sectors and at all parts of the production-processing chain. The political stability goals receive separate treatment below in the self-interest, the rent-seeking, and the protest sections. Last, the topic of macroeconomic stability showed up primarily as monetary policies, discussed in Baltzer (Chapter 2) and Bryan (Chapter 3), or in the quantitative levels of policy choice rather than the qualitative choice of which policies to choose.

The desire to reduce hunger implies that in most cases lower food prices are preferred to higher. Barrett (1999) provides a justification for equating governments' target to reduce food prices with maximizing social welfare. He constructs a structural model of coalition formation over food price policies. Small- to medium-scale farmers, landless rural labourers, and the urban population poor prefer low prices. Commercial farmers and agro-industrialists prefer high food prices.

Barrett (1999) is quick to point out that this is only a description of coalition formation, not of the complex policy processes that determine final policy outcomes. Barrett uses the model primarily to explain why countries with larger farms and more net food sellers prefer higher prices than countries with primarily small, subsistence farms. This is one reason why the USA, Brazil, South Africa, and Vietnam enacted fewer price decreasing policies. His paper also suggests that in studying food price crises, the important factor is that prices are high rather than that they are variable. Price stability is a less important target to achieving lower food insecurity than ensuring affordable prices, favouring the groups that prefer lower prices. However, as prices increase, variability raises costs and may become a more important part of policy processes going forward.

Empirically, most researchers find that lower food prices also help the poorest in rural areas because they tend to consume more food than they produce (e.g., Deaton 1989, for Thailand; Barrett and Dorosh 1996, for Madagascar; Klytchnikova, and Diop 2006, for Bangladesh; Mghenyi and Jayne 2006, for Kenya; De Janvry and Sadoulet 2010, for Guatemala). On the one hand, nearly all the rice Zambian farmers produce is for household consumption, so any increase in the price of imported rice is harmful in the short run (Chapoto, Chapter 8). On the other hand, most wheat in Zambia is produced by large-scale commercial farmers who benefit from higher wheat prices. Nearly two-thirds of the Kenyan crop and livestock producers are net food buyers (Nzuma, Chapter 9). According to Bangladesh's 2005 Household Income and Expenditure Survey, marginal farmers in Bangladesh must purchase 83 per cent of their rice from markets and even large farms acquire 20 per cent of their rice from markets (Raihan, Chapter 11). At the same time, however, these marginal farmers are selling 20 per cent of what they produce. This shows that price increases during harvest time will be welcomed by even the poorest, while price increases before it will harm even large, commercial farmers.

However, low food prices are not always preferred by poor farmers. In Cambodia, China, Madagascar, and Vietnam, the average farmer is a net food seller (World Bank 2007). Chinese academics argue that food inflation should be allowed in order to benefit the poorest Chinese (Huang, Yang, and Rozelle, Chapter 17). Even when farmers are net buyers, low food prices may not be in their best interests in the long run. Harriss (1979: 377) observes that, because most producers are net food consumers, they have favoured 'the very same cheap food policy that is causing their poverty in the first place since it is not in their interests to pay out higher prices for food'. However, low food prices discourage further investment in agriculture, keeping smallholders' production low. Numerous researchers argued before the food price crisis that small increases in food prices would help the same farmers in the long run. Similarly, Barrett (1999) shows that both higher and lower food prices create political coalitions to support the continuance of either one. Ravallion (2000) argues that higher food prices eventually generate increased agricultural wages which may offset the decrease in consumer welfare from higher prices. The Brazilian case makes use of this notion, showing that if food prices are fully passed through to increase wages—a big if—the poor in Brazil would be better off with higher food prices (Mueller and Mueller, Chapter 18). If there is only a 50 per cent pass-through, the poorest 10 per cent of the population is no worse off.

POLICY FAILURES

There are several significant factors which argue against taking the naive model of government action. For instance, economists typically assume governments identify and address specific market failures so that government intervention in pursuit of their goals can be efficiency enhancing. While roughly half the studies briefly mention speculative behaviour, hoarding, anti-competitive practices, or abuse of market power, very few of the governments took action to address the issues. In Ethiopia, the government merely warned firms not to hoard grain stocks (Admassie, Chapter 6). Egypt passed a law forbidding anti-competitive practices, but following the crisis it was deemed to be largely ineffective in addressing the problem (Ghoneim, Chapter 12). The three exceptions are: Bangladesh, where the government sealed warehouses to prevent hoarding (Raihan, Chapter 11); Malawi, whose government justified its trade restrictions and price bands on addressing hoarding problems (Chirwa and Chinsinga, Chapter 7); and South Africa, where a Competition Commission was established before the food crisis which increased prosecutions and fines for food companies engaging in anti-competitive behaviour (Kirsten, Chapter 19). Governments' relationship with the private sector will be discussed below.

No attempt was made to address other classic market failures, such as providing public goods, which would improve market integration or reduce spatial price variability (e.g., Vietnam). Instead, governments intervened when desirable outcomes were not being achieved by market forces in the short run, typically without regard for the long-run considerations.

More damaging to the naive model are the inefficiencies in the policy choices. Most of the governments did not target their food price policies to those facing hunger and food insecurity. The selected policies tended to be easier and quicker to operate and were either not targeted well or they targeted urban and middle-class citizens whose need was less. Kenya, for example, subsidized bags of processed maize meal which were too large for poor households to afford. India and Zambia, despite identifying reducing poverty as one of their top priorities, took no new actions to improve social safety nets or otherwise support the incomes of the poor. Despite the claim that the majority of the countries wanted to increase food self-sufficiency, most agricultural interventions were short-term only. While Mozambique has claimed to invest heavily in agricultural production and processing bottlenecks, food production has not increased since the crisis. Ganguly and Gulati (Chapter 16) complain that even though India is one of the few countries to increase investment in achieving a second green revolution, the budget allocations are so small that they are likely to have only symbolic impacts. Most of the important interventions are also quite expensive, working against the goal of macroeconomic stability.

In addition to the failures from inefficient policy choices, implementation failures may be found throughout the case studies. Policies are announced and then retracted within three to six months, usually for being ineffective, corrupt, or both. Subsidized foods did not get to the hungriest or poorest. Many policies were introduced too late to stop the rapidly rising prices. Most countries took many actions but had very little to show for it.

The success of the Chinese implementation stands in stark contrast to what happened in most countries (Huang, Yuang, and Rozelle, Chapter 17). China's primary goals were to increase national food self-sufficiency and provide macroeconomic stability. They certainly succeeded in creating food price stability. Regular government and public research centre reports were fed into a policy apparatus where trigger conditions for specific policies were already put in place. The bureaucratic system was ready to put those policies into operation quickly and efficiently. As a result, though rice and wheat prices did rise from 2005 to 2010, they did so at a steady rate that completely denied all international variation. The government credits the success to the combination of stock releases with gradually changing export subsidies into restrictions. If stocks were released without export restrictions, the subsidized grains would have easily made their way to other countries, as happened in the other countries. Since China imports all its soybeans, however, the domestic price fully realized all changes in the global prices. In the immediate aftermath, the majority of China's policies focused on the short-run impacts. Since then, new policies focusing on long-term agricultural development have been introduced.

There are multiple explanations for most countries' divergence from efficient policies, including fragmented government decision-making, path dependence, and self-interested decision makers. So far governments have been modelled as unitary decision makers with a single objective function. Relaxing this assumption, we can see that different factions, ministries, or individuals within government may have competing goals. The evidence on how fragmented government decision-making processes and uncertainty alter the policy mix and introduce delays and inefficiencies and the extent to which policy makers are constrained by past policy choices is discussed below. The 'public choice' model is then considered, which assumes that some or all of those factions may act in their own self-interest and not just for the national interest.

5.2.2 *Fragmented Government and Uncertainty*

> Claim 2: one primary cause of policy failure was fragmented government decision-making.

Thus far, the discussion has assumed that the government can be treated as one entity, capable of rational decision-making based on a known set of goals and constraints. In general, this will only be the case when most policy decisions are made by only one person or by a small group of like-minded people. China forms a distinct counter-example of a large government with many ministries involved in decision-making, yet unified around common goals directed from above (Huang, Yang, and Rozelle, Chapter 17).

Many of the studies, however, demonstrate that the simplifying assumption of unitary government decision-making masks essential dynamics. They reveal a pattern of poor coordination and tensions between different ministries—each with its own goals and maximands, special interest groups, targets, resources and constraints, biases, and influence—which slow policy formation, introduce inefficiencies, and result in sub-optimal outcomes. Roubini and Sachs (1989) are generally credited with introducing the study of fragmented government decision making to fiscal policy, examining whether single-party control of government changed budget deficits. Others have expanded the concept to include the number of decision makers (Kontopoulos and Perotti 1999) and their ideological cohesion (Volkerink and de Haan 2001). These authors also note that fragmentation will matter more during periods of crisis as the one currently being considered.

Fractures exist over who is in charge of decision-making. In Egypt, there was a great unity of purpose surrounding the bread subsidy, but outside of that one policy there was very little coordination or data sharing. The result was that each ministry used its own tools to accomplish its own goals, leading to both duplicated efforts and conflicting policies. In Bangladesh, by contrast, the ministry of commerce was nominally responsible for food market policies. However, it was unable to act without the consent and support of other ministries. Lack of coordination led to a widespread criticism of the ministry for failing its job in a time of crisis. One of the responsibilities of Bangladesh's ministry of commerce might have been to specifically take the blame for general government failures. Nhate, Massingarela, and Salvucci (Chapter 10) particularly mention the contention between government sectors over how much money to allocate to agricultural priorities in Mozambique.

In addition, fractures develop over what role different institutions are supposed to play. In South Africa, the finance ministry offered the ministry of agriculture 400 million Rands to improve food security. Agriculture's response, in one of the oddest inter-ministerial conflicts, was that their mandate covered increasing production and funding research, not food policy. The funding therefore went towards social development through another ministry. In India, the federal government structure complicated and slowed the decision-making process as the federal and state governments debated which was responsible for responding to the crisis.

Malawi seems at first an ideal counter-example: the president had a high level of control over government policies and—as a former minister of agriculture who installed a close friend as his successor in the ministry—he was deeply involved in creating and overseeing the primary agricultural policies. Public agencies that tried to act independently tended to be underfunded, encouraging all government bodies to act in concert with the president's wishes. However, when investigating why the price band failed, Chirwa and Chinsinga (Chapter 7) point, among other problems, to perennial institutional rivalry between the parastatal marketing board and the parastatal grain reserve board. Uncertainty about whether there was a crisis or not, with prices rising despite a record harvest, also slowed policy action. In Zambia, the late timing of government responses were due to conflicts between the ministry of agriculture and other ministries similarly reduced the country's ability to import enough grains to deal with the crisis.

The validity of the unitary government assumption depends on the policy being discussed. Significant government policies are largely determined by only one person or an elite group of like-minded individuals while other policies are left to large groups of diverse stakeholders inside and outside of government. Brazil's programmes to help smallholders are decided by a small group, while income and pricing policies are decided by large groups. In several countries, such as Egypt and Zambia, specific directives come from the highest level around which all policy makers must unify, but then ministries are left to follow other guidelines as they deem best. The survey results identify a slight tendency for the executive head to personally oversee policies relating to social or political unrest while agricultural policies tend to be made by larger groups of decision makers.

Claim 3: Uncertainty and incorrect forecasts significantly influenced government actions.

Analysts now have the convenience of being able to look back and see long time series of price data behind them. During the food price crisis, however, there was no telling how high prices might go, when they might come down again, or what was causing prices to rise so rapidly (Croushore 2011).

Uncertainty in Ethiopia over whether price increases were domestic or international delayed its monetary policy response.

The effects of a fragmented government could be magnified by uncertainty and incorrect forecasts. In Zambia the Disaster Management Consultative Forum watches for production shocks while the Ministry of Agriculture and Livestock focuses more on national food balance sheets. Thus, if there is no change in production, the committee trained to deal with disasters will not react to changes in the international market. Further, the disaster committee focuses on rural, smallholder, and poverty issues while the agriculture ministry responds more to the commercial farmers' needs. Private unions convinced the Minister of Agriculture in July 2008 that demand would be larger than the government estimated, and so it began importing earlier.

The interplay between uncertainty and fragmented government is best seen in the study on Vietnam. Vietnam's policy decisions were sparked by a March 2008 report from the Ministry of Agriculture and Rural Development (MARD) that claimed harvests would be lower than usual. The government felt it would be wisest to restrict exports. However, this decision was based on faulty predictions because Vietnamese farmers had a bumper crop. The minister apologized before the National Assembly for the wrong estimates that led to an export ban. This one bit of uncertainty in the report could therefore well be blamed for part of the crisis itself, to the extent that Vietnam's measures to restricting exports led to increasing global grain prices.

One hypothesis is that policy actions in India spilled over into Vietnam. The argument relies on imperfect information and uncertainty, with governments getting a signal about conditions in other countries based on their policies. When India restricted its exports, the Vietnamese government received a signal about the likely production of India and of the direction of future rice prices. Fearing that increasing prices would reduce consumer welfare, Vietnam began reducing its exports. As each government saw the other restricting exports, more restrictions were put in place.

The problem with the logic of this hypothesis is that the Vietnamese government viewed India as a competitor in the rice market (Nguyen and Talbot, Chapter 15). When India announced export restrictions, this signalled higher profits and foreign exchange to be earned by keeping markets open. Without the internal MARD report, the government would likely have not intervened in the export market. Rather than signalling a need to close borders, the Indian governments' actions gave the Vietnamese government a reason to keep them open. This is one reason Vietnam merely 'dabbled' in intervention, to use Bryan's (Chapter 3) classification.

While MARD was reducing export profits to protect consumers, the Ministry of Industry and Trade was tasked with protecting farmers and therefore introduced a price floor above the market clearing price. Put together, these conflicting policies meant that large amounts of rice were not sold domestically or abroad, prices rose despite the existence of surplus rice, and some households had less food access despite high food availability. Publicly held stocks increased rapidly. These examples highlight the importance of modelling governments as fragmented between different policy makers with different goals and constraints. Because of complex interactions, final outcomes may resemble the goals of none of these parts.

5.2.3 *Public Choice*

Claim 4: policy makers' private interests drove policy choice in select examples.

Unlike the naive model above, public choice theory assumes that policy makers also have self-interested motivations for what they do. In this chapter, I differentiate between two branches of public choice theory: the first I call the rent-seeking model and the other the 'self-interest' model. In the rent-seeking model used when we consider external factors, policy makers put more weight on the welfare of some stakeholder groups than others (e.g., urban versus rural consumers). In the self-interest model considered here, however, policy makers explicitly ask how they can personally benefit.

While there is some overlap between these branches, the fundamental question is why policy makers support a particular group: if it is for private gain, it falls under the self-interest model. In the self-interest model, policy makers do not attempt to reduce hunger and poverty purely out of altruism but because doing so also satisfies other, private interests. These private interests may include ensuring their continuance in power, personal financial rewards, increased power and influence, or achieving a place in history.

Consider first the desire to remain in power. Ganguly and Gulati (Chapter 16) report on the widely held belief in Indian political circles that elections have been lost on the basis of onion prices that skyrocketed the year before the election, and that the government's decision to forgive the debts of smallholder farmers was a populist sop before the 2009 elections. This supports the electoral business cycle theory, first put forward by Nordhaus (1975), in which politicians enact different policies near elections to secure their re-election (see also Vadlamannati 2008, for another application to India). Politicians have clearly learned to respond quickly to both preventing onion price increases and providing support when they do rise, lest they lose an upcoming election.

Nhate, Massingarela, and Salvucci (Chapter 10) and Resnick (Chapter 14) similarly argue that Mozambique and Senegal typically only begin implementing promised programmes just before elections. Efforts to prevent food price increases were therefore widely perceived as attempts to improve the government's re-election chances. Kirsten (Chapter 19: 422) indicates the few innovations South Africa enacted were based on 'the seriousness of the crisis in terms of political repercussions'.

Policies were not only chosen to secure electoral victory but to generate private wealth as well. For instance, the Grossman-Helpman (1994) 'pay to play' model assumes that governments maximize a weighted sum of social welfare and campaign contributions which can be thought of either as being used to stay in power or as private spending money. Practitioners then use data on trade barriers to measure government benevolence, with more open governments putting more weight on social welfare (e.g., Gawande, Krishna, and Olarreaga 2009). This explicitly assumes that some governments respond more to private incentives than others, and so we should expect the same in these studies.

Malawi and Zambia most closely exemplify the influence private incentives have on policy selection. The Malawian political system functions through a system of patronage, with votes and support bought using public resources doled out to favoured constituents. In part because of its importance to the diet and even more because of the food crises in 2001–2 and 2005, maize policies became the lifeblood of the political parties. The most important campaign element in the 2009 election for all parties was what to do with the extremely popular fertilizer subsidy which directly transferred resources to politically important farmers. Government officials admit that 'the government is only interested in controlling the price of maize because . . . there can be political backlashes' and is 'motivated largely by electoral considerations (Chirwa and Chinsinga, Chapter 7). Because of the importance of maize policies to government legitimacy, the president announced price policies and maize export bans at political rallies and functions.

The Malawian government granted one particular firm a monopoly in distributing and overseeing the fertilizer subsidy. That company was owned by the president. It was therefore very much in his private interest that the subsidy be expanded. Furthermore, Chirwa and Chinsinga (Chapter 7) argue that the reason the National Food Reserve Agency (NFRA) did not release grain stocks was that the major grain exporters to Zimbabwe were politicians who profited from the high international prices. This directly led to the implementation failure of the price band enacted through Agricultural Development and Marketing Corporation (ADMARC), the agricultural parastatal.

Political economists have posed two competing models for how a self-interested government should distribute scarce resources, such as fertilizer and seed subsidies, to their citizens and supporters. The 'swing voter' model says that governments should transfer resources to marginal constituencies to strengthen their loyalty (e.g., Lindbeck and Weibull 1993; Bates

2008). The 'core support' model, however, believes that governments should reward strong loyalty rather than tepid support, distributing resources to their strongest supporters (Cox and McCubbins 1986).

Empirical studies have found support for each model. Banful (2010) for instance finds that Ghana distributed more vouchers for subsidized fertilizer to districts where they lost the last election, evidence in favour of the swing model. The studies presented in this volume come down heavily in favour of the core support model. In both Malawi and Zambia, subsidized fertilizer vouchers are distributed as a reward for support in the previous election (Chapoto, Chapter 8). According to Mason and Ricker-Gilbert (2012), the average household receives 11 kg more fertilizer if it lives in a constituency that voted for the government party and that amount increases by 0.5 kg for every additional 1 per cent of the vote. Chapoto (Chapter 8) adds that stakeholder contributions were deliberately ignored to support policies with a higher political payoff.

In addition to winning elections and personal enrichment, decision makers' goals include seeking a place in history (Galeotti and Breton 1986). The Senegalese case study provides an interesting portrait of a leader compelled to make a name for himself in history. President Wade focused on very large projects, nearly all of them with his name emblazoned on top. Yet at the same time, these projects could be abandoned rapidly as ministerial responsibilities were shuffled to prevent anyone else from rising to the top.

Four of the study authors believe food policy goals were not pursued for their own sake but primarily in order to secure government power or legitimacy. Two further authors explicitly listed maintaining power as one of their governments' goals. They additionally confirm that this is standard operating procedure rather than a new factor. Where elections exist, they are universally ranked as one of the most important factors in determining when and how to respond to a food crisis. These answers and studies suggest that, while personal benefits accruing to policy makers influence governance and policy choice more in some governments than others, emergency situations do not alter governments' degree of self-interest or benevolence.

5.2.4 *Status Quo Bias and Path Dependence*

There are three possible ways that the food price crisis could change food policies: change governments' goals; introduce new policies used to achieve pre-existing goals; or adjust pre-existing policies (e.g., lower import tariffs).

Most of the changes witnessed were in the last category, evidence of status quo bias and path dependence.

> Claim 5: the responses to past crises are the best guides to predicting future actions.

Governments may suffer from a status quo bias for a number of reasons. One possible form of status quo bias would be if there are costs to enacting new policies. Governments would then maintain current policies until the forgone benefits are greater than the costs to change. Alternatively from accumulating evidence from behavioural economics posits that endowment effects and loss aversion mean that most individuals prefer the status quo to any change—effects which would afflict political decision makers as well (Tversky and Kahneman 1991). In particular, if it is unknown who will gain and lose from a particular policy, governments may hesitate to break from the status quo (Fernandez and Rodrik 1991). Tetlock and Boettger (2006) argue that if it is known who will lose from a particular policy, transparency will increase policy makers' status quo bias. These effects generate two possible hypotheses.

The first hypothesis is that governments should prefer policy changes with lower costs, such as changing the level of a currently existing policy rather than introducing a new policy.

Second, there should be relatively little government activity normally, but crises should impel government action in ways that would not be seen normally. Thus, we would expect to see larger and bolder policy experiments as a result of the food price shocks.

> Claim 6: the studies support the first hypothesis, but not the second.

The food price crisis did not change most countries' goals. Only two of the study authors believe that government goals and priorities shifted during the crisis: in Nigeria, where continued media pressure redirected at least some government attention to the neglected agriculture sector and in Egypt, where the 2005 change in election laws created new pressure on the government to address food policy issues. There has been some change in Ethiopia's goals after the crisis as well, as the prime minister indicated an increasing policy emphasis on food self-sufficiency and a reduced reliance on foreign food aid (Malone 2010).

Most governments seem to have felt that the policies they had in place or typically implemented were sufficient. The governments that typically intervene little did not change their history of non-involvement. The governments that typically have a single powerful decision maker let the person decide the food policy responses in ways that were largely predictable. Even though China changed direction from subsidizing exports to restricting them, it followed traditional policy processes in order to maintain impressive price stability, even without announcing a set price for rice or wheat. The global food price crisis only temporarily sped up India's right to food deliberations rather than changing their nature. Brazil and South Africa reacted in the most passive manner; their safety nets and policies were already in place for dealing with the crisis when it came. As a regional food exporter with significant safety nets in place, it is even questionable whether there was a food crisis in South Africa. Kirsten (Chapter 19: 424) adds the realities of fragmented government and considers

> The fact that the ANC in itself is not monolith and is intensely divided along many divisions it is no wonder that most spheres of government policy making—especially in agriculture, food, land and rural development matters are experiencing 'policy paralysis' or the inability to make important decisions.... This 'policy paralysis' can be ascribed to the fact that government (and the party) has succumbed to deep ideological divisions within the ruling alliance, which prevent any agreement on the way forward.

Even where new policies were introduced (roughly half the cases), they were most often a re-introduction, following historical precedent. Export-oriented countries that give significant support to agriculture were more likely to leave export borders open than the countries where consumer interests have typically received greater weight. Historically favoured farmers were more likely to receive farmer-friendly policies than farmers of less politically influential crops. Countries that have long been concerned about food self-sufficiency enacted policies to encourage that goal. These path-dependent policy choices may represent interest-group interactions (see next section), ideology, or a kind of myopia wherein the psychological costs of introducing new policies are higher than the costs of expanding current policies.

The most prevalent and first used policy changes were to adjust tariff and tax rates, add people to income or in-kind benefits and increase their value, or release stocks gathered in previous years. As Mueller and Mueller (Chapter 18: 399) point out for Brazil, 'the fact that these cash transfer programmes were already set up and running when the food price crisis hit in 2007 made it very easy for the government to use these channels to provide some compensating income to the poor'.

Citizens' willingness to protest the removal or reduction of a benefit acts as a significant constraint to the scope of policy choice. Ghoneim (Chapter 12: 256, 255) reports that 'removing one element of [Egypt's bread subsidy] can create a very dangerous domino effect' because it represents 'a powerful symbol for the social contract between the population and any governing regime'. Malawi's fertilizer subsidy and Brazil's *Bolsa Família* are showing a similar propensity.

There were relatively very few policy surprises: Brazil demonstrated that its relatively new institutional checks on executive power were more effective than would have been supposed. Egypt took advantage of the crisis to streamline many aspects of the ration card and bread subsidy system, reduce leakage to the black market, and speed the adoption of electronic ration cards to prevent fraud—though there was a desire to effect these changes already. Egypt also established an advisory board on food security to improve coordination of the various food and agricultural policies that straddle ministry divisions. The most common new policy was to introduce fertilizer subsidies which had been having a very good run in Malawi, both politically and in terms of agricultural production.

One of the best guides for identifying how governments would respond to the food price shock was how they responded to previous food crises or other disasters. Devaluation led to a food price shock in Egypt during 2001–3, which prompted the government to nearly double the size of the bread subsidy. The subsidy was again nearly doubled during the 2007–8 food price crisis. Malawi's fertilizer subsidy programme was developed in response to the two droughts and the food crises in 2001–5. Those food crises put the subsidy at the forefront of Malawi's political environment. Zambia established a system of national food balance sheets which would trigger an export ban in response to the 2001–3 and 2005–6 crises. South Africa similarly established a Food Price Monitoring Committee in response to the 2001 food price shock to improve the government's information set during crisis periods. Vietnam's transition to a market economy came about in part because of the food crisis of 1985–8, and the loss of food aid from once-communist countries starting in 1989.

Bangladesh is an interesting case in this regard. It had not suffered from food price crises, but had instead experienced several natural disasters during the 2000s. The government had established a network to deal with disasters, supplying food and other basic necessities wherever they were needed quickly. The food price crisis was therefore treated as if it was a natural disaster; as in the past, they went to buy rice from India. Given that there were also floods and a cyclone in 2007 on top of spiralling food prices, this seems a very reasonable interpretation. This also explains why Bangladesh was among Bryan's (Chapter 3) policy dabblers: it was another natural disaster and did not require a major policy shift to address. However, the caretaker government had a short time horizon for which it was planning and it failed to address long-term issues. When there was a delay before an agreement could be reached with the government of India to send rice to Bangladesh, it taught the government that stocks are needed to deal with natural disasters as well, leading to a renewed interest in national food self-sufficiency and stock building following the crisis (Raihan, Chapter 11).

Status quo bias may also exist because of the institutional backdrop within which policy elites work (e.g., Hager and Sullivan 1994). Brazil's institutional framework ensures that 'strong incentives' constrain the president 'irrespective of party or ideology. . . to pursue fiscally sound social inclusion' policies (Mueller and Mueller, Chapter 18: 385). Only 10 per cent of the budget is within the president's direct control, while at the same time the president must prevent inflation or be removed from the office. These institutional trappings of the presidency convinced even a left-leaning candidate like Lula da Silva—who advocated defaulting on Brazil's debt—to act like a fiscal conservative in office. The institutions, informed by electorate beliefs created during previous inflation crises, constrained the president's choice set. Mueller and Mueller (Chapter 18) also contrast Brazil's government's infrastructure with Argentina's where these checks and balances are not present, and attribute their varying policy choices (e.g., export ban in Argentina, none in Brazil) to that fundamental institutional difference.

India's goals did not shift during the crisis, but there was an institutional shift that began in 2001. Its Supreme Court ruled that the government's food-related programmes were legal entitlements (Srinivasan and Narayanan 2007). This shifted the government's policy priorities from poverty alleviation to fulfilling their people's right to food. Most of the long-term policies they enacted were already being discussed or in process of implementation before the crisis because of this institutional imperative. While Brazil's institutions shrank the scope of action, India's mandated increased action and attention to this area.

5.3 External Political Economy Factors

The first half of the chapter considered government largely in isolation from outside influences. To unify our discussion of policy makers' interactions with the rest of their countries, consider the Stigler–Peltzman rent-seeking model as generalized by Hillman (1982). The key insight it offers is that governments value the rents or the political support they receive from industry and consumers, as well as income from tariffs. The political support given is assumed to be closely related to group welfare, so we can say that governments have an incentive to increase the key groups' welfare. Producers' ideal price is that which maximizes industry profits: the monopoly price. Consumers' ideal price is that which would prevail under competitive conditions or the world price if the country imports. Depending on the weights governments place on these groups and tariff revenue, the government chooses tariffs and other policies to set industry prices. For instance, Senegal's Wade prominently introduced new policies immediately after meeting with different constituency groups in order to ensure their political support (Resnick, Chapter 14).

This half of the chapter considers the roles of various, overlapping special interest groups: urban citizens, donors, the private sector, and protestors.

> Claim 7: Policies tended to favour urban consumer groups over other stakeholders, but it is not clear that this represents a change in policy priorities.

Half of the country-study authors indicate that their governments' primary motivation was to maximize the welfare of particular, politically important groups of people. Chief among these politically important groups are urban consumers: only three authors say urban consumers' welfare was not considered by the government in making policy decisions. In Zambia it was mealie maize—consumed in cities and not in rural areas—that was subsidized rather than maize itself, so the benefits went to urban consumers rather than rural. Bangladesh similarly focused on subsidizing urban consumers' food through the rationing system rather than urban consumers.

Political economists and scientists have generally hypothesized that food price crises increase governments' urban bias. In terms of Hillman (1982), the additional weight governments place on urbanites' welfare is the underlying urban bias. Hillman (1982) demonstrates that if the world prices decrease, the governments would prefer to exactly offset the price decrease with an increase in tariffs to maintain the same domestic price. The same is true in reverse during a food price spike. This provides one partial explanation for the decrease in anti-agriculture policies documented by Anderson (2010) since the seminal Krueger, Schiff, and Valdes (1988) study: food prices had decreased and so anti-agriculture policies were reduced. Thus, policies designed to lower food prices may not be the result of a change in governments' preferences (i.e., the additional weight placed on urban consumers relative to agriculture) but merely attempts to preserve the existing balance. Future research will want to examine this possibility.

> Claim 8: foreign actors had no practical influence in most governments' decision-making processes.

With several of the sub-Saharan African countries relying heavily on international aid for budget support and food, given donors' historic interventions, it might have been expected that the international financial institutions and bilateral donors would have a significant influence on policies. This makes it surprising that donors took on a much more supportive role than the one with which they are usually credited. The authors regularly state that donor organizations helped fund government initiatives, but there is no evidence that they pressed for those initiatives to take particular directions. In Senegal and Malawi, multiple donor organizations did press for improved policy actions, but these calls went unheeded. The World Bank even helped to fund fertilizer subsidies in many countries which as recently as 2005 were against best practices.

For the most part, donor organizations and non-governmental organizations concentrated on expanding their own in-country programmes and alleviating the immediate hunger and poverty. It has been suggested this was due partly to a lack of experienced staff dealing with food and agricultural issues: no one was prepared for a sudden return to real prices not seen in twenty-five years. Since the crisis began, donor organizations increased their own capacity to deal with these issues, so they may be expected to play a more active policy role in future food price crisis (assuming different crises do not transfer the funding elsewhere).

There are several exceptions to the non-influence of foreign actors. In Bangladesh and Ethiopia, the International Monetary Fund claimed that the inflation they were experiencing was caused by domestic factors and that they therefore needed to employ tighter monetary policy. Raihan (Chapter 11) notes that the World Bank and other donors can have significant influence since they provide 55–60 per cent of the government budget, but no details are given for how or which policies they influenced. Egypt made use of donor admonition and help to introduce smart cards to their bread subsidy, improving efficiency and reducing corruption. The US indication that they would allow Japan to sell its rice stocks on the open market sent a powerful signal which is credited with reversing the price crisis, even though those stocks were never actually released.

5.3.1 *The Private Sector*

> Claim 9: insider business lobbyist groups played a pivotal role in policy formation, primarily in lower-level committees.
> Claim 10: lack of transparency fuels mistrust between the government and the private sector, leading to policy and implementation failures.

The relationships between governments and the private sector during the food price crisis are complex and fascinating in their contradictions. There are at least two types of stories repeated in the country studies: business lobby groups have significant access to government committees which grant them influence on policy decisions, but that influence is constrained by mistrust on both sides. Governments call firms saboteurs, accuse them of speculative hoarding designed to destabilize the country, and threaten them with fines and jail for performing temporal and spatial arbitrage. Firms are concerned about the uncertainty generated by policy reversals and lack of transparency. This combination makes policy making—not to mention efficient food markets and business development—a difficult process.

Lobbies' influence on politics can be readily seen. As only one example, Zambia's three main agricultural lobby groups represent large farmers, maize millers, and grain traders. While farmers' unions prefer to block grain imports, the largest millers prefer open imports and receive subsidized grain from the government. In January 2008 when these lobbies were in agreement over the direction policy should take, the stocks monitoring committee was happy to follow their suggestions. After that, however, the lobbies disagreed and because of their lack of unity the committee did nothing else until riots broke out, as discussed below.

This influence is heavily constrained by mistrust. Ethiopia's and Malawi's governments enacted specific policies to deal with distrusted private traders by restricting domestic grain trade. In Malawi's case, this was the only new policy crafted specifically for the price increase. In Ethiopia's case, the government largely relied on verbal censure, claiming businesses were deliberately trying to create unrest and instability. Admassie (Chapter 6) also refers to harassment and intimidation, but details are not known. In addition, the combination of fertilizer subsidies and closed borders led to smuggling in some cases, such as trading Kenyan subsidized fertilizers for Tanzanian maize.

In Bangladesh, the caretaker government's fight against corruption disrupted supply chains and decimated informal markets many people relied on for food access. This reduced supply and likely increased food prices in more remote areas. Even though Mozambique has created a forum for business concerns to be heard, their input was largely ignored in formulating the government's response to the food price crisis. India, the world's largest democracy with an impressive historical concern for human rights, can force private traders to liquidate their grain stocks within fifteen days or face jail time. Oddly enough, however, Vietnam has such a reverence for private property that the idea of seizing private stocks was not even debated.

The distrust the government has for the private sector also leads to a lack of policy transparency. Why tell people you mistrust what you are going to do? This creates uncertainty for market participants encompassing the prices at which the government will buy grains, the market price that will trigger government sales, the length of export or import bans, and the size and scope of subsidies. Farmers must make planting decisions without knowing government pricing plans and traders must import without knowing when governments will intervene. Each could potentially lose their entire investment. There is a persistent irony that smallholder farmers are verbally praised and largely forgotten during policy making while large commercial farms and processors are quietly subsidized and publically demonized.

For instance, when farmers begged the Kenyan government to reveal the price it would set for maize in the 2010–11 season, the government responded that that was not how markets worked—as if governments' price-setting policies were driven by market forces (Mugambi 2010). Egypt's export ban was announced for only six months, but then extended for six more. This generated uncertainty and increased price instability compared to a transparent system. India's agricultural trade regularly suffers from drastic policy changes and piecemeal policy making. Malawi follows the same pattern (Babu and Sanyal 2007).

The kind of policy gyrations witnessed in Nigeria, Kenya, Vietnam, and elsewhere impede the effectiveness of other policies because people cannot trust that other policies will remain in effect any longer than these. If a policy can change so rapidly, how can firms or consumers make informed decisions on investments?

Food price uncertainty contributed to the lack of transparency. Governments could not predict how long bans would need to be in place because they did not know what was going on in their own markets at the moment, let alone predict what would happen in the future. Ideally then, governments should establish clear guidelines about the conditions under which certain policies would be enacted—at what price thresholds bans would be put into place or taken down, how subsidies would vary with price, and so forth. This would promote both market and policy efficiency by enabling farmers and traders to make informed decisions.

In some cases, the problems stem from only partial market liberalization. The threat of government intervention through still-extant parastatal corporations keeps private firms from making the investments needed to create properly functioning, thick markets. The lack of well-established markets simultaneously tells the government they should not fully dismantle the parastatals. The end result preserves all the negatives of both market and control system while denying the benefits of both. Countries might be better off with either a more market-friendly system or a more controlled top-down system, rather than trying both and neither.

Resolving these concerns will require much greater transparency from government and trust between government and the private sector (Pinstrup-Andersen and Watson 2011). Unfortunately, as previously discussed, path dependence matters. Previous crises have built the distrust over decades and it requires a significant amount of time to change the culture of mistrust that exists. Jayne, Zulu, and Nijhoff (2006: 338) declare that:

> The phenomenon of subsidized government intervention in the market, or the threat of it, leading to private sector inaction, is one of the greatest problems plaguing the food marketing systems in the region. Effective coordination between the private and public sector would require greater consultation

and transparency with regard to changes in parastatal purchase and sale prices, import and export decisions, tariff rate changes and stock release triggers.

5.3.2 *Protests*

> Claim 11: protests and the threat of protests over food prices most often elevate food policy decision-making to a higher government level. Political protests have quite different impacts.

Bellemare (2012) convincingly demonstrates that food price shocks are significantly correlated with the risk of protests, but what leads some stakeholders to protest and others to work within the government processes? Insider/outsider models postulate that interest groups have different levels of access and influence over policy makers. The difference between the groups is variously identified as being one of access or of strategies, with insiders being able to and choosing to consult with the government while outsiders rely on other means, such as media or social protest to influence government decisions (e.g., Maloney, Jordan, and McLaughlin 1994). There is a hefty debate whether they are outsiders because they choose such tactics or whether they protest because they are denied inside access.

Protestors tended to be not the poorest, but middle-poor to lower-middle-income urbanites, often encouraged by opposition parties. Protestors hoped to sway policy toward their favour while opposition parties hoped to gain additional power in decision-making both at the time of the protests and at the next election (Vadlamannati 2008). These methods are significantly different from those of the insider business lobbies who try to become part of the decision-making process, providing the information and feedback on which governments rely.

Prior to the Zambian riots, which targeted retail shops rather than the government, the government had only acted when the major business lobbies acted in concert. After the riots, high-level officials took notice and the food policies 'became political' (Chapoto, Chapter 8). Huang, Yang, and Rozelle (Chapter 17) recall the Chinese proverb that when peasants are hungry, they rebel. In particular, the urban poor and university students were identified as the most politically sensitive group. Though there was an attempt to target subsidies to the poorest students, 'the students were included, of course, not fully because of poverty consideration, but the political power and their influences through demonstration' (Huang et al. 2013). Thus, even though the Chinese government's primary goals were related to its ongoing efforts to reduce poverty, desires for political stability played their role as well.

Ensuring political stability was one of Ethiopia's primary goals. Therefore reducing political instability was an essential element of Ethiopia's policy-making, despite the fact that there were no reported protests. Protests followed the 2005 elections that brought a large contingent of opposition candidates into the legislature. This accomplished several things. The instability that followed encouraged farmers to hold onto more of their produce, not bringing as much to the market. This decrease in marketed supply increased food prices before the international price spikes. At the same time, the government took several strategic actions—in addition to food policies—to reduce the possibility of further protests. Opposition leaders were accused of inciting the protests and were jailed. Freedom of assembly was curtailed in a number of instances in order to reduce the risk of protests. Food price policies were part of the policy response specifically to reduce the likelihood of protest: bringing down food prices and increasing food supply would reduce the pressures.

Admassie (Chapter 6) provides some confirmation for this version of events by noting that while the government's priority was reducing food prices, the reason for doing so was to ensure political and macroeconomic stability. He notes that 'the Ethiopian government took various measures to control rising food inflation since it did not want to take risks which might lead to another political instability' (Chapter 6: __). He further confirms that non-food policies were an important part of the government's food policy when he concludes that 'avoiding social unrest' was the first of the 'main factors that motivated the government to take these measures' (Chapter 6: 150).

In addition to being more frequent, protests seem to have been more effective in Senegal than in most other countries. With five major protests supported by opposition parties in 2007–8 alone, the government was pressured to improve vendor working conditions, agree to a new five year contract to import rice, introduce new rice subsidies, and to establish a new inter-ministerial task force to meet weekly with the head of the consumers union.

Political protests are different from food protests. The 2007–8 Egyptian riots were significantly smaller and more geographically constrained than the later 2010–11 protests. The primary complaint in the first riots dealt specifically with increasing food and fuel prices while any anti-government sentiment was largely a symptom of concerns about prices; the latter riots focused on poor government performance, low wage increases, and unemployment. When the government reaffirmed and increased the bread subsidy in 2008—a programmatic response to previous protests—the protestors largely dispersed. In that sense, these were similar to the 1977 riots which prevented a decrease in the size of the subsidy. In 2010, however, the riots and protests remained despite subsidy increases.

In Kenya, violence lowered the level of government addressing food policies instead of raising it. Kenya's chief executive was primarily concerned with the constitutional transformation following the election violence at the end of 2007; most food policy decisions were therefore made by the minister of agriculture. It is also interesting to note the similarity between South Africa in 1994 and Kenya in 2007–8. In both cases, the populace and government were intensely interested in political transitions that trumped attention to rising food prices. In South Africa's case this included the end of apartheid, the induction of Nelson Mandela as the first black president, and the 1995 Rugby World Cup win that overshadowed a 22 per cent food price spike. In Kenya, election violence and the changing constitution were more immediate concerns, leaving individual ministers free to set their own policies without much coordination.

5.4 Conclusions

This synthesis has made eleven claims about the political economy of food policies from the 2006–8 food price crisis:

1. Much of the common policy response can be explained by a social welfare function maximizing government.
2. One primary cause of policy failure was fragmented government decision-making.
3. Uncertainty and incorrect forecasts significantly influenced government actions.
4. Policy makers' private interests drove policy choice in select examples.
5. The responses to past crises are the best guides to predicting future actions.
6. Governments preferred policy changes with lower costs, such as changing the level of a currently existing policy rather than introducing a new policy.
7. Policies tended to favour urban consumer groups over other stakeholders, but it is not clear that this represents a change in policy priorities.
8. Foreign actors had no practical influence in most governments' decision-making processes.
9. Insider business lobbyist groups played a pivotal role in policy formation, primarily in lower-level committees.
10. Lack of transparency fuels mistrust between the government and the private sector, leading to implementation failure.

11. Protests and the threat of protests over food prices most often elevate food policy decision-making to a higher government level. Political protests have quite different impacts.

Remarkably, many of these factors can be seen in play in Nigeria. Data uncertainty led to significant government delays that were exacerbated by a lack of protests (Claims 3 and 11), which the government would have taken as a signal that the food price spikes were a cause for concern. Very few of the policy plans drafted were actually put into place, increasing business uncertainty about government actions and likely increasing rice hoarding (Claim 10). One reason cited for passing on a policy that would improve Nigeria's rice processing ability was the cost and the fact that its impacts would not have been seen for some months (Claims 4 and 6). When the federal government did release rice stocks to state government representatives (Claim 2), there were significant corruption charges against state representatives who used released stocks for political and personal gain (Claim 4 and self-interest model). Even though Olomola (Chapter 13) contends that the federal government's primary goal was reducing hunger, and was itself free of corruption in this episode (Claim 1), stocks were released to states not by population size but by political interest in particular regions' welfare (rent-seeking model). Agricultural credits were extended for political reasons (self-interest model). One reason for the ad hoc policy reactions, described by Olomola (Chapter 13) as panicked, was a lack of past experience with food crises; yet it is most likely we would see such ad hoc, stop and go actions again in another crisis because no long-term plan has been put into play to deal with the next crisis (Claim 5).

This synthesis has found three models of government behaviour to be particularly relevant to governments' decision-making during the global food price crisis of 2007–8. The broad commonalities between very different countries can be understood by appealing to a relatively naive model of political economy. Most governments interested in the short-run welfare of their people tend to favour policies that lower prices when international prices spike upwards: lowering import barriers while export barriers rise, and lowering taxes on food consumption while subsidies increase. Concerns about the food security of the poor will lead governments to increase the size and scope of social safety nets. Concerns about macroeconomic stability may moderate these policies but most governments demonstrated a willingness to forgo significant revenue in order to deal with the near-term crisis.

While the naive model is sufficient to uncover the broad similarities between policy packages, it is also apparent that this simple model is insufficient to explain much of the variance or the ways in which governments deviate from these simple predictions. Without strong leadership and clear direction from the executive, different ministries with different goals and instruments available not only act slowly, but enact directly contradictory policies (e.g., Vietnam). Even where governments have had a very clear, unified set of food and agriculture policies, severe swings in international prices may create or bring to the fore schisms that had not been politically relevant before (e.g., Egypt). Uncertainty led to significant policy delays and reversals (e.g., Vietnam, Nigeria). These factors combine to cause much of the policy implementation failure documented here and in Bryan (Chapter 3). Institutions, both formal and informal, constrain political choice and resources (e.g., Brazil, India).

Rent-seeking models that assume the governments care more about the welfare of particular groups implicitly underlie most of the cases and find significant support from them. Social safety net expansions were more likely to benefit urban consumers than rural (e.g., Bangladesh); governments did less to reduce price increases where farmers had large farms, were organized, and were politically connected (e.g., the USA, South Africa); and subsidies favoured groups more likely to protest and disrupt government legitimacy (e.g., Ethiopia, China). In some special cases, governments deviate even further, enacting policies in ways that are privately beneficial to the detriment of publically stated goals and targets (e.g., Malawi, Zambia, and Senegal). Politics matter.

Government relations with the private sector have also been shown to be of critical importance in some cases (e.g., Kenya). Mutual distrust between them has been paralysing for both investment and policy. Lack of government transparency and sudden policy shifts have led firms and traders to hoard and speculate, and farmers to invest more conservatively; those same responses support governments' beliefs that businesses will hoard and speculate, thereby promoting a lack of transparency and sudden policy shifts. This coordination failure is an essential component of policy failures in these countries and must be remedied to prepare for future crises.

The global food crisis also appears to have affected underlying policy processes much less than would have been hypothesized. Government/stakeholder relationships did not change, government goals did not change, and most countries responded not by introducing completely new policies but by either tweaking existing policies or responding to food price volatility with instruments they had used before. Most relevant institutional change happened in the five years prior to the food crisis, suggesting that it is the period between crises when governments are most susceptible to new policies and processes.

This suggests that now is the time to prepare for the next crisis rather than waiting for the next emergency to create an impetus for change. It is also likely that their responses to future global food crises will be similar to those followed during 2007–12. Among changes that would help resolve some of the challenges mentioned above is to establish automatic policy responses following important trigger variables. This would improve policy transparency and reduce the problems from policy delays and fragmented government.

References

Anderson, K. (2010). 'Krueger/Schiff/Valdes Revisited: Agricultural Price and Trade Policy Reform in Developing Countries Since 1960'. *Applied Economic Perspectives and Policy* 32(2): 195–231.

Babu, S., and P. Sanyal (2007). '"Persistent Food Insecurity from Policy Failures in Malawi". Case Study 7-2'. In P. Pinstrup-Andersen and F. Cheng (eds), *Food Policy for Developing Countries: The Role of Government in the Global Food System*. Ithaca: Cornell University Press.

Banful, A. B. (2010). 'Old Problems in the New Solutions? Politically Motivated Allocation of Program Benefits and the "New" Fertilizer Subsidies'. International Food Policy Research Institute (IFPRI) Discussion Paper No. 01002. Washington, DC: IFPRI.

Barrett, C. (1999). 'The Microeconomics of the Development Paradox: On the Political Economy of Food Price Policy'. *Agricultural Economics* 20: 159–72.

Barrett, C. B., and P. A. Dorosh (1996). 'Farmers' Welfare and Changing Food Prices: Nonparametric Evidence from Rice in Madagascar'. *American Journal of Agricultural Economics* 78(3): 656–69.

Bates, R. (2008). *When Things Fall Apart: State Failure in Late-Century Africa*. New York: Cambridge University Press.

Bellemare, M. F. (2012). 'Rising Food Price, Food Price Volatility, and Social Unrest'. APSA 2012 Annual Meeting Paper.

Cox, G., and M. McCubbins (1986). 'Electoral Politics as a Redistributive Game'. *Journal of Politics* 48(2): 370–89.

Croushore, D. (2011). 'Frontiers of Real-Time Data Analysis'. *Journal of Economic Literature* 99(1): 72–100.

Deaton, A. (1989). 'Rice Prices and Income Distribution in Thailand: A Non-Parametric Analysis'. *The Economic Journal* 99: 1–37.

De Gorter, H., and J. Swinnen (2002). 'Political Economy of Agricultural Policy'. In B. L. Gardner and G. C. Rausser (eds), *Handbook of Agricultural Economics*, Volume 2, Part 2, 1893–1943. Amsterdam: Elsevier.

De Janvry, A., and E. Sadoulet (2010). 'The Global Food Crisis and Guatemala: What Crisis and for Whom?' Mimeo.

Fernandez, R., and D. Rodrik (1991). 'Resistance to Reform: Status Quo Bias in the Presence of Indivdual-Specific Uncertainty'. *American Economic Review* 81(5): 1146–55.

Galeotti, G., and A. Breton (1986). 'An Economic Theory of Political Parties'. *Kyklos* 39(1): 47–65.

Gawande, K., P. Krishna, and M. Olarreaga (2009). 'What Governments Maximize and Why: The View from Trade'. National Bureau of Economic Research (NBER) Working Paper No. 14953. Cambridge, MA: NBER.

Grossman, G., and E. Helpman (1994). 'Protection for Sale'. *American Economic Review* 84(4): 833–50.

Hager, G. L., and T. Sullivan (1994). 'President-centered and Presidency-centered Explanations of Presidential Public Activity'. *American Journal of Political Science* 38(4): 1079–103.

Harriss, B. (1979). 'Going Against the Grain'. *Development and Change* 10: 363–84.

Hillman, A. (1982). 'Declining Industries and Political-Support Protectionist Motives'. *American Economic Review* 42(5): 1180–7.

Huang, J., J. Yang, and S. Rozelle (2013). 'The Political Economy of Food Pricing Policy in China'. WIDER Working Paper 2013/038. Helsinki: UNU-WIDER.

Jayne, T. S., B. Zulu, and J. J. Nijhoff (2006). 'Stabilizing Food Markets in Eastern and Southern Africa'. *Food Policy* 31: 328–41.

Karp, L., and J. Perloff (2002). 'A Synthesis of Agricultural Trade Economics'. In B. L. Gardner and G. C. Rausser (eds), *Handbook of Agricultural Economics*, Volume 2, Part 2, 1893–1943. Amsterdam: Elsevier.

Klytchnikova, I., and N. Diop (2006). 'Trade Reforms, Farm Productivity, and Poverty in Bangladesh'. Policy Research Working Paper No. 3980. Washington, DC: World Bank.

Kontopoulos, Y., and R. Perotti. (1999). 'Government Fragmentation and Fiscal Policy Outcomes: Evidence from OECD Countries'. In J. Poterba (ed.), *Fiscal Institutions and Fiscal Performance*. Chicago: University of Chicago Press.

Krueger, A. O., M. Schiff, and A. Valdés (1988). 'Agricultural Incentives in Developing Countries: Measuring the Effect of Sectoral and Economy-wide Policies'. *World Bank Economic Review* 2(3): 255–72.

Lindbeck, A., and J. Weibull (1993). 'A Model of Political Equilibrium in a Representative Democracy'. *Journal of Public Economics* 51(2): 195–209.

Malone, B. (2010). 'Is Ethiopia's Development Plan too "Ambitious"?' Africa News Blog, 13 August. Available at: <http://blogs.reuters.com/africanews/2010/08/13/is-ethiopias-development-plan-too-ambitious> accessed 12 April 2013.

Maloney W. A., G. Jordan, and A. M. McLaughlin (1994). 'Interest Groups and Public Policy: The Insider/Outsider Model Revisited'. *Journal of Public Policy* 14(1): 17–38.

Mason, N. M., and J. Ricker-Gilbert (2012). 'Disrupting Demand for Commercial Seed: Input Subsidies in Malawi and Zambia'. Indaba Agricultural Policy Research Institute (IAPRI) Working Paper No. 63. Lusaka: IAPRI.

Mghenyi, E., and T. Jayne (2006). 'Food Pricing Policy and Rural Poverty: Insights from Maize in Kenya'. Contributed paper prepared for presentation at the International Association of Agricultural Economists Conference, Gold Coast, Australia, 12–18 August. Available at: <http://ageconsearch.umn.edu/bitstream/25466/1/cp060596.pdf>.

Mugambi, K. (2010). 'Kenya: Maize Price Controls Rejected'. Available at: <http://allafrica.com/stories/201011020084> accessed on 19 June 2012.

Nordhaus, W. (1975). 'The Political Business Cycle'. *Review of Economic Studies* 42: 169–90.

Pinstrup-Andersen, P., and D. D. Watson II (2011). *Food Policy for Developing Countries: The Role of Government in Global, National, and Local Food Systems.* Ithaca: Cornell University Press.

Ravallion, M. (2000). 'Prices, Wages and Poverty in Rural India: What Lessons Do the Time Series Data Hold for Policy?' *Food Policy* 25(3): 351–64.

Roubini, N., and J. Sachs (1989). 'Political and Economic Determinants of Budget Deficits in the Industrial Economies'. *European Economic Review* 33(5): 903–38.

Srinivasan, V., and S. Narayanan (2007). ' "Food Policy and Social Movements: Reflections on the Right to Food Campaign in India". Case Study 11-1'. In P. Pinstrup-Andersen and F. Cheng (eds), *Food Policy for Developing Countries: The Role of Government in the Global Food System*. Ithaca: Cornell University Press.

Tetlock, P., and R. Boettger (2006). 'Accountability Amplifies the Status Quo Effect When Change Creates Victims'. *Journal of Behavioral Decision Making* 7(1): 1–23.

Tversky, A., and D. Kahneman (1991). 'Loss Aversion in Riskless Choice: A Reference-Dependent Model'. *The Quarterly Journal of Economics* 106(4): 1039–61.

Vadlamannati, K. (2008). 'Does Timing of Elections Instigate Riots? A Subnational Study of 16 Indian States, 1957–2004'. Working Paper No. 939. Ann Arbor, MI: William Davidson Institute.

Volkerink, B., and J. de Haan (2001). 'Fragmented Government Effects on Fiscal Policy: New Evidence'. *Public Choice* 109(3–4): 221–42.

World Bank (2007). *World Development Report* 2008: *Agriculture for Development.* Washington, DC: World Bank.

World Bank (2010). *Food Price Increases in South Asia*. Washington, DC: World Bank.

Part III

The Political Economy of Food Price Policy in Low-income Landlocked Countries

6

The Political Economy of Food Price Policy in Ethiopia

Assefa Admassie

6.1 Introduction

The world market prices of major staples such as wheat, maize, and rice doubled or tripled between 2007 and 2008 (UNCTAD 2008; FAO 2009). A combination of factors including export bans, structural and cyclical factors, and developments in international markets have been cited as the main causes of the price increase (Dewbre et al. 2008; Headey and Fan 2008).

There had also been a steady increase in the price of food staples in Ethiopia starting around 2004. For instance, the price of maize in 2008 was 130 per cent higher than the 2004–8 average (FEWS NET 2009). Several policy measures have been initiated by the Ethiopian government starting around 2006 in response to rising food prices. The policy measures include production subsidies, social safety nets for food insecure households, price controls, fiscal measures such as adjustments in tariffs, the release of grains from the strategic reserve, media campaign, and export bans on food products.

The purpose of this chapter is to assess the rational for adopting different policy measures and the role of different social groups as well as the likely impact of the policy measures. The chapter primarily relies on a synthesis of the available policy documents, research reports, newspapers, etc. Some consultations with experts were also organized to understand the policy processes and the role played by the various stakeholders during the design of the policy measures. Quantitative information on prices, production import and export, etc. was collected from the Central Statistical Agency (CSA), Ministry of Finance and Economic Development (MoFED), the National Bank of Ethiopia, and other internet-based sources.

6.2 Recent Staple Food Price Trends and Policy Responses

In Ethiopia, food production trends greatly affect staple food prices, which tend to rise during drought years and during the lean seasons (June–October) when most households run out of their own produced food stocks. What happed during the droughts in 1974/5 and 1984/5 are illustrations. The recent developments in food prices are briefly discussed next.

6.2.1 *Food Price Developments between 1998 and 2004*

Traditionally, Ethiopia has generally been a country with low inflation rates, and food inflation has not been a major challenge. For instance, the average month-to-month annualized cereal inflation before 1998 was hovering around 1 per cent. Several factors, such as prudent monetary and fiscal policies, general price controls, as well as the implementation of economic reform and stabilization programmes, have contributed to this.

In terms of food price developments, the last decade can be broadly categorized into five major episodes. Episode I represents the period from July 1998 to July 2000 that was characatrized by the Ethio-Eritrean war and localized drought in some parts of Ethiopia (see Figure 6.1). Episode II covers the period from July 2000 to July 2002, where the Ethio-Ertrian war was over. Deflationary situations were observed during this period partly due to the bumper harvest and partly due to the slow demand recovery from

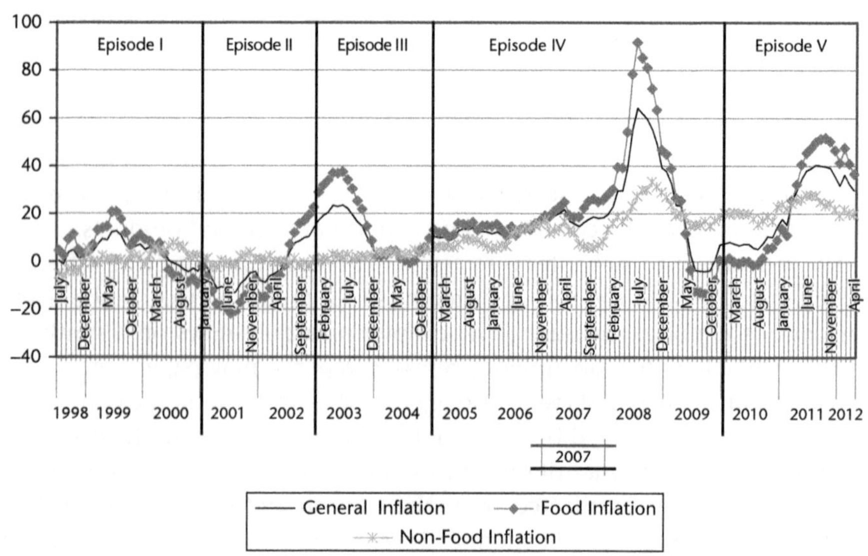

Figure 6.1 Inflation and time line of incidences

Source: computed using data from the Central Statistical Agency, general CPI (2000–11).

urban centres due to slow business activities in the aftermath of the Ethio-Eritrean war.

Episode III captures price developments between August 2002 and July 2004 when drought forced about 14 million people to depend on food aid and led to a 3.3 per cent decline in GDP in 2003 (EEA 2004). Weak and poorly functioning marketing and distribution systems and poor policy coordination were additional challenges. The Ethiopian government established a Disaster Prevention and Preparedness Commission and formulated a National Policy for Disaster Prevention and Preparedness, as well as a Food Security Strategy. In addition, the Emergency Food Security Reserve and the New Coalition for Food Security Programme were established towards the end of 2003 in collaboration with the donors.

6.2.2 *Food Price Developments between 2004 and 2008*

The period from August 2004 to July 2009 is captured by Episode IV, which was characterized by the 2007–8 global food price crises and the world financial and economic crisis. As pointed out earlier, Ethiopia was one of the countries with modest inflation rates except during drought and war periods. But, the story started to change around 2004 when Ethiopia started to experience high rates of inflation. Towards the end of 2004 and well before the rise in international food prices, nominal prices of grains started to rise in the Ethiopian markets as a result of strong demand- and supply-side factors.

Increased private consumption and increased investment in poverty-oriented sectors and improved purchasing power of farmers due to the injections of cash into the local economy through the Productive Safety Net Programme (PSNP) and microcredit services may explain the growth in aggregate demand. Supported by improved market information systems, road infrastructures, and storage facilities, farmers have gradually changed their trade practices, being able to hold some stocks in anticipation of better market opportunities. Increased remittances could be another important factor on the demand-side. On the supply-side, despite the good harvests obtained in the last several years, the amount of food marketed has not increased as expected. Household surveys complemented with market and cross-border trade surveys as well as analysis of large amounts of time series data have shown that the production estimates of cereals was roughly 30 per cent lower than the official estimates (Minot 2008).

Expansionary monetary policy, driven by a significant growth in money supply needed to meet the surge in credit demand for investment financing and the rising cost of imported intermediate inputs contributed to the increase in food prices. A World Bank (2007) study argued that during 2004–6, the money supply increased by 108 per cent, and real GDP increased by 48 per cent. In addition, the unit price of imports of petroleum soared by 145 per cent while the unit price of fertilizer increased by 254 per cent. The prices of imported food items including grains increased by 55 per cent.

Ethiopia had a national election in 2005 which was followed by serious controversies. Reduced budget supports by donors to the government due to disagreements on the handling of the post-election events and some social unrest following the election have contributed to the market instability. The government increased money supply to fill the gap created by the withdrawal of the donor support and to make credit available for investment in particular credit to the public enterprises.

The general inflation rate reached 12 per cent in 2006 resulting from a strong upward pressure on food (14 per cent), and non-food prices (7 per cent) (CSA 2010). The average month-to-month annual inflation for food and cereals during 2007 and 2008 was 41 per cent and 58 per cent, respectively. The overall annual inflation rate accelerated reaching an average rate of 46.1 per cent (based on 12-month moving average), while the national food inflation reached a record rate of 61.1 per cent in mid-2008. The food inflation rate in November 2008 stood at a record 58.7 per cent, with an increase of 37.4 per cent if compared to the same month in 2007.

The nominal prices of grains show a dramatic increase between June 2007 and June 2008. Similarly, between April and August 2008, nominal retail prices of wheat, teff and sorghum, and maize increased by 60 per cent, 80 per cent, and 90 per cent, respectively. The real maize price rose by about 80 per cent, real teff prices by about 40 per cent, and real wheat prices by about 20 per cent.

6.2.3 *Food Price Developments after 2008*

The last period representing the period starting around July 2009 and extending to the present is represented by Episode V in Figure 6.1. Several food price stabilization measures and strict monetary and fiscal measures were put in place to lower the rampant inflation. The National Bank imposed a credit ceiling on private bank lending in early 2009 with the intention of curbing food and general inflation. In May 2009 food inflation stood at 52.6 per cent, a decline of 8.5 percentage points since climbing to the record rate in 2008. Cereal prices started to decrease marginally also due to the arrival of the harvested crop on markets. In December 2009, the food inflation rate declined to about 6.1 per cent. However, while the food component of consumer price index (CPI) inflation has been declining fast, the non-food component of CPI inflation declined from 21.9 per cent by the end of December 2008 to only 18.2 per cent by the end of December 2009 (CSA 2010).

The declining trend in inflation was again reversed due to other policy interventions like the 20 per cent devaluation of the Birr against the US$ in September 2010 (see Figure 6.2). The government established price caps on essential food items which significantly destabilized the market and prices started again to rise. Accordingly, the month-to-month annualized general food and non-food inflation for May 2011 stood at 34.7 per cent, 40.7 per cent, and 26.2 per cent, respectively (EEA 2011). The government borrowing from the central bank as well as the significant increase in foreign exchange earnings contributed to the rise.

6.2.4 *Regional Price Trends for Major Food Staples*

A steady increase in food prices has been observed in all regions of Ethiopia. Some of the regions experienced much higher food inflation rates than the national average. The region of Harari (71 per cent), Dire Dawa (60 per cent), Gambella and Tigray (58 per cent) experienced the highest food inflation rates in 2008. After declining fast in 2009 and 2010, food inflation again picked up significantly in all regions and actually reached the 2008 levels; Benishangul Gumuz region recording the highest inflation in 2011. Often the different regions exhibit different food price trends. Usually Addis Ababa, Amhara, and Oromia markets share similar food price trends suggesting greater integration of markets in Amhara and Oromia with Addis Ababa.

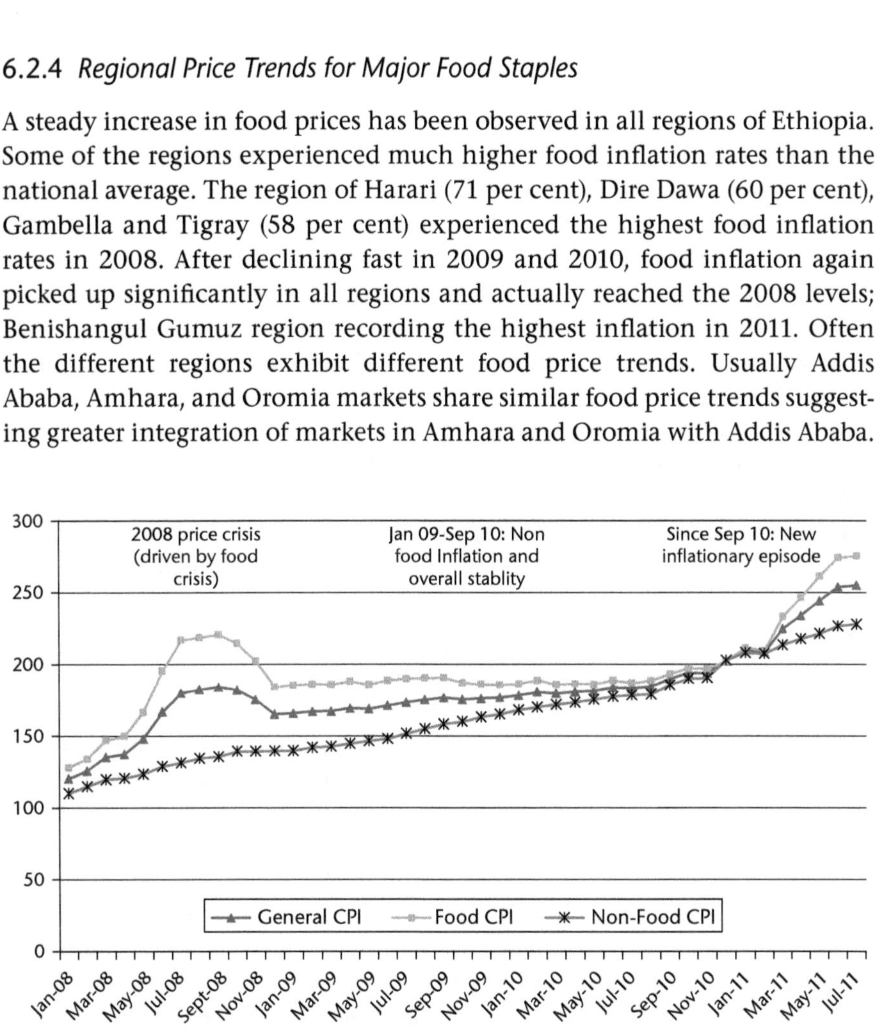

Figure 6.2 More recent trends in inflation

Source: computed based on data from the Central Statistical Agency, general CPI (2008–11).

The heterogeneity of regional food prices is partly explained by the limited regional market integration due to inadequate infrastructure and undeveloped food markets, restricting trade between food surplus and food deficit regions (World Bank 2007). In addition, weather conditions leading to differences in the performance of the agricultural sector across regions may explain some of the price heterogeneity across regions (Ulimwengu, Workneh, and Paulos 2009).

6.2.5 *Price Transmission from International Market to the Domestic Markets*

The price developments in the international market could have significant impact on local food prices if a country is highly integrated to the international market. However, according to Minot (2010) there could be a short-term transmission of only 8 to 9 per cent of the changes in international prices to local markets in sub-Saharan Africa. In the case of Ethiopia, the rising world food prices do not appear to have major implications for the domestic prices. Ethiopia is a relatively closed economy where imports are not more than 25 per cent of the GDP (Access Capital 2012). Moreover, about 75 per cent of food consumption in Ethiopia is comprised of local staples (such as sorghum and teff) that are not traded much internationally (World Bank 2007). Given the small share of imports in GDP and in the Ethiopian consumer basket, the inflation of imported items may have only marginal effects on domestic prices.

Commercial imports of food staples in Ethiopia are about 8 per cent of total consumption although this accounts for roughly 16 per cent of its foreign exchange earnings (World Bank 2007). Commercial import of maize was negligible. The commercial import of wheat was insignificant until 2008, but increased during the crisis. The largest amount of wheat import was in 2008, when the government imported 545,325 mt to stabilize the grain market. The impact of international food price increases can also filter through to domestic inflation if that domestically produced good is exported in large quantities since high prices in external markets become more attractive options for local producers and exporters pushing up domestic prices. And indeed, unit prices for some of Ethiopia's export commodities such as coffee and oil seeds have been increasing during the period. However, given the small weights of these commodities in the CPI, the net impact of such external price effects would not be expected to be significant on the overall domestic price index. In addition, the rise in world food prices was accompanied by a similar increase in oil price that led to higher costs for fertilizer, sea freight, and overland transportation, which could raise the cost of both domestically-produced and imported food. In the case of Ethiopia, unit price of imports for petroleum soared by 145 per cent and that of fertilizer increased by more than 254 per cent in 2008. Minot (2010) argues that landlocked countries face both higher costs, insurance, and freight prices of imported food and higher costs of overland transport. Thus, higher fuel costs may be an important contributing factor, but they are not enough to explain the full increase in staple food prices in Ethiopia.

Domestic prices in Ethiopia started increasing before the global food crisis and started increasing sharply long after world prices stabilized (see Figure 6.3). Ethiopian food prices also increased more rapidly than world food prices over the reference period. Moreover, local prices did not follow the downward trend in international prices after 2008, but continued to steadily rise.

A study by Ulimwengi, Workneh, and Paulos (2009) found that although all regions in Ethiopia have experienced drastic rise in food inflation since 2004, none of the Ethiopian regional maize markets had a long-term connection to the world market. The study found that the Ethiopian local maize markets do not share a common long-run trend in their respective price with the world maize market. The short-term impacts of a change in the world maize price on regional maize prices in Ethiopia are also limited and insignificant in most of the regions. Only border regions experienced higher and significant influence from the world maize price on local markets. Minot (2010) found that although the international price has a statistically significant effect on the domestic price of wheat, the coefficients suggest that the relationship is fairly weak.

In view of the above, it can be concluded that domestic rather than foreign factors were the most important determinants of Ethiopia's food price inflation during the crisis. As noted by Minot (2010), the domestic policy and production shocks such as the government's restrictions on imports and the purchase of foreign exchange must have been important contributing

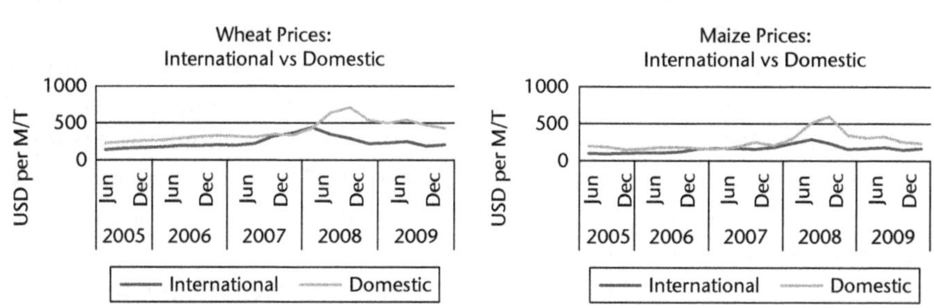

Figure 6.3 Domestic and world price of wheat and maize

Source: computed based on data from the Ethiopian Grain Trade Enterprise (2005–9) and IMF Database (2012).

factors. As indicated by the World Bank (2007) study and also emphasized by the study by Loening, Durevall, and Birru (2008) a supply shock may have contributed to higher real staple food prices in Ethiopia. In addition, although the rising inflation ought to be accompanied by a depreciation of the currency, the government imposed restrictions on imports and on the purchase of foreign exchange. While domestic prices rose about 70 per cent between June 2007 and June 2008, the exchange rate remained essentially unchanged. In early 2008, the national bank started rationing foreign exchange. So, as noted by Minot (2010) because of the fuel subsidies and restrictions on the foreign exchange market a shortage of foreign currency was created, preventing private traders from importing grain.

6.2.6 *Impact of the Food Crisis*

The price increases led to a reduction in the consumption of preferred foods and switching to cheaper foods. Reducing food and non-food consumption is a significant coping strategy by the most vulnerable households in Ethiopia (Bene, Devereux, and Sabates-Wheeler 2012). Teff is the most common staple grain consumed by most people, particularly in urban areas in Ethiopia. However, during the crisis many people resorted to relatively cheaper foods such as maize and sorghum. Anecdotal observation showed that people switched to eating twice a day instead of the usual three meals. According to the World Bank (2007), most poor people are net consumers implying that higher food prices could lead to increased poverty. Moreover, small farmers in Ethiopia both sell and buy food (it is estimated that more than 80 per cent of cereal producers purchase some cereals).

The result from a study on fifteen Ethiopian rural villages shows that the poverty level fell substantially (from 48 to 35 per cent) between 1994 and 2004 but increased to 52 per cent in 2009 and consumption per capita declined significantly (Dercon et al. 2011). Another study by Action against Hunger (2009) indicated that high prices were closely followed by an increase in malnutrition and under-five mortality rates. Ulimwengi et al. (2009) argues that a 50 per cent increase in grain prices would reduce urban caloric intake by 16 per cent and rural caloric intake by 24 per cent. Recently, Kumar and Quisumbing (2011) suggested that female-headed households in Ethiopia have experienced a higher food price shock in 2007/8. These studies suggest that the food price crisis indeed had significantly affected particularly the socially disadvantaged and poor people.

In addition to the significant effect on household welfare, the food crisis created serious balance of payment problems in Ethiopia. The worsening current account balance was accompanied by rising fiscal deficits. According to

IMF (2008), the impact of the 2008 food and fuel price increases has consumed more than 50 per cent of the international reserve for Ethiopia.

6.3 Policy Responses to the 2007–8 Food Crisis

The Ethiopian policy makers strongly felt that staple foods cannot be left to market forces alone and took several measures to stabilize food prices and to improve the purchasing power of the most affected segments of the population, mostly the urban poor. Like in many other countries, Ethiopia also took measures ranging from fiscal, trade, and monetary policy to social protection and safety net measures. Since the price transmission from the international market was limited, the policy responses were instigated by domestic price increases caused primarily by domestic factors.

6.3.1 *Export Bans on Cereals*

One of the first measures taken by the Ethiopian government was to restrict grain trade. The government banned the export of major food grains through several government circulars and directives based on the assumption that prices have increased because of the exports of tradable grains. Accordingly, the export of teff, wheat, maize, and sorghum was totally banned through a directive issued by the Ministry of Trade and Industry in December 2006. In June 2008 the ban was extended to all cereals.

6.3.2 *Fiscal and Monetary Measures*

Ethiopia removed value added tax and turnover taxes on food grains and flour through a directive issued in March 2008. The elimination was intended to help to control food prices particularly in urban markets. The government attempted to restrict the supply of monetary aggregates in the economy since increased money supply was suspected to have contributed to the crisis. The National Bank of Ethiopia raised the minimum reserve requirement from 10 to 15 per cent of net deposits in 2007 (National Bank 2007). In addition, the Bank issued another directive on 7 April 2008 in which it raised the minimum liquidity requirement to 25 per cent of the bank's total current liabilities (National Bank 2008). These directives are believed to have significantly reduced the lending capacity of commercial banks and thereby reduced the money supply in the economy. However, public spending has not been as such affected by the various national bank directives. The minimum interest rate on time and saving deposits was also raised.

6.3.3 *Administrative and Price Control Measures*

In addition to the above measures, the Ethiopian government suspended local procurement by the World Food Programme (WFP) and others and took several administrative measures on the domestic market. The most direct intervention was the price control, where the government prescribed the maximum prices to be charged for selling grains and placed directives on private traders to use price tags on their goods and to post the list of their goods for sale with the corresponding prices. Traders were warned not to hoard any grain. A task force was established with the mandate to take immediate action including the closing of illegal shops and stores without prior warning. Accordingly many traders were arrested for not respecting the directive (*Ethiopian Herald* 2008). The strategy seems not to have been effective.

6.3.4 *Releasing Reserve Grain Stocks and Grain Procurement Measures*

Ethiopia had maintained a strategic grain reserve for a long time although substantial market liberalization was implemented. The Emergency Food Security Reserve Administration was restructured and re-established in 2000 as a government organization to manage emergency food reserve as part of the preparedness strategy in the country's disaster management efforts. The government released food grain reserve stocks starting in late 2007. About 190,000 tons of wheat was released from the grain reserve stock. More than 5,000 tons of wheat was also distributed to flour mills (FAO 2011). In addition, the WFP and other non-governmental organizations (NGOs) on their part channelled about 200,000 tons of food aid during the crisis (FAO 2011).

The Ethiopian government also started to procure wheat from the international market and distribute to poor consumers at subsidized prices through consumers' associations and cooperatives. Thus, in 2008 Ethiopian Grain Trade Enterprise (EGTE) and WFP imported 520,000 and 515,000 tons of wheat and maize, respectively. The EGTE imports were distributed through the urban food rationing programme and through sales to flour mills at subsidized prices. This measure indeed helped to reduce the price of wheat in the domestic market. In order to finance the importation and sale of wheat at subsidized prices the government imposed a 10 per cent surtax on selected imported goods such as ready-made clothes, packed foods, electronics, beverages, perfumes, etc., which according to the government were luxury products in April 2007 (*Ethiopian Herald* 2008). The NGOs were also engaged in importing food.

6.3.5 *Productive Safety Net Programme*

Ethiopia, which had a long history of emergency food assistance in the form of relief aid, intensified its social protection interventions. It shifted its strategy of distributing food aid to a productive and development-oriented programme starting in 2005 by introducing the PSNP. The overarching principle of the PSNP was to facilitate 'a gradual shift away from a system dominated by emergency humanitarian aid to productive safety net system resources. The focus of this programme was to provide more reliable and timely support to chronically food insecure households by helping them to earn income (in kind or cash) through cash or food for work labour-intensive public programmes (MoFED 2007). Those households who have no labour or no other means of support, and who are chronically food insecure receive direct support. About 20 per cent of the beneficiary households in PSNP receive direct support (Kie-Song 2011).

The programme targeted about five million people when it started in 2005. However, the number of food insecure people increased to about eight million in 2008 and the government requested donors to increase their contribution in order for it to assist people in non-PNSP rural areas affected by the 2007/8 food price crisis. The number of people from non-PSNP areas that depended on the food assistance of various NGOs increased from 4.6 to 6.4 million people in 2008. Although WFP had planned in 2008 to provide food assistance to about one million people, it delivered assistance to more than eleven million people during the year. In addition, the government increased the daily wage rate (cash transfer for public works in the framework of the programme) from 6 ETB to 10 ETB per day. In many instances, households preferred to receive food assistance as opposed to cash during the food price crisis.

6.3.6 *Increased Investment in Agriculture*

Ethiopia took several measures to support domestic food production. Long-term investment in agriculture has been adopted as one of the viable options by the Ethiopian government starting in 2008 by offering attractive incentives for investors particularly from China and India. The Ministry of Agriculture transferred more than 3.5 million hectares (ha) of land to these investors and is in the process of transferring a similar amount in the next five years. However, there is much debate regarding these land investments and their food security implications (Desalegn 2011). It is argued that the acquisition of land that may be claimed by indigenous societies may lead to food shortage. Some also argue that foreign investors are acquiring land to feed their growing population and are leaving the local rural population without land or jobs. Nevertheless, the number of foreign investments that have started operation is still limited.

The Agricultural Transformation Agency was established to improve agricultural productivity and bring agricultural transformation by supporting existing structures of the government, the private sector and non-state actors. The agency is playing a coordinating role and aims to address the systematic bottlenecks in seeds, soil health, and fertility management, input and output markets, extensions and research, and cooperatives. The government is also committed to invest more in agricultural research, extension, irrigation and new technology development (Wodon and Zaman 2010). Improving farming practices, advising farmers to use water pumps, overcoming soil acidity, empowering farmers to get access to finance through microfinance institutions are examples. Investment in agriculture was also strengthened by improving infrastructure such as roads to make less densely populated areas more accessible to investors and investment.

Other measures to improve productivity through enhanced input delivery have been considered. For instance, donor assistance to cover around 50 per cent of the cost of fertilizer was requested in 2008 in response to the food price rises. The government has proposed to subsidize the cost of fertilizers by about 25 per cent. Schemes to improve and narrow the gap between the demand for improved seeds and actual supply and distribution through government-imported certified improved seeds have been designed. Increased resettlement programmes to reduce the pressure on overpopulated areas as well as increased family planning services with the view of reducing pressure on fragmented land holdings were additional measures taken. Introduction and support of agricultural insurance systems and microcredit services have been intensified. Measures were taken to support pastoralists by providing direct supply of feed and establishment of water points.

6.3.7 *Establishing a Commodity Exchange*

The Ethiopian government established the Ethiopian Commodity Exchange (ECX) in March 2008 to enhance market transparency and facilitate the use of long-term legally binding contracts between the agricultural commodities suppliers and traders and thereby reduce or manage risk. The intention is to create a new market place where all market actors (from farmers to traders to processors to exporters to consumers) can take advantage of more transparent market information and hedge against price risks through standardized contracts for immediate or future delivery. Although ECX trading started with four commodities, namely, maize, wheat, haricot beans, and sesame seeds, only some maize and wheat were traded initially through an agreement with WFP and government institutions, such as the military and universities. Currently, coffee and sesame are the main crops that are traded on the exchange. So, its contribution in stabilizing the prices of food staples is quite limited.

6.3.8 *Other Policy Measures*

The Ethiopian government has also attempted to create economic opportunities for the most vulnerable groups especially in urban areas by providing finance and working space. Several urban work programmes have been launched to engage the youth. The school feeding programme which started earlier was also expanded and strengthened to retain students in school (WFP 2008). The government, as well as non-state operators, also increased the salary of public employees.

6.4 The Rationale for Policy Interventions and the Role of Stakeholders

6.4.1 The Rationale for Policy Interventions

THE NEED FOR MACROECONOMIC STABILITY

The government has always claimed that achieving sustained economic growth by maintaining macroeconomic stability is one of its central objectives. Accordingly, the effort to lower the growth of money supply towards the end of 2008 was basically derived from the intention to maintain a level of inflation that is not detrimental to growth. For instance, the increased reserve requirements for private banks as well as the credit cap on lending by private commercial banks were direct responses to limit the growth of money supply. But, this action has seriously undermined the lending ability of private banks and had constrained import trade in particular as most of the short-term loans from the private banks were used to finance imports.

THE NEED TO AVOID SOCIAL UNREST

The 2007–8 food price crises occurred just two years after the national election in 2005. There have been some controversies about the result of the election and several protest actions were organized by the opposition political parties after the elections. The aftermath of the election created serious uncertainties and partly contributed to the upward pressure on prices. Some farmers were reluctant to sell their produce after the 2005 elections, due to these uncertainties. Members of the opposition political parties also often used the high food price inflation to show the weakness of the government. So, the Ethiopian government took various measures to control rising food inflation since it did not want to take risks which might lead to further political and social instability.

PROTECTING THE POOR (WELFARE CONCERNS)

The Ethiopian government has been extremely concerned about the implications of the food price rise on the food security status of the most vulnerable urban households and producers (*Ethiopian Herald* 2008). The importation and distribution of food grains at subsidized prices to poor people was a direct response to such concerns. The introduction of the food rationing programme suggests that the economic, human, and political costs that may be caused by price instability are a predominant government consideration in food policy in Ethiopia (Rashid 2010).

6.4.2 *The Role of Stakeholders*

THE CONFIGURATION OF THE DECISION-MAKING ORGAN

The Ethiopian system of governance recognizes three branches: the legislative, the executive, and the judicial branches and the system of political governance is based on a multi-party political configuration. Several political parties have been formed mostly organized along ethnic lines. However, most have been unable to win seats in the federal or regional parliaments during the successive elections in the country. In the entire history of the Ethiopian parliament only the 2005 election saw a sizable number of opposition political parties' representation, although several members of the opposition political parties refused to take their seats in parliament. However, in the most recent election in 2010 only one member of the opposition and one independent candidate were able to win seats in the House of Peoples' Representatives. The rest of the parliament belongs to the ruling party. So, the configuration of the political landscape is highly skewed towards the ruling Ethiopian People's Revolutionary Democratic Front (EPRDF) political party led by a powerful prime minister. The House of Peoples' Representatives, which is the legislative organ, is dominated by members of the ruling party which has easily reinforced the legacy of a one-party policy-making process. The power of the government is huge. It has several state-owned corporations involved in many critical economic sectors.

THE ROLE OF THE LEGISLATIVE AND THE EXECUTIVE ORGANS IN THE FOOD PRICE POLICY DECISIONS

Several key actors are created within the Ethiopian political landscape under the auspices of the space guaranteed by the constitution. The legislative, the judicial, and the executive branches of the government, the public and private media, civil society organizations, and academia are the major ones.

In addition, bilateral and multi-lateral international organizations such as the World Bank and International Monetary Fund (IMF) have a stake in the social and economic developments in Ethiopia.

The 2007–8 food price crisis was discussed by the House of Peoples' Representatives (lower chamber). The few members of the opposition political parties who took their seats after the 2005 elections were constantly requesting the government to provide explanations for the high food price increase, but consensus has not been reached on the causes of the rising food price and the policy responses. On the one hand, the government was arguing that the food price increase was the result of the growth process itself and, therefore, the solution is to intensify growth. According to the government, increasing supply will be the mechanism for meeting the imbalance between the demand for food and the supply as demand has grown faster than supply. On the other hand, the members of the opposition political parties were blaming the monetary and fiscal policies. It was only in 2009 that the government accepted the argument that its monetary policy is one of the sources of the problem and started to take measures to reduce the money supply in the economy. The imposition of credit ceilings on private commercial banks was an example of the measures.

While the persistent appeal by the opposition members of parliament at the time is believed to have marginally contributed to the adoption of various policy measures, the main initiator and driver of the policy measures with respect to the food price rise was the executive branch of the government. Most of the policy measures were drafted by the MoFED and the Ministry of Trade and Industry, discussed within the Council of Ministers, approved by the House of People's Representatives, issued as directives by the respective ministry and made public through the mass media. As the House of People's Representatives was dominated by the members of the ruling political party at the time, whatever was drafted by the executive branch often easily got endorsed by the House. The National Bank was mainly responsible for the monetary directives.

6.4.3 *The Contribution of Other National Stakeholders*

As discussed earlier the Ethiopian political landscape is dominated by a centralized and authoritarian executive branch which does not often respond to public pressure. Nevertheless, it is believed that some groups indeed had limited influence on the policy decisions. For instance, there have been several media reports regarding the high food prices; though it is not clear to what extent they have influenced the policy decisions. While the relatively strong public media invariably propagated only the government view and accused the private traders and developments in the international market for the food price rise, the relatively weak and less effective private media which is stifled by a restrictive press law was very emotional. Some of their arguments were not supported with evidence and focused mostly on condemning the government. So the views of the media in particular on the price crisis were often divided.

The private sector including the chamber of commerce had little influence on the food price policy decisions. The government has actually accused private traders of hoarding grains and causing the price escalation during the food price crises. As a result the private sector has often been harassed and intimidated by the government as the various statements issued by the government clearly show. Similarly, the role of civil society organizations in the food price policy decisions has been limited. The Ethiopian government has often stated that the attempt to influence policy by civil society organizations is not welcomed. There are not many consumers' and producers' associations in the country that can put meaningful pressure on the policy makers. There were some cooperatives and unions engaged in trading activities, which, according to some people, were contributing to the inflationary situation in urban areas as they bought grains from farmers and sold them at high prices. Apart from individual discontents and complaints, there has not been any major organized public riot or protest by the civil society groups.

There are a few national research institutions including the Ethiopian Economics Association, the Ethiopian Development Research Institute, and some university-based research units which were expected to provide evidence-based policy suggestions, but their contribution has been marginal as the culture of evidence-based policy decision is not strong within the Ethiopian system of governance. There are no references in the policy documents which show that the policy measures regarding the food price challenges were informed by the results of research undertaken by these institutions.

6.4.4 *The Role of External Development Partners*

It can be hypothesized that the multi-lateral institutions such as the World Bank, IMF, European Union (EU), Food and Agriculture Organization (FAO), WFP as well as the bilateral donors such as the UK's Department for International Development (DFID) or United States Agency for Interntional Development (USAID) might have some influence on the policy framework since Ethiopia is heavily dependent on these donors. However, the Ethiopian policy makers have often claimed that they have not been influenced and dictated by external partners. Nevertheless, some discussion forums focusing on the food prices have been organized and the government has accepted some of the recommendations although it has not openly acknowledged it in public. Some people say that the government was forced to cut back on some investment projects, or at least forced to delay them around 2008 as a result of the advice of the international bodies. In addition, some of the recommendations by international research organizations might have been considered by the policy makers, although there has not been any explicit reference to the studies.

6.5 Major Outcomes of the Policy Interventions

6.5.1 *Socioeconomic Impacts*

While studies have not yet established a clear link between changes in welfare and the policy measures in Ethiopia, it can be argued on the basis of limited anecdotal evidence that the measures have helped to reduce the potential negative impacts of the crisis on consumers. For instance, the FAO (2011) study showed that the number of undernourished people in Ethiopia in 2002 which was about 33 million remained the same in 2006–8. The same report actually stated that the proportion of undernourished people went down from 48 per cent in 2002 to 41 per cent in 2006–8. Another FAO (2009) study confirmed that malnutrition had continued to decline in 2008.

Similarly, official data from MoFED show that the food price rise does not seem to have reversed the decline in poverty. The proportion of the population below the poverty line which was estimated to be around 37 per cent in 2005/6 declined to 29.6 per cent in 2010 (MoFED 2012). It seems that the policy interventions have counter-balanced the potential negative effects of the food price rises and actually contributed to the poverty reduction. The release of emergency food stocks and the distribution of subsidized imported wheat to low-income urban families must have helped. The government sales of its wheat imports from July to October 2008 successfully reduced domestic market prices (Rashid 2010). Similarly the introduction of the productive safety net programme must have also helped to contain the impact. Although the PSNP was initially planned to benefit around 5.14 million people per year, MARD (2009) and Amdissa (2010), however, indicated that around seven million people have been able to meet consumption needs through food for work programmes and around one million as direct beneficiaries.

6.6 Conclusions

Inflation in general and food price inflation in particular was not a serious challenge in the past in Ethiopia except during drought years. However, the food price inflation rates portrayed a general upward trend starting around 2004. Though developments in the international markets indeed have some minor impact, the high food inflation was caused mostly by domestic factors including the increased monetization of the economy, the inefficient and poorly integrated market structure, as well as the speculative behaviour of market participants. Developments in the international market had little impact.

Recognizing the challenges brought about by the rising food prices, the Ethiopian government took several policy measures including the banning of cereal exports, reduction of import tariffs, raising the reserve requirement of commercial banks, administrative measures and releasing of grain stocks and most of all, distributing grains at subsidized prices to the urban poor starting in 2006. Although there has been some limited pressure by some interest groups, both domestic and external, most of the policy measures were initiated and implemented by the executive branch of the government. The main factors that motivated the government to take these measures include the desire to avoid social unrest, protect the urban poor, and maintain a stable macroeconomy.

These measures have indeed helped to control and reduce the potential negative impact of the food price increase particularly on the poorest segment of the population. The interventions helped to bring some level of macroeconomic stability, maintain the trend in poverty reduction, and improve the balance of payment position from a situation of one month's import to about 2.5 months import in 2009.

This chapter has clearly underscored the need for appropriate and well-targeted social protection programmes to reduce the impact during such crises. Buffer stocks and emergency reserves are also important instruments. In addition, the food price increases have also underscored the need for considering agricultural development as a priority for food security. Establishing monitoring mechanisms to reduce the negative consequence of food price volatility in the future could be useful.

References

Access Capital (2012). 'Agriculture Sector Review, Access Capital Research'. Available at: <http://www.accesscapitalsc.com/>.

Action against Hunger (2009). 'Feeding Hunger and Insecurity: The Global Food Crisis'. Briefing Paper. New York: Action against Hunger.

Amdissa, T. (2010). 'The Road for Long-term Social Protection: The Case of Amhara Region Productive Safety Net Programme'. In G. Alemu and D. Getachew (eds), *Proceedings of the First Regional Conference of the Amhara Regional State Economic Development*. Addis Ababa: Ethiopian Economic Association (EEA).

Bene, C., S. Devereux, and R. Sabates-Wheeler (2012). 'Shocks and Social Protection in the Horn of Africa: Analysis from the Productive Safety Net Programme in Ethiopia'. Working Paper 395. Brighton: Institute for Development Studies.

CSA (Central Statistical Agency) (2010). 'Country and Regional Level Consumer Price Indices'. Addis Ababa: CSA.

CSA (Central Statistical Agency) (2012). 'Monthly Consumer Price Index'. Available at: <http:///www.csa.gov.et/>.

Dercon, S., J. Hoddinott, and T. Woldehanna (2011). 'Growth and Chronic Poverty: Evidence from Rural Communities in Ethiopia'. Working Paper 2011-18. Oxford: Centre for the Study of African Economies.

Desalegn, R. (2011). 'Land to Investors: Large Scale Land Transfers in Ethiopia'. Addis Ababa: Forum for Social Studies.

Dewbre, J., C. Giner, W. Thompson, and M. Von Lampe (2008). 'High Food Commodity Prices: Will They Stay? Who Will Pay?' *Agricultural Economics* 39: 393–403.

EEA (Ethiopian Economics Association) (2004). 'Report on the Ethiopian Economy', Volume III. Addis Ababa: EEA.

EEA (Ethiopian Economics Association) (2011). 'Report on the Ethiopian Economy'. Addis Ababa: EEA.

Ethiopian Herald (2008). 'Promising Actions to Curb Inflation'. *Ethiopian Herald* LXIV(176): n.p.

FAO (Food and Agriculture Organization) (2009). 'FAO/WFP Crop and Food Security Assessment Mission to Ethiopia'. Special Report (Phase 2) Integrating the Crop and Food Supply and the Emergency Food Security Assessments. Rome: FAO.

FAO (Food and Agriculture Organization) (2011). 'Undernourishment around the World: Impact of the 2006–08 Price Shock'. Rome: FAO.

FEWS NET (Famine Early Warning System Network) (2009). 'Ethiopia Food Security Update'. Addis Ababa: FEWS NET.

Headey, D., and S. Fan (2008). 'Anatomy of a Crisis: The Causes and Consequences of Surging Food Prices'. *Agricultural Economics* 39: 375–91.

IMF (International Monetary Fund) (2008). *Food and Fuel Prices: Recent Developments, Macroeconomic Impact, and Policy Responses.* Fiscal Affairs, Policy Development and Review, and Research Departments Special Report. Washington, DC: IMF.

IMF (International Monetary Fund) (2012). 'IMF Primary Commodity Prices'. Available at: <http://www.imf.org/external/np/res/commod/index.aspx>.

Kie-Song, M. L. (2011). 'Integrating Public Works and Cash Transfers in Ethiopia: Implications for Social Protection, Employment and Decent Work'. Working Paper 84. Brasilia: International Policy Centre for Inclusive Growth.

Kumar N., and A. R. Quisumbing (2011). 'Gendered Impacts of the 2007–08 Food Price Crisis Evidence Using Panel Data from Rural Ethiopia'. Discussion Paper 01093. Washington, DC: International Food Policy Research Institute (IFPRI).

Loening, J., D. Durevall, and Y. Birru. (2008). 'Inflation Dynamics and Food Prices in an Agricultural Economic: The Case of Ethiopia'. Policy Research Working Paper 4969. Washington, DC: World Bank.

MARD (Ministry of Agriculture and Rural Development) (2009). 'Food Security Programme 20102015'. Addis Ababa: MARD.

Minot, N. (2008). 'Understanding Changes in Farm Level Crop Marketing'. Policy Brief 1 in EDRI-IFPRI Policy Workshop 'Market Dynamics and Cereal Availability in Ethiopia: Producers, Traders, and the Policy'. Addis Ababa.

Minot, N. (2010). 'Transmission of World Food Changes to African Markets and its Effects on Household Welfare'. Washington, DC: International Food Policy Research Institute (IFRPI).

MoFED (Ministry of Finance and Economic Development) (2007). 'Ethiopia: Building on Progress: A Plan for Accelerated and Sustained Development to End Poverty (PASDEP)'. Annual Progress Report 2006/07. Addis Ababa: MoFED.

MoFED (Ministry of Finance and Economic Development) (2012). 'Ethiopia's Progress towards Eradicating Poverty: An Interim Report on Poverty Analysis Study (2010/11)'. Addis Ababa: MoFED.

NBE (National Bank of Ethiopia) (2007). 'Reserve Requirement, 3rd Replacement Directive Number SBB/42/2007'. Addis Ababa: NBE.

NBE (National Bank of Ethiopia) (2008). 'Reserve Requirement, 4th Replacement Directives SBB/45/2008'. Addis Ababa: NBE.

Rashid, S. (2010). 'Staple Food Prices in Ethiopia'. Paper prepared for the COMESA Policy Seminar on 'Valuation in Staple Food Prices: Causes, Consequences, and Policy Options', held in Maputo, 25–26 January 2010.

WFP (World Food Programme) (2008). 'Standardized School Feeding Survey, Country Status Report: Ethiopia'. Rome: WFP.

Wodon, Q., and H. Zaman (2010). 'Higher Food Prices in Sub-Saharan Africa: Poverty Impact and Policy Responses'. *The World Bank Research Observer* 25(1): 204–21.

World Bank (2007). 'Explaining Sources of Food Price Inflation in Ethiopia: A Just in Time Policy Note'. Draft. Washington, DC: World Bank.

Ulimwengu, J. M., S. Workneh, and Z. Paulos (2009). 'Impact of Soaring Food Price in Ethiopia: Does Location Matter?' Discussion Paper No. 00846. Washington, DC: International Food Policy Research Institute (IFPRI).

UNCTAD (United Nations Conference on Trade and Development) (2008). 'Trade and Development Report: Commodity Price Hikes and Instability'. New York and Geneva: UNCTAD.

7

The Political Economy of Food Price Policy in Malawi

Ephraim W. Chirwa and Blessings Chinsinga

7.1 Introduction

This chapter examines the underlying political economy motivations of the government's policy responses to food price increases in 2007/8 focusing particularly on maize as the main staple crop. The main government policy responses to the food price spikes in 2007/8 were price control, and bans on domestic and international trade. We argue that although there has been increased openness in policy debates and dialogue relating to the question of food security since the transition to democracy in May 1994, the process continues to be unclear, dominated by presidential interventions, and tends to be highly motivated by electoral politics and considerations. Periodic food spikes are not a new phenomenon in Malawi, but the uniqueness of the 2007/8 experiences is that the country experienced sustained price increases when it had registered a record surplus of its maize harvest. The country reportedly recorded 1.3 million metric tonnes (MT) of maize over and above annual food requirements estimated at 2.8 MT (Dorward and Chirwa 2009). This has mainly been attributed to the Farm Input Subsidy Programme (FISP) which provides smallholder farmers with highly subsidized fertilizer and seed using a voucher system. Although the FISP was launched against fierce resistance among development partners, it turned out to be a huge success which, for several years, put Malawi at the centre of the global debates about the desirability of subsidies in reviving the fledging agricultural sector across the African continent (Chinsinga 2010).

Malawi has several food crops such as rice, cassava, and beans, the government's policy responses to the 2007/8 dramatic global food price spikes focused exclusively on maize. In addition to existing price support mechanisms such as input subsidies, safety nets, and strategic grain reserves, the government responded by introducing price control, domestic trade restrictions, and an export ban policy on maize. The government responded as such because maize is a very important political crop due to the fact that the legitimacy of politicians in government is closely linked to the availability and accessibility of maize to the people at the grassroots at prices they can afford, either through their own production or buying from the market (Harrigan 2003). According to one of the Ministry of Agriculture and Food Security (MoAFS) officials interviewed '... the government is only interested in controlling the price of maize because if it gets out of hand, there can be political backlashes since almost everyone depends on maize for subsistence'. He argued that both rice and beans are not grown by many farmers to the extent that 'apart from announcing the expected minimum prices for the farmers at the beginning of a growing season, the government does essentially nothing to intervene in the markets of these crops 'because even if their prices rise sharply, nobody will complain to the extent that it would become a public policy issue'.[1]

Food security in Malawi is defined primarily in terms of the availability and accessibility of maize. Maize is consumed by almost all Malawians on a daily basis and accounts for about 97 per cent of the total land area planted with crops. Consequently, food policy debates focus almost exclusively on policies relating to maize production, marketing, trade, and consumption (Chirwa 2009). The government's policy responses to the 2007/8 global food price crisis reveals that the president's direct involvement in food policy-making, national food security considerations as a key electoral issue, and vibrant private media were very important in influencing the shape, form, and nature of the government's reactions, actions, and strategies.

The key question is who are the key actors in the policy-making processes in Malawi? The identification of these actors is imperative because it would illuminate on their narratives, linkages, authority structures, and their political power and influence. However, this cannot be done effectively without understanding Malawi's political system and its recent political history. The point is that the political economy context of a country matters a great deal since policies' chance of success cannot be judged abstractly in their theoretical or technical attributes without considering the institutional, political, and cultural context in which they are applied.

[1] Interview with MoAFS official, 23 May 2012.

7.2 The Political System

Malawi returned to multi-party democracy in May 1994 after three decades of autocratic rule led by the Malawi Congress Party (MCP) under the leadership of the late Dr Hastings Kamuzu Banda (Banda 1998; Chirwa 1998). As a one-party state, power was centralized in the presidency which was buttressed by the 1966 republican constitution. This constitution abrogated the provision of the Bill of Rights and formally proclaimed Malawi a de jure one-party regime. This meant that the MCP regime systematically and strategically curtailed fundamental freedoms and human rights, cultivated a political culture of fear, docility, suspicion, and total loyalty and obedience to authority (Kaunda 1992 and Chinsinga 2003).

The centralized nature of the one-party state was further reflected in the nature of policy-making processes. The president almost entirely dominated the policy-making processes since the Office of the President and Cabinet (OPC) was effectively the centre for all public policies, planning, and implementation (Fozzard and Simwaka 2002). The main purpose of the parliamentary process in policy-making processes was largely to establish the legitimacy and the legal standards required for policy implementation (Chinsinga 2006). This amounted to a technocratic style of policy-making which is a huge impediment to democracy because the public cannot scrutinize decisions, yet scrutiny of this nature lies at the heart of democratic politics.

The transition to democracy in May 1994 fundamentally altered the nature of political and policy processes at least on paper. Malawi retuned to democracy with a liberal democratic constitutional order which opened up the political and policy processes and dispersed power to various public and private institutions including the citizens. The 1994 constitution explicitly states that legitimacy to govern derives directly from the people of Malawi and those privileged to govern continue to do so upon sustained trust of the people (Kanyongolo 2010). This implies that the transition to democracy represented opportunities for the renewal of the policy-making process.

Although the policy-making process is procedurally open and subjected to the influence of a diverse range of stakeholders, the presidency remains a dominant force (Banda 1998; Chinsinga 2010). For instance, following the fourth democratic elections, the policy space under President Bingu wa Mutharika was severely eroded and the presidency dictated most policy decisions. The dominance of the presidency is inevitable because it remains extremely powerful since the incumbent presides over an expansive patronage network. The incumbent has enormous powers of appointment to a wide range of senior positions in government without viable systems of checks and balances.

The relative autonomy of the incumbent president is further reinforced by the existence of the weak civil society and private sector. According to Harrigan (2001), the private sector exists in Malawi, but it is also owned by the state. This means that the survival of private sector enterprises is threatened as soon as they fall out of favour with the government. This is because the state is the major dispenser of lucrative contracts. Most of the civil society organizations are weak and have been captured by their founders mainly as instruments for livelihoods and they are mostly reactive instead of being proactive in their engagement with the state. Furthermore, most of the civil society organizations are urban-based without networks extending beyond the confines of the capital, yet they claim to speak authoritatively on behalf of the people (Chirwa 2000; Chinsinga 2006).

The main challenge for Malawi is that the one-party political culture has persisted without major modifications. The multi-party democratic dispensation is to a great extent shaped by the one-party political culture which has simply adjusted to the pressures of a multi-party political dispensation while remaining almost the same. The policy-making processes are essentially driven and underpinned by a neo-patrimonial logic (Cammack et al. 2007) where the government essentially functions as a transfer pump of resources by political leaders to their respective clients in return for their support. Thus, leaders and their opponents use both formal and informal rules, norms, and practices to gain legitimacy and advantage in a winner takes all competition for the control of the state.

7.3 Key Actors in the Policy-making Process

There are several key actors in Malawi's policy-making processes. Unlike in the one-party era, in principle, policy-making is no longer an exclusive preserve of the president; it is at least subject to the influence of a diverse range of stakeholders as shown in Table 7.1. These stakeholders include the following: political parties; civil society (the church, citizen groups, non-governmental organizations (NGOs), and professional associations); the media (print and electronic); international organizations (international financial institutions, and donor agencies); the three branches of government (legislature, executive, and judiciary); and the public at large.

The exact impact of these stakeholders in the policy processes varies from issue to issue. However, it is important to note that generally the enduring legacy of the strong presidency remains a huge impediment to subjecting the policy-making processes to the influence of a diverse range of stakeholders so that they become as participatory, transparent, and accountable as possible (Chinsinga 2006). With specific reference to food policy-making processes, there are several key stakeholders. These include the bureaucracy, the

Table 7.1 The roles of stakeholders in policy-making processes in Malawi

Stakeholder	Role in the Policy-Making Process
Media	Act as a sounding board in their interactive relationship with the public opinion. The media often call attention to issues on which political action and policy-making are required.
Political parties	Put forward interests, aspirations, and beliefs of their membership into coherent ideological platforms, policy initiatives, and programmes. They therefore provide a forum through which the grassroots can offer inputs and exert influence over the policy-making process.
Civil society	Offers the grassroots alternative channels of participation and influence in the policy-making process in their respective spheres of influence.
Judiciary	Determines and specifies not only what the government cannot do but also what it must do in order to meet legal and constitutional requirements for policy decisions.
Executive	Initiates and implements policies to be legislated on by the parliament.
Parliament	Legislates policies and provides oversight in the implementation of those policies.
Citizens	Exert influence over the policy-making process through various channels at their disposal, for example, through representation in the legislature, media, civil society, political parties, mass mobilization, demonstrations, etc.
International organizations	Influence the realm of economic policies by playing a key role since the country's economy is heavily donor-dependent. The national budget without donor support is hardly viable.

Source: authors' compilation.

presidency, media, civil society organizations, international development agencies, parastatal organizations, particularly the Agricultural Development and Marketing Corporation (ADMARC), the National Food Reserve Agency (NFRA), ordinary citizens, research institutions, and private traders.

The civil service, particularly the Ministries of Agriculture and Trade and Industry, plays key roles with reference to production, pricing, and trade control of agricultural produce. Besides being the head of the civil service, the president has an abiding interest in food policy processes due to the role they play in the country's electoral politics. The media reports on food policy processes, particularly in relation to food shortages and price trends. The manner in which the media reports on these policy issues depends very much on its perceived or actual political alignment. Private media tends to highlight challenges, whereas public media almost always attempt to paint a glittering picture of the food security situation in the country.

There are several civil society organizations that are prominent in the area of food policy processes. These include the Centre for Social Concern (CSC), Consumers Association of Malawi (CAMA), Farmers Union of Malawi (FUM), and National Association of Smallholder Farmers of Malawi (NASFAM). Both the CSC and CAMA keep track of the costs of the monthly food basket for the major cities across the country while FUM and NASFAM are farmers' organizations whose main interest is to promote and safeguard the welfare of farmers by lobbying for better returns on their produce and propagation of favourable policies for the agricultural sector more generally. The citizens are engaged in the food policy processes by articulating the impacts of deficient food policies on their livelihoods. The international development agencies play a particular role in influencing the nature of policies in the agricultural sector that have significant implications for food and price policy processes. There are often contestations between and among different international development agencies depending on their ideological orientations (Harrigan 2003). The major difference between and among the international development agencies relates to whether or not the market can be relied upon to guarantee food security at all times.[2]

The parastatals are used mainly for a price stabilization function in the food policy processes.[3] ADMARC serves as a marketing outlet for maize especially during periods of chronic food shortage and sudden price shocks. However, ADAMRC's roles have changed quite considerably over the years particularly following the implementation of structural adjustment programmes (SAPs) (Mvula, Chirwa, and Kadzandira 2003; Chinsinga 2011). The NFRA runs the country's strategic grain reserves, a function that was initially run by ADMARC. The main goal of the NFRA is to have adequate maize stocks in order to prevent the country from experiencing serious food shortages especially in the event of unforeseen disasters. Private sector players emerged following the liberalization of the agricultural sector. ADMARC is no longer the sole buyer of farm produce. It has to compete with private traders, both small and large. While ADMARC buys produce from farmers primarily as a social function, private traders are engaged in the exercise for profit.

7.4 Food Price Trends and Shocks

7.4.1 *Maize Price Trends*

Figure 7.1 shows the nominal and real prices for maize 2001–11, with price peaks in 2001, 2005, and 2008, with the 2001 and 2005 shocks attributed mainly to poor weather conditions. An interesting question is: why did the

[2] In this debate, the United States Agency for International Development (USAID) best represents the group of international development agencies that strongly believe that the market can guarantee food security in Malawi while FAO represents the group of international development agencies that believe in strong investment in domestic food production. There are some international development agencies that lie in between who basically argue for a strategic balance between these two polar extremes. The Department for International Development (DFID) is a very good example of such international development agencies.

[3] It is important to note that the managements of both ADMARC and NFRA are appointed on recommendation to the president. As such they are both not quite independent players in the food policy processes.

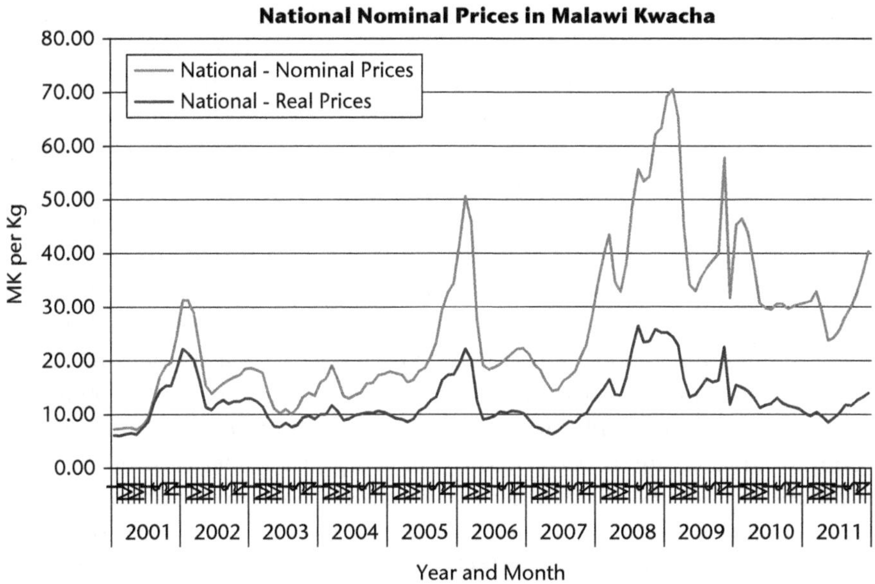

Figure 7.1 Trends in nominal maize prices, 2001–11

Source: based on Chirwa (2009) updated, using monthly retail prices published be the MoAFS between 2008 and 2011.

country experience high maize prices when it reported record maize surplus? Chirwa (2009) attributes the high maize prices to poor quality information about domestic supply from the government both in terms of domestic production and stocks in reserves. Why should the government be motivated to project a misleading picture? In the interviews, some stakeholders pointed out that 'the government was motivated to cook up impressive production figures because it wanted to maintain the grand success narrative of the FISP'.[4] The FISP had been endorsed as a success story even by 'the once pessimistic donors and nothing short of continued success would be welcome'.[5]

This claim of impressive productivity was invariably undermined by the apparent rise in prices of maize which in turn fuelled speculative behaviour among key players in the industry. This was further reinforced by the government's failure to export 400,000 MT of maize to Zimbabwe through NFRA. By the time about 300,000 MT were exported, the private sector was finding it difficult to source maize for export which sent signals that there were supply shortages and the prices began to rise substantially. Moreover, the behaviour of state agencies, ADMARC and the NFRA, by offering higher purchase prices

[4] Interview with the President of FUM, 28 May 2012.

[5] Interview with the National Coordinator of the Civil Society Network on Agriculture, 9 May 2012.

to farmers than the private sector, and through the government's action of imposing a ban on private traders and other desperate measures signalled that there were domestic supply shortages. Finally, the high international maize prices, amid continued surplus maize production, created speculation that the export market for maize would be lucrative, leading to stockpiling and purchasing maize from farmers at higher prices by the private sector.

The constant threat of inadequate domestic food supplies makes food price policies a priority issue for the government. This means that any slight indication of impending food shortages and increases in food prices are likely to trigger the government's intervention 'for it to be at least seen leading the efforts to guarantee food security otherwise it risks backlash from rural communities who constitute the bulk of voters and depend exclusively on maize for subsistence'.[6] He emphasized that the government does not worry much about urban consumers because they make up just 10 per cent of the total population. The urban constituents are mainly concerned with governance issues broadly defined. He argued that the protests in urban areas since the transition to democracy in May 1994 have focused on governance issues and not necessarily on food price policies per se.

7.4.2 *International Price Transmission*

The extent to which high food prices at international markets can have effects on domestic prices depends on the integration of markets through the price transmission mechanism. There is evidence that most of the maize markets in eastern and southern Africa are integrated with international markets as revealed by the co-movement of international and domestic maize prices in the long run (Rapsomanikis 2009). In the context of Malawi, earlier studies established a weak link between international and domestic maize and rice prices between 1980 and 2000 (Chirwa and Zakeyo 2006). Actually, Rapsomanikis (2009) notes that short-run effects of maize prices in Malawi and the international (and South Africa) prices are insignificant. The adjustment of domestic prices to international prices is also slow ranging from 4.7 months for the Karonga to 7.7 months for the Liwonde market.

7.4.3 *Policies for Management of Food Price Swings*

The government's policies to the 2007/8 price spikes were driven by the government's desire to project itself as playing a leading role in protecting citizens from the detrimental effects of price swings on their livelihoods. In

[6] Interview with the executive director of CAMA, 17 May 2012.

invoking these policies, the main government narrative advanced mainly by the late President Mutharika was that the government '...as a caring government was protecting the people of Malawi from ill-will forces that were driven by selfishness to profit from the high maize prices they were artificially creating by hoarding maize stocks when the country had registered record surplus maize'.[7] This narrative was clearly motivated by electoral considerations because food security is perhaps the only issue that features in Malawi's elections. The price spikes occurred a year before the general elections. Nevertheless, the policy responses to the 2007/8 global food price crises must be placed into a proper historical context in order to be fully understood.

7.4.4 *Price Controls*

In the wake of the 2007/8 global food price crisis, the government attempted to reinforce the price control policy for maize. The underlying motivation of this policy is to protect producers and consumers by making sure that producers and consumers generate adequate income from maize production and access maize at affordable market prices, respectively. This policy intervention is administered in the form of a price band which was first introduced in 1996. As the price of maize continued to soar, the government revised the price band upwards to MWK45 per kg as the producer price and MWK52 per kg as the consumer price from MWK20 and MWK30 per kg, respectively.

MoAFS officials described price controls as 'an automatic instrument we resort to or activate in the wake of price spikes either on our own or in consultation with the State House or upon a directive from the State House'.[8] The implementation of the price controls in 2007/8 followed a directive from the State House which MoAFS officials felt was triggered by 'persistent media reports that highlighted the escalating maize prices in local markets yet we had just recorded the historic maize surplus during that year'. According to these officials, the failure of the NFRA to satisfy the 400,000 MT maize export contract to Zimbabwe created panic at the State House. This forced the president to direct the revision of the price band upward for ADMARC to

[7] This narrative became a mantra that was recited at a very political rally at the peak of the global food price crisis. The main targets in this narrative were opposition politicians. The president argued that the opposition politicians were deliberately withholding maize to create artificial scarcity of maize in order to project him as a failure in managing food security with the idea of deceiving voters to vote for them in the May 2009 elections. The opposition politicians seized it accordingly, arguing that high maize prices amidst claims of the historic record maize surplus was a clear manifestation that the FISP's success had been exaggerated. They are the ones who are better placed to take it forward so that it guarantees food security on a sustainable basis.

[8] Interview with a MoAFS official, 22 May 2012.

compete with the private sector in buying maize from farmers. This maize was meant to stock the Strategic Grain Reserves (SGR) to avert a possible food disaster in case failure by the government to satisfy the maize export contract indeed indicated shortage of maize supply in the country to meet its subsistence requirements.

According to the president of the FUM, price controls do not attract any serious reaction from stakeholders because 'we know from experience they do not work in practice; prices continue to be dictated by the forces of demand and supply'. He argued that the government turns to price controls 'simply to be seen to be doing something about the escalating prices for political posturing and they know it'. The evidence indeed suggests that price controls have not worked effectively as depicted in Figure 7.2 which shows the nature of the maize pricing system's relative prices under private marketing. From 2008 through to March 2009 maize was trading at prices above the price band; this is also the period of high food prices. Maize production during this period was more than adequate but prices remained high and the price controls were ineffective in stabilizing maize prices during this crisis.

Chirwa (2009) attributes the ineffectiveness of the price band to several reasons which include: (1) the inability of the government to enforce the price band due to lack of relevant instruments; (2) the price band is often set

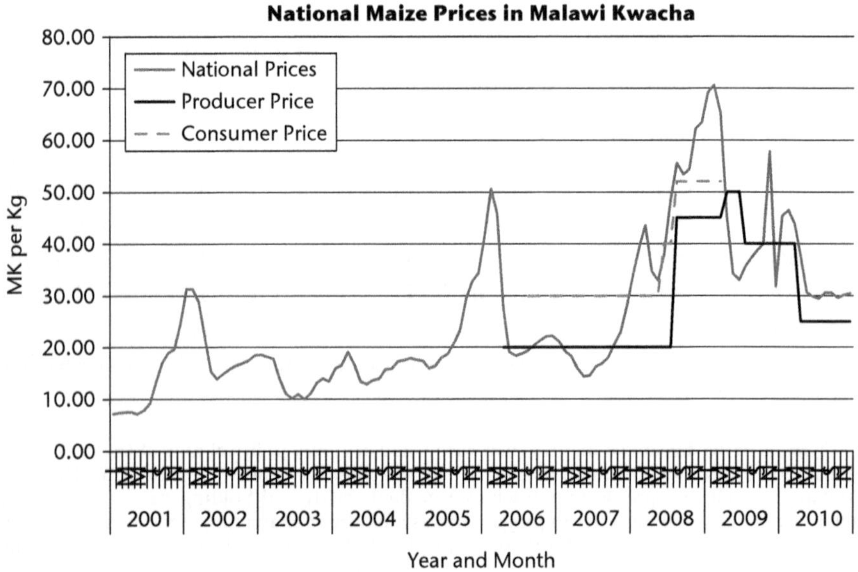

Figure 7.2 Price band and average maize prices, 2000–10

Source: authors' calculations based on MoAFS monthly retail prices between 2001 and 2010.

when maize prices are above the maximum price; (3) ADMARC lacks adequate financial resources to defend the price band effectively; (4) the price band is often too narrow offering very little margins to traders; and (5) there is no statutory provision for the strategic grain reserves for purposes of stabilization of prices. The conclusion of many officials interviewed particularly those from the Grain Traders Association of Malawi (GTAM) is that price controls do not often succeed because of limited management capacity worsened by institutional rivalry between ADMARC and NFRA. According to Chirwa (2009), NFRA had enough maize grain stocks estimated at 160,000 MT during the 2007/8 global food price spikes that could have been used to stabilize prices but did not release it into the market. Instead just like ADMARC, it proceeded to buy maize from farmers which increased the pressure on high maize prices as they both attempted to outbid the private sector in terms of the price offered to farmers which clearly signalled to the stakeholders shortages in domestic supply.

The institutional rivalry between NFRA and ADMARC is partly rooted in the history of the creation of the latter. NFRA's functions were before its formation performed by ADMARC but shed off to NFRA as an integral part of structural adjustment reforms (Mvula, Chirwa, and Kadzandira 2003). The purpose of the reforms was to make ADMARC more efficient by streamlining its functions to focus largely on buying and selling farm produce. However, in practice the roles of these two parastatal agencies have not been clearly spelt out and there are considerable overlaps which 'make effective and efficient coordination and implementation of mechanisms that would contribute to the stabilization of prices almost impossible'.[9] The paradox is that while politicians preach about food security, they are the very same people who undermine it. Most policy makers argued that while

> NFRA had enough maize stocks its management could not be allowed to release some of it to ADMARC markets to stabilize the prices because the majority of maize exporters to Zimbabwe were politicians with close links to the president...depleting the reserves would have jeopardized their deals once the situation somehow stabilized.[10]

The decision to let both ADMARC and NFRA buy maize from farmers at higher prices was not necessarily to ensure that 'the reserves were well stocked in order to avert possibilities of chronic food shortages but to fill the grain reserves so as to fulfil the export contract to Zimbabwe that was monopolized by politicians or their close associates'.[11]

[9] Interview with an NFRA official, 27 May 2012.
[10] Interview with a Ministry of Trade and Industry official, 26 May 2012.
[11] Interview with a Ministry of Trade and Industry official, 27 May 2012.

7.4.5 *Domestic Trade Restrictions*

The government imposed restrictions on the domestic maize trade as the prices of maize continued to soar. The domestic trade restrictions for maize were introduced in August 2008 but by mid-September 2008 they had been somewhat modified. In introducing the reforms, the MoAFS exempted small-scale traders operating in rural markets. The restrictions targeted mainly large companies that trade in maize or use maize as a raw material for manufacturing. According to Jayne, Mangisoni, and Sitko (2008) the justification for the trade restriction was that the private sector was deliberately hoarding maize, thereby creating shortages that fuelled price increases.

As a way to enforce the trade restrictions, ADMARC was designated as a sole buyer of maize from farmers and it was also given the exclusive mandate to sell maize to consumers at the prescribed government price. The political nature of the decision was evident from its justification. In reinforcing the ban, the deputy minister of MoAFS argued that 'maize is a protected crop and anybody buying it will be arrested'.[12] In this regard, ADMARC was instructed to purchase at least up to 50,000 MT of maize per year which it has not been able to do due to its perennial serious financial constraints.[13]

According to officials from the Ministry of Trade and Industry, the ban was relaxed as early as mid-September 2008 because of the fierce lobby of GTAM. They argued that 'most members of GTAM have close political connections and some politicians have stakes in companies that buy maize directly from farmers'. While politically plausible, it was quickly realized that 'an exclusive ban on large private sector companies would backfire because it would have led to the scarcity of manufactured maize products which can easily upset the rather docile urban consumers'.[14] Similar concerns were echoed by the FUM. Its main argument was that the policy did not make practical sense since 'it did not clearly define who a large trader was, it would not be enforced objectively'.[15] FUM further faulted the ban as 'infringing upon the rights of farmers by forcing them to sell their produce to ADMARC which does no longer have marketing outlets across the country and is often cash strapped'.[16]

These criticisms coupled with the stakes that some key politicians have in maize trade forced the government to somewhat modify the blanket ban on large-scale private sector involvement in maize trade in less than a month.

[12] See, 'Maize Prices Soar Again', *The Daily Times*, 24 April 2009.

[13] See, 'ADMARC Misses its Maize Target: Buys only 22,000 out of expected 50,000 tonnes', *The Nation*, 4 September 2009.

[14] Interview with CAMA's executive director, 17 May 2012.

[15] Interview with the president of FUM, 28 May 2012.

[16] Interview with the president of FUM, 28 May 2012.

While GTAM and FUM pushed for a total lift of the ban, the government opted for a modified version of the ban which allowed private sector traders to participate in maize trade as long as they were duly licensed to do so. This was highly strategic on the part of the government because it ensured that 'those who were licensed were either politicians or those with close connections to politicians... this cannot be hidden... some of us were licensed just to silence us'.[17] The decision to introduce an exclusive ban on private maize traders was justified as offering the government an opportunity to get an exact idea of the maize harvest so that 'we can keep enough for our consumption and how much to export'.[18]

The ban was not successful because ADMARC which was supposed to defend the price band could not purchase maize from smallholder farmers and was unable to sell maize to consumers at official prices due to its weak financial position. Jayne, Mangisoni, and Sitko (2008) note that the rapid rise in prices affected ADMARC's ability to buy maize from smallholder farmers as it initially offered to buy maize from smallholders at as low as MWK30 per kg when private traders were already buying maize at MWK60 per kg. As already noted, the financial stature of ADMARC has greatly diminished but the government continues to use ADMARC in this way 'merely as a desperate attempt to project an image of a caring government during times of hardship largely for electioneering purposes'.[19]

7.4.6 *International Trade Restrictions*

In reaction to the soaring maize prices, the government also imposed export bans on maize during the 2007/8 global food price spikes. It is, however, important to put into proper perspective the context in which the export ban on maize was instituted. Following the implementation of SAPs, Malawi phased out quantitative restrictions on international trade except for a few products whose restrictions are largely based on health, safety, and national security reasons (Chirwa and Ngalawa 2006). Although maize is not on the list of restricted products requiring import license, its import is subjected to heavy regulation which further underlies its sensitivity in the country's food security equation.

With respect to the 2007/8 food price crisis, the maize export ban was instituted in April by President Bingu wa Mutharika at a political rally. This ban was imposed when the export contract to Zimbabwe amounting to 400,000 MT had not yet been fully met. As already indicated above, the

[17] Interview with a chairperson of GTAM, 1 June 2012.
[18] See 'Maize Prices Soar Again', *The Daily Times*, 24 April 2009.
[19] Interview with a MoAFS official, 24 May 2012.

government issued maize export permits to Zimbabwe 'on the account that Malawi had registered a historic record maize surplus estimated at 1.3 million MT'.[20] However, most senior policy makers interviewed argued that the government was rather reluctant to impose the ban because 'it would undermine the grand success narrative of the FISP particularly during a season it had reportedly registered a historic maize surplus over and above the annual food requirements'.[21] The president was reportedly forced to impose the ban following media reports that indicated that maize prices had soared to as much as MWK90 per kg. In these stories, the media began to question the credibility of the claims that the country had enough maize 'yet the prices are soaring far much more than it is the case when the country is hit by drought'.[22] The media further highlighted the hardships that households were experiencing due to high maize prices.[23] This was seized by opposition political parties which argued that the price crisis amidst plenty 'simply suggested that Mutharika's government had failed to manage its own success to guarantee food security and as such it needs to be replaced at the next polls'.[24]

When he announced the maize export ban at a political rally, President Mutharika justified it as a means 'to stop unscrupulous traders, most of them allies of the opposition political parties, from depleting the country's grain reserves'. He argued that the ban would be lifted only when the government would be satisfied with the food security situation in the country. This was further justified as a way of dealing with speculation. He argued that business people were hoarding maize in their warehouses to create an artificial shortage in order to make supernormal profits out of maize either through exports or selling it locally at inflated prices.

The Ministry of Trade and Industry proceeded to gazette the maize export ban. This was fiercely protested by GTAM. According to GTAM's chairperson they protested 'because we knew that some politically connected traders or even politicians themselves would continue to export maize regardless of the export ban'. They further protested because most of the GTAM members had already invested considerable resources in arranging for their maize exports to Zimbabwe. The export ban was condemned by the United States Agency for International Development (USAID) and the IMF. They characterized the

[20] Interview with a MoAFS official, 22 May 2012.

[21] Interview with a MoAFS official, 22 May 2012.

[22] See, 'Disaster Looms as Maize Prices are about to Hit MK100 per kilogramme', *The Nation*, 22 March 2008.

[23] It is important to note that it was only the private print and electronic media which peddled these stories. The public media is heavily controlled by the state and carried stories that attempted to underplay the seriousness of the maize price crisis. It was essentially a mouth for the government to advance its narrative of sabotage as explaining the soaring of maize prices and that it was doing everything possible to deal with the culprits.

[24] Interview with an opposition member of parliament who at the time was sitting on the Parliamentary Committee on Agriculture and Natural Resources, 24 May 2012.

ban as retrogressive since it undermined Malawi's commitment to economic liberalization (Jayne, Mangisoni, and Sitko 2008). The argument is that donors were reluctant to engage forcefully with the government on these policy responses because at that time Malawi was widely seen as a success story in as far as the question of food security was concerned through the implementation of the FISP which they had fiercely opposed. They were thus afraid of making yet another 'mistake'.

However, regardless of the protest against the ban by GTAM and donors it remained in force until August 2010. Although the arguments presented by those who protested against it were generally sound, 'the government would not retreat for it was important for it to project itself as leading the efforts to protect the people especially since elections were just around the corner'.[25] He argued that in private, even the president recognized the negative consequences of these policy responses that entailed reversals without debate and discussion but 'considered them to be politically correct in terms of projecting his government as a caring government motivated largely by electoral considerations'.[26]

7.4.7 *Impact of the Policy Responses to Price Swings*

This section examines the impact of the policy responses implemented by the government to respond to the 2007/8 global food price crisis. The main question is: who were the winners and losers following the implementation of these policies? None of the policies that the government implemented were designed with a long-term orientation. They were driven by the desire to stabilize maize prices in order to make it affordable by vulnerable households while at the same time protecting them from food insecurity. The price band was invoked to prevent the prices of maize rising further; the restriction of domestic maize trade was implemented to boost the maize supply by making sure that private sector traders did not hoard maize to further fuel speculation; and the export ban was meant to ensure adequate supplies of maize were available in the domestic economy.

The main argument is that although the policy responses were justified as an attempt to protect both farmers and consumers, the main beneficiaries were maize traders with close political connections. For instance, when the large-scale private traders were banned from domestic maize trade, the politically connected traders managed to lobby for the implementation of a modified version of the ban in less than a month. This version allowed

[25] Interview with a chairperson of the Parliamentary Committee on Agriculture and Natural Resources, 2 June 2012.

[26] Interview with the executive director of CAMA, 27 May 2012.

large-scale traders to be involved in maize trade on condition that they were duly licensed and traded within the stipulated maize ban. According to some interviewees, the licensing requirement was exploited to exclude those traders that were not politically connected. The fact that ADMARC failed to enforce the price band meant that the privileged traders benefited from high maize which shot up to as high as MWK90 per kg. The very same people benefited when the export ban on maize was introduced in April 2008. According to key stakeholders interviewed, although the export ban was introduced, some privileged traders, mostly politicians and their associates, continued to export maize to Zimbabwe. Thus, traders without political connections lost out. They did not benefit from the soaring domestic maize prices since they could not be licensed and they incurred losses when the export ban was introduced quite abruptly. They had already invested considerable resources in the logistics related to the delivery of their export quotas to Zimbabwe.

The smallholder farmers who are mostly net buyers of maize and the poor urban consumers were the main losers as they disproportionately bore the brunt of the policy responses that the government implemented in the wake of the 2007/8 global food crisis. They suffered most because of the instability in maize prices fostered by the policies implemented by the government in order to address maize price spikes. While the government intervened in the maize markets by prescribing the floor and ceiling prices, it was unable to defend these prices for two main reasons. The government did not accurately estimate the actual production levels of maize which made it set the prices either too low or too high. This made it difficult for ADMARC to effectively defend them. The situation was often compounded by the failure of ADMARC to effectively defend the price band due to its weak financial position. It was neither able to buy maize from farmers nor sell it to consumers at the prescribed official price.

Consumers have also suffered from the effects of stockpiling maize supplies through ADMARC and NFRA. They did not release maize stocks into the market at all during the 2007/8 global food price crisis. They have often done so as part of their recycling strategy at times when there is too much maize in circulation. This has tended to depress maize prices quite substantially.[27] And in a drive to be competitive, ADMARC and NFRA have often slashed their prices. This means that farmers make severe losses which make further investment in maize less attractive. The overall net effect of maize

[27] See 'Malawi Maize Selling Low…NFRA is Offloading Maize as Part of the Agency's Grain Recycling Strategy', *Malawi News*, 2–8 April 2011; 'NFRA Maize Sale Oversubscribed', *The Daily Times*, 4 April 2011; and 'ADMARC Shocks ECAMA, Farmers: It is a Marketing, not Stocking Corporation', *The Nation*, 22 July 2009.

price instability is that it prevents smallholder farmers from graduating out of poverty and inhibits surplus production and investment in marketing infrastructure. The main drawback is that high price instability is detrimental to the poor constructing their own routes out of poverty since it increases the risk of failure to secure food from the market and reinforces a pattern of subsistence reliance on one or a few main food crops for household-level food security.

The government incurred substantial costs and losses resulting from the stockpiles of maize to which they added during the peak of the 2007/8 global food price crisis. Both ADMARC and NFRA incurred heavy costs of maintaining the stockpiles of maize that in some cases were almost five years old during this period. The enormous costs were inevitable because it is costly to maintain high-level quality maize for a longer period of time. As part of the recycling strategy, the NFRA incurred a loss of MWK390 million in disposing of the maize reserves that were procured at MWK1.05 billion way after the food price spikes were over. When the maize was offloaded, it fetched only MWK660 million. A similar story can be told about ADMARC. Having accumulated huge volumes of maize, ADMARC decided to dispose of the maize to create space for fresh reserves. As stated above, ADMARC had to slash down its prices in order to compete with private traders. Consequently ADMARC posted a MWK551 million loss against a projected net profit of MWK181 million.[28]

7.5 Concluding Reflections

The main purpose of this study was to assess how the government responded to the 2007/8 global food price spikes from a political economy perspective. The analysis demonstrates that the policy responses to the rising prices implemented by the Malawi government underpin the underlying political objectives and interests of the key stakeholders in the policy processes. As the single most important electoral battleground, the question of food security is central in determining whether those out of power can wrestle it from the incumbent or whether the governing party or coalition can maintain itself in power.

All the three major policy responses, namely: price control, domestic trade restrictions, and export trade ban were motivated by the desire for the government to maintain a semblance of food availability at all times. The main preoccupation is to fend off any perception of food scarcity as well as

[28] 'ADMARC Shocks ECAMA, Farmers: It is a Marketing, not Stocking Corporation', *The Nation*, 22 July 2009.

unaffordability to the majority of smallholder farmers and consumers. The policy interventions to ensure that ADMARC and NFRA hold enough maize stocks were meant to ensure that maize would be readily available even when there is some slack in production in a growing season. It is for this reason that ADMARC was mandated to act as a primary buyer of farmers' produce often at higher prices than those offered by private traders in order to outbid them. Both the NFRA and ADMARC have since the 2005/6 growing season accumulated maize reserves which are supposed to be released into the market when there are indications of scarcity, but the evidence suggests that they were not able to do this effectively during the 2007/8 global food price spikes.

The maize export ban and the regulation of who is involved or not in the maize trade were implemented in the same spirit. When there are apparent signs of scarcity the government has moved in to effect an export ban of maize. An export ban on maize trade was introduced in April 2008 when it became apparent that the country was short of maize. The ban remained in force until August 2010 when the government authorized that up to 300,000 MT of maize be exported to Zimbabwe. The maize export ban was further complemented by the ban on private traders' involvement in maize trading activities leaving ADMARC as the only legitimate buyer and seller of maize.[29] In a modified version of this policy intervention, only those who were duly licensed were allowed to get involved in maize trade. The justification for the drastic policy interventions was to protect farmers as well as consumers from unscrupulous traders who are primarily obsessed with making supernormal profits.

A critical assessment of the underlying dynamics of the policy responses show that there is no real commitment to ensure that the policies actually succeed. The real beneficiaries of these policies were not necessarily smallholder farmers and consumers but rather maize traders who are politically connected. This was mainly the case because the low transparency in the policy-making process related to food policies created a certain level of uncertainty in the food markets which further led to speculation pushing food prices even higher to the advantage of those who were still able to engage in maize trade under these circumstances.

The traders who were licensed following the implementation of a modified version of the domestic trade restriction in maize benefited from high maize prices as a result of the failure of ADMARC to defend the price band. Some of the traders continued to export maize to Zimbabwe even when the

[29] See, 'Cost of not Exporting Surplus Maize: Reflecting on Forex Shortage, High Storage Costs', *The Nation*, 12 August 2010; 'Malawi Strategizes on Excess Maize... ADMARC to be Sole Buyer', *The Daily Times*, 15 April 2009; 'ADMARC Misses its Target: Buys only 22,000 out of Expected 50,000 Tonnes', *The Nation*, 4 September 2009.

export ban was in force. There is thus absolutely no political will to ratchet technical competence relating to the estimation of food needs, food supply, national food reserves, and impact evaluation of policy change(s) vital to managing the food economy effectively and to increase the benefits of polices and reduce their cost. These weaknesses are further reinforced by the inherent institutional rivalry between NFRA and ADMARC. The capacities of the relevant stakeholders entrusted with the implementation of the policies are so weak that the policies themselves are not fully implemented or monitored at all.

Why then are these policies implemented when there is clearly no political will to ensure that they deliver? The policy makers interviewed acknowledged as much about the inevitable failure of the policies but they are nonetheless implemented for sheer political expediency. This underlies the centrality of maize in the politics of Malawi. Although both policy makers and politicians know that the policies are not effective at all they still proceed to implement them because they project a government's commitment to the citizens' welfare by attempting to ensure the availability of adequate food supplies at all times and its affordability since it forms part of the social contract between the state and its citizens.

Although the food policy-making processes are theoretically subjected to the influence of a diverse range of stakeholders, few are dominant. The president was clearly dominant in initiating policy processes although this was not necessarily followed up with firm political commitment to ensure that the policies succeeded. The history of Malawi generally shows that the presidency dominates policy processes relating to matters of food policy and pricing. This is attributed to its uniqueness due to having a single dominant staple, maize, which suggests that Malawi is relatively homogenous ecologically (Poulton 2011). This, combined with a history of chronic food shortages and insecurity, has transformed maize into a political crop whose influence in electoral politics and in the social contract between Malawians and their government has become extremely important.

The government's responses to the global food price spikes further demonstrate that while moments of opportunities often triggered by crises exist when other actors as identified above could have the potential to influence the shape and form of policy processes, their effect is rather limited. The resultant policies often reflect the government's interests which are to a great extent motivated by desire to maintain a tight grip on the ruling coalition. The ordinary people are essentially on the receiving end of the policy processes. Except through the ballot box once every five years opportunities, moments, and channels for the ordinary citizens to influence the nature, form, and shape of policy processes hardly exist (Cammack 2010). Thus, although there has been increased openness in the policy debate and dialogue relating to food security, the process continues to be unclear, dominated by presidential interventions and tends to be highly motivated by electoral politics and considerations.

References

Banda, J. (1998). 'The Constitutional Change Debate of 1993–1995'. In K. Phiri and K. Ross (eds), *Democratization in Malawi: A Stocktaking*. Blantyre: Christian Literature Association of Malawi (CLAIM).

Cammack, D. (2010). 'The Politics of Chameleons Revisited: The Burden of Malawi's Political Culture'. In M. Ott, and E. Kanyongolo (eds), *Democracy in Progress: Malawi's 2009 Parliamentary and Presidential Elections*. Balaka/Malawi: Montfort Media.

Cammack, D., F. Golooba-Mutebi, E. Kanyongolo, and T. O'Neil (2007). 'Neopatrimonial Politics, Decentralization and Local Government: Uganda and Malawi in 2006'. ABIA Working Paper 2: London: Overseas Development Institute (ODI).

Chinsinga, B. (2003). 'Lack of Alternative Leadership in Democratic Malawi: Some Reflections Ahead of the 2004 General Elections'. *Nordic Journal of African Studies* 12(1): 1–22.

Chinsinga, B. (2006). 'Public Policy Making'. In N. Patel, and L. Svasand (eds), *Government and Politics in Malawi*. Balaka/Malawi: Montfort Media.

Chinsinga, B. (2010). 'Seeds and Subsidies: The Political Economy of Input Programmes in Malawi'. Future Agricultures Working Paper 13. Brighton: Future Agricultures Consortium.

Chirwa, E. W. (1998). 'Fostering Private Food Marketing and Food Policies after Liberalisation—The Case of Malawi'. In P. Seppala (ed.), *Liberalized and Neglected? Food Marketing Policies in Eastern Africa*. Helsinki: United Nations University World Institute for Development Economics Research (UNU-WIDER).

Chirwa, W. (2000). 'Civil Society in Malawi's Democratic Transition'. In M. Ott, K. Phiri, and N. Patel (eds), *Malawi's Second Democratic Elections: Processes, Problems and Prospects*. Blantyre: Christian Literature Association of Malawi.

Chirwa, E. W. (2009). 'Sustained Increases in Food Prices: Effect and Policies in Malawi'. Paper presented at the FAO Regional Workshop on Policies for the Effective Management of Food Price Swings in African Countries held on 2–3 April, Dar es Salaam, Tanzania.

Chirwa, E. W., and H. Ngalawa (2006). 'The Extent and Impact of Import Surges in Malawi: The Case of Maize, Sugar and Milk'. Paper submitted to Food and Agriculture Organisation. Rome: Food and Agriculture Organisation (FAO).

Chirwa, E. W., and C. Zakeyo (2006). 'Malawi'. In H. Thomas (ed.), *Trade Reforms and Food Security: Country Case Studies and Synthesis*. Rome: Food and Agriculture Organisation (FAO).

Dorward, A. R., and E. Chirwa (2009). *The Agricultural Input Subsidy Programme 2005 to 2008: Achievements and Challenges*: London: School of Oriental and African Studies (SOAS).

Fozzard, A., and C. Simwaka (2002). 'How, When and Why does Poverty get Budget Priority: Poverty Reduction Strategy and Public Expenditure in Malawi'. London: Overseas Development Institute (ODI).

Harrigan, J. (2001). *From Dictatorship to Democracy: Economic Policy in Malawi 1964– 2000*. London: Ashgate.

Harrigan, J. (2003). 'U-Turns and Full Circles: Two Decades of Agricultural Reform in Malawi 1981–2000'. *World Development* 31(5): 847–63.

Jayne, T. S., J. Mangisoni, and N. Sitko (2008). 'Malawi's Maize Marketing System: A Rapid Appraisal Study'. Report to the World Bank. Lilongwe, Malawi.

Kanyongolo, F. (2010). *Back to the Courts: Legal Battles and Electoral Disputes, Democracy in Progress: Malawi's 2009 Parliamentary and Presidential Elections*. Balaka: Montfort Media.

Kaunda, J. (1992). 'The Administrative Organization and Processes of National Development Planning'. In G. C. Z. Mhone (ed.), *Malawi at the Crossroads: The Postcolonial Political Economy*. Harare: SAPES Books.

Mvula, P. M., E. W. Chirwa, and J. Kadzandira (2003). 'Poverty and Social Impact Assessment in Malawi: Closure of ADMARC Markets'. Final Report submitted to Social Development Department, World Bank, and Economic Section/PRSP Support, GTZ. Lilongwe.

Poulton, C. (2011). 'Democratization and the Political Economy of Agricultural Policy in Africa'. London: School of Oriental and African Studies (SOAS).

Rapsomanikis, G. (2009). 'The 2007–2008 Food Price Swing: Impact and Policies in Eastern and Southern Africa'. FAO Commodities and Trade Technical Paper 12. Rome: Food and Agriculture Organisation (FAO).

8

The Political Economy of Food Price Policy in Zambia

Antony Chapoto

8.1 Introduction

Like many countries in the world, ensuring food security is at the centre of Zambia's agriculture policy. Unstable and high prices for food staples such as maize, wheat, and rice have severe economic, social, and political consequences.[1] The global food price crisis of 2007 and 2008 raised fears about the impacts of higher and more volatile food prices for the urban and rural poor in Zambia.

Recent large price swings for the major staple food, maize, reinforced the general perception that food prices are far too strategically and politically important to be left to the market. They may expose poor farmers and consumers to unacceptable price spikes and collapses (Chapoto and Jayne 2009). Rapidly increasing retail prices for maize meal triggered food riots in Kitwe, a mining town in the Copperbelt province, which pushed the government to take action and attempt to respond to the global food crisis of 2007 and 2008.

The policy response strategies were similar to those used in past drought-induced food crises including an immediate maize export ban/restriction without looking at implications on regional trade; agreement on the quantity of maize to be imported, and how much each of the different stakeholders should import; request for import duty waivers from the Ministry of Finance and National Planning (MoFNP), and the provision of subsidized maize grain to millers for onward transmission to consumers. The outcome of using this package was not effective in solving the crises because the agreed

[1] See Newberry and Stiglitz (1981); Timmer (2000); Dehn, Gilbert, and Varangis (2005); Byerlee, Jayne, and Myers (2006); Chapoto and Jayne (2009); and Govereh (2009).

implementation plan was fraught with problems. With the existing high levels of mistrust between government and the private sector, opposing self-interests among the key interest groups and some vested interest amongst certain individuals in both the public and private sector led to inertia in dealing with the problem.

While the causes of past global food crises have been studied, there is little knowledge of the policy processes and the related political economy issues. A few studies have helped to catalogue events and responses in the country, for example, Govereh (2009), Chapoto and Jayne (2009), and Jayne et al. (2009). These studies outlined in detail the timeline of events and responses although political economy issues were not at the centre of the analyses. International non-governmental organizations (NGOs) in Zambia also helped to raise awareness of the likely impact of the global food price crisis on the poor and vulnerable households by outlining how they were positioning themselves to respond to the impending crisis. Unfortunately, most of their reports or analyses were done at the height of the global food crisis and tended to overstate the crisis and its impact since their main focus was to attract funding to support their humanitarian efforts in the country. On the other hand, press reports covering the local food price crisis tended to be driven mostly by what was going on outside of Zambia. This failed to take into account local conditions and political economy issues pertaining to the government responses to the impending crisis. The local media started to pay more attention to the domestic situation only after the crises had deepened.

This country study uses political economy analysis framework to better understand how the Zambian government responded to past food price escalations with special emphasis on the most recent global food crisis. Indeed, Zambia saw price escalations of wheat, rice, and soybeans in 2007 and 2008, whilst maize prices rose in 2008 and 2009. Maize, as the main staple crop, continued to attract the most attention from the government, hence the response strategies focused on maize grain and maize meal.

8.2 Country Context

Despite the rapid growth of gross domestic product (GDP) in the past decade, poverty rates in Zambia remain very high at about 60 per cent of the population. General economic growth has not reduced poverty (Tembo et al. 2010; Chapoto et al. 2011). Addressing high rural poverty rates remains a government priority in the national development programmes, but solutions have proven elusive. The main impediment is not simply a lack of technical knowledge concerning what needs to be implemented, but realizing that such knowledge cannot be translated into action unless the policy process is capable of allocating scarce public resources in ways that reflect this knowledge. Chapoto et al. (2011) argue that political economy and associated governance problems are increasingly recognized as crucial.

Like most countries in Africa, white maize in Zambia is a strategic political crop. After independence, maize became the cornerstone of an implicit and sometimes explicit 'social contract' between the government and the Zambian people (Jayne and Jones 1997). The social contract meant that the government had to ensure that smallholder farmers received higher producer prices whilst consumers accessed cheaper food. To achieve these two opposing objectives, the Zambian government adopted a controlled marketing system, run by the government's National Agricultural and Marketing Board (NAMBOARD) and later through the Zambia Co-operative Federation until the system became financially unattainable (Govereh 2009; Tembo et al. 2010).

With market liberalization in 1991, the government of Zambia stopped subsidizing production and consumption of maize, immediately causing the prices of basic food commodities including maize to sharply increase. Consumers resorted to rioting, so food pricing policy became highly politicized under the new multi-party democratic system. Due to this pressure, the Movement for Multi-party Democracy (MMD), the political party that was in government, decided to revert back to some government controls on the food market. This resulted in the establishment of the Food Reserve Agency (FRA) in 1996. Unlike its predecessor, NAMBOARD, which was the sole buyer and seller of grain in the country, FRA was originally conceived to hold buffer stocks to dampen price variability and, when necessary, provide liquidity in the maize market during the initial years of market liberalization while the private sector was establishing itself (Jayne and Jones 1997). Due to the recurring drought induced food crises, the government through the FRA decided to increase its participation in the maize market via state restrictions on the private export of maize, and unpredictable changes in trade tariff rates, quantities traded, and prices offered and paid by FRA. Ostensibly, these state activities have been in response to perceived failings of the private sector to provide reliable markets and stable prices for smallholder farmers' surplus maize production (see Nijhoff et al. 2002; Chapoto and Jayne 2009; Tembo et al. 2010).

8.2.1 *Key Decision Actors in Food Policy Issues*

Food policy in Zambia is formulated at both the technical and political level. During the food crisis, the policy-making process was overwhelmingly dominated by the political level. Technical operatives had limited input into the decision-making process. The major stakeholders, farmers, and millers had direct access to policy makers at very high levels.

The executive branch of government comprises cabinet ministers and is chaired by the president of the Republic of Zambia. The secretary to the cabinet is the head of the civil service and ultimately all policy positions that originate from ministries pass through his/her office. Each ministry is responsible for generating its own policy positions which are submitted to the permanent secretary, and finally to the minister for approval. Once approved, the documents are sent to the policy analysis and coordination section in the secretary to the cabinet's office. After approval, the cabinet memorandum is finally sent to the cabinet for debate and approval.

Ultimately, all power in the cabinet is vested in the head of State. Although a minister can lobby for policy change, his/her limits are set by policy statements made by the political party in power. For example, during the food crisis of 2008 and 2009, the executive branch did not openly veto any policies but in most cases the aspirations of the political party in power and recommendations of lobby groups with access to the cabinet were prioritized. Also, the fact that the minister of agriculture is a member of the cabinet meant the executive branch was briefed about the situation and considered recommendations coming from various stakeholders. The policy responses that were chosen tended to ignore the technical input from the relevant ministry or research organizations in favour of input from very powerful interest groups.

Zambia's parliament has an oversight role on government policy implementation, although some of the issues not requiring changes or enactment of new laws are dealt with at cabinet level and not taken to parliament for ratification. However, from time to time, the parliamentary committee on agriculture, for instance, makes requests for briefings and updates on various policy implementation issues. One of the major weaknesses of this system is that a policy can be radically changed by the cabinet disregarding technical input. This is especially crucial given that powerful interest groups often directly lobby cabinet members.

The main policy tools that are at the disposal of Ministry of Agriculture and Livestock (MAL) include: issuance of import and export permits based on the crop forecast results; stock monitoring through the stocks committee; recommendations to the cabinet on the level of market participation by FRA; and dealing with plant and phyto-sanitary matters and the issuance of appropriate importation and exportation clearance for agricultural commodities. Cross-border trade policy is administered through the Zambia Revenue Authority, which has the mandate to manage all customs functions with MAL's phyto-sanitary officers stationed at most of the major borders. Internal marketing policy is generally implemented through FRA.

Recently, the maize monitoring committee chaired by MAL permanent secretary was transformed into the stocks committee, an inter-ministerial and private sector technical body that routinely meets to discuss the national food security status (stocks), specifically focusing on the major cereals, maize, wheat, and rice.[2] Although transparency is often emphasized in dealing with food crises, the decision-making is characterized by high information asymmetry amongst major stakeholders. For instance, Millers Association of Zambia (MAZ) does provide consolidated information on stocks held by its members. However, competition amongst the individual milling companies means that they are often very hesitant to share accurate stocks information even to the association. This makes policy-making very difficult. For instance, in December 2009, millers reported lower than expected stocks. But, when the government offered a price subsidy to millers, the reported quantity of available stocks increased significantly. The lack of transparency among the players in the milling industry is partly due to the way the industry is organized. Due to the high cost of credit in Zambia most mills are not able to keep significant inventory of grain for processing. The implication of this has been that mills with the highest inventory are able to influence the market prices more than mills with lower inventory. Consequently, inventory information is a very closely guarded secret. This has proven to be one of the biggest challenges in the grain market decision-making process. In years of cereal deficits, inventory information is also used by the milling industry to lobby government for intervention; this introduces considerable issues of information asymmetry.

INTEREST GROUPS

The two biggest interest/lobby groups in Zambia are the Zambia National Farmers Union (ZNFU) and Millers Association of Zambia (MAZ). The Grain Traders Association of Zambia (GTAZ) has increasingly gained some prominence over the last five years or so. However, the organization has very limited membership and the wide scope of consumer issues has made the association relatively less effective when dealing with specific food policy issues. Other lobby groups include the Zambia Consumer Association (ZACA) and the Jesuits Centre for Theological Reflection (JCTR). ZACA has been in existence since 2000 and is supposed to be the major advocacy group representing consumers instead of MAZ when it comes to maize meal prices. JCTR has

[2] The stocks committee comprises: MAL, MoFNP, Central Statistical Office (CSO), Zambia National Farmers Union (ZNFU), MAZ, Zambia Farm Growers Association, Zambia Peasant Small-scale Farmers Association, FRA, Grain Traders Association of Zambia (GTAZ), National Food and Nutrition Commission, Bank of Zambia, Indaba Agricultural Policy Research Institute (IAPRI) (formerly Food Security Research Project), Agricultural Consultative Forum FEWS NET Zambia, Zambia Agricultural Commodity Exchange, and Zambia Co-operative Federation.

been instrumental in highlighting issues affecting the poor in the country via their monthly consumer bulletin. However, they do not carry the same influence as the ZNFU and MAZ.

The ZNFU represents the interest of farmers with members drawn mostly from the commercial farming sector. Although the membership of the union is not publicly announced, the total number of large-scale agriculture holdings in Zambia numbers no more than 2000 (MAL 2011). On the other hand, the country has over 1.5 million small- and medium-scale agricultural households who can become members of the ZNFU through any small-scale farmers' associations.

Generally, ZNFU is very vocal on pricing and trade issues for the staple grains (maize, wheat, and soybeans) and inputs (fertilizer, fuel, and electricity). With the exception of maize, which is mostly grown by the smallholder farmers, the union is very active on issues that address the commercial farming sector in the country. Some critics from the peasant farmers association think that ZNFU does not fully represent the interests of the small-scale farmers because it was formed initially to represent commercial farmers. Their argument is that issues of the small farming sector are more complex and require different lobby mechanisms. ZNFU's agenda for the small-scale farmers has been to fight for higher maize producer prices and more fertilizer subsidies under FISP. Unfortunately, the union chooses to ignore the empirical evidence regarding maize production and marketing characteristics of smallholder farmers and facts about the effectiveness of the government entitlement programmes in terms of resource use and effect on overall agriculture development, especially when these subsidy/entitlement programmes result in under-funding of the key agriculture drivers, such as irrigation, roads, and research and development.

The second most influential lobby group is the MAZ, a self-financing association formed to represent millers in Zambia with a production capacity of 1.5 metric tons per hour or more.[3] Since 2001, MAZ has increased its influence on maize issues in Zambia through its ability to influence government's policy on maize and maize meal prices during food crises. The association has long been plagued by allegations of collusion in price setting. These allegations have always been denied by the association. During the past food price crisis, MAZ was able to convince government to intervene by allowing FRA to sell subsidized grain to them in order to reduce the consumer prices.

[3] MAZ's objectives are: (i) to promote the interests of the milling industry in Zambia; (ii) to assist the Zambian government with the country's food security; (iii) to foster international and regional trade for the industry; (iv) to create dialogue with the government on behalf of the millers on trade policies and budgetary allocations; and (v) to provide a ready market for maize growers in Zambia.

Donors and cooperating partners in Zambia are important in providing assistance to the Zambian government whenever there is a food crisis especially by helping to finance food aid importation for vulnerable groups. However, in most cases, the donors' role in the agricultural sector has mainly been limited to an advisory one through the Troika (World Bank, Netherlands, and United States). During the food crisis, Food and Agriculture Organization of the UN (FAO) funded a number of meetings to encourage stakeholders to discuss how to deal with the global food prices.

8.2.2 *Past Food Crises, Price Trends, and Price Transmission*

In the past decade, Zambia has experienced four episodes of food crises, in 2001–2, 2002–3, 2005–6, and 2008–9 marketing seasons. The first three episodes were caused by severe drought conditions in the country. Zambia's agriculture is mainly rain-fed, so crop production in the country is vulnerable to weather shocks.

LESSONS LEARNED FROM PAST FOOD CRISES

Zambia has not learned from past experiences how to plan and quickly respond to food crises. With similar and less successful response strategies in the past, one wonders why the government in collaboration with the relevant stakeholders does not put together a standard operation strategy on how to deal with future food crises. The answer lies in the political economy surrounding food issues in the country, a subject that is central to this study.

The common characteristics of the past food price crises that hinder the successful implementation of the agreed upon plan are as follows:

1. The government through MAL has always been open to the stakeholders' input before the onset of a food crisis. However, the execution of the agreed plan is fraught with problems resulting in the crisis worsening before serious action is taken.
2. A high level of mistrust exists between the government and the private sector. The private sector seems to be always uncertain about government actions especially regarding imports. This is because the government has in the past sanctioned the FRA to release its stocks at subsidized prices to a few selected millers hurting traders and/or millers who would have imported maize.
3. Once the alarm bell is sound through the crop forecast and national food balance sheet about an impending crisis, the government always imposes ad hoc export restrictions/ban. The effectiveness of such a response is highly contended because informal exports will continue

to flow out of Zambia illegally. Also, ad hoc export bans have made the country become an unreliable regional grain supplier thereby curtailing the growth of the private sector participation in regional trade.

4. The refusal and delays to grant duty waiver requests by the MoNFP shows lack of inter-ministerial dialogue with the MAL and other related government agencies, especially when the country requires them to respond quickly to a food crisis.

8.2.3 *Policy Responses to the 2007–9 Global Food Crisis*

Policies in response to the rising food prices in 2008 and 2009 fall into three categories: trade-oriented, consumer-oriented, and producer-oriented policy responses.

TRADE-ORIENTED POLICIES

Export restrictions/ban: The food security update by FEWS NET at the end of December 2007 reported localized maize and maize meal price escalation in some parts of the country especially the flood ridden southern province. In January 2008, Zambia like Malawi and Tanzania imposed export bans as a safeguard from likely shortfalls and to curb further food price increases. There is no evidence that this was done in a coordinated way. Each country was trying to protect itself from the looming food crisis triggered by the global events. This response was a result of the continued pressure from politicians, consumer groups, and press reports warning the government to respond to the impending food crisis due to floods and the global food crisis.

Maize export restrictions are a common feature in Zambia and date back to the 1960s. Whenever the country experiences a maize production deficit, export ban/restrictions through the non-issuance of export permits is invoked. Since the region has the same growing season, a drought in Zambia usually means a drought in most of the neighbouring countries. Therefore, the decision to restrict exports is made out of fear that the millers and traders in search of higher prices will export most of the local stocks thereby exacerbating the food problem. Unfortunately, such restrictions have not worked well in the past because any ban requires strict policing, something that is not possible in Zambia, a country sharing borders with eight countries. Illegal exports tend to increase during this time and are hard to detect and the treasury forgoes revenues from export taxes. When the situation improved, there was a delay in lifting the ban because the government feared public backlash.

MAIZE IMPORTS AND IMPORT DUTY WAIVER

At a meeting held on 25 July 2008 between the government and the agriculture stakeholders and chaired by the Minister of Agriculture, MAZ, GTAZ, and ZNFU disputed the national balance sheet for maize grain announced in May 2008 indicating a surplus of 200,000 MT for the 2007/8 agricultural season. They argued that the annual maize consumption of 50,000 MT was understated given the growth of the breweries and the stock feed sector. At this meeting, the FRA declared having maize stocks amounting to 150,000 MT, MAZ, 55,000 MT, and GTAZ, 25,000 MT. From these stocks, it was ascertained that precautionary measures needed to be taken by the private sector through buying futures on South African Futures Exchange (SAFEX).

However, given past experiences when government through FRA released stocks on the market to selected millers at a time when private sector imports were just hitting the market, traders wanted guarantees from government that this was not going to happen. On the other hand, the farmers wanted to make sure that maize imports by traders did not disadvantage local farmers who were still selling their maize. All parties agreed to have a memorandum of understanding (MOU) drawn up and signed by all parties.

As a requirement, the MAL had to send the draft MOU for vetting by the Ministry of Justice. Unfortunately, the Ministry of Justice indicated that two clauses included in the MOU were not favourable to the government. In particular, the clause that would allow the private sector to re-export the maize if at the time of importation there was enough maize in the country. In addition, traders wanted an import duty waiver. Unfortunately, the latter was outside the jurisdiction of the MAL but required the MoFNP to make a ruling. The idea of the private sector locking into contracts on SAFEX was abandoned. In the meantime, as these discussions were progressing, maize prices were increasing and the ZMK had lost ground to the US$—from 3,500 ZMK to 5,000 ZMK (Figure 8.1). This meant maize imports were going to be more expensive, irrespective of who the importer was going to be—government or private sector. The private sector requested the MoNFP to peg the exchange rate at July rates of US$1 to 3,500 ZMK to facilitate their maize imports. However, this request was also not granted.

In October 2008, there were reports of a food riot in the Copperbelt province targeting retail shops because of the high prices of maize meal. This was a wakeup call for the government to effectively deal with the rising food prices. With maize meal outlets targeted, the government's concern was to find immediate solutions to quickly reduce maize meal prices and re-engage stakeholders on the issue of maize imports.

As of November 2008, neither the government nor the private sector had arranged to import maize and maize stocks held by FRA, MAZ, and GTAZ were reported to be 208,000 MT in mid-November, a 16 per cent decrease

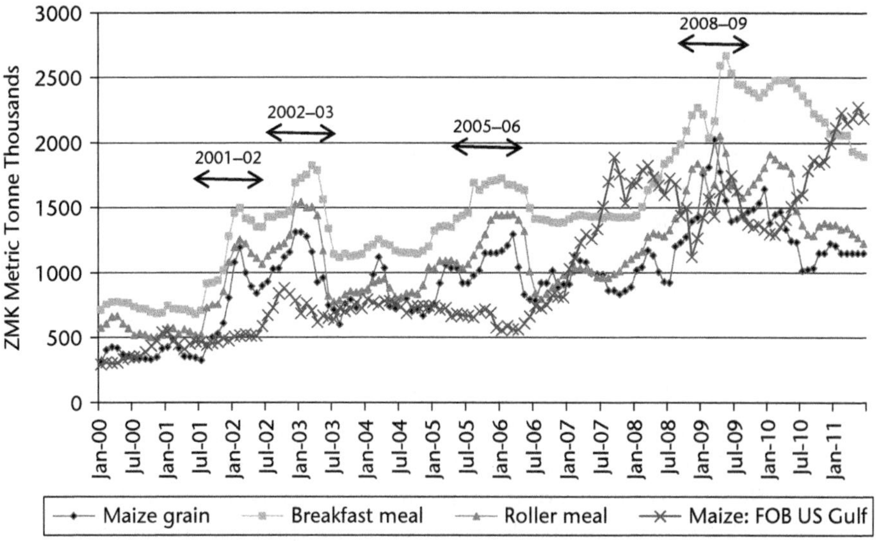

Figure 8.1 Zambia's exchange rates and inflation rate, 2001–11
Source: based on Central Statistical Office (various years).

from 250,000 MT in July. The retail maize prices were now in the range of US$350 to US$400 per MT compared to US$176 per ton on the SAFEX exchange. Maize prices had risen above the import parity price from South Africa.[4] On 24 November, 2008 a select committee of cabinet ministers mandated the FRA to urgently import 100,000 MT of maize wherever it could be found. This was an indication that the decisions about the food crisis were now being made by the president's office.

As the FRA arranged to import this maize, there were reports of increased local maize stocks and the traders were calling for the government to stop purchasing more expensive stocks from outside since they had enough stocks locally. According to the grain traders, maize stocks that were pre-contracted to millers and not included in the uncommitted stocks was now available on the market since millers were now getting subsidized maize from FRA. Also, millers who were not members of MAZ challenged the stocks that MAZ reported to the stocks monitoring committee in July as they were never consulted. After further consultation the government revised its import requirements to 35,000 MT.

On 5 December 2008, the Minister of Information and Broadcasting Services and chief government's spokesperson, General Shikapwasha,

[4] Import parity prices are calculated as the sum of the FOB price, transport charges from source to Lusaka, and an additional 10 per cent to cover handing and insurance cost at the source price.

announced at a press briefing that the government had set up a high-level task force to deal with the rising food crisis. This committee was different from the technical committee that was set up at the onset of the crisis. The task force was to be chaired by the Minister of Agriculture with a mandate to urgently come up with a national action plan to deal with the situation. This marked a turning point in how the country was going to deal with the escalating food prices, in particular maize meal.

CONSUMER SUBSIDIES

To cushion consumers from the rising maize meal prices, the government after meeting with stakeholders decided in December 2008 to subsidize maize grain to millers, requiring them to pass along lower maize meal prices to consumers. FRA was to release 30,000 MT of maize per month for four months to selected millers at US$275 per MT, and millers would then blend an equivalent amount of commercial stocks at market prices that ranged between US$410–420 per MT. The millers would then guarantee a low retail price of 53,000 ZMK per 25 kg bag instead of the market price of 65,000 ZMK per 25 kg. Unfortunately, retail maize prices remained above the 53,000 ZMK mark, so the government reconsidered its position and unilaterally decided to release 100 per cent subsidized stocks at US$220 per MT to be processed into maize meal without blending with commercial stocks. This meant FRA had to double its supply per month to 60,000 MT. Since FRA stock releases were inadequate to cater for millers' requirements, the government was compelled to sign a legal instrument to procure the maize stocks held by the millers at a price of US$385 per MT and releasing the maize at a price of US$220 per MT in December 2008. This innovation also failed to influence countrywide maize meal price reductions. Worse still, not all millers were able to access the cheaper maize provided by FRA and thus could not reduce their prices (Tembo et al. 2010). At the same time, there was a big outcry from grain traders who were now failing to sell their more expensive stocks. After protracted negotiations, FRA agreed to purchase 70,000 MT of maize from the traders in two parts, 40,000 MT at the time of signing the agreement and 30,000 MT in March 2009 at a price of US$405.95.

The release of subsidized maize grain to selected large-scale millers with a guarantee that they would in turn reduce maize meal prices by 23 per cent from 65,000 ZMK to 53,000 ZMK, did not work well. With the continued price escalation, the press and other stakeholders began to blame the millers. The Minister of Agriculture threatened to push for the removal of the subsidy to millers as the programme was not benefiting the consumers. On the other hand, millers were threatening to increase maize meal prices if this happened. Eventually in March 2009, the government reduced the subsidy rate from 50 per cent to 40 per cent with maize meal prices remaining very high.

The upshot of these results is that the government of Zambia needs to seriously review its policy of providing consumers with price relief through subsidizing maize grain to a few large-scale millers. As in the past, this policy has failed the country, although general subsidies are easier to implement, but they fail to meet their goal of reducing prices; instead they distort the market and the big winners will be those millers who are able to access the subsidized grain. The government should have offloaded maize to the open market so that the poor consumers had access to low cost maize that could have been milled cheaply at local hammer mills as well as other small-scale mills (Chapoto and Jayne 2009).

PRODUCER-ORIENTED POLICIES

Input subsidy: The main government response to the food crisis of 2008 involved mostly supply-side policies. These included ramping up FISP, targeting more smallholder farmers. A major reason for focusing on supply-side interventions is that the support base for the then ruling MMD party overwhelmingly comprised rural farming households. After the death of President Levy Mwanawasa in August 2008, fertilizer subsidies and higher maize producer prices became a campaign issue during the elections to replace him. Results from a study by Mason, Jayne, and Myers (2012) shows that the amount of fertilizer distributed was highly correlated to the election outcomes.

Since 2001, Zambia has provided smallholder farmers with subsidized fertilizers. With the rising food and fertilizer prices in 2007, the government increased those subsidies. Initially, farmers eligible for subsidized fertilizers were required to pay only 50 per cent of the fertilizer market price but were now required to pay only 25 per cent. In February 2008, the Zambian parliament approved the 2008 budget with a planned spending of 187 billion ZMK for fertilizer subsidies (approximately US$42 million). Two months after the budget was approved, fertilizer prices further increased by more than 60 per cent compelling the government to seek an additional 305 billion ZMK (US$68 million) to cover the increased procurement costs. The total expenditure on fertilizer subsidies released from the 2008 budget amounted about 33 per cent of the total amount spent by the whole Ministry of Agriculture. In addition, the number of beneficiary farmers increased from 120,000 to 200,000. However, the implementation of the FISP programme continued to suffer from corruption, poor delivery, poor targeting, leakages, lack of training, and absence of monitoring and evaluation. The elite argue for the continuation of the fertilizer programme through government procurement and distribution via a handful of preferred companies that have a track record working with the government. The resistance to reform the programme is likely driven by the vested interest of people who derive personal benefits from the programme. Research has recommended the use of an e-voucher to deliver the subsidy, thereby eliminating the need for government to tender and distribute inputs while including the private sector and encouraging competition.

Producer price support through FRA: With the continuing desire to promote smallholder maize production, the government through FRA buys all its stocks from the smallholder farmers at prices above the market price. This is mainly due to pressure exerted by ZNFU and members of parliament. Unfortunately, this policy only benefits about 35 per cent of small-scale farmers with the top 2–5 per cent of the well-endowed farmers benefiting the most because they are able to sell 50 per cent of all the marketed maize. In 2008 and 2009, there was extensive political pressure for FRA to announce its floor price even before the crop forecast and the national food balance sheet were announced by the Ministry of Agriculture. This was due to the allegations that millers and traders were ripping off farmers by buying maize early at below market prices.

In June 2008, the FRA announced a buying price of ZMK 45,000 per 50 kg bag (about US$260/ton), an increase of 16 per cent from the previous season. On the other hand, anticipating higher returns later in the year due to the global food crisis, millers, and other private players started the 2008–9 marketing season by aggressively buying maize at a price higher than FRA floor price, something that was uncommon at that time of the year. FRA tried to counter this by raising its price to ZMK 55,000 per 50 kg bag (about US$304/ton) but due to the tight maize supply in the market, they failed to reach their target of 88,000 MT. Instead FRA managed to procure only 72,000 MT at the end of an extended buying season in October 2008. The argument for raising the FRA purchase price above market price in a deficit period was that smallholder farmers needed this incentive to keep producing maize for the country to remain food secure. Figure 8.2 shows an increase in maize and maize meal prices attributed to the stiff competition between the private sector and FRA as well as from some smallholder farmers holding grain off the market in anticipation of higher prices later in the season (FEWS NET 2008).

Tax changes: Some of the tax proposals made by the high-level task force were adopted in the 2009 budget. In order to promote agriculture production through mechanization, the government, through the national budget of 2009, announced that all agricultural equipment including small tractors, ploughs, pumps, and sprayers would be free of VAT. The tax policy changes were intended to reach the small- and medium-scale farmers. Also, the 25 per cent duty on gypsum imports was scrapped in order to promote local fertilizer production. With the rising transportation costs due to the rising fuel costs, the government also removed customs duty on commercial trucks.

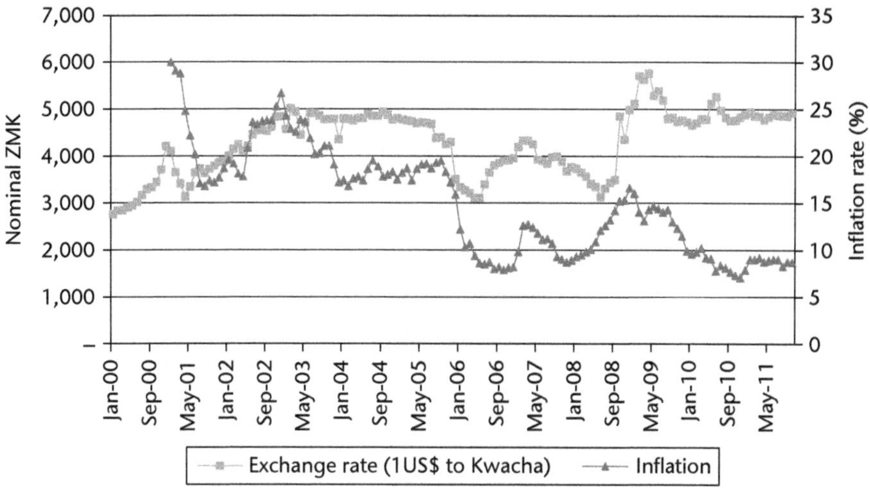

Figure 8.2 Nominal price trends 2001–11: Lusaka maize grain, breakfast meal, roller meal, and FOB US maize gulf prices, in ZMK
Source: based on CSO (various years) and <http://www.sagis.org.za>.

The impacts of these measures have not been subject to any scrutiny but it is reasonable to assume that they would support the agriculture sector to better withstand production shocks.

8.2.4 *Relationship between World Food Prices and Zambia Food Prices*

Results from price transmission models showed that that there was no statistically significant long-run relationship between local maize prices and the US Gulf freight on board (FOB) maize prices and South Africa, SAFEX maize prices. This may not be very surprising because Zambia is a landlocked country that has in the recent past been able to produce maize surpluses and only imported maize from South Africa in drought years. The caveat to this finding is that domestic policies and trader actions in Zambia were largely trigged by what was happening on the international market despite the fact that the country was not in an import position.

During the global food crisis, maize prices in Zambia started to escalate in July 2008, a time when global maize prices were trending downwards (Figure 8.1). This was mainly due to speculative maize purchases by the traders and millers and general bidding up of prices by both government and private sector over the limited maize surplus at the beginning of the marketing season. Prices continued to rise until March 2009 when the new harvest had started hitting the market.

On the other hand, global maize prizes started to increase again in November 2008 and continued to increase beyond March 2009 when maize prices in Zambia had started to decline. The price trends showed in Figure 8.2 support the results from the transmission model that no long-run relationship existed between local maize prices and the US Gulf FOB maize prices and South Africa. Instead, the rising maize prices in Zambia were driven primarily by what was happening domestically than driven by global maize prices. However, the general inflation in the country was rising due to the increase in prices of inputs such as fertilizer, diesel, labour, and transport. The rising inflation was also accompanied by the depreciation of the ZMK against the US$, from 3,186 ZMK per 1 US$ to 5,500 ZMK between June 2008 to July 2009 making imports more expensive (Figure 8.3). Figure 8.3 shows the US$ denominated prices and it is apparent from this graph that Zambia grain prices did not skyrocket.

8.3 Impacts on the Poor

The increase in food prices is a big threat to the welfare of the poor, both urban and rural, who also constitute the majority of the Zambian population.

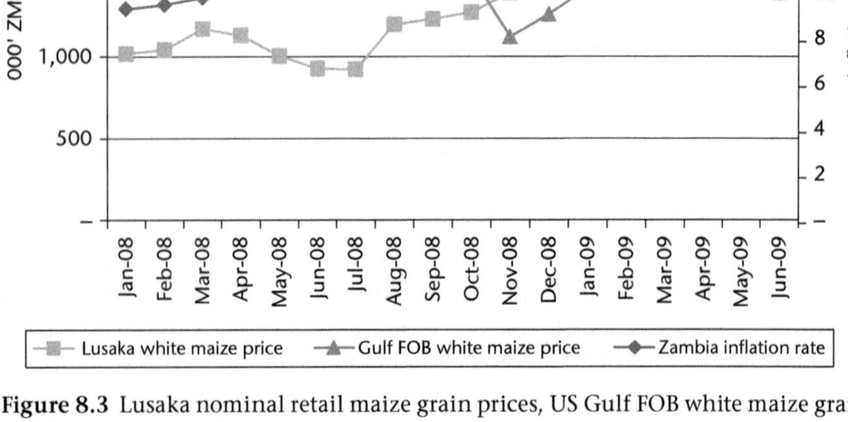

Figure 8.3 Lusaka nominal retail maize grain prices, US Gulf FOB white maize grain prices and Zambia general inflation rate

Source: based on CSO (various years) and <http://www.sagis.org.za>.

However, the impacts will vary depending on the characteristics of different households (Govereh 2009; Jayne et al. 2009).

Amongst the rural households, net sellers (28 per cent) are likely to have gained from the surge in food prices especially for maize whilst net buyers (49 per cent) were disadvantaged. The urban consumers and 49 per cent of the rural population, who are net buyers of maize, were negatively affected by the escalating maize and maize meal prices. The greatest impact was felt in the hungry season when prices rose above import parity.

Unfortunately, government marketing activities and policy decisions during normal and abnormal years have thus far been largely unresponsive to these statistics. For example, the FRA and the private sector usually attempt to purchase the entire marketed maize surplus, leaving virtually nothing for purchase by rural farmers during the lean season. The grain is instead bought and hauled to urban centres, where it is sold to millers thereby disadvantaging the majority of the poor rural households, who are net buyers of grain.

Furthermore, FRA's sale of subsidized grain to large millers, who sell relatively expensive maize meal, further disadvantages the poor in urban areas who would prefer to purchase grain from the market and send it to small and cheaper grinding mills. Evidence indicates that many of the urban and rural poor rely on these less expensive ways of procuring their maize meal as long as grain is available in local markets for purchase (Mwiinga et al. 2002; Mason et al. 2011). However, when the supply of grain in local markets dries up, consumers are forced to switch to more expensive packaged maize meal, or cut the number of meals they eat per day. Mwiinga et al. (2002) estimated that low-income urban households could save roughly 7–20 per cent of their monthly income if they were able to purchase grain and mill it into roller meal (*mugaiwa*) at a local grinding mill, rather than relying on more expensive commercial alternatives. Mason and Jayne (2009) showed that a lot of poor households are not able to buy a 25 kg bag of maize meal, hence resort to buying small repacks *pamelas* at a price per kg that is about 30 per cent higher.

Government policies and strong lobby groups continue to ignore empirical evidence regarding the impacts of various past policy choices, not because they are insensitive to the plight of the poor, but because of other goals. Lobby groups, whose desire is to serve their own constituency, tend to pressure the government to implement policies that may not be beneficial to the poor. For example, the ZNFU has continued to lobby for higher subsidies to farmers, higher FRA buying prices and a ban on wheat imports. Whilst, on the other hand, the MAZ has in the past used their access to high government officials to influence FRA to offload maize to its members at subsidized rates with the promise of reducing maize meal prices to consumers, asking for the removal of export bans whilst pushing for open borders for wheat flour. Such a tug of war that exists amongst the key lobby groups tends to force the government to choose policies that are politically popular ignoring their costs to the country and the impact on the poor. Political expediency in dealing with past food crises has always resulted in unintended consequences to the poor.

8.3.1 *Impact to the Treasury*

The level of government intervention was costly and exacerbated the degree of uncertainty in the market, something that could have been avoided with good planning. With the adequate warning provided to government as early as July 2008 regarding the impending maize shortages, early planning for imports could have saved the government 230 billion ZMK (approximately US$50 million). In addition, the sale of maize by the FRA should have started much earlier and would have prevented the prices from climbing to above import parity prices. The timely planning for imports would have ensured that moderate imports were purchased with the help of the private sector at a cheaper price and arriving before the start of the lean season in November 2008.

8.3.2 *Mistrust between Government and Private Sector*

The attempt to deal with the rising food prices reinforced the mistrust between government and the private sector. The government accused private traders of acting as saboteurs who only cared about their interests and profits whilst poor people suffered. On the other hand, the traders accused the government of favouring the interests of a few stakeholders.

8.4 Conclusion and Recommendations

In Zambia, the effect of the rising global food prices was not felt until late 2008 and early 2009. This study argues that failure by the government and other stakeholders to quickly respond to the global food crisis was the leading cause of the escalation of maize prices in the country rather than being driven by what was happening on the international scene. Like in the past, the implementation of government policy responses to deal with the rising food prices, especially for the major staple crop maize, were delayed due to ineffective response policies, protracted discussions, and inaction amongst key agriculture stakeholders.

This study exposes a number of key areas that need to be addressed if the government is to be successful in dealing with future food crises. First, the high level of mistrust between government and private sector, especially for the maize sector, should be recognized and reduced.

Second, strong lobby groups with access to high political officials should be discouraged from overriding recommendations by the main technical committee tasked to deal with food policy issues. Procedures need to be established beforehand and all parties should be compelled to stick to them. Third, the government needs to review its policy of providing consumers with price relief through a few large-scale millers. The policy is easy to implement in the short run but past attempts to use this strategy failed to have a meaningful effect on retail maize meal prices. Instead, the government should consider off-loading maize to the open market so that the poor consumers have access to low cost maize. Local hammer mills and other small-scale mills can be utilized rather than forcing consumers to buy more expensive super refined maize meal from the commercial mills.

Since the government co-exists with the private sector, a rules-based market system will benefit the country because the market will become more predictable. It is not realistic to assume that the Zambian government will let market forces deal with food crises. However, as this study has shown, past unpredictable behaviour by the government tends to make the private sector seek guarantees before making any investments. If the government insists on participating directly in agricultural markets, predictable and transparent rules governing state involvement should be established to reduce market risks.

As in the case of rice, avoiding government intervention in exports and imports for maize may be an important part of an overall maize long-term policy because it would reduce the impact of droughts on domestic prices. However, there is fear that allowing external market shocks to be transmitted into local markets will cause unbearable pain to the poor in the country. This could be true in a static environment, but regional trade may be able to encourage private investment into technologies and institutions that broaden the scope of the market to better absorb price shocks. Policies that fail to include empirical evidence about the characteristics of the people they are trying to serve usually fail to achieve their intended results. The country should move towards a situation where politicians or policy makers should embrace empirical evidence rather than shy away from research results that deviate from the conventional wisdom. Depoliticizing government subsidy programmes is a good place to start. This may be one of the toughest recommendations to be adopted because of the power of some civil servants and politically linked private companies with vested interests who tend to resist recommendations to reform politically popular, but less effective programmes in favour of short-term personal gains. Good examples include the two most popular programmes in the country, the maize producer price support via FRA and fertilizer subsidy under FISP. Despite study results that have revealed the shortcomings of these two programmes and their negative impact on long-term government investments on key agricultural drivers, the programmes have remained a top priority for most politicians. It may be true that elections can be won through these programmes but it is very irresponsible for public officers and interest groups to push for programmes that only benefit a few. With similar and less successful response strategies in the past, the government in collaboration with other relevant stakeholders should put together a standard operation strategy on how to deal with future food crises rather than waiting for a crisis to happen. An effective early warning system is required to trigger the response strategy with all players playing their part as per the operational strategy. This may be one of the ways to start dealing with the mistrust that exists between government and private sector thereby helping to quicken the policy responses to future food crises.

Last, the MAL should make every effort to have the Agricultural Marketing Act enacted. The draft Agricultural Marketing Bill agreed upon by the stakeholders in 2010 and revised in 2011 provided guidance on the involvement of the government in the fertilizer, seed, crops, and livestock markets. In particular, it proposed: the formation of an independent marketing council to help the country deal with food crises; limiting the role of FRA to only handling strategic grain reserves as well as requiring FISP to be reformed, particularly with regards to not limiting the coverage of the subsidy to mostly fertilizer but requiring the use of an electronic voucher to include the private sector dealers in the procurement and distribution of inputs. Implementing that proposal would be a step in the right direction.

References

Agriculture Consultative Forum (ACF) (2010). 'Wheat Value Chain Study'. Consultant Report. Lusaka: ACF.

Byerlee, D., T. S. Jayne, and R. J. Myers (2006). 'Managing Food Price Risks and Instability in a Liberalizing Market Environment: Overview and Policy Options'. *Food Policy* 31(4): 275–87.

Chapoto, A. and T. S. Jayne (2009). 'Effects of Maize Marketing and Trade Policy on Price Unpredictability in Zambia'. Working Paper No. 38. Lusaka: Food Security Research Project.

Chapoto, A., D. Banda, S. Haggblade, and P. Hamukwala (2011). 'Factors Affecting Poverty Dynamics in Rural Zambia'. Working Paper No. 55. Lusaka: Food Security Research Project.

Central Statistical Office (CSO) (2006). '2006 Living Conditions Monitoring Survey Report 2004'. Lusaka: Government of Zambia.

Central Statistical Office (2011). 'Preliminary 2010 Census Results Report'. Lusaka: Government of Zambia.

Dehn J., L. C. Gilbert, and P. Varangis (2005). 'Agricultural Commodity Price Volatility'. In J. Aizenman and B. Pinto (eds), *Managing Economic Volatility and Crises: A Practitioner's Guide*. Cambridge: Cambridge University Press.

FEWS NET (2008). 'Zambia Food Security Update July 2008 Report'. Lusaka: Famine Early Warning System Network.

Govereh, J. (2009). 'The 2007–2008 Price Swing: Impact and Policies in Zambia'. *Project on Policies for the Effective Management of Food Price Swings in Africa*. Rome: FAO.

Jayne, T. S., and S. Jones (1997). 'Food Marketing and Pricing Policy in Eastern and Southern Africa: A Survey'. *World Development* 25(9): 1505–27.

Jayne, T. S., A. Chapoto, I. Minde, and C. Donovan (2009). 'The 2008/09 Food Price and Food Security Situation in Eastern and Southern Africa: Implications for Immediate and Longer Run Responses'. MSU International Development Working Paper No. 96. East Lansing, MI: Michigan State University.

MAL (Ministry of Agriculture and Livestock) (2011). 'Crop Forecast Results'. Lusaka: Government of Zambia.

MAL (Ministry of Agriculture and Livestock) (various years). 'National Food Balance Sheets'. Lusaka: Government of Zambia.

Mason, M. N., and T. S. Jayne (2009). 'Staple Food Consumption Patterns in Urban Zambia: Results from the 2007/2008 Urban Consumption Survey'. Working Paper No. 42. Lusaka: Food Security Research.

Mason, M. N., T. S. Jayne, A. Chapoto, and C. Donovan (2011). 'Putting the 2007/2008 Global Food Crisis in Longer-Term Perspective: Trends in Staple Food Affordability in Urban Zambia and Kenya'. *Food Policy* 36(3): 350–67.

Mason, M. N., T. S. Jayne, and R. J. Myers. (2012). 'Smallholder Behavioral Responses to Marketing Board Activities in a Dual Channel Marketing System: The Case of Maize in Zambia'. Selected Paper prepared for Presentation at the International Association of Agricultural Economists Triennial Conference, Foz do Iguaçu, Brazil, 18–24 August.

Mwiinga, B., J. Nijhoff, T. S. Jayne, G. Tembo, and J. Shaffer (2002). 'The Role of Mugaiwa in Promoting Household Food Security: Why It Matters Who Gets Access to Government Maize Imports'. Policy Synthesis 5. Lusaka: Food Security Research Project.

Newberry, D., and J. Stiglitz (1981). *The Theory of Commodity Price Stabilization: A Study in the Economics of Risk*. Gloucestershire: Clarendon Press.

Nijhoff, J. J., T. S. Jayne, B. Mwiinga, and J. Shaffer (2002). 'Markets Need Predictable Government Actions to Function Effectively: The Case of Importing Maize in Times of Deficit'. Policy Synthesis 6. Lusaka: Food Security Research Project.

Tembo, G., A. Chapoto, T. S. Jayne, and M. Weber (2010). 'Fostering Food Market Development in Zambia'. *Zambia Social Science Journal* 1(1): 39–60.

Timmer P. C. (2000). 'The Macro Dimensions of Food Security: Economic Growth, Equitable Distribution, and Food Price Stability'. *Food Policy* 25(3): 283–95.

Part IV

The Political Economy of Food Price Policy in Low-income Countries with Limited Dependence on Food Imports

9

The Political Economy of Food Price Policy in Kenya

Jonathan Makau Nzuma

9.1 Introduction

This chapter evaluates Kenya's food price crisis over 2002–11 using a political economy approach. Kenya's food prices have been high and volatile relative to world food prices. Moreover, domestic food markets are highly integrated while about 30 per cent of the changes in world market prices are transmitted to domestic markets in Kenya. The study finds a relatively slow speed of adjustment of domestic food prices in Kenya of between three to five months. In response, the government implemented both supply-side and demand-side policies. However, the implementation of these policies has not been fully institutionalized and relies on the most part on the executive. These findings lend credence to calls to institutionalize the policy-making process in Kenya.

Domestic food prices within Eastern and Southern Africa (ESA) countries show a different pattern from world food prices (Meijerink, Roza, and van Berkum 2009). While global food prices rose sharply and peaked in the first half of 2008, food prices within the ESA region increased too, but at lower rates (Karugia et al. 2009). Although global commodity prices slumped in the second half of 2008 and stabilized throughout 2009, food prices within the ESA region defied the international food price trends. In 2010 and 2011, food prices within the ESA region have continued to rise in tandem with world food price trends. While high food prices may no longer be making headlines in rich economies, the food price crisis has remained a topical issue in the policy arena of ESA countries, in particular Kenya. The food crisis has worsened the food security situation of most Kenyan households since a majority of these households are net food buyers. Estimates from the recent Kenya

Integrated Household Budget Survey (KIHBS 2006) indicate that about 63 per cent of crop and livestock producers are net buyers. In addition, food purchases constitute about 60 per cent of total expenditures of farming households. For these households, any food price increases negatively affect their food security status. Moreover, high and volatile food prices are not a new phenomenon to such households (Chambers, Longhurst, and Pacey 1981).

Commercial farmers, who can respond to the increase in prices by increasing production, can potentially benefit from the price boom, provided that changes in the prices are transmitted to them through the value chain (Okello 2009). The rising food prices put the country at risk of a reversal in gains made towards the attainment of the Millennium Development Goals (MDGs) especially MDG 1 on reducing hunger and poverty. The impacts of the high food prices in the country are complicated by unstable macroeconomic conditions and other regional factors such as persistent droughts and political conflicts that keep food prices high.

In response to the food price crisis, Kenyan policy makers adopted a broad spectrum of policy responses broadly classified into demand-side (food safety nets and tax reductions) and supply-side policies (subsidies and price support). The most common responses aimed at ensuring an adequate and affordable food supply for the majority of consumers. Safety nets are provided for the most food insecure and the vulnerable. They also aim at fostering a positive agricultural supply response. The food price crisis re-affirms the need for adequate investments in the agricultural sector, with a focus on the increasing productivity through improved access to inputs and markets so that farmers are less vulnerable and capable of responding to production incentives.

9.2 Study Approach

The conflicting interests of producers and consumers of a commodity in an economy are fundamental problems for government policy decisions (Timmer, Falcon, and Pearson 1983). The behaviour and dynamics of visible and invisible actors within the food sector therefore can only be understood in terms of their power and class position in the larger social system. In practice, however, economists rely on two frameworks, namely: public choice and the traditional political economy approach (De Gorter and Swinnen 2002).

This study employs the political economy framework in seeking to understand why governments choose a certain policy option over others in attempting to respond to food crisis. The study focuses on the price trends and policies of three major staple food crops in Kenya, maize, wheat, and rice. It explores prices at the wholesale and retail levels and describes the policy context within the food sector. The price data used in this study are compiled from the Ministry of Agriculture, the Kenya National Bureau of Statistics (KNBS), and the East Africa Grain Council.

9.2.1 *Recent Political History*

The key salient features of Kenya's recent political history are the reintroduction of multi-party democracy in 1992 and the recent enactment of a new constitution in 2010. The first two administrations under Jomo Kenyatta (1963–78) and Daniel Arap Moi (1978–2002) exercised control over both the state and markets. Policy decisions were basically made by the executive even though multi-party democracy was allowed under President Kenyatta. After an attempted coup in 1982, President Moi concentrated state authority by making Kenya a single party state. The state pursued inward looking policies mainly meant to protect food producers but at the same time subsidize urban consumers.

The state controlled food production and marketing by subsidizing production and administering controlled product prices. Official crop prices were gazetted and announced by the Agriculture Minister before the crop was planted each year. Decisions to import or export food were made by the cabinet and enforced through a monopoly state enterprise, the National Cereals Produce Board (NCPB). The price controls tended to benefit large-scale food producers, processors, and urban consumers who had the power to lobby the state.

After a decade of single party rule, multi-party elections were held in 1992, creating an opportunity for the opposition to check on the executive in policy decision-making. The advent of multi-party politics coincided with the era of market reforms where state control on marketing and trade of food commodities was reduced, while the private sector was allowed a greater say in markets and trade.

The key policy-making institutions in the multi-party era have continued to be the finance and agriculture ministries, wherein the ministers and permanent secretaries are key policy actors. A new constitution was enacted in Kenya on 27 August 2010. The new constitution devolves decision-making to county governments rather than concentrating it on the central government. This would encourage wider participation of stakeholders. In the recent past, producer associations under the umbrella of the Kenya National Producers Federation have been lobbying government before the national budget is read in parliament. Similarly, the parliamentary budget committee has been allocated wider powers in budget-making. These recent developments have tended to widen stakeholder participation in policy-making.

AGRICULTURAL POLICIES SINCE INDEPENDENCE

The first independent government weathered a period of protectionism that saw a lot of external pressure yield to structural reforms in the second administration that were enhanced by trade liberalization and the current multi-lateral trading systems. Thus, agricultural policies in independent Kenya can be grouped into two distinct categories. (1) Policies whereby direct government controls and participation dominated agricultural production and marketing—the era of government controls from 1963 to 1980. (2) Those whereby government participation was reduced and market forces and private individuals or organizations have played major roles in agricultural production, marketing, and investment—liberalized period.

ERA OF CONTROLS

After independence, agricultural policies were underpinned on Sessional Paper No. 10 on 'African Socialism and its Application to Planning in Kenya' that focused on problems of transition (Kenya 1964). The immediate concern was Africanization of land ownership with financial support sought from various sources, resettlement of the landless and selection of suitable forms of organization. This typified the Kenyatta regime and saw the resettlement on one million acre schemes probably the greatest policy success this far. Farm organizations adopted the existing forms of national farms, cooperatives, companies, partnerships, and individual farms. Land use was to be closely monitored to prevent mismanagement and idle farms. Appropriate legislation and land use policy was proposed under the 1970–4 planning period. In addition, a policy of placing statutory management orders on mismanaged farms was reinforced and the reform of customary land tenure systems into a modern legal system was started.

Kenya inherited several statutory marketing institutions from the colonial regime. Virtually all important commodities had state boards, which regulated their production and marketing. These included The Sisal Board of Kenya, Kenya Sugar Authority, Coffee Board of Kenya, Tea Board of Kenya, Pyrethrum Board of Kenya, Kenya Dairy Board, the Cotton Board of Kenya, the Dairy Board, and the Kenya Meat Commission. Smallholder production and marketing was organized under cooperatives to assist in the procurement of production inputs and in the marketing of produce. A majority of these cooperatives were affiliated to the Kenya National Farmers Union. A number of state-run farmer organizations were also set up to support the production and marketing of most commodities. These included Kenya Tea Development Authority (KTDA) for tea, Kenya Co-operative Creameries for milk, NCPB for cereals, National Irrigation Board (NIB) for irrigated crops, Horticultural Crops Development Authority for horticulture.

Similarly, price controls that predated the Second World War and covered virtually all sectors drawing legal basis from the Price Control Ordinance of 1956 that was later renamed Price Control Act of 1972 were applied. Price controls operated at both the production and retail levels depending on the commodity, mainly maize, wheat, and milk, which were considered essential foodstuffs. In the 1970s producer prices were set based on parity prices to discourage export surpluses during this period when Kenya was a net exporter of wheat and maize. Subsidized agricultural credit was availed through the Agricultural Finance Corporation (AFC), Land Agricultural Bank (LAB), and cooperatives. Later on LAB was absorbed by AFC once most transfer of land had been finalized.

The policy on research inherited at independence over-emphasized cash crops and a few food crops. After independence research efforts were geared towards both small and large African farmers. The government increased expenditure on agricultural research and extension. The policy on extension was to retain existing staff and expand their numbers and as such Egerton College was expanded to train increased staff. However, most of the extension agents were primary school graduates with little or no technical training. These problems were recognized in 1970 and a new policy was formulated to recruit school certificate graduates and train them for two years at agricultural training institutes.

The 1980s to early 1990s were a period of policy reforms in Kenya. The policy reforms were aimed at reducing the involvement of government in economic activities and therefore letting the country move towards a free market economy. Market liberalization policies started from the 1980s under the structural adjustment programmes of World Bank and International Monetary Fund. The impetus of the reforms, however, gained momentum in 1982 with the requirements of the World Bank for removal of distortions in the economy as a conditionality for the disbursement of the World Bank's loans. However, it was not until 1986 that the government officially spelt out the wide range of policy reforms for the whole economy in Sessional Paper No. 1 on 'Economic Management for Renewed Growth'.

The liberalization period also coincided with multi-party politics in Kenya and a period after an attempted coup in 1982 that shook the administration under President Moi. There was a complete failure in policy formulation and such efforts were disjointed and uninformed by local conditions. After the second multi-party elections, donor support was withdrawn on governance grounds and the government lost interest in agriculture. There was insufficient money voted to agriculture. Moi's interest in agriculture was exercised through patronage on maize, milk, and tea with negative effects on coffee. In the last days of the Moi regime, an attempt was made to save the regime's image by composing a team of technocrats popularly known as the 'dream team' to tame corruption and spearhead policy formulation. However, they happened to arrive at the scene a bit too late after the horse had bolted and as expected they did not get the necessary political good will to formulate and implement policies.

The third political administration rode to power on promises of ridding the country of corruption and has made an attempt to institutionalize policy formulations by appointing qualified technocrats to positions of policy-making and giving them autonomy to do so. The new administration under President Kibaki that came to power at the end of 2002 wanted something to be identified within the agricultural sector. The ministers for agriculture and livestock therefore asked their respective permanent secretaries to prepare a strategy document (political expediency) towards this goal. Tegemeo Institute was asked to assist in the crafting of the document while United States Agency for International Development (USAID) was also willing to assist. The team borrowed heavily from the Kenya Rural Development Strategy (KRDS) to develop the Strategy for Revitalization of Agriculture (SRA).

KRDS had been prepared earlier in year 2000 with efforts spearheaded by Professor Shem Migot-Adholla, a member of the so called 'dream team' in President Moi's era. KRDS was broad in coverage and extensively participatory unlike SRA that was not fully accepted by stakeholders. The SRA mainly related to the organizational/institutional reform of ministries (downsizing) rather than agricultural sector policies. Nonetheless, the SRA has now been developed as a strategy for the next ten years as a sectoral implementation of the ERS. The focus is on raising productivity of agriculture mainly through providing support (public goods), private sector development, and democratization of policy-making. There is renewed emphasis on improving the institutional governance of stakeholder organizations and groupings.

However, the culture of ministries is still very much personality-driven by the permanent secretary. Moreover, the design of much of the legislation has vested too much power in the directors of agriculture and livestock, hence making other decision makers irrelevant or having to accept the director's decision (even the PS in this position on some issues). Each line ministry now has a Central Planning Unit (CPU). Heads of planning departments who head the CPU's are seconded from the Ministry of Planning as are many staff under the Economics Scheme of Service. However, there are insufficient staff and capacity from this source so the planning departments have staff with agricultural economics training seconded from the 'technical' departments to assist in the work and provide technical expertise, which provides new synergies.

At the CPUs, a new policy preparation process has been devised where documents are passed from the ministry to a cabinet committee after which they may or may not be sent to the attorney general for legal interpretation depending on the seriousness of the issue at hand. After this stage the policy is then sent to parliament for debate. Again there is a high staff turnover in the Economics Scheme of Service with a lot of staff joining policy research institutes. The ten-year government embargo on employment led to a decline in this scheme's staffing levels and permission was given to recruit a hundred graduate economists. It is hard to retain officers within government terms, which has led to the 9 am to 5 pm mentality that has demoralized the service. Clearly there is a need to retain and strengthen CPU for institutional memory. There is also need to build capacity among officers on negotiating skills with regard to international trade issues such as World Trade Organization. Moreover, the civil service within ministries in the Kibaki administration has been weakened and demoralized by the retention of retired officers as key decision makers. There is also a return of ethnicity and corruption in public sector recruitments.

9.3 Food Price Trends and Shocks

This section analyses the food price trends in Kenya using wholesale market prices relative to the international prices for the period 2007–11. The wholesale price data used in this study are collected from the agriculture ministry and KNBS.

9.3.1 *Food Price Trends*

Food prices in Kenya rose gradually when global food prices surged in 2007, but defied the global food price trends to continue rising throughout 2009–11 and remained high relative to the world food prices (Figure 9.1). The Kenyan food price movements are heavily dependent on rainfall patterns since Kenyan agriculture is largely rain-fed.

Underlying the domestic food price volatility are price increases in key staple crops such as maize, wheat, and rice. Maize is a major staple crop in Kenya and food security in Kenya is equated to the availability and lack of maize. It carries a weight of about 13 per cent in computation of food inflation and is the highest proportion attributable to a single food commodity. Unlike the international maize prices which fell in the second half of 2008 and stabilized throughout 2009 and the first half of 2010, maize prices in Kenya rose throughout much of 2007, 2008, and 2009 (Figure 9.2). The stable global maize prices persisted up to July 2010 when prices began to climb and have been on an upward trend up to the fourth quarter of 2011. In contrast, maize prices in Kenya have remained relatively high but fell in the last quarter of 2010 but rose sharply since the start of 2011 (Figure 9.2).

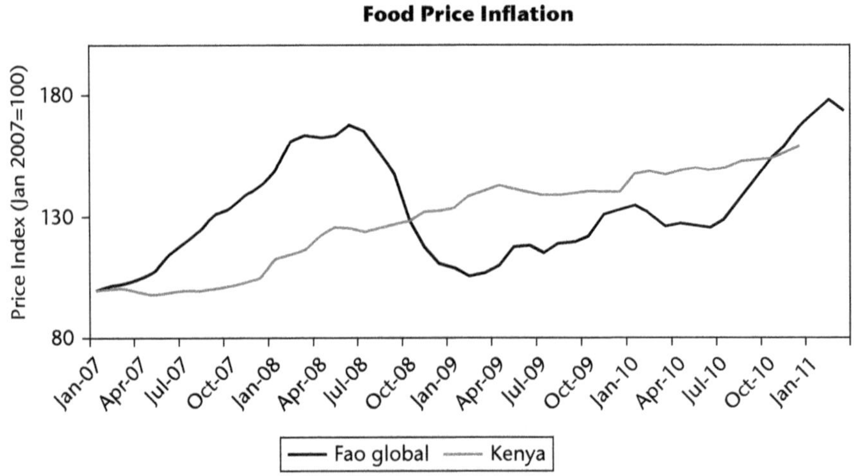

Figure 9.1 Monthly trends in food prices, 2007–11 (January 2007=100)
Source: FAOSTAT (2000–9) and KNBS (2007–11).

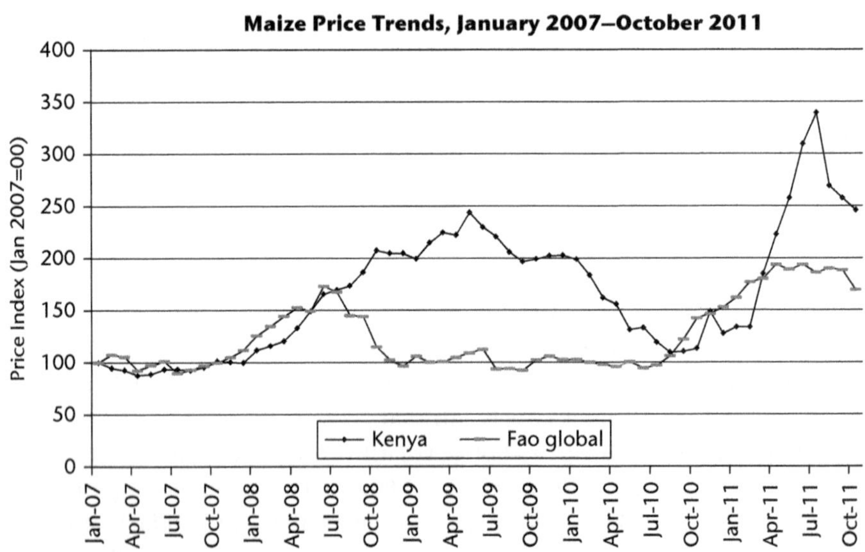

Figure 9.2 Maize price trends, Kenya
Source: FAOSTAT (2000–9) and KNBS (2007–11).

The rise in maize price can be attributed to a less than optimal maize harvest for three consecutive long rains harvests during 2007–9.

The food price pressures in Kenya could also stem from price-induced consumption shifts from traditional food staples, such as maize, to other imported commodities such as rice and wheat which are readily available on the international market. Between January and May 2008, international rice prices rose to unprecedented levels. Over the same period, rice prices in Kenya were lower than the global prices but also rose to reach their peaks three months later in September 2008. In the second half of 2008, international rice prices fell to stabilize in early 2009, a trend that has persisted throughout 2010 and well into 2011. In tandem with the global trends, rice prices in Kenya remain stable over the 2008–11 period.

On the other hand, wheat prices in Kenya rose sharply relative to the international wheat prices throughout 2009 and 2010. In the second half of 2010, international wheat prices began to climb and have been on an upward trend up to March 2011. However, domestic wheat prices within Kenya have exhibited mixed trends over the same period. Between 2009 and 2011, wheat prices in Kenya have been on a downward trend but have been characterized by high volatility as indicated by the frequent price swings. A key observation with regard to the domestic wheat prices within Kenya is that they increased at a higher rate than the international wheat prices, suggesting the existence of protectionist domestic policies.

During the period February 2007 to February 2008, the volatility of domestic food prices in Kenya, as measured by month on month percentage changes in the price indices, was lower than the volatility of international food prices (Figure 9.3). However, the food price volatility in Kenya over 2009–11 was higher than the volatility experienced in world market prices. The most volatile food prices in Kenya were those for wheat and maize while the price of rice was relatively stable. These food price trends indicate a

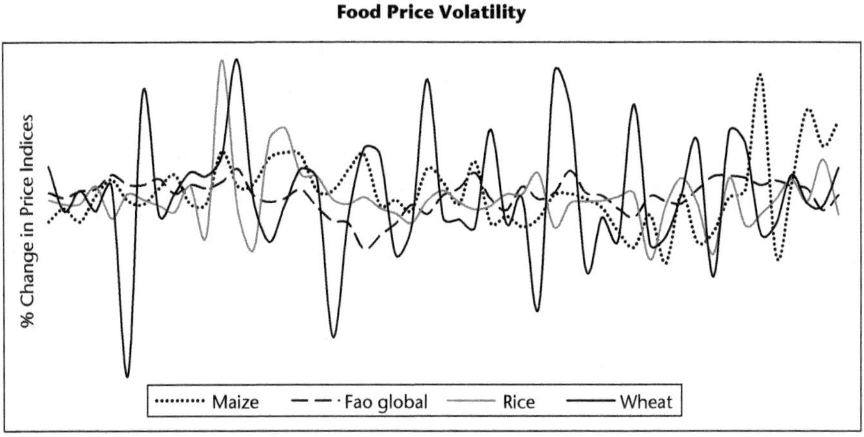

Figure 9.3 Percentage changes in food price indices, Kenya
Source: author's computations.

destabilizing food price scenario in Kenya, which could adversely affect the food security status of the country.

Of particular concern from a food security perspective are indications that prices in Kenya remain persistently high in 2009 despite the precipitous decline in international prices. These persistently high food prices indicate a poor degree of price transmission from international markets to domestic markets in Kenya. Price transmission effects provide insights into the nexus between domestic and international food prices (Karugia et al. 2009). They indicate the extent to which domestic markets are integrated into global markets and therefore the degree to which changes in global prices might influence domestic prices.

The links between international prices and local prices are complicated; the first determinants of how international prices translate into site-specific prices relate to exchange rate movements and a country's net trade position. Furthermore, the existing domestic trade policies, and the manner of their implementation, often determine the extent to which individual producers are able to respond to market signals. Local price movements, meanwhile, reflect a multitude of factors, ranging from weather conditions, shifts in local production, disease and consumption shocks, inflation, changing informal trading patterns among others. However, that said, a cursory review of monthly price movements in Kenya reveals a trend of puzzling persistently high and increasingly variable food prices, which have a negative effect on the country's food security.

9.3.2 *International Price Transmission*

An enterprise content management of price transmission was estimated using monthly domestic wholesale maize prices for five markets (Nairobi, Mombasa, Nakuru, Eldoret, and Kisumu) and the South African Futures Exchange (SAFEX) white maize price for the period January 2002 to December 2011 (Table 9.1).

The results show that out of the five markets, only two (Nairobi and Mombasa) have a significant long-run relationship with SAFEX maize prices. This is expected given that Kenya is a net maize importer that regularly imports maize through the port of Mombasa that is well-connected to Nairobi by both road and rail. However, the transmission of international prices to other domestic markets might be hampered by infrastructural constraints. The elasticities of price transmission in these two markets were about 0.3 (Table 9.2). Although no significant long-run relationships existed between SAFEX prices and other market prices in Kenya, the elasticities of price transmissions were in the range of 0.2 to 0.3 implying that between 20 and 30 per cent of the changes in SAFEX maize prices are transmitted to Kenyan markets.

Table 9.1 Transmission of SAFEX maize prices to domestic prices in Kenya

Market	ADF	PP	Johansen Test (Co-integrated)	Speed of Adjustment	Short-run Adjustment	Long-run Adjustment
Nairobi	No	Yes	Yes	−0.305***	0.103	0.304***
Mombasa	No	No	Yes	−0.287***	0.114	0.287***
Nakuru	Yes	Yes	No	−0.428***	0.047	0.212***
Eldoret	Yes	Yes	No	−0.350***	0.253***	0.259***
Kisumu	Yes	Yes	No	−0.191***	0.024	0.368***

Note: ***significant at the 1% level.
Source: author's computation from KNBS data (2006–11).

Table 9.2 Timeline of government responses to the food price crisis

Year	Policy Action	Remarks
2002–5	NCPB intervention in the operation of a strategic grain reserve	Stabilized market prices
2002–5	Import tariffs	Tariff reduction to increase import access
2002–5	Zero rating of imports from East African Community and Common Market for Eastern and Southern Africa	Deepening of regional integration
2008	Export ban on maize	Retaliation from neighbouring countries
2008	NCPB maize importation	Arrival of imports delayed by 3 months
2008	NAAIAP launched Kilimo pus Kimlimo Biasha Partners, Equity Bank, AGRA, FAO, IFAD	Fertilizer and seed subsidy
2008	Irrigation subsidy	Economic stimulus package
March 2008	NCPB procures 30% of national fertilizer requirement	Fertilizer subsidy
June 2008	Reduction of wheat import tariff from 35 to 10%	Prices rose owing to a surge in world prices
June 2008	Zero rating of maize, wheat, and milk	Prices rose owing to a surge in world prices
December 2008	Urban consumer price subsidy on maize meal (prime minister)	Poor targeting, inaccessible to the poor, food riots, flawed distribution
December 2008	NCPB producer price subsidy of KES 200/90 kg bag	Farmers decline to release stocks
February 2009	Consumer subsidy policy reversal	Maize meal subsidy withdrawn
February 2009	Food price taskforce formed	Multi-sector task force on food prices formed
March 2009	Cash for work programme launched by the prime minister	Poor targeting
March 2009	Fertilizer price subsidy announced by the president	Poor targeting

Source: author's compilation.

Similarly, the speed of adjustment of domestic prices to the long-run relationship across the five markets was in the range of 0.2 to 0.3 (Table 9.1). The implication that can be drawn is that domestic maize prices take about 3 to 5 months to fully adjust to changes in world prices. The findings of this study are comparable to earlier transmission studies undertaken in the country. Rapsomanikis (2009) finds a relatively slow adjustment of domestic food prices in Kenya to international prices with domestic prices taking 11 to 7.7 months for the SAFEX white maize price. While reliance on rain-fed agriculture and therefore, weather shocks, is one cause of price volatility, poor infrastructure is another contributing factor.

Poor roads especially, in isolated producing and consuming regions within a country lead to increases in price variability. It has also been argued that poor infrastructure may, however, insulate domestic markets from international shocks. Rapsomanikis (2009) shows evidence of a strong long-run co-movement between prices in major Kenyan markets with the international price. Maize price in Eldoret (the main producing market) and Kisumu at the western part of the country, strongly directly co-move with both the international yellow maize price and the SAFEX white maize price. Strong co-movement suggests that international maize upturns would, in the long run, likely affect white maize in these markets.

Apart from poor infrastructure, rapid international price transmission may be hindered by state involvement in the procurement of both domestically produced and imported maize, and the subsequent release of the same at predetermined price. This may partly be responsible for the weak relationship (moderate co-movement) between the SAFEX white maize price and the Nairobi and Mombasa maize prices.

9.4 Policy Responses

The government of Kenya has used a combination of policies to respond to the food price crisis. The policies pursued have included both supply- and demand-side policies. Table 9.2 provides a timeline of these policy interventions while the discussion that follows categorizes these actions into market-oriented interventions, safety nets, and supply response stimulation policies.

9.4.1 *Market-based Interventions*

Market-based policies attempt to reduce the cost of food, and increase its availability. Such policies change the market conditions and therefore potentially affect all households. Prior to the 2007/8 food price crisis, the government of Kenya intervened in markets through the operation of the NCPB and the imposition of import tariffs on food imports. Though charged with the responsibility of maintaining a strategic grain reserve, its food procurement activities have the effect of stabilizing market prices. On the other hand, the imposition of food import tariffs that were in the range of 25 to 50 per cent over the 2000 to 2005 period has the effect of limiting imports and increasing domestic prices.

After the 2007/8 food price crisis, the Kenyan government implemented export restrictions on maize in 2008 while at the same time embarking on an aggressive importation of maize through the NCPB to build up stocks for the national strategic grain reserve. At the start of 2008, the government had licenced large-scale traders to export maize to neighbouring countries such as South Sudan. Much of these maize exports were procured from trader stocks and the NCPB strategic grain reserve. On realizing that the national strategic reserve was depleted while supply was constrained by the impacts of the post-election crisis and a drought, the government imposed an export ban on maize. In response to the drought experienced throughout most of east and southern Africa, Kenya, Malawi, and Tanzania imposed maize export bans. The maize export bans in countries such as Tanzania and Malawi limited the country's ability to increase supply and curb the price surge through quick imports.

As the crisis worsened, and the imports failed to arrive on time, the government turned to domestic procurement through the NCPB largely as a result of pressure being exerted by consumers following high maize meal prices. Although the government set a high price of KES 1,750 per 90 kg bag, farmers held on to their stocks in anticipation of higher market prices later in the season. They demanded a 20 per cent increase to KES 2,200 per 90 kg bag. The government over the same period increased the producer price from KES 1,750 per 90 kg bag to KES 1,950, but directed the NCPB to sell the same to millers at KES 1,750. This translated to a producer subsidy of KES 200 per 90 kg bag.

The government maize imports did not arrive until March 2009. Moreover, there were flaws in the distribution of the subsidized maize to millers. The NCPB imports were sold to briefcase traders posing as maize millers who were licensed to procure grain from NCPB in an effort to support a maize meal subsidy programme pioneered by the prime minister (see discussion under consumption subsidies). This undermined the effect of the subsidy programme. In addition, NCPB sold the subsidized maize only in bundles of 50 kilogrammes making it unaffordable to the poor.

The export restriction may have been ineffective given the existence of substantial informal cross-border trade with its neighbours. Despite the export ban on agricultural commodities in Tanzania, substantial volumes of maize were exported into Kenya in 2009 (LEI 2008). Although export restrictions are aimed at protecting consumers by keeping the price low, they potentially increase transaction costs through the informal trade routes, effectively hurting the consumers. Jayne, Myers, and Nyoro (2005) observe that export bans increase smuggling costs, depress producer prices, and raise consumer prices.

Other trade policies that were adopted included the reduction of import tariffs and taxes on maize and wheat. In June 2008, import duty on wheat was reduced by 25 per cent (from 35 to 10 per cent) while that of maize was zero-rated following the intervention of the Ministry of Agriculture. Other fiscal measures included zero-rating value added tax on wheat and maize flour, and milk. Despite these efforts, the price of maize continued to rise and by October/November 2008, the government shifted its strategy to a direct protection of consumers through food subsides. This decision followed near food riots in Nairobi owing to pressure from urban populations.

9.4.2 *Consumption Subsidies and Safety Nets*

While universal food subsidies are ideal as a quick response in improving access to food and in mitigating the initial impacts of a price surge, they are costly and often fail to target those most in need. In December 2008, the Kenyan government adopted a direct consumer price subsidy by introducing a dual pricing system for maize meal. This urban maize meal subsidy programme was the brain child of the prime minister, whose urban constituency covers Kibera, the largest slum in Nairobi. The Ministry of Finance and Planning initially opposed the maize meal subsidy programme, but later on grudgingly accepted. A 2 kg packet of maize meal was supposed to sell at a commercial rate of KES 72 and a subsidized rate of KES 55. The latter was supposed to benefit the poor. The subsidy programme was largely supported by the milling industry that was licenced to procure maize from NCPB, mill it, and sell it at subsidized prices but later on apply for rebates from the Ministry of Finance and Planning.

Other than transporting the subsidized meal to the informal settlements and other low-income neighbourhoods, there were no other targeting criteria. Furthermore, the subsidized pack was retailed in 5 kg bags which made it inaccessible to the poor. Within a short period, the urban maize meal subsidy programme became untenable owing to financing and distribution bottlenecks and was eventually discontinued. The subsidy programme raised some political overtones given the composition of the grand coalition government where the prime minister, who supported the programme came from one wing of the coalition while the minister for finance, who came from another wing of the coalition, opposed it.

The cost of the scheme was estimated at KES 23.4 billion (US$334 million) in subsidy and tax foregone in the fiscal year (FY) 2008/9. After a critical analysis, the cabinet withdrew the scheme in February 2009 and a commitment was made to develop an alternative, more effective scheme. In the meantime, the price was left to market fundamentals. In addition, the cabinet directed the relevant ministries to work with interested donor agencies to develop a comprehensive food subsidy programme.

Consequently, a multi-sectoral taskforce was formed in February 2009 to facilitate this process. The membership of the task force covered the Ministry of Agriculture, Ministry of Finance and Planning, Ministry of Livestock Development, Ministry of Special Programmes, Kenya Federation of Agricultural Producers, Parliamentary Committee on Agriculture, and various lobby groups on maize, wheat, and livestock. The taskforce designed a cash transfer programme initially targeting the poor informal settlements in Nairobi on a pilot basis. Where improved access to food is the objective, cash transfers would work efficiently where food markets function well. The implementation of this initiative was, however, shelved by the cabinet due to design flaws.

Another initiative implemented by the government was a cash-for-work programme named Kazi Kwa Vijana (KKV) that was mooted by the prime minister. In an environment of increasing food prices, such public work programmes increase the income of the poor and improve their access to food. The large number of unemployed youths made such an intervention very attractive. The KES 15 billion (US$214 million) KKV programme was launched in March 2009 and aimed at creating 300,000 jobs within six months of its launch. The programme engaged the unemployed youth in infrastructure works (mainly roads) and environmental conservation exercises such as tree planting and river cleaning efforts. The programme, although bedevilled by payment problems, was successful in building some assets, notable being the clean-up of the Nairobi river.

9.4.3 *Stimulating Food Supply Response*

During the post-liberalization period, the government through NCPB, entered into farm inputs (fertilizer, maize seeds) markets in the year 2000 with an aim of boosting the board's revenue and stabilizing the fertilizer prices in the local market. However, following the surge in fertilizer prices in 2008, the government undertook to procure 163,000 MT or 40 per cent of the national fertilizer requirement at a cost of KES 6.2 billion (US$89 million). This excluded the tea fertilizer bought by KTDA worth KES 1.6 billion.

In March 2009, the president announced that diammonium phosphate fertilizer would be sold at a reduced price of KES 2,500 while calcium ammonium nitrate fertilizer would retail at KES 1,650 per 50 kg bag from a high of KES 6,000. The price of seed was also reduced by KES 50 and KES 10 per 10 kg packet and 2 kg packet, respectively. Just like the interventions in the maize market, the implementation of the input subsidy also encountered governance challenges. Once again, some unscrupulous traders procured the fertilizer from NCPB, repackaged it and sold it to unsuspecting farmers at higher prices than those recommended by the government. This was in addition to the potential disruptions of the fertilizer business. Smuggling was rife at the Kenya–Uganda border as fertilizer prices were higher in Uganda than in Kenya.

In realization that resource poor farmers, especially those in the lowlands may not have the know-how or cannot afford purchased inputs, the Kenyan government embarked upon a National Accelerated Agricultural Input Programme. The programme was aimed at promoting food security and poverty reduction. Initially planned to subsidize fertilizers and maize seed for a limited number of districts, it was subsequently expanded to national coverage with plans to provide 2.5 million farmers with maize seed and fertilizers for one acre each, with vouchers issued to targeted farmers (with less than 2.5 acres) and subsequent redemption through private input sellers who would also be eligible for trade credit guarantees. Farmers under this input grants popularly known as *Kilimo* Plus.

Starter kits are supposed to be linked to extension, cereal banks, warehouse receipts, and participation in farmer groups. These farmers are supposed to graduate after two years into another programme: *Kilimo Biashara* (farming as a business). The expected graduation is yet to successfully materialize due to the poor harvest in late 2007 and 2008. The programme received a financial boost from Food and Agriculture Organization (FAO) and the World Bank in 2008 in response to the high food prices. *Kilimo Biashara* was launched in May 2008 as a US$50 million (KES 3 billion) loan project. Probably encouraged by the Malawi successful experience with fertilizer and seed subsidies, the Kenyan government in partnership with the Alliance for Green Revolution, International Fund for Agricultural Development and Equity Bank launched the project with the aim of targeting small-scale farmers and enterprises in the agricultural value chain.

The Alliance for a Green Revolution in Africa (AGRA) catalysed the project by setting up a US$5 million (KES 400 million) 'cash guarantee fund'. The fund buffers the Equity Bank's risk of lending money to farmers and small agricultural businesses with little or no collateral. The loans carry a 12 per cent interest rate applied when the loans fall due, a rate well below the bank's standard lending rate of 18 per cent (as per 2008). Under the programme, farmers also receive training on improved farming techniques and business management in addition to government vouchers that enable them to purchase new farming inputs. Another government response came in the form of an economic stimulus to agriculture through revival of the stalled Hola irrigation scheme in the lower Tana Delta. In September 2008 the president and the prime minister launched a KES 2 billion National Economic Stimulus Programme on food production in the irrigation scheme. However, there seems to have been no plans to market the output as extensive post-harvest losses were recorded in February 2010.

9.5 Conclusions and Policy Recommendations

Over the last four years, international food prices have witnessed unprecedented increases. FAO's FPI rose by 57 per cent between March 2007 and March 2008 as compared to an increase of 9 per cent in 2006 (FAO 2008). However, food prices began to fall in July 2008 and trended downwards until the start of 2009 when food prices began to rise again albeit marginally but surged throughout 2010 to reach an unprecedented peak in January 2011. In contrast, food prices in Kenya rose gradually when global food prices surged in 2007, but defied the global food price trends to continue rising in the second half of 2008 and throughout 2009 to 2011.

Of particular concern from a food security perspective are indications that prices in Kenya remain persistently high despite the precipitous decline in international prices. These persistently high food prices might be indicative of a poor degree of price transmission from international markets to domestic markets in Kenya. The findings of a market integration analysis seem to suggest that domestic food markets in Kenya are highly integrated. Markets close to each other, such as Eldoret and Kisumu, show higher correlation coefficients, as do markets that are connected by better transport infrastructure, such as between Nairobi and most of the other markets. The results seem to support the generally accepted notion that shorter distances and improved infrastructure among markets lead to lower transaction costs, making arbitrage profitable and thus enhancing integration of such markets.

Moreover, price transmission analysis finds that about 30 per cent of the changes in world market prices are transmitted to domestic markets in Kenya. However, the study finds a relatively slow speed of adjustment of domestic food prices in Kenya of between three to five months to their long-run relationship with international prices. The results of the econometric analysis do not give a clear picture to explain why market prices in Kenya remain high, the evidence of highly integrated markets and a slow speed of adjustment to the world prices notwithstanding. The political economy approach adopted offers better insights.

In response to the food price crisis, the government of Kenya implemented both supply-side and demand-side policies. However, the design and implementation of these policies has not been fully institutionalized and relies mostly on the executive. This is best illustrated by the 2009 reversal of the 2008 urban maize meal subsidy programme and the challenges facing other subsidy programmes. These political economy findings lend credence to the calls to institutionalize and strengthen the policy-making process in Kenya while the slow adjustment of domestic markets to international markets could best be addressed through infrastructure developments.

References

Chambers, R., R, Longhurst, and A. Pacey (eds) (1981). *Seasonal Dimensions to Rural Poverty*. London: Frances Printer.

De Gorter, H., and J. Swinnen (2002). 'Political Economy of Agricultural Policy'. In B. L. Gardner and G. C. Rausser (eds), *Handbook of Agricultural Economics* Edition 1, Volume 2. Amsterdam: Elsevier.

FAO (Food and Agriculture Organization of the United Nations) (2008). *The State of Food Insecurity in the World 2008: High Food Prices and Food Security: Threats and Opportunities*. Rome: FAO.

FAOSTAT (Food and Agriculture Organization Statistics Division) (2000–9). Data. Available at: <http://faostat.fao.org/faostat/>.

Jayne. T. S., R. L. Myers, and J. Nyoro (2005). 'The Effects of Government Maize Marketing and Trading Policies on Maize Market Prices in Kenya'. WP Series. Nairobi: Tegemeo Institute of Agricultural Policy and Development.

Karugia J., M. Waithaka, A. Freeman, R. Prabhu, B. Shiferaw, S. Gbegbelegbe, S. Massawe, M. Kyotalimye, J. Wanjiku, and E. Macharia (2009). 'Responding to Food Price Crisis in Eastern and Southern Africa: Policy Options for National and Regional Action'. ReSAKSS Working Paper. Washington, DC: ReSAKSS-Eastern and Central Africa.

Kenya National Bureau of Statistics (KNBS) (2002–11). 'Kenya National Bureau of Statistics Reports'. Nairobi: Government Printer.

Meijerink, G., P. Roza, and S. van Berkum (2009). 'East African Governments' Responses to High Cereal Prices'. Report 2009/102. The Hague: LEI Wageningen UR.

Ministry of Agriculture (2004). 'Strategy for the Revitalization of Agriculture 2004–2014'. Nairobi: Government Printer.

Okello, J. J. (2009). 'The 2007–2008 Food Price Swings: Impact and Policies in Kenya'. FAO Discussion Paper Series. Rome: Food and Agriculture Organization (FAO).

Rapsomanikis, G. (2009). 'The 2007–2008 Food Process Episode: Impact and Policies in Eastern and Southern Africa'. Rome: Food and Agriculture Organization (FAO), Trade and Markets Division.

Timmer, C. P., W. Falcon, and S. Pearson (1983). *Food Policy Analysis*. Washington, DC: World Bank.

10

The Political Economy of Food Price Policy in Mozambique

Virgulino Nhate, Claudio Massingarela, and Vincenzo Salvucci

10.1 Introduction

Mozambique heavily relies on imported food and fuel, which makes it vulnerable to international price shocks. As a consequence, Mozambique experienced reduced exports, more expensive imports, and increased food and oil prices.[1] This may have contributed to the stagnant poverty rates registered by the 2008/9 Mozambican Household Budget Survey (GoM 2010b).

This chapter attempts to analyse the relation between international and domestic food prices, and the policy responses adopted by the Mozambican government to stabilize the impact of price shocks in the domestic market.

10.2 Background

Despite the high gross domestic product (GDP) growth experienced by Mozambique in the past, poverty has not declined. According to official statistics, the Mozambican economy continued to grow at a 6 per cent rate even after the crisis had reached its peak in 2008 (GoM 2008a). GDP per capita increased from US$236 to US$453 from 1997 to 2009 (GoM 2008a, 2008b, 2010a, 2010b, 2010c). But poverty rates, after a steep decline from about 69 per cent in 1996/7 (GoM 2010b), have remained steady at about 55

[1] The export value of cashew nuts declined from MZN 20.5 million to MZN 10.8 million; sugar from MZN 71.4 million to MZN 49.4 million (GoM 2007); tobacco from MZN 109 million to MZN 45.2 million (GoM 2008a). MZN=Mozambican Metical (exchange rate, 7 March 2013: 1 US$=29.5 MZN).

per cent between 2002/3 and 2008/9. A possible explanation for the stagnation of poverty is that food price shocks have severely affected the poorer socioeconomic groups.

As a response to these shocks, the government implemented a mixture of policies aimed at containing the influence of international food prices and avoiding chaos on the domestic markets. The main government goals included increasing local food production and reducing dependence on imports, while enhancing productivity to improve competitiveness with imported foods. Measures for fuel subsidies and the construction of granaries for the storage of agricultural surplus were also implemented. It is likely that the government's desire to be re-elected in the upcoming 2010 elections was one of the motivations for implementing these policies. Nevertheless, the subsidies and other measures helped to maintain the retail price of commodities such as rice and bread stable, thus avoiding greater social struggle.[2] However, the effect of these (costly) policies on the macroeconomic framework is less clear. In what follows, we try to understand, first, whether international price shocks were transmitted to the Mozambican economy; and, second, whether governmental policies succeeded in reducing the negative consequences of the price shocks on the economy.

10.3 Main Facts of the Mozambican Economy and Agricultural Sector

Mozambique has slightly more than 20 million inhabitants. Agriculture is the most important sector, with about 80 per cent of the population dependent on agriculture for their livelihoods (Cunguara and Hanlon 2010). However, its contribution to GDP is stagnant, approximately 25 per cent (Magaua, Hong, and Massingarela 2011). Subsistence agriculture is predominant despite the availability of fertile and irrigable land, and smallholders account for 99 per cent of total farms (Cunguara and Hanlon 2010). The agriculture budget share has always ranged between 3–4 per cent of total GDP, even though there is an ongoing pressure to increase it. Donavan and Tostão (2010) find that the average cultivated land for smallholders, who constitute 99 per cent of total rural households, is less than one hectare (ha) (0.9 ha), and most rural households are net buyers of food staples. This is also due to a paucity of granaries for the storage of staple crops, which prevents the build-up of domestic production surpluses, reduces food security, and increases vulnerability to international food price crises.

[2] The increased price of food and fuel did lead, however, to violent riots and demonstrations in 2008 in Maputo, the capital city.

Furthermore, almost 70 per cent of total household expenditures in Mozambique are devoted to food. Thus, a major upsurge in food prices such as the one experienced in 2008/9 can potentially affect large sectors of the population, especially lower income and urban households (GoM 2010b). Arndt et al. (2008) estimate that as a consequence of price increases in 2008, poverty increased by 0.5 per cent. At the same time, the 2008/9 agricultural season was not successful due to poor weather conditions that caused droughts in some parts of the country and heavy storms and floods in others (GoM 2010b). This resulted in either reduced or null food surpluses for most farmers, who thus were unable to benefit from higher domestic prices. Food access and food security are recognized as the country's major unsolved issues.

10.3.1 *Staple Food Consumption and Production*

Thirty-six per cent of all calories consumed in the country come from cassava and another 22 per cent from maize. Wheat and rice account for 7 per cent each. Wheat and rice are mainly imported, but are increasingly preferred by both urban and rural households (Donovan and Tostão 2010). Figure 10.1 presents wheat imports and consumption for the years 1996–2006.

Thus, in order to study the transmission mechanism between international food prices and domestic prices, we focus in the following on wheat and rice. The analysis is based on three markets (Maputo in the south; Beira in the centre; Nampula in the north). Most imported food products are delivered to regional markets from these three main marketing centres. The

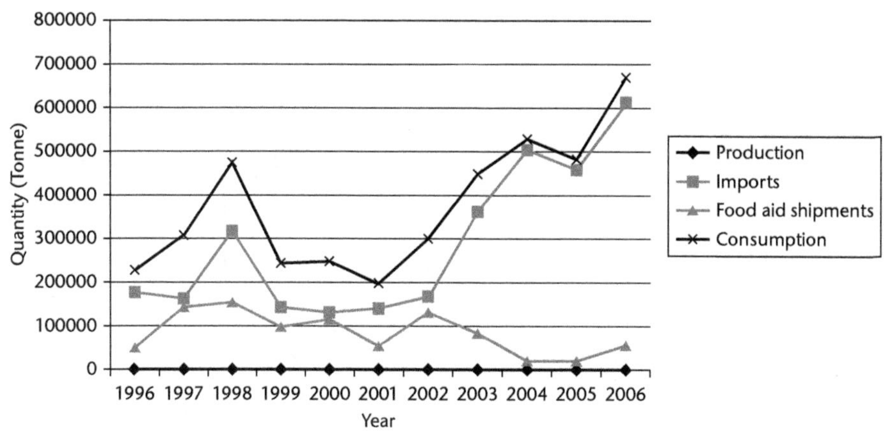

Figure 10.1 Wheat imports and consumption, 1996–2006
Source: based on Cachomba (2010).

prices recorded in Maputo, Beira, and Nampula are also used by the National Institute of Statistics to compute the official Mozambican consumer price index.

RICE PRICES

Figure 10.2 shows rice price trends both domestically and at its origin (the price of rice in Thailand is taken as a reference) for the years 2000–9. The price of rice has been following a slightly increasing trend both domestically and at the origin from 2002 until mid-2007 (Figure 10.2). In October 2007, it started to increase, reaching its peak in mid-2008. Thereafter, it went down again in the world market but remained high in Mozambique until the end of 2009. In January 2009 the price declined slightly only in Beira, but in general it never returned to its pre-crisis levels. Despite the international price exhibiting a few extraordinary peaks, these were not reflected in the domestic price. This may be the result of different forms of subsidies introduced by the government, and of a substitution effect in consumption shifting towards locally produced staple crops.

WHEAT PRICES

With regard to wheat, the reference international price (Gulf of Mexico) started to rise in the second half of 2007, reaching its peak in the first quarter of 2008 (Figure 10.3). As observed for rice, the international price upsurge directly affected the domestic price for wheat. However, domestic price did not revert to the pre-crisis levels even though the international price did. On the contrary, it slightly increased, especially in Maputo and Nampula. This un-arrested increase in the domestic price of wheat—and hence of bread—was among the main causes that led to massive demonstrations in Maputo

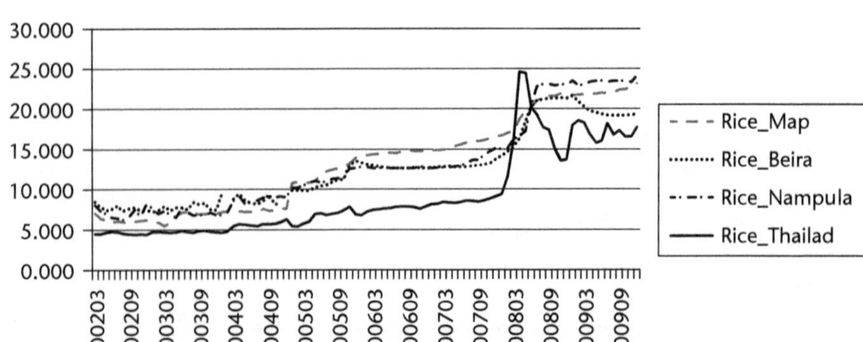

Figure 10.2 Rice price trends, 2002–9

Source: authors' calculation.

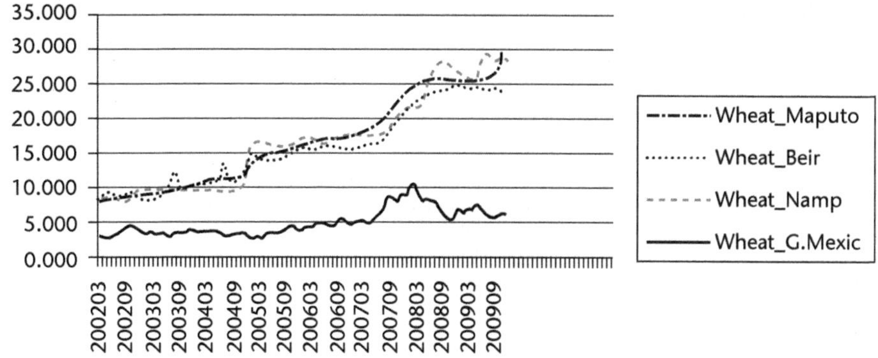

Figure 10.3 Wheat price trends, 2002–9
Source: authors' calculation.

at the end of 2010. To contain these occurrences, the government decided to implement additional price control measures.

10.4 The Degree of Price Transmission

In this section we perform a co-integration analysis to assess the degree of transmission between international and domestic prices for wheat and rice. The degree of transmission between prices in Maputo and prices in Beira and Nampula is subsequently also studied. As is standard in this kind of analysis, we (i) test for the presence of a unit root; (ii) check for the existence of a long-run relation; and (iii) assess the speed of adjustment, and the long- and short-run adjustment (Minot 2010; Traub et al. 2010).

The results are presented in Table 10.1. The Augmented Dickey-Fuller (ADF) and Phillips-Perron unit root tests almost always agree on the non-stationarity of the series analysed. A co-integrating relation exists only between the international rice price and its price in Nampula. This might be due to the fact that the northern region of Nampula is where most cassava is produced and consumed. This would imply that a cheaper alternative to rice exists locally and high mark-ups on the import price of rice do not last long. The test performed finds no co-integration between international and domestic prices of wheat. As displayed in Figure 10.3, the gap between international and domestic prices of wheat is wide. In particular, domestic prices followed the rise of international prices but did not follow their subsequent decline. This may be due to the lack of competitiveness in the local markets, but also to the population's increasing preference and demand for wheat derivatives, especially bread. Thus, it would seem that wheat and rice prices in

Table 10.1 Transmission of international rice and wheat prices to domestic markets in Mozambique

		Unit root in domestic price?		Long-run relationship	Error correction model (if long-run relationship confirmed)		
Location	Commodity	ADF test	Phillips-Perron test	Engle Granger test	Speed of adjustment	Short-run adjustment	Long-run adjustment
Maputo	Rice	Yes	Yes	No	–	–	–
Beira	Rice	Yes	Yes	No	–	–	–
Nampula	Rice	Yes	No	Yes	0.112*	0.18*	0.13
Maputo	Wheat	Yes	Yes	No	–	–	–
Beira	Wheat	Yes	No	No	–	–	–
Nampula	Wheat	Yes	Yes	No	–	–	–

Note: * $p<0.05$.
Source: authors' calculations.

Mozambique are only weakly linked to international prices, especially when these decline. This would confirm that Mozambique is still a fairly small economy weakly integrated with international markets (Simeone 2010).

10.4.1 *The Degree of Price Transmission among Domestic Markets*

Maputo, the capital, is the most important economic centre of the country and the most populous city. Thus, most of the imports pass through its port, for delivery to the rest of the country. Therefore, here we investigate whether a co-integration relation exists between Maputo and the other two main markets (Beira and Nampula), concerning food price transmission. The results presented in Table 10.2 show that the price of rice and the price of wheat in Maputo and Nampula are co-integrated. This might seem puzzling, given that Nampula is about 2,000 km away from Maputo. However, it needs to be noted that Nampula is still a developing market, and that it serves the country's most populated province of about four million inhabitants. Hence, part of the food sold in Nampula is imported from Maputo and then transported to this local market.

Also in this case, the ADF and Phillips-Perron unit root tests agree on the non-stationarity of the series analysed. Moreover, the Johansen procedure found that the prices in Maputo and Nampula exhibit long-run relations for both rice and wheat despite the existence of imbalances in the short run. The degree of rice price transmission between Maputo and Nampula was estimated at 0.03, i.e., only 3 per cent of the change in price in Maputo is transmitted to

Table 10.2 Transmission of food prices in Maputo to other markets in Mozambique

		Unit root in domestic price?		Long-run relationship	Error correction model (if long-run relationship confirmed)		
Location	Commodity	ADF test	Phillips-Perron test	Johansen test	Speed of adjustment	Short-run adjustment	Long-run adjustment
Beira	Rice	Yes	Yes	No	–	–	–
Nampula	Rice	Yes	Yes	Yes	0.03	0.01	0.09*
Beira	Wheat	Yes	Yes	No	–	–	–
Nampula	Wheat	Yes	Yes	Yes	0.07	0.11	0.24*

Note: * p<0.05.
Source: authors' calculations.

Nampula. The disequilibrium in the prices that is observed in the short run is corrected in about one month and the series revert back to the long-run relationship in about nine months. For wheat, the elasticity of transmission is about 7 per cent. The short-run disequilibrium is corrected in eleven months, while the long-run relationship is re-established in about two years (twenty-four months).

10.5 The Political Economy of Food Prices

The direct and indirect policy responses to the food price crisis in Mozambique are analysed and discussed in this section. The direct responses included various measures to smooth the impact of food price increases on domestic prices, while the indirect ones were aimed at reducing the impact of higher fuel prices on other sectors, including food production and distribution. Mozambique has a long history of price control and direct public participation in the markets as buyer and seller of key agricultural commodities. Alfieri, Arndt, and Cirera (2007) describe how during the 1980s and early 1990s the government frequently bought and sold key staples in the markets—especially maize—through Agriculture Competences (AGRICOM) and later through the Institute of Cereals of Mozambique (ICM). In this manner, the government sought to maintain food prices low for the consumers. However, the ICM was restructured in 1996 and is no longer active in any staple crop sales or purchases; currently it owns just granaries which are rented out to the private sector. Thus, the private sector has been largely free to set prices since 1997, although the government continues to issue indicative (non-binding) prices. In 2008/9, government policies were adopted mainly in the agricultural and trade sectors.

10.5.1 *Promotion of Increased Agricultural Production and Productivity*

In the aftermath of the 2008 price shocks, the government introduced the Plan for Action for Food Production (PAPA 2008–11), which was meant to secure food to the entire population. The PAPA operational plan was mainly targeted to the production of rice, wheat, and poultry, but also aimed to reduce the dependence on the imports of similar products. In addition, it proposed the application of different mechanisms to enhance food storage and distribution, and setting up basic conditions in rural areas to develop food processing using local inputs. Furthermore, in July 2008 the Ministry of Trade and Industry promoted the construction of granaries for the storage of cereals. As mentioned earlier, the storage of agricultural surpluses is one of the main problems for the Mozambican agricultural value chain. Given the high transportation costs, producers frequently sell their surplus locally and immediately after the harvest, missing the opportunity of higher profits. The granary initiative was intended to create a domestic production surplus that would improve food security and reduce the impact of international food price crises. Notwithstanding these policies, agricultural productivity did not exhibit any considerable improvement. Cunguara and Hanlon (2010) show that maize productivity was lower in 2008 than it was in 2002 and 2003, while Mosca (2011) compares agricultural productivity in the 1950s with recent figures and concludes that the production structure and agricultural productivity show no significant improvement over time. Figure 10.4 displays the growth rate for agricultural production and all sector production from 2006 to 2010, both series showing a slightly decreasing trend.

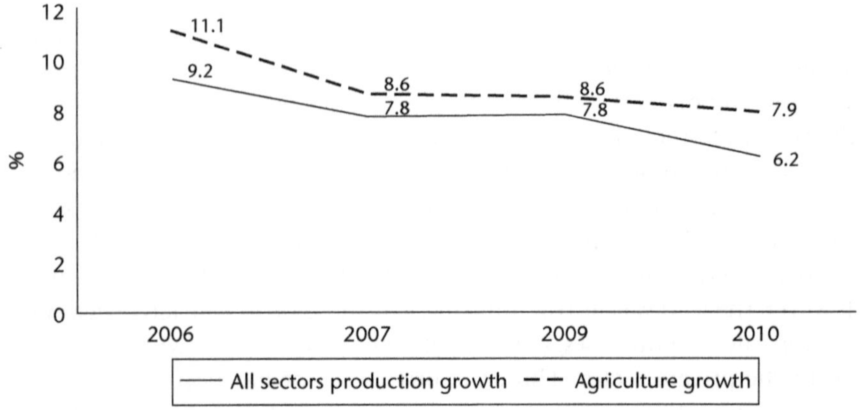

Figure 10.4 Trend of growth of the economy in Mozambique
Source: authors' calculations based on Banco de Moçambique (2012).

10.5.2 *Trade Policy Measures*

To mitigate the short-term effects of increasing global food prices, the government reduced import tariffs in early 2008, cutting the tariffs of maize, wheat, and rice from 25 to 2.5 per cent. Moreover, after the 2008 increase in food and fuel prices, a specific committee was activated to search for possible strategic responses. The committee interacted with different stakeholders, such as companies that had intended to increase certain domestic prices. The increase of domestic fuel prices in response to the increase of international prices was also discussed first within a specific inter-ministerial committee. The government also adopted policies to maintain an overvalued exchange rate, while subsidizing fuel prices and freezing any increase in tariffs for public utilities. Whereas the policies adopted for the agricultural sector did not have the expected results, it seems that such trade policy measures were generally effective in reducing the international price shock impact.

10.5.3 *The Rationale for Policy Interventions*

As introduced in previous sections, there are several reasons why the Mozambican government decided to step in during the 2008/9 fuel and food price crisis, and implement a series of measures to mitigate the most negative effects of the crisis.

PROTECTING THE POOR

First of all, the need to protect the poor was at the centre of the governmental agenda, as it appears from the main strategic documents in the country (GoM 2005, 2010b). Since most of the poor depend on agriculture for their livelihood, then part of the implemented policies obviously concerned the agricultural sector. However, the 2008/9 poverty assessment shows that the headcount ratio did not decrease from its 2002/3 levels (55 per cent). Cunguara and Hanlon (2010) also find that the median income was 10 per cent lower in 2008 than it was in 2002, and was lower for most income groups, concluding that poverty has been increasing rather than decreasing. Nonetheless, increased food prices and declining terms of trade cannot entirely explain the stagnation of consumption levels over time. The 2008/9 poverty assessment stresses that at least two other factors contributed to that outcome: (i) very slow growth rates in agricultural productivity, especially with respect to food crops; (ii) weather shocks that impacted the harvest of 2008, particularly in the central provinces (GoM 2010b). As previously discussed, notwithstanding the agricultural strategies to increase the levels of agricultural production and productivity, there is not enough evidence that these instruments have been successful in helping the country's poor. The country is still a net importer of agricultural commodities and the vulnerability of the agricultural sector to shocks does not seem to have been reduced (GoM 2011).

THE GOVERNMENT DESIRE TO BE RE-ELECTED AND AVOID SOCIAL UNREST

The 2008/9 food and fuel price shocks occurred immediately before the Mozambican presidential elections, and this certainly influenced the government decision to stabilize the impact of price shocks in the domestic market, especially in order to avoid a generalized social unrest. The revenue losses and huge increase in public debt that the government incurred in 2008/9 can also be explained in the light of its desire to be re-elected. However, such costly measures left no room for adopting additional policies after 2009. By then the government had used almost all available resources to avoid a general price upsurge, and had the international fuel prices continued to increase, there would have been very limited capacity to keep smoothing the impact on the domestic market. The government desire to be re-elected in the upcoming 2010 elections was then among the main motivations for implementing subsidies and other greatly incisive but costly trade policy measures.[3] Indeed, such interventions were gradually abandoned in 2010.

MACROECONOMIC STABILITY

Another goal of the government for intervening during the crisis was to maintain a low inflation rate and the stability in the exchange market. This was accompanied by a reduction in tariffs, which resulted in an increased import capacity and helped to avoid the increase of domestic food prices. However, the annual growth rate of tax revenue as a share of GDP from 2007 to 2008 was below the 1.4 per cent target, and the decrease was mainly driven by the reduction of taxes on goods and services. Moreover, public debt increased 42 per cent after the crisis, and external debt increased 17 per cent. According to GoM (2010c), subsidies increased so that the primary fiscal deficit passed from 2 per cent of GDP in 2008 to 5 per cent of GDP in 2009. This huge increase was largely due to the payments to fuel retailers and to millers and bakers.

Given the quantity and complexity of the different responses implemented by the government during and after the food and fuel price crisis, it is difficult to accurately assess the impact of the adopted policies. While the adopted policy responses broadly fulfilled the goal of ultimately preserving the consumers from a massive price increase, their effect on macroeconomic

[3] See also: <http://blogs.worldbank.org/africacan/on-the-riots-in-mozambique-are-subsidies-the-solution>.

stability is less clear. Some of these policy adjustments came at a very high cost, especially those that deprived the government of important sources of revenue, thereby preventing future investments.

Some sectors were more adversely affected by the price shocks: namely, transport and communications, tourism, and manufacturing. Other sectors, like agriculture, financial services, water and electricity, and construction seemed to be more immune to the crisis shocks (Castel-Branco and Ossemane 2010). The limited impact of the price shocks on consumers can then be explained largely by both the country's weak integration with international markets (Simeone 2010) and by the interventions of the central government in the economy.

10.6 Conclusion

The food and fuel price shocks occurred in 2008/9, immediately before the general elections which led the central government of Mozambique to intervene in order to stabilize the impact of price shocks in the domestic market. A mixture of subsidies and other measures helped to keep the retail price of food commodities stable, and thus to avoid greater social struggle. Nonetheless, such policies turned out to be extremely costly in terms of lost revenue and increased debt, so that their effect on the macroeconomic framework and on poverty reduction is less clear.

Using a standard co-integration procedure, we find that domestic prices for rice and wheat followed the international trends only partially, and that they remained high even after international prices had declined. This chapter concludes that a significant price transmission mechanism existed only between the international price of rice and the price of rice in Nampula, and between wheat and rice prices in Maputo and Nampula. Such a transmission mechanism did not seem to be in place for the market of Beira in the central region.

Mozambique is a fairly small economy, with weak linkages to international markets and prices, but it increasingly depends on imported food commodities and fuel. This makes Mozambique vulnerable to international price shocks, also because the economy in the past had been unable to create the conditions needed for increasing agricultural productivity and food production, and for storing post-harvest agricultural surplus efficiently. Price shocks affected some sectors as well as some socioeconomic groups more than others, but the overall effects of these seemed to have been limited. This can be explained largely by both Mozambique's weak integration with international markets and by central government's deep interventions in the economy, which could have been more severe had the government not intervened.

References

Alfieri, A., C. Arndt, and X. Cirera (2007). 'Distortions to Agricultural Incentives in Mozambique'. DNEAP Working Paper No. 54. Maputo: National Directorate of Studies and Policy Analysis, Ministry of Planning and Development.

Arndt, C., R. Benfica, N. Maximiano, A. Nucifora, and J. T. Thurlow (2008). 'Higher Fuel and Food Prices: Economic Impacts and Responses for Mozambique'. IFPRI Discussion Paper No. 00836. Washington, DC: IFPRI.

Banco de Moçambique (2012). 'Base de dados da balança de pagamentos'. Maputo: Mozambique.

Cachomba, I. (2010). 'Impacto económico da redução da importação do trigo em Moçambique'. II Simpósio de Investigação Agrária, Mozambique. 15–17 September 2010.

Castel-Branco, N., and R. Ossemane (2010). 'Mozambique Phase 2'. Global Financial Crisis Discussion Series Paper No. 18. London: Overseas Development Institute.

Cunguara, B., and J. Hanlon (2010). 'Poverty is not being Reduced in Mozambique'. London: Crisis State Research Centre, London School of Economics and Political Science.

Donovan, C., and E. Tostão (2010). 'Staple Food Prices in Mozambique'. Paper prepared for the COMESA Policy Seminar on 'Variation in Staple Food Prices: Causes, Consequence, and Policy Options'. Maputo: Mozambique.

GoM (Government of Mozambique) (2005). 'Programa quinquenal do governo 2005–2009'. Maputo: Mozambique.

GoM (Government of Mozambique) (2007). 'Balanço do plano economico e social'. Maputo: Mozambique.

GoM (Government of Mozambique) (2008a). 'Balanço do plano economico e social'. Maputo: Mozambique.

GoM (Government of Mozambique) (2008b). 'Plano de Acção para a Produção de Alimentos 2008–2011'. Maputo: Mozambique.

GoM (Government of Mozambique) (2008c). 'Cenário fiscal de médio prazo 2009–2011'. Maputo: Mozambique.

GoM (Government of Mozambique) (2010a). 'Programa quinquenal do governo 2010–2014'. Maputo: Mozambique.

GoM (Government of Mozambique) (2010b). 'Terceira avaliação nacional da pobreza em Moçambique'. Maputo: Mozambique.

GoM (Government of Mozambique) (2010c). 'Relatório de execução orçamental'. Maputo: Mozambique.

GoM (Government of Mozambique) (2011). 'Balanco do Plano Economico e Social'. Maputo: Mozambique.

Magaua, M., V. Hong, and C. Massingarela (2011). 'Natural Resource Endowment of Vietnam and Mozambique'. Mimeo.

Minot, N. (2010). 'Transmission of World Food Price Changes to African Markets and its Effect on Household Welfare'. Paper prepared for the COMESA Policy Seminar on 'Variation in Staple Food Prices: Causes, Consequence, and Policy Options', held 25–26 January in Maputo, Mozambique.

Mosca, J. (2011). *Politicas agrarias y cambios en la agricultura de Moçambique (1975– 2009).* Maputo: Mozambique.

Simeone, F. (2010). 'A crise económica mundial. Implicações e impacto em Moçambique no primeiro semestre de 2009'. Discussion Paper No. 65P. Maputo: National Directorate of Studies and Policy Analysis, Ministry of Planning and Development.

Traub, L. N., R. J. Myers, T. S. Jayne, and F. H. Meyer (2010). 'Measuring Integration and Efficiency in Maize Grain Markets: The Case of South Africa and Mozambique'. Paper presented at the Joint 3rd African Association of Agricultural Economists (AAAE) and 48th Agricultural Economists Association of South Africa (AEASA) Conference, Cape Town, 19–23 September.

Part V

The Political Economy of Food Price Policy in Low- and Middle-income Countries Heavily Dependent on Food Import

11

The Political Economy of Food Price Policy in Bangladesh

Selim Raihan

11.1 Introduction

The Bangladeshi government moved beyond the public sector-led development strategy to a private sector and market-oriented development strategy through the implementation of different structural adjustment programmes (SAPs) during the 1980s and 1990s. In response to donor suggestions the government adopted the Poverty Reduction Strategy Papers (PRSP) in 2005. It emphasized a greater role of private sector investment and providing appropriate fiscal and other incentives to achieve that. The strategy highlighted the importance of agricultural and rural development and focused on the intensification of major crops (i.e., cereals), the diversification to high-value non-cereal crops (i.e., vegetables and fruits), the development of non-crop agriculture (i.e., fishery, poultry, livestock), and the promotion of rural non-farm activities (i.e., rural construction, transport, and services). The strategy also put emphasis on the expansion of micro-credit and importance of the safety net programmes. A national food policy was formulated in 2006, which called for several agricultural development and extension services. The second PRSP was formulated in 2009, which emphasized enabling the macroeconomic environment for pro-poor economic growth. The Awami League (AL) government in 2010 abandoned the PRSP and reintroduced the Sixth Five-Year Plan for the period 2011–15 which identified a number of core targets in line with the vision and objectives of the Perspective Plan as well as the Millennium Development Goals. These targets are related to a considerable rise in economic growth, significant reduction in poverty, significant improvement in human resource development, water and sanitation, energy and infrastructure, gender equality and empowerment, environment sustainability, the widespread use of information, and communications technology.

11.2 Food Price Trends and Shocks

11.2.1 *Previous Crisis Episodes and Policy Responses*

Over the last forty years after independence in 1971, Bangladesh faced a number of man-made and natural calamities which threatened food security of the poor and marginalized population. These calamities include a famine in 1974, floods in 1987 and 1988, a cyclone in 1991, and a flood in 1998.

During the 1974 famine the food price rose sharply when rising inflationary expectations raised the demand for food while the supply of food decreased as farmers and traders released less food in the market. According to Drèze and Sen (1989) the famine was due to entitlement failure, rather than the per capita availability of food. The government tried to ensure subsidized food to all the urban people on a priority basis through the rationing system. The government's famine relief efforts were limited and disorganized and the government was inadequately prepared to face the challenge.

In 1987 and 1988 the country experienced disastrous floods. The government undertook various disaster management programmes. Food aid and increased imports of rice and wheat were the major steps. All the international development partners supported a project entitled Flood Action Plan from 1990 to 1996 to formulate a national flood and water management strategy.

The 1991 Bangladesh cyclone was among the deadliest tropical cyclones on record. The government and the international community launched a major response to the cyclone disaster which included food aid and large scale reconstruction.

In 1998, over 75 per cent of the total area of the country was flooded. It was similar to the catastrophic flood of 1988 in terms of the extent of the flooding. The government responded to the crisis by supplying food for immediate relief efforts during the floods and by helping to coordinate food aid commitments and deliveries. At the same time, as part of its price stabilization strategy, the government encouraged private sector imports, a policy that helped avoid a food supply shortage following the floods (del Ninno et al. 2001).

11.2.2 *Price Trends for Key Food Crops and Price Transmission*

As shown in Figure 11.1, the domestic retail price of rice had been higher than the import cost, insurance, and freight (CIF) price of rice until 2003–4. Though, since 2004–5, both the domestic retail price and import CIF price of

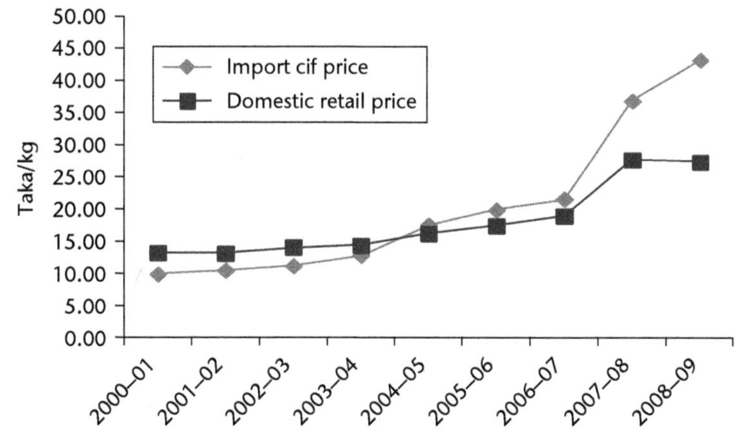

Figure 11.1 World price and domestic retail price of rice during 2001–9
Source: Department of Agricultural Marketing (<http://www.dam.gov.bd/jsp/index.jsp>) and Indexmundi (<http://www.indexmundi.com>).

rice began to rise considerably, the domestic retail price had been much lower than the import CIF price until 2008–9. This is a reflection of the fact that in recent years, Bangladesh has become less dependent on import of rice and therefore, the world price had little effect in determining the domestic price.

Bangladesh is heavily dependent on the import of wheat and therefore, the domestic retail price of wheat had always been higher than the import CIF price. The gap between these two prices widened during 2003–4 and 2007–8, suggesting that the domestic retail price of wheat increased more than the rise in world price of wheat. In 2008–9, the gap between these two prices narrowed (Figure 11.2).

11.2.3 *Causes of the Price Hike*

There are several explanations for the food price hike during 2007–8. Some of them were domestic and some were related to the effects generated at the global level. Raihan and Fatema (2007) identified eight reasons.

1. Bangladesh had been one of the high growth performing economies over the last ten years. The high growth rate of per capita gross domestic product (GDP) contributed to a demand-pull inflation.
2. Bangladesh had been a net food importing country. As a result, any rise in food prices in the world market pushed the domestic prices of those commodities to increase.
3. The Bangladesh government increased fuel prices in April 2007 in order to make domestic prices of fuel closer to the international market prices.

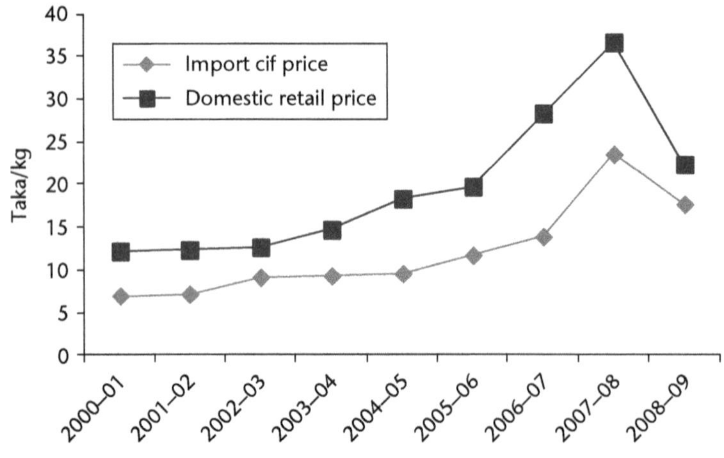

Figure 11.2 Wholesale and retail prices of wheat flour during 2001–9

Source: Department of Agricultural Marketing (<http://www.dam.gov.bd/jsp/index.jsp>) and Indexmundi (<http://www.indexmundi.com>).

Though fuel constituted a very small share in the basket of commodities used for the calculation of the consumer price indexes, the rise in fuel prices had some indirect impacts on the prices of commodities by rising cost through two major channels: the high prices of fuels led to high costs for irrigation, which raised the costs of agricultural production, and high fuel prices increased the cost of transportation, which also raised the prices of essential items transported from remote villages to urban areas.

4. Since 2002 the Bangladeshi taka had depreciated much against the US$ while the Indian rupee has been appreciating. This resulted in a major depreciation of the Bangladeshi taka against the Indian rupee. India had been one of the major sources of Bangladesh's imports, as imports from India constituted more than 20 per cent of Bangladesh's total imports comprising many essential food items.
5. Though there was no concrete evidence of established syndicates in the markets of essential commodities taking advantage of the weak consumer protection laws, there were some short-term alliances among the suppliers of these goods to influence supply and prices. This might have some impact on the rising prices of essential items.
6. Due to the anti-corruption drive by the military backed caretaker government many businessmen contracted their usual business activities with the fear of legal actions. Furthermore, many informal marketplaces, both in rural and urban areas, were wiped out by law enforcing agencies on legal grounds. Such actions resulted in a disruption in the 'established' supply chains, which exacerbated the inflationary trend.

7. There was a declining trend of growth in agriculture over time, especially of the crop sector in Bangladesh. This resulted in less domestic production relative to the domestic demand. Slower growth in agriculture, and especially of the crop sector, was due to failures in the timely supply of fertilizer, seed, and pesticide to the farmers, increased cost of irrigation because of a rise in diesel price, and the decline in the availability of cultivable land because of population growth and rehabilitation. Severe floods during July–August 2007 also exacerbated the situation.
8. Bangladesh was experiencing a steady rise in remittance inflow until the mid-2000s. In 2006–7, the growth of remittances was 24.49 per cent. Such inflow also contributed to some demand-pull inflation in Bangladesh.

11.3 Broad Impact on Stakeholders as a Result of Price Shifts Associated with the Crisis Period

The impacts of food price shocks on different categories of households would depend on the extent by which the households are integrated to the market. In the case of rice and wheat it appears that while farmers source around 80 per cent of their consumption needs from own production and the remaining 20 per cent from the market, marginal farmers procure more than 80 per cent of their consumption needs from the market and the remaining 20 per cent from own production. The small farmers can source around 56 per cent of their consumption need from own production and the remaining 44 per cent from the market. This suggests that large farmers may gain from rice price increases while small and marginal farmers would lose. Non-producing households such as rural landless households, rural non-farm low-income households, and urban low-income households are extremely vulnerable to price shocks.

Several studies assessed the impact of food price increase on the level of poverty in Bangladesh. According to the World Bank (2008), a reduction in poverty by 5 per cent, between 2005 and 2008, was expected in Bangladesh resulting from the strong GDP growth during that period. However, the study instead projected around a 3 per cent increase in the incidence of poverty from the baseline rate of 40 per cent in 2005 as a result of the increase in food prices. Therefore, the net impact on poverty, from the combined effects of economic growth and the inflation of food prices, was to result in a decline of about 2 per cent; from 40 per cent in 2005 to 38 per cent in 2008. Rahman et al. (2008) showed that in the fifteen-month period from January 2007 to March 2008 the gross income of poor people plummeted by 36.7 per cent. The income erosion of up to 30.5 per cent alone resulted from paying for the high food bill, the predominant item in the rather bare purchase list of the poor. In consequence, 8.5 per cent of people comprising 2.5 million households fell below the poverty line.

Raihan (2009) explored the impact of the rise in food prices on the food consumption and education of children in the poor and vulnerable households in Bangladesh. The study showed that during early 2008 the prices of rice, pulses, and edible oil increased exceedingly which threatened the status of food security of these poor and vulnerable households in Bangladesh. As a result of the price hike, a significant percentage of households were forced to cut their consumption of rice, pulses, and edible oil.[1] The households who could maintain the same level of consumption of rice could do so at the cost of reduced consumption of other non-rice food items and/or by reducing the non-food expenditure, i.e., expenses on their children's education.[2]

11.4 Policy Responses

11.4.1 *Increased Agricultural Production through Input Subsidies, Investment, and Enhanced Extension*

The government took a number of initiatives for the development of the agriculture sector in the light of the PRSP, National Agriculture Policy, and Millenium Development Goals. Discussions with the policy makers suggest that many of these initiatives were reinforced in the context of rising food prices in the global market. These included subsidy on fertilizer, a rehabilitation programme for flood and cyclone, endowment funds for agricultural research and development, diesel subsidy to the small and marginal farmers, cash incentives for exporting agricultural products, rebate on electricity bills to the entrepreneurs of agro-based industries, reduction of the rate of interest for disbursement of loan for the production of pulse, oil-seed, and spices, and pursuing distribution programmes of agriculture and rural credit

[1] Raihan (2009) reported that more than 25 per cent of sample households in the rural areas were forced to reduce their consumption of rice while the corresponding figure was about 19 per cent in the urban areas. However, the extent of fall in the consumption of rice was relatively higher in the urban areas compared to that in the rural areas, since for the urban households, who experienced a fall in consumption of rice, on average, decreased by around 22.8 per cent, while the corresponding figure was 21.6 per cent for the households in the rural areas.

[2] Raihan (2009) also reported that high dropout rates among the children of these vulnerable households were observed because of the price hike of food items as most of the households could not continue to bear the expenses of their children's education. On average, 58 per cent and 56 per cent of households in the rural and urban areas, respectively, experienced a dropout of their children from school. A significant proportion of these dropped out children were engaged in different jobs for contributing to their household income.

through state-owned commercial banks. The allocation for these programmes increased during 2007 and 2008 (*Economic Review* 2008).

The Bangladesh Bank (BB) undertook several initiatives to streamline higher and balanced flow of agricultural credit as well as the distribution of subsidies on agricultural inputs. It was made compulsory for all local and foreign banks to disburse agricultural credits to facilitate agricultural production. The BB introduced a 'revolving crop credit limit system' for a three-year period to ensure access of farm loan to farmers continuously engaged in agricultural production.

11.4.2 *Domestic Price and Trade Policies*

Tariff rates on essential imported food commodities, such as rice and wheat, were brought down to zero in 2007–8. Also, operative tariff rates on other food items were reduced drastically during 2007–8. There was the withdrawal of the provision of an annual renewal fee of value added tax (VAT) registration by commercial importers.

The government also directed the BB to encourage the banks to provide credit facilities on softer terms to new importers, to ease the letter of credit (L/C) margin for food items, and to extend the time for customer facility. In order to curb inflation, the BB stated that it would continue following an accommodative monetary policy.

11.4.3 *Social Safety Nets*

In the face of escalated food prices in the domestic market, the national budget of 2007–8 expanded the existing food grains distribution through various social safety net programmes. There was also increased coverage and amount of individual grants under those programmes. Some additional programmes, such as Bangladesh Rifles (BDR) 'Dal-Bhat' (Pulses-Rice) programme, were undertaken. The national budget of 2008–9 continued these measures and expanded the open market sale (OMS) of food grains at subsidized price.

11.4.4 *Procurement and Stocking Policies*

In 2007–8, though the government decided to intensify internal procurement of food grains, in reality, total procurement was much lower than the targeted procurement. This was due to loss in production caused by natural disasters and higher prices prevailing in the market compared to the procurement prices set by the government. The government could also not meet the shortfall in domestic procurement through higher imports from the international market due to the fact that in October 2007 India imposed a ban on rice exports, and the international market price of rice was much higher than the domestic price during that period, which discouraged private importers from importing.

One important observation made by Dorosh (2009) was that though the government in Bangladesh mostly relied on private sector imports to supplement any shortfalls in domestic production, it also traditionally held public stocks of cereals. The public stock of rice began to decline in 2004–5 reaching a low level in 2006–7 after which it doubled by 2008–9. The public stock of wheat in 2006–7 became almost one-third of its level in 2001–2 and dropped further by 2007–8. It almost doubled between 2007–8 and 2008–9. Dorosh (2009) suggested that the export bans that many traditional grain exporting countries imposed in reaction to the 2007–8 food crisis created concerns among Bangladesh's senior policy makers that international trade might be disrupted at times when the country needed to import. As a result, the government set a high public stock target of rice and wheat for 2008–9. The increased stock was attributed to lesser off-take and increased domestic procurement and import (FPMU 2008).

11.4.5 *Other Policies and Interventions*

The national budget of 2007–8 announced the establishment of a task force at the national and district levels to review prices of essential commodities regularly. The country at that time was run by a 'civil' caretaker government backed by the military. The activities of the political parties were very limited. The demand for establishing task forces to review prices didn't come from the political parties; rather the civil society organizations, non-government organizations, and consumer groups were the pioneers in raising that demand. However, discussions with the stakeholders indicate that very little achievements were made in terms of establishment of task forces, and their operations were limited and were mostly ineffective. The inter-ministerial monitoring committee was formed to analyse the price situation of essential commodities. A legal framework was proposed to protect consumer rights which later in 2009 took the shape of a Consumer Protection Act. The civil society organizations, including the Consumers' Association of Bangladesh, were very active in pursuing the Consumer Protection Act. Also, in the Ministry of Commerce (MoC), there was support for this act, especially due to the fact that the MoC was usually criticized for its 'failure' in monitoring and curbing prices and there was a general perception among the high officials in the MoC that the enactment of the Consumer Protection Act would provide them with the necessary instruments to take measures against any anti-competitive practices which prevailed in the markets of essential commodities.

The national budget of 2008–9 announced medium-term measures such as an increase of production and distribution of food grains through creation of wholesale markets in various places including Dhaka and taking initiatives for introducing a Consumers' Rights Protection Ordinance. The measures related to boosting agricultural production had some positive effects as reflected in an increased production of agricultural commodities in the subsequent years. However, the enactment of the Consumer Protection Act had little effect in containing the prices of essential food items since the government lacked required machineries, personnel, and capacity to effectively implement this act.

11.4.6 *A Timeline of the Events and Responses*

Table 11.1 provides a brief summary of the timeline of the major events and responses during 2007 and 2008. The timeline suggests that the government's major success was raising the boro rice production and on targeted safety net programmes. A significant rise in rice production during April/June 2008 helped the government to increase the public stock of rice.

11.5 Political Economy Context

11.5.1 *The Role of Ministries*

The MoC and the Ministry of Food and Disaster Management (MoFDM) were at the centre of discussion related to government's actions against the food price hike during 2007–8.

On 18 March 2007 the MoC, as part of its action to keep the prices of essential commodities within the purchasing power of the common people, announced it would set up a Price Monitoring Cell (PMC) in line with the proposed Consumer Protection Act to monitor the prices of essentials on a day-to-day basis. This PMC was successful in collecting data on prices of essential food items on a daily basis. However, because of the lack of required machineries, personnel, and capacity, PMC also failed to exert any influence over the market prices. The MoC urged the Federation of Bangladesh Chambers of Commerce and Industry (FBCCI) to set up a monitoring cell and display price lists at the wholesale and retail outlets. FBCCI's monitoring cell was ineffective, and the MoC's instruction to display price lists at the wholesale and retail outlets was largely disobeyed by the traders because of lack of monitoring capacity of the MoC.

The MoC was instrumental in pursuing the Ministry of Finance (MoF) to cut down the tariffs on food imports. According to a report published in

Table 11.1 A timeline of the events and responses

Year	2007				2008			
Quarter	Jan/Mar	Apr/Jun	Jul/Sep	Oct/Dec	Jan/Mar	Apr/Jun	Jul/Sep	Oct/Dec
Events			Two rounds of severe floods Spike in global fuel prices	Super cyclone Sidr (mid-Nov). India bans rice exports	Uncertainties about rice import from India and other major exporting countries	Boro rice harvest 17% up on previous year		
Responses	- Import duty on rice and wheat withdrawn - OMS initiated	Bank credit for private food import eased	- First round of major safety net operations - Agricultural rehabilitation	- Second round of major safety net operations - Intensifications of OMS operation	- Massive support for boro rice harvest - Continuation of OMS operation - Announcement of highest ever farm price support - India agrees special dispensation for exports of 0.5 million tonnes of rice	Procurement drive for stock build-up	Targeted continuation of safety nets	OMS operation scaled down

Source: Wiggins et al. (2010). Reproduced under ODI Creative Commons Licence (CC BY-NC 3.0).

the newspaper on 19 March 2007,[3] businessmen welcomed the government initiative of exempting taxes on wheat and rice imports. They also suggested going for the same step regarding import of other food items like soybean oil, milk, lentils, etc. The same report mentioned that some high officials of the Commerce Ministry and the National Board of Revenue (NBR) held the view that the reduction of L/C margin would not play any role in reducing the prices of commodities and only businessmen would benefit from such provision.

Price hikes of essential food items during the month of Ramadan had been a regular phenomenon in Bangladesh. In the months of Ramadan during 2007 and 2008, the MoC had been consistently maintaining that the stocks of essentials were sufficient and thus there was no cause for a price hike. Also, in 2009, when the food prices in the international market were decling, the MoC had been calling the businessmen to reduce food prices in the domestic market. However, the businessmen were arguing that because of the the rise in international commodity prices local prices were getting pushed up. An article published in a British daily newspaper did not find valid reasons for the soaring local prices as the current stocks had been procured when the international market prices were lower.[4] The same article also mentioned that despite calls from the commerce minister to the business community to avoid stockpiling and hoarding, especially during Ramadan, as this would create artificial scarcities and thus manipulate prices upward, such practices were still observed in the retail community.[5]

There were also some debates within the MoC with regard to involving the Trading Corporation of Bangladesh (TCB), an organization under the MoC, as a market player during the times of price hike. TCB is a public organization and it used to have some roles in the past when after the independence the government could intervene in the market through imports of essential commodities using the TCB. However, with the growing dominance of the free market philosophy, the importance of the TCB gradually declined and currently it has become an organization with insufficient funds and manpower. There are some interesting political economic issues related to the debate whether to make TCB effective or not. There was a 'public' demand for making TCB effective in the sense that TCB with some sizeable volume of imports of essential food items could put some downward pressure on the prices of essential food items in the domestic market. However, there was resistance from the business community and their lobbys in the government not to extend the operation of TCB. During the episodes of price hike in 2007,

[3] *The Daily Star*, 19 March 2007.

[4] *The Daily Star*, 9 August 2009.

[5] *The Daily Star*, 9 August 2009.

2008, and 2009, there were regular features in the national dailies related to this debate.[6]

During 2007 and 2008, the MoFDM set high targets of public food distribution and building up of the government's food reserve. However, there were concerns in the media with regard to the failure of the MoFDM in achieving those targets. Quoting a food ministry official, *The Daily Star* reported that the stocking and distribution of food grains through government programmes had not been satisfactory. That the newspaper also mentioned that the government invited tenders for importing rice 36 times during 2007 and 2008 but the response to the tenders was not good as the import cost of rice became higher than what had been quoted in the tender bids.[7]

It should, however, be mentioned that the MoC and MoFDM didn't have any direct power to influence the prices in the domestic market. For example, the MoC didn't have any direct authority to lower the duties on import of food items. They had to request the MoF to undertake such a decision. Also, to expand the operation of the TCB in terms of increased manpower and increased fund for a larger volume of imports of food items could only be possible through the endorsement of the MoF, which was not straightforward. A number of studies (such as Raihan, Khondker, and Uddin 2010) identified some important non-economic reasons for a food price hike in the domestic market, such as extortion and unofficial payments in the transportation, distribution, and marketing conduits of food. This required actions from the Ministry of Home. The caretaker government, through the Ministry of Home, took a number of measures to combat the non-economic factors and also drove actions against 'illegal' or 'informal' supply chains. Though some of the measures against extortions were effective, many of those actions against 'illegal' or 'informal' supply chains were

[6] An article in *The Financial Express*, 3 October 2012, mentioned that the commodity markets in Bangladesh were characterized by monopolies, duopolies, oligopolies, etc., and frequent price manipulations. Though a significant volume of food requirements is met by import from the international market, the prices of imported food had been much higher in the domestic markets than in the international markets. The report thus highlighted the importance of reactivating TCB. In the early years after its establishment, TCB was used to establish competitive prices in the domestic market as it had a large share in total imports. For example, in 1972–3, it imported 63 commodities and its share of total import was 24.84 per cent. Also, during the period between 1972 and 1977, TCB imported as many as 70 commodities. However, from late 1970s the role of TCB has been curtailed, and in recent years the organization has hardly managed the import of three products (sugar, edible oil, lentils) from the international market. Also its share in total imports has been even less than 1 per cent. The organization has been inactive since the early 1980s, with the beginning of privatization and liberalization of the economy following prescriptions by the World Bank and the International Monetary Fund. The number of TCB employees has been reduced quite drastically over the years—in 1996 the number was reduced from 1,390 to 714, and again in 2002 the number was further reduced to 225. The article highlighted that the TCB has been currently suffering from a shortage of efficient manpower, legislative inflexibility, resource mismanagement, difficulties in its decision-making process, and lack of leadership.

[7] *The Daily Star*, 6 April 2008.

counter-productive. CPD (2008) mentioned that strict law enforcements by the joint forces and the eviction of many roadside markets adversely affected the food inflation situation in Bangladesh. Demolition of local hat and bazars did not help either.

11.5.2 *Role of Business Associations*

The Metropolitan Chamber of Commerce and Industry (MCCI), Dhaka urged the central bank to consult the leaders of private sector businesses and industries and collectively evolve a strategy for controlling inflation. In a statement, published in a newspaper,[8] on the fourth mid-year Monetary Policy Statement (MPS) of the BB announced on 12 July 2007, the leading chamber body of the country said the MPS which hinted at a tighter monetary policy in the near and the medium term should not aim at increasing interest rates and effecting a hike of statutory liquidity ratio and cash reserve requirement (CRR) of banks. The MCCI also urged the BB to ensure that the administrative prices of fuels, utilities, and fertilizers not to be increased and ensure that the borrowings of the government be reduced. MCCI opposed BB's tight monetary policy as it might raise the cost of borrowing for the entrepreneurs, curb the enthusiasm of genuine businessmen to invest in the formal economy, and subdue economic growth. However, such call from the business community didn't have any impact on the BB to reverse its stance on monetary policy.

The MCCI also urged the government to strengthen the price-monitoring cell. Since the MCCI was the country's prestigious and elite trade body, they wanted to uphold the clear image of the business people through such actions. They also suggested that the hoarders or syndicates should be given exemplary punishment. Furthermore, they asked for a clear definition of 'hoarding' and 'artificial crisis' so businessmen could distinguish between what was allowable and what was not. The MCCI also suggested the government turn the TCB into a public limited company and give it enough autonomy to function independently.[9] Such a call from the MCCI could appear to contradict its self-interest, since TCB would presumably compete with the private traders. However, as mentioned before, TCB had always been neglected by the government, and it was a common perception among the business people that TCB would never be operationalized effectively. And in fact, despite such a call from the MCCI, TCB was not made functional.

The FBCCI in May 2008 commissioned a task force comprising top traders, ministry officials concerned, and members of the joint forces to monitor the price situation.[10] The task force was supposed to collect information on

[8] *The Financial Express*, 19 July 2007.

[9] *The Daily Star*, 6 January 2010.

[10] *The Daily Star*, 8 May 2008.

the prices, demand and supply, stock and market trends of essentials, and to come up with a set of recommendations to contain the prices. The task force was supposed to meet once every fifteen days and three major chambers—Chittagong, Khulna, and Jessore—would provide daily information for its cell. A website on the task force was also supposed to be lauched. Complaining against the government's anti-hoarding drive, the FBBCI also demanded a food and hoarding policy, changes to the present food procurement policy, and immediate measures to create a better business climate.

A newspaper report in July 2008, however, mentioned that the FBCCI price monitoring task force was yet to gather pace two months after its launch in May.[11] It thus appears that, though a few top leaders of FBCCI were eager to set up the price monitoring task force, they didn't receive any support from the larger business community.

In September 2008, the FBCCI president urged business people to keep prices of basic commodities within people's reach by not making unreasonable profits during the month of Ramadan.[12] He urged the wholesalers to give vouchers to the retailers for transparency in pricing of the commodities. However, in reality, there was no authority to monitor whether this was practised by the traders.

FBCCI formed a ten-member committee to investigate the sugar scam in October 2009 and recommended possible ways to control the prices of sugar and other essentials.[13] Meanwhile, backtracking from its earlier stand to arrest the unscrupulous sugar traders, who manipulated the sugar price during the month of Ramadan, the government in September 2009 decided to form two separate committees to conduct an 'extensive investigation' into the sugar price spiral.[14] The committees submitted the reports, though the reports were never made public and there were no effective actions against those unscrupulous sugar traders.

In August 2010, the FBCCI urged the government to make a commodity price control policy to tackle irrational price spirals in the market.[15] The policy should deal with the issues that affect prices and should define clear strategies and

[11] *The Daily Star*, 7 July 2008.

[12] *The Daily Star*, 11 September 2008. [13] *The Daily Star*, 1 October 2009.

[14] An article in *The Daily Star* on 30 September 2009 mentioned that those committees were set up at a time when eight sugar traders had been trying to escape from being arrested as they were alleged to have manipulated sugar prices in the local market. Though the commerce minister persistently stated that legal actions would be taken against those responsible for destabilizing the sugar market, the business leaders were denying the allegations and held the soaring international price responsible for the local price hike. The government's attempt to arrest the alleged sugar traders created fear among many traders in the large wholesale markets, and some even kept their businesses shut. The article also mentioned that the Consumers' Association of Bangladesh (CAB) was alarmed that some dishonest members of the business community were trying to create a new sugar crisis to put pressure on the government, and that some business leaders were trying to save business syndicate members. The CAB reminded the government that the commerce minister's declaration to arrest these syndicate members had not yet been implemented and asked for immediate action.

[15] *The Daily Star*, 23 August 2010.

guidelines on the pricing of commodities at various levels of commodity supply chains. FBCCI called for continued action from the government in its drive to check food adulteration, deploring the misdeeds of an unscrupulous section of the business people, who tarnish the image of the whole business community. The FBCCI president suggested that the inconsistencies in supply chain could be removed by adopting appropriate measures, including guidelines for tackling the issues affecting commodity pricing, not only during Ramadan but all the year round. The FBCCI chief also called for the abandonment of the demand order (DO) system for sugar and edible oils and replacing it with appointment of dealers, claiming that the latter would better address the price spirals evident in the market. Underpinning the need for using the latest information technology systems to track commodity prices, the FBCCI president mentioned that the prices of all commodities at all levels of the supply chain should be put on the website. He also mentioned that FBCCI would recommend the wholesalers to write out sales slips or receipts for each transaction they would make and ask retailers to display the price lists of the commodities to ensure transparency. The FBCCI, however, noted that a section of the business community and traders were still trying to manipulate prices through their attempts to create an artificial crisis of commodities. However, most of the suggestions of the FBCCI president did not materialize. Only the DO system for sugar and edible oil trade was replaced by the dealership system in October 2010.

11.5.3 *Other Institutions*

By 19 March 2007, the BDR[16] set up 'free markets' at seventeen places in the capital, as a part of the government's efforts to stabilize the soaring prices of essentials.[17] These 'free markets' sold essential commodities at fair prices to help the lower- and middle-income groups facing hardships due to price spiralling. By 23 March, there were another eight 'free markets'.[18] The products sold at the BDR 'free markets' were cheaper than those at the regular markets since BDR could charge very low retail margins. However, such operations were limited in terms of scale and thus had little effect in curbing the market prices.

The government also continued with the OMS. This was part of the government's subsidized food distribution programmes. According to the newspaper article, in Chittagong there was a huge demand for the OMS on the first day with huge crowds thronging from early morning. However, many consumers returned home empty handed as the stalls ran out of rice stocks very quickly.[19]

16 A para-military border security force.

17 *The Daily Star*, 19 March 2007.

18 *The Daily Star*, 23 March 2007.

19 *The Daily Star*, 23 March 2007.

The BB intervened in the foreign exchange markets, directly and indirectly, to keep a stable exchange rate against the US$. The BB continued following a moderate contractionary monetary policy. During early 2010, in a seminar, the governor of the BB announced that the government would soon launch the value added agricultural project in collaboration with the Asian Development Bank (ADB) to ensure better prices for growers.[20] In May 2010, the central bank raised the cash reserve requirement[21] for banks in a bid to contain inflation. However, economists and businessmen thought that would make the businessmen's access to bank finance difficult, and would also sag the investment.[22] The World Bank welcomed the monetary policy stating that as a cautious policy stance.[23] In December 2010, the BB took new steps to control the credit flow in an effort to contain inflation. The central bank issued two separate circulars. One of them directed the banks to take back the loans given to rice-mill owners and traders every thirty days, which was forty-five days earlier. In another circular, BB asked the banks to set the loan equity ratio at 50:50 for consumer loans. Earlier, there was no guideline for the loan equity ratio for consumer finance. According to the BB, it was done to curb the credit flow to unproductive sectors.[24]

The International Monetary Fund (IMF) in July 2008 suggested the Bangladesh government execute tight monetary policy and termed the existing policy too expansionary to deal with the soaring inflation. The IMF suggested that the monetary policy should be less expansionary to contain the already high inflationary pressures.[25] It seemed that BB listened to such advice during 2008 and in later years, though this policy suggestion was not welcomed by the business community.

11.5.4 *Civil Society*

The Centre for Policy Dialogue (CPD), a leading private sector think tank in Bangladesh, praised the government's step to fix the procurement price for

[20] *The Daily Star*, 22 March 2010. The ADB also confirmed that it would extend financial assistance to Bangladesh to grow high-value crops including vegetables, spices, and fruits that would boost incomes for poor farmers and support the nation's food security. A loan of US$40 million equivalent from ADB's concessional Asian Development Fund was being provided for the Second Crop Diversification Project. It would be used to support the development of high-value crops in 27 districts in the South West and North West of Bangladesh—including some of the poorest, least developed, and most climate-vulnerable areas in the country (source: <http://www.adb.org/news/adb-40-million-loan-boost-food-security-farm-incomes-bangladesh>).

[21] The reserve requirement is a central bank regulation that sets the minimum reserves each bank must hold against customer deposits. The reserve ratio is sometimes used as a tool in the monetary policy, influencing the country's economy, borrowing, and interest rates. Any rise in CRR means mopping up excess liquidity from the money market by using the instrument as part of demand management to curb inflation.

[22] *The Daily Star*, 5 May 2010.
[23] *The Daily Star*, 20 July 2010.
[24] *The Daily Star*, 16 July 2008.
[25] *The Daily Star*, 30 December 2010.

paddy and rice, called for increasing the capacity of rice milling and storage capacity, and also called for widening the scopes for social safety net programmes.[26]

As inflation continued to rise in 2009 mainly because of soaring food prices, civil society organizations and experts blamed volatility in the international commodity markets for the rise in the inflation rate. The suggestion was that the government should monitor the global market on a regular basis so that the government could make a buffer stock by importing essentials when the prices were low in the international market. Also, suggestion was for the government to reduce fertilizer prices to minimize production costs.[27] The government reduced the fertilizer prices in the subsequent months.[28]

Dr Akbar Ali Khan, the former finance adviser to the caretaker government, mentioned that the subsidy and reduction of import duty on essentials would help the government get a grip on the price inflation. He sugggested that, if necessary, the government would have to allocate funds from other sectors of the budget. He also held the view that various initiatives of the government in tackling the price hike including the sealing off of numerous warehouses to prevent illegal hoarding and harassment of business leaders were not appropriate. He advised the government to increase the supply of commodities in the market and, at the same time, enhance its own stockpile and suggested the government import more essentials and undertake a massive essential goods distribution programme for the poor. He suggets that above all, the government would have to put emphasis on food management for overcoming the enduring problem.[29] The caretaker government eventually backtracked from its position to conduct drive against 'corruption' of businessmen, which was alleged to be responsible for disrupting the 'normal' supply chain of essential commodities.

11.5.5 *Newspapers*

The newspapers played some vital roles in publishing key news, information, and analysis during the period under consideration. Newspapers were

[26] Rahman et al. (2008). [27] *The Daily Star*, 15 September 2009.

[28] An article in *The Daily Star* on 23 October 2010 mentioned that the government for the third time in its tenure, to provide incentive to farmers to grow more winter crops, decided to reduce the prices of non-urea fertilizers—muriate of potash (MoP) and diammonium phosphate (DAP)—by 40 and 3 per cent, respectively. This led to the prices of all non-urea fertilizers being reduced by almost half by 14 January 2009. The report, quoting an official at the agriculture ministry, mentioned that the size of the fertilizer subsidy by the government in that fiscal year would be Tk 22,000,000,000.

[29] BBC Sanglap (Discussion), published in *The Daily Star*, 16 September 2009.

the major means for disseminating the government's decisions and policy actions, and the reactions of the stakeholders. A news report on 8 March 2007, for example, revealed that the interim government, in a meeting with high officials of the BB and the armed forces, decided to cut import duties on commodities, ensure increased supply commodities in the market, and ask the joint forces to coordinate their drives targeting the corrupt and dishonest businesses only.[30] The report also mentioned that the BB officials in the meeting drew attention to various negative impacts of the ongoing anti-corruption drives by the joint forces. They observed that the drives panicked genuine traders. The meeting decided to ask the law enforcers to coordinate their drives against hoarding and corrupt businesses and take assistance for the drives from government departments concerned—NBR, Anti-Corruption Commission, and BB. The meeting also decided to intensify import of essentials through the state-run trading agency, TCB, to reduce the prices of essentials.[31]

Another report on 19 March 2007 indicated that the commerce ministry did virtually nothing to control the market during the tenure of the immediate-past government (the government during 2001–5). There were two changes of commerce ministers, reportedly for their failure to exercise enough influence in the market to halt the rise in prices. The report added that the recent unbridled rise in prices was attributed to some factors, which included shortages of essentials in the market, caused by jitters owing to the crackdown by businessmen who refused to import the essentials, leaving the entire supply chain disrupted. The report hailed the CTG as it made a major move to reduce prices of foodstuffs by lifting import duties on rice and wheat and allowing banks to open LCs on liberal terms. The CTG also decided to start an open-market sale of some essentials, and also ordered the opening of the sealed food storages across the country as a way of keeping the supply available in the market. The report suggested the CTG take utmost care so that the benefit of duty concessions could really reach the consumers. The report also called for an effective activation of the TCB. The TCB, established in 1972, was tasked with intervening in the market when the prices of essentials rose. But the immediate past government closed down the TCB in March 2002 with a view to leaving business to the private sector, mostly to its coterie. The report held the view that the TCB, in the past, had played a very vital role in foiling the machinations of the price syndicates and cartels by going into competition with the private sector importers of essentials. The

[30] The anti-corruption drive against the dishonest businessmen by the caretaker government created fear among the business community as a whole which disrupted the 'normal' business practices.

[31] *The Daily Star*, 8 March 2007.

reactivation of TCB was thus urgently required for a let-up in the price spiral. The report added that the government's steps in the recent past, to vend some widely used commodities through the TCB and BDR personnel, brought positive results in containing the price spiral. Such vending should be restarted soon. The report opined that the erratic market behaviour clearly evinced that the syndicates and cartels were still very much active, and were trying to blackmail the CTG. The report mentioned that there was no policy for regulating the storage of foodstuff and other commodities, which led to hoarding. The report suggested the CTG possess effective tools for market intervention, and create a monitoring system that would deter syndicates and cartels from market manipulation.[32]

11.6 The Policy-making Process

The constitution of Bangladesh is at the centre of all public policy-making processes. It provides the required fundamental guidelines for the formulation of public policies, which includes setting the goals, objectives, and strategies of national development. All these categorically emphasize the issue of meeting the basic needs of the people.

In Bangladesh, since independence, there have been several forms of government. In the early years after independence there was a parliamentary form of government, where the prime minister with his cabinet was responsible for taking major policy decisions. The country was run by military dictators for one and a half decades until 1990 when the policy decisions were taken by the military dictators with their chosen set of people from both military and civil bureaucracies. The parliamentary form of government was reinstated in 1991 and until now this system has continued with the exception of 2007 and 2008 when the country was run by an interim government backed by the military.

Under the parliamentary democratic system the cabinet is a small body of senior ministers responsible for directing the policy administration of the state. As per clause 4(ii) of the rules of business 1996, no important policy decision shall be taken except with the approval of the cabinet. In other words, the cabinet is the ultimate authority of approving a policy. It should, however, be mentioned that during 2007 and 2008, since there was no parliament, the interim government did not have any ministers and a formal cabinet. Instead of a prime minster, the government was run by chief advisor of the CTG and there were several advisors in place of the ministers. These

[32] *The Daily Star*, 19 March 2007.

advisors looked after the operations of different ministries. It is understood from discussions with different stakeholders that though there was no formal cabinet, the chief advisor of the CTG used to take advice from some senior advisors and in particular from the chief of army.

As per the constitution of Bangladesh, a minister is in charge of formulating policies and their implementation. The minister is also responsible for conducting the business as well as is accountable for the actions of the ministry in the national parliament. Since there was no parliament during the rule of CTG, the advisors, in charge of different ministries, were not accountable for their actions in any people's forum.

The secretary, a senior bureaucrat, is the official head of a ministry and is responsible for administration and related businesses. The secretary also plays an important role in the policy-making process. During the rule of the CTG, the secretaries in the MoC, MoF, and MOFDM were very active in formulating and executing policies targeted at curbing inflation.

According to the constitution of Bangladesh, the MoF, and the Ministry of Law, Justice, and Parliamentary Affairs play very important roles in both the formulation and approval process of public policy. Clause 13(4) of the Rules of Business clearly sets out that the Finance Ministry should be consulted on all economic and financial questions arising out of any case, particularly in matters of the (a) preparation of export and import policy; (b) negotiation of trade and barter agreement; (c) determination of tariff policy; (d) determination of pricing policy; (e) determination of investment policy; and (f) determination of labour policy. Similarly, consultation with the Ministry of Law, Justice and Parliamentary Affairs is obligatory in matters of (a) all proposals for legislation; (b) all legal questions arising out of any case; (c) preparation of any contracts, international agreements, international conventions, and modifying international law; (d) the interpretation of any law; and (e) before authorizing or the issue of a rule, regulation, or bylaw. Therefore, when the MoC wanted to cut down the duties of the imported food items and to expand the operation of TCB, it had to get the endorsement from the MoF.

National Economic Council (NEC) is the highest political authority for consideration of development activities reflective of long-term national policies and objectives in Bangladesh. It serves as the economic mini-cabinet, consisting of the main economic ministers of the cabinet and headed by the prime minister. The ministries are responsible for adopting their policies, plans, and programmes according to the objectives and priorities set by the NEC. Members of the planning commission and the secretaries in charge of all ministries/divisions are expected to attend its meetings. In addition, other important officials who are required to attend the NEC's meetings include the cabinet secretary and the governor of BB. The Planning Commission is assigned to provide secretarial services to NEC. During the rule of the CTG, the functions of the NEC were limited.

The Planning Commission is the central planning body of the country. It is entrusted to prepare national plans and approve development programmes of the national budget. During the CTG, the planning commission was not involved in preparation of any national plans.

Article 76 of the Constitution provides for the constitution of a number of standing committees composed of the members of the National Parliament. In addition, the parliament also can appoint other standing committees, and a committee so appointed is to examine legislative proposals, or review the enforcement of a law, or investigate or inquire into the activities/administration of a ministry, or any matter of public importance. As mentioned before, in the absence of any parliament during the CTG these standing committees were dysfunctional. However, during the elected government after 2009, many of these standing committees became active in the policy-making process.

It is also important to note the providers of foreign aid play a significant role both in the development and formulation of plans/projects and the management in Bangladesh. Bilateral donors such as the USA, the UK, and India have important stakes in Bangladesh's national policy-making. Multilateral donors such as the World Bank, the IMF, ADB, and the European Union also have significant influence over the policy-making process. On average about 55 to 60 per cent of development expenditure in the national budget is supported by foreign donors and agencies. The donors also play an important role in injecting policy ideas and recommendation of different policy interventions.

11.7 Conclusion

This study has explored the political economy of food price policy in Bangladesh. The analysis suggests that the food price hike during 2007 and 2009 had a profound impact on the welfare of the households in Bangladesh. The then government undertook several measures to contain the overall inflation rate generating mainly from the food inflation. Since the country was then run by an undemocratic, interim, and military-backed government, there was little accountability for its actions. Even under a democratically elected government there was a lack of coordination among different ministries and government institutions. It has also been seen that though the major focus of containing food prices is the MoC, they have very little power and tools in hand to influence the market prices. The power and tools are in the hand of other ministries, such as the finance ministry, though they are not the major focus of such discussion.

References

del Ninno, C., P. A. Dorosh, L. C. Smith, and D. K. Roy (2001). 'The 1998 Floods in Bangladesh: Disaster Impacts, Household Coping Strategies, and Response'. Research Report No. 122: 80–92. Washington, DC: International Food Policy Research Institute.

Dorosh, P. (2009). 'Price Stabilization, International Trade, and National Cereal Stocks: World Price Shocks and Policy Response in South Asia'. *Food Security* (1): 137–49.

Drèze, J., and A. Sen (1989). *Hunger and Public Action*. Oxford: Clarendon Press.

Economic Review (2008). 'Bangladesh Economic Review 2008'. Dhaka: Ministry of Finance, Government of Bangladesh.

Economic Review (2009). 'Bangladesh Economic Review 2009'. Dhaka: Ministry of Finance, Government of Bangladesh.

FPMU (Food Planning and Monitoring Unit) (2008). 'Bangladesh Food Situation Report, October–December, 2008'. Dhaka: Food Planning and Monitoring Unit, Ministry of Food and Disaster Management, Government of Bangladesh.

Rahman, M., D. Bhattacharya, W. B. Sadat, and U. K. Deb (2008). *Recent Inflation in Bangladesh: Trends, Determinants and Impact on Poverty*. Dhaka: Centre for Policy Dialogue.

Raihan, S. (2009). 'Impact of Food Price Rise on School Enrolment and Dropout in the Poor and Vulnerable Households in Selected Areas of Bangladesh'. Dhaka: Department for International Development.

Raihan, S., and K. Fatema (2007). 'A Critical Review of the Current Hypotheses on Inflation in Bangladesh'. *Bangladesh Economic Outlook* 1(1).

Raihan, S., I. Haque, E. Khan, and R. Chowdhury (2008). 'Updating Poverty Estimates in Bangladesh: A Methodological Note'. *Bangladesh Economic Outlook* 1(4): 1–3.

Raihan, S., B. H. Khondker, and H. Uddin (2010). 'Price Monitoring of Selected Commodities in Dhaka City'. A Report prepared for the Ministry of Commerce, Government of Bangladesh.

Wiggins, S., J. Compton, S. Keats, and M. Davies (2010). 'Country Responses to the Food Price Crisis 2007/08: Case Studies from Bangladesh, Nicaragua and Sierra Leone'. London: ODI, http://www.odi.org.uk/publications/5097-country-responses-food-price-crisis-200708-case-studies-bangladesh-nicaragua-sierra-leone>.

World Bank (2008). 'Poverty Assessment for Bangladesh: Creating Opportunities and Bridging the East-West Divide'. Bangladesh Development Series, Paper No. 26. Falls Church, VA: Bangladesh Development Research Centre.

12

The Political Economy of Food Price Policy in Egypt

Ahmed Farouk Ghoneim[*]

12.1 Introduction

This chapter elaborates on the global food crises in the Egyptian context, focusing on the period 2004–9, while highlighting the main features of the period of food crisis of 2006–8 and how it affected the different socioeconomic variables. The chapter's main focus is on the political economy context of the food price policy formulation. The effectiveness of policies adopted is also evaluated, and the chapter touches upon the 25 January 2011 revolution in relationship to food price policy and anticipating future prospects.

The research utilizes a mixture of data analysis and a number of selected interviews with senior government officials and other main stakeholders to try to understand the political economy dynamics of setting the food price policy in Egypt.

12.2 Setting the Scene: An Overview of the Economic and Political Set-ups, Agriculture Sector, and Food Policies

12.2.1 *General Overview*

The government of Egypt (GOE) has extended subsidies, especially in the energy sector, as a means to protect the population against rising living costs.

[*] The research assistance of Asmaa Ezzat, Noura Abdel Wahab, and Heba El Deken is highly acknowledged. The author would like also to thank Per Pinstrup-Andersen, Kenneth Thomas Baltzer, Danielle Resnick, Robert Paarlberg, Finn Tarp, Phil Abbott, and Henrik Hansen for comments on earlier versions of this chapter.

During the period 2001/2–2010/11, subsidies represented more than 20 per cent of total government expenditures. During the period of the study (2004–9) fuel subsidies reached skyrocketing amounts accounting for EGP 70 billion in 2007/8 (the exchange rate is shown in Appendix Table 12.A1) (Ministry of Finance 2011) leading to a sharp increase in the budget deficit. Food subsidies, relatively less in terms of fiscal burden, have also remained a significant element of the subsidy system. The food subsidy system has been suffering from increasing inefficiencies associated with corruption, waste, and lack of right targeting. Piecemeal reforms undertaken to fix it remained incomplete and insufficient to tackle the roots of the system inefficiency.

Poverty in Egypt has remained high and vulnerable to changes in gross domestic product (GDP) growth rates. By February 2009, it was estimated that almost 21 per cent of the population (approximately 13.5 million) was below the national poverty line (EGP 120 per capita per month).[1] According to World Bank (2009), the incidence of poverty decreased between 2004/5 and 2008, whereas the poverty gap and the severity of poverty increased slightly. Moreover, there is a high sectoral concentration of the poor (40 per cent) in agricultural activities, construction, and the informal sector (World Bank 2009). The food subsidy system represents an important pillar in the social safety net and although costly and inefficient, it provided an important indispensable safety net to the poor (Ahmed et al. 2001; Aboulenein et al. 2010).

The political scene in Egypt has remained stagnant over the last twenty years. The remaining of ex-President Mubarak in power for more than thirty years, the revolving of the whole governing regime around him, and the increasing domination of power by the ruling party (the National Democratic Party—NDP) implied that there is a high degree of concentration of power, and little room for real democracy (despite the existence of twenty-four parties before the January 2011 revolution). The domination of power of the NDP was increasing in the last ten years carrying the seeds of the succession procedures of the son of the ex-president and trying to enforce the hegemony of the NDP on both the legislative and local council elections (ECA 2008). The policies committee in the NDP, created in 2006 and headed by the son of the ex-president, dictated policies to the government and influenced all aspects related to economic, social, and political life. The 2010 parliamentarian elections were viewed to be a fraud as the NDP won 81 per cent of the 420 seats (Wikipedia 2011), despite the heavy and significant presence of other political powers, namely the Moslem Brotherhood. Such political turbulences under

[1] World Bank (2009) puts the figure of poor in Egypt at 28 million people in 2005 representing 40 per cent of the population. World Bank (2009) considers 13.6 million (19.6 per cent) in absolute poverty or ultra-poverty (spending less than the minimum to cover their basic food requirements or less than EGP 1,423 per year per capita) and 14.5 million (21 per cent) in near poverty (spending between EGP 1,424 and 1,854 per year per capita).

the surface, accompanied by the increasing level of corruption where Egypt's rank in Transparency International worsened from seventy-second (out of 158 countries) in 2005 to 111th (out of 180 countries) in 2008 (Transparency International 2005, 2008). The feeling of an increased level of poverty and lack of fair income distribution have been among the main reasons that ultimately led to the January 2011 revolution. The fear from social unrest and the desire to push forward with the son of the ex-president as the future president of Egypt implied, at least during the course of our study, that any serious reforms to the food subsidy system (e.g., by better targeting, or reduction) could not be undertaken. Food subsidy has remained extremely important for enhancing political stability in Egypt constituting a powerful symbol for the social contract between the population and any governing regime (Ahmed et al. 2001).

12.2.2 *The Agricultural Sector and its Role in the Egyptian Economy*

Agriculture contributes around 15 per cent of GDP and provides 27 per cent of employment. However, the agriculture sector is not likely to generate sizeable additional employment due to limited land and traditional methods of production (Abou-Ali and Kheir-El-Din 2010). Nevertheless, enhancing growth in the agriculture sector has an important role to play in poverty reduction due to the concentration of poor in this sector (El-Ehwany and El-Megharbel 2008).

Egypt remains highly vulnerable to international food price risk as it relies on food imports for around 50 per cent of domestic consumption and food accounts for more than 15 per cent of all imports (Aboulenein et al. 2010). Among the important crops for Egypt are wheat, rice, and maize (their importance arises from playing a paramount role in the diet of Egyptian consumers as well as their economic aspects (e.g., significant impact on government budget, exports' proceeds, etc.)).

12.2.3 *Short Historical Review of Food Price Policies*

The history of the Egyptian food subsidy programme dates back to the mid-1940s when the first programme was initiated to provide everyone (not just target groups) with necessities such as sugar, kerosene, edible oil, and tea. Since then, the food subsidy system has passed through several changes and remained an integral element of the Egyptian political, social, and economic systems. During Nasser's regime, budget allocations for food subsidies were modest, and the ration card system aimed at protecting all Egyptians, without targeting, from commodity shortages. The system grew during Sadat's era where more commodities were introduced to the subsidy system reaching eighteen products. The budget allocations for the food subsidy programme increased significantly, and its share in government expenditure soared in the 1970s. In an effort to reduce expenditures, the GOE, following the recommendations of the International Monetary Fund and the World Bank, announced a drastic reduction in food subsidies, including the *baladi* bread subsidy, in January 1977. This measure resulted in massive popular riots, and as a result the measure was reversed. By 1980/1, total expenditures on food subsidies jumped to 14 per cent of total government expenditures, compared to only 0.2 per cent in 1970/1. During Mubarak's era several reforms were undertaken, while avoiding any type of political or social unrest similar to the one that took place in 1977 (Ahmed et al. 2001). The reforms included the reduction of the number of commodities on ration cards, introduction of two tier ration card systems (fully subsidized, and partially subsidized), as well as other reforms which continued until the time of the crisis (World Bank 2010). However, reforms remained of piecemeal nature and were never able to tackle the roots of inefficiency. As put by the World Food Programme (WFP) (2008b: 7), 'It is therefore important to understand that the subsidy system represents a core feature of the entire economy and that removing one element of it can create a very dangerous domino effect, politically, socially and economically'. Moreover, the nutrition aspects of the food policies have not been explicitly considered even though malnutrition was widespread with 26.7 per cent of children suffering from stunting and 10 per cent suffering from wasting in 2007 (WFP 2008a).

The procurement policy is also one of the main policies adopted by the government to preserve food security and reduce vulnerability to food price fluctuations. In fact, the government has been the largest buyer of wheat (around 30 per cent of wheat production) and hence the price it sets is a leading price for other buyers. The General Agency for the Supply of Commodities (GASC), affiliated to the Ministry of Social Solidarity, is the key body in the procurement process. Yet, such practice has suffered from corruption. It was found that influential people (e.g., the secretary of the ex-president) had their private companies engaged in such tenders and was involved in manipulating prices of imported wheat.[2] The government does not only subsidize food commodities, but also production inputs such as irrigation water, which is provided free of charge and subsidized or price controlled fertilizers (mainly through subsidizing energy requirements for public factories producing them, and ensuring that they sell them at certain prices). The government provides each farmer with a certain entitlement of subsidized fertilizers, which in turn has affected positively the agricultural output and sustained

[2] See *Youm El Sabia* (newspaper), 12 February 2012.

the living of many poor farmers who own small plots of land (WFP 2008b). The subsidized fertilizer scheme has always been suffering from problems associated with distribution bottlenecks, lack of sufficient fertilizer entitlements to farmers, and selling in the black market.

Around 20 per cent of the Egyptian population in urban areas and 24 per cent in rural areas are food insecure (WFP 2011). Following the latest available household budget survey of 2008/9 it was found that the budget share for food is around 53 per cent for the lowest decile and 33 per cent for the richest decile, with an average of 44 per cent. This corresponds to a 40 per cent weight allocated to food in the consumer price index (CPI).

12.3 Food Price Trends (2004–11)

The relationship between food domestic prices and international prices is shown in Figure 12.1. The spikes (downturns) in domestic prices are preceded by significant increases (decreases) in international prices. The correlation is relatively high (correlation coefficient is equal to 0.83) with the international prices being higher than domestic prices. Moreover, the extent of decrease in prices following international price reductions is low. At the domestic level, food inflation increased by 47 per cent between 2005 and 2008 whereas the overall CPI increased by 31 per cent (IAAM1 2009). The extent of integration with the world market prices remains evident although not very strong (Figure 12.2).

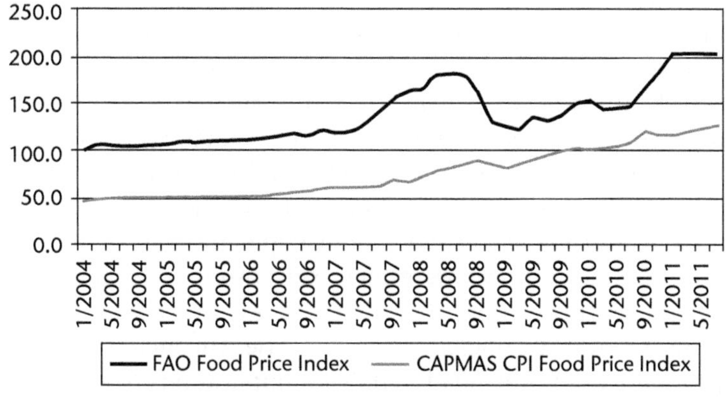

Figure 12.1 Food inflation in domestic and international markets

Notes and source: FAO food price index data is available at: <http://www.fao.org/worldfoodsituation/wfs-home/foodpricesindex/en/>, while CAPMAS CPI Index data is calculated by the author from CAPMAS disaggregated CPI data. Data available at: <www.capmas.gov.eg>.

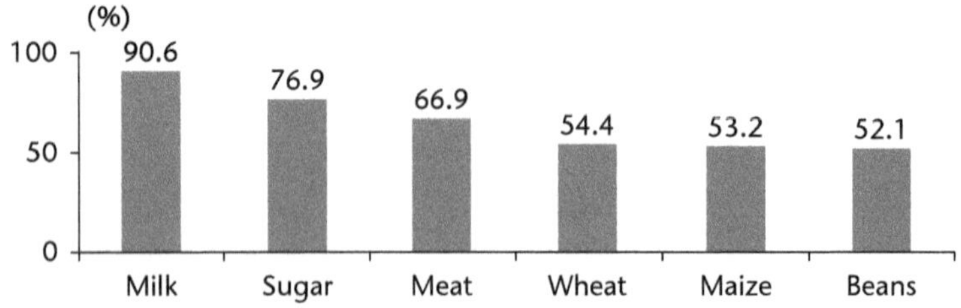

Figure 12.2 Increase in Egypt's food import prices (percentage change, over the period July 2006–June 2008)
Source: Abouelenien et al. (2010).

Yet, domestic price changes are not caused solely by changes in international prices as there are other factors that have contributed to the change of prices in the domestic market. The existence of highly concentrated markets with anti-competitive behaviour prevailing in some markets could have resulted in higher prices at the domestic level. The fact that the pass-through effect is evident in the upturns of prices but less evident in the downturns (Figure 12.3) suggests the prevalence of anti-competitive behaviour[3] (for a similar argument, see McCorriston 2011). The heavily subsidized system for a large number of food crops (due to government monopoly in their supply chain) forced the retailers and wholesalers to operate mainly in non-subsidized food products such as vegetables and fruits, and the fragmented nature of the local markets implied significant differences in price levels. Moreover, the subsidized inputs (e.g., irrigation water and fertilizers), as well as subsidizing a wide array of food products, have also affected the price of food staples in the domestic markets sometimes positively by lowering prices of final products and sometimes negatively where inefficiency in the system caused supply bottlenecks and created black markets. Hence, there are two opposing forces, one which contributes to price increases on the domestic level including the fragmented markets and anti-competitive behaviour, and one that could have helped to lower prices such as subsidies for food staples, water, and fertilizers. These forces have contributed to a lower price transmission between international and domestic prices. There is a correlation between international and domestic prices, however not *very* strong. For example, in the case of rice, during the crisis while world prices were increasing (April 2008) domestic prices were decreasing. This was not the case for wheat where international price increase was followed by domestic price increase. The increase in food prices in the aftermath of the crisis had significant implications. The risk of *extreme*

[3] For example, the Minister of Social Solidarity announced in September 2011 that trade in a number of food products including rice and oil has been controlled by a handful of traders. This has also been confirmed by interviews with senior government officials.

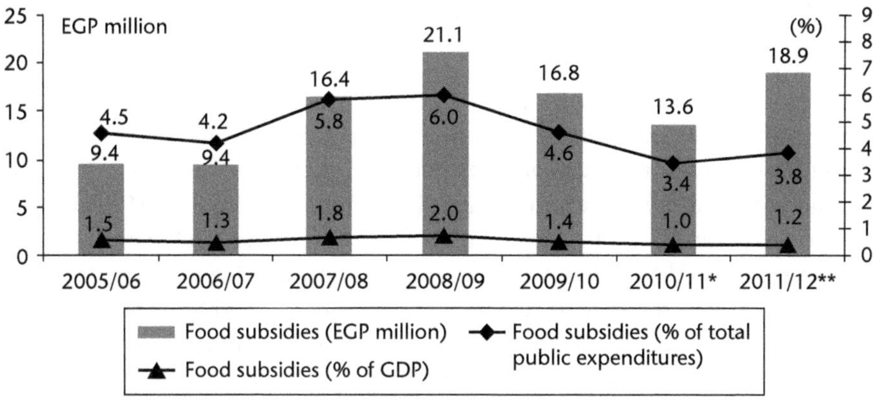

Figure 12.3 Food subsidies in Egypt during the period 2005/6–2011/12

Note: *Preliminary,**budget.

Source: Ministry of Finance (2010), Monthly Statistical Bulletin, Section Four, Fiscal Sector, October, available at: <http://www.mof.gov.eg/English/publications/Reports%20and%20Indicators/Pages/TheFinancialMonthly-October2010.aspx>.

poverty (inability to meet basic food needs) increased by almost 20 per cent in February 2008 and affected about 6 per cent of the population in Egypt (World Bank 2009), hence emphasizing the importance of food prices and their crucial importance in affecting the level of poverty in the country. As evidence of the significance of increased food prices, there has been a limited scale of protests in the aftermath of the crisis, yet with some severe injuries and fatalities (*BBC News* 2008).

To sum up, the pass-through effect is difficult to measure due to the existence of several variables that could have affected the domestic price level. This is in line with other studies. World Bank (2011b) estimated a pass-through coefficient of 0.4, and Al-Shawarby and Selim (2012) identified that the pass-through effect is between 12 and 36 per cent. Moreover, and as argued by Abbott (2009) the policy measures adopted by any government could break the link between international and domestic prices which has been the case for Egypt where the wide use of price controls, kind subsidy, and other policy measures have relatively shielded the Egyptian consumer from a full pass-through effect (UNDP 2008).

12.4 Policy Responses to the Crisis

We classify the policy responses undertaken by the GOE into five types including (a) agriculture production policies; (b) trade policies; (c) safety nets; (d) procurement and stocking policies; and (e) other policies e.g., monetary and fiscal policies.

12.4.1 *Agricultural Production Policies*

The government adopted strict monitoring of land cultivated rice. The government set a maximum area of 1.2 million feddan (480,000 hectares (ha)) where production of rice requires a permission from the Ministry of Water Resources and Irrigation, however, in practice, before the crisis, the area actually cultivated reached 2.2 million feddan (0.92 ha). After the crisis the cultivated area of rice was reduced by 18 per cent between 2009–10 as farmers shifted to other crops due to the ban on rice exports, and the enforcement of a regulation setting a certain quota of water for rice farms. Domestic prices decreased when the government first interfered by restricting exports, at the time when international prices were increasing, but soon started to reverse trend and increase, and in some cases the rate was higher than the rate of increase in international prices. As explained by WFP (2008b), this was mainly due to traders holding stocks, which happened in October 2008 when international prices started to decrease, anticipating that prices would rise again and hence they could profit more by restricting supply.

12.4.2 *Trade Policies*

Two main trade policies were adopted by the government to deal with the crisis: an export tax followed by an export ban on rice and tariff reductions.

In the case of rice, several decrees by the Minister of Trade and Industry were issued by the end of 2006 and during 2007 and 2008 to impose export taxes (levies). The aim of export taxes was to shield the local market from the soaring world prices, and to reduce the costs incurred by GASC when purchasing rice. When such export taxes proved to be ineffective as they were circumvented by traders, a ban was imposed in April 2008. In fact, prices in the domestic market decreased after the rice export ban and then tended to rise again. The reason was that traders decided to store rice until the export ban ended and then export what they had stored at the international prices which at that time were almost double the domestic price even after the imposition of the export ban (*Al Ahram* (newspaper) of 2 June 2008; Ghoneim 2008). In 2009 the decision to ban export of rice was relaxed on the condition that an equivalent amount of rice was provided by rice exporters to GASC. Such a system was manipulated by rice exporters, and hence the government introduced a heavy export levy and then a licence auction system for exporters depending on the type of rice. Finally the system of licence auctioning was abandoned in 2011 and a ban was imposed again until October 2012. Up until 2012 the ban was not lifted as the harvest of rice that was supplied to GASC through the Principal Bank for Development of Agricultural Credit

(PBDAC) was not enough to cover the needs of the food subsidy programme in 2011.

The export ban had negative repercussions on the production and trade of rice since many large private rice mills have specialized in the production of export quality rice, and could not profitably switch to the milling of local rice. Traders also reduced their supply and held large inventories to keep domestic prices high (WFP 2008b). The continuation of imposing such an export ban reduced the incentive for producing rice.

The government abolished import tariffs in April 2008 on a number of food items including soybean oil, cheese, rice, milk for infants, and milk substitutes, and reduced it to 5 per cent on butter and dairy products. Yet such reductions did not have a significant impact due to its low marginal effect having started from an initially low tariff.

12.4.3 *Safety Nets*

The social safety net schemes ranged from bread subsidies, to ration cards, to school feeding programmes, to cash transfers, to other community support type of schemes. The crisis resulted in an increase in government allocations of food subsidies entitlements for bread and ration cards; the widening of beneficiaries from ration cards; and increase in cash transfers and governmental wages and salaries.

The government allocations for food subsidies increased dramatically in 2007–8 (Figure 12.3) whether in absolute terms or as percentage of total public expenditure or GDP.

Beginning in 2004 several reforms of the ration cards were undertaken to reduce fiscal costs. A massive revision to the ration card system was undertaken in light of the food crisis in January 2008, where additional allocations were provided to overcome the negative impact of the food crisis (a significant retreat from the reforms that started in 2004).

Subsidies allocated to ration cards do not constitute more than 25 per cent of food subsidies entitlements (including sugar, rice, and edible oil) and less than 4 per cent of total subsidies provided (ECES 2010). From a food price policy perspective, an increase of the commodity basket for subsidized food and additional beneficiary registration have effectively shielded poor households from the impact of rising international food prices (World Bank 2010). Yet, the system suffers from massive leakages. The poorest quintile gets less than its proportional share in subsidized products, with the exception of wheat (Table 12.1). The system of subsidized food has been inefficient in terms of targeting the rural poor. For example, as put by WFP (2010), 33 per cent of subsidized *baladi* bread is distributed to low expenditure rural households as compared to 31 per cent to middle and 36 per cent to high

Table 12.1 Distribution of total benefits across quintiles, 2008/9

	Per capita expenditure quintile (%)				
	1 (poorest)	2	3	4	5 (richest)
Subsidies for:					
Baladi bread	16.69	18.30	19.93	22.31	22.77
Rice	17.08	19.66	20.49	21.10	21.67
Wheat	39.02	25.83	16.64	11.81	6.70
Oil	15.99	18.75	20.40	22.15	22.70
Sugar	18.26	19.72	20.65	21.15	20.22
All subsidies	18.66	19.29	19.85	21.19	21.02

Source: Aboulenein et al. (2010).

expenditure households. Similarly, only 28 per cent of the ration card commodities are allocated to low-expenditure rural households compared to around 31 per cent allocated to middle expenditure and around 41 per cent allocated to high expenditure households (WFP 2010). WFP (2008a) found also that 15–20 per cent of the poor do not benefit from the existing system. World Bank (2010) found that in 2008/9 Cairo and other metropolitan governorates received about 38 per cent of bread subsidies, while their share of the poor population was only 14 per cent. Adding to that corruption associated with the value chain of bread production and distribution has been a major concern.

There are several other reasons for the inefficiency of the food subsidy system including the lack of cash among the poor which implied that not all the commodities considered in the ration cards are bought. Moreover, as mentioned above, the system suffers from weak targeting and lack of coverage where a substantial number (no exact figures available) for poor and vulnerable groups to food insecurity do not possess ration cards due to their inability to obtain the necessary documents to obtain such government assistance. According to El Laithy and Armanios (2011) and following the system adopted by the Ministry of Social Solidarity in identifying the poor who deserve the ration card, 23 per cent of the people who deserve to hold the ration card according to the criteria set by the Ministry of Social Solidarity do not have one, whereas 64 per cent of the people who do not deserve it have a ration card. World Bank (2010) argues that around 28 per cent of food subsidies (EGP 5.5 billion) in 2008/9 did not reach intended consumers, with *baladi* bread accounting for 68 per cent (EGP 3.7 billion) of the leakage and cooking oil for 20 per cent (EGP 1.1 billion). Table 12.1 shows that the richest quintiles benefit more from subsidies when compared to the poorest quintiles. Finally, the inefficiency of logistics in terms of transport, storage, and handling has been considered a major culprit accused of leakages and waste. It was estimated that between 15–35 per cent of wheat and grain losses are associated with inefficient logistics, and the estimates were even higher as put by the government reaching 70 per cent for some perishable products.

The government introduced a new type of 'smart cards' in 2008. Those cards contain data on the household head's monthly quota of subsidized goods. The new cards allow the government to trace the distribution and consumption of subsidized goods by recording transactions electronically. By December 2010 smart cards replaced paper cards all over Egypt (World Bank 2010; UNDP and MOED 2010).

While school feeding programmes and other social assistance programmes did not experience any significant change in response to the food crisis, cash transfers and governmental and public sector wages did. Regarding cash transfers, the number of beneficiaries[4] of social pension schemes has increased from 650,000 beneficiaries in 2005 to one million beneficiaries in 2007 and its value doubled. Moreover the value of the cash transfers provided to families as an education grant increased in 2008. In addition, and as a reaction to the food crisis, and specifically in 2008 the annual increase in salary of public sector employees was 30 per cent, compared to a usual 10 per cent increase in previous years.

12.4.4 *Procurement and Stocking Policies*

The wheat price GASC used to offer to farmers was less than that offered by private traders. However in 2008 it increased the price over that offered by private traders. This policy has helped to increase the prices of wheat produced domestically. However, many of the farmers still preferred to sell to local traders for three main reasons. The first reason is that private traders collect wheat at the farms whilst in the case of GASC farmers are required to deliver it to the mills. Adding to that the absence of nearby places for collection from farmers set by PBDAC had lowered the positive impact of the announced policy. The second reason is related to the cheap loans for production provided by traders (WFP 2008b). In October 2008 wheat prices started to fall rapidly in the world market. The third reason is related to the delay in announcing the purchasing price by the government which always took place during the harvest or growing seasons, and not before the planting season. The stocking policy did not change in light of the crisis, due to the limited availability of silos used for wheat storage. Yet the government began building new silos in 2010 to allow it to handle more volumes of stored wheat.

[4] Ministry of Social Affairs programmes available at: <http://www.mss.gov.eg>.

12.4.5 *Other Related Policies*

To overcome the leakage problem of wheat bran which is highly associated with corruption (where the bakeries sell their assigned quotas of subsidized flour from the government in the black market), the government adopted a new system of separating production of the subsidized bread from its distribution. It established a new company to distribute *baladi* bread in greater Cairo, while in other governorates home delivery for *baladi* bread is done by NGOs (WFP 2010). The monetary policy was geared to achieve food policy objectives. In light of the food crisis and its negative impact on the balance of payments, devaluation could have taken place to restore the balance of payments. However, the fear from inflationary pressures, which were already significant at that time, made the Central Bank reluctant to undertake any devaluation. The fiscal policy was adjusted to count for the increase in allocations of food subsidies and increase in wages and salaries, where the sources of financing such outlets were financed through reduction of some energy subsidies, increase of taxes on cigarettes, seizing tax exemptions on energy intensive industries in free zones, etc. (Kandil 2010).

Finally, the government during the crisis has asked for the military to help with distribution, while at the same time increasing the capacity of bakeries managed by the military (but owned by the government) to face the increasing demand on bread.

12.5 Political Economy Dynamics of Food Policy in Light of the Food Crisis

The key stakeholder groups include governmental institutions, particularly the Ministry of Social Solidarity, but also the Ministry of Agriculture and Land Reclamation, Ministry of Trade and Industry, Ministry of Irrigation and Water Resources, Ministry of Health, and Ministry of Finance.

The Ministry of Social Solidarity was the main responsible governmental body during the food crisis responsible for handling food subsidies as it oversaw the ration card system, *baladi* bread subsidy, cash transfers and other consumer subsidy programmes, other than the fuel subsidy (with the exception of liquefied gas cylinders which fell under its mandate). The Ministry of Agriculture and Land Reclamation played an important role in handling the policy of fertilizer subsidy, together with PBDAC which is affiliated with the Ministry. The Ministry of Irrigation and Water Resources played an important role regarding some crops such as rice where it sets the quota of water per cultivated area as well as other irrigation-related rules and regulations. The Ministry of Trade and Industry influences inputs' prices as fertilizers when sold from public firms to the farmers, and finally the Ministry of Finance has an important role in determining the amount of subsidies allocated in the budget whether to consumers or producers. The interaction between such ministries, the level of coordination, and the political influence of their ministers has played a paramount role in formulating and implementing food policy.

The other stakeholders include public companies, cooperatives, and export commodity councils. Several holding companies and public companies exist which play an important role in the production of fertilizers and chemicals, and in commodity trade and storage. The cases of the shortage of fertilizers produced by the public firms and the quota system where every farmer is assigned a limited amount of subsidized fertilizers prove the inefficiency of the system as it led to black market and smuggling. Wheat and maize procurement, as well as fertilizers and certified seeds provision, are functions that cooperatives (semi-governmental institutions) play an important role in and can play an effective role in overcoming the related marketing distribution problems. Such organizations represent the link between the Egyptian farmers and government policies. Finally, so-called export commodity councils are semi-governmental entities financed mainly by exporters and their secretariats and are hosted by the Ministry of Trade and Industry. There are eighteen export commodity councils. One is for agricultural crops and another for processed food products. The members of those commodity councils are major exporters and representatives of small and medium exporters of the products. Among the other stakeholders associated with food policy are many think tanks and research institutions (Handoussa et al. 2009). Among the most important research institutions is the Egyptian Food Security Information Centre which was established in 2007 with the support of Food and Agriculture Organization (FAO) and WFP, and has been affiliated with the Ministry of Agriculture and Land Reclamation. The coordination committee of the Food Safety Information Center consists of representatives from several related ministries and agencies, with involvement of related donors.[5] Also among the important research bodies dealing with food security is the Information and Decision Support Centre of the cabinet (IDSC).[6] IDSC established the Egyptian Food Observatory which provides tools for monitoring and evaluating the situation of main agricultural crops and food commodities. In addition, the Observatory develops early warning tools which predict future food crises whether they are triggered domestically or internationally. Food security information is also collected by the Ministry of Social Solidarity.

[5] http://www.efsic.com/index.html.

[6] The IDSC is an influential research institute as it feeds data to the cabinet, and accordingly helps in shaping the decision-making process.

The ministry has been using Geographic Information System to create vulnerability maps with WFP support. These maps are focused on vulnerability to food insecurity, where wheat quota allocated to bakeries, bakeries locations, as well as population relative distribution to the village level are mapped in several layers, which provides useful information (Handoussa et al. 2009).

There is also a series of international food-related organizations dealing with food policy that operate in Egypt. The most important of these are the WFP, and FAO, in addition to bilateral and multi-lateral donors such as World Bank, United Nations Development Programme (UNDP), World Health Organization (WHO), the International Fund for Agricultural Development (IFAD), United Nations Population Fund (UNFPA), and others (Handoussa et al. 2009). The role of the think tanks and international organizations in influencing food policy has remained substantial yet not always recognized. Different ministries have depended mainly on the studies undertaken by such organizations in drawing policy and initiating reforms.

Finally, several local and international NGOs play an important role, though not highly publicized, in addressing issues of food security and providing help to farmers (Handoussa et al. 2009). Food policy has gained increased importance in Egyptian policy-making circles in the last fifteen years for several socioeconomic and political reasons. Although the governing regime was dominated by one person backed by the NDP, opposing parties represented a real threat. Other important reasons forcing the governing regime to pay greater attention to food policy include the change of the process of choosing the president from national referendum to open elections in 2005 (Transparency International 2009) and the desire of the ruling regime for succession of the son of the president to his father. Hence, reforms were always postponed. The sensitivity of the food subsidies and the alarming signals of long bread queues in streets (associated with violence) did not leave any room for the GOE to reduce the subsidy allocations. In other words, the fear of the governing regime from the political and social consequences of any substantial reform made it always prefer status quo, while undertaking small adjustments that in fact added to the fiscal burden and dealt with the occasional symptoms of the food price policy problems, but never tackled the roots.

As for the role of cooperatives, their role has been disappointing for several reasons including the lack of appointed employees by the governments, the lack of awareness among the farmers involved in its functioning, corruption, existence of black markets (employees in some cases insist on selling additional fertilizers for farmers in order to allow them to obtain their entitlements of modestly priced fertilizers),[7] and the extremely insufficient

[7] *Al Ahram* (newspaper), 19 December 2011.

capital needed to allow such cooperatives to function properly. During the period of study (2004–9) the private sector was very influential in affecting policy-making. Nevertheless, favouritism was highly evident in the selection of donors' projects that serve the interests of the private sector (with little attention for its impact on consumers) as well as the lack of enforcement of competition law. Favouritism was also evident where a number of wheat flour mills were owned by members of the parliament. Moreover, influential people (e.g., the secretary of the ex-president) owned private firms which handled the importation of wheat. There was a clear conflict of interest where members of the legislative and/or executive bodies also acted as traders.

International organizations have been influential in shaping the food policy by identifying the main problems and suggesting policies to solve them; and exerting pressure to tackle neglected issues such as the nutritional dimension. The implementation of their recommendations in many cases is undertaken, yet not with the speed expected (due to bureaucracy and slow reactions by the government). Think tanks and research institutions have also been playing an important role in affecting food policy in Egypt.

The media's role has been significant during the food crisis in two respects; namely, intensifying the pressure on the government to take fast action; and pinpointing the corruption cases, especially in terms of smuggling wheat flour. The media has always echoed the voices of the urban population more than the rural population. Also the military's role has been evident during the crisis where it has utilized the massive production capacity of the bakeries managed by it to increase its bread production, as well as helping in overcoming distribution bottlenecks. It has been evident that the military was able to handle the crisis. Despite such significant efforts to address food security, a coordinated approach remained lacking which is attributed mainly to the lack of political will to drive the reforms. During the crisis, some institutional set-ups for enhancing coordination emerged including ministerial committees, but the political will remained absent.

The fragile institutional set-up governing domestic trade with no competition law until 2005, and ineffective implementation after that year, implied that anti-competitive behaviour prevailed. The importance of food subsidies arises also from strengthening the Egyptian capability of meeting the Millennium Development Goals, especially those related to poverty and hunger reduction. Relevant food subsidy programmes, if expanded on an efficient basis, can help to achieve such goals (UNDP and MOED 2010). This was reflected in the January 2011 revolution where among its main causes and slogans was achieving social equity and overcoming the proliferated corruption. The establishment of the food security policy advisory board in 2010, affiliated to the Ministry of Agriculture, with the aim of developing a strategy for food security, which includes senior representatives of the ministries involved in food policy and other related domestic and international organizations including FAO and WFP, helped to improve the coordination process. The policy advisory board depends on old data for analysis which throws doubt on its ability to draw the right strategy. However, such a board, despite all such negative aspects, still remains a positive step in the coordination process. In addition, the prime minister issued a decree for forming a ministerial committee to deal with food policy in 2007. The Social Solidarity Minister and the Agriculture Minister were on one side whereas the Finance Minister and the Trade and Industry Minister were on another side, which was felt during the crisis when the Social Solidarity and Agriculture Ministers were asking for increasing subsidies' allocation and imposing a ban on rice exports whereas the Finance and Trade and Industry Ministers were against such demands. Contradictory objectives have been evident and in many cases the overriding concern of the negative effects of the food crisis led to the surrender of the Finance and Trade and Industry Ministers. An incident of conflict was also raised where it was found that rice production in 2012 exceeded the domestic market requirements, and hence there was a suggestion to allow exports based on certain conditions. However, such a proposal by the Ministry of Trade and Industry was not highly welcome by Ministry of Irrigation and Water Supply, implying that conflicts of interests prevail, where in many cases the national interest remains missing. Yet, during the food crisis, no conflict arose (despite strong negotiations between different ministries for increasing food subsidies versus reducing budget outlays and enhancing exports), maybe due to the overriding political importance of the issue at that time. Also the governing regime had to respond in a faster way to urban consumers, which gave the (false) impression of urban consumers being prioritized in the agenda of the government. This has not been the case in reality. However, the relatively stronger bargaining power of urban consumers who can arrange protests, access media channels, and exert pressures on parliament members in a more efficient way when compared to rural producers and consumers, made their voice heard loudly when compared to rural consumers.

The food crisis resulted in food price policy affecting several other policies (agriculture, irrigation, fiscal, monetary, and trade). In the case of agriculture policy, the crisis did not result in conflicting objectives or measures. In fact the decision to ban rice exports was imposed after the crisis coincided with the agricultural and irrigation policies which have for a long while set a limit on the land that can be rice cultivated, yet was not strictly enforced. In other words, at the national level the social and political concerns coincided with the interest of the Ministry of Agriculture. Moreover, the desire to increase self-sufficiency from wheat, which intensified during the crisis, has always been one of the main national goals. Food policy and agricultural as well as irrigation policies might have different objectives, yet they were rarely contradictory. For example, even in the case of the rice planted area which had to be reduced in the aftermath of the food crisis, such reduction did not affect the food security aspect, due to the over-supply of rice, and it helped to serve the irrigation policy due to the nature of rice being a heavy consumer of water, which is already scarce in Egypt. However, this has not been the case with other policies such as fiscal and trade policies. In the case of fiscal policy, the food crisis and the widening of coverage of the ration card system to a larger number of households as well as maintaining the *baladi* bread price implied additional fiscal burden which has been reflected in the allocations of food subsidies in the years 2007 and 2008 that increased dramatically as aforementioned. Such a trend is likely to continue after the revolution where social aspects including achieving social equity remain among the most important indispensable objectives. This has been reflected in the budget set after the revolution for 2011/12 where food subsidies remained high at EGP 18.9 billion compared to EGP 13.6 billion in the 2010/11 budget for food subsidies and to EGP 14.1 billion for food subsidies in the 2009/10 budget (Ministry of Finance 2011). Moreover, the reduction of tariffs on food staples in the light of the food crisis affected negatively the tariff revenues, though in an insignificant manner due to the low tariffs imposed on food products and the wide array of free trade area agreements that Egypt is engaged in. The possibility of lessening the fiscal burden of food policy in the aftermath of the January 2011 revolution is not likely to take place through reduction of subsidies by any means, even though the economy is in bad shape and the government has announced austerity measures where real GDP growth rate has been extremely modest after the revolution.

12.6 Conclusion and Policy Implications

The government's response to the crisis is deeply embedded in the country's socioeconomic context. The importance of quick actions undertaken to make the bread available and control its price was evident. The responses to the food crisis have certainly lessened the crisis' negative social effect on the majority of the population. But this has been costly as exemplified by the increasing outlays for social safety nets. The core of government reactions focused mainly on bread availability and prices, which is by nature the central theme of the food subsidy system in Egypt. Other policies were enacted including the change of the commodity mix in the ration card system while increasing the number of beneficiaries. Moreover, cash transfers and wages of government and public sector employees were increased as were pension holders' transfers. Given the high correlation between food prices and the level of poverty in Egypt—Egyptians spend on average 44 per cent of their income on food and the poorest spend on average 53 per cent—the poor in Egypt are vulnerable to any increase in food prices. Trade policies were changed including the reduction of import tariffs on a number of commodities and the imposition of the export ban on rice. These trade policies, particularly the rice export ban might have helped to solve the bread problem by keeping domestic rice prices lower than they would otherwise have been. Yet, such policies affected negatively export prospects of rice and the price of rice was kept stable and below the international price level. The high fiscal cost and the strong demand for social services raise concerns about the sustainability of such policies and whether from a macroeconomic perspective the current and future governments are able to carry on with the burden of such policies. The relatively small amount of subsidies allocated to food when compared to fuel subsidies could imply that the burden of food subsidies is expected to be contained by the government for a while, especially that the focus of the current regime after the revolution and the future regimes will be on achieving social equity and lessening poverty. However, hard budget constraints could also imply a need for reform, at least to prevent leakage and attain better targeting on income and geographical levels.

The political economy of food policy in Egypt has proven to be highly complex. The negative social and political repercussions that can arise from any serious economic reforms implied a preference of the political leadership for the status quo. The interaction of poverty aspects with food security dimensions and the high vulnerability of a relatively large portion of the population to fall into the poverty trap if food prices increase added to the difficulty of undertaking any reforms. Lack of sincere political will, weak coordination among different stakeholders, proliferation of corruption, inefficient pricing system, modest logistics, and heavily distorted market because of the subsidy system all implied more difficulties for reforming the food security system.

A policy towards reducing the waste and leakages resulting from production and distribution inefficiencies is highly needed. This can be achieved by reforming the pricing system and improving the logistics. The government should also start applying hedging for the strategic commodities, which is in fact applied by some of the large private corporations importing directly in Egypt by taking the necessary monetary measures in case of exchange price change. The institutional set-up (laws and regulations) is not conducive to including this type of activity, implying the need for an institutional reform. Changing the mix of commodities considered on the ration cards can help to avoid problems associated with obesity and improve the nutritional requirements (WFP 2011). Yet, there is also a need to simplify the registration process to make the system more effective in terms of reaching the needy people.

Diversification of main suppliers of wheat by relying on other main producers, besides Russia, can help in securing wheat procurement from other countries such as the Netherlands, from which Egypt should increase its wheat imports. However, GASC remained constrained by its organizing law that does not allow it to trade in futures, and hence it has to buy wheat on the spot market (where delivery takes place within two months from the date of purchase). Reducing leakages and shortcomings of the subsidy system cannot be attained by substituting cash transfers for in-kind transfers due to the absence of a full database of poor people, and fear from induced inflation (WFP 2008a, 2010). In order to pursue better coordination, a supreme council of food policy security should be established. It should not be under a specific ministry, and should have overriding power over related ministries and agencies. It could be headed by the prime minister or his deputy and should meet on a frequent basis. It should be guided by a serious political leadership providing it with clear signals on directions of reform.

Finally, announcing purchasing prices by the government of major commodities such as maize and wheat has always been problematic. For example, regarding maize, the Ministry of Agriculture and Land Reclamation has tried to encourage maize production by expanding its cultivated area through announcing a purchasing price set prior to the plantation time only in 2010 and set on a par with the price of rice (the competing crop). Yet, such policy suffered from similar drawbacks to those associated with wheat where farmers still preferred to sell to the private sector and not the government due to transport facilities offered by the private sector and avoiding problems associated with PBDAC. Hence, the change of maize policy can be considered a long-term policy in light of the crisis that was enacted after a relatively long while.

The features of the Egyptian political system after the 25 January 2011 revolution are still unclear. There has been a rising trend of new parties which represent all ideological backgrounds, and the NDP was dissolved. The role of Islamic-oriented parties, and especially the Moslem Brotherhood affiliated party, has been evident. Yet, and concerning the focus of this chapter, it is clear that all parties are refusing the adoption of the free market economy policies as has been the case in the previous era where free market policies were adopted without establishment of the right institutions that monitor anti-competitive behaviour and conflict of interest. Reviving the role of the government in achieving social equality and reaching better income distribution is widely discussed, yet without a clear strategy still announced. Despite the fact that the government as well as the existing parties emphasize such aspects, it is still not clear how the modalities and polices needed to achieve such goals will be designed and adopted. One of the main issues that has been raised lately has been the subsidy system and the need to reform it. More emphasis has been put on energy subsidies, but less emphasis has been devoted to the issue of food subsidy reform. What is clear is that any political system that will evolve will pay considerable attention to social aspects including equity and income distribution, while creating the right institutions that avoid conflict of interest and fight corruption.

Appendix Table 12.A1 Exchange rate between the EGP and US$, 1985–2010

Year	Official exchange rate (EGP per US$, period average)	Year	Official exchange rate (EGP per US$, period average)
1980	0.70	1996	3.39
1981	0.70	1997	3.39
1982	0.70	1998	3.39
1983	0.70	1999	3.40
1984	0.70	2000	3.47
1985	0.70	2001	3.97
1986	0.70	2002	4.50
1987	0.70	2003	5.85
1988	0.70	2004	6.20
1989	0.87	2005	5.78
1990	1.55	2006	5.73
1991	3.14	2007	5.64
1992	3.32	2008	5.43
1993	3.35	2009	5.54
1994	3.39	2010	5.62
1995	3.39	2011*	5.93

Notes: *Average for the period (Jan 2011–Nov 2011).

Source: Ministry of Finance (2011), Monthly Statistical Bulletin, December 2011. Available at: <http://www.mof.gov.eg/MOFGallerySource/Arabic/Reportes/2011/12/allparts.pdf>; World Bank (2011a).

References

Abbott, P. (2009). 'Development Dimensions of High Food Prices'. Food, Agriculture and Fisheries Working Paper No. 18. Paris: OECD Publishing.

Abou-Ali, H., and H. Kheir-El-Din (2010). 'Economic Efficiency of Crop Production in Egypt'. Working Paper No. 155. Cairo: Egyptian Center for Economic Studies.

Aboulenein, S., H. El-Laithy, O. Helmy, H. Kheir-El-Din, and D. Mandour (2010). 'Impact of the Global Food Price Shock on the Poor in Egypt'. Working Paper No. 157. Cairo: Egyptian Center for Economic Studies.

Ahmed, A., H. Bouis, T. Gunter, and H. Loefgren (2001). 'The Egyptian Food Subsidy System: Structure, Performance and Options for Reform'. Research Report 119. Washington, DC: International Food Policy Research Institute.

Al-Shawraby, S., and H. Selim (2012). 'Food International Price Pass-Through in Egypt's Inflation'. Paper presented at the Economic Research Forum Annual Conference, Cairo, 25–27 March 2012.

BBC News (2008). 'Egypt Army to Tackle Bread Crisis', 17 March. Available at: <http://news.bbc.co.uk/2/hi/middle_east/7300899.stm> (accessed 23 February 2012).

Economic Commission of Africa (2008). 'Governance Report on Egypt'. Unpublished Report. Addis Ababa: Economic Commission of Africa.

Egyptian Center for Economic Studies (ECES) (2010). 'Policy View Point 25'. Cairo: ECES.

Egyptian Food Safety Information Center (2011). Available at: <http://www.efsic.com/index.html> (accessed 14 January 2012).

El-Ehwany, N., and N. El-Megharbel (2008). 'Employment Intensity of Growth in the Egyptian Economy Growth with focus on the Manufacturing Industries'. Working Paper No. 130. Cairo: Egyptian Center for Economic Studies.

El-Laithy, H., and D. Armanios (2011). 'Targeting of Poor in Egypt: Identifying the Alternative Means of Living: with Application on Ration Cards'. Cairo: Social Contract Center, the Observatory of Development Justice.

Ghoneim, A. F. (2008). 'Can Trade Policy Save Egypt from the World Food Crisis?'. Paper submitted to Social Contract Center Project, Information and Decision Support Center. Cairo: Cabinet of Prime Minister.

Handoussa, H., D. Abdou, A. T. Awny, and V. Kirk (2009). 'Exploring Research Options on the Impact of Food Price Fluctuations in Egypt'. Scoping Survey Final Report submitted to IDRC. Ottawa: International Development Research Centre (IDRC).

IFPRI (International Food Policy Research Institute) (2008). 'High Food Prices: The What, Who, and How of Proposed Policy Actions'. Policy Brief. Washington, DC: IFPRI.

Kandil, M. (2010). 'Reforms of Public Finance in Egypt: Energy and Food Subsidies'. Price Subsidies in Egypt: Alternatives for Reform. Presentation delivered at the Egyptian Center for Economic Studies, Cairo, 5 October.

McCorriston, S. (2011). 'Commodity Prices, Government Policies and Competition'. Paper presented at the WTO-CUTS Symposium on Trade in Primary Product Markets and Competition Policy, Geneva, 22 September.

Ministry of Finance (2010). 'Monthly Statistical Bulletin'. Section Four, Fiscal Sector, October. Available at: <http://www.mof.gov.eg/English/publications/Reports%20and%20Indicators/Pages/TheFinancialMonthly-October2010.aspx> (accessed 10 September 2011).

Ministry of Finance (2011). 'The State's General Budget for the Fiscal Year 2010–2011'. Available at: <http://www.mof.gov.eg/MOFGallerySource/Arabic/Mwazna2010-2011/Financial_statement10-11.pdf> (accessed 10 September 2011).

Transparency International (2005). 'Corruption Perceptions Index'. Available at: http://www.transparency.org/policy_research/surveys_indices/cpi/2005 (accessed 15 September 2011).

Transparency International (2008). 'Corruption Perceptions Index'. Available at: <http://www.transparency.org/policy_research/surveys_indices/cpi/2008> (accessed 15 September 2011).

Transparency International (2009). 'National Integrity System Study: Egypt 2009'. National Integrity System Assessments: Reports by Country'. Available at: <http://www.transparency.org/policy_research/nis/nis_reports_by_country> (accessed 15 September 2011).

UN Inter-Agency Assessment Mission on Soaring Food Prices: Government of Egypt, FAO, WFP, World Bank, IFAD, and NEPAD (IAAM1) (2009). 'Macro-economic Analysis and Review of Poverty in Egypt'. Working Paper 1. Available at: <http://neareast.fao.org/Publications> (accessed 6 November 2011).

UNDP (United Nations Development Programme) (2008). 'Food Security and Agriculture in Arab Countries: Facts, Challenges and Policy Considerations'. Cairo: UNDP and League of Arab States.

UNDP (United Nations Development Programme) and MOED (Ministry of Economic Development) (2010). 'Egypt's Progress towards Achieving the Millennium Development Goals'. Cairo: UNDP and MOED.

Wikipedia (2011). 'Egyptian Parliamentary Election, 2010'. Available at: <http://en.wikipedia.org/wiki/Egyptian_parliamentary_election,_2010> (accessed 5 February 2012).

World Bank (2009). 'Economic Growth, Inequality, and Poverty: Social Mobility in Egypt between 2005 and 2008'. Report No. 48093. Washington, DC: World Bank.

World Bank (2010). 'Egypt's Food Subsidies: Benefit, Incidence, and Leakages'. Report No. 57446. Washington, DC: World Bank.

World Bank (2011a). 'World Development Indicators CD-ROM 2011'. Washington, DC: World Bank.

World Bank (2011b). 'MENA Facing Challenges and Opportunities: Regional Economic Update'. Washington, DC: World Bank.

World Food Programme (WFP) (2008a). 'Vulnerability Analysis and Review of the Food Subsidy Program in Egypt'. Cairo: World Food Programme.

World Food Programme (2008b). 'Marketing of Food in Egypt'. Cairo: World Food Programme.

World Food Programme (2010). 'Analysis of Consumer Profiles and Behavior Patterns of Food Subsidy Recipients: An Approach to Targeting'. A study prepared for the Ministry of Social Solidarity, Cairo.

World Food Programme (2011). 'WFP Strategy in the MENA Region 2011–2014'. Cairo: WFP Regional Bureau for the Middle East, North Africa, Eastern Europe, and Central Asia.

13

The Political Economy of Food Price Policy in Nigeria

Aderibigbe S. Olomola

13.1 Introduction

Nigeria is a net importer of food. Therefore, any crisis that occurs in the international food market will be felt in Nigeria. It is in the context of the international dimensions of the 2008 food crisis that the nature, impact, and policy responses in Nigeria can be understood. Although the prices of many commodities slumped during the first couple of years of the new millennium, some commodities (coffee, cotton, sugar, rubber, cocoa, rice, etc.) started to witness a rebound thereafter. The main causes include the shifting fundamental trends in supply and demand, poor harvests, policy changes, episodic shocks arising from climatic fluctuations, and a variety of other natural and political factors. As in 2006, the increases in commodity prices in Africa were regarded as a commodity boom being driven by growth in other developing countries, especially China and India, influence of taste and preferences, climatic fluctuations, conflicts in crop producing countries, high energy costs, and price speculation (Olomola 2007). By 2008, however, the price rises have assumed crisis dimensions in food markets across the developing world, including Nigeria. The crisis actually came to a climax during the first three months of 2008 and the implementation of policies to mitigate the effects started during the first week of May.

In Nigeria, the crisis followed a period of renewed growth in the agricultural sector and the concerted effort to modernize the sector. Thus, initially it was felt that since there was no food scarcity of any significant proportion the food crisis could be regarded as mere media propaganda. On the realization of the fact that Nigeria is a net food importer and that a price escalation would reduce access to food for the majority of the people who already were precariously food insecure, the government made frantic efforts to address the situation. But what prompted the government to agree to take actions? What is the impact of the food crisis in Nigeria? What measures were adopted by the government to reduce the impact? Why did the government respond the way it did? How effective were the policy responses? What lessons can be drawn to forestall or to remedy the situation in case of future occurrence? These are the issues being unravelled in this chapter. Specifically, the objectives of the chapter are to (i) examine the agricultural commodity price trend and determine the effects of the 2008 food crisis in the country; (ii) identify the types and time horizon of the policy measures adopted to address the food crisis; (iii) analyse the political economy context of the policy responses in terms of determining the role of key actors and the factors circumscribing the adopted policies; (iv) analyse the dynamics of decision-making among the various actors in the policy process; and (v) assess the socioeconomic consequences of the policy responses.

From the analysis of data gathered through interactions with policy makers and major stakeholders and from official documents, we found that price transmission internationally and within the local supply chains played a considerable role in the food crisis. The nation faced severe shocks arising from sharp and simultaneous increases in the international prices of food and crude oil in 2008. Critical supply shortages arising from inclement weather conditions, investment-unfriendly macroeconomic environment, and poor implementation of projects exacerbated the price transmission effects. The supply response demonstrated by farmers was clear and remarkable. Younger farmers were attracted to the agricultural sector.

However, consumers were worse off. Those on low incomes witnessed a substantial increase in the proportion of their income that was spent on food. There was also deterioration in their intake of calories and protein as they engaged in unhealthy food consumption patterns. The government—executive and legislature—farmers' associations, and other stakeholders including the mass media rose up to the challenge and came up with some policy actions to remedy the situation. The measures included (i) a release of grains from the strategic reserve at appropriate intervals to mitigate the impact of high food prices on consumers; (ii) the provision of the sum of NGN 80 billion (US$712 million) for the import of 500,000 metric tons (MT) of rice from Thailand and other parts of the world within five months to be sold locally at a subsidized rate; (iii) some adjustments in tariff measures on food import to ease transaction; and (iv) a campaign to sensitize Nigerians to the looming dangers of food shortage and the need to conserve food.

These responses generated mixed effects. In the short term it was possible to reduce the spike in food prices and to introduce a guaranteed minimum price as a safety net to stabilize producers' income. But the release of food from grain reserves was badly managed as were the financial innovations for agricultural commercialization. The initial momentum in the implementation of projects was lost along the line and some of the projects were uncompleted due to the lack of commitment to release funds on a timely basis.

13.2 Food Price Trends and Shocks

In spite of production variabilities and fluctuations in prices and weather conditions, the country has not witnessed famine or food riots; neither has it been a beneficiary of food aid. Thus, the soaring food prices and the accompanying hysteria witnessed in 2008 seem to be unprecedented. It is, therefore, not surprising that it took some considerable controversy before the soaring food prices of 2008 could be considered as a food crisis. In general, the prices of many commodities have followed an increasing trend but skyrocketed between 2007 and 2008, especially in the case of rice, sorghum, cassava, soybean, maize, millet, and wheat. Even after 2008, prices of many crops continued to rise with the exception of rice (Figure 13.1).

The continued rise in prices beyond 2008 is partly due to demand pressures from neighbouring countries as Nigeria's importance in regional (cross-border) trade in the Sahel region became more prominent in terms of its involvement in ensuring food security through export of dry grains such as millet, maize, and sorghum. For instance, in the aftermath of the production shortfall in Niger Republic in 2009 which degenerated into a demand-supply gap of about 400,000 tonnes of grains, exports from Nigeria effectively bridged the gap and helped to stabilize prices. An assessment of the situation as at February 2010 shows that between 80 and 100 per cent of markets in Niger Republic were supplied each week with about 4,300 tonnes of grains from

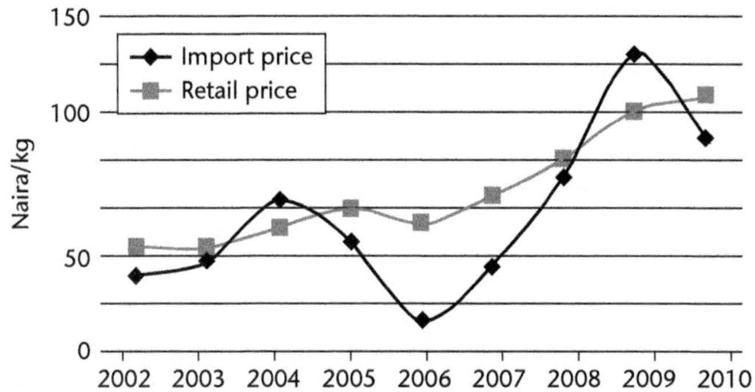

Figure 13.1 International wheat price transmission in Nigeria
Source: author's illustration using data from NBS (2011).

Nigeria, 1,750 tonnes from Benin, and 240 tonnes from Burkina Faso and this continued until around August that year (Diao 2010).

The fact that the prices of various commodities like rice, sorghum, cassava, soybean, maize, millet, and wheat surged between 2007 and 2008 irrespective of whether they are tradeables or non-tradeables is an indication of the complex nature of the drivers of the food price crisis in Nigeria. Ordinarily the international market prices of rice and wheat could be held responsible for the soaring prices experienced during the period. The fact that the prices of other commodities were rising at the same time, however, suggests that other factors might also be contributing. In this regard, there are three possibilities. First, sorghum, millet, and beans could face a higher regional demand as neighbouring countries and other West African countries where food riots have been reported might be sourcing the food staples from Nigeria as mentioned earlier, thus transforming their trade configuration as they gained entry into the region formally or informally. The possibility of cross-border trade in the case of sorghum, millet, and beans cannot be ruled out. Second, is the substitution effect of the 2008 food crisis. Consumers in Nigeria and indeed in many West African countries turned from the consumption of rice and bread to the consumption of other food staples such as cassava products, yam, and maize; a trend that has been observed in Guinea, Liberia, Sierra Leone, Ghana, Benin, and Nigeria together with an increase in the production and trade of cassava farina in West Africa since 2008 (NISER 2009; SWAC 2011). The third possible source of price increase is the high cost of transportation in Nigeria during the period, particularly occasioned by the increase in the international price of petrol occurring simultaneously with the soaring of international prices of rice and wheat. As Nigeria was also importing fuel during the same period, such increase in the price of petrol would be transmitted to the domestic economy leading to an escalation of transportation cost.

13.2.1 *International Price Transmission*

Graphical illustrations of the co-movements between the import prices and domestic retail prices of the commodities for annual data from 2002 to 2010 show strong evidence of transmission of international prices (Figures 13.1–13.3). Furthermore, a correlation analysis reveals that the co-movement is strongest in the case of wheat ($r = 0.84$), followed by rice ($r = 0.70$), while in the case of maize, the movement is also in the same upward direction, but the correlation is weak ($r = 0.37$).

The shock in world food prices in 2007–8 should be expected to generate extraordinary effects because the rise in prices coincided with sharp increases in the prices of petroleum products (including petrol) imported into Nigeria which followed the same trend as the price of crude oil in the international

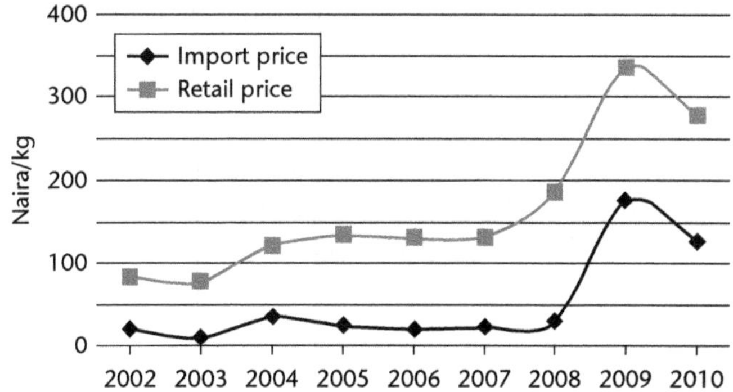

Figure 13.2 International rice price transmission in Nigeria
Source: author's illustration using data from NBS (2011).

Figure 13.3 International maize price transmission in Nigeria
Source: author's illustration using data from NBS (2011).

market. Prices of refined petroleum products, fertilizer, and other agricultural inputs imported into the country increased, resulting in a substantial rise in prices of both imported and domestically produced food.

The weak exchange rate which continued to depreciate up until 2010 also fuelled the hike in food prices especially in view of the fact that the country is highly import-dependent for the supply of its agricultural inputs. In Nigeria, the Nigerian naira (NGN) exchange rate to the US$ continued to depreciate from 2005 to 2010. It was NGN 132.9 in 2005, NGN 137.4 in 2007, and NGN 139.27 in 2008. It depreciated further to NGN 148.9 in 2009 and NGN 150.3 in 2010. Moreover, the inflation rate which stood at a single digit before the crisis, rose considerably from 6.6 per cent in 2007 to 15.1 per cent in 2008 and 12 per cent in 2009. To date, the inflation rate has not reverted to the pre-crisis single digit. The domestic inflationary pressure, inadequacies of the foreign currency market and imported inflation through massive imports of petroleum products (which jerked up transportation and production costs) were partly responsible for the food price crisis in Nigeria. This situation also partly accounts for the observed trend in which domestic food price increases actually exceeded world food price increases.

Apart from the transmission of international prices there are other factors which accounted for the soaring of food prices in Nigeria from 2008 to 2010. They included food supply shortages, macroeconomic environment with high interest rate, the weakness of the Nigerian currency, poor implementation of projects, as well as high transportation cost.

13.2.2 *Broad Impact of the Price Shifts on Stakeholders*

PRODUCTION IMPACT

Although the small-scale farmers may not be able to fully capitalize on price rises due to limited access to markets and key production inputs such as seed, fertilizer, knowhow, irrigation facilities, and credit they are still expected to be encouraged to increase production in response to the rising product prices. The production trend for major commodities from 2004 to 2009 increased (Figure 13.4), varying widely among commodities. There is continuous expansion in the production of cassava and yam even up to 2009. The rice producers have not increased output significantly and this resonates with the unimpressive price regime in the aftermath of the import of rice in 2008 which effectively reversed the upward swing in price and dampened farmers' enthusiasm to cultivate the crop during the following cropping season. The slight production increase has been spurred by incentives provided by the government in the form of credit facilities and availability of modern inputs.

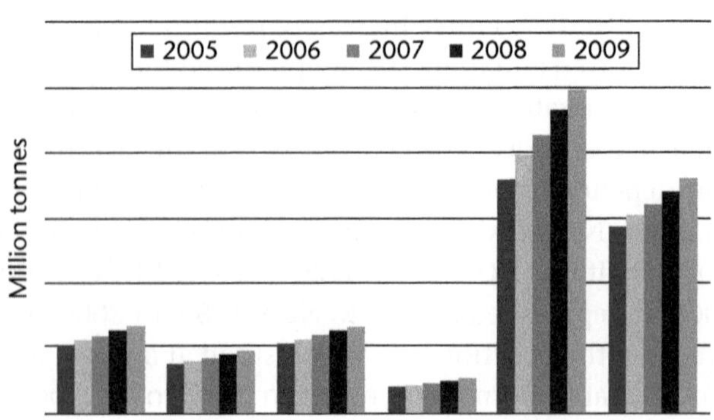

Figure 13.4 Production trend of food staples in Nigeria, 2005–9

Source: author's illustration using data from Federal Ministry of Agriculture and Rural Development (2010).

EFFECTS ON FOOD CONSUMPTION PATTERNS

The effects of the 2008 food crisis on food consumption can be gleaned from the study conducted by Nigerian Institute of Social and Economic Research (NISER) (2009) which examined the budget share various food categories consumed at homes across the six geo-political zones in the country. The study revealed that cereals, root, and tubers as well as vegetables account for a larger share of the total food budget in both the rural and the urban sector. On the other hand, the budget shares of meat, fish, and beverages are smaller. The high food prices changed the share of food budget in favour of cereals in both the urban and the rural sectors. Similarly, between 2007 and 2008, the results show an increased share of roots and tubers in the food budget in some areas (NISER 2009). The share of meat and beverages in the food budget declined between 2007 and 2008 in most of the zones. Household expenditure on food increased from around 50 per cent in 2007 to about 75 per cent in 2008.

13.3 Policy Responses to the Crisis

In Nigeria, the policies adopted can be categorized into short-term, medium-term, and long-term policies. In what follows we present details of the various policies.

13.3.1 *Short-term Measures*

RELEASE OF GRAINS

The federal government released 65,000 MT of various grains and garri to the public, which led to a reduction of prices of some tradable and non-tradable food items such as maize, sorghum, millet, and garri. The states were enjoined to do the same but this took place at an insignificant level given the low stock levels. The intervention buying operation of the federal government was aimed at increasing the supply of rice within the next three months (May–July 2008) and sustain it for the following three months in the first instance (August–October 2008). This was expected to cause a significant reduction in the market price for rice, based on evidence that it had risen much faster than the current price at the border with Benin Republic. The incremental import would be sold to the general public at a subsidized price, with a view to bringing the price down.

MOPPING UP OPERATION

This involved purchasing the current stock of imported rice in the country from local stores in different parts of the country. It was established that about 110,000 MT were available to be mopped up at the prevailing market price to be sold to the consuming public at subsidized prices. Although this was achieved within the short term, the quantity available was too small to generate any perceptible impact.

DISTRIBUTION OF SMALL-SCALE MACHINES

The government considered the option of processing the paddy in storage based on the quantity confirmed to be available. Rice Farmers Association of Nigeria (RIFAN) had claimed that about 4 million MT of paddy would be available in the short term, comprising present stock level in July 2008 (2.5 million MT) as verified by the Federal Ministry of Agriculture and Water Resources (FMAWR) plus new harvest (1.5 million MT) in the following season in October 2008. However, the problem of processing was underscored, in terms of low capacity of small-scale processors and poor quality of domestically milled rice in Nigeria. Thus, small-scale machines could be distributed to processors in the short run for the purpose of milling the paddy to be made available in October 2008. Therefore, the government made an attempt to place an order for small-scale rice processing machines from abroad. About 1,000 small-scale milling machines were to be purchased which would need one month to install in all parts of the country. This was expected to reduce the rice price by at least 30 per cent. It was also to have favourable socioeconomic implications including creation of jobs for processors, engineers, and others. The fact that farmers would be encouraged to produce rice made this option particularly attractive. The option did not go beyond the level of conceptualization. It failed as a short-term measure because about two or three months would be required for the import of machines and putting up the factory buildings.

TARIFF WAIVERS

The federal government approved the suspension of all levies and duties on rice imports with effect from 7 May to 31 October 2008, which stimulated the private sector to place an order for rice import to the tune of almost 10 MT. The actual rice import was only 172,518 tons, which led to a 45 per cent fall in prices. In addition, the cross-border trade in rice probably increased. The socioeconomic implication was in terms of increased business among rice traders and consumers in the short run, which of course was at the expense of low morale of farmers in the long run.

13.3.2 *Medium-term Measures*

Subsequently the ordeal of soaring food prices was converted to an opportunity for Nigeria to institute medium- to longer-term measures for improved agricultural development. Thus, the federal government set up an implementation committee comprising ministers of agriculture and water resources, finance, commerce, and industry. A number of medium-term measures emerged to address the looming food crisis.

FOOD PRODUCTION

An allocation of 1.68 per cent of the federal budget was made to the Natural Resources Development Fund during 2008–11 for boosting the domestic production of food crops, the development of the agro-allied industry, and research and development (R&D) on seed varieties. As discussed below, not all the amount was actually spent due to bureaucratic delays and untimely disbursement of funds.

AGRICULTURAL CREDIT

NGN 10 billion was made available from the rice levy account as a credit scheme at a concessionary interest rate, in support of the local rice processing capacity in the country. However, many small-scale producers and processors could not access the funds. A major complaint was that the selection of beneficiaries was politically motivated. Furthermore the Central Bank of Nigeria resolved to raise NGN 200 billion funds from the commercial banks in two weeks. The fund would be used for commercial agriculture to be disbursed by accredited banks. The credit under the scheme was to be disbursed for crop and livestock production, the processing and marketing including storage and input supplies. The commercial agricultural credit scheme was not targeted at financing the establishment of rice mills. Thus, despite the introduction of this scheme the issue of inadequate rice processing mills remained unresolved. The implementation of the scheme was inequitable as small-scale farmers who produced over 80 per cent of the agricultural output in the country received little or nothing from the credit scheme while large-scale producers benefitted immensely. Smallholders also face far more restrictions in terms of access to formal credit than the large-scale farmers.

FOOD RESERVE AND STORAGE FACILITY

The federal government decided to complete the outstanding storage projects before the end of 2008 in order to increase the national strategic food reserve capacity from 300,000 to 600,000 MT. The state governments were encouraged through moral suasion to step up their buffer stock operations, which involve at least 10 per cent of food output in their respective domains. It was envisaged that up to two million MT silos capacity would be required for the country. Efforts were made to complete seventeen silos which were already at various stages of completion across the country. The federal government also decided to start up the building of eleven others in various states of the country. A sum of NGN 15 billion was earmarked for this purpose. To date, however, many of the silos remain uncompleted and the target capacity has not been met due to poor budget implementation especially non-release of appropriated funds.

CROP PROCESSING

A decision was taken by the government to increase the rice milling capacity by an additional 88,000 MT per annum and create about 8,000 direct and indirect job opportunities. The mills were to be located in the major rice producing states to take advantage of proximity to raw materials. The local capacity for the operation and maintenance of rice mills and the fabrication of spares was to be gradually built thereby creating employment for youth. Commitment to this decision seems to remain on course. The federal government is making arrangements to secure international financing for the establishment of a hundred rice mills across the country. The target date for the completion of the project has been put at 2015. As it turned out, the issue of importing rice processing equipment which failed as a short-term measure has been shifted to the medium-term horizon and even then it has been difficult to achieve mainly due to scarcity of investment funds and the lack of confidence on the part of private investors that the policy environment will protect their investment if they provide the necessary funds. There was also emphasis on the physical development of markets for livestock and birds, physical development of grain markets and the introduction of a guaranteed minimum price (GMP) scheme. This is to serve as a safety net measure for the farmers in terms of providing remunerative prices and stabilizing their income. The GMP was actually introduced but its implementation has not been effective.

13.3.3 *Long-term Measures*

Later in 2009, the federal government produced a food security strategy document which prioritized a number of measures in the long term. The policy thrust behind this includes a number of desirable attributes, namely the value chain approach to agricultural development, commodity focus in providing support to producers, the visibility of the private sector, successor farmer generation, and provision of safety net. In this regard, the aspects of the policy response in the long term include (i) the promotion of large-scale commercial agriculture of between 500 and 3,000 hectares (ha) that is intended to have a direct linkage to the small-scale farmers with a target of 10,000 ha for a period of four years; (ii) the construction of 60 specialized warehouses that will increase storage capacity; and (iii) the setting aside of 1.68 per cent of the Natural Resources Fund for agricultural research.

13.4 Political Economy Context

The 2007–8 food crisis was widely reported by the Nigerian mass media and this generated responses from all strata of the society—the executive, parliament (National Assembly), non-governmental organizations, producer associations, development partners, scholars, and activists. This section examines the actual policy process that took place, the actors involved, their roles, and the type of links and interactions among them as well as the timing of responses and the factors influencing the adopted policy actions.

13.4.1 *The Policy-making Process*

A diverse group of stakeholders (government, donors, research community, farmers' associations, media organizations, and the private sector) was involved in the debate surrounding the food crisis and policy responses in Nigeria. The policy-making process did not follow the conventional linear model with a unidirectional flow from an agenda setting phase to the decision phase and implementation phase which actually had been flawed in the literature (Sutton 1999). A major characteristic of the food crisis policy (response) process is that it involved the participation of a variety of stakeholders dominated by the government (policy makers), politicians, the mass media, and producers' associations. The policy process can best be described as one of disjointed incrementalism or muddling through (Lindblom 1980). Indeed, muddling through a 'time bomb' which never exploded offers an intriguing experience. Discussions about the nature of the crisis and possible solutions were going on simultaneously but a considerable length of time was taken to build consensus. It was difficult for the stakeholders to promptly prescribe the policy agenda because of the political colouration and connotation implied by the controversy surrounding whether or not Nigeria was actually facing a food crisis. As the price hike was becoming increasingly burdensome for consumers and food supply shortages were being reported and intensively analysed in the media, the National Food Reserve Agency (NFRA)—a more or less technical arm of the Federal Ministry of Agriculture and Water Resources (as the ministry was then known) claimed that the country was not facing any risk of food crisis. This position was unpopular in the country and took some time before it was reluctantly vacated. It effectively created a lull in policy response and put the executive arm of the government on the defensive rather than staying at the forefront to study the situation properly and provide the rallying point to set the policy agenda to tackle the crisis. The government was later to be stampeded by criticisms from opposition parties (politicians), civil society organizations, and media reports of the dire consequences of soaring food prices in other countries including deadly riots and threats to the stability of governments.

Consequently, the process witnessed the pronouncement of decisions by the government even when consensus had not been reached and hurriedly identified solutions which turned out to be unimplementable within the stipulated time. Such a panicky process was exemplified by the initial announcement of the direct import of rice to the tune of NGN 80 billion. The basis for this was the fear that the soaring food prices in the world market could introduce significant shocks into the Nigerian food market, given the status of Nigeria as a net food importer wherein rice and wheat predominate among others in the food import bill of US$2.8 million per annum. Following sharp criticism by RIFAN and opposition parties the policy had to be moderated by another commitment of NGN 10 billion for the provision of credit to farmers to boost food production. This way, the government was able to assuage the apprehensions of both consumers and producers. This is a demonstration of the fact that producers' associations could have a significant influence on the policy processes. The government continued to muddle through the process but had to work out incentives for the benefit of producers in tandem with what the consumers will benefit from cheap imports of rice. Another example was the attempt the government made to import small-scale rice processing machines to be installed within one month in all parts of the country. The idea failed when it was later realized that the process of importing and putting up the factory buildings would require up to three months. Further details of what worked and what else failed to work can better be understood as we characterize the process by examining the role of the decision-making actors as well as the stakeholders who influenced the process, timing of responses, policy choices and effects, as well as the factors that circumscribed the selection of policies implemented.

13.4.2 *Decision-making Actors*

LEADERSHIP ROLE OF GOVERNMENT IN SETTING THE AGENDA

Of the three tiers of government in Nigeria (federal, state, and local) the federal government maintained the leadership role in organizing and implementing policy responses to the 2008 food crisis. And in the same vein, the executive and legislative arms of government played prominent roles. The response of the executive arm of government (led by the president) came mainly through the FMAWR while in the National Assembly (parliament), the House of Representatives and Senate organized public hearing, debates, and investigations through their respective committees on agriculture. The FMAWR was the fulcrum around which the policy process revolved. It has the responsibility to liaise with other stakeholders including the parliament, the Federal Executive Council (FEC), the private sector, farmers' associations, and development partners, package the policy measures for necessary approval by the government and implement such policy response measures. During the period, approval of executive actions followed the normal procedure in which the FEC comprising all cabinet ministers and chaired by the president, examines the policies brought before it by the relevant minister and arrives at a consensus after thorough consideration of the merits and demerits.

As part of the consensus building process, the minister of agriculture convened a stakeholders' meeting which took place at Abuja on 3 May 2008. The stakeholders in attendance included directors of various departments in the Federal Ministry of Agriculture, representatives of the National Food Reserve Agency, Agricultural Research Council of Nigeria, development partners, representatives of agribusiness firms, and the Rice Farmers' Association of Nigeria. The agenda of the meeting was to examine the food situation in the country and to obtain the commitment of stakeholders towards implementing the proposed policy decisions. The sole objective of the policy response in the short term was to bring the domestic price of rice down quickly having jumped by about 100 per cent in a couple of months prior to that time. It was established that the rice output in 2007 was 3.4 million MT out of which only 1.4 million MT was milled leaving 2.0 million MT of rice paddy unprocessed because of inadequate processing capacity. It was also established that the requirement of the country for paddy rice for its 140 million people at 30 kg per caput consumption was 6.5 million MT or 4.2 million MT milled rice equivalent at 65 per cent recovery rate; and that the harvest of paddy in 2008 was estimated at 3.94 million tonnes.

The timing of the legislative and executive actions taken between October 2007 and November 2008 in response to the crisis attests to the role of both houses of parliament (Senate and House of Representatives) as policy champions (Table 13.1). The legislature demonstrated a better understanding of the problem and wielded considerable influence in setting the policy agenda and in ensuring effective delivery of services at the implementation stage. This was done through organizing public hearings and conducting debates to ensure appropriate policy implementation was neither delayed nor derailed.

A major political dimension in the policy process in Nigeria was the involvement of the thirty-six state governors as part of the key decision actors especially in view of the federal nature of the country with a multi-party democracy and multi-layered governance structure. All the governors met with the president on 29 April 2008 to examine the policy response measures. The following week, 5 May, the measures were tabled before the stakeholders for validation prior to presentation before the FEC

Table 13.1 Policy process of the Nigerian 2007–8 food crisis response

Time line	Issues addressed and measures taken
25 October 2007	Through resolution No. 37 of 25 October 2007 the Senate alerted the nation to the drought in some parts of the country. This alert was mainly due to the devastating effects of droughts especially in view of the need to ensure national food security. The Senate further resolved that the Federal Ministry of Agriculture should immediately brief the house on the status of the nation's strategic grains reserve. The strategic grains reserve is the mandatory storage by the Federal Government of about 5 per cent of grains harvested nationwide. This reserve is to ensure continuous availability of food even in the time of famine.
25 April 2008	The Committee on Agriculture of the House of Representatives alerted the federal government to the growing food shortages and the attendant soaring of prices of grains. The legislative chamber thereafter invited the Federal Ministry of Agriculture to a meeting to discuss in detail the status of food security in Nigeria.
29 April 2008	Based on the above articulated concerns the president convened an emergency meeting with all the 36 state governors to review the situation and take necessary actions. The meeting extensively discussed the food security situation in the face of the global food crisis arising from the shortage in the aggregate world food output and resolved that very urgent measures be put in place to protect the populace and develop the agricultural sector.
3 May 2008	A stakeholders' meeting was convened in Abuja at the instance of the minister of agriculture. The agenda of the meeting was to examine the food situation in the country and to obtain the commitment of stakeholders towards implementing the proposed policy decisions.
14 May 2008	Some of the measures proposed during the meeting with the state governors were considered and approved by the FEC. The FEC approved inter alia that: (i) the sum of NGN 10 billion be provided from the rice levy account for a credit scheme to support local rice processing capacity. Credit granted under the scheme was to attract 4 per cent interest rate, a repayment period of 15 years, and a five-year moratorium; (ii) all outstanding food storage projects should be completed before the end of 2008 to significantly increase the national food reserve capacity from 300,000 to 600,000 MT; (iii) the funds accruing to the Natural Resources Development Fund (May 2008 to 2011) be utilized as Special Intervention Fund Agriculture to boost domestic production of food crops and development of agro-allied industries as well as R&D for the production of improved varieties of seeds.
8–14 November 2008	In its annual retreat held in Kano (north west Nigeria) the Senate held sessions on 'Desertification, Climate Change and Challenge of Poverty' and 'Ensuring Food Security in Nigeria' as part of the key issues of concern during the retreat. The food crisis was widely discussed. The speakers and discussants at these sessions were distinguished academics drawn from various parts of the country. The whole nation was sensitized regarding the need to address the main causes of the crisis and the need for the government to take effective measures to address the crisis.

Source: author's compilation.

for approval on 14 May 2008. Thus after the initial loss of time as mentioned earlier, the executive evolved a participatory process of taking decisions about the type of policy instruments to deploy in tackling the food crisis. Following the approval, the process moved into the implementation stage with the FMAWR being at the core of the administrative procedures. Even at this stage some of the key actors continued to play an active role in various ways.

CATALYTIC ROLE OF THE MASS MEDIA

The mass media did not stop at drawing the attention of policy makers to the need to take urgent steps to address the soaring food prices. When the palliative measures were being implemented, a repentant NFRA urged the media to appeal to Nigerians to remain calm as the government was already taking measures to address the food crisis. The media monitored the process and reported cases of abuses and inequity in the distribution of grains that were released from the reserve. The parliament responded by setting up a panel to investigate all the issues involved. Other active participants in the decision-making process are the development partners who have to align their programmes and projects with the policy measures put in place by the government to tackle the food crisis.

SUPPORTIVE ROLE OF DEVELOPMENT PARTNERS

Many of the development partners started to address the consequences of the food crisis through the re-allocation of resources in existing programmes, the mobilization of new funds to ensure delivery of food assistance, nutritional care and support, supporting social safety nets for the most vulnerable groups, and the supply of seeds, fertilizers and other basic inputs to smallholders. The FAO, the International Fund for Agricultural Development (IFAD), United States Agency for International Development (USAID), the African Development Bank (AfDB) played crucial roles in this regard. In addressing the enormous challenges facing African agriculture and its major role in attaining the MDGs and poverty reduction objectives, the FAO took the initiative to mobilize key development partners in the establishment of Nigeria's Food Security Thematic Group (FSTG).

The FSTG provided technical support for discussions and actions related to the soaring food prices in Nigeria including the development of the National Food Crisis Response Programme (NFCRP). By and large, the involvement of these agencies was largely in terms of strengthening their ongoing projects to achieve the medium-term objectives. They did not have any significant influence on the short-term measures taken by the government in response to the food crisis in 2008, neither were they directly involved in the design and implementation of the policy measures earlier discussed.

ADVOCACY ROLE OF PRODUCERS' ASSOCIATIONS

When the idea of importing rice to address the supply shortages was mooted, All Farmers Association of Nigeria (AFAN) and the RIFAN launched their opposition. They criticized the move arguing that it would be better to invest the funds in expanding domestic production. Some concerned members of the public even suggested massive imports of food to remedy the situation whereas representatives or sympathizers of food producers argued otherwise claiming that uncontrolled imports would dampen enthusiasm of farmers and constrict food production. The Association of Master Bakers of Nigeria threatened to stop the production of bread unless the price of wheat flour was brought down through massive imports of wheat. These arguments were going on up till May 2008 when the Federal Executive Council met to take the decisions highlighted earlier. The chairman of Lagos state chapter of the Association of Master Bakers and Caterers of Nigeria met with top government officials to ask them to reduce or cancel wheat tariffs or subsidize bakers but claimed to have received no response. The association therefore embarked on a one-week nationwide strike beginning from 5 May 2008 arguing that flour mills have been increasing their prices almost every week. The millers and government blamed the soaring price of flour on increases in international wheat prices. Many consumers supported the bakers' grievances especially in urban areas where all dwellers consume bread virtually on a daily basis. A similar strike action by bakers took place in August 2007 after the government increased taxes on flour by 100 per cent. The price of bread then rose by about 25 per cent. Whereas the bakers' association could not succeed in pressurising the government to subsidize the wheat industry, the AFAN and RIFAN were able to influence the government in setting up a NGN 10 billion loanable fund to boost rice production and processing capacity.

The producers' associations were also not in support of a tariff waiver associated with the rice import policy. As the countdown to the 31 October 2008 deadline for the removal of the rice import duty waiver commenced, mixed reactions trailed the measure. Farmers' associations and rice millers who were originally against the waiver continued to advance reasons why it should not be extended while traders and consumers who were in support continued to canvass reasons for its extension. Some state chapters of AFAN regarded the waiver as a disincentive to local rice production as it has deprived local farmers of the income to engage in rice production. It was claimed that the waiver had adversely affected local rice production and had further impoverished the country's rice farmers. Besides, rice farmers from one state had to transport their produce to other states covering great distances for processing; a situation which has greatly discouraged local rice production. With regard to RIFAN some state chapters especially from the north east argued that continued rice import was discouraging local production, adding that local rice farmers were unable to produce enough due to lack of credit facilities and low investments in the sector and that tariff waiver would compound the problem. They complained that even though the waiver was temporary, it has succeeded in rendering the local producers jobless and if sustained, it will destroy the local rice production completely. The rice millers were also against the policy, claiming that efforts should have been made to establish new mills given the critical shortage of milling machines in the country. The solution proposed by the farmers' associations to address the food price crisis is that the government should empower domestic rice producers through the supply of improved seeds and other modern inputs. The only alternative to the waiver according to them is the provision of at least 50 per cent subsidy to local rice farmers for tractor hiring services and for the procurement of fertilizers and improved seeds. The government was not convinced by these views; the waiver was considered to be necessary when it was suspended in May and the suspension had to be lifted in October as scheduled. In the end the views of the policy makers and interest of consumers prevailed as far as the waiver policy was concerned. The policy was a short-term response in the interest of the generality of the consumers. The waiver was terminated as scheduled at the end of October after it had helped to reverse the dramatic price hike around the middle of 2008.

13.4.3 *Key Decision-making Factors*

A close observation of the policy process, its political, administrative, and social dimensions as well as the role of actors shows clearly that the internal considerations weighed more heavily than external factors in deciding which policy response measures were to be adopted. Given the fact that globalization can trigger the inflow of food crisis oppositions it is instructive for the government to take urgent steps to resolve the crisis. However, there are equally compelling reasons why the policy decisions had to be taken in Nigeria. Altogether, the decision-making factors are five-fold.

RISING UNCERTAINTY ABOUT FOOD SECURITY

It was recognized that the increase in price has the tendency to affect food adequacy as well as the accessibility and affordability of basic needs of Nigerian households. Arising from the global food shortage and soaring prices, food became an increasingly worrisome item in households' budgets in Nigeria where it created rising uncertainties about food security. It was a very contentious issue because of its diverse consequences on different stakeholders in the country. Thus, how to cope with the global food crisis and enhance increased access by consumers in both rural and urban sectors to adequate variety of food became a new challenge and concern of the Nigerian government.

SOARING FOOD PRICES CAN FURTHER IMPOVERISH THE MASSES OF THE PEOPLE

In Nigeria, the rise in food prices is particularly worrisome because food price inflation hurts the poor most and it may have tremendous consequences on economic growth and poverty. Concomitantly, the public spending on the basic investments needed for agriculture and rural economic transformation has remained grossly ineffective and inefficient to bring about adequate food production. Agriculture is expected to form the fulcrum for the growth of the economy because it provides employment for about 70 per cent of the working population and has prospects for development by its size and spread. However, while agriculture has shown remarkable improvement, with a yearly contribution of nearly 42 per cent to the gross domestic product, poverty remains endemic and pervasive in the sector and in the country in general. To date, food insecurity remains a serious challenge to achieving the millennium development goal of halving the proportion of population who suffer from extreme poverty and hunger by the year 2015. A particular reason for concern about the impact of high food prices arose from the fact that the consumers' income being spent on food has been rising with deleterious effects on the financing of children's education and healthcare.

NEED TO AVOID POLITICAL DESTABILIZATION

The surge in food prices witnessed during the first three months in 2008 precipitated thunderous public discourse but there seemed to be no easy agreement on the best ways to resolve the issues. At the level of the executive, government actions were characterized by stampede and ad hockery with some of the panicky measures drawing criticisms from the media and the parliament from time to time. Understandably, an explosive food crisis was what the government could ill-afford at that time. The food crisis came at a point when the government in power was barely one year in office having been inaugurated on 29 May 2007. The elections that brought many of the political office holders to power were also being heavily contested in various election tribunals across the country. Clearly therefore, the government could not ignore the concerns being expressed in the media about the soaring food prices. The government had to muster the necessary political support and adopt a participatory policy process to provide interventionist measures to address the food crisis. This derives from the understanding of the lack of a cohesive action to stem the tide of persistent food insecurity and the concern and discontent often expressed by the poor and highly vulnerable groups in this regard. It was felt that the food crisis has the potential to derail not only past achievements but ongoing pro-poor programmes aimed at reducing the incidence or breaking the cycle of poverty.

UNSUSTAINABILITY OF PERSISTENT FOOD IMPORT

Decisions regarding the termination of a tariff waiver and a number of the medium-term and long-term measures were based on the fact that the country could not afford to continue with the level of food imports recorded during the period. This is in view of the requirement of foreign exchange for development in other critical sectors of the economy especially infrastructure and energy. Since reliance on import is not fiscally sustainable there must be efforts to boost domestic production hence not only short-term palliatives were decided upon but also medium- and long-term strategies were designed to transform and modernize the agricultural sector.

PHOBIA OF FOOD RIOT CONTAGION

Unpleasant consequences of the global food shortages have already been widely reported in many countries in terms of high prices of food, people eating less and less well, protests, strikes, and riots in the wake of dramatic rises in the prices of wheat, rice, corn, oils, and other essential foods. Furthermore, the food price shock has been destabilizing governments, igniting street riots, and threatening to send a new wave of hunger rippling through the world's poorest nations. In Africa, fourteen out of fifty-three countries have witnessed mass disturbances following abrupt spikes in food prices in 2007–8. Some of the countries (Burkina Faso, Senegal, Guinea, Côte d'Ivoire, and Mauritania) are in West Africa. In February 2008, a severe riot also broke out over soaring food prices in Cameroon—a neighbouring country to Nigeria. If food riots in Egypt, Morocco, Tunisia, and Zimbabwe could be said to be far away, that of Cameroon was close enough to serve as a warning to Nigeria not to take the food crisis for granted. Thus, all the stakeholders agreed that the problem must be quickly nipped in the bud.

It could be puzzling to external observers why riots never broke out in Nigeria in spite of the price hikes and level of urbanization. The reasons are not far-fetched. First, Nigeria has no tradition of food riot comparable to other African countries and developing countries in other parts of the world. Second, Nigeria's political landscape had witnessed considerable improvement since the return of democratic governance in 1999. Third, is the fact that Nigeria has been witnessing unparalleled press freedom for quite some time. The mass media in the country is one of the most unfettered in the world. Indeed, the media organizations have been providing opportunities for stakeholders to express their opinions, especially on food security—thus making the alternative of street protest on food issues unattractive.

13.5 Conclusions and Policy Implications

The soaring food prices of 2008 have international and national dimensions. The transmission price effects were exacerbated by simultaneous increase in international oil price. The situation was complicated by food supply shortages occasioned by climatic fluctuations, investment-unfriendly macroeconomic environment and poor implementation of agricultural projects. The food crisis received considerable attention but inflicted notable impact on producers and consumers in Nigeria. The production trend for major commodities from 2004 to 2009 reveals that the impact on production is positive. There is also a positive impact on enterprise profitability as gross margin increased in 2008 in respect of all the commodities with the exception of millet and cowpea. In general, the consumers were worse off. The high food prices induced a change in the pattern of food consumption. For instance, there was a general shift in the share of food budget in favour of cereals in both the urban and the rural sectors in most of the zones. In terms of the effect on nutrition and food security we found that both the rural and urban dwellers consume less than the recommended minimum per capita daily protein and calorie intake implying worsening malnutrition among Nigerians in both the urban and the rural areas between 2007 and 2008.

A response policy was packaged to address the impact but the implementation yielded mixed results. The major problem which arose in the implementation of the short-term measures was the attempt to scuttle the flow of benefits by unintended beneficiaries. This was evident in the allocation of the grains released for distribution to various markets to cushion the effect of the price hikes. At the stage of implementing the palliative measures, individual and group interests overshadowed the interests of the targeted consumers thus undermining the effectiveness of the policy measures.

In the light of the foregoing, a number of lessons and policy implications can be drawn from Nigeria's experience in managing the food crisis policy responses. First, the implementation of the NFCRP should have had provision for its continued implementation and for necessary review at a stipulated time. This should have made it impossible for policy makers and relevant actors to abandon the programme or starve it of necessary funds and political will to drive the process to a logical conclusion. The programme did not also emphasise the value chain approach which came up as an innovation in the National Food Security Programme Document prepared in 2009. Second, to avoid the distortion of targeting for personal or political purposes, there is a need for high transparency regarding the process and conditions of distribution of resources (grains, credit, inputs, etc.) to identified target groups. Third, proper design and implementation of safety nets and other forms of support will improve with participation and consultation of key stakeholders. Therefore, a participatory approach should always be adopted when incentives are being designed to assist the farmers. Fourth, efforts should be made to intensify the registration of farmers across the country for proper targeting of support and inclusion of farmers in key decision-making processes from time to time.

References

Diao, M. B. (2010). 'Nigeria's Role in Niger's Food Security'. *Grain de Sel, Special Issue: Nigeria—A Look at the Agricultural Giant of West Africa* 51: 25–26. Paris: Inter-Reseaux Développement Rural.

Federal Ministry of Agriculture and Rural Development (2010). 'Report of the 2009 Agricultural Production Survey'. Abuja: National Programme for Agriculture and Food Security.

Lindblom, C. E. (1980). *The Policy-Making Process*. Englewood Cliffs, NJ: Prentice Hall.

NBS (National Bureau of Statistics) (2011). Data obtained from NBS. Abuja: NBS. <http://nigerianstat.gov.ng/>.

NISER (Nigerian Institute of Social and Economic Research) (2000). 'Strategic Issues'. In O. Ajakaiye and B. Akinbinu (eds), *Nigerian Development in a Globalizing and Liberalizing World*. Ibadan: Nigerian Institute of Social and Economic Research.

NISER (Nigerian Institute of Social and Economic Research) (2009). 'The Global Food Crisis; Impact and Policy Implications in Nigeria'. Final Research Report by the Agriculture and Rural Development Department of NISER, submitted to the National Fadama Office, Abuja.

Olomola, A. S. (2007). 'Strategies for Managing the Opportunities and Challenges of the Current Agricultural Commodity Booms in SSA'. In 'Seminar Papers on Managing Commodity Booms in Sub-Saharan Africa: A Publication of the AERC Senior Policy Seminar IX'. Nairobi: African Economic Research Consortium.

Sutton, R. (1999). 'The Policy Process: An Overview'. Working Paper No. 118. London: Overseas Development Institute.

SWAC (Sahel and West Africa Club Secretariat) (2011). 'The 2008 Rice Crisis: Shock and New Challenges'. West African Challenges, No. 2. Paris: OECD, SWAC.

14

The Political Economy of Food Price Policy in Senegal

Danielle Resnick

14.1 Introduction

In mid-2008, one of Africa's most stable democracies descended into a period of economic depression and growing social discontent. The sentiments of one taxi driver, who noted that 'If things continue like this, we'll have to eat sand', captured the anxiety of many Senegalese as the price of rice continued to skyrocket.[1] Between January 2007 and September 2008, the consumer price of imported Thai A1 rice, which is the country's main food staple, increased by more than 100 per cent in the capital of Dakar. The rise in the price of rice and other key commodities resulted in a level of inflation not seen since the country was forced to devalue its currency, the Communauté Financière Africaine (CFA) franc, in 1994. In fact, Senegal was one of the worst affected by the 2007/8 global food price crisis, with food prices 24 per cent higher than the African average (Ndione 2008).

Senegal's historic dependence on external markets to supply its food needs, coupled with two seasons of poor domestic cereals production, made it especially vulnerable to global food price rises. While the high level of price transmission from the international to the domestic market impacted the rice sector most severely, other affected commodities included wheat and milk. Yet, there were a variety of long-term structural factors that contributed to Senegal's vulnerability. These included the lack of a visionary agricultural strategy for promoting greater domestic production and commercialization of local goods as well as the country's high level of urbanization and the long-standing preference of urbanites for imported food.

[1] Cited in Sylla (2008: A11).

The government's initial response to the crisis was slow and characterized by a diverse array of interventions. After first suspending custom duties and value added taxes (VAT) in July 2007, the government subsequently provided consumer subsidies. These were accompanied by a diverse range of social protection schemes and the launch of a high-profile agricultural initiative known as the Grand Agricultural Offensive for Food and Abundance (GOANA). The cumulative impact of these interventions in protecting the most vulnerable was relatively small, while the burden on the public finances became extraordinarily heavy.

Why and when did the government choose these particular policies? And what key factors limited their ultimate success? I argue that the policies emerged from the confluence of a strong, diverse civil society placing disparate pressures on a government increasingly centralized around the personality and populist impulses of the former president Abdoulaye Wade. Having ascended to the presidency with the support of urbanites, Wade was loath to alienate this constituency. The decision to implement, and then often to rescind, short-term policies reflected the variable pressures exerted by different groups. Both high levels of ministerial instability under Wade and the desire to please different interest groups resulted in inadequate targeting and implementation of policy measures and a lack of long-term planning to weather the crisis. In the face of competing demands by various stakeholders, schizophrenic policy outcomes emerged.

14.2 Contextualizing Senegal's Agricultural Sector

Although agriculture has long represented an important sector for the Senegalese economy, the country imports about 60 per cent of its food (Ba et al. 2009). Rice in particular constitutes about 5 per cent of total imports and almost 70 per cent of total cereal imports (Cabral, Cissé, and Diagne 2009). The reasons for this high food import dependence are due to the historic promotion of peanuts, key structural constraints, a series of ineffective agricultural reforms, and rapid urbanization.

Challenges for the agricultural sector were further exacerbated when Senegal, along with other members of the CFA zone, devalued its currency in January 1994 by 50 per cent, meaning that the cost of imports purchased on the international market with the CFA franc increased by 100 per cent.[2] While the devaluation temporarily reduced the country's import dependence, the domestic agricultural sector did not experience a large boost in

[2] The CFA was devalued from a ratio of 50 CFA francs to 1 French franc to a ratio of 100 CFA francs to 1 French franc. By halving the currency, imports became twice as expensive.

exports due to the increased cost of imported inputs. Consequently, many rice producers diversified into other crops. An escalation of civil conflict during the mid-1990s in the Casamance region, which is one of the main rice-producing areas, further hurt local production.[3] At the same time, the devaluation concentrated the market structure for imported rice; while there were forty-three importers in 1996, there were only seven importers in 2000, four of which controlled 63 per cent of the total volume of imported rice (Ba et al. 2009).

Spurred by both the impact of the devaluation as well as Senegal's entry into the West African Economic and Monetary Union (UEMOA), the government adopted in 1994 the Structural Adjustment Programme for the Agricultural Sector (PASA).[4] PASA aimed to further liberalize the distribution and price of all agricultural products, privatize the rice sector and eliminate subsidies to the production of local rice, and progressively reduce tariffs with the goal of ultimately adopting a regime of general custom tariffs under UEMOA (IIED 2002).

14.3 Policy and Politics during Wade's First Term (2000–7)

Senegal's gradual economic liberalization occurred in parallel with a number of political reforms that paved the way for multi-party democracy in the mid-1990s.[5] These reforms culminated with the victory of Abdoulaye Wade, leader of the Parti Démocratique Sénégalais (PDS), in the 2000 presidential elections and ended forty years of Parti Socialist du Sénégal (PS) rule. Much of Wade's initial support came from the country's urban poor. Retaining the support of this constituency while also trying to expand his appeal to rural voters partially explains Wade's erratic approach to the agricultural sector.

Early on in Wade's tenure, Senegal adopted the Common External Tariff (CET) imposed by its membership within UEMOA. The CET was established in 2000 in order to harmonize member countries' customs duties on third-country imports and required imposing a 10 per cent levy on cereal imports from countries outside of the UEMOA area. In many ways, this increased the scope for greater rice imports since the previous customs duty was 20 per cent (Baris 2009). At the same time, UEMOA allows every member

[3] The Casamance civil war began in 1982 when then-President Leopold Senghor reneged on a promise to make the region independent. Subsequently, the Movement of Democratic Forces of Casamance launched a secessionist rebellion, which has now become a low-level conflict.

[4] UEMOA consists of eight francophone, African countries: Benin, Burkina Faso, Côte d'Ivoire, Guinea Bissau, Mali, Niger, Senegal, and Togo.

[5] Senghor paved the way for political liberalization in 1976 by allowing two additional parties besides the PS to compete in elections. However, it was not until constitutional changes in the early 1990s when full restrictions on multi-party competition were lifted.

state to choose seven categories of products that are exempt from VAT if they are consumed in large quantities by the poor. The Senegalese government chose to exempt groundnuts, cereals/manioc, fresh vegetables, fresh meat, fresh and frozen fish, eggs, and potatoes and onions (see IMF 2008).

Besides regional trade issues, Wade attempted to put his own mark on agricultural issues. Starting in 2005, Senegal increased the share of government expenditure on agriculture from 4.4 to 14.1 per cent (see Fan, Omilola, and Lambert 2009). This exceeded the target advanced under the Comprehensive Africa Agriculture Development Programme (CAADP) whereby African governments committed to spending at least 10 per cent of their budgets on agriculture. But, instead of having a consolidated vision for the agricultural sector, much of Wade's tenure was characterized by a variety of scattered interventions that lacked long-term planning. For instance, in 2003, Wade announced a 'plan for maize' that envisioned Senegalese farmers producing one million tons annually. Yet, the plan was announced right before the growing season, with little attention to the seed, fertilizer, or land requirements to achieve this goal (see Antil 2010). This was followed by a 'plan for manioc', 'plan for sesame', and then a 'plan for bissap'. None of these initiatives were very successful, and they involved minimal engagement with other stakeholders.

The one exception was the Agricultural, Forestry, and Livestock Act (LOASP), which provided a framework for reducing poverty and diminishing inequalities between rural and urban populations over a twenty-year time horizon. To do so, the LOASP primarily was concerned with increasing agricultural exports and generating incentives for private investment in rural areas (Stads and Sène 2011). After drafting the initial version of the LOASP, the Ministry of Agriculture interacted closely with other government agencies and with the National Council of Rural Consultation and Cooperation (CNCR) in order to refine the LOASP. Established in 1993, CNCR is a federation of twenty-eight small-scale producers' associations and due to its broad representation, CNCR has become the main civil society organization that interacts with the government on issues of agricultural policy. As such, CNCR organized almost 50 consultative meetings throughout the country to discuss an existing draft of the LOASP.

Another agricultural initiative emerged in November 2006 in the wake of increasingly frequent attempts by young, unemployed Senegalese to emigrate to Europe. A series of high-profile deportations by the main destination countries, Spain and Italy, led to widespread anger in the months preceding the 2007 elections. Wade therefore responded by launching the Return to Agriculture programme (REVA), which aimed to integrate the youth into pilot farming centres of excellence in order to combat unemployment by creating 300,000 new rural jobs (see Antil 2010).

None of these fragmented initiatives amounted to a clear and coherent agricultural and rural development strategy. This was both a result of, and exacerbated by, the institutional landscape. Due to the increasing centralization of power around the presidency under Wade, he frequently shifted his cabinet to prevent the emergence of political competitors or to reflect a new perspective on how his government should be organized (see Mbow 2008). For instance, the portfolio of the Ministry of Agriculture was consistently changing during Wade's first seven years in office. It shifted from being responsible for agriculture and livestock under Pape Diouf from 2000 until 2003, to agriculture and water under Habib Sy from 2003 until 2006, and then to agriculture, water, and food security under Farba Senghor in 2006. This persistent shift in ministers undermined policy continuity. Furthermore, these circumstances prove highly problematic for the vast donor community in the country concerned with issues of rural development. As noted by an agricultural specialist at the United States Agency for International Development (USAID), 'the fundamental problem for USAID is that there is no interlocutor to discuss agricultural strategy' (interview with Badiane 2012). Likewise, the director of the Food and Agricultural Office (FAO) in Senegal noted, 'There is a lot of instability within the agricultural ministry since 2002, and there have been at least seven ministers over the last six years. These changes are often accompanied by a change in the directors as well and this makes our communication less efficient, and this is honestly a problem' (interview with Ouattara 2012).

A similar dynamic characterized policy in other important sectors, such as social protection. Between 2001 and 2007, the main ministry in charge of social protection had its main mandate and portfolio of operations changed seven times, shifting from the Ministry of Social Development to the Ministry of Family, National Solidarity, Female Enterprise, and Micro-Finance by the end of 2007. Not surprisingly, this institutional instability prevented the Department of Social Assistance, which has been housed in these various ministries, from implementing durable social protection programmes (Samson and Cherrier 2009). At the same time, a number of other ministries, ranging from education, labour, agriculture, and health, are also involved in social protection activities, leading to challenges with coordination.

Historically, Senegal's social protection regime has been extremely limited. However, in 2005, the government adopted the National Social Protection Strategy (NSPS), which aimed to extend health insurance coverage from 20 to 50 per cent of the population, and to implement a social protection regime to protect those most vulnerable to shocks. Yet, there has been little ownership of the NSPS, and yearly reviews of the Poverty Reduction Strategy Paper reveal that this is the component which has the weakest implementation (interview with Pigois 2012).

14.4 Evolution and Manifestations of a Crisis

The above context, characterized by weak social protection measures, the lack of an agricultural strategy, continued food import dependence, and high levels of ministerial instability, provided the backdrop to the food price crisis in Senegal, which began in 2007 and continued through 2008. The immediate cause of the crisis was twofold. First, Senegal experienced especially poor agricultural yields during both the 2006/7 and 2007/8 production periods. In 2006/7, a shortage in seeds and other inputs and a late start to the rainy season shortened the plant cycle and caused cereal yields to decline. In December 2006, the FAO was already warning of a crisis and noted that net domestic production could only meet 48 per cent of the country's grain needs (FEWS NET 2006).

Torrential rainfalls in late August and September further limited output from the 2007/8 harvest (EIU 2007). Second, the crisis in domestic production only increased Senegal's dependence on food imports. High levels of exposure to external markets proved particularly dangerous due to global price increases in 2007 for key commodities that Senegal imports. In fact, food price inflation increased 1.4 to 7.3 per cent between 2006 and 2007 (WFP 2008a).

14.5 Government Responses to the Food Crisis

Senegal therefore faced a crisis for a variety of major consumer products, in addition to rising costs for fuel, kerosene, and butane gas, which are critical for cooking and electricity. Yet, the government's response to the crisis initially was quite slow, hindered by the priorities of the February and June 2007 presidential and parliamentary elections, respectively.[6] Indeed, the director of the FAO office in Senegal observed, 'Six months before the crisis in 2007, the previous [FAO] director tried to attract the attention of the president and his ministers to the fact that there was a looming crisis by showing them our statistics and early warning system. The former director wrote a communiqué noting that the government needed to be careful

[6] Wade was re-elected as president in 2007 with 55 per cent of the vote, with strong levels of support from both rural and urban areas. His PDS party also obtained the majority of seats in the 2007 legislative elections.

because a food crisis was looming because we could see that the global food stocks were going down. The government was not very convinced' (interview with Ouattara 2012).

By mid-2007, radio stations increasingly were emphasizing the implications of rising food prices as the period of Ramadan approached. Due to growing social pressures, the government ultimately responded with a combination of trade and fiscal measures, social protection policies, and production support. The broad and variegated level of interventions reflected the influence of various interest groups, who each in turn convinced the government to support their particular cause. Figures 14.1 and 14.2 elaborate on the chronology of events and policy decisions over 2007 and 2008, which are detailed in the subsequent sub-sections.

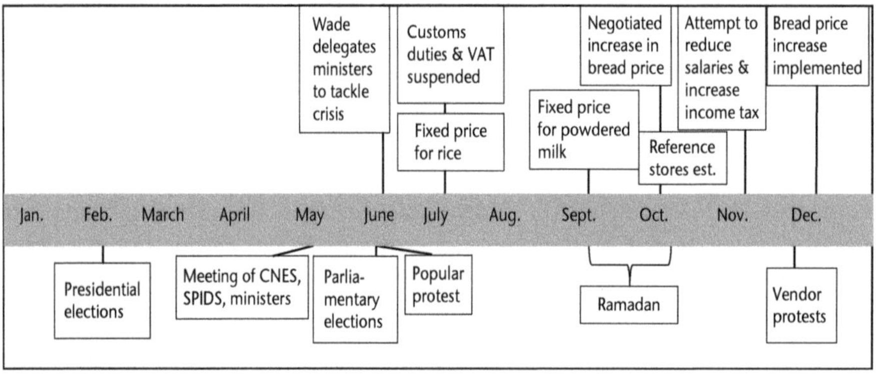

Figure 14.1 Timeline of events, 2007
Source: author's compilation.

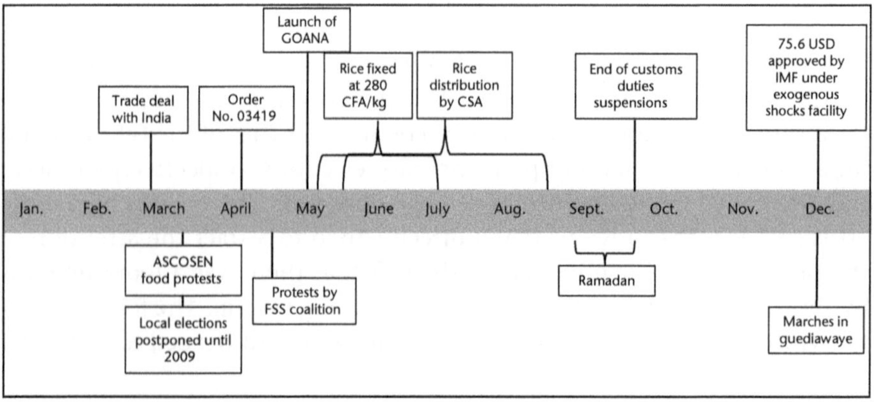

Figure 14.2 Timeline of events, 2008
Source: author's compilation.

14.5.1 *Trade and Fiscal Measures*

Some of the initial impetus for the government's response to the food crisis emerged from the National Confederation of Senegalese Employers (CNES) who sent a declaration to the Ministry of Economy and Finance in early 2007 demanding the removal of custom duties and VAT taxes on powdered milk. By May 2007, the CNES met with the Ministry of Finance, the Ministry of Commerce, the Ministry of Livestock, importers, and producers of milk-based products affiliated with the Union of Professionals of Industries and Mines (SPIDS). Most stakeholders involved in the meeting disagreed with CNES, and subsequent studies by the Ministry of Finance revealed the negative fiscal impact that such measures would have (Dia et al. 2008).

The following month, a range of important consumers groups and trade unions organized demonstrations in which they accused traders of benefiting from the price rises and the government of failing to care about consumers. In turn, during a meeting of his ministers later that month, President Wade delegated the Ministry of Commerce to find a way to tackle the food crisis (Dia et al. 2008). In July and August, the Ministry of Economy and Finance subsequently announced the suspension of customs duties of 10 per cent for rice, 5 per cent for wheat, and 5 per cent for powdered milk that it typically implements as part of the CET with UEMOA. The 18 per cent VAT under UEMOA was also lifted on powdered milk (IMF 2008). The latter measure was opposed by domestic milk processors and producers who believed that the VAT should be maintained and re-invested into the local dairy sector (Dia et al. 2008).

To compensate for the revenue losses created by these interventions, the government attempted to undergo further fiscal policy changes. In early November 2007, the government announced it would reduce public sector salaries and introduce a progressive tax of between 1 and 30 per cent for both private and public sector salaries. Not surprisingly, these measures were heavily unpopular and ultimately reversed. Yet, it motivated many of the country's trade unions and opposition parties to announce a march on 22 November to protest against the rising cost of living and to demand higher salaries. The march coincided with a heavily violent riot in Dakar by street vendors, who were forced off the street by police in an effort to gentrify the city centre to prepare for Senegal's hosting of the eleventh summit of the Organization of the Islamic Conference. The government eventually quelled tensions by focusing more specifically on improving working conditions for vendors (EIU 2007) rather than addressing the concern over high food costs. However, it did prompt President Wade to sign an agreement with the Government of India in March 2008 to send approximately 600,000 tons of rice to Senegal annually for the subsequent five years (OBG 2009).

14.5.2 *Social Protection Policies*

Besides these trade and tax measures, the Ministry of Commerce implemented a series of price ceilings, or implicit consumer subsidies, which tended to have only minimal sustainability. For instance, in November 2006, wheat flour was added to the homologation regime, resulting in a fixed price for both wheat and wheat flour (Ministry of Commerce 2007; Ndiaye 2007a).[7] Yet, the world price and import price of wheat slowly increased over the summer of 2007, leading both large-scale importers and millers to demand that the government amend its price ceiling, noting that they were losing money as the price of flour and bread remained fixed. Philippe Steffan, the director of *Grands Moulins de Dakar*, which is the largest importer of wheat and miller of flour in Senegal, alerted the government in October 2007 that his factory would begin firing millers if the prices were not re-adjusted (see Flipo 2007). Bakers, however, wanted to continue retaining a profit margin from their sale of bread while major consumers' organizations insisted that the government maintain price stability. Ultimately, the government sided with the millers and bakers by agreeing in late October to raise the price of bread by November, strategically ensuring that this increase occurred after the end of Ramadan.

In July 2007, the price of scented, broken rice was set at CFA 225, down from the CFA 250–75 national average. Yet, due to a lack of enforcement, most rice retailers eventually abandoned the price ceilings (Ndiaye 2007b). The price of milk and milk powder was not fixed until right before the start of Ramadan in September 2007 (Ndiaye 2007b). However, as noted in more detail below, the concentration of milk consumption among wealthier Senegalese meant that this measure did not have a large impact on protecting the poor.

In late March 2008, the government faced even greater pressure to confront the food crisis as a result of a demonstration by the largest and best organized consumer union, the Association of Senegalese Consumers (ASCOSEN), and supported by many key opposition parties. Since many participants wrote on their T-shirts *On a faim, ça suffit* (We are hungry, that's enough!), this march was ultimately labelled in the media as the *Emeutes de faim* (Food riots) (interview with Ndao 2012). Due to the participation of opposition groups, President Wade claimed that the rally was only an attempt by the opposition to gain attention. Instead, he announced publicly 'There is no famine in Senegal. There are no hunger riots in Senegal' (cited by Sy 2008).

Subsequently, however, Wade invited the leader of ASCOSEN, Momar Ndao, to explain why he organized the protests. After explaining their concern with

[7] Homologation is a price setting mechanism that requires the government to consult with relevant stakeholders before taking decisive action and choosing a price.

reducing consumer prices and the organization's own solutions to this problem, 'Wade called the prime minister and said "These people have some interesting solutions and I ask you to organize a meeting every week in order to exchange ideas about how to deal with the food prices". The State organized a type of task force, quasi inter-ministerial, presided over by the prime minister and with all the relevant ministries' (interview with Ndao 2012).

Consequently, in April 2008, the government stated it would offer a subsidy to rice distributors in order for them to maintain the price at a maximum of CFA 280 a kilogram (WFP 2008a). This, however, led to a rationing of rice supplies because the government could not pay many distributors the subsidies on time. In turn, 200,000 tons of rice were stockpiled in warehouses around Dakar by early May 2008 and caused the retail price in Dakar to inch closer to CFA 300 per kg (Sylla 2008).

Indeed, the powerful National Union of Traders and Industrialists of Senegal (UNACOIS), which includes large-scale rice importers as members, believed the subsidies were a mistake. According to the organization's secretary general, 'During the crisis, we [UNACOIS] did tell the Ministry of Commerce that we are in a free market and the government needs to have the courage to say that to the population... We opposed the government's decision to introduce subsidies but, the government ignored us because it was under so much pressure and protests. But, we didn't think this was a sustainable policy' (interview with Lo 2012). The subsidy on rice was discontinued in July 2008 due to budget constraints. In fact, the policy had cost the government CFA 11.5 billion (Daffé, Cissé, and Diène 2011), even as many importers and traders still remained unpaid for this consumer subsidy in the form of tax rebates and direct payments (Ndiaye 2009).

The crisis also demanded a greater role for the Commission for Food Security, which holds the country's cereal stocks and provides price and supply information on a regular basis for millet, sorghum, rice, maize, peanuts, and beans. The main response of this agency to the crisis occurred in May 2008 through its Assistance au Monde Rural (AMR) programme. The AMR involved the purchase of more than 20,000 metric tons of rice in order to target vulnerable consumers in rural areas. By August 2008, when the annual rains began, the distribution of rice was halted (interview with Sèye 2012).

Arguably, a more developed social protection programme would have represented the best approach for protecting vulnerable Senegalese from food price shocks in the short term. Despite the country's weak social protection system, a range of donors in the country, including USAID, UNICEF, the World Food Programme, the World Bank, and the FAO have shown an interest in supporting greater protection of the vulnerable. For instance, a school feeding program was established in Dakar in 2008 that assisted approximately 80,000 children between the ages of 3 and 12 (Daffé, Cissé, and Diène 2011).

Another project, entitled 'Targeted Child Nutrition and Social Transfers', has provided vulnerable mothers of children aged 0–5 with a financial subsidy. A programme of food vouchers, costing approximately CFA 1.9 billion, was also established in 2008 for 17,400 households in a suburb of Dakar and in the southern region of Ziguinchor (Daffé, Cissé, and Diène 2011). Probably one of the clearest modes of social protection occurred through overseas remittances, which increased from CFA 400 to 560 billion between 2006 and 2008 before falling in 2009 (see Daffé, Cissé, and Diène 2011).

14.5.3 *Production and Commercial Support*

The centrepiece of the government's response to the food crisis was GOANA, which was launched in May 2008. The announcement followed another march on 26 April against the rising cost of living that was organized by the opposition coalition known as *Front Siggil Senegal*. Food self-sufficiency represented GOANA's main objective. The mechanisms for doing this included irrigating and cultivating unused land in the River Valley, providing subsidies for seeds, fertilizers and phytosanitary products, assisting with rice commercialization, reinforcing the capacity of producers, and introducing new varieties of rice, such as the New Rice for Africa. Overall, GOANA aimed to create, on an annual basis, 500,000 tons of rice, 2 million tons of maize, 3 million tons of manioc, 2 million tons of other cereals, and 400 million litres of milk (Antil 2010).

The announcement of GOANA received only a lukewarm reception from both domestic stakeholders and international donors. While large-scale investments in the agricultural sector were widely supported, the specific aim of attaining food self-sufficiency was deemed unrealistic. Moreover, like REVA and previous agricultural plans, the initiative reflected Wade's tendency for short-term, populist projects rather than a long-term agricultural strategy. According to one report, many government ministers were completely surprised by the announcement of GOANA (see Antil 2010).

The CNCR in particular denounced the abandonment of the LOASP, which had involved large-scale stakeholder consultation, while GOANA had involved none. Furthermore, given that the CNCR includes many of the country's small-scale producers, the organization's members did not understand how GOANA's goals could be feasibly achieved: 'CNCR and its members are surprised by the extremely ambitious quantitative objectives, which they consider impossible to achieve in the given time frame. The experiences and failures of special programmes of production for maize, manioc, sesame, and bissap confirm that these objectives are not realistic' (CNCR 2008). Indeed, the cost of expanding rice production by the desired 500,000 tons for just one year was estimated by experts to cost US$335 million, which was equivalent to the entire total budget for the agricultural sector during the previous four years combined (Ndiaye 2009).

Although the FAO provided US$1.5 million to buy inputs for the most vulnerable smallholders during the crisis, it has had no affiliation with GOANA. In fact, the organization had been working with the government on elaborating a national policy document called the National Programme to Support Food Security, which had a five-year time horizon and involved a diverse range of long-term interventions. Without consulting the FAO, the government abandoned the document and soon thereafter announced GOANA. According to the national FAO director, 'GOANA is not a sustainable programme. In fact, you see every year GOANA I, II, III. If this was a good programme, it would have been oriented towards the medium and long term rather than changed every year' (interview with Ouattara 2012). Representatives of USAID felt similarly, noting that GOANA lacked structural support and sustainability and should have instead been embedded within a larger agricultural programme (interview with Badiane 2012).

A second and less controversial initiative undertaken specifically by the Ministry of Commerce was the establishment of Reference Stores. Although originally adopted by the government in July 2001, this project was not implemented until October 2007 after a consultation with the president's council of ministers. The objectives of this programme were threefold. The first was to better integrate the food distribution network so that retail sellers would be more directly linked with purchasing centres, thereby reducing transaction costs and creating competition among retailers in order to improve prices for consumers. The second was to promote local agricultural production through supporting goods in the Reference Stores such as iodized salt, local rice, milk, sugar, oil, tomatoes, onions, and soap. A final objective was to promote greater employment, particularly among the youth, by creating more retail jobs. Three private promoters (Easy Boutiques, Prista, and Référence Boutique) were responsible for implementing this programme with the support of CFA 3 billion in finance from the Ministry's Economic Promotion Fund (Ministry of Commerce 2011).

Collectively then, the government encountered a broad range of well-organized and vocal interest groups who each possessed distinct preferences on various policy mechanisms (see Table 14.1). The type and design of the interventions the government ultimately took illustrated three key elements of policy-making under Wade. First, even though a well-targeted social targeting programme combined with a legitimate, long-term agricultural strategy would have been the most appropriate response to the crisis, the government clearly was concerned with attempting to satisfy as many groups as possible. Second, many of these initiatives were reactionary, had short time-horizons, and were not well-planned. Third and relatedly, they

Table 14.1 Identifying key domestic stakeholders and policy preferences

Stakeholder Group	Organization	Preference	Key Government Interlocutor
Consumers and labour unions	ASCOSEN, CNES	Reduction of customs duties and VAT; Provision of consumer subsidies	Ministry of Commerce, Ministry of Finance
Producers	CNCR	Implementation of LOASP, rejection of GOANA, broader view of the agricultural sector	Ministry of Agriculture
Importers and traders	UNACOIS (including seven rice importers)	Opposed consumer subsidies for rice	Ministry of Commerce
	Grands Moulins de Dakar, Nouvelle Minoterie Africaine, and Moulins Sentenac	Opposed price fixing for wheat flour and bread	Ministry of Commerce
Processors	SPIDS (Nestlé, Saprolait, Senlait, Mamelles Jabot, etc.)	Opposed removal of VAT for powdered milk	Ministry of Livestock
Opposition parties	Front Siggil Senegal	Advocated supporting consumers and producers simultaneously	Not applicable

Source: author's compilation.

also were the outcome of presidential interference in the policy process, reflecting the increasing centralization and personalization of power around Wade that already manifested during his first term.

14.6 Impact of the Crisis and Government Responses

By the end of 2008, many of these policies had not quelled social discontent. Nevertheless, the collective impact of both the crisis and the government's response was increasingly clear in three key domains: (1) macroeconomics and trade; (2) poverty, malnutrition, and household welfare; and (3) production and commerce.

14.6.1 *Macroeconomics and Trade*

Both the crisis and the government's reaction placed a huge burden on the country's public finances. The rising cost of imports resulted in a trade deficit increase from 17.1 to 25.6 per cent of gross domestic product (GDP) between 2006 and 2008. During the same period, the external current account deficit rose from 9.8 to 14.7 per cent (Daffé, Cissé, and Diène. 2011). Some of this burden was alleviated in December 2008 when the International Monetary Fund (IMF) approved a one-year arrangement of US$75.6 million under the exogenous shocks facility (ESF) to enable Senegal to finance the balance of payments impact of higher food and energy prices. This allowed Senegal to immediately obtain US$37.8 million from the IMF and to receive an equal amount upon completion of the first review under the ESF arrangement.[8]

The government's collective response to the crisis resulted in a tremendous loss of public revenue. According to the IMF (2008), elimination of customs duties on rice, wheat, and milk powder, which were finally re-instated in September 2008, cost the government a total of CFA 12 billion during 2007. Similarly, the removal of the VAT on wheat flour and milk powder resulted in a loss of CFA 5 billion and 12 billion, respectively.[9] Collectively, these revenue losses were equivalent to 0.5 per cent of GDP in 2007. During 2008, the cost of the trade and fiscal measures increased to CFA 36 billion (FAO 2009). After considering the cost of other social protection policies as well as subsidies that the government allocated for electricity and gas, the government's overall response to the crisis amounted to CFA 374 billion (US$748 million) (Diouf 2011).[10]

Besides causing the government to lose substantial revenue, the reduction of the VAT on rice in particular further augmented the appeal of importing rice, thereby exacerbating one of the main structural weaknesses at the heart of the crisis (David-Benz et al. 2010).

14.6.2 *Poverty, Malnutrition, and Household Welfare*

The crisis demonstrated notable impacts on incomes and consumption within urban areas, across the rural and urban milieu, and among different rural regions of the country. Households engaged in a variety of strategies to cope with the crisis. In urban areas, households often shifted their diets to cheaper but more affordable goods or reduced their number of daily meals. In rural areas, households often depended on assistance from neighbours and family or bought food on credit (WFP 2011).

The poverty rates of rural households are estimated to have risen slightly between 2005–6 and 2009. In rural areas, Cabral (2008) found that farmers who combined subsistence agriculture with livestock breeding were more protected from the crisis than those who relied on subsistence agriculture alone. Indicators of child malnutrition generally worsened in the years after the crisis, even in urban areas. One of the main exceptions to this trend was in St. Louis where child stunting in particular decreased over time. St. Louis is

[8] See <http://www.imf.org/external/np/sec/pr/2008/pr08334.htm>.

[9] For the powdered milk, Dia et al. (2008) have further estimated that the loss in public revenue in 2008 was CFA 10.76 billion.

[10] This excludes the cost of GOANA. Subsidies for butane gas and electricity comprised some of the largest outlays by the government, estimated at around CFA 75 billion (see FAO 2008).

the centre of domestic rice production and as many Senegalese shifted to consuming domestic varieties of rice when imported rice became too expensive, access to such varieties were higher in this region than elsewhere. Moreover, domestic rice production experienced a boost during the 2009 and 2010 seasons.

Within urban areas, informal workers and casual labour were hurt much more than salaried professionals by price rises. A study on urban malnutrition following the crisis revealed that residents in both Pikine, which is the most densely populated area of Dakar, and in Ziguinchor were more likely to be unable to meet their food needs than those in Kaolack, which is the center of millet production (WFP 2008b). Even though it is the second main rice producing region, Ziguinchor had the highest rates of food insecurity during the crisis (WFP 2011), a phenomenon tied to poor infrastructure connecting the region to the rest of the country and continuing low-level civil conflict in the broader region of the Casamance.

The VAT removals and suspension of customs duties by the government had disparate effects on the rural and urban segments of the population depending on the commodity under consideration. Estimates by the IMF (2008) revealed that the use of these measures in 2007 to contain the price of rice benefitted the two poorest quintiles of the population and those in rural areas more, especially given that these commodities comprise a larger share of the food budget for these groups. By contrast, richer Senegalese benefitted from the measures targeted at powdered milk. The tariff removals for bread were most beneficial for the urban poor, who consume a higher share of this commodity than their rural counterparts. Overall, the IMF (2008) concluded that by the end of 2007, almost 55 per cent of the benefits accumulated from the trade and fiscal measures accrued to households within the top 40 per cent of the welfare distribution.

A similar trend emerged with respect to the government's various social protection policies. According to the Commission for Food Security, its efforts to distribute rice through the AMR were not very successful for numerous reasons. First, the government reduced the Commission for Food Security's requested budget for the programme, from CFA 10 billion to 7.9 billion, during a series of modifications within the National Assembly. Second, these resources were released to the Commission for Food Security forty-five days behind schedule, delaying the purchase of rice from UNACOIS and the organization of vehicles and technical capacity to deliver the rice. Third, while the Commission for Food Security wanted to target so-called 'red zones', which indicate the highest level of vulnerability, the government preferred to target everyone. Above all, the director of the Commission for Food Security argues that his unit's ability to function has been hindered by high levels of ministerial instability: 'We've been in the office of the president, the office of the prime minister, the Ministry of Agriculture, and now in the Ministry of the Family... We are moving all the time, like a suitcase. In the same way, many other agencies and their bosses are moving' (interview with Sèye 2012).The political disincentive for targeting is exacerbated by a lack of both technical capacity within the government and a database for identifying beneficiaries, the absence of a governmental body in charge of social protection, and little consensus on targeting (e.g., community based vs. means tested) even among the donor community (interview with Pigois 2012).

14.6.3 *Production and Commerce*

The impact of the main initiative to support production, GOANA, was positive in the short term but with few long-term benefits. On the one hand, Gergely and Baris (2009) estimate that the country achieved its objective of 500,000 tons of rice production during 2008/9, mostly because of favourable rains, the expansion of cultivated land, and planting during the both the dry and wet seasons. Much of these production gains occurred in the River Valley around St. Louis, which accounted for approximately 70 per cent of the increase in production. As a consequence of this increased production as well as a substitution to maize, the average level of dependence on rice imports decreased to 65 per cent in 2010, compared with an average of 82 per cent over the period from 2001–10 (WFP 2011).

On the other hand, rice production fell again to 406,000 tons by the 2010/11 growing season, suggesting that the brief period of production gains was due more to good rains than to the structure of GOANA. Ndiaye (2009) also notes that the political pressures for GOANA to succeed have prevented an objective assessment of crop surveys and the implementation of key famine early warning mechanisms. Furthermore, GOANA does not address processing and commercialization, and therefore increased production does not necessarily translate into increased food security for the broader population (OBG 2009). Therefore, while the intention underlying GOANA was laudable, the plan appears to have been too focused on short-term production goals rather than structural changes critical for ensuring the country's long-term food security.

REVA has likewise demonstrated ambiguous results in terms of enticing young people to farm. As of 2010, a total of 600 jobs, rather than the anticipated 300,000, have been created within the fruit and vegetables sector (Daffé, Cissé, and Diène 2011). According to a study conducted by Sall (2012), REVA resulted in young people learning new farming techniques, including ways of farming during the typical dry season. However, a number of participants have still complained about the low incomes from agriculture, and some farms experienced noticeable dropout rates by youth from Dakar who found it difficult to adjust to living conditions in rural areas. Most significantly,

REVA's focus on horticultural, export-oriented agriculture appears to conflict with the food security objectives embedded within GOANA and previous agricultural plans, such as the LOASP (see OECD 2007).

The Reference Stores created by the Ministry of Commerce resulted in the establishment of 170 stores by 2011, 119 of which were in Dakar. But, this has not proved to be a very sustainable programme due to the inability to retain store managers beyond a year or so. Many have migrated, either to other areas of Senegal or overseas, and some used the money they received from the state for other means than to purchase goods from local markets. The three networks managing the stores complained that part of the reason for the lacklustre success of this programme was the lack of support from the state (interview with Diouf 2012). The continued operation of the programme and its expansion to the rest of the country depends heavily on further investment in resources by the government (Diouf 2010).

14.7 Conclusions: Beyond 2007/8, beyond Wade

The 2007/8 food price crisis dramatically highlighted the unsustainability of Senegal's longstanding consumption and production patterns. The preference of Senegal's large urban population for imported rice, powdered milk, and wheat-based bread represented the country's Achilles heel as such goods became increasingly expensive. Although the preference for imported goods was inherited from the colonial period, successive governments have done little to ameliorate this skewed pattern. Large-scale discontent, particularly in Dakar, manifested in no less than five major protests during the crisis period. For the former president Wade, who rose to power in 2000 by tapping into urban disgruntlement under his predecessor, the food price crisis represented a threat to his presidential legacy. The crisis emerged at a time when he had already increasingly centralized power around the executive, launched a variety of short-term but high-profile plans within the agricultural sector and elsewhere, and reshuffled his cabinet multiple times. The resultant high levels of ministerial instability prevented more long-term strategic planning within the agricultural and social protection sectors as well as closer engagement with the donor community. Simultaneously, however, Senegal's vibrant democracy resulted in the emergence of a broad range of well-organized interest groups advocating for specific policy mechanisms. In order to satisfy as many groups as possible, the government forfeited the opportunity to devise a well-targeted social protection programme and a long-term agricultural strategy. Instead, the government's initiatives were reactionary, myopic, and resulted in significant policy volatility, including the retraction of unpopular salary taxes and the termination of consumer subsidies only three months after their implementation.

These patterns were not just limited to the 2007/8 period. By 2012, the price of food became heavily politicized due to presidential elections scheduled for February. Wade's key opponent in those elections, Macky Sall, argued on the campaign trail that food prices would again increase if Wade were re-elected for a third time (Dione 2012). To avoid attracting scorn on his government's attempts to handle the 2007/8 crisis, Wade failed to respond to growing warnings by the donor community that a second crisis was possible within the Sahel. In late 2011, the FAO noted that a decline in cereal and agro-pastoral production in a number of West African countries, including Senegal, posed a new threat to food security. With a level of cereal production that could meet only 39 per cent of the Senegalese population's cereal consumption needs, the Commission for Food Security, USAID, the WFP, and the FAO all publicized the possibility of a new crisis but received no response from Wade's government (interview with Seye 2012). Indeed, for the FAO, electoral motives were clearly a prime reason for this decision: 'Another crisis is looming but in the electoral period, the government has said nothing and not asked the FAO and WFP to help because if it declares that a famine is possible, the opposition could then blame the government for this' (interview with Ouattara 2012).

Ultimately, Sall ousted Wade, obtaining almost two-thirds of the national vote. Widely viewed as a technocrat who lacks Wade's penchant for short-term populist policies, there is the potential for greater bureaucratic decision-making on issues of agriculture, trade, and social protection.[11] Thus, if another global crisis occurs, hopefully the impact will not only be less severe but also the policy responses will target the poorest without requiring exorbitant outlays of government revenue or sowing so much discontent among Senegal's various stakeholders.

References

Antil, A. (2010). *Les 'émeutes de la faim' au Sénégal. Un puissant révélateur d'une défaillance de gouvernance*. Paris: International Food Policy Research Institute (IFPRI).

Ba, C. O., B. Diagna, P. Nouhine Dièye, I. Hathie, and M. Niang (2009). *Changements structurels des economies rurales dans la mondialisation. Programme RuralStruc-Phase II*. Washington, DC: World Bank.

[11] Since coming to office, Sall's government has promised to conduct an audit of GOANA to assess whether the programme should continue.

Baris, P. (2009). 'Quels outils de régulation pour relancer la riziculture au Sénégal?' *Grain de sel* 48: 5–6.

Cabral, F. J. (2008). 'Insécurité alimentaire en milieu urbain et rural au Sénégal. Les mêmes causes créent-elles les mêmes effets?'. Working Paper No. 08-12. University of Sherbrooke: Groupe de Recherche en Economie et Développement International.

Cabral, F. J., F. Cissé, and A. Diagne (2009). *Croissance agricole et options d'investissement pour la réduction de la pauvreté au Sénégal*. Dakar: CRES.

Conseil National de Concertation et de Coopération des Ruraux (CNCR). 2008. 'Déclaration sur la GOANA et le Programme Agricole 2008/09'. Dakar: CNCR. Available at: <http://www.cncr.org/spip.php?rubrique32>.

Daffé, G., F. Cissé, and M. Diène (2011). *Evaluation des impacts des crises et des réponses politiques mise en œuvre au Sénégal. Situation des enfants et simulations de politiques de protection sociale*. Dakar: CRES.

David-Benz, H., A. Diallo, F. Lancon, V. Meuriot, P. Rasolofo, L. Temple, and A. Wane (2010). *L'imparfaite transmission des prix mondiaux aux marchés agricoles d'Afrique subsaharienne*. Montpelier: CIRAD.

Dia, D., Y. Ngom, V. Duteurtre, P. Nouhine Dièye, G. Duteurtre, and C. Broutin (2008). *Etude de l'impact de la hausse des cours du lait et des produits laitiers sur les producteurs et les consommateurs*. Dakar: ISRA and Montpelier: CIRAD.

Dione, B. (2012). 'Macky Sall aux populations de Louga. Si vous réalisez Wade, les prix vont encore flamber'. *Le soleil*, 13 March.

Diouf, El H. A. (2011). 'La formation des prix intérieurs dans les pays importateurs de denrées alimentaires'. Dakar: Ministry of Commerce.

Diouf, M. M. (2010). 'La politique de baisse des prix des denrées de première nécessité par les magasins de référence'. *Revue de l'amicale des commissaires aux enquetes economiques*, 14–15.

Economist Intelligence Unit (EIU) (2007). 'Country Report: Senegal, November'. London: EIU.

Fan, S., B. Omilola, and M. Lambert (2009). 'Public Spending for Agriculture in Africa: Trends and Composition'. ReSAKSS Working Paper No. 28. Washington, DC: International Food Policy Research Institute (IFPRI).

FAO (Food and Agricultural Organization) (2008). 'Sénégal. Initiative en réponse à la flambée des prix des denrées alimentaires'. Rome: FAO.

FAO (Food and Agricultural Organization) (2009). *Initiative on Soaring Prices in Senegal: Inter-Agency Consultative Mission with the Government and Development Partners*. Rome: FAO.

FEWS NET (Famine Early Warning Systems Network) (2006). 'Senegal: Monthly Food Security Update, December', Rome: Food and Agriculture Organization (FAO).

Flipo, B. (2007). 'L'Afrique Face à la flambée du blé'. *Jeune Afrique*, 22 October.

Gergely, N., and P. Baris (2009). *Étude sur la compétitivité du riz de la Vallée du Fleuve Sénégal sur les marchés nationaux et régionaux*. Paris: GLG Consultants.

IIED (International Institute for Environment and Development) (2002). *Pour le développement d'une agriculture régénératrice au Sénégal*. London: IIED.

IMF (International Monetary Fund) (2008). 'Senegal: Selected Issues', IMF Country Report No. 08/221. Washington, DC: IMF.

Mbow, P. (2008). 'The Return of Personalism'. *Journal of Democracy* 19(1): 156–69.

Ministry of Commerce (2007). 'Decret n 2006-1246 du 13 Novembre 2006 modifiant l'Article 3 du Décret n 95-77 du 20 Janvier 1995 portant Application des Articles 44 et 64 de la Loi n 94-63 du 22 Août 1994'. *Journal Officiel* No. 6342, 28 April. Dakar: Ministry of Commerce. Avalaible at <http://www.jo.gouv.sn/spip.php?article5856>.

Ndiaye, M. (2007a). 'Senegal Agricultural Situation Country Report 2007'. Global Agricultural Information Network (GAIN) Report. Washington, DC: USDA Foreign Agricultural Service.

Ndiaye, M. (2007b). 'Senegal Agricultural Situation: Domestic Market Price and Policy Update 2007'. Global Agricultural Information Network (GAIN) Report. Washington, DC: USDA Foreign Agricultural Service.

Ndiaye, M. (2009). 'Senegal Agricultural Situation: Agricultural Situation Update 2009'. Global Agricultural Information Network (GAIN) Report. Washington, DC: USDA Foreign Agricultural Service.

Ndione, M. (2008). 'Contraintes d'une croissance inégalement répartie, No. 10'. *Magazine du Bureau Régional de la Banque Mondiale à Dakar*: 22–3.

OECD (Organisation for Economic Co-operation and Development). 2007. 'Country Report: Senegal'. *African Economic Outlook*. Paris: OECD.

Oxford Business Group (OBG). 2009. *The Report: Senegal 2009*. London: OBG.

Sall, M. (2012). 'The REVA Plan in Senegal: Does Modern Farming Change the Minds of Young People about Agriculture?' Paper prepared for the Conference on 'Young People, Farming, and Food', held in Accra, Ghana, 19–21 March.

Samson, M., and C. Cherrier (2009). *Etude de faisabilité pour un programme de transferts sociaux monétaires comme instrument majeur d'une protection sociale centrée sur l'enfant au Sénégal*. Dakar: UNICEF.

Stads, G.-J., and L. Sène (2011). *Private-Sector Agricultural Research and Innovation in Senegal: Recent Policy, Investment, and Capacity Trends*. International Food Policy Research Institute (IFPRI), Rutgers University, and McGill University.

Sy, H. T. (2008). 'Senegal: Debate Rages Over Whether Country Faces Famine'. *The Daily Nation*, 30 April. Available at: <http://allafrica.com/stories/200804300061.html>.

Sylla, C. (2008). 'Senegal Suffers from Food Crisis, Nation is Reliant on Others to Import most of its Edible Resources'. *Nanaimo Daily News*, 17 May: A11.

WFP (World Food Programme) (2008a). 'Rapport d'analyse de marché Sénégal. Commerce du riz'. Rome: WFP.

WFP (World Food Programme) (2008b). 'Impact de la hausse des prix sur la sécurité alimentaire des populations en milieu urbain. Sénégal-Pikine-Kaolack-Ziguinchor'. Rome: WFP.

WFP (World Food Programme) (2011). 'République du Sénégal. Analyse globale de la vulnérabilité, de la sécurité alimentaire et de la nutrition (AGVSA)'. Rome: WFP.

Interviews

Badiane, Dr. Aminata Niane. *Agricultural Expert, USAID*. Dakar, Senegal, 13 March 2012.

Diouf, Makhfou Mahécor. *Head of the Legislative and Entrepreneurial Assistance Department*, Department of Interior Commerce, Ministry of Commerce. Dakar, Senegal, 13 March 2012.

Guèye, Cheikh. *Geographical Researcher, Enda Tiers-Monde*. Dakar, Senegal, 19 November 2008.

Lô, Moustapha. *Secretary General of UNACOIS*. Dakar, Senegal, 15 March 2012.

Ndao, Momar. *President of the Senegalese Association of Consumers (ASCOSEN)*. Dakar, Senegal, 15 March 2012.

Ouattara, Amadou. *FAO Representative for Senegal*. Dakar, Senegal, 14 March 2012.

Pigois, Rémy. *Chief of Social Policy, UNICEF*. Dakar, Senegal, 14 March 2012.

Seye, Colonel Issa. *Director, Commission for Food Security*. Dakar, Senegal, 16 March 2012.

Part VI
The Political Economy of Food Price Policy in Large Exporters

15

The Political Economy of Food Price Policy in Vietnam

Nguyen Manh Hai and Theodore Talbot

15.1 Introduction

It is difficult to overstate the importance—cultural and nutritional—of rice to Vietnam's economy and society. As such, policies that influence rice production and prices provide a lens through which to understand broader agricultural policies both in Vietnam and other low- or middle-income economies where agriculture remains one of the major components of national income. This paper sheds light on the political economy of rice price policy in Vietnam by discussing the government's response to a rapid escalation in food prices. We document how agricultural policy and market incentives caused domestic production and prices to deviate from market-clearing equilibrium values, and draw broader lessons for agricultural policy in Vietnam and beyond.

This is an opportune moment to develop an understanding of how domestic political processes interact with market forces to determine prices. First, as in many low-income countries experiencing a combination of economic growth and rapid urbanization, Vietnam's arable land is under pressure: rising land prices and high prices for crops that can be produced with approximately the same inputs increase the opportunity costs of rice production. Second, the structural transformation of the Vietnamese economy is moving a large number of households away from agricultural production into higher value added activities, creating a large, growing, and politically influential group of net food consumers whose real incomes are compromised when food prices rise. Third, despite the primacy of industrial policy, agricultural policies—particularly food price policies—remain an important focal point for the Vietnamese government, particularly in light of dramatic 150 per cent increase in real agricultural prices between 2000 and 2010. Although the share of the agricultural sector in the Vietnamese economy is slowly declining to 21 per cent of gross domestic product (GDP) in 2010, 69.8 per cent of the total population continues to live in rural areas where rice is either a major income source, a large component of the household consumption basket, or both (GSO 2011a). Finally, understanding how food prices are determined has become particularly urgent in light of countries' vulnerability to food price shocks revealed by a global run-up in food prices during 2007–8. The Vietnamese experience was, of course, not unique in this respect.[1] Prices reflect the interplay of market forces and government policies, and the agricultural price shock has made policy formulation in low- and middle-income countries an important contemporary research area. While traditional economic analysis provides partial explanation of overall price movements, a full account of price dynamics requires understanding the political economy of food price policy. This study fills a gap in the literature by focusing on the case of rice prices in Vietnam. Specifically, we argue that observed prices reveal significant market intervention by the state, and that this intervention appears internally inconsistent because it reflects the competing demands of two distinct constituencies: net rice producers and net rice consumers.

15.2 Country Context

Most authors date the end of Vietnam's era of central planning to 1986, when the government implemeted the *Doi Moi* (commonly translated as 'reform' or 'renovation') process, a series of market-oriented industrial and agricultural reforms reversing collectivization and successively introducing measures ranging from privately-held land use rights to decreased import taxes, including on key agricultural inputs like urea and fertilizer. During the 1970s, the country exhibited chronic low levels of agricultural production and, as a consequence, low levels of food consumption per capita, including localized instances of famine. As in many post-collectivist economies, liberalization generated significant increases in yields, culminating in the current situation in which Vietnam is the world's second largest rice exporter by volume, with seven million tons of rice exported in 2011, second only to 8.5 million tons exported by Thailand (VFA 2012). Vietnam's green revolution is remarkable, but should be contextualized. While a large exporter, Vietnam's total rice production remains lower than that of countries such as China, India, and Indonesia, and while the country accounts for about one-fifth of annual world rice exports by volume, it accounts for only around 5 per cent

[1] See, for example, Cudjoe, Breisinger, and Diao (2008), de Janvry and Sadoulet (2009), Wondon and Zaman (2009), Minot (2010), Phung (2011), and Wright (2011).

of total exports by value, indicating a combination of lower quality and lower value added rice exports. Vietnam's macroeconomic performance has also delivered remarkable increases in average living standards. Higher agricultural yields have been accompanied by dramatically higher rates of economic growth. From 2000 onwards, Vietnam's real (purchasing power parity- (PPP-) adjusted) per capita income has grown at 6 per cent per year.

While the economy continues to expand, there have been chronic structural and macroeconmic problems. Vietnamese agriculture has increased yields and total output but has not been able to substantially increase quality or value added. Further expansions in agricultural production are possible, but remain stymied by small, fragmented cultivation areas that prevent investment in agricultural equipment or exploiting economies of scale in crop production. The country is ranked ninety-eighth out of 183 in the World Bank's Doing Business index in 2011 (IFC 2012), indicating significant administrative and bureaucratic barriers, including corruption. Along with high growth rates, the country has experienced persistent and volatile inflation and, since 2009, a decline in investment, generating sufficient concern for the government to introduce a macroeconomic stabilization package in 2008. Finally, as a price taker in agricultural markets and an oil producer (oil contributes arpproximately 20 per cent to the country's GDP), Vietnam's current account is heavily exposed to international price movements.

15.2.1 *Socioeconomic Context*

The state sector's share of GDP has decreased from 35.9 per cent in 2007 to 33.2 per cent in 2009, reflecting increasing prominence of the private sector, including through privatization (referred to as 'equitization') and mergers and acquisitions of state-owned enterprises (SOEs).

Vietnam weathered the global financial crisis relatively well: growth rebounded from earlier slumps to reach 6.78 per cent in 2010. But the agriculture, forestry, and fishery (AFF) sector continues to face serious challenges, with estimated growth rates of value added around 3 per cent in 2010, indicating serious structural issues and persistent vulnerability to price shocks.

How inclusive has this growth been? While some groups have not benefited from macroeconomic growth, overall poverty has declined dramatically. The share of Vietnam's population living beneath the national poverty line more than halved between 1998 and 2009, from 37.4 per cent to 14.2 per cent, much of which has been driven by a decline in rural poverty, which decreased from 35.6 per cent in 2002 to 17.4 per cent in 2009, while urban poverty rates have been relatively static: 6.6 per cent in 2002, and 6.9 per cent in 2009 (MOLISA 2011). Due, in part, to the financial crisis in 2008–9, the poverty rate increased from 13.4 per cent in 2008 to 14.2 per cent in 2009.

While the overall trend for poverty is steeply negative, there is some fluctuation around this trend, and microeconomic evidence points to localized areas of persistent poverty, particularly in the north of Vietnam and amongst ethnic minority populations (Tarp and McKay 2011).

15.2.2 *Political Structure*

Since 1975, Vietnam has been a Socialist Republic governed by a constitution promulgated in April 1992 that replaced the previous document drafted in 1980. The constitution establishes the country as a single-party state governed by the Communist Party of Vietnam (CPV), whose stated objectives include growth-oriented policies to increase welfare and the delivery of social services. A unicameral legislative system means that all laws are passed by the National Assembly (NA) of Vietnam. Nominally, the executive and judicial branches of government are subservient to the NA, which has a constitutional mandate of 'close co-operation and co-ordination' with the CPV. Government ministers and senior officials are largely drawn from the membership of the NA. Figure 15.1 illustrates the policy-making process in Vietnam.

Despite its formal status as a one-party state, a form of electoral competition exists because members must be elected to the NA through locally-contested elections, while the Party Congress provides an opportunity for critique of existing policies and the introduction of radically new ones.[2] As with most contested political competitions, the Government's incentives to minimize economic volatility increase around the time of the Congress or elections to the NA. For the former, price volatility or inept economic management can result in dramatic changes in economic policy. For sitting representatives in the NA, economic mismanagement may prevent re-election. These 'electoral' cycles therefore create additional pressure for the state to move market prices.

The combination of a strong, centralized bureaucracy and a single-party system has resulted in a relatively stable political environment. The tone of CPV's policy is increasingly oriented towards liberalization and, having previously prioritized economic growth, emphasis is shifting towards macroeconomic resilience and stability.

15.2.3 *Key Decision-making Actors*

The key political bodies are the NA, the state president, and the government, led by the prime minister. The NA is the most senior decision-making body,

[2] The 1986 CPV congress, for example, formally endorsed Vietnam's departure from central planning.

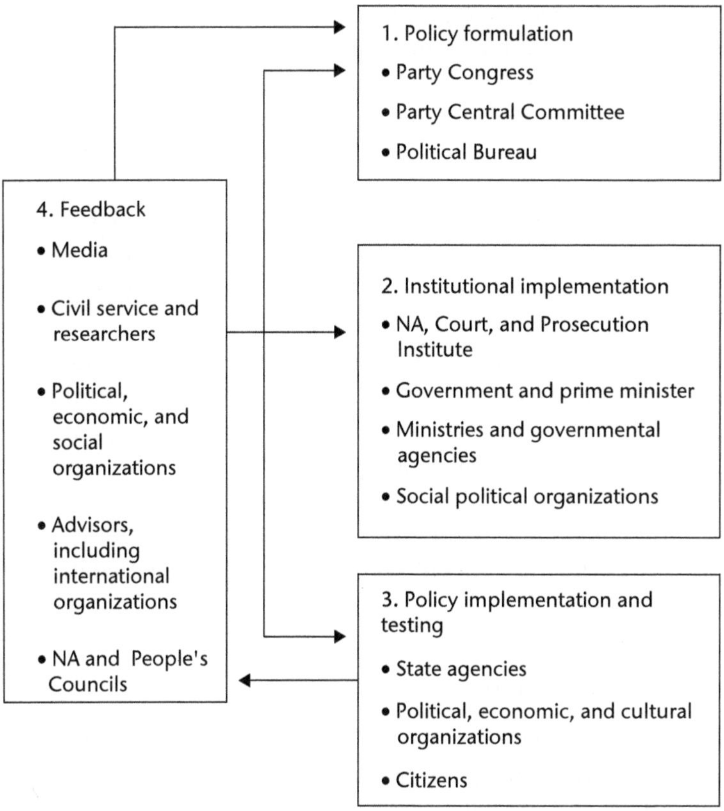

Figure 15.1 The policy-making process in Vietnam
Source: adapted from Cong (2001) and McCarty (2002).

determining domestic and foreign policy, including national defence and state security. The NA is also the only body able to revise and approve the constitution and draft legislation. (Vietnam has numerous, highly specific legislative tools, such as codes, decrees, decisions, laws, and resolutions, each with subtle differences in scope and authority.)

Article 4 of the Vietnamese constitution defines the role of the CPV as '. . . the leading force of the state and society'. While the CPV and the NA are theoretically distinct, 90 per cent of NA members are also on the membership rolls of the CPV, as are the majority of senior government officials, including the prime minister and the cabinet (ISOS 2013).

The NA has significant power over political appointments, and collectively selects the president. Candidates for this office are drawn from the elite deputies of the NA, and the holder of this office has a mixture of legislative and executive responsibilities. According to Article 103 of the 1992 constitution, the president promulgates legal documents adopted by the NA, has command of the armed forces, holds the office of chairman of the National Defence and Security Council, and appoints or proposes the appointment of vice presidents, the prime minister, the chief judge of the Supreme People's Court, and the head of the Supreme People's Procuracy.[3]

Policies decided by the NA under the leadership of the president are implemented by the government, and senior government officials are typically party members. The government is accountable to the NA, in particular to the standing committee and the office of the president. The most senior executive officers of the government are the prime minister, deputy prime ministers, ministers, and the heads of ministerial level agencies.

As the head of government, the prime minister is the head of the cabinet and responsible for delegating authority to line ministries through their respective ministers. A minister or a head of a ministerial agency is directly responsible to the prime minister and the NA for his or her respective sector (CIEM 2011). While ministries' authority is ultimately mandated to them by the NA, these mandates often overlap in scope and authority, an issue we highlight here in the inconsistent set of policies implemented in response to volatile rice prices in 2008.

15.2.4 *Non-political Actors*

More open political discourse began following the *Doi Moi* era, creating space for several non-political actors to influence government policy, including independent and official research institutes, civil society, international organizations, and the media. To various degrees, each of these actors influenced the government's actions to stabilize rice prices during the price shock of 2008.

Government research institutes have a formal consultative role in the policy process, and are mandated to report to ministers or senior officials. The research agenda is often set by the government, but significant flexibility means research institutes have been able to develop their own research themes, including through cooperation with researchers outside Vietnam. The Central Institute for Economic Management (CIEM) in the Ministry of Planning and Investment, amongst others, has a direct reporting role about economic policies, including food prices and agricultural policies.

Legal civil society has also emerged and has been empowered by better communication tools, especially widespread internet access. These organizations are distinct from mass political organizations such as the Vietnam Fatherhood Front that are closely aligned with the government or the CPV. In

[3] This term dates to the Soviet era. The Supreme People's Procuracy of Vietnam is tasked with ensuring the legal compliance of the Vietnamese state, including the military.

2008, the NA passed a law formalizing such civil society organizations' right to comment on draft legislation (CIEM 2011), an important step forward in formalizing civil society's role in policy formation.

In addition to domestic civil society, there is extensive engagement with the international donor community. A consortium of donors, including the World Bank, the United Nations (UN) System, and several national aid agencies such as AusAID, remain active in Vietnam despite the country's recent graduation from low- to middle-income status. Notably, the UN and World Bank publicly argued against restrictions on rice exports, contradicting the government's policy to impose this restriction in the second quarter of 2008.

Finally, increased space for public discussion has resulted in an increase in media freedom, which has increased the accountability of policy makers. Food prices, both international and domestic, were extensively covered during the crisis, and national media outlets directly and publicly questioned senior officials about the policies implemented.

15.3 Rice Production and Prices

15.3.1 *Rice Production*

Collectivization of land, lack of key agricultural inputs, and a shortage of mechanical agricultural equipment caused chronic rice shortages until 1989, forcing Vietnam to import 300,000–500,000 metric tonnes of rice annually between 1985 and 1988 to meet domestic demand (Luu 2002), with much of the shortfall between domestic subsistence consumption and production met through food aid from the USSR. This aid was cut off shortly after the Soviet collapse in 1989, making agricultural reform an urgent priority.[4] In April 1988, Resolution 10 of the Politburo assigned agricultural land to individual households for up to fifteen years, effectively privatizing production. The march towards private ownership (accompanied by increases in yields) continued with the land laws of 1993 and 2003 that granted farmers private 'land use rights'.

The cumulative effect of these reforms has been a consistent increase in rice production from 1989 to the present, enabling the country to satisfy internal demand and sell surplus production internationally. While the total area under cultivation has remained roughly static, paddy rice

[4] Some tentative reform efforts in fact pre-dated the collapse of the USSR. In 1981, the 'Directive 100' policy assigned agricultural land to farming groups or individuals through a system of agricultural cooperatives, under which farmers directed production while cooperatives had a monopoly on sales; farmers received payment on rice based on how much they produced (Marsh, MacAulay, and Hung 2006).

production has increased from 2000–11 by almost 3 per cent per year (GSO 2011b), largely through mechanization in some areas and planting hybrid rice varieties in preference to traditional open pollination varieties. In 2009, Vietnam's exported rice value reached 5.95 million tonnes (nominal US$3.23 billion).

Despite the centrality of rice to the traditional Vietnamese diet, it has a negative income elasticity of demand: wealthier households substitute away from rice consumption, with the effect that per capita consumption is decreasing (as in many other high growth Asian economies) while aggregate consumption has increased due to a combination of population growth, demand for feedstock, and increased demand from secondary processing industries.

As shown in Figure 15.2, rice exports have persistently increased in terms of volume and value since measurement began in 1989, and the share of rice in total export value in 2011 was around 3.6 per cent,[5] which has been increasing since 2008 due to the high export demand. In 2008, Vietnam exported 1.7 million tonnes of rice to the Philippines, the single largest buyer by volume (USDA 2011); this strong demand for rice exports is predicted to continue to 2030 (MARD 2006).

15.3.2 *Rice Prices*

Vietnam's economy has achieved gains in spatial integration, but considerable regional price dispersion remains and indicates the persistence of transportation costs and other frictions. There is a systematic difference in rice prices between 2008 and 2009 as markets priced-in the global increase in

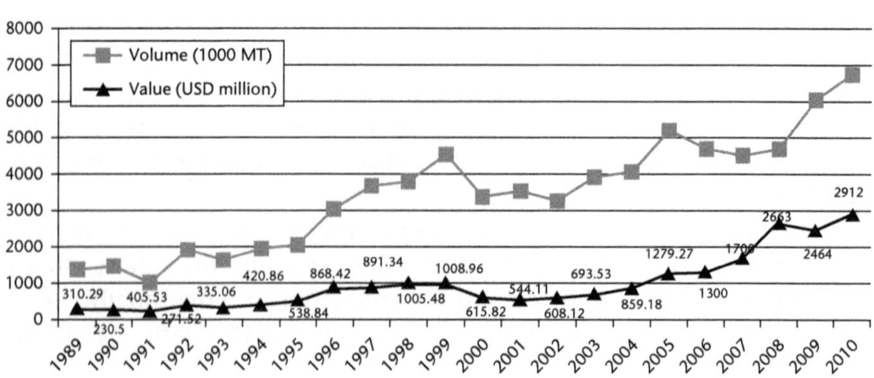

Figure 15.2 Rice exports, 1989–2010

Source: authors' calculation based on data from VIFAP (2011).

[5] Estimated from the data of VFA (2012) and VCO (2012).

rice prices and the data show a persistent but unstable price wedge between domestic and international prices.

The spatial differences in rice prices across Vietnam are relatively large and increasing, indicating high transaction costs: the price gap for paddy rice between the highest priced region and the lowest rose from 15.5 per cent over 1996–9 to 26.8 per cent in 2000–2. More recent data (MARD 2006) show the percentage gap between rice prices in the Red River Delta and Mekong River Delta has doubled from 10.3 per cent to 20.2 per cent (MARD 2006). The overall picture is one of significant price dispersion across Vietnam, due to the interaction of transaction costs that create frictions for cross-province arbitrage and regional differences in production costs and efficiency.[6]

Due to the impact of the global price shock in agricultural commodities, domestic rice prices were much higher in 2009 than in 2008 (Figure 15.3).

During the 2008 food price shock, the average domestic rice prices increased quickly, while regional rice prices varied substantially. For example, the Mekong River Delta had the smallest year-on-year increase in prices, in contrast to significant increases in urban and peri-urban areas. Prices in the productive Mekong River Delta area increased by 36 per cent, while Ho Chi Minh City and Hanoi experienced a doubling of rice prices. These price differentials are driven by asymmetries in agricultural efficiency, endowments,

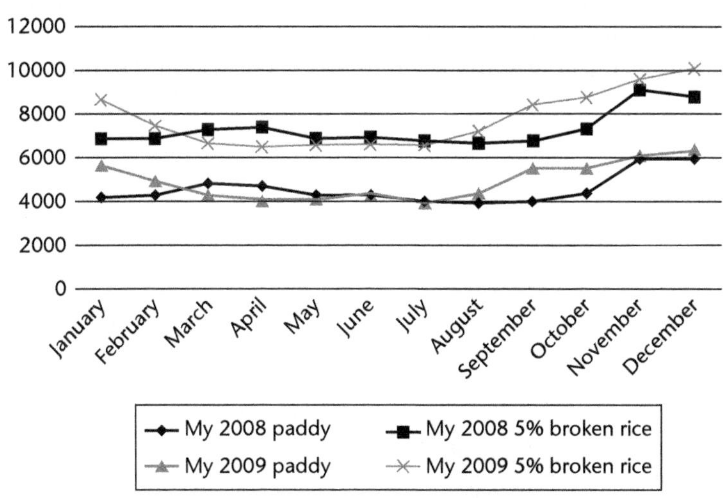

Figure 15.3 Price trends: paddy and milled rice, 2008 and 2009
Source: USDA (2011).

[6] The Red River Delta and Cuu Long River Delta are the main sources of rice, accounting for 66 per cent of total rice production area, and 70 per cent of total paddy output.

and transaction costs, particularly the cost of transportation from the south to the north.

Luu (2002) shows that rice price movements are co-integrated across Vietnam, so while the level of rice prices may be different due to differences in rice production and transportation costs, changes in prices are roughly consistent over time. Domestic cost differences, where they exist, arise mainly from different geographical conditions, with substantially higher transportation costs in highland and mountainous regions (for example, Lao Cai province, bordering China). Figure 15.4 shows this informally by tracking prices over time based on available time series data.

The ratio of the domestic to international prices provides further evidence of market imperfections due to price differentials. In an integrated market with no changes in frictions like import tariffs, the market structure of importing firms, or, as we argue here, state-sponsored market interventions, the ratio of domestic prices to world prices should be approximately stable over time, since changes in the world prices would pass one-for-one into domestic prices. In fact, this ratio fluctuates dramatically (Figure 15.5).

The world prices for Vietnamese rice showed modest fluctuation from early 2009 to the fourth quarter of 2010, and the ratio of domestic to world prices is flat. Before that, increases in world prices accompany a less-than-proportional increase in domestic prices (the ratio falls below one); after that, increases in domestic prices exceed increases in world prices (the ratio rises above one). Even when world and domestic prices move in the same direction, the sizes of the relative price changes are different and inconsistent. Despite significant

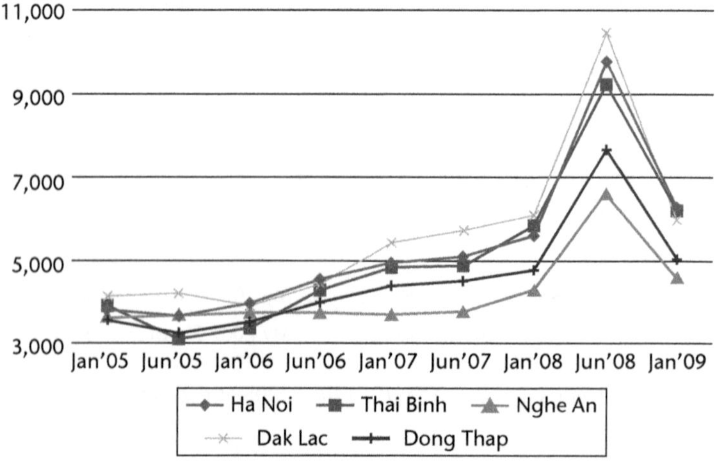

Figure 15.4 Local rice prices (nominal Vietnamese dollar) per kilo, 2005–9
Source: authors' calculations from GSO (2011b).

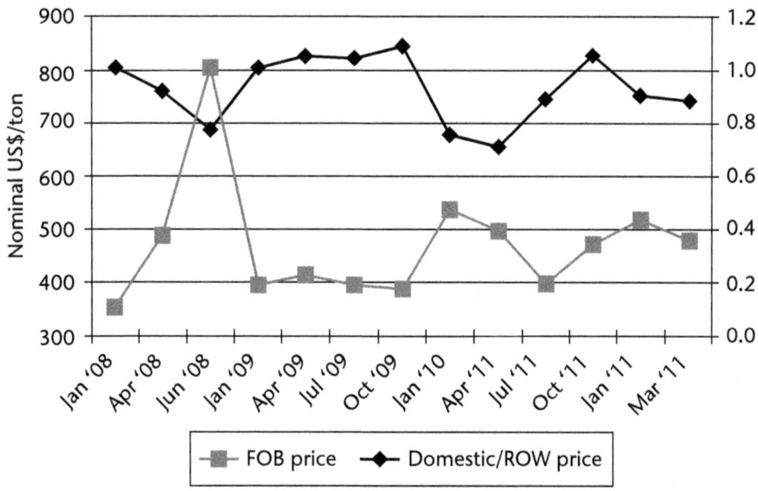

Figure 15.5 Free on board rice prices: pass-through relative to the world market prices
Source: authors' calculation based on data from ASEAN Secretariat (2010) and GSO (2011b).

steps towards market integration, some form of friction that is not stable over time evidently affected the transmission of price signals from international to domestic markets.

15.4 From Prices to Policies

The previous section argued that in addition to regional price dispersion within Vietnam, rice prices diverged from world prices during the relevant period. Two wedges could have caused observed prices to be different from (unobserved) equilibrium prices: market integration and price intervention policies. The previous section argued that price dispersion across Vietnam roughly reflects transaction costs. At the same time, domestic prices exaggerated world price movements, and moved in the *opposite* direction to world prices during the crisis of 2008.

Food price policies distort market prices. In some cases, distortionary policies are defensible on grounds of equity or food security; in others, they create opportunities for rent extraction. We do not take a position on how 'good' it is for the state to move rice prices. Rather, we argue that these price movements can be understood by examining changes in government agricultural policy over this horizon, and that these policies were motivated in turn by a desire to cater to the competing demands of distinct domestic constituencies of net-producers and net-consumers. We start by examining the set of available policy measures to influence rice production and rice prices.

15.4.1 *Domestic Policy Space*

Policies can be implemented through the passage of legislation or through instruments such as decrees that govern the interpretation or implementation of existing legislation. We group the policies designed to affect rice prices (though not necessarily only rice prices) into two categories: long-term policies to increase yields and short-term policies to respond to price fluctuations.

To understand short-term deviations from world prices beyond those explained by transaction costs, we turn to a set of government policies that enable the state to intervene directly in markets by setting export levels and domestic prices when prices are high or volatile.

While investment incentives and other fiscal policies are designed to tilt production towards increasing agricultural output, the focus of short-term policies is to directly move market prices. Price decreases benefit consumers. Since rice is part of every household's consumption basket, lower prices increase rice consumption or enable substitution towards other foods or non-foods. Symmetrically, lower rice prices are a negative income shock to net rice producing households.

The incompatible objectives of keeping prices low to benefit consumers while keeping them high to benefit producers gives rise to inconsistent price stabilization policies that combine procurement and price interventions with quotas. When rice prices are low, the central government provides state-owned firms with capital to buy rice from producers, putting upward pressure on prices. When world prices are high, the government is able to impose an export quota. When world prices are above domestic equilibrium prices, the export quota effectively reduces prices, harming farming households while benefiting net rice consumers.

There are two tools to move rice prices: direct intervention through purchasing rice and trade policy to limit rice exports. Direct intervention is enabled by the 'Ordinance on Prices' drafted by the NA in 2002 which theoretically subjects a range of agricultural products to price stabilization by the state; Article 6 of this ordinance allows the government to set minimum purchase prices that large state-owned buyers and the Vietnam Food Association (VFA) pay for rice.

These large purchases by the state can be timed to coincide with price decreases to raise profits to farming households. Decision No. 1518/QD-TTg dated 22 September 2009 of the prime minister, for example, released government funds to increase rice stockpiles.[7] Using strategic stockpiling to move

[7] The legislation theoretically enables the government to compel private companies or traders to sell rice or other agricultural products to the government at prices set by state agencies; fortunately, this provision is very rarely used.

market prices will likely remain an aspect of the Vietnamese agricultural policy over the medium-run: the state has invested heavily in storage capacity, and a government resolution in 2009 earmarked funds to upgrade a four million ton rice storage facility and begin construction of a new 2.8 million ton storage facility. To contextualize this, the state's export target for rice through 2020 is around four million tons per year.

Recent government policies further institutionalize the state's ability to determine market prices through controlling exports. In 2010, Decree No. 109/2010/ND-CP was issued with the nominal goal of increasing 'export efficiency'. According to the decree, exporting firms have to meet extensive minimum requirements, for example owning at least one specialized warehouse with a minimum capacity of 5,000 tonnes and a rice milling facility with a minimum capacity of ten tonnes rice/hour. The net effect was to push smaller exporters out of the market. A reasonable recommendation, therefore, is that a better quality control system be implemented to replace the current licensing regime that reduces competition in the rice export market.

The government's most effective tool for moving market prices remains trade policy. Intervention in markets is implemented through the VFA and the Ministry of Industry and Trade (MOIT). From 2000–10, the government enacted numerous export measures, including several during the period of record increases in world agricultural prices.[8]

15.5 From Policies to Prices

Having established a set of tools available to the state that can plausibly affect market prices, we move to arguing that they were used to responding to world price movements during the period in question. While domestic markets are relatively well integrated, the price of rice is determined at the margin, so domestic prices reflect any manipulation of export quantities or prices. The balance of this chapter explores how government policies generated these price inconsistencies by examining the rice price crisis of 2008 and the set of policies that generated this crisis as well as the responsible actors and relationships between them, and the efficacy of the state's overall response. These short-run policy responses provide a unique laboratory in which to understand the domestic political pressures on agricultural prices.

During non-crisis periods, price signals are transmitted relatively efficiently. Internal differences exist, but are driven by unequal endowments,

[8] In addition to export controls that are sometimes implemented, taxes on rice imports remain in place, but these mainly target imports of small quantities of high quality rice varieties that are not available domestically.

productivity, and transportation costs, while an export monopsony (only state-owned firms and a few private companies can export) drives a wedge between world and domestic prices. Within these constraints, prices are set by bidding between exporters in light of world prices and domestic demand.

During periods of high food prices such as 2008, however, the price transmission was significantly distorted by a temporary restriction on rice exports, motivated by concerns about domestic food security. The government's desire to protect the welfare of net rice consuming households therefore caused the implementation of a policy that effectively taxed rice producers by depriving them of windfall profits.

In the first quarter of 2008, a combination of speculation on commodity exchanges and expectations of supply shortfalls drove up world rice prices across all quality classifications. Domestically, rice harvests were forecasted to be low. The combination of high world prices and low expected rice yields generated significant concern in the Vietnamese agricultural policy community about a potentially destabilizing contraction in the quantity of rice available to domestic consumers.

In response, as global food prices rose steeply in 2008 and rice reserve stockpiles were depleted (Pham 2009), and based on advice from the Ministry of Agriculture and Rural Development (MARD), the government issued Announcement No. 78/TB-VPCP, revising its export target of 4.5 million tonnes down to 3.5 million tonnes. A temporary restriction for rice exports was also applied, with a ban on signing further contracts for rice exports imposed between May and July of 2008. In non-crisis periods, rice prices are determined by the interplay of supply and demand, and world and domestic prices move together. However, steep increases in rice prices create domestic winners and losers. Because world prices are higher than domestic prices under autarky, exporting results in higher domestic prices; the export ban and binding quota therefore reduced domestic prices and export quantities, effectively subsidizing domestic consumers by taxing producers.

In fact, Vietnamese rice yields (particularly in the southern provinces) were exceptionally high in the first quarter of 2008, while world rice prices for the highest quality grain reached US$1,000 (nominal 2008 prices) per tonne, a windfall profit above production costs that was not available to many farmers due to the export ban; the government's export restriction effectively deprived producers of above-average profits. At a meeting of the NA, the minister of MARD admitted responsibility for the pessimistic harvest forecast and the resulting imposition of an export quota (Khanh 2008). Notably, once the export quota was imposed, it was not revised to reflect new data about agricultural production or high world prices.

Following the boom in global rice prices in early 2008, commodities markets began to bid down contract prices, creating a sharp reduction in rice prices across quality grades. In an effort to protect farmers from this collapse in rice prices, a secondary set of government actors intervened. The purpose and remit of the VFA are clarified by its original name: the Vietnam Food Import & Export Association. Hierarchically, the VFA is part of MOIT, retaining the power to set a price floor for rice exports. By mid-2008, the VFA, acting on policy advice from the MOIT rather than MARD, contradicted these signals from the international markets and established a price floor of US$600 per tonne, raising this to US$650 in mid-August of 2008.

With world prices now below this price floor, Vietnam's community of rice exporters were not able to clear the domestic market, a textbook case of a price control creating a mismatch between supply and demand at a non-market price point. Establishing a price floor was therefore ultimately highly inconsistent: manipulating external trade policy lowered prices while setting a price floor—if it became binding—would raise prices above their new equilibrium level.[9]

The first intervention, by MARD, effectively reduced export profits while world prices were high, while the second, by the VFA, prevented the market from clearing when world prices were low. In both cases, lower domestic prices may have increased net consumers' real incomes, but at substantial and potentially offsetting costs imposed on net rice-producing households. A key element of the mismatch of policies, problems, and policy instruments is that controls were implemented by two distinct sets of actors with two distinct objectives: in the first case, to insulate domestic consumers from high rice prices, in the second case, to ensure profits for rice producers.

15.5.1 *Timing of Market Interventions*

Twenty-seven agricultural policies were issued between 2000 and 2011. Tracking the introduction of new policies over time suggests that political pressure and policy innovation are correlated. As rice prices increased, the number of agricultural policies to indirectly or directly affect rice prices increased dramatically. Figure 15.6 shows the number of new policies introduced, and informally indicates that rising prices put pressure on the political establishment to act.

Relevant policies can be broadly grouped into those that affect land issues, infrastructure investment, agricultural extension, taxation and tax incentives, direct intervention through state rice purchases, and export quotas. Figure 15.7 dates these innovations relative to rice price movements. The intention is not

[9] The office of the prime minister reacted by ordering Vietnam's rice exporters to buy paddy rice based on a floor price that would ensure profits of around 40 per cent for farmers, but could not or did not specify what this price floor should be.

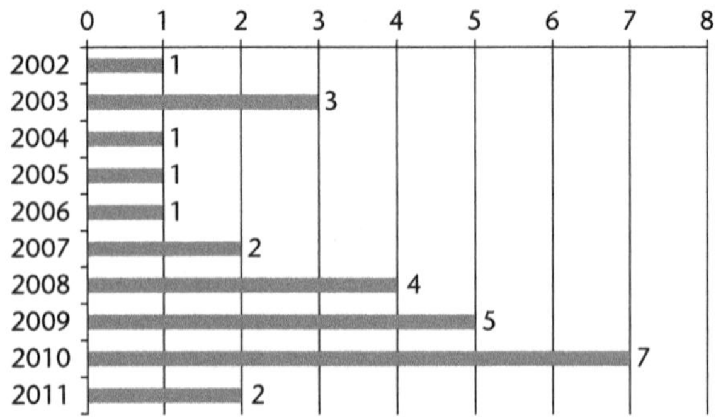

Figure 15.6 Timing of policy interventions
Source: authors' compilation.

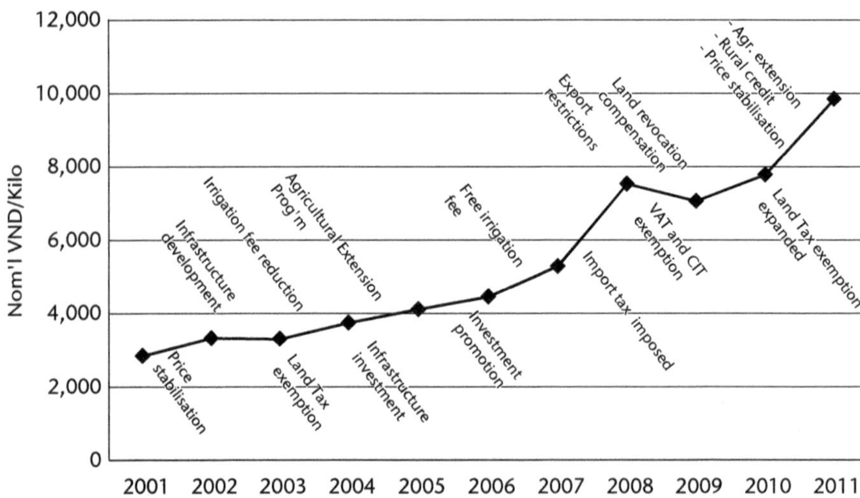

Figure 15.7 Rice price policies, 2001–11
Source: authors' compilation.

to formally (i.e., econometrically) establish a causal relationship, but to provide suggestive evidence that the government resorted to a wide range of policy tools in reaction to movements in market prices, and that the use of diverse policy instruments increased dramatically following the crisis period 2008.

15.5.2 *Evaluating the Policy Response*

On balance, market intervention kept domestic prices below what they would have been without interventions, but not enough to prevent significant hardship amongst rice consuming households, particularly the urban poor. As rice prices increased, the hardest hit amongst the poor were urban, low-income households. In the absence of a behavioural response (for example, substituting away from rice), we estimate that these households experienced real income reductions of 10–18 per cent. Since rice prices continued to rise despite government intervention, it is reasonable to conclude that the full set of policy tools were not used effectively to stabilize prices or protect the real incomes of net rice consuming households.

While net rice producing households benefited from higher prices, affecting about 37.4 per cent of Vietnamese households, most of these households were in the rice producing regions of the Red River Delta and Mekong River delta. Most of them were already above the national poverty line in 2008, and non-poor households enjoyed, on average, twice the increase in income of poor households (Phung 2011).

On the other hand, banning rice exports harmed rice producers by preventing them from benefiting from dramatically higher world prices. During the ban, rice exporting firms agitated for a lift in the ban because of indications from rice-producing regions of a bumper crop.[10] As mentioned above, the MARD acknowledged this at the end of May 2008 but continued to comply with the suspension of rice exports.[11]

The export restriction was combined with a price floor that, while intended to support rice producers with higher purchase prices by the export sector, in fact simply prevented the domestic rice market from clearing. The form and timing of policy interventions reflect the overlapping authority and competing interests of ministries and agencies within the government, which sought to simultaneously satisfy the competing constituencies of rice consumers and producers.

The net effect of these inconsistent policy interventions was a smaller decrease in real incomes of urban rice consumers relative to the counterfactual (full pass-through of world prices to domestic prices) achieved through the introduction of several price stabilization policies, and an effective tax levied on rice producers.

15.6 Conclusions

We have argued that the observed time path of policies is not consistent with a social planning model of policy-making. Rather, it can be explained

[10] Truong Thanh Phong, general director of the Southern Food Corporation, stated that although rice was scarce elsewhere in the world, Vietnam, particularly the Mekong Delta, would not experience shortages (*Vietnam News*, 21 May 2008).

[11] 'The signing of rice-export contracts may continue after the 30 June deadline for them to stop', according to Cao Duc Phat, Minister of Agriculture and Rural Development (*Vietnam News*, 21 May 2008).

by a political economy narrative in which the state attempted to balance the competing interests of consumers and producers. While Vietnam's markets are increasingly liberalized, the state continues to have, and use, a large set of policy instruments that move market prices.

The issue of rice prices in 2008 suggests two potential areas for reform in the domestic policy-making process. First, the set of policy instruments should be streamlined and made more transparent. The nature of Vietnam's political system is that numerous actors can issue decisions with varied levels of relevance, policy coherence, and coverage. This introduces substantial uncertainty amongst producers and consumers, and, in the case of rice prices, generated mutually incompatible policies that were not easy to reverse. Second, coherent policy formulation requires a large set of actors to act collaboratively and communicate clearly. In the case of market intervention in rice prices, relevant stakeholders were represented at the Ministry level by, variously, the MARD, the Ministry for Industry and Trade, the Ministry of Finance, the VFA, and others. It will be important for future agricultural policies to be shaped by input from each of the relevant decision-making actors.

Vietnam's economic prognosis is generally positive. The country enjoys a growing economy with rising capital intensity, which has regularly delivered high rates of economic growth. To maintain this growth path, the state ultimately needs to develop a clear set of tools for market intervention and a clear framework for discussion between relevant political and non-political actors about which policy instruments should be used, and when. Effective governance will balance the competing claims of winners and losers from unexpected price shocks, and ultimately increase the set of feasible policy responses, for example funding safety nets that prevent households from slipping into debt or poverty due to price shocks. Vietnam is poised to realize significant returns on market-oriented reforms and investments in education, public health, administration, and infrastructure, and the gains made so far from continued, broad-based growth highlight the importance of getting policy formulation right.

References

ASEAN Secretariat (2010). 'ASEAN Agricultural Commodity Outlook'. No. 4. Jakarta: ASEAN Secretariat.

CIEM (Central Institute for Economic Management) (2011). 'Governmental Transformation in Vietnam: Renewal and Renovation'. The Capacity Study on the Government of Vietnam. Vietnam. Hanoi: CIEM.

Cong, V. H. (2001). *The Public Policy Process and its Characteristics in Vietnam*. Hanoi: Ho Chi Minh Political Academy.

Cudjoe G., C. Breisinger, and X. Diao (2008). 'Local Impacts of a Global Crisis: Food Price Transmission and Poverty Impacts in Ghana'. Technical Report. Washington, DC: International Food Policy Research Institute (IFPRI).

de Janvry, A., and E. Sadoulet (2009). 'The Impact of Rising Food Prices on Household Welfare in India'. Mimeo. Berkeley, CA: University of California at Berkeley.

General Statistics Office (2009). 'Updating CPI Calculation Method in the Period 2009–2014'. Press Release: Hanoi: GSO.

General Statistics Office (2011a). *Statistical Yearbook 2010*. Hanoi: Statistics Publishing House.

General Statistics Office (2011b). 'Gross Output of Agriculture at Constant 1994 Prices by Province'. Available at: <http://www.gso.gov.vn/default_en.aspx?tabid=469&idmid=3&ItemID=11779> (accessed 10 November 2012).

International Finance Cooperation (2012). Data. <http://www.doingbusiness.org/rankings> (accessed 13 September 2012).

ISOS (Institute for State Organisational Sciences) (2013). 'Results of 13th NA and People Councils at different levels 2011–2016'. (Vietnamese original). Available at <http://isos.gov.vn/Thongtinchitiet/tabid/84/ArticleId/296/language/vi-VN/B-u-c-d-i-bi-u-Qu-c-h-i-khoa-XIII-va-d-i-bi-u-H-i-d-ng-nhan-dan-cac-c-p-nhi-m-k-2011-2016-M-t-b-c-xa.aspx> (accessed 30 April 2013).

Khanh, C. (2008). 'Minister Cao Duc Phat Would Receive any Form of Discipline'. Viet Nam Express. Available at: <http://vietbao.vn/Xa-hoi/Bo-truong-Nong-nghiep-Toi-chiu-trach-nhiem-va-xin-nhan-ky-luat/11082598/157/>.

Luu, T. D. H. (2002). *The Organization of the Liberalized Rice Market in Vietnam*. Groningen: Rijksuniversiteit Groningen.

MARD (Ministry of Agriculture and Rural Development) (2006). 'Summary of the Vietnamese Rice Sector'. Hanoi: Information Centre for Agriculture and Rural Development—Institute of Policy and Strategy for Agriculture and Rural Development, MARD, Hanoi. Original in Vietnamese.

Marsh, S. P., G. MacAuley, and P. V. Hung (eds) (2006). *Agricultural Development and Land Policy in Vietnam*. Sydney: Australian Centre for International Agricultural Research.

McCarty, A. (2002). 'The Policymaking Process in Vietnam'. Public Administration Reform Study. Hanoi: Mekong Economics Group, ADB.

Minot, N. (2010). 'Transmission of World Food Price Changes to African Markets and its Effects on Household Welfare'. Paper presented at the Comesa Policy Seminar 'Food Price Variability: Causes, Consequences, and Policy Options', held in Maputo, Mozambique under the Comesa-MSU-IFPRI African Agricultural Markets Project, 25–26 January.

MOLISA (Ministry of Labour, Invalids, and Social Affairs) (2011). 'Poverty Rates by Region and Province / City'. Available at: <http://www.molisa.gov.vn/docs/SLTK/DetailSLTK/tabid/215/DocID/5282/TabModuleSettingsId/496/language/vi-VN/Default.aspx> (accessed 1 November 2012).

Pham, B. D. (2009). 'Analysing Scientific Bases of Policy Recommendations for Income Compensation for Rice Farmers in Specialized Rice Growing Zones

Ensuring National Food Security'. A Scientific Project Report to the Ministry of Agriculture and Rural Development (MARD). Hanoi. Original in Vietnamese.

Phung, D. T. (2011). 'The Impacts of Food Price Crisis on Poverty and Welfare of the Vietnamese Households'. Paper presented at IRC's Development Seminar Series 7, held in Hanoi, Vietnam, 15 September.

Tarp, F., and A. McKay (2011). 'Welfare Dynamics in Rural Vietnam, 2006 to 2010'. Hanoi: Central Institute of Economic Management.

USDA (United States Department of Agriculture) (2011). 'Grain and Feed Annual Vietnam'. Prepared by T. Quoc Quan, A. M. Vigil, and R. J. Taylor. (VM1034. 5/6/2011). Washington, DC: USDA.

VFA (Vietnam Food Association) (2012). 'Rice Exporters Results'. Available at: <http://www.vietfood.org.vn/vn/default.aspx?c=52&n=5908> (accessed 13 September 2012).

Vietnam Custom Office (2012). 'Customs Procedures for Goods Export Trade'. Available at: <http://www.customs.gov.vn/lists/tinhoatdong/> (accessed 24 September 2012).

VIFAP (Vietnamese Initiative for Food and Agricultural Policy) (2011). Data. Available at: <http://www.vifap.org/archives/311> (accessed 19 October 2012).

Wondon, Q., and H. Zaman (2009). 'Higher Food Prices in Sub-Saharan Africa: Poverty Impact and Policy Responses'. *World Bank Research Observer* 25(1): 157–76.

Wright, B. D. (2011). *The Economics of Grain Price Volatility*. Oxford: Oxford University Press, on behalf of Agricultural and Applied Economics Association.

16

The Political Economy of Food Price Policy in India

Kavery Ganguly and Ashok Gulati

16.1 Introduction

In the context of the global food price crisis of 2007–8, India took some big decisions: adopted a very restrictive export policy for essential food articles (e.g., banning exports of wheat and common rice) and not allowing the domestic fertilizer prices (especially urea) to increase in line with global prices. This helped India to contain the food price rise in 2007–8 remarkably well (within 5 per cent to 7 per cent only). But this food price stability did not last long. From mid-2009 on, India's food prices started rising in the wake of (a) the severest drought in 2009 that India had experienced since 1972; and (b) India injected high doses of 'fiscal stimulus' as a part of a synchronized strategy adopted by Group of 8 (G8) and major emerging economies to avert global economic recession in the aftermath of the financial crisis of 2008. High food inflation in India continues until today (December 2012), hovering between 8–12 per cent in most of the quarters (since mid-2009) with occasional easing out in certain months and picking up spikes (even going up to 20 per cent) in some other months. But the composition of food inflation changed from cereals-led in 2009 to the one led by high-value foods (fruits and vegetables, and protein foods) in 2010 and 2011. This changing complexion of food inflation suggests increasing demand pressures emanating from rising incomes.

India as an emerging economy with a growing population is likely to experience increased demand for food. India being the second most populous country and home to a large number of poor in the world (41.6 per cent of the Indian population or 456 million people lived on less than US$1.25 a day in 2004–5 (Chen and Ravallion 2008)) faces a challenge of bringing down its food price inflation to economically and politically acceptable levels. In the context of this multi-country study, it is of interest to understand the politico-economic underpinnings of food price policy in India as it may have ramifications not only for neighbouring countries but also for global prices. As Timmer (2011) rightly observes, political dynamics play a powerful role in determining the policy responses particularly in times of rising food prices, and it cannot be truer than in a country like India with a vibrant democracy, and where the government is based on multi-party coalition.

The overarching food policy in India has been driven by the objective of food security for a large and growing population. For this, India has followed the path of attaining almost self-sufficiency in the production of key staples like rice and wheat, and making them available to economically weaker sections at affordable (highly subsidized) prices. The food price policy, therefore, has twin instruments, remunerative minimum support prices (MSPs) for rice and wheat farmers, and subsidized prices through public distribution systems for poor consumers. The export basket of Indian agriculture has been expanding and diversifying. While India is a net exporter of cereals, it is a major importer of edible oils and pulses. However, overall food availability (through domestic production and imports) is reasonably comfortable, and increasing over time in per capita terms. The challenge is more on the distribution front, especially for the poor. Despite highly subsidized staples being distributed through the public distribution system, consumption and nutrition levels of the poor remain low and a cause for much concern. The recent food price crisis has infused even greater urgency to address the food and nutrition security concerns through strategic policy actions placed over the short, medium, and long term.

16.1.1 *Overall Economic Performance and Macroeconomic Trends*

Despite robust economic growth and significant achievements on many other key economic indicators, India has not been as successful in addressing its concerns related to poverty and food and nutritional security of a large number of vulnerable people. The number of people living below the poverty line (as per the national definition of poverty line) as a per cent of the total population has declined from 55 per cent in 1973–4 to 36 per cent in 1993–4 to 27.5 per cent in 2004–5 and further to 22 per cent in 2009. However the number of poor people has decreased only slightly from 320 million in 1973–4 to 302 million in 2004–5 (as per national estimates, GoI 2010), indicating that India still has a huge burden of poverty, concentrated in less developed states.

Although India achieved high rates of overall gross domestic product (GDP) growth, its agri-GDP growth remained very low. During the last decade of the 2000s, agri-GDP growth hovered around 3 per cent per annum, despite the fact that each Five-Year-Plan during this period was targeting at least 4 per cent. Boosting agricultural growth to 4 per cent plus will be critical in reducing poverty even faster given that agriculture employs nearly 58 per cent of the workforce and a larger number of people are dependent on agriculture. While the expenditure on food subsidy is likely to touch US$20 billion with the introduction of the proposed National Food Security Act, approximately US$8 billion on the employment programme, and a fertilizer subsidy bill of US$15 billion, public investments in agriculture remain pitiably low at less than US$5 billion. The major concern with huge welfare and social safety net programmes is the ability to deliver services to the targeted population.

16.1.2 *Major Food Crops: Production, Trade, and Consumption*

Rice and wheat are the major cereal crops in India accounting for 57 per cent of the area under food grains and 75 per cent of the overall food grain production. Augmenting the availability of food grains has been a policy priority in India arising from food security concerns that emanated in the 1950s and 1960s when India witnessed several episodes of hunger and famine. Although the food grain production has increased manifold and per capita availability of food grains improved, there continues to be an over-emphasis on attaining self-sufficiency and a surplus in food grains, which poses considerable financial and fiscal strain.

Food accounts for a large part of the total monthly budget of an average Indian, although its share has been declining over time and as per the 2009–10 survey estimates, it is still almost 50 per cent of the monthly per capita expenditure (NSSO 2011). However, the low expenditure classes (bottom 30 per cent) spend more than 60 per cent of their monthly expenditure on food. National survey estimates suggest that the demand for cereals has been declining over time driven by changing consumption preferences. The consumption patterns are diversifying towards high-value commodities across rural and urban areas and also across expenditure groups. Rising income levels, changing lifestyles and trends in urbanization are among the key drivers of this change. India has been a net exporter of cereals, especially rice and corn, of meat and fish, of cotton, of oilseeds cake, and a wide variety of other commodities. Its imports of agri-commodites are largely concentrated in edible oils and pulses.

Driven by food security challenges, there have been several policy hiccups in liberalizing grain markets since the 1990s. Although India has moved away from import controls and quotas there still exist knee jerk reactions taking recourse to export controls and bans to augment domestic supplies.

16.2 Food Price Crisis

16.2.1 *Crisis Episodes: Trends and Patterns*

Since 1947, India witnessed the highest inflation (measured in terms of wholesale price index) in September 1974, when overall inflation reached 33.3 per cent.[1] November 1973 to December 1974 has been the worst period of inflationary pressure when inflation did not drop below 20 per cent. Inflation hovered over and above 30 per cent for four consecutive months starting June 1974 (Basu 2011).

A headline inflation accelerated in the second half of 2009–10, and continued to remain high in 2010–11.[2] Inflation in India has also undergone structural changes with food inflation being an important driver to begin with in mid-2009 and then outpaced by increasing energy prices post economic crisis (RBI 2011a). India experienced lower food price volatility/spikes in the domestic market in 2007–8. When world prices of food commodities touched new peaks, and domestic food prices, especially for staples, in several countries went up by 20–40 per cent, food price increase in India remained within 5–6 per cent. But the relief was not long-lasting and in 2009, India was hit by a severe drought that set food prices soaring. The increase in food prices was further fuelled by somewhat loose monetary and fiscal policies emanating from the need to provide fiscal stimulus in the wake of averting global recession. Price transmission effects of international prices on domestic prices have been somewhat muted in the context of India, given the continuing ban on exports of rice and wheat during 2007–11, raising the fertilizer subsidy bill to contain the shocks arising from global price spikes in fertilizers. Rather populist measures, like loan waiver, expansion of Mahatma Gandhi national rural employment guarantee scheme (MGNREGS), raising agricultural subsidies, announced ahead of the 2009 general elections, were all dubbed as fiscal stimulus.

The food price index here is defined as the weighted average of the wholesale price index of food articles and manufactured food products. Inflation measured in terms of the change in monthly wholesale price index of commodities year on year has been highly volatile after having touched unprecedented levels. Domestic food prices started flaring up to mid-2009 onward crossing the 10 per cent mark in June 2009, the 15 per cent mark in November 2009, touched a peak of more than 20 per cent in February 2010. Though it slid from those high levels, yet until November 2011, it has remained largely

[1] The monthly inflation is measured as percentage change of the wholesale price index of the month in the current year over the same month in the previous year.

[2] The headline inflation measures the overall inflation within an economy and is significantly influenced by sudden price spikes in food or energy sectors.

in double digits, lately hovering around 10 per cent, attracting a major debate in parliament (Figure 16.1). During this period nearly all food commodities registered a price spike, their contribution varying over a period of time.

The pressure has been on food articles which witnessed a consistent 20 per cent and more inflation during December 2009 until June 2010.[3] Flaring up of prices of manufactured food products was relatively short-lived attaining a peak of 19 per cent for two consecutive months, December 2009 and January 2010, and prices started cooling off thereafter.[4] However, prices of manufactured food products are once again on an upward swing from 2.4 per cent in March 2011 to more than 8 per cent since June 2011. During the course of the recent price spikes the contribution of individual food items and groups has been varying. To begin with, manufactured food products contributed the most to the rising inflation on food; 56 per cent in the first quarter of 2008, followed by food grains at 23.4 per cent. Over time, the contribution of manufactured food products declined substantially to 3.5 per cent in the first quarter of 2011 and thereafter zoomed to more than 32 per cent over

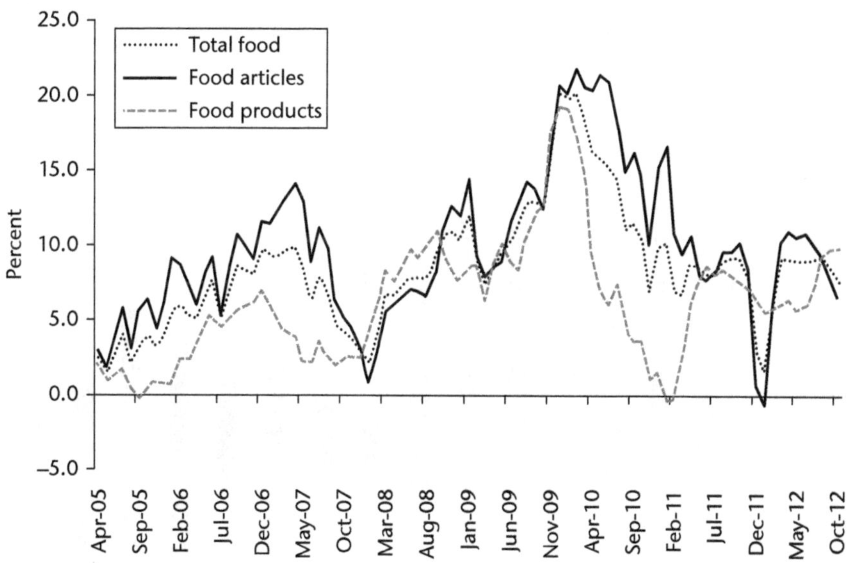

Figure 16.1 Percentage change in wholesale price index of food articles and manufactured food products (per month this year over same month in the previous year)
Source: GoI, OEA (2012).

[3] Food articles include food grains, fruits and vegetables, milk, eggs, meat and fish, condiments and spices, tea and coffee.

[4] Manufactured food products include dairy products, grain mill products, bakery products, sugar, khandsari and gur, common salts, sugar and confectionary, edible oils, oil cakes, processed tea, coffee, cattle feed, and malted foods.

the second and third quarter of 2011 (Figure 16.2). The pressure on manufactured food is coming from the rising wholesale price index of edible oils at 16.2 per cent and 14.4 per cent during the second and third quarters of 2011. Within food articles, the contribution of cereals in total food inflation has come down from 30.2 per cent in the first quarter of 2008 to 5.3 per cent in the fourth quarter in 2010 and has risen to over 8 per cent in the last two quarters of 2011. High-value commodities such as fruits, vegetables (highly fluctuating), milk, meat, and eggs are contributing significantly to total food inflation.

It is quite evident that the pressure on food inflation is arising from high-value commodities in the sub-group of food articles. This is perhaps explained in terms of the growing demand for these commodities (considering the structural changes in consumption patterns) and the lack of adequate supply responses. This in turn is affected by domestic production, import patterns to fill up the gap, and also fragmented supply chains. This offers an insight into the current policy thinking that holds food grains as the key to food and nutrition security of the nation. With the price pressure lingering on and even worsening in the case of high-value commodities, there is need to address the demand-supply gap.

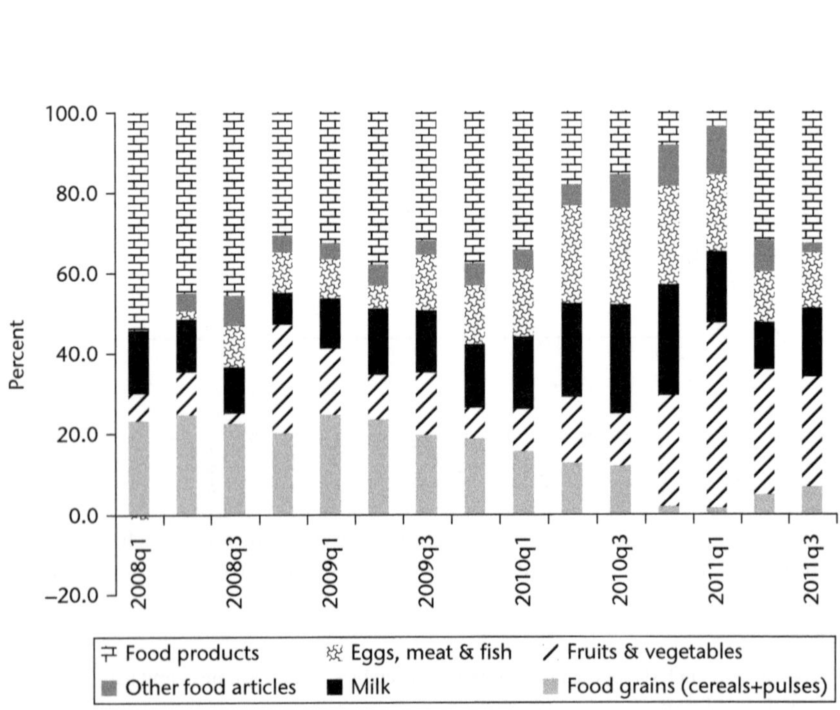

Figure 16.2 Contribution of various commodities in total food inflation
Source: GoI, OEA (2012).

16.2.2 *Price Trends for Key Food Crops*

Rice is the staple crop in India, production of which increased at a rate of 1.0 per cent per annum during 1999–2000 to 2009–10. During the same period, area under rice reduced at a rate of 0.52 per cent while productivity increased at a rate of 1.28 per cent annually. A large part of the total rice production is procured by the Food Corporation of India (FCI), together with state agencies. Rice exports from India reached a peak of 6.5 million tonnes in 2007–8, when a ban on exports of common rice was imposed. During 2010–11, India exported 2.28 million tonnes of rice (basmati) worth US$2.4 billion. Common rice exports were opened in September 2011, and during the one year from October 2011 to September 2012; India exported ten million tonnes of rice valued around US$6 billion, becoming the largest exporter of rice in the world.

The wholesale price index of rice started increasing after July 2006 (over the corresponding months of the previous year). This upward movement in monthly rice prices continued until the end of 2008, and thereafter it started declining (Figure 16.3). However, month to month increases (of the same year) in prices of rice was much lower, and Indian rice prices remained much more subdued in relation to international prices of rice (Figure 16.4). This was primarily due to the ban on exports of common rice and increasing production and stocks at home. The domestic prices started rising again in December 2011 in the wake of the opening-up of rice exports in September 2011.

Wheat prices witnessed periods of high growth in some parts of 2006, and then again from July 2009 to end of 2009, and therafter precipitously falling

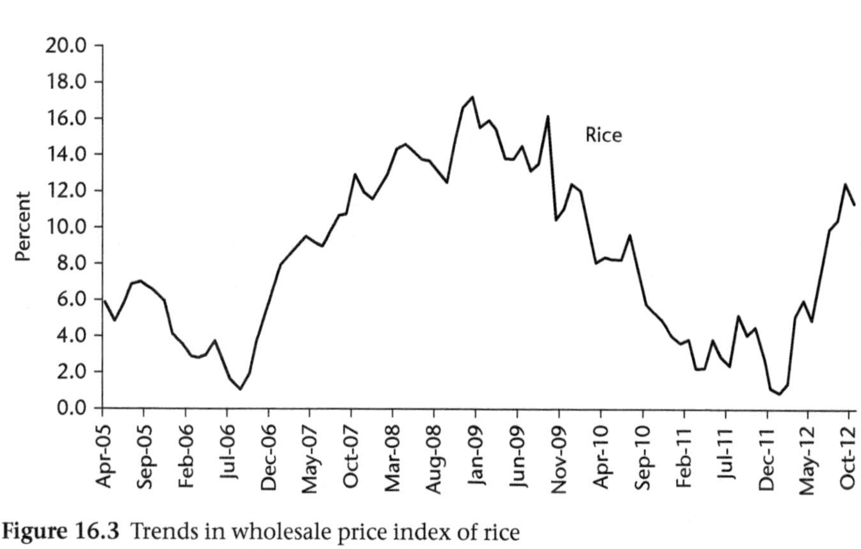

Figure 16.3 Trends in wholesale price index of rice
Source: GoI, OEA (2012).

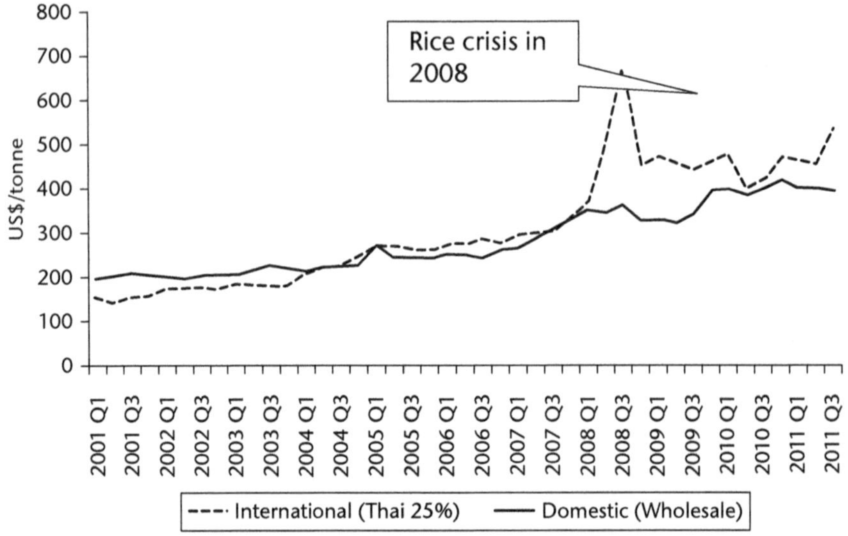

Figure 16.4 International and domestic price movements of rice

Note: International prices are of Thai Rice, 25 per cent broken, FOB Bangkok. Domestic prices have been calculated by averaging monthly data across government regulated market yards (known as *mandis*) in all states available from DES.

Source: GoI, CACP (2011).

to price decreases (Figure 16.5). The export ban on wheat and also increased import of wheat together with favourable production helped contain the price rise. But since July 2012, wheat prices have increased by 15 to 20 per cent over the corresponding months of previous year. This has happened despite the government having stocks of more than 40 million tonnes (in November 2012) compared to a buffer stock norm of 14 million tonnes. The large scale procurement of wheat to the tune of 38 million tonnes in the marketing season of 2012–13 (April to June) has left very little in the open market, which is putting pressures on market prices.

Domestic price of wheat is largely in line with international prices except for certain periods of extreme swings in international prices during the last two quarters of 2007, the last quarter of 2010 and first quarter of 2011. After almost remaining flat from 2001 until 2005, the minimum support price of wheat has increased signifcantly.

Maize prices have been fluctuating during this period and hovered around double digit inflation and since January 2011 prices have spiralled rapidly (Figure 16.6).

Domestic prices of maize have been relatively stable as compared to periodic fluctuations in international prices of maize. The minimum support price has been moving in tandem with the international prices. In 2008 the

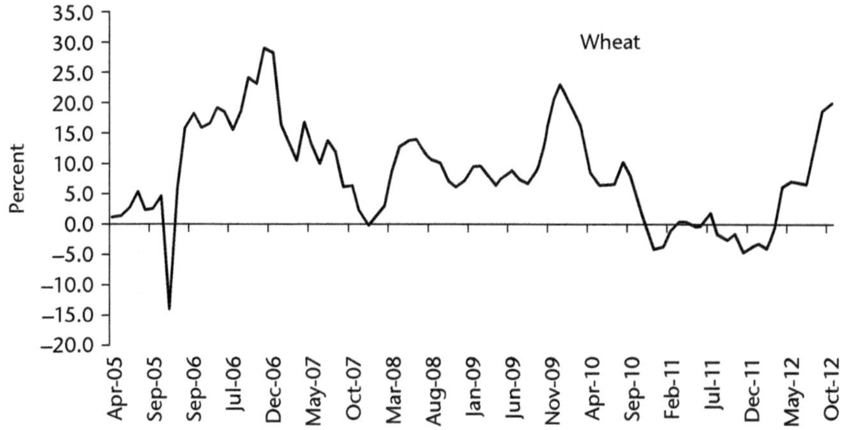

Figure 16.5 Percentage change in monthly wholesale price index of wheat
Source: GoI, OEA (2012).

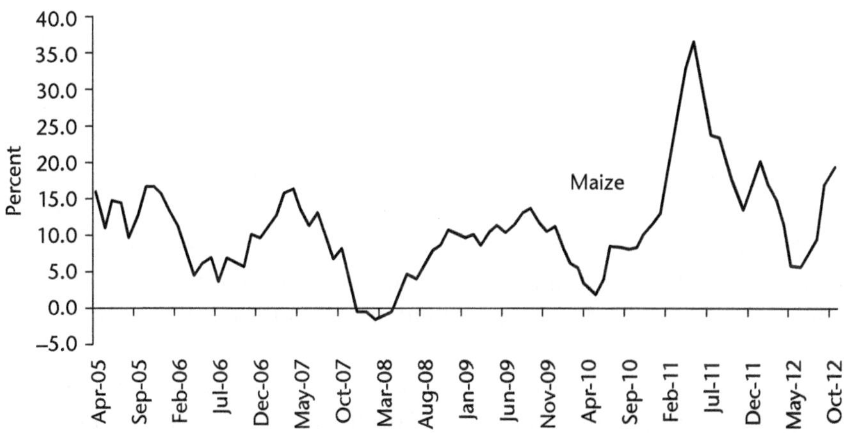

Figure 16.6 Percentage change in monthly wholesale price index of maize
Source: GoI, OEA (2012).

domestic price of maize was below international price and there was a significant increase in the export of maize during that year.

16.2.3 *Price Transmission: Causes and Impact*

The degree of price transmission among cereal crops has been influenced by the government through its various policy interventions such as export controls, imposition of minimum export prices, and varying tariffs. But to say that international price movements have no impact on Indian prices will be far from the truth. Nevertheless, policy packages safeguard the consumers and producers from the brunt of price spikes and troughs in global prices. For example, during 2007–8 when global prices were surging, India did not witness large price spikes. Support prices were increased to help farmers tide over increasing costs of production as well as to catch up with global price trends (not spikes), though with a little lag. In the case of increasing global prices of fertilizers, the government contained the spiralling of domestic prices by increasing the fertilizer subsidy bill which cost nearly US$16 billion in 2008–9.

Chand (2008, 2009, cited in Acharya et al. 2012) states that India successfully restricted the snowballing of abnormally high international prices in 2007–8 on domestic prices. Although rice and wheat witnessed high price inflation, it was lower than that observed in their global prices. The lack of a strong price transmission effect is largely attributable to a robust domestic production (except 2009–10 when the production was hit due to a severe drought), timely intervention by the government to control price rise in domestic markets, and the containing rise in cost of production due to a rise in global prices of crude oil and fertilizers. As observed by Dasgupta et al. 2011 (cited by Acharya et al. 2012), the domestic price of wheat is weakly and only moderately impacted by international prices due to the policy intermediation of the government (export bans, lowering duties to import and also incentivizing production through an increase in minimum support price). Co-integration test results from Acharya et al. (2012) do not show any co-integration between international and domestic prices of rice. In the case of wheat, the wholesale domestic price and international price are somewhat co-integrated—the speed of adjustment in response to change in international price was 4 per cent.

Although the prices of rice and wheat increased in late 2009, the increase was less than the international prices. The global price inflation on rice fluctuated between 206 per cent in April 2008 and 4.7 per cent in March 2009. In contrast, domestic inflation on rice ranged from 8.7 per cent in April 2008 to 17.1 per cent in February 2009. In the case of wheat, global inflation declined to negative in March 2009 from 83 per cent in April 2008 whereas domestic inflation on wheat hovered between 7 per cent and 5 per cent during the above period.

The price surge in 2009 can be partly attributed to the bad agricultural year when food grain production suffered a set-back. It was the worst drought year since 1972. Nearly 59 per cent of the Indian districts received deficient/scanty rainfall. The actual rainfall was 23 per cent less than the normal monsoon rainfall (GoI 2010). Although the government took immediate steps to augment supply from existing stocks, and through publicly managed distribution centres, high food inflation persisted. It drove the government to look at medium- to long-term measures much through the existing public programmes geared toward augmenting productivity (for example, Rashtriya Krishi Vikas Yojana, National Food Security Mission, Second Green Revolution).

16.2.4 *Key Drivers of Food Price Inflation*

Food inflation is being driven more by non-cereal commodities and the phenomenon is largely demand-driven. Although there are supply-side issues that need to be addressed, increasing income levels are fuelling food prices. The soaring prices of protein rich food (meat, fish and eggs, milk and milk products) reflect the rise in demand owing to rising income levels and changing lifestyle. The price spikes in fruits and vegetables can be attributed to a large extent to fragmented supply chains and less so to supply constraints, although a detailed study on what is actually driving up prices of fruits and vegetables in not available. There is a widening gap between the prices received by farmers and that paid by the consumers due to a large number of intermediaries and fragmented supply chains, High taxes on agricultural commodities, market fees, and high fees charged by the commission agents in government-regulated markets and increasing fuel prices further fuel prices.

In brief, the food inflation in India has been driven by both supply and demand factors, depending upon the commodity under consideration. For commodities like edible oils, and pulses, there are clearly serious supply constraints, and rising demand is being met by huge imports. Wheat and rice have been largely insulated from global spikes, and it is largely the domestic policies (MSP, procurement, stocking, and distribution) that influence their prices. For fruits and vegetables, supply is not as much an issue, but fragmented supply chains have often contributed to the price spikes.

16.3 Key Policy Responses

Anti-inflationary policies adopted by the Government of India typically involve fiscal and monetary measures, the rationalization of excise and import duties on key commodities to safeguard the interests of the consumers, the use of liberal tariff and trade policies to manage demand-supply situation of key commodities, and the strengthening of the public distribution system to improve availability and accessibility of food. In addressing the broader issue of food and nutrition security, reforming the existing social safety net programmes (improving the delivery mechanism, moving from physical transfer to cash transfers), procurement and stocking policies have been on the policy agenda. Long-term policy measures with a focus on boosting agricultural production in a sustainable manner has been emphasized, along with reforming agricultural marketing practices to cut down the marketing margins.

16.3.1 *Domestic Price Policies (Consumer Prices, Minimum Support Prices (MSPs))*

Increasing retail prices have invited varied responses. For example, when prices of pulses shot up, the government took measures to make available other varieties of low-priced pulses through government managed retail outlets. The issue price at which subsidized food grains are distributed to people under the public distribution system did not undergo any change during this period.

MSPs of cereal crops have seen a significant increase in order to incentivize production given the rising cost of production. After six million tonnes of wheat import in 2006–7, and fast rising international prices of wheat and rice in 2007–8, the MSP of wheat was increased by more than 30 per cent in 2007–8 over 2006–7. The MSP of rice, maize, and pulses increased by 30–50 per cent in 2008–9 over 2007–8, to catch up with rising global prices and compensate farmers for rising costs of production.

16.3.2 *Trade Policies (Export Bans, Import Tariffs, Exchange Rate Policies)*

The price control measures taken by the government included selective bans on exports as observed in the case of rice and futures trading in food grains, zero import duty on selected food items, among other measures pertaining to key food items. Larger quantities of rice and wheat were released from buffer stocks to ease pressure on domestic prices.

In response to rising global prices of food grain, the government banned wheat exports in February 2007 and common non-basmati rice exports in October 2007. About three months later, an export quota was opened for Bangladesh followed by very small export quotas of both rice and wheat for a number of other South Asian and African countries honouring the existing commitment. These highly restrictive export policies mostly remained in place until early September 2011. The rice export restrictions (which did not apply to existing export contracts) began to affect physical exports in a major way around March–April 2008. The government finally lifted the ban on wheat and non-basmati rice exports up to two million tonnes each (as in September 2011). While estimates for the financial year (April to March) 2011–12 show that rice exports have reached 6.75 million tonnes, wheat exports are not more than one million tonnes given the lower international prices.

16.3.3 *Increased Agricultural Production (Input Subsidies, Investment, Enhanced Extension)*

Input and food subsidies outpace investments in agriculture (Figure 16.7). Food and fertilizers account for the giant share of total agricultural subsidies and both have been spiralling over time. Food, fertilizer, power and irrigation subsides together account for 15.1 per cent of agricultural GDP in 2009–10 up from 7.8 per cent in 1995–96. Food and fertilizer subsidies account for the larger share of agricultural subsidies and their share peaked to 74.3 per cent in 2008–09, when world prices of food and fertilizers peaked.

In order to protect farmers from rapidly increasing fertilizer prices in the world market, the government provided subsidies of about US$16 billion in 2008–09.

In February 2008, the finance minister announced a relief package for farmers which included a complete waiver of loans given to small and marginal farmers. The US$ 14.9 billion agricultural debt waiver and debt relief scheme included the total value of the loans (US$12.4 billion) to be waived for thirty million small and marginal farmers and a one time settlement scheme (OTS) (US$2.5 billion) for another ten million farmers. This loan waiver scheme has been criticized widely as a populist measure

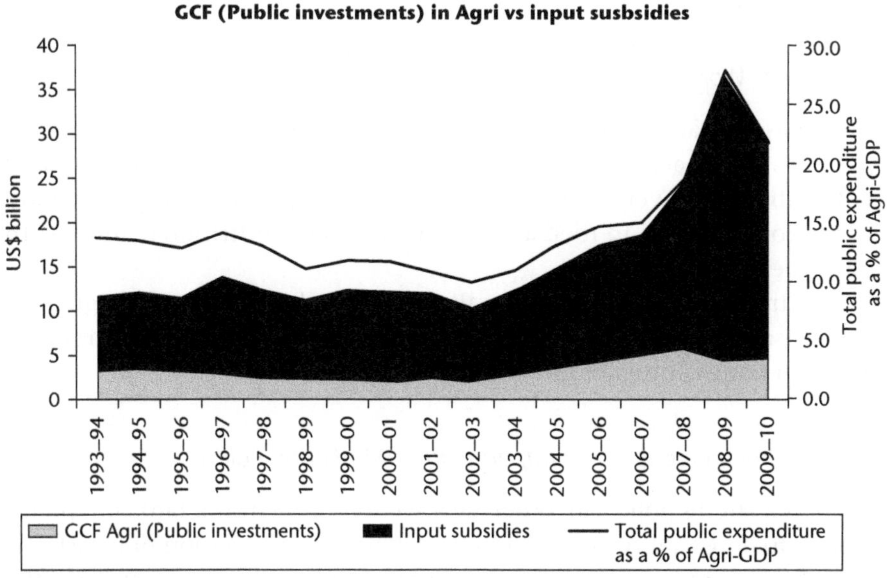

Figure 16.7 Composition of public expenditure in agriculture: 1993–4 to 2009–10
Source: GoI, CACP (2012).

ahead of the 2009 general elections in India and also for the fact that this scheme did not include a large number of farmers who depend on informal sources of credit.

16.3.4 *Larger Public Programmes to Boost Agricultural Productivity*

The urgency to boost agricultural productivity particularly food grains resulted in the launching of the National Food Security Mission (NFSM) 2007–8, a flagship programme aimed at boosting the production of rice (by ten million tonnes), wheat (by eight million tonnes), and pulses (by two million tonnes) by 2011–12. The geographical coverage includes the potential districts with a heavy representation of the eastern states. During 2008–9 nearly 50 per cent of the NFSM-rice districts, 50 per cent of NFSM-pulses districts, and 33 per cent of NFSM-wheat districts have recorded a 10–20 per cent increase in productivity compared to 2006–7 (GoI 2010). The Rashtriya Krishi Vikas Yojana (RKVY) or the National Agricultural Development Programme (NADP), with an outlay of Indian rupees (INR) 250 billion for five years, has provided the much needed impetus to strengthen state outlay for agriculture. The Second Green Revolution aims at shifting the cereal basket to the eastern region, which is largely rain-fed in nature and with lower yield levels providing scope for expanding the production frontier.

16.3.5 *Safety Nets (Public Distribution System, Food for Work, Cash Transfers)*

India has a legacy of social safety net programmes to help improve people's economic access to food with a particular focus on the poor and vulnerable. However, these programmes have not been very successful in improving access to food and hence improving nutritional and health outcomes.

Cash transfer programmes as an alternative to physical transfer of grains is being discussed along with a reform of the existing public distribution system and cash transfer programmes.

16.3.6 *Procurement, Stocking, and Other Marketing Policies*

There is a strong policy advocacy by a section of the think tank and policy makers to decentralize and eventually downsize the operation of parastatals in India learning from some of the international experiences (within the Asian region). Agricultural markets particularly that of food grains have been closed to market competition and highly distorted given the controls and regulations (for example: procurement at minimum support price often less than the market price, compulsory levy on rice millers). Procurement levels have increased over time and have reached unprecedented levels in recent years. From 11.2 million tonnes of rice and wheat in 1980–1, procurement has increased to 56.5 million tonnes in 2010–11. Procurement of wheat in particular more than doubled in 2008–9 at 22.7 million tonnes from eleven million tonnes in 2007–8 (Figure 16.8).

With a record production of food grains, an export ban on rice and wheat and increasing procurement, the grain stocks are much in excess of the buffer stock requirement. India had accumulated 64.7 million tonnes of rice and wheat in June 2002, which it had to later dispose by an export subsidy. The stocks plummeted to 12.4 million tonnes in October 2006 only to increase to sixty-four million tonnes in July 2011 against a buffer norm (including strategic reserves) of thirty-two million tonnes (Figure 16.9). As in June 2012, grain stocks have reached a record high of eighty-two million tonnes.

The large food grain stocks pose a huge financial burden on government and there are reports of grain damage owing to lack of proper and adequate storage facilities. Despite structural changes observed in consumption patterns from cereals to high-value commodities, food grains continue to be the mainstay of food security in India. There is very little scope for private sector participation in grain marketing given the controls that are in place arising out of food security concerns. It is difficult to liberalize the grain markets extensively owing to food security concerns and political

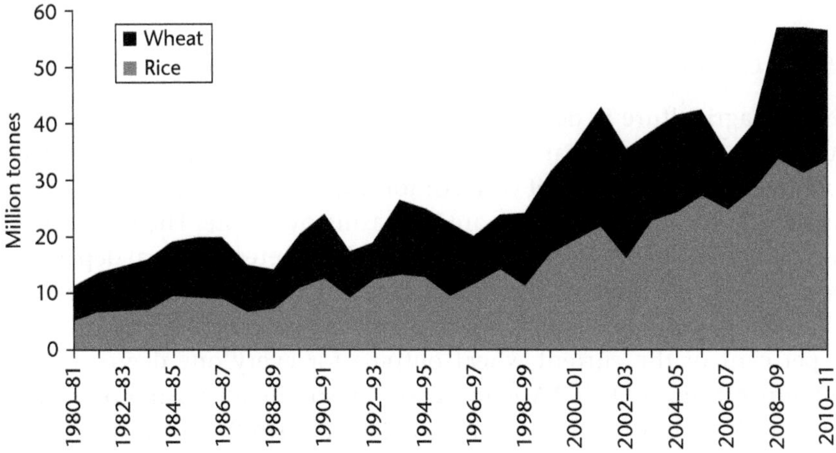

Figure 16.8 Procurement of rice and wheat for the central pool

Source: Food Corporation of India (2011).

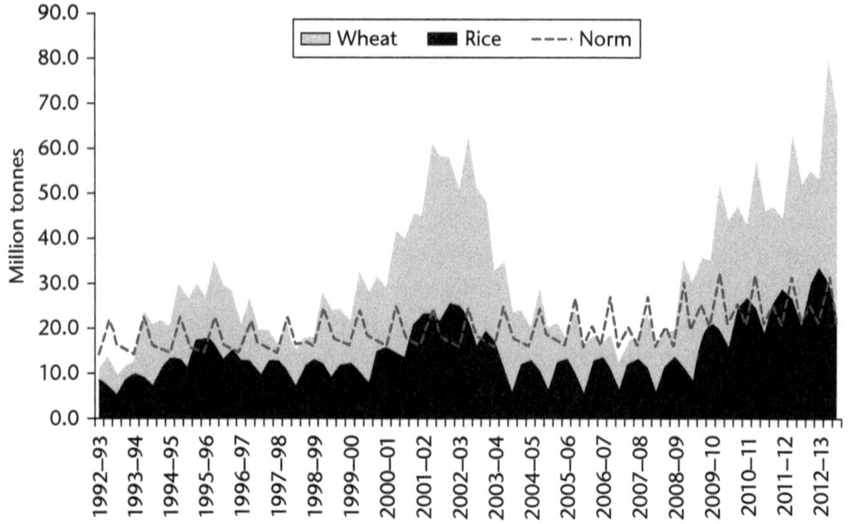

Figure 16.9 Stocks of rice and wheat with the central pool (up to October 2012)
Source: Food Corporation of India (2011).

will driven by the mandate to provide food for all. Efforts are on to liberalize high-value commodity markets such as fruits and vegetables which do not directly and largely impact the food security concerns. In a recent move (September 2011), the central government has asked states to lift all restrictions on the movement of fruit and vegetables, in order to eliminate intermediaries, reduce wastage, and tame the stubbornly high food inflation (Sikarwar 2011).

16.3.7 *Other Policies (Environmental Policies and Land Acquisitions)*

Because agriculture is dependent on monsoons and natural conditions, increasing environmental stress and climate change impacts on sustainable food production are of concern for India. The frequency of droughts and erratic climatic conditions are increasing over time. The inter-governmental panel on climate change and the India meteorological department reports a 2 to 4 degrees increase in mean temperatures (FAO-GOI Mission 2009). Production losses in wheat are likely to be around six million tonnes (7 per cent of the current wheat output) for every one degree increase in temperatures (AO-GOI Mission 2009). Also, the increasing pressure on water and soil in the cereal growing states in north India has necessitated taking the second green revolution to eastern India, which is water abundant and where environmental conditions are more favourable.

16.4 Political Economy Context

16.4.1 *Key Decision-making Actors*

India has a coalition government. The executive office of the Prime Minister is responsible for the day-to-day functioning of the government. Given the parliamentary form of government, all major policy decisions that require legislative clearance are tabled in the parliament. The central government together with the Ministry of Food, Consumer Affairs, and Public Distribution and the Ministry of Agriculture in consultation with state governments and other ministries are at the helm of agriculture and food price policy-making. In his address at the Second Annual Conference of Chief Secretaries on 4 February 2011, the prime minister emphasized the need to augment agricultural productivity together with a paradigm shift in institutions to contain escalating food prices. He pointed out that the state governments need to be proactive in bringing about these changes—particularly reviewing the scope of the amended Agricultural Produce Market Committee Act, feasibility of waiving market and other taxes. He also reiterated the need to reform the public distribution system, and create adequate storage facilities for increasing stocks of cereals. Rising food prices indicated gaps in supply chain management which need to be strengthened by creating a level playing field for the organized retailers (GoI, PMO 2011). The cabinet approval to foreign direct investment (FDI) in multi-brand retail (that includes food retail) in September 2012 was long overdue. This is held as a break away from the policy paralysis that the ruling government has been criticized for by various stakeholders both national and international. Implementation of the policy is likely to facilitate enhanced FDI inflows, generate employment opportunities, usher in global best practices, which altogether have the potential to benefit consumers and farmers and invoke greater supply chain efficiencies in the agricultural sector and development of critical backend infrastructure.

States have a distinct role to play in the area of agriculture policies given that agriculture is a state subject under the provisions of the Constitution of India. The states have the authority to impose taxes and levies (compulsory selling to the state agencies) on marketing of agricultural commodities and this includes rice and wheat. Punjab imposes statutory levies (taxes) of 14.5 per cent on wheat, which has driven the private sector away from markets, and hence the state has almost a monopoly over procurement. For rice millers, there has been an indirect taxation given that they have to sell 50 to 70 per cent of the milled rice to state agencies at pre-determined prices. Also, in Madhya Pradesh, a bonus of INR 100/quintal over and above the MSP resulted in a record production and procurement of wheat in the state resulting in an overflow of wheat stocks in the state.

The Reserve Bank of India also plays a critical role. It reversed its expansionary monetary policy stand beginning October 2009 by raising the cash reserve ratio by a hundred basis points and the policy rate or the repo rate by a cumulative 275 basis points; the effective tightening was about 425 basis points (RBI 2011b).

The Ministry of Finance continuously monitors the food price situation, and one of the critical steps is to rein in the rising fiscal deficit, which in many ways is responsible for the flaring up of prices. A road map to bring it down to manageable levels of 3 to 4 per cent from its current level of more than 5.5 per cent, over a period of five years has been a policy priority. But given the high fuel prices, and the impending National Food Security Bill, it remains challenging to see how and when it can be done.

The Planning Commission has also been actively involved in suggesting measures to contain price surge and tame inflation. The opposition political parties play an important role in putting pressure on the government to be more proactive in controlling rising food inflation. In the context of the recent petrol price hike, one of the key alliance partners threatened a pull out if the government did not roll back the hike in the interest of the common man. Within a week of the prime minister stating no roll back, petrol prices were slashed.[5] Over the period of the food crisis, opposition parties have staged protests against rising prices mobilizing common people around the country, demanding government action on containing rising food prices. The National Advisory Council (comprising the political representatives, policy makers, think tanks, and academia) has been quite influential in pushing the National Food Security Bill (which is now pending with the Parliamentary Committee to be examined) which gathered momentum in the wake of high food inflation. Research institutes (national as well as international) have been involved in analysing the trends in food prices, engaging in dialogue with the government, policy makers, and also the media to understand the situation and brain storm on the potential ways of containing high prices and smoothening them over time.

In the wake of high food price inflation, the Confederation of Indian Industry (CII) National Council on Agriculture has sought structural changes to augment growth in the farm sector, linking the farmers directly to the retailers and processors. It also recommended an introduction of input stamps whereby the farmers have the choice to avail the input subsidy that they require. CII has also suggested reforming the land lease markets in agriculture to enable the leasing of land and benefit from the economies of scale.

[5] 'Petrol price cut by Rs 2.22'. *The Hindu*, 15 November 2011. Available at: <http://www.thehindu.com/news/national/article2630325.ece>.

It considers opening up multi-brand retailing to FDI will be critical in developing supply chains, and facilitating direct firm-farm linkages (Menon 2011).

While there have been no reports of major riots over increasing food and fuel prices in India, there was a report of public furore over rising prices in Bihar.[6] There have been mass protests organized by farmers and other lobbies in various parts of India, and also those organized by the opposition political parties, demanding the government to be proactive and committed to protect the interests of the common man/woman and not subject him/her to the onslaught of rising prices.[7] The issue of high food inflation led to a disruption of the parliament proceedings several times over the past few years by the members of the opposition parties.

The media has been active in reporting increasing food prices and the reaction across various segments of the society. International institutions like the World Bank, the Food and Agriculture Organization (FAO), the Asian Development Bank, and others have been continuously tracking the global trends in prices and the forces behind them. The views expressed by international think tanks have had their impact on the policy-thinking in India as observed in their being more cautionary and having a protectionist approach with respect to trade (export controls and bans) and in general procurement and stocking policies with respect to grains (resulting in record procurement and surmounting stocks of rice and wheat).

16.5 Conclusions

The period of high food prices since mid-2009 has raised concerns and challenges, although for India as a developing country and home to a large number of poor and malnourished people, ensuring food and nutrition security has always ruled the policy domain. The policy makers have been confronted with the difficult task of balancing higher economic growth and improving the social welfare of the masses. The ruling coalition government is committed to ensuring inclusive growth wherein people from different economic and social backgrounds are part of the economic growth process. It is met with fierce criticism and disruption of parliamentary proceedings by the opposition parties, putting pressure on the government to control surging prices. Rather than providing an actual solution to the problem of rising food prices, the opposition was more vocal to downgrade the efficacy of

[6] 'India Faces Food Price Discontent Violent Protests'. Reuters, 28 January 2010.

[7] 'India opposition parties strike over high food prices'. *BBC News*, 27 April 2010. Available at <http://news.bbc.co.uk/2/hi/8645725.stm> and 'Thousands protest against high food prices in Delhi'. *BBC News South Asia*, 23 February 2011. Available at <http://www.bbc.co.uk/news/world-south-asia-12549050>.

the ruling government, failing to protect the interests of the common man/woman. Policy decisions to hike transport and cooking fuel prices were met with severe criticism as these were seen to further fuel food prices. High food and fuel inflation is seen to thwart the high economic growth that India has achieved despite the fragile global economic scenario.

While short-term measures were undertaken to address the prevailing crisis, emphasis was given to medium- to long-term policies to increase food supplies and access. The international food price increase did not change the Indian agricultural and food policy which was already geared towards ensuring sustainable agricultural production to ensure food security of the masses, although it provided the extra momentum. Immediate measures like offloading stocks in open markets, reducing tariffs on imported food commodities, raising price support or imposing export controls and bans are the general course of action taken time and again when prices were flaring up beyond tolerable limits.

As illustrated by the National Food Security Bill, perhaps the period of high inflation and increasing vulnerability of poor people to food price shocks prompted the speeding up of food security deliberations. The proponents of the Act had more reason to push for the enactment of the bill without taking into consideration the fiscal and financial implications. Reforming the public distribution system versus replacing it with other alternatives such as cash transfer, coupons/stamps are also being debated in the country. Recent research also reveals that the existing public distribution system has a leakage of around 40 per cent. Given this, a strategic move towards conditional cash transfer can be a real game changer. But some have expressed suspicion of the ability to do cash transfers in a society where financial inclusion of the poor remains a major challenge. However, under the Aadhar project, there are plans to install one million micro-automated teller machines (ATMs) all over the country and use finger prints and Aadhar's unique number to widen the financial inclusion, and the government has already taken a bold decision to move towards cash transfers for twenty-nine schemes. Although the food and fertilizer subsidy is not currently in this scheme, the Commission for Agricultural Costs and Prices (CACP) has recommended piloting a food subsidy at a hundred places, to be transferred through cash. This is a potential weapon to contain leakages in the system and enhance the effectiveness of social safety programmes. While the objective of seeking the food and nutrition security of the masses remains the same or is rather more highlighted due to the crisis, the means of achieving it is still debated. There have been suggestions of downsizing public procurement and storage of grains, particularly the operations of the Food Corporation of India, and allowing greater private sector participation and also allowing markets to operate. The current inflationary trends in India are observed to be a mix of demand-driven factors and also supply factors that resulted in spikes and fluctuations in price movements. Erratic supply conditions owing to weather and climatic changes resulted in rapid price fluctuations. On the other hand, large scale food subsidies have resulted in the accumulation of large stocks of wheat and rice. While the evidence is weak, it appears that poverty levels have been declining. One finding is that despite rising food prices during 2007–12, real farm wages have increased at 6.8 per cent per annum. Given that landless labour is generally at the bottom rung of the economic ladder, this is heartening news to policy makers.

India is home to a rising middle-class population which has been driving demand patterns. This phenomenon to a large extent has fuelled the price inflation in high-value and protein-rich commodities. The pressure is on prices of non-cereal commodities driven by demand expansions and weak and fragmented supply lines. The focus, therefore, is on streamlining the supply chain, reducing the marketing margins and ensuring adequate supply response to increasing demand. Some of the policy measures that India adopted (largely populist in nature and part of the election manifesto) which helped address the concerns arising from the food and financial crisis resulted in inflating the fiscal deficit and adding to the inflation concerns. Increasing the subsidy bill (notably fertilizer) and loan waiver scheme resulted in a ballooning of the fiscal deficit from 4.1 per cent in 2007–8 to 8.5 per cent and 9.5 per cent in 2008–9 and 2009–10, respectively (RBI 2011b).

The nature and extent of food price inflation in India has been less severe than in many other developing countries. Although met with severe criticism by the opposition political parties, the flagging of issues by the media, and protests by civil society groups and people in general, the situation did not result in riots or major clashes. As for grains (rice, wheat, and maize), domestic prices have been fluctuating but their contribution to overall food inflation has eased out over time. Rising energy prices also contributed to a rise in inflation. The period of high food inflation has brought food security concerns to the forefront and there is a renewed interest among the representatives of the government, and the policy think tanks to devise strategies to control prices and smooth out the impact of these price spikes on consumers. While immediate actions were taken to control price spikes, some of the medium- to long-term policy actions are aimed to ensure sustainable growth in agricultural productivity and food production. In the wake of the crisis, this policy stand has been further strengthened although a consensus on the strategic approach is missing. Indian agriculture and food policy measures have been conservative. While the trade restrictions and building up of stocks helped contain flaring up of grain prices on the domestic front, India has been criticized for having adversely affected the global situation.

Overall, it seems the policies and political debates have ensured that there is ample food in the country, that the real wages of farm workers have gone up, and now the challenge is to bring down food inflation by controlling fiscal deficits, retaining somewhat tight monetary policy, improving the supply chains, and honing the social safety net programmes, besides improving productivity and overall food production in the country, and releasing more from the public stocks.

References

Acharya, S. S., P. S. Ramesh Chand, S. K. Birthal, and D. S. Negi (2012). 'Market Integration and Price Transmission in India: A Case of Rice and Wheat with Special Reference to the World Food Crisis of 2007/08'. Rome: Food and Agriculture Organization.

Basu, K. (2011). 'Understanding Inflation and Controlling It'. Paper. Available at: <http://finmin.nic.in/WorkingPaper/understanding_inflation_controlling.pdf> (accessed 14 November 2011).

Chen, S., and M. Ravallion (2008). 'The Developing World is Poorer than We Thought, But No Less Successful in the Fight against Poverty'. Policy Research Working Paper No. 4703. Washington, DC: World Bank Development Research Group.

FAO-GoI (Food and Agriculture Organization–Government of India) (2009). 'The Impacts of Climate Change on Wheat, Food, Agriculture, and the Environment'. Discussion Paper No. 29. Washington, DC: International Food Policy Research Institute (IFPRI).

Food Corporation of India (2011). 'Data on Procurement. Food Corporation of India'. New Delhi: Food Corporation of India. Available at: <www.fciweb.nic.in>.

GoI (Government of India) (2007). 'Agricultural Statistics at a Glance 2007'. Ministry of Agriculture, Government of India, New Delhi.

GoI (Government of India) (2009). 'Agricultural Statistics at a Glance 2009'. Ministry of Agriculture, Government of India, New Delhi.

GoI (Government of India) (2010). 'Agricultural Statistics at a Glance 2010'. Ministry of Agriculture, Government of India, New Delhi.

GoI (Government of India) (2011). 'Report on Price Policy for Kharif Crops of 2011–2012 Season'. New Delhi: GoI.

GoI (Government of India), Commission for Agricultural Costs and Prices (CACP) (2012). 'Report on Price Policy for Rabi Crops for Marketing Season 2013–2014'. New Delhi: GoI.

GoI (Government of India), OEA (Office of Economic Advisor) (2012). 'Wholesale Price Index Database'. New Delhi: GoI.

GoI (Government of India), PMO (Prime Minister's Office) (2011). 'Handbook of Statistics on Government of India'. (2011). Available at: <http://pmindia.nic.in/speeches.htm> (accessed 25 July 2012).

Menon, B. D. (2011). '"Exempt Horticulture from APMC Act", says CII Farm Panel Chief'. *Business Line,* 23 January. Available at <http://www.thehindubusinessline.in/2011/01/24/stories/2011012451030200.htm> (accessed 26 October 2011).

NSSO (National Sample Survey Organization) (2011). 'Key Indicators of Household Consumer Expenditure in India, 2009–10'. Report No. NSS KI (66/1.0). New Delhi: GoI: Central Statistical Organization, Ministry of Statistics and Programme Implementation.

RBI (Reserve Bank of India) (2011a). 'Striking the Balance between Growth and Inflation in India'. Speech by Subir Gokarn Gokarn. New Delhi: RBI. Available at: <http://www.rbi.org.in/scripts/BS_ViewBulletin.aspx?Id=12426#C4> (accessed 14 October 2011).

RBI (Reserve Bank of India) (2011b). 'First Quarter Review of Monetary Policy 2011–12 by Duvvuri Subbarao, Governor, Reserve Bank of India'. Available at: <http://www.rbi.org.in/scripts/BS_ViewBulletin.aspx?Id=12415> (accessed 10 November 2011).

Sikarwar, D. (2011). 'Centre to States: Lift all Restrictions on Fruit and Vegetables Movement'. *The Economic Times,* 29 September. Available at: <http://economictimes.indiatimes.com/news/economy/agriculture/-centre-to-states-lift-all-restrictions-on-fruit-and-vegetables-movement/articleshow/10164055.cms> (accessed 20 October 2011).

Timmer, P. (2011). 'Managing Price Volatility: Approaches at the Global, National, and Household Levels'. Paper prepared for Center on Food Security and the Environment. Stanford Symposium Series on Global Food Policy and Food Security in the 21st Century, Stanford University.

17

The Political Economy of Food Price Policy in China

Jikun Huang, Jun Yang, and Scott Rozelle

17.1 Introduction

Although China is often cited as one of several countries that have successfully dealt with the food crisis and food price volatility, there is a dearth of information on how China responded to the crisis and whether or not the counter-measures taken were successful. This chapter seeks to understand China's economic and political environment, its response to the food crisis, what the policy-making process involved, and the effectiveness of the policy responses. In addressing these questions, the chapter tries to explain why the government of China, in responding to the crisis, chose a specific set of policy measures that included the release of the government's grain reserves in the beginning of the crisis, long-term future/forward contracts with trading firms in exporting countries, provision of subsidies and insurance to producers, cancellation of support for storage and transport of export grains, increased subsidies on grain production and input, and enhanced social protection for urban consumers. As in many other countries, however, China also used wider measures at the border to protect domestic prices from international food price fluctuations. Furthermore, China adjusted its long-term development strategies on biofuel development and strengthened the commitment to invest in agriculture.

17.2 Country Context

17.2.1 *Economic Growth and Ability to Respond to External Crises*

Over the past two decades, China has exhibited considerable capacity to respond to external economic shocks, as exemplified by the Asian financial crisis in the late 1990s. While the shock did affect economic growth (from 9.7 per cent over 1985–95 to 8.2 per cent over 1996–2000), recovery thereafter was rapid. This was largely due to the fact that the government took decisive action to combat sluggish growth, which created the perception of stability, and re-established producer and consumer confidence. Fiscal spending (mainly on infrastructure), for example, was raised by 100 billion yuan to stimulate demand and increase the efficiency of the nation's business environment in the second half of 1998. Other stimulating measures were implemented in 1999.

More recently, like many other countries, China was also seriously affected by the global financial crisis. After a 14.2 per cent growth rate in 2007, growth fell sharply to 9.6 per cent in 2008 and 9.2 per cent in 2009 (NSBC 2010), and the drop of 4.6 percentage points between 2007 and 2008 was the largest of any major country. However, despite the serious effects of the global financial crunch, the economy was able to recover quickly as a result of China's rapid and massive response. As the financial downfall took its toll, in order to maintain economic growth, the country initiated an aggressive stimulus and monetary expansion package for 2009 and 2010 valued at four trillion yuan (US$586 billion), accounting for 14 per cent (or nearly 12 per cent) of China's GDP in 2008 and 2009, respectively.

While there was concern over the long-term impact of these expansionary policies, China's massive and rapid response to the external crisis was quite effective—and unique. Decisions could be made quickly at the central level of government and implemented without any major resistance from the public and other stakeholders. Thus, based on China's past responses to the Asian financial crisis in the late 1990s and the recent global crunch, it will not be difficult to understand its similar reaction in the face of the global food crisis.

17.2.2 *Political Regime and Development Goals*

Based on the national constitution, the Communist Party of China (CPC) is the country's sole political party in power. This fact has ramifications with regard to the decision-making process on national policies, including food policy and the government's response to global commodity crisis. Under the national constitution, all rights are vested with officials who exercise their power through the National People's Congress (NPC) and local congresses at all levels. The State Council is the highest administrative body of the government.

Democratic centralism guides the decision-making principle. The CPC's most powerful policy- and decision-making entity is the Politburo, comprising the Party's two dozen or so national leaders and its Standing Committee. Generally, members of the Politburo and its Standing Committee simultaneously hold state positions with functions and tasks similar to their personal Politburo appointments. The role of the Politburo is mainly to decide on long-term development strategies and short-term policies related to political and social crises. China is also strongly committed to agricultural and rural development.

Policy formulation for agricultural and food economy is largely vested with the State Council, the highest government administrative body and the cabinet of the Chinese government. National food and agricultural policy decisions are made by the premier and a vice-premier in charge of agriculture. These two top leaders[1] consider agriculture to be a fundamental sector for overall economic growth, and have expressed particular interest in agricultural growth, farmer income, and rural development. Grain security, however, is priority number one among the national leaders.

17.3 Food Price Transmission

To understand the political economy of China's food pricing policy during the global food crisis, it is useful to have an overview of the performance of the nation's food market and its functions.

17.3.1 *Trends, and the Transmission of International and Domestic Food Prices*

TRENDS IN DOMESTIC AND INTERNATIONAL PRICES

Figure 17.1 gives the annual prices of major foods in China and on the international markets at border for the years 2000–10. Prior to the global food emergency, domestic food prices moved with border prices. However, the domestic and international price co-movement weakened during 2007–9 for all food products analysed with the exception of soybean. When international prices for rice, wheat and maize increased sharply in 2007–8, domestic prices for these commodities increased only moderately, an indication of the likely impact of China's policy responses to the global food crisis. Soybean is the exception because it has been fully liberalized and there is no policy tool that could be used to arrest price transmission between international and domestic markets.

PRICE TRANSMISSION FROM INTERNATIONAL TO DOMESTIC PRICES

To find statistical evidence of, and to evaluate, the price transmission from international to domestic price, we apply the cointegration analysis method

[1] At the time of writing, these were Wen Jiabao and Hu Liangyu.

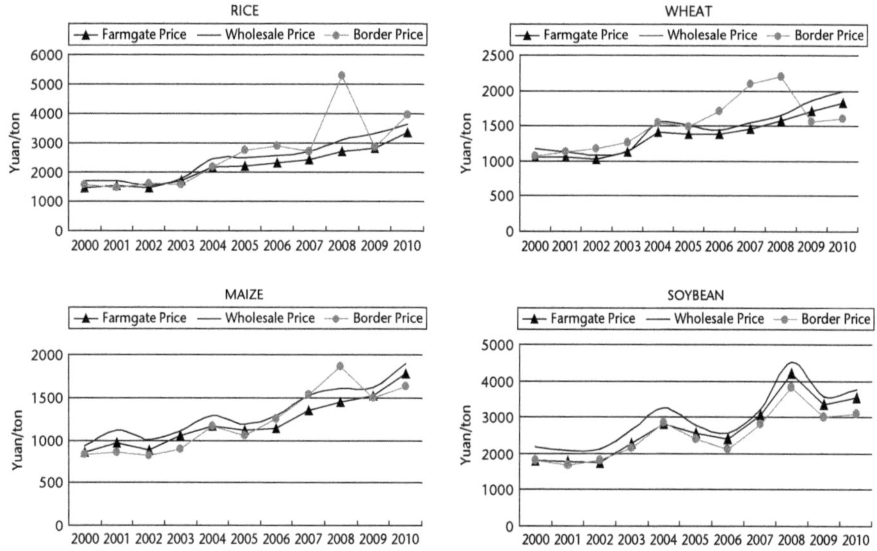

Figure 17.1 Rice, wheat, maize, and soybean prices in China and the international markets (at border), 2000–10

Source: Computed by authors based on farm-gate price from the NDRC; wholesale price from the MoA; border price from the MoC.

and the error correction model (ECM). The analyses are based on monthly domestic wholesale market price and international price for the commodities examined here (rice, wheat, maize, and soybeans) for the period January 2003 to December 2008. Domestic data are taken from the Wind database, and international prices are from the International Monetary Fund (IMF) database.

Both the cointegration analysis and ECM analysis show that China's domestic agricultural prices were affected significantly by international prices in 2003–6 (a period prior to global food crisis in 2006–9). The cointegration analysis reveals that there was a long-run transmission of international prices to China's domestic prices, with a statistical significance at the 1 per cent level for all four commodities in 2003–6. The estimated long-run adjustment parameters indicates that the domestic price of rice, wheat, maize and soybean would increase by 0.54 per cent, 0.25 per cent, 0.50 per cent, and 0.84 per cent, respectively, in the event of a corresponding international price increase of 1 per cent.

Similar results are found with the ECM analysis. Estimated speed of adjustment was statistically significant for all four commodities, ranging between –0.02 for rice to – 0.16 for soybean. The results also show that short-term effects for soybean and maize were larger than those for rice and wheat. A 1 per cent international price increase for soybean and maize would directly lead to 0.22 per cent and 0.15 per cent increase in domestic prices for these crops. For wheat and rice, the short-run adjustments are 0.07 per cent and 0.04 per cent, respectively, for a 1 per cent increase in their international market price. The higher impacts in the short term and quick adjustment speed imply that the time needed to transfer international price changes to the domestic market would be much shorter particularly for soybean, but also for maize.

17.4 Food Price Shocks and Policy Responses

17.4.1 *The Threat—Rising Prices in World Food Markets*

The 2006–9 global food crisis, like similar situations in the early 1970s, came on fast. After a long period of falling prices, international food prices began to rise in 2006, accelerating in 2007 and early 2008. Although prices fell sharply after May 2008 after the global financial crunch, international commodity prices remained high, with significant fluctuations.

As prices of major commodities in international markets rose, three aspects of China's food economy became critically important. First, food still accounts for more than 35 per cent and 41 per cent of consumer budgets in urban and rural regions, respectively. In 2010, the bottom 10 per cent of urban population (measured in per capita income) spent more than 46 per cent of total household expenditures on food. Second, given this high share for food expenditure, any substantial price increase on foodstuff would almost certainly have implications for national price stability and overall consumer price inflation. Third, as the trade of many food commodities is not restricted across China's borders and domestic markets are highly integrated (Huang and Rozelle 2006), international food prices are easily transmitted to domestic markets. By mid-2007 when international food price increases started to accelerate, officials were concerned that rising prices were becoming a problem that could threat China's food economy and overall price inflation (Wen 2008).

17.4.2 *Short-term Responses*

With the rapid rise in food prices on the international market, particularly for imported soybean, edible oils and other foods, China recognized that this could become a threat to domestic food security and undertook a series of policy responses in late 2007 to mid-2008.

AGRICULTURAL POLICIES

The first agricultural policy response was the grain reserve scheme in late 2007, which released rice, wheat and maize from government reserves. This was a major measure commonly used by China in the past to maintain domestic grain price stability. Grains that had been stored mainly as a precaution against natural disasters and to control seasonal price fluctuations were now released through the National Development and Reform Commission (NDRC) and the State Grain Administration (SGA) in consultation with Ministry of Agriculture (MoA) and other relevant ministries. The size of China's grain stocks is not generally known, but Premier Wen Jiabao's (2008) press announcement in March 2008 indicated that even after several months of sales, China still had between 150 and 200 million tons of grain available for stabilizing domestic prices.

The second short-term response in agricultural policy was the effort to find external sources for grain and meat during the last quarter of 2007. As grain reserves declined, the NDRC officials, in consultation with the Ministry of Commerce (MoC) and MoA, authorized the China National Cereals, Oil and Foodstuffs Import and Export Corporation (COFCO) to sign long-term future and forward contracts for grain (and meat) with exporting countries. In late 2007, escalating domestic prices for pork also triggered a policy response from NDRC to provide subsidies (and insurance) to producers. When it became clear that China would not be able to import large volumes of food due to high world prices, government action in the second half of 2007 focused on efforts to increase domestic supplies, and to try to hold down local prices.

Third, short-term measures were taken to create a disincentive for cereal exports late in 2007. As international food prices continued to rise, the NDRC and the MoC undertook increasingly strong action to prevent the cereal released from domestic stocks from being exported. International prices had increased to such an extent that domestic grain traders (mainly national and provincial grain reserve agencies and COFCO) were beginning to recognize the benefits of shipping the relatively low priced grain to global markets. Maize was the first target, as it had historically been exported in large volumes, and government (NDRC) measures made it increasingly expensive to continue to do so.[2] In November 2008, subsidies for the storage and transport of export-destined maize were suspended. But as international grain prices continued to mount through the first part of 2008, the NDRC and the Office of the State Council decided to cancel valued added tax (VAT) rebates. At the same time, there was also apprehension over rice and wheat. As no transport or storage subsidies had been applied to the export of these grains, China recalled the policy on VAT reductions. A mere month later, to further dampen export incentives for wheat, maize and rice, China assigned a 5 per cent export levy on all shipments, except those destined to Hong Kong, Taiwan and Macao.

[2] Ministry of Finance and General Administration of Customs of China (2008), and personal interviews with officials from the SGA.

The fourth short-term policy reaction to the dire global food situation came late in the winter of 2008. Even after the release of stocks and cancellation of export subsidies (and introduction of export levies), national leaders and NDRC decision makers were not convinced that the measures were enough to offset the continuing surge of international food prices. Stronger measures were needed, and the nation's top leaders announced a total ban on the export of food and feed commodities. Wen Jiabao (2008) proclaimed that 'in order to control rising food prices, China will strictly restrict the use of food by industry and for grain exports'. Chen Xiwen (2008), one of the chief architects of China's agricultural policy, sanctioned the ban, emphasizing that the restrictions, which would be in effect only for 2008, were necessary in order to keep up domestic supplies. Thus, between the period from summer 2007 to March 2008, China had shifted its stance from exports subsidization to levies and quantitative restrictions on exports; it clearly did not want traders buying domestic grain to sell on export markets.

Fifth, the government turned its attention to fertilizers in February 2008. Similarly to the rise in global grain prices in late 2007, international fertilizer prices also increased significantly, and this increase was largely transmitted to China's domestic markets in 2007 and 2008. For example, the rising international chemical fertilizer and energy prices meant an increase of more than 40 per cent between July 2007 and June 2008 (NBSC 2008). The extra cost of fertilizers lowered demand particularly from grain producers, posing a further threat to production, and therefore to the increasing food prices.

In response, in early 2008 the Chinese leaders approved the NDRC and MoA proposal of export taxes on fertilizers. Phosphate fertilizers were first, and on 15 February 2008 all exports of phosphate fertilizers and any chemical fertilizers containing phosphates were to be taxed. In April, an additional 30 per cent was applied to triple super phosphates, and in May, 35 per cent on urea exports. Finally, in an effort clearly designed to halt all chemical fertilizer exports, a 100 per cent export levy was announced in mid-May. These policies were in effect until the end of 2008 when international food and fertilizer prices fell significantly because of the global financial crisis.

CONSUMERS AND SOCIAL PROTECTION

Consumer and social protection targeted to low-income groups has been enhanced in recent years during and after the global food crisis in 2006–9. Although most of China's poor live in rural areas, the share of food expenditures in 2008 for the urban population in the bottom 5 per cent of the income scale was as much as 49 per cent (NBSC), making these people highly vulnerable to increasing food prices. Fortunately, prior to the crisis, China already had in place a comprehensive safety and social protection system (e.g., *Chengshi Dibao* programme) that extended basic living allowances to the urban poor. This system was enhanced during the global food crisis period by increase of food subsidies.

17.4.3 *Long-term Responses*

BIOFUEL POLICY

Faced with the growing dependency on oil imports and the need to improve energy security, in the early 2000s China began to formulate an ambitious biofuel programme that was aimed at producing ten million tons of bioethanol and two million tons of biodiesel annually by 2020. Several supporting policies were implemented to ensure the achievement of these goals. By 2006, China produced 1.3 million tons of bioethanol. Maize is the primary feedstock of the biofuel firms in the northeast, and wheat is the other important feedstock for bioethanol in Henan, the nation's top wheat production province.

However, after 2007 the policies supporting biofuel expansion shifted dramatically. Concerns about rising food prices and national food security triggered a moratorium on the building of the new biofuel programme. By the end of 2007, China decided to revise its biofuel development strategy and decreed that: (i) biofuel production should not compete with grain for land; (ii) biofuel expansion should not vie with humans for food; and (iii) feedstock for biofuel should not compete with livestock over feed. While existing biofuel plants could continue production, their expansion was to be based on the use of alternative feedstock such as sweet sorghum, sweet potatoes, cassava, and other non-grain products.

AGRICULTURAL DEVELOPMENT POLICY

The global food crisis also prompted China to increase commitment to agriculture and rural development. China normally dedicates the first policy document of the Central Committee of CPC, often called the Number-One Policy Document, to the country's most significant issue. To re-affirm the commitment to agriculture and rural development, the Number-One Policy Document in 2004–6 underlined these issues. While the continued emphasis on agriculture for 2007–12 in the Number-One Policy Document is mainly indicative of China's national development policies, the rising concern for food security triggered by the global food crisis may also have contributed.

Two recent reports among these Number-One Documents are worthy of mention as they are directly related to food security: (i) the 2011 document which outlined plans to invest about US$630 billion in water conservancy over the next ten years to ensure food and water security; and (ii) the 2012 document which specifically highlighted innovation in agricultural science and technology for boosting farm productivity and substantial increases in investment in agricultural technology. The annual growth rate of public agricultural research and development expenditure increased in real terms from an average of 16 per cent in 2000–9 to more than 20 per cent in 2010–11. This is expected to become higher in the coming years.

17.5 Political Economy Context

Why and how was China able to apply policy responses to the global food dilemma so quickly? In addition to the country's political regime and development goals that were briefly discussed earlier, this section reviews the background of its political economy with a special focus on the framework and partners that make up the decision-making process in agricultural economy.

17.5.1 *The Decision-making Framework for Long-term Development Strategies and Law*

Three political bodies are vital with respect to agricultural policy and the relevant laws. The State Council is the highest body of government; the CPC central committee decides the basic principles and mandates of agricultural policy, and the National People's Congress (NPC) is in charge of the constitution and the laws and thus, in theory, has an important voice in supervising and auditing the state's fiscal budgets. Each of these three bodies carries out its mission in collaboration with other relevant organizations. Under the State Council, the MoA, the NDRC, the Ministry of Finance, and several other ministries related to agriculture are the major organs that formulate the annual five-year and long-term plans and policies on agricultural development. Within the National People's Congress, there are nine special committees, three of which[3] are important in setting laws related to agriculture. They also have a supervisory and a consultancy role with regard to implementation.

Normally, the general procedure for policy-making is as follows: The CPC central committee in conjunction with the State Council decides the issues to be considered by NPC. Based on the outcome, the State Council then prepares the implementation plan for approval by the NPC. The NPC then authorizes the State Council to implement the plan.[4]

[3] The Committee of Agriculture and Rural Development, the Committee of Finance, and the Committee of Environment and Natural Resources.

[4] For example, the fifth session of the sixteenth CPC central committee adopted as its theme the modernization of agriculture and the steady promotion of the development of a new socialist countryside. This was outlined in the 'Suggestions on the 11th Five-Year Plan of the National Economy and Social Development'. Based on documentation, the State Council drew up 'the Outline (draft) of the 11th Five-Year Plan for the National Economy and Social Development' and sent it to the 4th session of the 10th NPC for discussion, recommendations, and approval. After ratification by the NPC, the plan was implemented by the State Council.

17.5.2 *Key Actors of the Decision-making Framework within Food and Agricultural Policy*

OVERALL PROFILE

In China the major actors embodied in the decision-making process are the CPC and various government organizations as well as major research institutes. These include the State Council and two inter-ministerial governance organs under CPC jurisdiction, known as the 'leading groups' (one specializing in finance and economy, the LG-FE, and one on rural works, the LG-RW). Other entities such as the NDRC, MoA, and the Ministry of Commerce are included as well. Key research institutes and think tanks also have a vital say in the national decision-making mechanism. The role of the private sector is limited. Political lobby is not a common phenomenon. However, views and interests of the private sector and the public with respect to national food policy can be aired at least partly through the media, which is expected to have indirect effect on national policies.

THE STATE COUNCIL

The State Council, as the cabinet of the government of China, is responsible for all major policies on social and economic development. It meets approximately once a month to decide on current matters of national significance, agriculture included. The top body within the State Council is its standing committee. Comprising the premier, four vice-premiers, and five state councillors, the daily administration of the government is handled by the State Council's standing committee. Agriculture and food is handled by one vice-premier.

THE LEADING GROUPS OF THE CPC

The leading groups are inter-ministerial governance bodies. Each leading group has an executive office headed by an official at the level of a minister. Under the jurisdiction of the CPC and the State Council, the LG-FE led by the premier and the LG-RW (one of the few sector- or area-specific LGs) led by a vice-premier play a vital role in decision making of China's agricultural policy. The executive offices of these leading groups prepare national policy documents, coordinating with the relevant ministries and various tiers of government. Currently, the LG-RW executive office is headed by Chen Xiwen who is also deputy head of the executive office of LG-FE.

THE MoA

The MoA is primarily responsible for agricultural production. Contrary to other countries, responsibility for agricultural input and output marketing as well as international trade policies is vested with NDRC, the Ministry of

Commerce, and SGA. But MoA does submit policy suggestions on matters affecting agricultural input and output prices, tariff adjustment, marketing, rural credit, taxation, rural financial subsidies, and rural economic reform.

NDRC AND OTHER RELEVANT MINISTRIES

The NDRC is a key player in the formulation of development plans and responding to crises in all sectors, including agriculture. One of its major functions is to find a balance between the interests of the different ministries or sectors. The NDRC is also in charge of the state reserve of strategic commodities and materials; it handles and supervises the collection, utilization, rotation, management, and price fluctuation of agricultural products and inputs.

RESEARCH INSTITUTES AND THINK TANKS

Research institutes[5] and leading economists and scientists have an important role in proposing, consulting, and preparing national policy. Policy research institutes and think tanks under the auspices of the government (e.g., NDRC and MoA) normally mirror the stance of the supervising authorities. Agencies affiliated with academia have greater autonomy to express their views.

MEDIA

Although the media in China has traditionally been run by the state,[6] independent media coverage is emerging. Since 2000 the internet has emerged as an important communication medium, and there were more than 485 million internet users in China in 2010. While politically related issues are often censored, news on economic development and food security face less regulation. The role of the media in the decision-making mechanism has been growing.

In order to analyse the media coverage given to, and its likely role in, China's policy responses to the global food crisis, we selected the following four widely distributed newspapers: two are run by the state (*People's Daily*, the most influential official newspaper in China, and *Farmers' Daily*), and two are independent, commercial papers (*South Weekend* and *21st Century Business Herald*). These papers were reviewed daily from 1 January 2007 to 31 December 2008, and the major content of each report noted.

[5] Major research institutes and think tanks that have influenced agricultural policies include the Policy Research Department of CPC, Development Research Center of the State Council, Academy of Macroeconomic Research of NDRC, Center for Chinese Agricultural Policy of the Chinese Academy of Sciences, and Rural Economic Research Center of MoA.

[6] For example, Xinhua, CCTV, and *People's Daily*.

Figure 17.2, giving the average number of reports related to food prices during 2007–8, clearly illustrates its increasing appeal among China's media. Interestingly, the trend of media coverage in Figure 17.2 resembles the trend in global food prices, except for the break in February 2008 (coinciding with the Chinese Spring Festival). The number of articles rose significantly in March–April 2008, but as global food prices fell after May 2008, so did media coverage.

17.6 The Policy-making Mechanism Guiding the Responses to the Global Food Crisis and their Policy Impact

17.6.1 *The Policy-making Process on Major Policy Responses*

Faced with rising global food prices, recognizing the threat of transmission of international food prices to domestic market, and overheating and high inflation in the late 2007, the State Council quickly decided to take counter-measures to stabilize domestic food prices. Given the one party-rule and a decision-making mechanism based on internal democratic centralism, it is not difficult to understand how China was able to make such quick decisions when the economy faced a challenge. China's massive and effective responses (discussed early) to financial crises, first in Asia in the late 1990s and then more recently in 2008–10, may also help to understand its rapid response to the recent global food crisis and its decision-making mechanism.

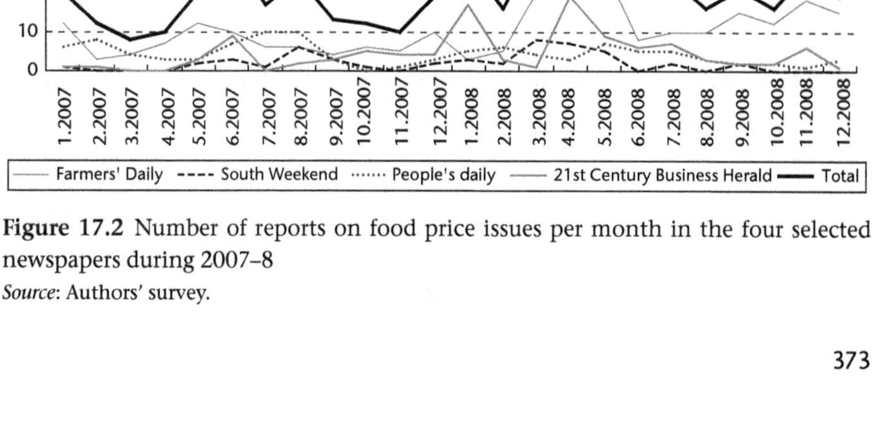

Figure 17.2 Number of reports on food price issues per month in the four selected newspapers during 2007–8

Source: Authors' survey.

THE POLICY-MAKING PROCESS RELATED TO SHORT-TERM POLICY RESPONSES

As policy decisions in the short term do not affect long-run national development strategies, institutions, or laws, the State Council and relevant ministries are the key decision-making organs. While it is not easy to determine who initiated this policy process, we were told that NDRC and LG-FE played an important role in securing approval from the State Council for introducing the stabilizing counter-measures. Once the State Council decided to contain food price inflation in late 2007, each relevant ministry had to identify its own approach for achieving this aim. In designing the detailed counter-measures to be implemented in various stages during 2007–8, major think tanks were also invited to several policy consultant meetings for comments and suggestions.

One major initial change in policy was to release the government's grain reserve. Recognizing the threat posed by the global food situation, particularly after the number of food reports in the media continued to climb in the second quarter of 2007 (Figure 17.2), the State Council, NDRC, and LG-FE convened several times to discuss the likely future trends of international and domestic prices and whether China should start to control its food prices. In late 2007, the State Council made a final decision to release grain reserves for the market—as its first effort to deal with the likely significant grain-price hike before the end of the year.

The decision to open the government's grain reserve met no resistance. NDRC and the SGA are major governmental departments in charge of grain reserves and were thus the decision-making actors to have directly influenced the State Council (or the premier) to adopt this recourse. This was necessary because of the pressure from escalating domestic prices as border prices increased. Furthermore, grain stock adjustments had been a standard approach in the past. There was no opposition from the farmers as China does not have a national or regional or any large-scale farmers' association.

Once the State Council had decided to take steps to counter food inflation, each relevant ministry decided on its own proposal for stabilizing domestic prices. Based on its mandate of increasing agricultural production and farmer income, the MoA would have favoured a moderate rise in farm prices but the ministry has little authority in the control of domestic food prices. In general, MoA follows the decisions made by the State Council, and by NDRC in particular. Thus, the ministry proposed a plan for expanding the production of grain and other foods through non-price methods such as better technological service and measures for controlling natural disasters. It also recommended a subsidy on swine to increase pork production. Supported by NDRC and the Ministry of Finance, this proposal was approved by the State Council for implementation in late 2007. A decision was also taken within the MoC to authorize China's largest oil and food importer and exporter, COFCO, to sign forward contracts with grain trading firms in exporting countries. All these decisions were made within a couple of months.

When domestic inflation topped 6 per cent in late 2007, climbing to more than 8 per cent in early 2008, and international food prices were still rapidly climbing, the State Council undertook further action to improve existing policy implementation and explore new stabilizing measures in 2008. Policy responses included: limiting and later banning the exports of maize and other grains, restricting fertilizer exports, increasing input subsidies to farmers, revising existing plans on biofuels, and supporting low-income urban consumers and students. During this period, major government-affiliated policy think tanks frequently participated in the decision-making mechanism. Given the need for speed in the policy-making procedure, academic think tanks had no major role except to provide information on the current economic situation and likely future trends.

At this time, NDRC and LG-FE, working closely with the ministries of commerce and agriculture, the SGA, the People's Bank and other government authorities under the State Council, coordinated directly with the national leaders. This is only natural, because contrary to other ministries, the jurisdiction of NDRC and LG-FE is not restricted to a special sector or field, which makes these organs key players in the face of any emerging economic issue. The restriction on grain was easy because international trade of rice, wheat and maize is managed by state-owned enterprises. The limitation on fertilizer exports, however, did invoke some opposition from the industry, but this was dampened by the significant increase in domestic fertilizer prices in 2007–8. The policy outlining extra input subsidies for farmers was applauded by all ministries because it complemented the goals of the NDCR, MoA and LG-FE for improved farmer income, although it was now up to the Ministry of Finance to find the budget to do so. Based on the division of governmental functions, support to low-income urban consumers is the responsibility of local government. Despite the resulting budgetary implications for the local government, their commitment to the central government to maintain a 'harmonious society'—i.e., local social and political stability—and to avoid unruly demonstrations or rebellious acts was more important

Local government and industry played a very minor role in China's policy-making process. For example, the ban on maize exports initially did raise protests from the local government in the northeast (China's major maize production zone) and from maize exporters. This did not alter the situation, although agricultural subsidies were nevertheless increased (covering nearly all farmers in addition to maize growers) in 2007 and 2008 (Huang et al. 2011). The chemical industry was aware of the proposed policy to limit fertilizer exports and appealed for compensation, but without results because domestic fertilizer prices had also increased significantly, albeit less than on the international market.

Experts had a two-sided role in the decision-making framework that worked either to facilitate or impede the process. Policy research institutes and think tanks continued to provide information and comments on stabilization policies but opinions among the experts differed. Debates centred mostly around the issue of whether or not China should let grain prices trend up, a topic widely examined in the media and internal reports. On the one hand, arguments favoured rising grain prices because (i) higher prices meant greater incentive for grain production, thereby promoting food security; (ii) improvement in the income of poor farmers and grain producers was more important than food price inflation or urban consumers, as these were covered by social protection programmes; and (iii) inflation in 2007–8 was also partially due to macro-investment and monetary policies. On the other hand, arguments supporting the control of prices included (i) apprehension over high inflation; (ii) increasing living costs for low-income consumers in urban areas; and (iii) the need to avoid social instability.

Media reports reflect the level of concern among the different stakeholders. As Table 17.1 shows, comments in the media were frequently from the journalists themselves (33 per cent), then from officials (30 per cent), and experts/scholars (18 per cent). As can be expected, comments by officials were largely supportive of all food-price control measures; on the other hand, opinions of the experts differed. The agriculture-oriented think tanks were strongly in favour of farmer benefits, while macroeconomic analysists supported consumer interests. Agricultural think tanks reported on the causes of food price increases, including the role of biofuel expansion in the rest of the world. Articles by the journalists themselves concentrated on food price increases in the domestic and international markets, or at times, outlined their newspaper's stand on national policies.

Table 17.1 Views and opinions reported in four selected newspapers in China, 2007–8

	Views expressed by:						
	Officials	Experts	Consumers	Farmers	Companies	Journalists	Total
Total	30	18	2	5	11	33	100
People's Daily	39	7	2	7	7	39	100
Farmers' Daily	29	17	1	2	7	44	100
South Weekend	17	20	10	3	13	37	100
21st Century Business Herald	31	28	1	7	22	9	100

Source: Compiled from authors' survey.

There is some divergence among the views and opinions reported by the four papers. The *People's Daily* is the top newspaper owned by the central government, and journalists' views mirror the official stance, accounting together with the *Farmers' Daily* for 78 per cent of the reports. *South Weekend* and *21st Century Business Herald*, as commercial newspapers, reported the viewpoints of experts and of companies more frequently. Interestingly, except for *South Weekend*, consumer views were almost non-existent. Farmer voice in the media was minimal, and accounted for only 2–7 per cent of all reports.

THE POLICY-MAKING PROCESS OF LONG-TERM POLICY RESPONSES

The response to the global food crisis generated two major long-term policy modifications to China's biofuel development plan and agricultural commitment.[7] The nature of these policy changes, which were introduced as long-term development strategy and short-term modifications, suggests that the relevant decisions were taken at the central level of government by the highest decision-making bodies, the CPC central committee and the State Council. It was clearly announced on several occasions that there was to be no trade-off between biofuels and food, and that increasing agricultural productivity through investment was the primary tool to ensure the country's food security.

These decisions, although quickly made, were based on a round of consultations. The same was true for biofuel. Discussions with experts as well as the media reports on the likely impact of biofuel on global and domestic food security convinced the national leaders that renewable energy or biofuels utilizing grain as feedstock, even though vitally important for the country's future energy security, had no role to play. However, the existing biofuel plants that utilized maize and wheat as feedstock for ethanol protested. Negotiations between the biofuel industry and NDRC eventually led to a compromise: existing biofuel firms using grain as feedstock could continue to operate and produce bioethanol up to the 2007 production level, but future expansion would have to depend on non-grain feedstocks.

China's commitment to improve national food security and investment in agriculture were pre-existing policy stands but additional measures were taken after the global food crisis. Key decision makers were members of the policy document preparation team coordinated by LG-FE. These included representatives from the major think tanks and different ministries.[8]

[7] This was communicated through several Number-One Policy Documents (see Section 17.4).

[8] For example, in drafting the Number-One Policy Documents on agriculture and rural development for approval by the CPC central committee and the State Council, the LG-FE works closely with NDRC, Ministry of Science and Technology (MOST), the Ministries of Finance, of Agriculture, and of Water Resources as well as others related to agriculture. These policy documents, together with the 12th Five-Year Plan (2011–15) in agriculture, as prepared by the MoA and approved by the State Council, have become the national guidelines for agricultural policy and investment.

17.6.2 *Impacts of Policy Responses*

IMPACTS EXAMINED WITH A GRAPHICAL ANALYSIS

To assess the effect on domestic agricultural prices of China's counter-measures in the face of the global food crisis, we need to trace the monthly food price fluctuations on international and China's domestic markets. The results are presented in Figure 17.3, which shows that China did well in keeping domestic prices from rising as much as international prices. Between January 2005 and December 2008 the trajectories of domestic and international prices differed distinctly. While international prices of the three cereals increased steeply starting in 2007, domestic prices went upward only gradually (Figure 17.3).

Why were China's grain-price trends so different from those on the international markets? The explanation is, of course, the policy responses introduced. Although trade liberalization policies had allowed domestic prices to move towards international prices before the middle 2000s (Huang et al. 2009), the pattern was broken when China released grain stocks onto domestic markets and closed its borders. This forced domestic prices to fall below world market prices after 2007.

The trends in soybean prices, however, reveal another interesting story. China is the world's largest importer of soybean, more than three-quarters of the domestic soybean consumption is imported. As shown in Figure 17.3, domestic and international soybean monthly prices moved very closely because, unlike grains, soybean is not a state-traded product, and was thus subjected to only a 3 per cent tariff and 13 per cent VAT. China had no policy measures in place to force down domestic prices in the short run. Importantly, the relation between China's grain prices and those on the international market was restored roughly two years after the onset of the financial crunch. For example, the domestic price of rice moved slightly upward and has been approaching the international level since late 2008. Prior to 2006, the price of wheat in China corresponded roughly to the global level, but during the crisis, world market price surpassed China's. Since late 2008, the two price trajectories have moved in parallel. The price development of maize is similar. By the end of 2010, the price difference between China and international markets reflected just international transportation costs plus value-added tax at the border.

IMPACTS EXAMINED WITH A SIMULATION MODEL ANALYSIS[9]

Impacts of the major factors affecting China's grain prices in 2005–8 have been quantitatively analysed in our recent study (Yang et al. 2008). Yang et al. (2008) finds that rising international oil prices and the biofuel expansion had

[9] This part of the discussion is mainly based on the earlier study by Yang et al. (2008).

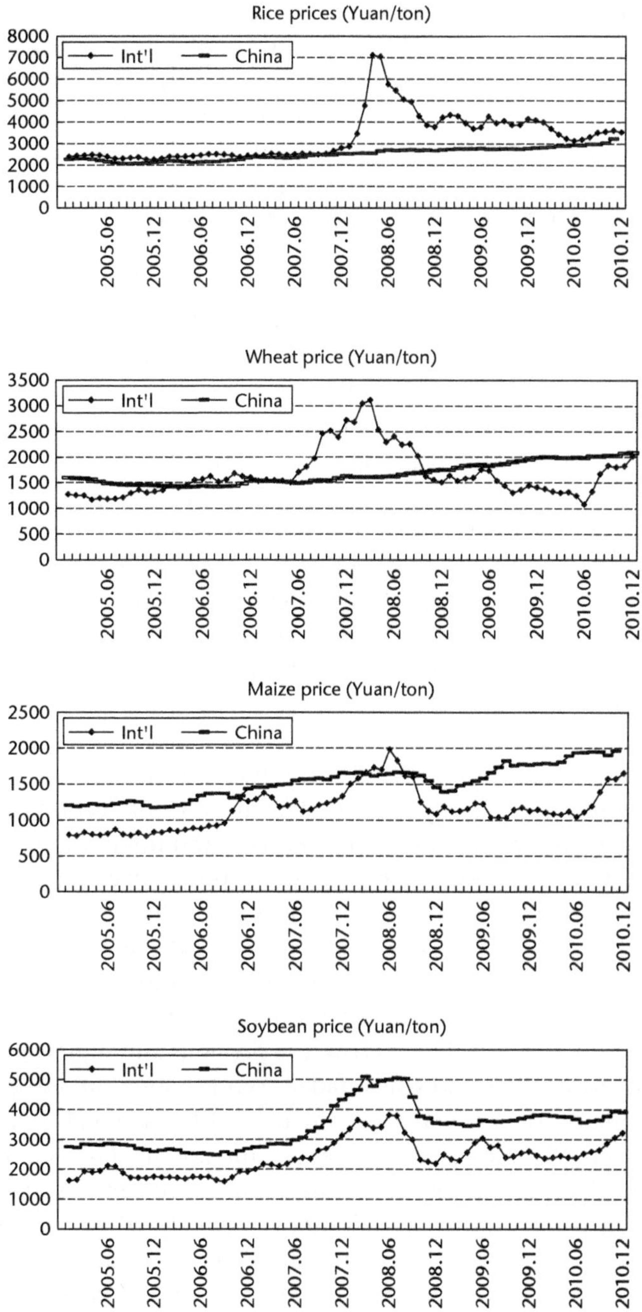

Figure 17.3 Graphical analysis of international and domestic monthly prices of rice, wheat, and maize, January 2005–December 2010

Source: International prices are from International Monetary Fund (2011). Domestic prices are from China's MoA's wholesale market price database.

affected grain prices in China. Had there been no other effects, the higher international price of oil would have pushed up the price of rice, wheat, and maize from 16.6 to 27.9 per cent (Yang et al. 2008). This would have been enough to account for 85 per cent of the actual price increase in rice. Similarly, had there been no other factors, the price of wheat and maize within China would have risen by 190 per cent and 105 per cent, respectively, while in reality these rose by 11.2 per cent for wheat and 26.5 per cent for maize. The price of oil would have also forced up soybean price by 39 per cent. We also find that the emergence of the global biofuel production added a similar upward pressure on China's grain prices. All other factors being equal, biofuel expansion in 2005–8 would have pushed up the price of rice by about 16 per cent, maize 20.6 per cent, and soybean 24.5 per cent.

The results also find evidence of the effectiveness of China's price stabilization policies during the global food crisis. Although other factors may have had some role, it is likely that the government's policy responses did lower the price of rice by 16.6 per cent. Given the actual 19.5 per cent increase during 2005–8, this implies that had it not been for government measures, the upsurge would have been 35.1 per cent. Likewise, wheat would have increased by an additional 29.6 per cent and maize 27.7 per cent. The results on soybean also show that domestic policy does not matter for fully liberalized commodities (Yang et al. 2008).

IMPACTS BASED ON PRICE TRANSMISSION ANALYSIS

The price transmission analysis presented in previous sections shows that China was fully integrated into world markets and international prices had been transmitted to domestic markets prior to 2006. However, based on recent data, our analysis finds that the above results either disappear or become considerably weaker in 2007–8. The results further indicate that China's policy responses were important and that they were effective in preventing price transmission from international to domestic markets.

During the 2006–8 global food crisis, the previous and significant long-run correlation between rice and wheat faded. While a long-run association still existed for maize, the estimated parameter (0.18) was much smaller (0.50) than in 2003–6.[10] The short-term price transmission in 2007–8 did not affect rice and wheat, and even for maize, the degree of price transmission in the short run fell from 0.15 to 0.08. Moreover, the speed of adjustment was not statistically significant. Over time, however, the transmission of price seems to have become pronounced, as the long-run cointegration coefficient increased from previous 0.84 to 0.99. The short-term price transmission for

[10] For a comparison with the pre-food crisis period, see Table 17.1.

soybean also speeded up somewhat, from – 0.16 to – 0.18. Greater change occurred in the short-run adjustment parameter, which increased from 0.22 in 2003–6 to 0.90 in 2007–8. This is as expected because (i) China's soybean imports have increased significantly in recent years (rising from about one million tons in 1996 to more than 52 million tons in 2009) (NBSC 2000–10); (ii) China's soybean market has been fully integrated in the world market; and (iii) no policy instruments existed that could have effectively intervened, as was discussed earlier.

17.7 Concluding Remarks

Given China's unique characteristics—its economic and political environment, the nature of the agricultural market, the national goal of food security, the large share of food expenditure in consumption budget, the country's past experiences in responding to external economic shocks—it is not surprising that the government's reaction to the global food crisis was swift and decisive. Counter-measures were introduced in the early stages of the crisis and covered a wide ranges of domestic and border policies. Short-term counter-measures, implemented with considerable speed, were comprehensive, and extended to domestic grain supply, demand, and trade. Moreover, fulfilment of the national goal of improved food security was further boosted through modifications to the biofuel development strategy and strengthening of the nation's commitment to agricultural development and food security. Investment in agriculture, particularly agricultural technology and water, has increased significantly in recent years and is expected to continue to increase further.

The decision-making process in China reflects the country's unique characteristics. The decision on the overall direction to stabilize domestic food prices and ensure national food security in the short term was made by the CPC and the State Council in the fall of 2007. The NDRC and the LG-FE as well as some major government-sponsored think tanks played an important role. Media reports had some influence as they collated information and options from different stakeholders. Once the overall policy direction had been set by the CPC and the State Council, each relevant ministry established its own path for promoting the policy goals in the short term.

There was no significant resistance from the relevant stakeholders to either the decisions or implementation. Again, China's political system—decision-making based democratic centralism and balanced policies—directed the different stakeholders. The primary focus of agricultural policies is food security, and this objective was commonly sanctioned by all ministries. Although there were debates among scholars over grain price control and the trade-off between producers and consumers, the decision to stabilize food prices and concurrently to increase subsidies to producers and low-income consumers was made by the national leaders. Furthermore, even though limiting fertilizer exports for a few months delayed its upward price trend, the chemical industry did benefit from price increases on the domestic market. All stakeholders related to agriculture, including farmers and consumers, will benefit from China's renewed commitment to invest in food and agriculture.

Policy response impacts were impressive. With the exception of soybean which was fully liberated, domestic grain price increased only moderately. After the global financial crunch, grain prices in relation to the international trend returned to levels that had existed prior to the global food crisis. Soybean and edible oil prices increased, and consumers faced higher prices on several commodities, but fortunately most of China's poor live in rural areas. This means that they might have some land for subsistence farming and there are few truly destitute residents. On the other hand, China has significantly increased investment in agriculture, and this will have important implications for long-term food security.

China's food price stabilization policies have helped the nation to reach its food security goals by safeguarding domestic grain prices from the increasing trends seen on international markets, but it is worth noting that this does not imply that all of these policies are beneficial for the world. China's counter-measures to keep domestic food prices down might also have helped to exacerbate the difficult global food situation, as the levy of export tariffs prevented major grains and fertilizers, agricultural commodities and other inputs from reaching world markets. Of course, China did not act alone: 28 other countries (World Bank 2008) responded to rising international prices with measures to levy export taxes or to prohibit exports. To deal with similar emergencies in the global food supply, it is essential there is a new global governance system, which can effectively coordinate action among major food importers and exporters.

References

Chen, X. W. (2008). 'China Will Stop the Grain Export'. *The Beijing News*. Available at: <http://www.farmer.gov.cn/ReadNews.asp?NewsID=621>.

Huang, J., and S. Rozelle (2006). 'The Emergence of Agricultural Commodity Markets in China'. *China Economic Review*, 17(3): 266–80.

Huang, J., Y. Liu, W. Martin, and S. Rozelle (2009). 'Changes in Trade and Domestic Distortions Affecting China's Agriculture'. *Food Policy* 34(5): 407–16.

Huang J., S. Rozelle, and M. Chang (2004). 'The Nature of Distortions to Agricultural Incentives in China and Implications of WTO Accession'. *World Bank Economic Review* 18(1): 59–84.

Huang, J., X. Wang, H. Zhi, Z. Huang, and S. Rozelle (2011). 'Subsidies and Distortions in China's Agriculture: Evidence from Producer-Level Data'. *The Australian Journal of Agricultural and Resource Economics* 55(1): 53–71.

Ministry of Finance and General Administration of Customs of China (2008). 'The Regulation of Temporarily Increasing the Export Tariff on Certain Fertilizer Products'. Available at: <http://news.xinhuanet.com/newscenter/2008-02/18/content_7625695.htm>.

NSBC (National Bureau of Statistics of China) (various years). *China Rural Statistical Yearbooks, 1985–2011*. Beijing: China Statistical Press.

NSBC (National Bureau of Statistics of China) (various years). *International Statistical Yearbook*. Various years, 2000 to 2011. Beijing: China Statistical Press.

NSBC (National Bureau of Statistics of China) (various years). 'China Monthly Economic Indicators'. Various issues, 2005 to 2008. Beijing: Office of China Monthly Economic Indicators.

Wen, J. B. (2008). 'Government Report of People's Republic of China'. Available at: <http://www.news.xinhuanet.com/misc/2008-03/18/content_7813043.htm>.

World Bank (2008). 'Double Jeopardy: Responding to High Food and Fuel Prices'. Available at: <http://www.worldbank.org/html/extdr/foodprices>.

Yang, J., H. Qiu, J. Huang, and S. Rozelle (2008). 'Fighting Global Food Price Rises in the Developing World: the Response of China and Its Effect on Domestic and World Markets'. *Agricultural Economics* 39(Supplement): 453–64.

18

The Political Economy of Food Price Policy in Brazil

*Bernardo Mueller and Charles Mueller**

18.1 Introduction

This chapter examines the impact of and the reactions to the world food crisis of 2007–8 in Brazil. It shows that the reactions by society and by the government were relatively subdued as compared to many other countries. It is argued that this outcome is surprising as there are good reasons to expect the government to be particularly concerned with the potential impacts of a shock of this nature. These reasons are related to the political incentives faced by the government, and particularly the president, to pursue social inclusion subject to monetary and fiscal discipline. The chapter traces the emergence of these incentives to a pair of beliefs that emerged after Brazil redemocratized in 1985. The first is a belief that policy must pursue social inclusion as a primary concern. It emerged as a reaction to the historic inequality in the country and the trauma from the authoritarian period from 1964 to 1985. The second belief is a fear of inflation that arose from the ten-year experience with hyperinflation from 1985 to 1994. Together these beliefs constrain government policy to prioritize fiscally sound social inclusion. Given these incentives, the food crisis of 2007 and 2008 posed a dual threat, as it undermined both social inclusion and price stability. The absence of any great reaction by the government is therefore somewhat of a puzzle.

* This chapter benefited from the comments and suggestions of Kenneth Baltzer, Antônio Márcio Buainain, Aercio S. Cunha, Per Pinstrup-Andersen, Danielle Resnick, Pedro Zuchi, as well as participants at the workshop on the Political Economy of Food Price Policy at Addis Ababa, 24–25 February 2012.

The main purpose of the chapter is thus to explain this puzzle. This is done by first describing the sharp transformation undergone by the country's economy and polity in the past two decades. In the economic realm Brazil has tamed inflation, reached investment grade in 2008, accumulated over US$350 billion in reserves, become an agricultural powerhouse, discovered extensive oil reserve, reduced poverty and for the first time in its history significantly reduced inequality. It is true that in this period economic growth was lacklustre and many economic problems persisted, yet it remains the case that an impressive transformation has taken place.

In terms of political institutions the country has also experienced a dramatic transformation, with a clear consolidation of democracy. The chapter argues that despite the fact that political institutions give the Brazilian president substantial powers, they simultaneously provide for a series of checks and balances which constrain that power to be used for the greater good rather than to pursue private interests. The upshot is that the president (irrespective of party or ideology) faces strong incentives and constraints to use those powers to pursue the agenda of fiscally sound social inclusion described above.

Given this economic and political background the chapter proceeds to describe the circumstances that mitigated the impact of the food crisis when it hit in 2007–8, so that only minor policy adjustments were needed. The first of these circumstances is the fact that Brazil is a major producer and exporter of agricultural goods. Ferreira et al. (2009) show that although this shock did in fact reduce household welfare hitting the poorest the hardest, the compensating effect of income from labour in agriculture, together with transfers from governmental social programmes, mitigated that impact considerably. This was especially true for the poorest deciles, which were thus spared from the brunt of the crisis.

Brazil already had in place, prior to 2007, an extensive system of social protection through which the government realized transfers to the poorest cohorts of the population. These programmes, headed by the *Bolsa Família* conditional cash transfer schemes, have managed to redistribute resources without generating perverse work incentives or other major distortions. When the food crisis hit the country the pre-existence of these mechanisms meant that only parametric changes to the level of benefits were needed, as opposed to having to set up a new programme. In the same vein the government was able to use its networks of large public banks to increase the level of credit in the economy as a reaction to the concurrent financial crises, thus also contributing to insulate consumers and the economy from the potential hardships of food price increases. The upshot was that the pass-through of higher world food prices to inflation and the exchange rate was relatively limited, not endangering either of the government's core concerns: inflation and social inclusion.

The chapter also discusses the Brazilian biofuel programme in the light of the criticism that such use of agricultural resources could be a cause of the food crisis. It is argued that the Brazilian programme, based on alcohol made from sugar cane, is energetically efficient and given the availability of land and water in Brazil does not crowd out the production of food crops.

18.2 Country Context

Brazil has recently undergone such a dramatic process of change that it is in many respects a much different country than it was a couple of decades ago. Understanding these changes is crucial to understand why Brazil was affected in the way it was by the food price crisis and why the different actors reacted as they did. This section will simply describe the changes, leaving to a later section a political economy analysis of how and why these changes came about.

From 1913 to 1980 Brazil was one of the fastest growing countries in the world. It industrialized over that period through a process of import substitution with high levels of state dirigisme. During this period Brazilians came to believe that this process of intense growth would lead the country to developed nation status. Endowments in the form of land, natural resources, climate, geography, population, and a huge potential internal market seemed to provide the necessary conditions for continued prosperity. Yet this confidence in the future did not last. Starting in the mid-1970s the country stagnated with falling levels of productivity and near-zero economic growth until the end of the century, an experience which substituted the confidence and optimism with an obstinate cynicism and disbelief about the country's ability to ever get back on track.

The defining mechanism through which this perverse situation was reached was the period of severe hyperinflation that started after the demise of the military dictatorship in 1985. That regime had steered the country through the 'Brazilian miracle' of 1968–73, but gradually lost power as a deteriorating economy added to the dissatisfaction due to the political repression. With redemocratization there came to dominate a rejection of anything associated with the old authoritarian ways, ushering in a dominant belief in inclusion, democracy, participation, transparency, citizenship, and other similar values. Far from being innocuous statements of intent this belief became a crucial determinant of many political choices that shaped the country's path to the present day. We will argue below that these beliefs are key for understanding the impact of the food price crisis in Brazil.

One of the first consequences of this belief was a rejection of the fiscal and monetary austerity of the last decade of the military dictatorship. In the new regime policies had to be inclusive and open. Notwithstanding the merits of such values, the lack of concomitant forces for assuring the fiscal viability of these new policies resulted in a prolonged process of hyperinflation. Brazilian history in the twentieth century had been a succession of recurring periods of high inflation interspersed with a brief periods of reprieve. But what the country experienced from 1985 to 1994 were several orders of magnitude more painful and disrupting, with average annual inflation at 1,050 per cent and a maximum of 2,012 per cent in 1989. This was an experience that severely traumatized the Brazilian people. As one government plan after another failed to improve the situation, there came to prevail a sense of hopelessness and a feeling that inflation and all its perverse consequences were an integral part of Brazilian life.

In 1994 inflation was finally tackled with the creation of a new currency, the Real, instituted by a plan lead by Fernando Henrique Cardoso who would be the president of Brazil until 2002. Yet despite the success on the monetary front, few people at that time would have predicted the changes that the country would go through in the following years. At that point the country had been through a political opening, with a massive extension of the franchise, and was in the midst of economic liberalization, with removal of trade barriers, privatization, and a reduction of the state's role as a producer. Nevertheless, both the economy and the polity remained in many ways so dysfunctional and suffered from so many seemingly intractable problems, that even the most optimistic analysts would not have dared dream of the transformation that was to come.

The key to understanding this transformation is the rise of a new belief that complemented in a crucial way the belief in inclusion, both of which remain active to the present day. This new belief is a strong aversion to inflation, that is, recognition by policy makers, politicians, voters, and society in general of the perils of inflation. It translates into an unwillingness to accept policies and choices which may lead to short-term benefits at the risk of sparking of a renewed process of inflation. Perhaps the best evidence of the real constraining force of this belief was the surprising conversion of President Lula once in office in 2003, reneging the leftish policy agenda his party had defended for years in the opposition, only to continue the fiscally disciplined macroeconomic policies of his predecessor.

It is the conjugation of these two beliefs, inclusiveness and fiscal discipline, that has been the determining force of policy-making in Brazil in the past decade and a half. It thus follows that consideration of these constraining forces is essential to understand how policy makers reacted to the food price crises in Brazil. Note that an increase in food prices has the potential to directly affect issues which lie at the core of both of these beliefs: (i) rising food prices overwhelmingly affect the poor and excluded; and (ii) food price increases are a direct threat to inflationary expectations. Therefore, there are very good reasons why policy makers and society in general would have been concerned with the crises and willing to take measures to dispel their perverse potential effects. What measures were effectively taken will be addressed in the following sections, as will a political economy argument that explains why that was the chosen line of action. Before this, in the rest of this section we will briefly describe the transformation that has taken place in Brazil.

When the Brazilian economy was hit by a crisis in 1999 that forced a massive devaluation of its currency, there were suspicions that the hard-earned price stability would be lost. Staving off this fate would require a level of fiscal discipline that many doubted the country could muster. Nevertheless, since then macroeconomic policy has been centred on stringent primary surplus targets that have prioritized fiscal discipline and monetary stability over all other policies and goals. This is quite a remarkable accomplishment as the cuts required to meet those targets go against the natural instincts of politicians who typically have short political horizons.

The benefits of this line of macroeconomic policy have not yet been reflected in particularly high rates of growth of gross domestic product (GDP), which has been rather average. The new circumstances have, however, laid a foundation of stability and order that has been crucial for other transformations that not only reflect important achievements but should also facilitate future growth. Perhaps the most conspicuous sign of this transformation was the achievement of 'investment grade' in 2008, which has improved the country's access to international capital markets. This promises to have a big economic impact as the lack of savings is often recognized as one of the major constraints on growth in Brazil (Hausmann 2008). Partly as a consequence of this change Brazil has lately been one of the major recipients of foreign direct investment in the world. Together with high commodity prices this has led to an unprecedented level of foreign reserves, which has provided considerable financial security to the country in the midst of the current global crisis. This level of reserves is currently higher than the country's external debt, which has always been perceived by Brazilians as evidence of their country's weakness and vulnerability. In this sense the fact that in 2010 Brazil became a creditor to the International Monetary Fund (IMF) and has, in 2011, offered to help out financially with the European crisis, has been particularly symbolic. Another sign of the new times has been inclusion of Brazil in the Brazil, Russia, India, China, and South Africa (BRICS) group of large emerging nations, and with it the status of being a key player in international fora, in contrast to the very marginal position it held just a few years back. Similarly the choice of Brazil to hold the 2014 World Cup and 2016 Olympics reflects the country's new-found prestige.

Two other changes that are of extreme importance for the analysis of the impact of food price increases in Brazil are the recent falls in the level of poverty and of income concentration. Poverty rates have been halved since 1993 (from 43 per cent to 21 per cent of the population) and income concentration has fallen almost every year since 1995 (Gini index of 0.601 to 0.543). These changes have been brought about by, among other factors, the end of inflation, conditional cash transfer programmes, and real increases in the minimum wage (Barros et al. 2007), which in turn are consequences of the dual beliefs in fiscally sound inclusion. These changes are unprecedented and highly consequential. Brazil has traditionally been one of the most unequal countries in the world, a position that until very recently has been impervious to all the policies that sought to rectify that situation. These changes have given access to millions of new consumers to markets that used to be beyond their reach, dramatically expanding the extent of the internal market and its future growth possibilities.

Even in education, an area where Brazil has always been most vulnerable, there have been important improvements in recent years. Although it remains low in international rankings, the past decade has seen persistent improvements. More importantly, these improvements have been the result of extensive and innovative reforms based on a willingness to measure, evaluate, and benchmark performance at many different levels (OECD 2010). These reforms have focused not only on funding but also on testing, community participation, completion rates, teacher wages and training, and increases of the school day/calendar/curriculum among other areas. Over half a million graduates and 10,000 PhDs are now produced every year and the share of published scientific papers among all countries has risen from 1.7 per cent to 2.7 per cent since 2002.[1]

A final area where dramatic improvement has materialized in the past decade has been agriculture. Brazilian agriculture has historically been plagued by distortions and inefficiencies that have impeded the full potential of its natural endowments from being realized. Problems such as excessive concentration of land ownership, low productivity, poor infrastructure, and thin markets have often been exacerbated by the very policies that sought to address them (Rezende 2006). Perverse subsidies and ill-conceived land and rural labour reforms have led to inverted price signals for capital and labour relative to the country's natural endowments of these factors.

[1] *The Economist*, 6 January 2011.

Rather than achieving redistribution land reform has weakened property rights and distorted land use decisions, for example leading to an underuse of tenancy (Alston and Mueller 2010). Up until the mid-1990s the standard diagnostic of Brazilian agriculture was that severe structural change, through a real land reform and greater government involvement, was the only way to set the sector on the right path. It is thus surprising that by the mid-2010s Brazil had, with barely any such structural change, become one of the world's agriculture powerhouses. Today Brazil is either the major or one of the major, producers and exporters of a long list of products such as coffee, sugar, orange juice, beef, pork, chicken, soybeans, maize, cotton, and a major player in an even longer list. This achievement has been reached through investment in high-level agricultural research and innovation. The *Economist* (28 August 2010) has even suggested that the recent Brazilian model of agriculture could be a template to help solve African agricultural problems. Additionally Brazil is currently one of the few countries in the world that still has a viable expanding agricultural frontier, even without including the Amazon. Similarly the availability of water and great scope for growth as infrastructure improves, means that Brazilian agriculture will likely occupy an even more prominent place in the production of food and fuel in the future.

While in many ways Brazil is undergoing the positive transformation described above, a myriad other constraints on the country's economic growth and the improvement of the population's quality of life still persist or are getting worse. Infrastructure is crumbling or lacking, corruption is high, taxation is excessive, social security marches towards insolvency, etc. This section has not argued that Brazil has overcome all the major problems it faces, but rather that it has undergone a fundamental and unexpected transformation in recent years. It is thus a much different country than it was just a decade ago and as such the impact and reaction to the food price crisis has been much different than it would have been in the absence of this transformation.

18.3 The Evolution of Food Prices in Brazil

18.3.1 *The Impact of the Food Crisis on Internal Prices in Brazil*

Figure 18.1 shows the annual change in the general price level in the Brazilian economy and the variation in the food component of inflation. Because of its hyperinflationary past the price index is closely followed by policy makers. Unexpected upward variations can trigger immediate policy responses. The figure shows that in 2007 and 2008 the inflation of food

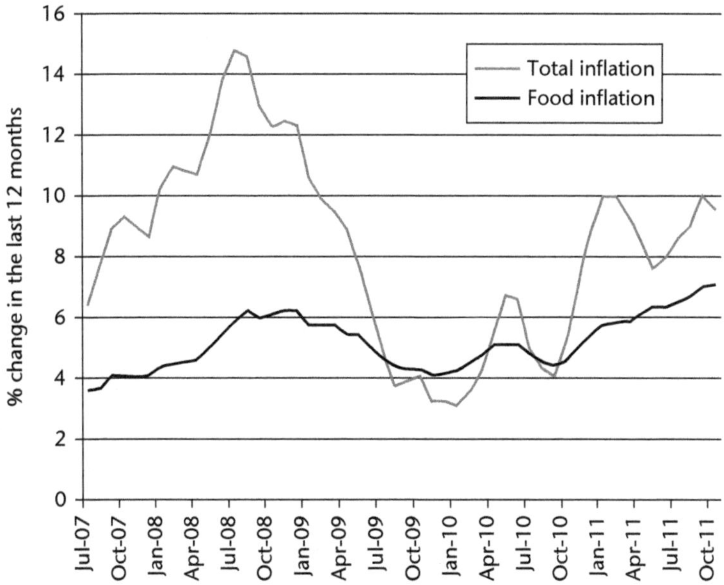

Figure 18.1 Total inflation and food inflation, 2007–11

Source: IBGE Índice Nacional de Preços ao Consumidor (INPC), indices available at <http://www.ibge.gov.br>.

items increased dramatically, suggesting a strong transmission from international markets. The effect of food inflation was felt in total inflation contributing to a rise of approximately 2 per cent from early 2007 to mid-2008. Although this was not enough to derail the Central Bank from its official target, it was certainly enough to raise concerns. In Figure 18.2 we show the changes in food prices at a more disaggregated level. The increases were not homogenous across food items. Of the six items we show, cereals suffered the greatest variation, having reached price increases of approximately 60 per cent in mid-2008. Similarly the price of meats and milk exhibited sharp increases, whereas vegetables, which are not typically tradable, actually fell over most of 2007.

As shown in Figure 18.3, although there is some pass-through from world market prices for staples, the volatility is significantly less in the domestic market. Finally, Figure 18.4 shows the evolution of the price of a basket of staples that is deemed the minimum necessary for an average family to survive for one month. This is a common index of the cost of living that is often used in Brazil. The data shows a sharp increase in early 2007 above the trend. This is a good indication that the cost of living was directly affected by the world food crisis and that it was felt by the poor that normally spends a large fraction of its income on food.

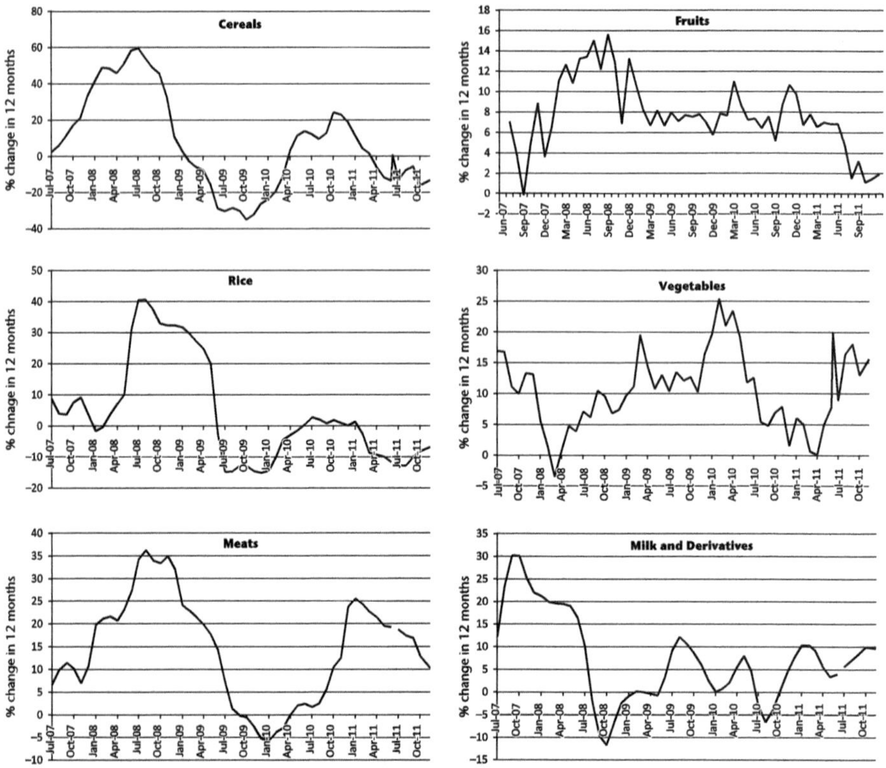

Figure 18.2 Consumer price increase for selected food items
Source: IBGE Índice Nacional de Preços ao Consumidor (INPC).

18.3.2 *Political Institutions, Policy-making Process, and Policy Outcomes in Brazil*

In this section we provide a brief description of political institutions in Brazil. We have already described the intense economic and social transformations that have taken place in Brazil in the past two decades. Here we analyse the concomitant political changes that have been both cause and consequence of those transformations. The focus is on describing who are the main actors, what are their motivations, how they interact and what are the characteristics of the policies that emerge from these political transactions.

The most important aspect of political institutions in Brazil is the overwhelming power of the president. The Brazilian president has a series of powers and prerogatives that in essence have allowed him/her to closely control the agenda in congress, such as strong decree power, line-item veto, monopoly of proposal in some specific areas, and a series of political currencies with

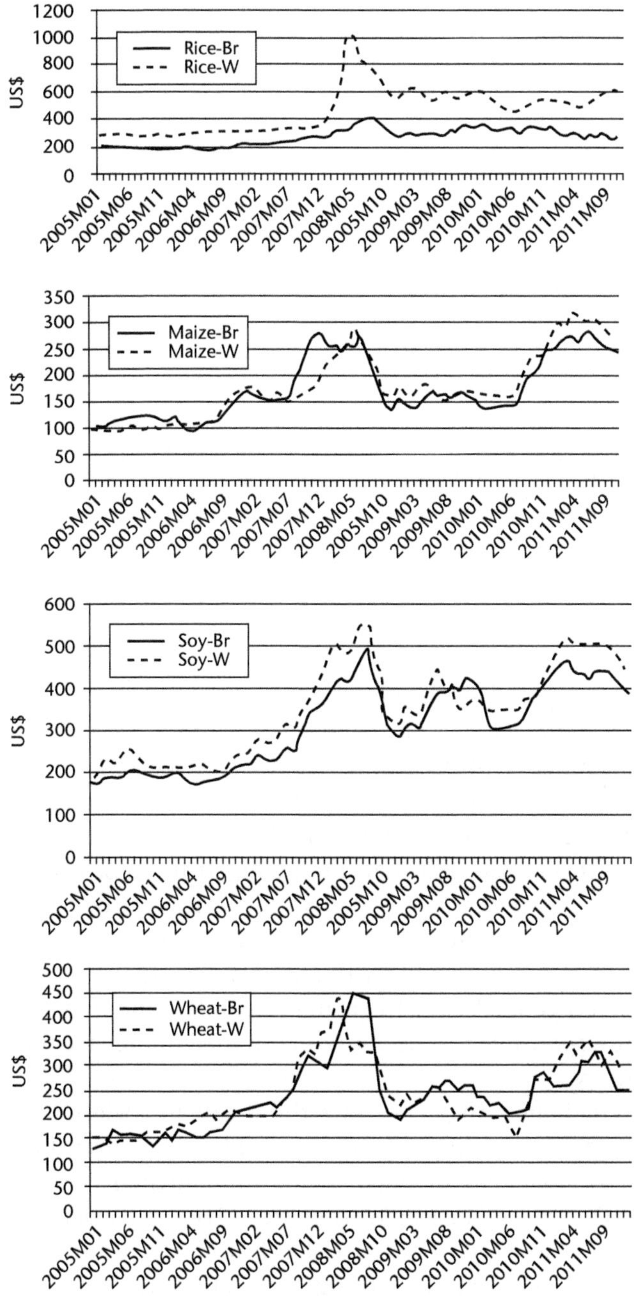

Figure 18.3 Prices received by farmers in Brazil vs. world market prices

Source: Prices received by farmers in Brazil from Instituto de Economia Agrícola (<http://www.iea.sp.gov.br/out/index.php#>). The original data in Brazilian Reais for a 60 kg sack was transformed into US$ per metric ton. World market prices from IMF Primary Commodity Prices in dollars per metric tons: <http://www.imf.org/external/np/res/commod/index.aspx>.

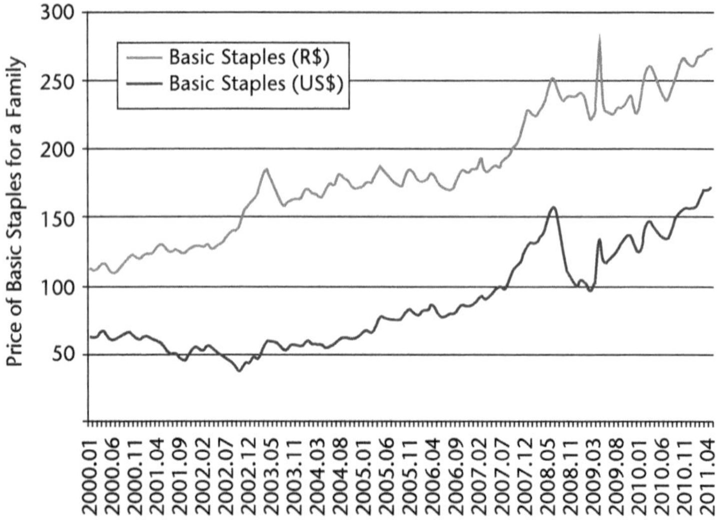

Figure 18.4 Price of basic staples for a typical family
Source: Dieese (<http://www.dieese.org.br>) nominal prices.

which to buy support.[2] The upshot has been high levels of governability and the ability to approve much of the president's reform agenda. Given the history in Latin America of poor outcomes associated with strong executives, this characteristic of Brazilian political institutions might seem like cause for alarm. However, contrary to most Latin American cases of *caudillos, juntas,* and populist strongmen, Brazilian presidents in the past two decades have increasingly faced a series of constraints and incentives that have checked the power of the executive thus restricting the use of that power towards directions generally more compatible with public welfare than with that of private groups. This has gradually led to greater rule of law and inclusiveness and is in great part responsible for the above mentioned impressive transformation in the economy.

The two key beliefs that permeate the Brazilian society influence what kind of policies emerge. Together they provide a bias toward fiscally sound inclusion that affects policy-making in a fundamental way and constrain the president's choices, shaping his/her incentives. In particular, every president in Brazil today is acutely aware that if inflation returns he/she will be punished by voters who rightly recognize that the end of monetary stability was due to a failure of the executive. Similarly, globalized international

[2] For greater details on Brazilian institutions and how the current arrangements evolved through recent history, see Alston and Mueller (2006); and Alston et al. (2008).

markets would punish the country almost automatically if fiscal discipline even started to slide. That represents a credible threat and an important constraint for the president's choice of macroeconomic policy given that Brazil has highly evolved and internationally integrated financial markets and thus much to lose if credibility is undermined. The discipline provided by these electoral and financial constraints have been manifest through an unwavering policy of high primary surpluses since 1999, under presidents of very different ideological lines, which in turn has led to the hard-earned credibility epitomized in the raising of the country's sovereign debt to investment grade status.

The beliefs in inclusion and monetary stability do not imply that policy and its outcomes are generally efficient or that they always achieve their intended goals. Because achieving inclusion generally involves redistribution, especially in such an unequal country as Brazil, those groups that stand to lose from policy changes resist and use their political and economic power to avoid losing rights, privileges, and transfers. Some redistribution and inclusion is realized, but at the same time distortions, inefficiencies, and wastefulness are generated. To most observers, including much of the Brazilian population and academics studying the country, these distortions are glaringly apparent and given that there are so many superior alternative ways of organizing policy and socioeconomic relations, it simply seems absurd that things are done this way. The insistence on such inefficient behaviour is often written off as some form of irrationality or a cultural trait. In reality, these outcomes are driven by the beliefs that constrain policy in this way. An important result is that together with the highly visible distortions some hard to observe inclusion also takes place. While the distortions have immediate impact, the inclusion is silent and often only has impact in the long term. Nevertheless there is a large literature that argues that political and economic openness has been the key determinant of economic growth historically. We argue that much of the improvement in Brazil in the past decades is rooted in the inclusion that has silently taken place over this period. Clearly it would be preferable to have the inclusion without the distortions, but given the way things work in Brazil you cannot have one without the other. This is a process which we call 'dissipative inclusion'.

A quintessential example is land reform which has, over the past half century, given incentives for land invasions, violence, rural conflict, deforestation, and undermining of property rights (Alston, Libecap, and Mueller 1999, 2010). At the same time an area of land equal to France and Portugal has been redistributed to landless peasants providing access to land, credit, and citizenship. That is, there has been dissipation of rents and also inclusion and it is not readily apparent what is the net effect. Alston et al. (2011) show that dissipative inclusion is not limited to land reform but is rather a ubiquitous characteristic of policy-making in Brazil. In the next section we will show that this process also affects policies related to food prices.

One of the main mechanisms through which the powers of the executive are constrained is the existence of a series of checks and balances that together constrain and incentivize fiscally sound pursuit of social welfare by the president. These checks and balances involve an independent judiciary including a Supreme Court that routinely goes against the interest of the executive; a free, combative, and high quality press; a diverse civil society that has carved several institutionalized entry points into the policy-making process; independent and legally savvy public attorneys that view their mandate to protect society from the failings of government, among others. Even congress, where the executive always manages to build a majority governing coalition serves as a check of extreme behaviour by the president (Alston and Mueller 2006).

What are the characteristics of policies that emerge from such a system? Alston et al. (2008) argue that there are four related categories of policies in the Brazilian policy-making process. The first is a series of policies that aim to assure monetary stability, based on fiscal discipline, stringent primary surpluses, inflation targets and high levels of taxation, among others. These policies form a fiscal imperative that takes precedence over all other types of policies. That is, if inflation starts to rise, all other policies will be cut or put on hold to assure the fiscal imperative.

The second category involves a series of policies which the executive uses to purchase political support in congress and across political parties. This is a process of the exchange of 'pork for policies' which involves the distribution of relatively small concessions of pork and jobs in the federal government structure to coalition partners (small compared to the level of pork in the US Congress). These exchanges give the president the political governability to do whatever it takes to maintain the fiscal imperative.

The third category of policies is composed of those which have been hardwired into the country's budget and are thus insulated against opportunistic changes by politicians including the president. These policies make up more than 90 per cent of the budget and are composed mostly of social security, civil service, education, and health. These are mandatory expenditures over which the executive has very little discretion and can thus not be cut to help with the fiscal imperative.

The final category includes all the remaining policies, which are not hardwired and over which the president has full discretion. These residual policies include investment in infrastructure, social policies such as anti-poverty programmes, environmental policy, land reform, etc. Importantly for the purpose of this chapter, many policies which would typically be used to address a shock in food prices are included in this category. Residual policies tend to be volatile for two reasons. The first is that when the fiscal imperative is threatened, this is where the cuts will happen to re-establish monetary stability. The second is that these policies are funded by the small slice of the budget which is not hardwired and over which the president has full discretion (less than 10 per cent of the budget) so that whenever the officeholder changes many of these policies and programmes also change.

18.4 The Political Economy of the Food Price Crisis in Brazil

18.4.1 *Introduction*

Figure 18.5 shows a timeline for events that are relevant to the food price crisis in Brazil. What stands out the most from the timeline is the relative absence of major governmental or societal reactions to the crisis. Although there are some government policies that are related to the impact of higher food prices especially on the poor, these are all quite minor adjustments of programmes and policies that were already in place, motivated by the overarching belief in social inclusion. The *Bolsa Família* programme, for example

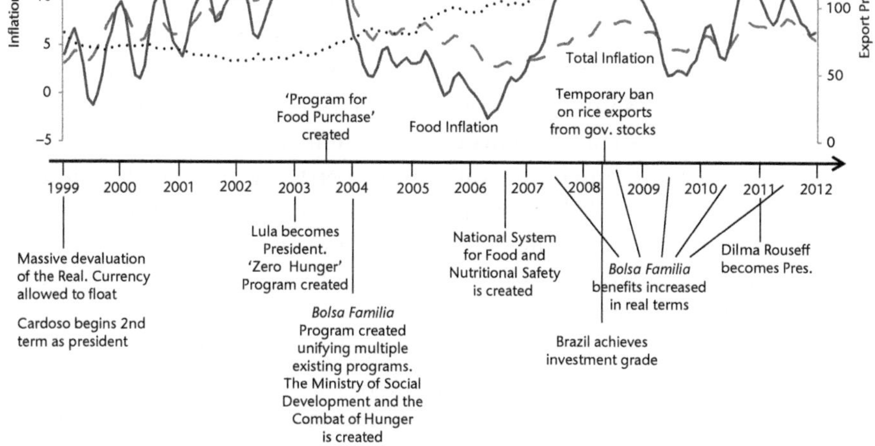

Figure 18.5 Timeline of the food crisis in Brazil

Source: Total and food inflation from IBGE Índice Nacional de Preços ao Consumidor (INPC). Export prices from Boletim Funcex de Comércio Exterior (<http://www.ipeadata.gov.br>).

(discussed in greater detail in the next two sub-sections) was instituted in 2004 by unifying several other social programmes that were already in place, some since the mid-1990s. The increase in benefit levels (in real terms) that took place as a reaction to the increase in food prices in 2007 and 2008 was just the fine tuning of a policy instrument that was already in place and working. Another remarkable fact shown by the figure is that Brazil had already been through a food price shock in 2002 and 2003. This shock was in fact greater than that experienced five years later but was motivated instead by the political uncertainty and exchange rate devaluation associated with the coming to power of a left-wing government for the first time in the country's history. This experience with a drastic price shock before 2007–8 may have helped prepare the country to deal with that subsequent shock.

18.4.2 *The Impact of the 2007–8 Food Price Shock Across Households*

In order to analyse the political impact of the increase in food prices it is necessary not only to have a measure of the magnitude of that shock but also of its incidence across different types of households. If we want to understand the response by government to the food price crisis it is necessary to consider explicitly how different social groups, and particularly the poor, were affected.

A recent study by Ferreira et al. (2011) seeks to measure the impact of food price increases across percentiles of income classes. This study not only measures the effect on households' expenditures, but also the countervailing impacts of increased wage income for those engaged in food production as well as the increases in social transfers by the government as direct measures to mitigate the impact of the crisis on the poor. The net measured effect is thus the result of the sum of three related components, an expenditure effect, a market income effect, and a transfer income effect.

Taking into account the countervailing effect on wages is particularly important in a country like Brazil that is deeply integrated in international agricultural markets and that thus stands to gain from commodity price increases. The results are presented using an assumption of 50 per cent pass-through of agricultural prices to wages.

In the same manner changes in official social protection programmes must be taken into account as they can mitigate the impact of increased food expenditure for the lower income percentiles. In Brazil this effect is potentially large as more than 11 million families (approximately 23 per cent of the population) receive transfers through the federal government's flagship programme *Bolsa Família*, and more are benefited by other assorted programmes.

This amounts to a transfer of approximately 0.4 per cent of GDP. Brazil was one of the pioneering countries to adopt means-tested programmes in the late 1990s and today the *Bolsa Família* is the largest conditional cash transfer programme in the developing world.

The fact that these cash transfer programmes were already set up and running when the food price crisis hit in 2007 made it very easy for the government to use these channels to provide some compensating income to the poor. Because these programmes work through electronic cards that can be used in automated teller machines (ATMs) across the country, the transfers are more finely targeted at the beneficiaries avoiding being captured by local political intermediaries as was often the case in assistential programmes in the past. The government increased the benefits of the *Bolsa Família* and other programmes at both the intensive and extensive margins as an explicit response to the increase in food prices in 2008 (Neri 2011). According to Ferreira et al. (2011: 13) citing the Minister of Social Development, the average benefit of the *Bolsa Família* was increased in 2008 by 8 per cent with the stated 'objective of improving the purchasing power of low-income families in the midst of the world food crisis'.

The final equation that is estimated explains the overall proportional change in household welfare b^h due to the food price shock, as:

$$\Delta b^h = -\Sigma_i\, \omega_i^h \frac{\Delta p_i}{P_i} + \frac{\Delta w^h}{y^h} + \frac{\Delta \tau^h}{y^h} \tag{1}$$

where ω_i^h are the budget shares for each commodity i, p_i is the price of commodity i, w^h is the market component of non-farm income, and τ^h is the transfer received by household h. Thus equation 1 explains the change in household welfare due to the food price shock as the sum of the three terms on the right hand side, respectively the expenditure, income, and transfer effects.

Figure 18.6 shows the results for the entire country. The expenditure effect is negative for all households but affects the poor considerably more than the rich. Households at lower percentiles suffered a welfare drop of approximately 12 per cent while the households at the higher percentiles lost only around 2 to 3 per cent. The average reduction in welfare across all households was of 7.5 per cent. However, once the labour income and transfer effects are added to the analysis the net impact changes considerably. The benefits of higher food prices accrue especially to the poorer households, especially in rural areas (Figure 18.7). The price incidence curve now takes an inverted U-shape with the very poor and the rich suffering little welfare loss and those from the tenth to the eightieth percentile suffering a loss of approximately

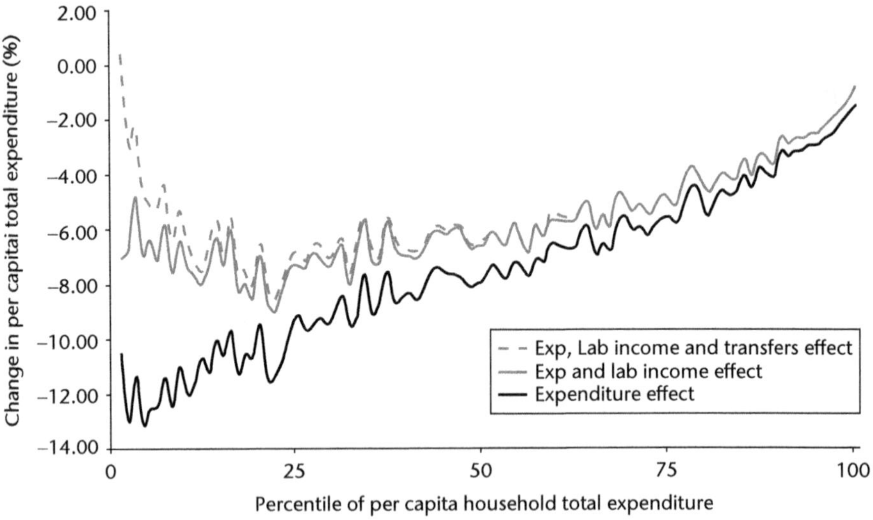

Figure 18.6 Price increase incidence curve: net effect, Brazil

Note: This figure uses 50% pass-through of commodity prices to agricultural wages.

Source: Ferreira et al. (2011) with data from IBGE Household Survey (POF) 2002/3.

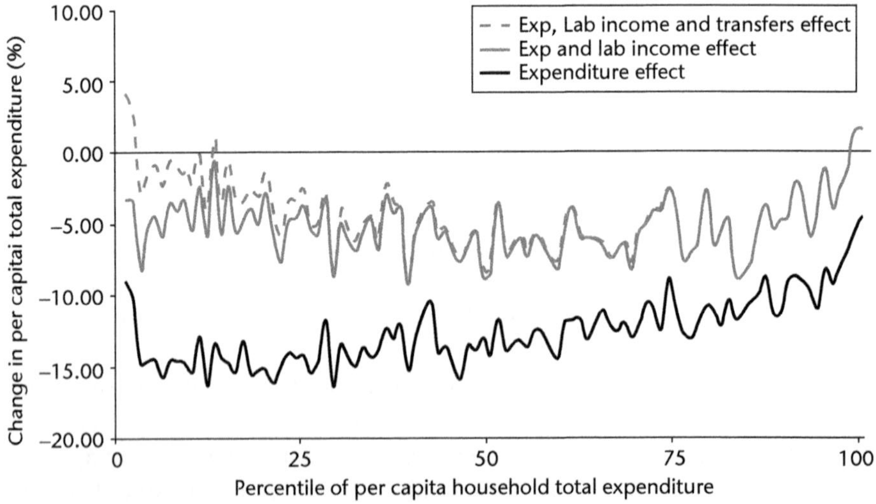

Figure 18.7 Price increase incidence curve: net effect, rural areas

Note: This figure uses a 50% pass-through of commodity prices to agricultural wages.

Source: Ferreira et al. (2011) with data from IBGE Household Survey (POF) 2002/3.

7 per cent on average. The transfer effect also improves household welfare, although the impact accrues mostly to the poorer twenty percentiles and is much smaller than the labour income effect.

The negative expenditure in rural areas was stronger than for the country as a whole, but once the other two effects are taken into account, the impact of the shock is significantly mitigated, with the poorest 10 per cent suffering almost no loss of welfare. The compensating effects of labour income and transfers were particularly important in rural areas. The expenditure effect in urban areas is smaller than in rural areas but the compensating income effect is also smaller, as there is little agricultural activity (Figure 18.8). The net effect is regressive with the poor faring worse than the rich, except for the very poor (the lowest 5 per cent), which receives a significant boost in welfare from governmental transfers (Figure 18.9).

These results help us understand why the response to the food price crisis was limited to an adjustment of existing programmes. Only a marginal increase of the transfers in social programmes was needed. The benefits from the increased value of agricultural production also had other indirect positive effects. A report by Federação da Indústria do Rio de Janeiro (FIRJAN) (2011) that calculated an index similar to the UN's Human Development Index for each Brazilian municipality found that especially in the Centre West, where commercial agriculture is expanding greatly, increased income

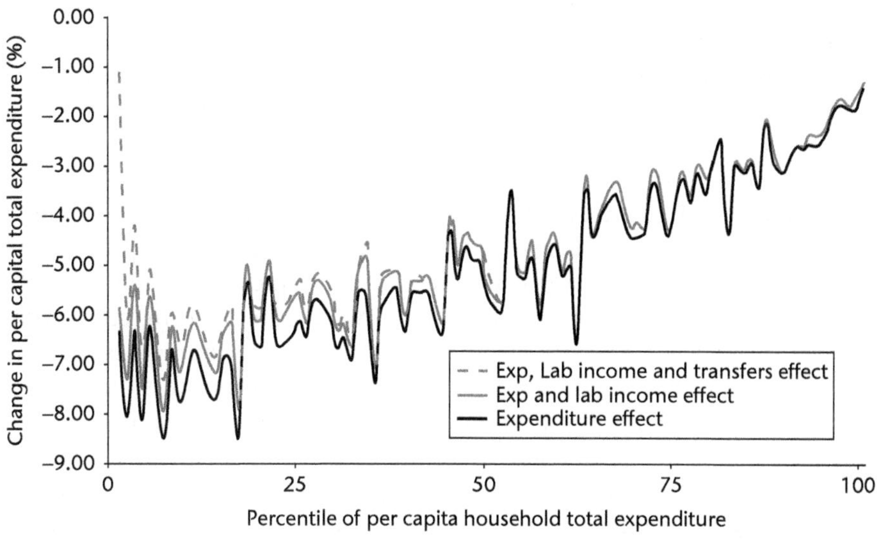

Figure 18.8 Price increase incidence curve: net effect, urban areas

Note: This figure uses a 50% pass-through of commodity prices to agricultural wages.

Source: Ferreira et al. (2011) with data from IBGE Household Survey (POF) 2002/03.

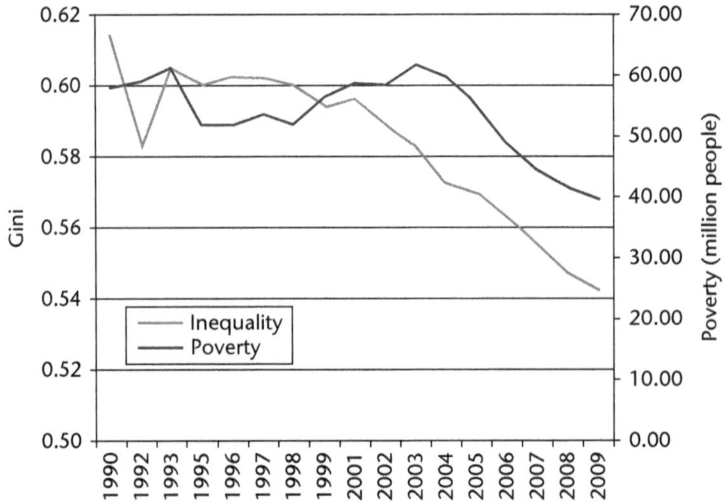

Figure 18.9 Poverty and inequality in Brazil, 1990–2009
Source: IPEADATA (<http://www.ipeadata.gov.br/>).

from agriculture lead to higher tax receipts by municipal governments that in turn offered better public services to the population.

18.4.3 *The Role of Social Programmes in Mitigating the Food Price Crisis*

In 2003 when President Lula came to office the flagship programme of his government was the 'Zero Hunger Programme'. Because this was the first time in Brazilian history that a left wing party had made it to the presidency, there were great expectations that social programmes would be given an absolute priority so as to set right what was seen as a historic social debt towards the poor and excluded. An Extraordinary Ministry of Food Security was created to administer the 'Zero Hunger Programme' in 2003. Keeping in the tradition of being inclusive and fostering participation, the programme is accompanied by a National Council of Food and Nutritional Security which has fifty-seven seats, thirty-eight of which are filled by representatives of civil society and nineteen representatives from ministries and the federal government. In the spirit of dissipative inclusion, this broad level of participation makes the process open and democratic but at the same time often leads to paralysis and irrelevance. This programme did not really create the means-tested cash transfer programmes in the *Bolsa Família* but rather brought together and expanded on a series of separate programmes that had already been created by the previous government as well as other sub-national governments. One of the sub-programmes within the 'Zero Hunger Programme' is the Programme for Food Acquisition which has the objective of simultaneously strengthening small scale agriculture and providing food to the extreme poor. The idea is to link these social groups by purchasing the produce from family farms that find it hard to participate in regular markets and distributing it to vulnerable social groups, such as public schools, day care centers, asylums, soup kitchens, etc. According to Chmielewska and Souza (2011: 18) more than US$1.5 billion where used in this programme between 2003 and 2009 to purchase 2.6 million tons of food. In 2009 this benefited 138,000 family farms and provided food for approximately 13 million people.

The point to be stressed here once again is that these programmes were already in place when the food price crisis hit in 2007–8, reflecting a deep existing concern with poverty and food security. The ready availability of these policy instruments together with the mitigating effect of higher agricultural labour income described in the previous sections, meant that the reaction to the crisis could take place by simply strengthening actions that already existed.

18.4.4 *Public Banks and Anti-cyclical Credit Expansion*

While social programmes and gains in agricultural labour income were important compensating mechanisms that helped to mitigate the impact of the food price crisis on the poor, it was also the case that the crisis did not have a very significant impact on the rest of the population that is not directly affected by those mechanisms. One important reason for this was the anti-cyclical policy adopted by the federal government to counteract the financial crisis that took place almost simultaneously with the food price crisis. Contrary to much of the developed world, where interest rates were close to zero, Brazil had much leeway for monetary policy given one of the highest interest rates in the world. The government also expanded its Programme for Growth Acceleration to counteract the effects of the global depression. In addition, as a complementary instrument against the effects of the financial crisis the government promoted a strong expansion of the availability of public credit making up for the retraction of credit from the public national and foreign banks. This policy was very effective in propping up the level of economic activity, avoiding unemployment, and generally deflecting many of the debilitating symptoms of the financial crisis (IPEA 2011). As private credit diminished in the wake of the crisis public credit increased, avoiding a fall in total credit. This policy could be quickly deployed because Brazil has a very highly developed system of public banks composed of a development bank (Banco Nacional do Desenvolvimento (BNDES)), a commercial bank (Banco do Brasil), and a savings and loans bank (Caixa Econômica Federal). Regardless of the merits and demerits of having such a large state presence in the banking system (and there are lots of controversies over this structure of the banking system in Brazil) the fact is that in the recent crisis it provided the government with a quick and effective instrument to counteract the effects of the global depression. Together with other measures, including reductions in various taxes on durable goods, these policies propped up the level of economic activity and consumption, with the result that consumers in Brazil were largely oblivious to the real extent of the world crisis. As a result of these policies millions of consumers made first-time purchases of goods such as refrigerators, cars, computers, as well as services such as airplane trips and holidays. The impact of these anti-cyclical policies also played an important role in counteracting the harmful effects of the food crisis and helps explain why the country was so lightly affected.

18.4.5 *Biofuels and the Food Price Crisis*

The use of agricultural land to produce biofuels is one of the main culprits listed in almost any discussion of the determinants of food price hikes.[3] Because Brazil is one of the most advanced countries in the production and use of biofuels—practically all cars sold today can run on both gasoline and ethanol—it is worthwhile to consider to what extent this suggested link actually holds in the Brazilian case. We will just make two points about this issue. The first is to note that the nature of biofuel production in Brazil is significantly different than in most other countries, where the criticism is more applicable. According to *The Economist* (24 February 2011):

> Not all ethanols are the same. Brazil, the world's second-largest producer, makes its fuel mainly from sugar. Processing plants can go back and forth between ethanol and crystallised sugar at the flick of a switch, depending on prices. Brazil gets eight units of energy for every unit that goes into making it, so the process is relatively efficient and environmentally friendly. In contrast, American ethanol produces only 1.5 units of energy output per unit of input, but its inefficiency is underwritten by government subsidies and high tariff walls.

The second point to note is that although the area dedicated to sugar cane and other crops used for producing biofuels has grown significantly in the past decade in Brazil, this has not led to much displacing of the production of food crops. Brazil has over 400 million hectares (ha) of arable land, of which less than 40 million are currently in use; while the United States, with slightly less than 400 million ha of arable land, already uses approximately half that area (*The Economist*, 28 August 2010). In addition Brazil also holds access to

[3] See Runge (2010) for a review of the scientific research finding against the environmental merits of biofuels and making the link to higher food prices. In 2007 a UN expert called biofuels a 'crime against humanity'.

more water than practically any other country, though it is true that other inputs such as roads and ports are still constraining. Although the issue is clearly more complex than the two points raised here, they should at the least suggest that also when it comes to the issue of the link between food prices and biofuels, compared to most other countries there are several mitigating circumstances in the Brazilian case.

18.5 Conclusions

This chapter portrayed the subdued reaction by the Brazilian government and other players to the food price crisis of 2007–8 as a paradox. Given the incentives inherent in the country's political institutions one would have expected that the threat presented by significantly higher food prices to have elicited a more rambunctious reaction. The chapter has shown that although the threat was indeed real, such a response was not needed. This was so partly because the crisis presented several benefits to the Brazilian economy that mitigated the effects on the poor and on inflation. Additionally, incentives in political institutions had, even before the crisis, led to the creation of several programmes and mechanisms to promote social inclusion and to maintain price stability, so that when those pressures emerged from the international hike in food prices, those objectives were already insulated or could be easily defended. These circumstances were not a coincidence or a stroke of luck, but rather structural characteristics of the Brazilian economy and political institutions, so that if food prices continue to increase, as seems likely to be the case, the analysis in this chapter indicates that Brazil will be well-placed to respond.

References

Alston, L. J., M. A. Melo, B. Mueller, and C. Pereira (2008). 'On the Road to Good Governance: Recovering from Economic and Political Shocks in Brazil'. In E. Stein, M. Tommasi, C. Scartascini, and P. Spiller (eds), *Policymaking in Latin America: How Politics Shapes Policies*. Harvard, MA: Harvard University Press.

Alston, L. J., and B. Mueller (2006). 'Pork for Policy: Executive and Legislative Exchange in Brazil'. *The Journal of Law Economics and Organization* 22(1): 87–114.

Alston, L. J., and B. Mueller (2010). 'Property Rights, Land Conflict and Tenancy in Brazil'. Working Paper Series No. 15771. Cambridge, MA: National Bureau of Economic Research (NBER).

Alston, L. J., G. Libecap, and B. Mueller (1999). *Titles, Conflict and Land Use: The Development of Property Rights and Land Reform on the Brazilian Amazon Frontier*. Ann Arbor, MI: The University of Michigan Press.

Alston, L. J., G. Libecap, and B. Mueller (2010). 'Interest Groups, Information Manipulation in the Media, and Public Policy: The Case of the Landless Peasants Movement in Brazil'. Working Paper No. W15865. Cambridge, MA: National Bureau of Economic Research (NBER).

Barros, R. P., M. Carvalho, S. Franco, and R. Mendonça (2007). 'A Importância da Queda Recente da Desigualdade na Redução da Pobreza'. Texto para Discussão 1256. Rio de Janeiro: IPEA.

Chmielewska, D., and D. Souza (2011). *The Food Security Policy Context in Brazil*. Brasilia: United Nations Development Program, International Policy Center for Inclusive Growth.

The Economist (2010). 'Briefing: Brazilian Agriculture'. 28 August.

The Economist (2010). 'Plagued by Politics: Biofuels are an Example of What not to do'. 24 February.

The Economist (2011). 'Science in Brazil: Go South, Young Scientist'. 6 January.

Ferreira, F. H. G., A. Fruttero, P. Leite, and L. Lucchetti (2011). 'Rising Food Prices and Household Welfare: Evidence from Brazil in 2008'. Policy Research Working Paper No. 5652. Washington, DC: World Bank.

FIRJAN (Federação da Indústria do Rio de Janeiro) (2011). *Índice FIRJAN de Desenvolvimento Municipal: Ano Base 2007*. Rio de Janeiro: Federação da Indústria do Rio de Janeiro.

Hausmann, R. (2008). 'In Search of the Chains that Hold Brazil Back'. Working Paper No. 180. Cambridge, MA: Harvard University, Center for International Development.

IPEA (2010). 'The Agricultural Policy in Brazil: A Long-term Outlook'. *Revista de Política Agrícola* (Special edition): 9–23.

IPEA (2011). 'Banco do Brasil, BNDES e caixa econômica federal. A atuação dos bancos públicos federais no período 2003–2010'. *Comunicados do IPEA No105*. Rio de Janeiro: IPEA.

Neri, M. (2011). 'Superação da pobreza rural?' *Conjuntura econômica*. Rio de Janeiro: Fundação Getúlio Vargas.

OECD (Organisation for Economic Co-operation and Development) (2010). 'Strong Performers and Successful Reformers in Education: Lessons from PISA for the United States'. Paris: OECD.

Rezende, G. de Castro. (2006). 'Políticas trabalhista, fundiária e de crédito agrícola no Brasil. Uma avaliação crítica'. *Revista de economia e sociologia rural* 44(1): 47–78.

Runge, F. E. (2010). 'The Case against Biofuels: Probing Ethanol's Hidden Cost'. *Yale Environment 360:* 11: Opinion.

19

The Political Economy of Food Price Policy in South Africa

Johann F. Kirsten

19.1 Introduction

The South African agricultural and food economy is characterized by some stark realities. On the one hand, there is a large productive agricultural and agribusiness sector ensuring national food security. On the other hand, 52 per cent of households experienced hunger in South Africa in 2005 while almost fourteen million, or about 35 per cent, of the South African population are generally considered to be food insecure and categorized as poor. Given the fact that the affordability of food should be an important political issue in South Africa, it is important to understand the structure of the agricultural and food industry and to evaluate the policies and programmes the government has introduced in this sector to deal with the broader issue of food security.

For almost sixty years during the twentieth century South African agricultural and food markets were controlled and regulated by the government. Several parastatals performed a number of functions such as import control, price control, and issuing of licences, quotas, and permits on behalf of the state. This era of controlled food marketing came to an end in the mid-1990s and since then South Africa had a liberalized agricultural and food market with limited, if any, border controls and no control over the behaviour of farmers, traders, food companies, and retailers in the food value chain. The spirit of liberal capitalism was in full operation. Since the period of deregulation South Africa experienced two periods of food price crises: in 2002/3 and again 2007/8. As will be shown later the 2002/3 crisis was largely caused by a sharp depreciation of the South Africa exchange rate but was amplified by staple food shortages in neighbouring countries in the Southern African

Development Community (SADC) region. In 2007/8 global commodity price trends were dominant factors in the South African food price inflation.

The main objective of this chapter[1] is to understand the food price trends during these two periods and to unpack the political reaction and policy responses to the food price crises. We will show in this chapter that agricultural and food policy in South Africa remained largely unchanged with no controls or regulations introduced. The policy of unregulated agricultural and food markets continues although the Competition Commission increased the number of investigations into uncompetitive behaviour in food supply chains resulting in heavy fines for a number of food companies.

19.2 Country Context

19.2.1 *South Africa's Political Dispensation Post-1994*

South Africa's recent political history is characterized by the advent of democracy in 1994 and the various policies and government programmes introduced to rid South Africa of its racial injustices and its deep poverty, extreme inequality, and high unemployment. The African National Congress (ANC) is the ruling party since 1994 and attracts around 66 per cent of the popular vote and thus dominates the national assembly as well as the legislative assemblies in the different provinces (except the Western Cape Province). The policies of the government over the last seventeen years have mainly focused on the delivery of basic services, reducing poverty and expanding the payment of social grants to poor communities. The ideology of 'growth-with-redistribution' dominated for more than a decade after 1994 but in the last five years or so more policy decisions are now framed in terms of South Africa's political ambition to build a 'developmental state' (Gumede 2011). The policy framework for a 'developmental state' focuses on a strong role of the state to improve the socioeconomic conditions of the population and the strong believe that only the state can deliver development. As a result many government programmes are focused on the delivery of basic services, infrastructure, education, and health.

The key policy-making institution in South Africa is the policy conference of the African National Conference that takes place every five years. The policy resolutions taken at this conference shape the 'programme of work' for the government, as well as the legislative programme of parliament.

[1] Research assistance was provided by Jurre Hartwigsen, Marlene Labuschagne, and Babatunde Abidoye.

Various sectors have undergone dramatic reform over the twenty-year period of democratic government in South Africa. Included here, and relevant for this chapter, are water reform (a new Water Act), land reform, and liberalization of the agricultural sector. The latter involved the abolishment of all market controls and all agricultural control boards and the liberalization of prices and import controls. A bias against the so-called privileged and protected commercial farmers, as well as believing that food can be cheaper if imported, informed the political support for the liberalization of agricultural markets. This exposed South African agriculture to all the volatilities of the international commodity markets. South African agriculture has since 1994 been fully integrated in global agricultural commodity markets with the majority of tariff lines carrying a zero tariff.

19.2.2 *Agriculture in the National Economy of South Africa*

Primary agriculture contributes 3 per cent of South Africa's gross domestic product (GDP) while the broader more inclusive definition of the agricultural, food, and fibre sector contributes between 8 and 10 per cent of the national economy with around 10 per cent of workers employed in this sector (National Department of Agriculture 2009). The two most important features of the South African agricultural economy are its dualistic structure and the process of deregulation of commercial agriculture that has taken place over the past two decades. These features have to be seen against the background of the country's resource endowment. Of the 100 million hectares (ha) of agricultural land, only some 14 per cent receive enough rainfall for arable farming, while the remainder is used for extensive grazing. Only 1.35 million ha of the arable land is irrigated, yielding at least one-third of total agricultural output (National Department of Agriculture 2009).

Some 40,000 commercial farmers (or farming units) occupy almost 87 per cent of the total agricultural land in the country, and produce more than 95 per cent of marketed output. Only 7 per cent of these farms—or 2,900 units—are considered large-scale units. In contrast, African smallholder farmers are found mostly in the former homeland areas, which make up some 13 per cent of the agricultural land (National Department of Agriculture 2009). These areas were established under the notorious Land Acts of 1913 and 1936, and are characterized by traditional forms of land tenure, which were regulated by a series of laws and regulations, mostly proclaimed in terms of the Black Administration Act of 1927.

Deregulation of the agricultural output market has increased productivity (Vink and Kirsten 2003) and the change in trade policy has expanded market access and caused a shift from field crops to horticultural and animal products (Vink and Kirsten 2003).

Over the past fifteen years, the value of imports of agriculture products have been growing by an average rate of 13 per cent per annum, while the value of exports have grown, on average, by 12 per cent annually. Strong growth in agriculture imports can be attributed to significant increases in the value of processed agriculture imports. The top ten imported commodities account for around 70 per cent of total agricultural imports in 2010 and include wheat and rice.

Since stock levels do play an important role in inflationary trends and outlooks it is important to review the opening stocks of maize, wheat, and sunflower seed (all kept by private agribusiness firms). This is presented in the two panes in Figure 19.1 below. The low maize stock levels in 2002 and 2008 are noteworthy.

19.3 Food Price Trends and Shocks

19.3.1 *Previous Food Price Crises*

Before the food price changes in the 2007–9 period can be analysed it is important to have a more long-term perspective on food inflation in South Africa. South Africa experienced a number of food prices crises between January 1991 and January 2011. The periods of extreme food inflation were 1991/2; 1994/5; 2002/3; and then again in 2008/9. We now provide a brief overview of the main causes of the last two spikes in food price inflation.

South Africa experienced two periods of sharp increases in food prices during the period from 2000 to 2010 and they were not caused by a national drought as was the case in 1991/2. The first period of food price increases occurred towards the beginning of 2002, when the prices of staple food commodities skyrocketed, and kept on increasing throughout 2002. As expected, food retail prices were not long to follow, and double-digit inflation rates seemed once again to be the order of the day. As an immediate response the government appointed on 28 November 2002 a Food Pricing Monitoring Committee (FPMC) to investigate the sharp increases in food prices. While FPMC was busy implementing its mandate during 2003, food price levels improved and food inflation remained low for most of 2004, 2005, and 2006.

During its investigations the committee established that higher local commodity prices (helped by world prices and the exchange rate) were largely responsible for increases in retail food prices during 2002. The exchange rate which depreciated from around R8 to the US$1 to around R12 to the US$1 had a profound impact on local prices since international commodity prices are now fully transmitted to local markets (see Figure 19.2).

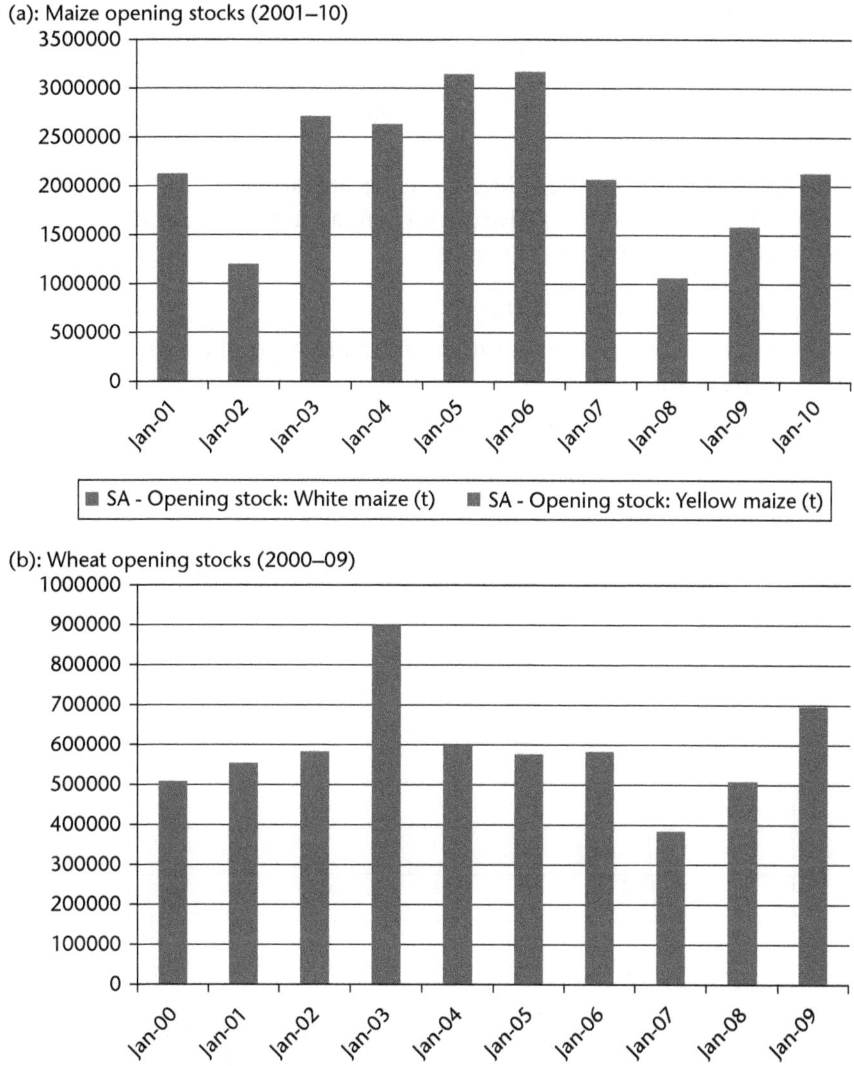

Figure 19.1 Opening stocks for maize and wheat

Source: South African Grain Information Service, available at <http://www.sagis.org.za>.

Although it was clear that the depreciation of the South African currency had the biggest effect on the local market, some suspicion remained about the role of futures market traders and speculators in driving commodity prices to these high levels. Later criminal procedures against one such trading group confirmed these suspicions. Several measures to regulate the trader behaviour on the Johannesburg Stock Exchange were subsequently introduced following the recommendations of the FPMC and following the outcome of the court case against the specific trader. It is worth noting that this process was pursued by the financial services board (that regulates financial markets in South Africa) and the governing board of the Johannesburg stock exchange. It is not evident that there was any political pressure responsible for this.

The investigations by the FPMC as well as an earlier report by Kirsten and Vink (2002) for the National Treasury summarized the main drivers of the food price shock in 2002 as follows:

(a) increasing international prices;

(b) a lack of competition in the supply chain beyond the farm gate, especially at the retail level;

(c) a fast and severe depreciation in the value of the currency;

(d) a shortage of maize in the SADC region; and

(e) a climate of uncertainty, created specifically by the unfortunate circumstances surrounding the land reform programme and the election in Zimbabwe, and more generally by the instability in parts of central and southern Africa.

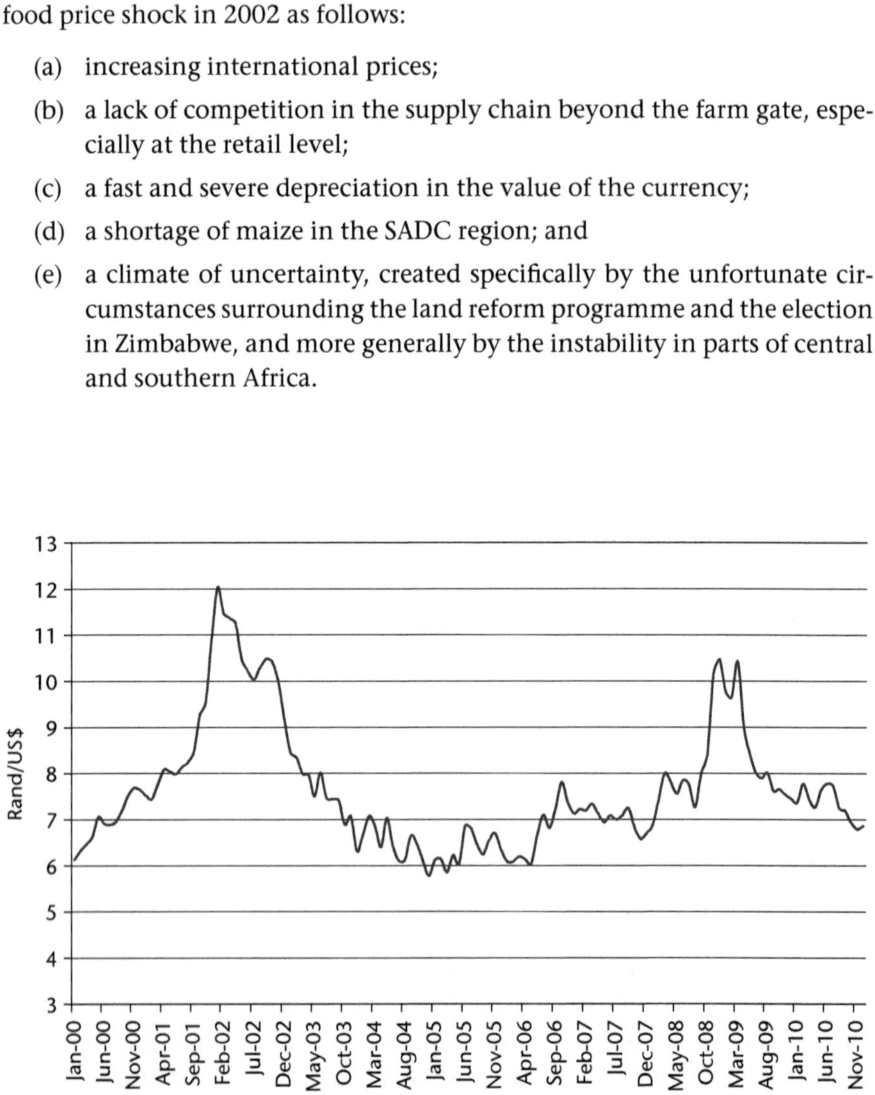

Figure 19.2 The exchange rate of the South African Rand against US$, January 2000–December 2010

Source: own calculations based on South African Reserve Bank exchange rate database.

These factors jointly caused the maize and therefore other food prices to rise substantially. It is generally believed that the depreciation of the exchange rate was dominant. Commentators generally ascribed the deprecation of the exchange rate to a number of events in the global currency market and the limited confidence in emerging economies as well as several political decisions in South Africa that reduced investor confidence.

The second period of rapid food price increases happened during the 2007–8 period with food price inflation peaking at 18.5 per cent in July 2008. Food inflation remained above 10 per cent for the rest of 2008 and first half of 2009. During 2010 food prices at retail level remained high but the rate of price increases was significantly lower than that experienced in 2009. During 2010, food and non-alcoholic beverages inflation contributed less to headline inflation in 2010 compared to its contribution in 2008 and 2009. The details of this price shock are discussed in the detailed analysis below.

19.3.2 *Price Trends for Key Food Items*

Although we had access to retail and commodity prices for a large number of agricultural and food products we limit our discussion on price trends to maize, wheat, and rice. It was important to include rice since it is one of South Africa's major imports and a key component of the dietary intake of South African consumers.

The price of maize meal (processed from white maize) is the most important food price in South Africa's food economy. Maize meal is the main food item in the diet of the poorest 40 per cent of the population and the dominant starch for most of the majority black population group.

With urbanization and increased affluence bread becomes the preferred starch. The price of bread is therefore just as politically sensitive as that of maize. Since South Africa has always been a net importer of wheat and therefore the local commodity price for wheat has since the period of deregulation been at import parity levels and therefore depending on the international price of wheat and the value of the South African currency. Ever since the spike in food prices in 2002 the retail price of bread has continued its upward trajectory. Price only stabilized for short periods of time but never got back to the levels of the year 2000.

South Africa produces no rice but imports large quantities from Thailand, Malaysia, and China. It is therefore expected that the value of the South African currency versus other currencies and the levels of international rice prices will impact directly on the retail price of rice.

During the 2002 food price crisis the analyses of the FPMC showed how the exchange rate influenced prices. In the case of rice, international commodity prices plus the exchange rate directly influenced the retail price. The specific manufacturer (mainly doing cleaning and packaging) of the Tastic Rice brand increased the retail price in 2002 in response to the rising landed cost of rice. As the exchange rate appreciated, prices improved immediately. By late 2003 prices were back to their 2001 levels confirming that with limited processing costs within South Africa, prices will track international prices and exchange rate influences.

Without going into the detail of the analysis on food price trends we summarize the main developments in the decade long time line to illustrate the main break points in the prices time series. This is summarized in Table 19.1. The table also presents the different price levels in different time periods and thus provides a comprehensive review of the speed of change in the different price trends. The information also helps to provide important time lines for the discussions to follow on media reporting and policy responses.

19.4 Policy Responses and the Policy-making Process

19.4.1 *Introduction*

There have been very few policy responses following the food price crises of 2002/3 and 2007/9. The timeline presented in Figure 19.3 provides a useful perspective on all the policy repsonses during the specific ten-year period. Apart from the appointment of the FPMC in 2003, some partial responses in the form of immediate relief for the most needy and poorest households, and aspects related to market information and anti-competitive behaviour by food manufacturers and retail chains, no real substantive changes in government food and agricultural policy or in the social welfare programmes were announced. The same happened during 2007–9. These facts were at first verified through a review of government policy statements and key announcements but were confirmed through interviews with senior government officials in leadership positions in the National Department of Agriculture during the two crisis periods.

19.4.2 *Policy-making Process and Policy Impact*

South Africa is still, after twenty years of democracy, largely a divided society and only a few people and institutions outside the inner core of the ruling party are trusted with policy-making and drafting policy positions. Parliament therefore acts only as a rubber stamp and any large differences between politicians are usually swept away by majority vote. Sometimes new legislation that contravenes principles of the constitution is challenged by the opposition through the constitutional court. Despite the 'right to food' being listed

Table 19.1 Time line of price changes on selected food items

Commodity	Prices began increasing in:	Price at start of increase	Months when prices rose fastest	Month-on-Month per cent increase	Prices peaked in:	Peak price	Prices came down in:
International maize price	April 2006	US$107.72	June 2008	17.93	June 2008	US$287.11	July 2008
	July 2010	US$163.76	Sept. 2010	17.26	Dec. 2010	US$250.38	
Spot price of white maize	May 2001	R755.09	Nov. 2001	20.95	Mar. 2002	R2,006.89	Apr. 2002
	April 2005	R545.95	Mar. 2007	23.89	June 2008	R2,005.75	July 2008
Maize meal (1 kg)	Feb. 2002	R3.14	Apr. 2002	10.88	May/Jun. 2003	R4.36	July 2003
	May 2006	R3.39	Apr. 2008	8.13	July 2008	R5.72	Aug. 2008
International wheat price	June 2002	US$132.03	Sep. 2002	16.48	Oct. 2002	US$190.32	Nov. 2002
	June 2007	US$223.04	Sep. 2007	25.73	Mar. 2008	US$439.72	Apr. 2008
Wheat	Dec. 2006	R1,728.06	Feb 2008	18.31	Jun. 2008	R4,071.63	Jul. 2008
White bread (700 g)	Dec. 2006	R4.89	May 2008	7.60	Feb. 2009	R7.92	Mar. 2009
Brown bread (700 g)	Dec. 2006	R4.42	May 2008	9.70	Feb. 2009	R7.29	Mar. 2009
International rice price	Sep. 2007	US$330.00	Apr. 2008	50.92	Apr. 2008	US$1015.21	May 2008
Rice (1 kg)	Feb. 2008	R8.46	July 2008	21.71	Feb. 2009	R17.52	Mar.2009

Source: Own estimates from NAMC and SAFEX data.

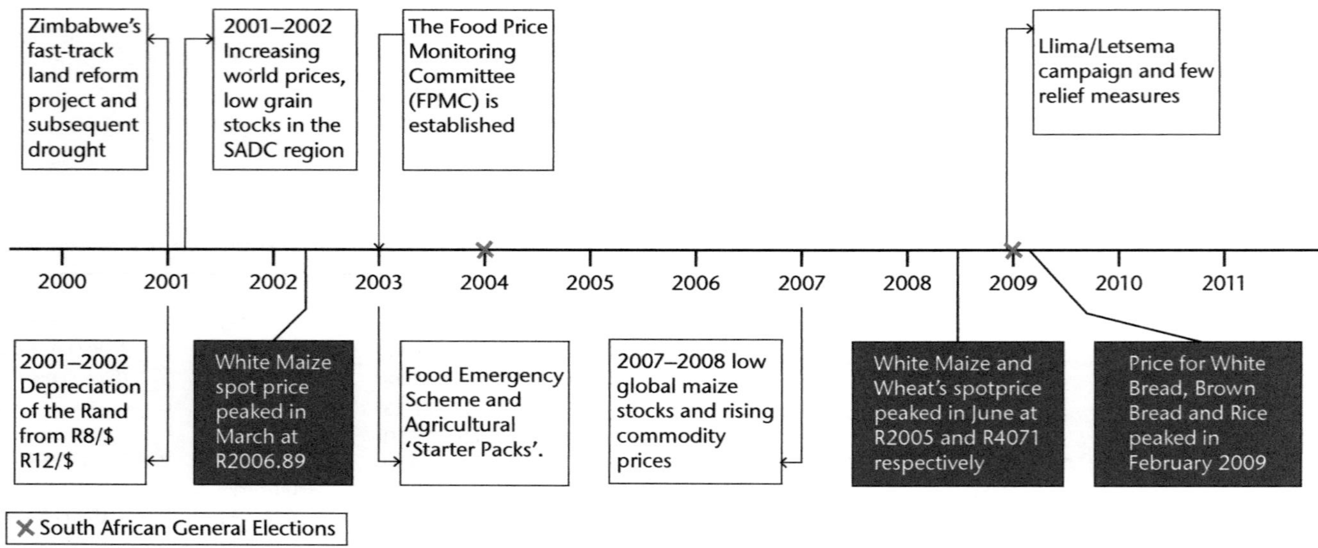

Figure 19.3 A timeline showing price peaks and policy responses between 2000 and 2011

Source: own interpretation based on personal recollection and media reports.

in the bill of rights in the constitution, agriculture and food issues are never major debates in parliament and in society. It is hardly ever contentious bar the issue of land and land reform.

Food security was nevertheless included as a priority policy objective in the Reconstruction and Development Programme (RDP)—which was the main policy framework guiding the reconstruction of post-apartheid South Africa in the years immediately after 1994. As a result, the government re-prioritized public spending to focus on improving the food security conditions of historically disadvantaged people. That policy brought about increased spending in social programmes of all spheres of government such as school feeding schemes; child support grants; free health services for children between 0–6 years, for pregnant and lactating women; pension funds for the elderly; working for water; community public works programmes; provincial community food garden initiatives; and more. The national school nutrition programme was one of the programmes implemented by the government in post-apartheid South Africa to deal with hungry and malnourished children at primary schools and was one of the presidential-led projects under the RDP. By 2005/6 the programme was feeding approximately 4.5 million primary school learners. The programme has later on been augmented by a school food gardens project, implemented with the support of the Department of Agriculture, local authorities, and non-governmental organizations.

Food Security initiatives in the various South African government departments were too fragmented without coherent strategy and in 2000 changes became necessary to improve this unsatisfactory situation. As a result, the cabinet decided to formulate a national food security strategy that would streamline, harmonize, and integrate the diverse food security programmes into the integrated food security strategy (IFSS) (FAO 2004). The cabinet finally in July 2002 endorsed the IFSS as a priority programme of the social sector cluster action plan with the specific instruction that an implementation programme be developed. The social cluster of departments has been mandated by the cabinet to ensure that the IFSS is effective. The integrated food security and nutrition programme, later on the IFSS, was developed based on five programmes forming the pillars: (1) food production and trade; (2) food safety and nutrition; (3) community asset development; (4) social safety net and food emergencies; and (5) food insecurity vulnerability information and mapping system. Despite these good intentions this strategy never got funded and was never comprehensively implemented.

Given the fact that the policy-making process in South African agriculture is rather non-transparent this section was rather tricky to deal with since most researchers and technocrats are not members of the inner core of the ruling party. Nevertheless the interviews with the directors general of agriculture who were leading the department during the time of the two food crises confirmed our initial hypotheses, as well as the anecdotal evidence.

19.4.3 *Policy Responses Following the 2002/3 Crisis*

The responses of the South African government following the food price spike in 2002/3 did not really include major policy changes but as mentioned earlier the response was mainly targeting short-term measures. The FPMC report of 2003 provides a detailed overview of the immediate government responses in 2002 (FPMC 2003: 39–42) and can be summarized as follows:

The immediate government responses during the 2002/3 crisis were mainly focussed on a number of initiatives to provide relief to the most vulnerable communities. The most important were:

- Poverty relief measures to cushion the effect of rocketing food prices on the country's poor in the form of cheaper maize meal and welfare increments (known as the food emergency scheme).
- Agricultural 'starter packs' distributed by the government among poor rural farmers. These packs include: seed; fertilizer; information packs; basic tools, such as hoes and hand tools; day-old chicks; point-of-lay chickens; pregnant cows; and bulls.

The food emergency scheme was launched to provide emergency food parcels for a period of three months by which time the agricultural starter packs would have enabled households to produce their own food. The emergency scheme was plagued by lack of coordination, long delays in issuing starter packs, and also problems relating to the identification of beneficiary households. All in all the government response seemed to be rather superficial covering only a small portion of the most needy households and with little coordination between departments within the social cluster. Capacity issues in government, availability of finance, and non-compliance with the public tender and procurement system limited the further and continuous roll out of this programme.

The appointment of the FPMC in 2003 was in itself an immediate government response to the food price crisis of those years. One can argue that the committee's appointment in some way focussed public attention on the food price issue but at the same time reduced the possibility for opportunism during the period of rising prices. The FPMC made a number of important recommendations following its investigations of the 2002/3 food price crisis:

1. The implementation of a reliable and consistent food price monitoring network.
2. Improvement in the accuracy of crop estimates by means of better technology, expertise and dedicated funding.

3. Increased budgetary allocation for agricultural information and statistics.
4. The government should introduce a statutory measure compelling all grain traders to report on a weekly basis on realized and planned (i.e., a finalized contract) imports and exports of whole grain and grain products.
5. An annual publication, to be known as the *South African Food Cost Review,* should be published by the National Department of Agriculture to disseminate information on food costs and trends in retail prices and farm-retail price spreads as widely as possible.
6. School feeding programmes should be expanded.
7. The competition commission should be requested to conduct a thorough investigation into the market structure of the food industry, as well as the agricultural input industry.

A number of the recommendations dealt with the issue of information given since it was argued that not enough information was around in the market regarding stocks, crop estimates, export trends, and the size of the harvest in other countries of southern Africa. In the grain markets of southern Africa it is often argued that one of the main drivers in formulating prices is the estimation of the local crop, as well as the regional crops. The underestimation of the maize crop by one million tons during 2002 was considered to be one of the main drivers of the spike in maize commodity prices. The improvement of the crop estimates in South Africa and the southern African development community could contribute substantially towards household food security. Intervention to improve the accuracy of crop estimates would cost the government far less than strategic stock holding and would contribute substantially towards household food security.

Certain of the FPMC recommendations were implemented:

- National Agriculural Marketing Council (NAMC) and Statistics South Africa (STATS SA) and provincial departments of agriculture formed a food price monitoring network.
- The NAMC issue quarterly food price monitoring statements and since 2005 an annual 'Food Cost Review' has been published by the NAMC.
- Crop estimates have been improved largely through support by the private sector.
- The Competition Commission implemented a number of investigations into anti-competitive behaviour in the food chain and has found a number of large food companies guilty of price collusion. Some of these investigations were concluded during the most recent food price spike.

All the monitoring work and the large volume of information made available in the aftermath of the FPMC's tenure and a much more vociferous Competition Commission have not prevented the 2007–9 price increases. It could be argued that the openness of the South African market and the strong transmission of world prices into the South African market made it rather difficult for the South African government to shield the poorest households from these price spikes. It, however, also suggests a limited understanding of the global and national food economy but also clearly illustrates a limited appreciation by top officials of the importance of analytical evidence.

19.4.4 *Policy Responses Following the 2007–9 Crisis*

The political statements during the 2007–9 period were not really committing any firm 'new' policy responses or any change in the general policy direction. In early 2008 the then Minister of Finance suggested that public policy responses to rising food prices should focus on two main areas—income support to the most vulnerable and efforts to increase production. This was also the position in 2002/3 and summarizes the South African government's position on food price inflation. It is in this regard that the 'social relief of distress grant' was introduced as a temporary social grant aimed at dealing with precisely these types of emergencies. He then went on to mention other options to mitigate the effects of rising food prices such as (a) increase the coverage of school feeding schemes; (b) increase support to non-governmental organizations and community-based organizations that run soup kitchens and similar feeding schemes; and (c) broaden the social security net by raising the threshold on means tests and by extending the grant. Here again only options were presented but nothing substantial was committed.

The notions presented here by the Minister of Finance correspond to the points made by the government officials who were interviewed but also show little deviation from the responses in 2003. It furthermore illustrates the lack of urgency despite acknowledging that the poor will be negatively impacted by the increase in food prices. The treasury—which to a large extent influences the government policy because it holds the purse—rejected the possibility of introducing any form of price controls or any other form of government intervention in the market economy. The interviews also confirmed that the option of controls or any form of market intervention was never considered by any of the ministries.

It seems clear now with having the benefit of hindsight and the collective memory of government officials that the treasury was driving the government's policy response to the food price crisis. Proposals on food reserves (more specifically a virtual food reserve) were circulated and debated in 2002/3 and again in 2008. The costs involved in such a scheme were considered to be too high and therefore never implemented resulting in money being allocated for immediate relief programmes for the neediest.

In light of this policy context the process of dealing with the increasing rise in food prices in 2008/09 has been a major challenge for the South African government. The National Department of Agriculture introduced the *Ilima/Letsema* campaign to promote household food production by accelerating and improving agricultural crop production. The campaign was launched nationally in eight provinces (excluding the North West Province) in pursuit of national and household food security to mobilize communities to leverage land as a resource to fight poverty and hunger. As part of the campaign, agricultural starter packs (similar to those provided in 2003) were provided for household vegetable production and promotion of food gardens.

Additional funds were also allocated for production projects such as mass food production, investments in production-enhancing infrastructure, including irrigation schemes and soil reclamation. Obviously these programmes were not blanket interventions and were only applied in selected communities.

One of the provincial governments, Gauteng, argued that one of the best ways to deal with high food prices and the unaffordability of food was to develop community gardens. The province established a total of 29,579 homestead food gardens between 2004/5 and the 2007/8 financial years. Additionally, over R108 million was spent on establishing 2,447 community food gardens.

The perceived lukewarm approach by the South African government to the crisis can partly be explained by the comprehensive social welfare system that has been in place since 1998 and managed by the Department of Social Development. The welfare and safety net programmes are central to the 'developmental state' paradigm in South Africa. The numbers below report the extent of these programmes in 2007—just at the time the second period of high food price inflation was observed. Income transfers to households, mainly through social assistance grant programmes, stood at R77 billion in 2007. In April 2007, 12.1 million South Africans were receiving social assistance grants, amounting to R5.1 billion. Grants are disbursed in the following categories (April 2007 figures) (Department of Social Development 2007):

- foster care grant: 405,813 recipients (R620 a month)
- care dependency grant: 98,690 recipients (R870)
- war veterans' grant: 2,317 recipients (R890)
- old age grants: 2,194,066 recipients (R870)
- disability grant: 1,425,105 recipients (R870)
- child support grant: 7,910,748 recipients (R200)
- grant-in-aid: 32,280 recipients (R200)

These grants amount to some R61 billion a year, about 3.3 per cent of GDP, and contribute more than half of the income of the poorest 20 per cent of households. This is obviously an important state intervention but in the context of this chapter it should be mentioned that these programmes have been in place for a number of years and no major budgetary increases related to these programmes were introduced during the crisis period of 2008–9. It can therefore with reasonable certainty be argued that South Africa's well-developed safety net programme for all practical purposes prevented a major crisis in the wake of rapid food price inflation in 2008.

19.4.5 *Summary*

The government response during the two periods of rapid food price inflation can typically be classified as responses in the so-called 'second class' of interventions (see Watson 2011). The second-class actions target the poorer populations in an attempt to mitigate the negative effects of price changes and include elements such as welfare payments, school feeding programmes, food parcels, and related interventions. These responses did not require any regulatory or legislative changes but were possible in terms of current government mandates and only required additional funding from the treasury. This additional funding was small compared to the 3.3 per cent of GDP that has already been allocated to social welfare payments in years prior to the 2008–9 crisis. The funding for the additional small interventions was made available fairly quickly given the seriousness of the crisis in terms of political repercussions. Note should be taken that 2004 and 2009 were election years in South Africa and distributing food parcels or providing food relief thus useful instruments to show that the government was looking after its people! Nevertheless, South Africa has a well-funded social safety net programme in place which provided an important cushion during the periods of high food prices.

19.5 Political Economy Context

19.5.1 *Introduction*

As mentioned above, the South African government did not implement any major policy changes in the aftermath of the two periods of food price inflation. Most responses were in the category of responses introduced to mitigate the impact of food price inflation on the poorest communities. South Africa had, as part of the developmental state paradigm, already in place a comprehensive social welfare programme that served as an important buffer during the relevant crisis periods.

South Africa therefore did not experience any food riots, civil unrest, and did not introduce any mechanism to control food reserves and food trade. Given the history of the political economy related to agriculture, land and food, there are important political dimensions to be considered. Why, then, did the food crises not lead to civil unrest or any political instability in the country during the height of the food price crises. The following sections endeavour to provide an answer.

It should, however, be mentioned that a few months after the completion of the initial phase of the research for this chapter—during the period November 2012 to January 2013—the main agricultural export crop producing regions of the Western Cape experienced large farm labour unrests as a result of demands for higher wages. The Department of Labour set the minimum wage for farm labour and this rate was not up for review for at least another year. It is now clear that the increased cost of living, perhaps inflated by higher food costs, contributed to the demands for a doubling of the farm worker wage. There were however a number of anecdotal stories of political opportunism and criminality that were the main factors behind the unrest. Nevertheless high cost of food is a fact and poverty is rife and therefore provided fertile ground for any revolutionary ideas.

19.5.2 *Political Institutions in the Context of Food and Agricultural Policy*

Since 1994 South Africa has been a democracy based on the principle of majority rule but with an element of proportional voting also entrenched in the way members of parliament are elected. The ANC has since the first democratic elections in 1994 secured just under two-thirds of the votes in all the general elections in 1999, 2004, and 2009. As such the party and its officials play an important role in policy formulation and execution. It is also a well-established fact that the National Executive Committee, the highest organ of the ANC, is the most important policy-making institution in South Africa that produces documents and policy positions. In the years between the National Conference that takes place every five years the National Executive Committee convenes a policy conference, as a recommendation-making body on any matter of policy. The National Executive Committee has to convene a national policy conference at least six months before the national conference to review policies of the ANC and to recommend any new or to amend any present policy for consideration by the national conference (last policy conference took place in June 2012).

The National Executive Committee makes recommendations on the deployment of 'cadres' to ministerial and public servant positions and thereby ensures that policy positions of the party are carried into all organs of state.

Many of these positions do not really pass through parliament. Policy positions and programmes have to be confirmed by cabinet which is preceded by agreement in the economic cluster of ministries.

Food and agricultural policy forms part of the economic cluster and therefore necessitates a discussion on the country's economic policy in broad terms. The economic policy adopted by the ANC is often criticized by analysts and observers arguing that the promise of the struggle has been sacrificed to a market-oriented economic policy that is tailored to the demands of national and global capital. Authors like Terreblanche (2002) offer interesting analyses and explanations of how the ANC was attracted to the benefits of business and global capitalism during the transition years between 1991 and 1994. He argues that this led to a behind the scenes compact between business and the political elite of the ANC which led the ANC to dispense with an emphasis on state-led growth and social expenditure in favour of the pro-business growth, employment and redistribution programme, betraying the ANC's core constituency, the working-class poor.

Terreblanche's detailed analysis of the South African political economy unpacks this alliance between South African capital and business and the governing party and how it influenced and directed the economic policy. Economic policy was therefore typically embedded in the Washington Consensus of liberal market capitalism steering thus a non-interventionist role of the state. This economic policy made it difficult for the government to deal with the structural problems of the post-apartheid state and to make meaningful contributions to alleviating poverty and most likely also informed many of the decisions in the aftermath of the food price crises.

It is quite astonishing that this blend of economic policy is so well-entrenched in government policy despite the fact that the ANC is strongly aligned with the Confederation of South African Trade Unions (COSATU) and the South African Communist Party (SACP) in what is known as the tripartite alliance (ANC-SACP-COSATU) and which typically represents workers and left wing interests. Add to this the fact that the ANC in itself is not monolith and is intensely divided along many divisions it is no wonder that most spheres of government policy-making—especially in agriculture, food, land, and rural development matters—are experiencing 'policy paralysis' or the inability to make important decisions. This situation of paralysis is present in land reform policy, general agricultural policy, but was certainly also present during the food price crises. This 'policy paralysis' can be ascribed to the fact that government (and the party) has succumbed to deep ideological divisions within the ruling alliance, which prevent any agreement on the way forward. It may well be that officials and minsters really do not know what to do or it could be that any sensible policy proposal is considered to be too controversial so it seemed easier to appoint a committee or to commission a study.

This paralysis was not present when the new democratic government introduced sweeping and quick agricultural policy reforms in the late 1990s when all state support, subsidies and guarantees to commercial agriculture (mainly white farmers at the time) were abolished. Although agricultural economists argued for these changes for many years in order to improve the efficiency in the sector, it is now clear that the ANC stalwarts thought by removing all farm policy benefits to white farmers it would encourage farmers to sell out and thereby speed-up the process of land reform. At the same time it was believed land values would drop to be closer to productive values and thereby assist the state to acquire land for land reform purposes. Given the racial history of South Africa it was considered critical to remove all privileges to whites.

Removing the privileges and importing cheap food was considered to be a useful policy to bring cheaper food to the working class and the impoverished groups. The ruling party only after 2002 realized that relying on imported food does not necessarily bring cheaper food and gradually brought a stronger appreciation for the role of commercial agriculture in South Africa. The crisis in 2008/09 emphasized this point and with a new global recognition of the role of agriculture following the World Development Report in 2008 (World Bank 2008) it became apparent to policy makers in the ANC and government that agriculture should not be neglected. Local food production and ensuring a positive agricultural and food trade balance became an important national objective. Despite this acknowledgement, support to agriculture did not increase but at least there was no anti-agriculture bias any more.

More evidence of this new appreciation of the role of agriculture in the South African economy and specifically in the challenge of alleviating poverty and creating jobs was to be found in the National Development Plan—Vision 2030 released by the National Planning Commission (2011). The document highlights the importance of agriculture in growing the rural economy and recommends a set of policies and programmes to ensure that agriculture creates an additional one million jobs.

Koch (2011) also argues that political support for food security is now high. He bases this conclusion on the fact that the ruling party needs the political support and votes of the white commercial farmers to maintain a healthy and successful tripartite alliance between the ANC, trade unions, and the SACP. By politicizing agriculture and food security the ANC managed to ensure high political support of agriculture and food security. This was also emphasized in the 2009 election manifesto of the ANC.

As an illustration of the limited 'direct' action by government during the different food price crises we have reviewed different statements of the South African cabinet on the issue of high food prices. The various extracts confirm our interpretation and views throughout this chapter. Before this can be done it is important to understand that any cabinet decision would have been prepared by the individual government departments and after which it would be discussed at the economic and employment cluster and then prepared for submission to cabinet.[2] To some extent this process confirms the limited role of the parliament. The parliament has a legislative mandate and also has oversight over the expenditure and programme design of the different ministries. But most policy decisions are rooted in the National Executive Committee of the ruling party and within the cabinet and its various clusters.

Most of the cabinet statements illustrate the non-interventionist and rather neutral approach by the government. The statements have not indicated any major policy shifts and thus confirm our initial hypothesis of no or limited policy response. The social welfare programmes have, since they already take a large chunk of the budget, not been boosted as a result of the crisis. There were only small areas of targeted interventions by different ministries. The government, however, refrained from intervening in any of the agricultural commodity markets or changing its trade policy.

19.5.3 *Pressure Groups, Public Uprising, and Food Riots*

In South Africa the various labour unions, specifically COSATU, were very vocal while the different consumer lobby groups also made a lot of noise during the two periods of sharp food price increases. Most of these institutions blamed the food manufacturers and then later on the retailers for the sharp food price increases. The same line of critique was presented by the ANC's alliance partner, the SACP, in a press statement issued in October 2002 (available at: <http://www.sacp.org.za/>).

The pressure from COSATU, the SACP, the Consumer Union, and NGOs as well as some suspicion within government circles increased the concern that there is collusive behaviour in some sectors of the economy, particularly in the food industry. These concerns as well as specific complaints lodged at the Competition Commission led to several investigations by the Commission into the conduct of several food companies. A number of them were found guilty of misconduct and fined large penalties.

At the same time the media used the food price crisis to stir sensation and hype while academics, commodity traders and farmers' groups tried to explain the trends on the basis of market fundamentals and supply chain realities. We compiled a simple analysis to track the number of media reports related to the different periods of high food prices to assess the media hype and sensation

[2] The economic and employment cluster is a meeting of the minsters and their directors general from the following departments: rural development and land reform (chair); science and technology (deputy chair); agriculture, forestry and fisheries; communications; economic development; finance; higher education and training; labour; mineral resources; public enterprises; rural development and land reform; tourism and trade and industry.

around the topic. Figure 19.4 presents this very rough review of articles carrying an issue on food prices over the last decade. We only reviewed the major print media to get a sense of whether what the media was reporting corresponded with periods of high food prices. The 2008/9 crisis received much more coverage in the local media than was the case in the 2002/3 period.

Although the media covered the food price crisis during 2008 heavily it did not really have much impact. Most of the articles were informed by international media reports and furthermore only reported on the cabinet statements mentioned earlier or highlighted the information released by NAMC through its quarterly food price reviews. The numbers presented by the NAMC showed sharp retail price increases and provided useful material for the media in a period where other news was very stale and uninteresting. It was also good material to highlight the plight of the middle class and the poor in the run-up to the general election in May 2009.

Apart from the farm labour unrest in the Western Cape at the end of 2012–13—years after the last food price crisis—South Africa had no civil unrest and/or riots that could directly be linked to the food price crisis. It therefore played no role in framing the policy responses during the two periods in question.

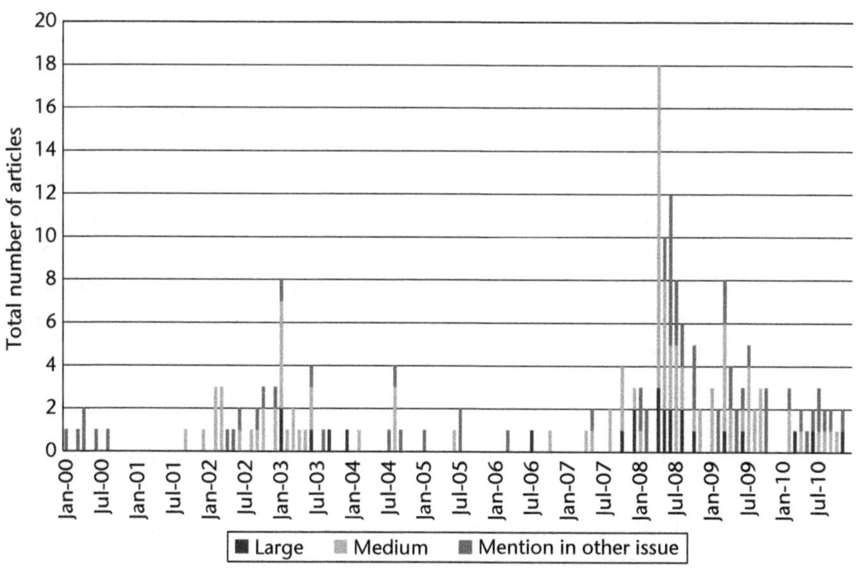

Figure 19.4 Newspaper articles on food prices in South Africa, January 2000–December 2010

Source: own calculations based on a recording of articles in the main daily newspapers.

19.6 Conclusion

Since the period of agricultural market deregulation, South Africa experienced two periods of food price crises: in 2002/3 and again 2007/8. The 2002/3 crisis was largely caused by a sharp depreciation of the South Africa exchange rate but was amplified by staple food shortages in the SADC region. In 2007/8 global commodity price trends were dominant factors in South African food price inflation.

The main objective of this chapter was to understand the food price changes during these two periods and to unpack the political reaction and policy responses to the food price crises in these two periods. Our personal recollection of events during the past decade, interviews with former politicians and state officials as well as a thorough investigation of all cabinet and government documents released during the specific years provided us with the conclusion that there were no major policy responses or changes in policy direction following the two periods of rapid food price inflation. It could be argued that the comprehensive social welfare programmes that were in place since 1998 would have provided a sufficient safety net for the most vulnerable suggesting to government decision makers that there is no need for substantive policy response. What the crisis did, however, is bring about a greater appreciation amongst politicians and members of the ruling party of the role of a domestic agricultural sector and how important it is not to depend on international trade for domestic food needs. This new 'understanding' did, however, not bring about specific policy changes.

We established that the policy of neo-liberal capitalism is so well-entrenched that it was difficult for the cabinet or bureaucrats to contemplate radical interventions in the market for agricultural commodities and food products. The fairly neutral response by government happened despite the call for action by the trade unions, the South African Communist Party and some strong media reporting. The evidence clearly suggests that the government's response was more focussed on the line of statements and comments by senior politicians and a few pockets of government programmes introduced to deal with the negative consequences of the crisis within the neediest communities. The social safety net programme by the government that reaches about fourteen million people also provided some reassurance that the poorest people are already protected by substantial government programmes. At the same time the government made sure that any possible collusion by agribusiness firms and food companies was dealt with effectively by the Competition Commission.

We have shown in this chapter that agricultural and food policy in South Africa remained largely unchanged with no controls or regulations introduced. The policy of unregulated agricultural and food markets continues although the Competition Commission increased the number of investigations into uncompetitive behaviour in food supply chains resulting in heavy fines for a number of food companies.

Taking into account all the government responses during the two periods of rapid food price inflation, the South African government implemented actions that can typically be classified as responses in the so-called 'second class' of interventions that mostly target the poorer section of the population in an attempt to mitigate the negative effects of price changes and include elements such as school feeding programmes, food parcels, etc. In the South African government these responses did not require any regulatory or legislative changes since they could be taken care of under the existing social welfare system and were thus possible in terms of current government mandates and in some cases only required additional funding from the treasury. This was made available fairly quickly given the seriousness of the crisis in terms of political repercussions. Note should be taken that 2004 and 2009 were election years in South Africa and distributing food parcels or providing food relief were thus useful instruments to show that the government was looking after its people. Nevertheless, South Africa had a well-funded social safety net programme in place prior to the crisis period and thus provided an important cushion during the periods of high food prices.

In closing it is worth noting that South Africa still does not have a comprehensive food security policy in place. The oversight role for food security is allocated to the National Department of Agriculture, Fisheries and Forestry, and specifically to a weak directorate in the department. This in essence prohibits the South African government from introducing a comprehensive and coordinated food security strategy. It could well be argued that the current social welfare payments are insufficient and that much more coordinated and well planned food security interventions are needed in the neediest communities of South Africa. This, however, is part of an ongoing debate in South Africa and not necessary following from the crises in 2008–9.

References

BFAP (Bureau for Food and Agricultural Policy) (2009). 'South African Agricultural Baseline, 2009'. Pretoria: University of Pretoria.

Department of Social Development (2007). 'Annual Report of the Department of Social Development'. Pretoria: Department of Social Development.

FAO (Food and Agriculture Organization) (2004). 'Republic of South Africa: Integrated Food Security Strategy'. Available at: <http://www.fao.org/righttofood/inaction/countrylist/SouthAfrica/IntegratedFoodSecurityStrategy_2002.pdf>.

FMPC (Food Price Monitoring Committee) (2003). 'Final Report'. Pretoria: National Agricultural Marketing Council and Department of Agriculture.

Gumede, W. (2011). 'Developing a Democratic Developmental State in South Africa'. Policy Brief 1. Midrand: Development Bank of Southern Africa.

Kirsten, J. F., and N. Vink (2002). 'Pricing Behaviour in the South African Food and Agricultural Sector. A Report to the National Treasury'. Available at <http://www.sarpn.org/documents/d0000327/P280_Pricing.pdf>.

Koch, J. (2011). 'The Food Security Policy Context in South Africa'. Country Study 21. Brasilia: UNDP, International Policy Centre for Inclusive Growth.

May, J. (2012). 'Smoke and Mirrors: The Science of Poverty Measurement and its Application'. *Development Southern Africa* 29(1): 63–75.

National Department of Agriculture, South Africa (2009). 'Overview of South African Agriculture'. Available at: <http://www.nda.gov.za> (accessed June 2009).

National Planning Commission, South Africa (2011). National Development Plan: Vision 2030. Available at: <http://www.npconline.co.za>.

Terreblanche, S. J. (2002). *A History of Inequality in South Africa*. Durban: University of Natal Press.

Vink, N. (2003). 'The Influence of Policy on the Role of Agriculture in South Africa'. Paper presented at TIPS/DPRU Forum 2003 'The Challenge of Growth and Poverty: The South African Economy since Democracy', Johannesburg, September.

Vink, N., and J. F. Kirsten (2003). 'Policy Successes and Policy Failures in Agriculture and Land Reform in South Africa: The 1990s'. *The South African Journal of Economic History* 18(S 1 and 2): 96–117.

Vink, N., and J. van Rooyen (2009). 'The Economic Performance of Agriculture in South Africa since 1994: Implications for Food Security'. Development Planning Division Working Paper Series No. 17. Midrand: Development Bank of Southern Africa.

Watson, D. D. (2011). 'A Review of Unanswered Political Economy Questions in Food Policy'. Mimeo. Ithaca, NY: Cornell University.

World Bank (2008). *World Development Report 2008: Agriculture for Development*. Washington, DC: World Bank.

Part VII

The Political Economy of Food Price Policy in High-income Countries

20

US Policy Contributions to Agricultural Commodity Price Fluctuations, 2006–12

Gordon C. Rausser and Harry de Gorter

20.1 Introduction

The recent food commodity price boom and bust follows the pattern of those that preceded it, with broad and sharp co-movement of commodity prices. Such booms and busts have the heaviest economic and social impact on developing nations, where agriculture accounts for a sizable portion of economic activity, households spend a large share of their disposable income on food commodities, and economies depend heavily on food commodity trade. Typically, food commodity price spikes—and volatility in general—resonate with populists and affect social welfare more dramatically than most (if not all) other asset price volatility or spikes.

For storable food commodities, price spikes and volatility result from a sequence of supply and/or demand shocks that reduce inventories to low levels.[1] Although the specific factors that cause each dramatic increase in volatility and/or price are nuanced they include the dynamics of commodities stockholding and speculation; macroeconomic phenomena observed through nominal interest rates, real interest rates, and exchange rates; cross-commodity linkages or general equilibrium effects through factor substitution and input costs; and governmental policies. When such events combine with macroeconomic fiscal and monetary policies that result in disequilibria between nominal and real rates of interest, the incentives for stockholding change. Moreover, export quotas and other trade restrictions can aggravate (and have aggravated) the

[1] The linkages between supply and demand shifts, inventory situations, and commodity price changes are described in more detail in Hochman et al. (2011), Wright (2011), and Carter, Rausser, and Smith (2012).

volatility of food commodity prices and send the wrong price signals to domestic markets (Carter, Rausser, and Smith 2011). To the extent that such price volatility is not temporary, the cross-commodity linkages through competition for land allocation and demand substitutability often create spill-over effects from one food commodity to another. Still another causal force that has emerged over our recent history is the growing global demand—sourced with higher income levels in emerging markets—for higher quality sources of protein.

Public policy responses frequently amplify the consequences of these internal and external market forces. In this chapter, we demonstrate how US public policies have contributed to recent global price spikes and volatility. We examine agricultural and macroeconomic policies, which have always played a significant role in generating grain price volatility. But we also focus on new causal mechanisms that have emerged since 2006 in the form of energy and environmental policies. These policies have made biofuel and food grain prices interdependent. We also highlight the ways in which various US biofuel policies have interacted both with each other and with biofuel policies in the rest of the world. For example, US biofuel policies contributed to the 2007–8 episode of food price volatility (which was magnified by both US fiscal and monetary policies). Since biofuel policies in the USA and other Organisation for Economic Co-operation and Development (OECD) countries interact with fossil fuel energy markets, the level and variability of crop prices are highly susceptible to changes in oil prices and macroeconomic conditions, especially those that cause major shifts in transportation fuel demand.

The net effect of these new causal mechanisms is that US biofuel policies have ultimately increased rather than lowered world prices (without reducing volatility). High oil prices elevated crop prices in 2006–8; lower oil prices in 2008–9 helped make crop prices plummet. Lately, crop prices have risen again almost to their 2008 peak levels, and some studies have even argued that oil prices have led increased food grain commodity prices (e.g., Baffes and Haniotis 2010). In short, the economics of commodity price volatility have recently become more complex. Interaction effects now depend not only on the source of the shock (oil prices versus crop supply/demand shocks), and on which biofuel policy determines the world biofuel market price (e.g., tax credit versus mandate), but also on the interactions across the various environmental, energy, and agricultural policy instruments within a country as well as across countries.

US biofuel policies were a critical factor in instigating the increase in food grain commodity prices that began to emerge in 2006 (Carter, Rausser, and Smith 2012),[2] as were biofuel policies in the rest of the world, especially in the

[2] We focus on the USA, the European Union, and Brazil because the USA accounts for 42 per cent, Brazil for 24 per cent, and the European Union for 14 per cent of total 2012 world biofuel production.

European Union and Brazil. US biofuel, agricultural, and macroeconomic policies contributed substantially to the rise in food grain commodity prices that emerged in 2008.[3] From that point forward, US fiscal and monetary policies, combined with US biofuel policies, generated the roller-coaster ride that lasted from 2008 through 2012. For example, when the USA negotiated the release of Japanese rice stocks, this move allegedly caused rice prices to begin to decline from their peak in 2008 (Slayton 2010). But US monetary and fiscal policies that were devised in order to respond to the 2008 financial crisis—which itself was induced by failed regulatory and financial policies—substantially affected commodity prices and thus volatility.

US energy and environmental policies have also played a role in the evolving political-economic landscape in which traditional agricultural policies are determined. In one clear instance, the deliberations concerning the upcoming US Farm Bill have been substantially tilted towards revenue insurance programmes (in place of direct and countercyclical payments) and allowed farmers to be subsidized by high prices (Zulauf and Orden 2012; Babcock and Paulson 2012). The expiration of the ethanol tax credit and import tariff at the end of 2011 could also be described as a policy response to high and volatile crop prices. Although these policy changes had little immediate impact, there are longer run consequences.

20.2 US Food, Agricultural, and Biofuel Policies

Since 1985, the Farm Bill legislation that defines US agricultural policy has slowly been transformed into a 'food bill'. The Food Security Act of 1985 included programme commodity provisions that focused on loan programmes, target prices, deficiency payments, acreage reduction, and public grain stock reserves. Export provisions in this legislation included food aid and cargo preferences. Conservation reserve programmes were introduced with the stated intent of removing highly erodible land and wetlands from production and thus, indirectly, managing supply response (Rausser 1992). This Act also authorized three alternative market promotion programmes and continued food stamp programmes.[4]

After the Uruguay Round concluded, the 1996 Farm Bill (the Federal Agriculture Improvement and Reform Act) replaced the previous target price

[3] Many papers in the literature have noted the influence of biofuels on commodity prices. For excellent surveys of this literature, see Abbott, Hurt, and Tyner (2008), Hochman et al. (2011), and Zilberman et al. (2012).

[4] After this 1985 legislation was passed, export subsidies from both the European Union and USA created a prisoner-dilemma global competition, with the net effect of decreasing world food commodity prices (*Economic Report of the President* 1987).

deficiency payments with fixed 'production flexibility contract payments' over the course of seven years. Both the crop basis and the acreage reduction programmes were eliminated. For the first time, farmers participating in US government programmes were allowed to make their own planning decisions, free of government regulations (with minor restrictions). In the political economic process that influenced this legislation, various commodity organizations and agribusiness interests coalesced, in the hope that a more market-oriented agricultural policy would develop. Political economic forces squelched this hope with the passage in 2002 of the Farm Security and Rural Investment Act. Over a six-year period, this new Act budgeted almost US$40 billion for commodity programmes and almost another US$10 billion for conservation.

In the movement from legislation that had focused largely on agriculture to legislation focusing on food consumption, more than 50 per cent of the allocations made in the 2002 Act (US$149.6 billion) were directed to food stamps and other nutrition title programmes. This trend accelerated with the passage of the 2008 Food, Conservation, and Energy Act. In this most recently implemented legislation, 'nutrition' subsidies accounted for more than 75 per cent of the outlays for authorized programmes. The total budget authority over five years for this act amounted to US$284 billion (Congressional Budget Office 2008).

In the current century, the USA—and the world—has shifted from chronic excess supply (due to greater growth in farm productivity than in demand) to chronic excess demand and rising real food prices. The USA's agricultural sector has become, on average, more prosperous relative to the rest of the economy, so that the distributional justification for many agricultural policies in the USA has ceased to exist (Gardner 1992). In this sense, continued agricultural subsidies were rewarding rent-seeking and political muscle. As the agricultural industry realized the value of developing new sources of demand for agricultural commodity that has a higher price elasticity, biofuels became increasingly attractive.

It is not surprising, then, that the most recent agricultural policy legislation includes energy. Although the 2008 Act explicitly budgeted only a small amount for energy expenditures (approximately US$643 million over a five-year period under Title IX), when combined with US renewable energy legislation,[5] the increased legislative support for US biofuel policies becomes evident. One of the major economic motives for the renewable

[5] Although the Renewable Fuel Standard (RFS) was not enacted until 2005, bills containing variants of the RFS were repeatedly debated by the US Congress (in 1978, 1987, 1992, 2000, 2001, 2003, and 2004). All were strongly supported by the corn lobby. These lobbying efforts led the RFS for corn ethanol to be doubled in 2007. The 2007 RFS specifies minimum renewable fuel production each calendar year from 2007 through 2022: the 2022 standard is four times that of 2008.

energy legislation—and for resulting US biofuel policies—was that they led to increases in prices of corn, oilseeds, and wheat as feedstocks. A second motive was the widespread political desire to reduce highly visible programme commodity subsidies (e.g., deficiency payments). Such legislation and the policies it spawned have led to increased demand for corn, oilseeds, and wheat as feedstocks for biofuel production: between 2003 and 2012, US ethanol production increased sevenfold. Meanwhile, EU biodiesel production also increased sevenfold, and Brazilian ethanol production increased threefold.

The political economic landscape underlying US biofuel policies has been shaped by a broad spectrum of energy-, agricultural-, and environmental-policy objectives. Here, we focus on energy security, farm policy, and environmental goals.

20.2.1 *Energy Security Goals*

The US government first implemented tax credits for ethanol fuel blenders and import tariffs for foreign ethanol producers in 1978 and 1980, respectively. Proponents justified these measures by citing the need to improve energy security and to counter oil supply disruptions such as those that had occurred in the 1970s. The tax credits and tariffs were designed to reduce dependence on oil in order to address rising public concern about dwindling oil supplies and rising and unstable oil prices.

20.2.2 *Farm Policy Goals*

After oil prices declined in the mid-1980s, the farm lobby continued to use ethanol policy for its own purposes. The farm lobby claimed that fostering ethanol production via mandates, tariffs, and tax credits would help achieve farm policy goals by improving farm incomes and promoting rural development. In the meantime, the higher prices farmers received for their crops (especially corn) meant lower costs to taxpayers of price contingent government farm subsidies. However, the complex links among biofuel policies, farm income, and rural development produce novel effects. For example, an implicit tax on value added agriculture (such as the livestock, dairy, and poultry sectors), in the form of higher prices for corn and other feedstocks, can reduce the incomes of these farmers. This result would ultimately defeat the same US farm policy goals that supposedly justify ethanol support. Ethanol support measures can also constrain economic growth in rural areas, even if biofuel production brings in increased revenue for some rural farmers or processors. Since ethanol production is capital-intensive, its primary effect on rural development is to increase land prices, which is unlikely to benefit many farmers.

20.2.3 *Environmental Policy Goals*

Concern among the American public about greenhouse gas emissions has prompted more vigorous efforts to strengthen environmental policy. However, protecting the environment became a political driver in Washington only after energy security concerns and farm policy goals had been articulated. In contrast to the European Union, where concern about greenhouse gas emissions has been one motivation for energy policy for several years, US policy makers have, in general, become motivated only very recently to advocate measures that will reduce greenhouse gas emissions. Moreover, corn producers' lobbying groups were one of the first groups to promote biofuels based on projected greenhouse gas reductions.

20.2.4 *Types of US Biofuel Policies and their Effects on Grain Prices*

The US biofuel policies that were implemented during the period 2006–12 include the following:[6]

- biofuel consumption subsidies, such as the tax credits (implemented in 1978) that expired at the end of 2011;
- formal ethanol mandates such as the Renewable Fuel Standard, which took effect in 2005 (and was revised upwards in 2007);
- de facto mandates that ethanol be used in fuel to satisfy environmental regulations, such as provisions of the Clean Air Act in the 1990s resulting from the banning of methyl tertiary-butyl ether (MTBE);
- production subsidies for both biofuels and feedstocks;[7]
- import tariffs and tariff rate quotas, such as the US$0.54/gallon (gal) ethanol import tariff (implemented in 1980) that expired at the end of 2011; and
- 0, 1 sustainability standards: the standard that 1 gal (energy equivalent) of corn ethanol must reduce greenhouse gas emissions by 20 per cent relative to the 1 gal of gasoline it is assumed to replace.[8]

Although each type of policy affected corn prices, it did so through various channels at various times and magnitudes. The key to understanding how these biofuel policies affect grain commodity prices is to recognize the links between ethanol prices and corn prices:[9] ethanol prices are indirectly linked

[6] Many of the federal incentives, subsidies, and mandates listed here have been complemented by similar state measures.

[7] In addition to direct production subsidies for biofuels, many federal and state 'infrastructure' subsidies were created, such as subsidies for alternative vehicles and fuelling stations.

[8] It is '0, 1' in that if greenhouse gas emissions for corn production are below the threshold, ethanol is not eligible for tax credits or to be counted toward the mandate.

[9] This price link must be adjusted for ethanol production subsidies.

to gasoline prices (through mandated premiums above the tax credit), and gasoline prices are a direct function of oil prices.[10] The corn ethanol price transmission elasticity is the key driver for corn prices (de Gorter and Just 2008), and hence, as we will show later, for all grain prices.[11]

US biofuel policy began to noticeably affect food grain commodity prices in October 2006. Until that date, as Figure 20.1 reveals, corn prices held steady even though oil prices steadily increased (and even crossed the US$40/barrel threshold in mid-2004).[12] Since the products that initially competed with ethanol as gasoline additives (oxygenated and octane enhancers, particularly MTBE) were petroleum based, ethanol prices followed crude oil-derivative gasoline prices (Figure 20.1). As one state after another banned MTBE, continued upward pressure was exerted on ethanol prices. When a federal court failed to grant immunity against lawsuits for firms using MTBE in July 2006, ethanol prices reached their all-time highs. Until that date, corn markets were relatively stable (Figure 20.2a), even though rising ethanol prices were leading ethanol plant capacity to escalate (Figure 20.2b).[13]

Beginning in October 2006, the corn price finally reacted to higher oil and ethanol prices.[14] Coupled with the de facto ban on MTBE, high oil prices activated the otherwise dormant ethanol blenders' tax credit by providing a premium on ethanol over gasoline prices. Ethanol prices soared to a peak of US$3.65/gal in July of 2006 (Figure 20.1).[15] By September 2007, corn and ethanol prices had become tightly linked (Figure 20.3), and corn ethanol markets reached equilibrium. Between October 2006 and September 2007, markets were in adjustment, from the disequilibrium situation depicted in Figure 20.1 to the equilibrium linking corn to ethanol prices.

Meanwhile, soybean prices (in the USA) and rapeseed oil prices (in the European Union) became tightly linked to biodiesel prices. Like corn

[10] An indirect link between oil and corn prices always exists through input costs, since corn uses energy-intensive inputs. This factor has been characterized as a major driver of commodity price increases. See, e.g., Abbott, Hurt, and Tyner (2008) and Baffes and Haniotis (2010).

[11] The links between rapeseed, soybean, and palm oil prices and biodiesel prices, and between biodiesel and diesel gasoline prices, are equally important, as is the link between sugarcane, sugar, and ethanol prices in Brazil. Note that ethanol production creates a large distillers' grain market, which, owing to the high protein content, serves to displace soybean meal consumption and drive down soybean price and production.

[12] In the 2005–6 crop year, the US farm price of corn averaged only US$2/bu, even though world commodity trade had been increasing sharply for years, following the fastest-ever growth of emerging economies.

[13] As Carter, Rausser, and Smith (2012) show, by mid-2006, corn stockholding was beginning to expand in anticipation of demand from ethanol plants.

[14] Enders and Holt (2012) determine a structural break in corn prices for October 2006 using sophisticated econometric techniques, confirming our analysis in Figures 20.1 and 20.2a, and 20.2b that October 2006 was an important month.

[15] Ethanol prices have never regained this peak. As of this writing (April 2012), the ethanol price is US$2.12/gal. Meanwhile, the recent oil prices were close to their all-time monthly average high of US$133/barrel (June 2008).

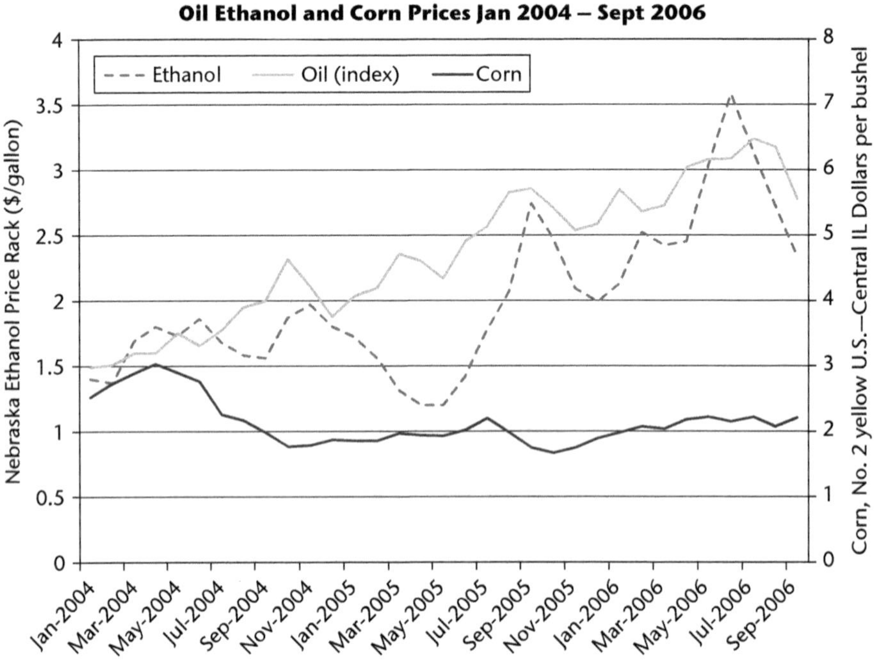

Figure 20.1 Oil, ethanol, and corn prices, January 2004–September 2006

Source: Authors' computation, based on data as given below:

Corn price = No. 2 yellow US—Central IL $/bu (available at: <http://www.ers.usda.gov/data-products/feed-grains-database/feed-grains-yearbook-tables.aspx>).

Ethanol price = Nebraska rack $/gal (available at: <http://www.neo.ne.gov/statshtml/66.html>).

Oil price = World Bank Pink Sheets (available at: <http://www.econ.worldbank.org/WBSITE/EXTERNAL/EXTDEC/EXTDECPROSPECTS/0,,contentMDK:21574907~menuPK:7859231~pagePK:64165401~piPK:64165026~theSitePK:476883,00.html>).

Ethanol capacity and under construction (million gal) (Renewable Fuel Association) (available at: <http://www.ethanolrfa.org/pages/statistics#C>).

ethanol production, non-corn ethanol biodiesel production also affects prices. Although the volume of total biofuels production in OECD countries (excluding US corn ethanol) is only half that of US ethanol production, this non-US OECD biodiesel production requires much more land area per gallon of biofuel yielded (e.g., wheat for ethanol or rapeseed and soybeans for biodiesel). As a result, non-corn ethanol biodiesel production has a disproportionate impact on food grain prices. Because soybean and corn are largely substitutable on land in the USA, and because prices among alternative oilseeds are directly linked because of very high substitution in demand, any change in land use for biodiesel production will have one-to-one impacts on oilseed and corn prices (and vice versa for corn ethanol production on oilseed prices). Owing to competition for land and substitutability in demand, we would expect wheat to be tightly linked to both

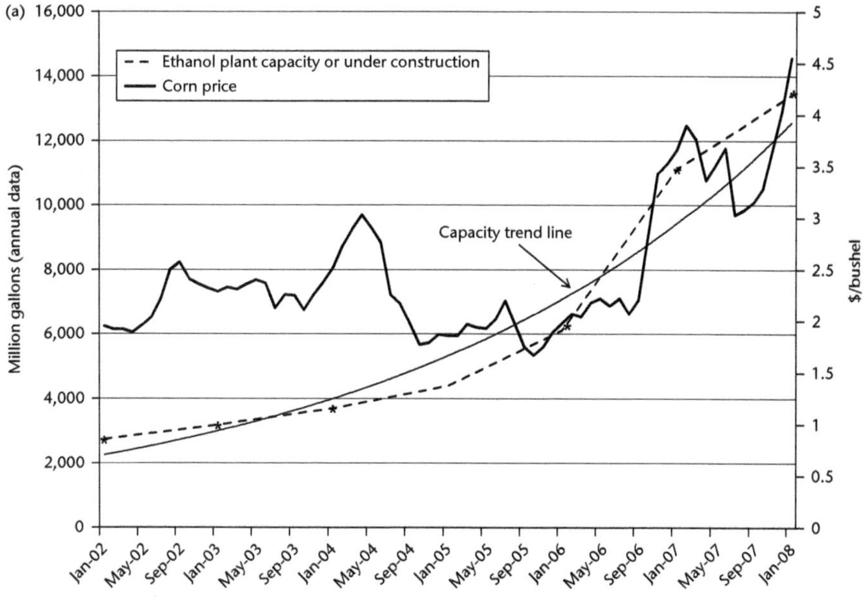

Figure 20.2(a) Corn prices catching up to ethanol production capacity

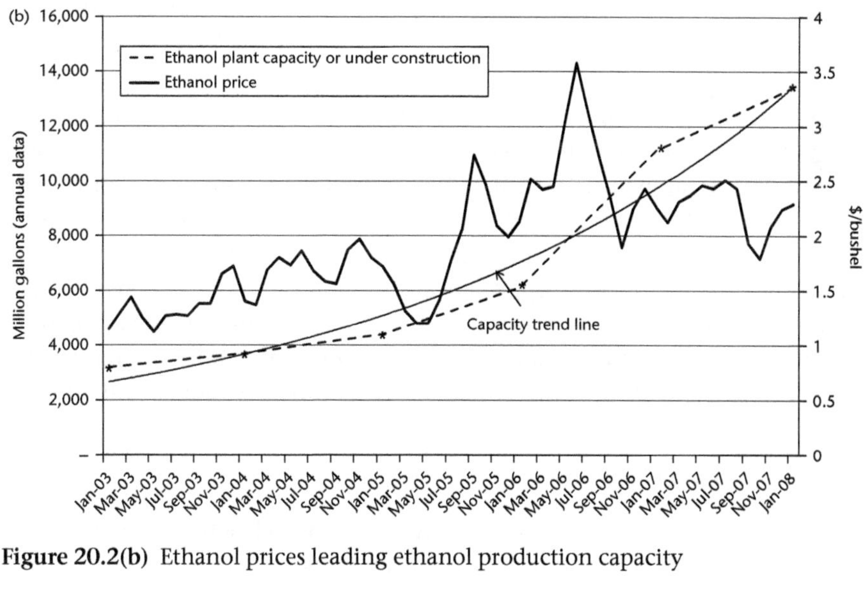

Figure 20.2(b) Ethanol prices leading ethanol production capacity

corn (and coarse grains in general) and oilseed prices. In contrast, we would expect the rice price to be less closely related to coarse grain and oilseed prices in the short run, since there is no need for the rice price (in contrast to corn and oilseed prices) to respond to crude oil prices (and hence corn and oilseed prices).

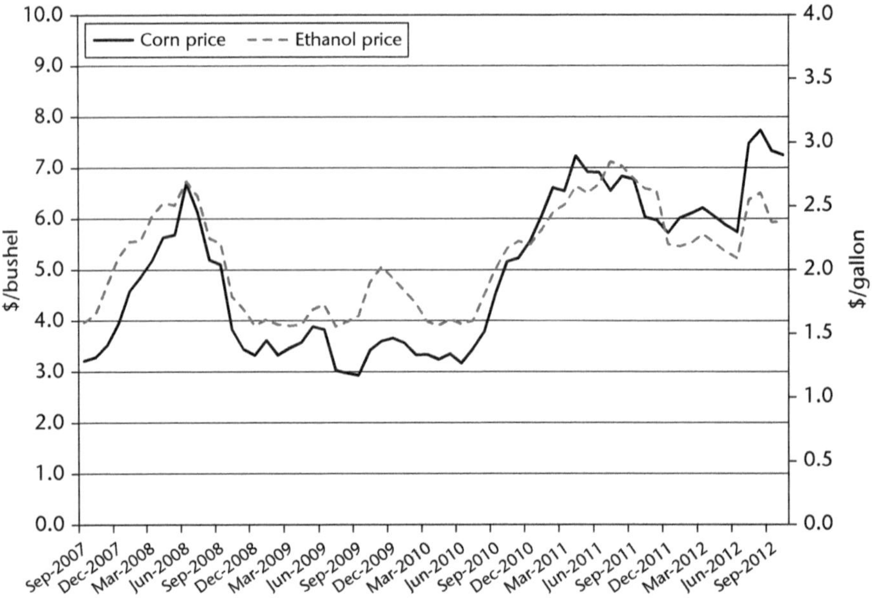

Figure 20.3 US corn and ethanol prices

Source: Authors' computation, based on corn price Iowa farm US$/bu and ethanol price Iowa US$/gal, data sourced from: CARD, Iowa State University (available at: <http://www.card.iastate.edu/research/bio/tools/hist_eth_gm.aspx>).

The environmental and renewable energy policies of the USA, in combination with those of other OECD countries, have evidently also been critically important in establishing the link between food grain commodity prices and biofuel prices (Tyner 2008) and for supporting the surge not only in corn, oilseeds, and other coarse grain prices but also in wheat and rice prices during 2006–8. As oil prices dropped in 2008–9, biofuel policy moderated the ensuing decline in food grain commodity prices. Ever increasing biofuel price premiums over gasoline and diesel prices and the subsequent rise in oil prices in 2011 resulted in all-time high prices for corn and other grains and oilseeds.

20.2.5 *A Domino Effect*

Once corn and oilseed prices had become more closely linked to crude oil prices through ethanol and gasoline markets, and crude oil prices had increased, corn and soybean prices inevitably followed suit. In contrast, although wheat is used for ethanol production in Canada and Europe, there is no evidence that wheat prices follow ethanol prices. Nonetheless, wheat is related to other grains because of competition for land and demand substitution as well as other external events (such as monetary policy and exchange rates). Like wheat prices, rice prices are not directly linked to biofuels, but in India, rice competes for land with wheat, and in many parts of the world, rice is substitutable in demand for both wheat and corn. It is therefore not surprising that all four price categories (coarse grains, oilseeds, wheat, and rice) rose to their peaks in mid-2008, at about the same time when crude oil prices peaked (Figures 20.4, 20.5, and 20.6). Similarly, prices for all of these commodities rose again in 2010.

The month of October 2006, when corn prices increased, is pivotal to understanding this domino effect. The central Illinois farm price for corn increased 88 per cent between August 2006 and February 2007 (Kansas City 2 No. 2 white corn prices increased 107 per cent in the same time period). Although world wheat production was down by 3.9 per cent in 2007, overall grain production was essentially unchanged that year. But wheat prices were pulled up by the sudden increase in corn prices (Figure 20.4). India and

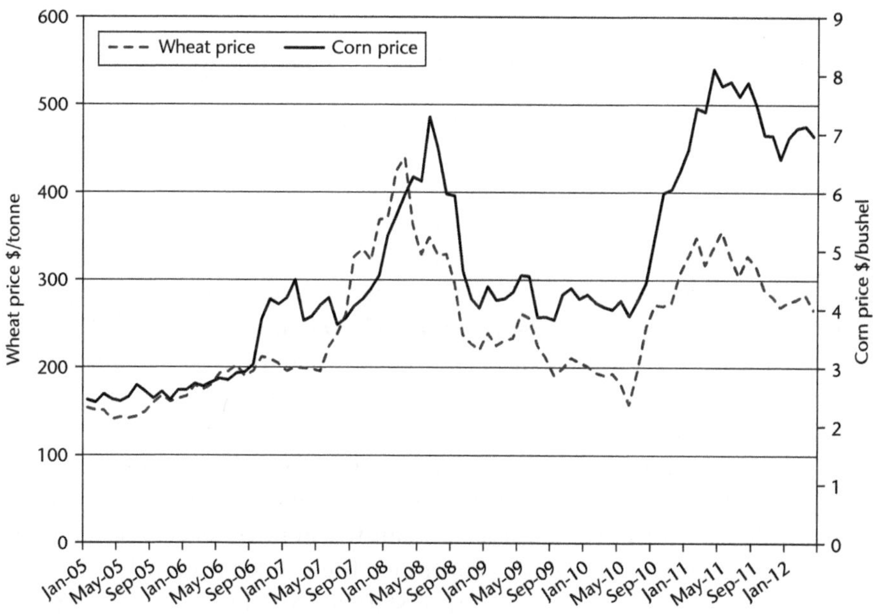

Figure 20.4 Corn and wheat price developments

Note: Wheat price = US$/tonne [(US), no. 1, hard red winter, ordinary protein, export price delivered at the US Gulf port for prompt or 30 days shipment].

Corn price = US$/bu [Maize (US), no. 2, yellow, free on board (FOB) US Gulf ports] (Figures 20.5 and 20.6).

Rice price = Rice [(Thailand), 100% broken, A.1 Super, government standard, FOB Bangkok].

Source: Computations by authors, based on data from: World Bank Pink Sheets (available at: <http://www.econ.worldbank.org/WBSITE/EXTERNAL/EXTDEC/EXTDECPROSPECTS/0,,contentMDK:21574907~menuPK:7859231~pagePK:64165401~piPK:64165026~theSitePK:476883,00.html>).

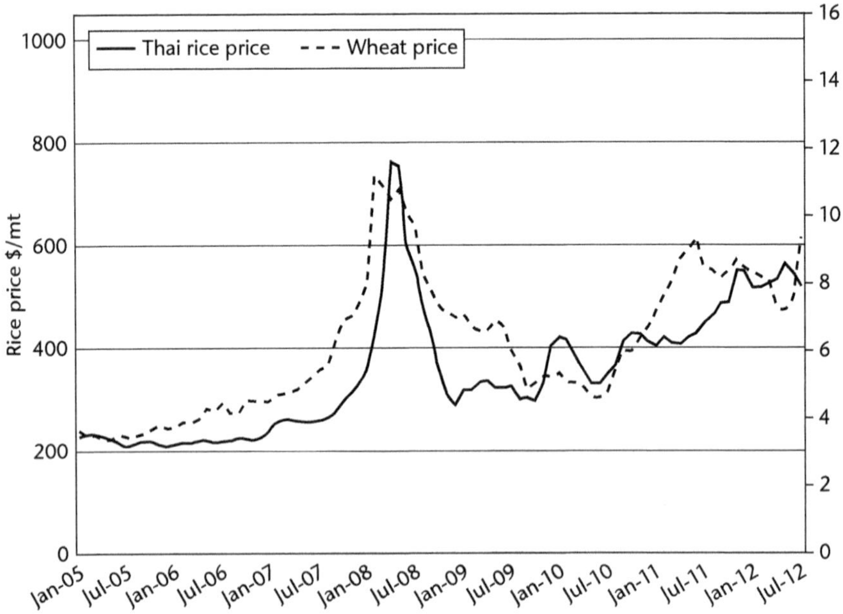

Figure 20.5 Wheat and rice price development
Note and Source: See Figure 20.4.

Ukraine's export bans on wheat occurred immediately after corn prices finally reacted to high oil prices and skyrocketed to their interim peak in February 2007. Immediately following these two wheat export bans, increases in the price of wheat (which had risen about US$3/bu since January 2005) actually overtook the corn price increase. Wheat price increases began the last leg of their ascent (basically straight up) after the October 2007 rice export ban by India, moving from US$7 to US$11/bu in a very short period. Wheat prices peaked before corn prices and also began to come down before corn did (although wheat prices blipped up again two months before corn's price peak, while corn prices were still rising). But wheat prices declined again one month before corn prices did and continued their slide for months.

Thus, biofuel policies and corn markets started a ball rolling that spilled over into the wheat market and subsequently into the political decision-making of Asian governments. Their policy responses set off speculation, including hoarding, which caused rice prices to spike.[16] As Figure 20.3 shows, once corn prices

[16] No major supply or demand shocks occurred at this time in the rice market: 'Rice market fundamentals were not the cause. The rice crisis was not caused by adverse shocks to rice production or low rice stocks. The world rice to stock ratio was roughly constant in the three years preceding the crisis. World rice trade in the first four months of 2008 ... was 20 per cent higher than in the first four months of 2007. The favourable situation as regards production, stocks and trade strongly suggests factors other than basic market fundamentals were at work' (Dawe and Slayton 2010).

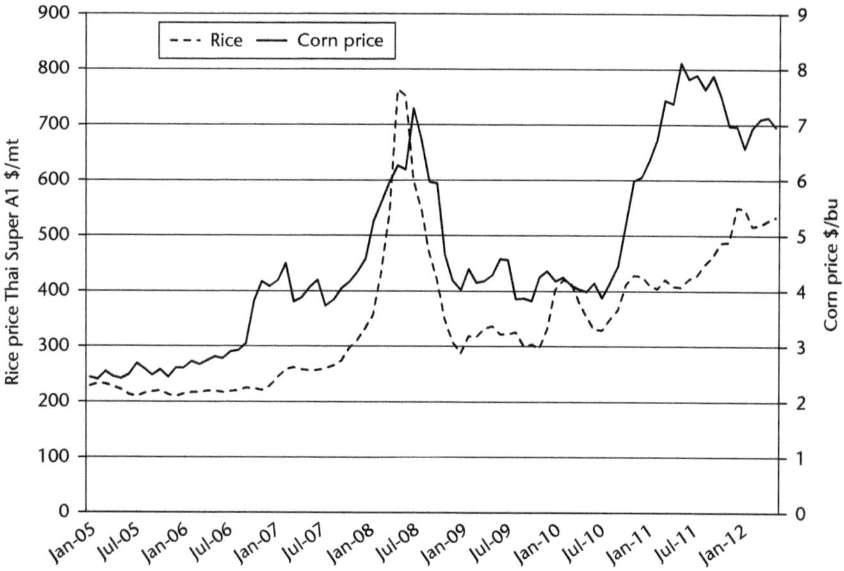

Figure 20.6 Rice and corn price development
Note and Source: See Figure 20.4.

were finally linked to ethanol prices (August 2007), corn (and oilseed) prices began to follow oil prices. Contrary evidence in the literature (Zilberman et al. 2012; Serra 2012) on these links between the ethanol, energy, and corn price is largely based on reduced-form time series analysis. But our analysis shows that although these links were not visible prior to October 2006 (and remained in flux for nearly another year), beginning in September 2007, ethanol and corn prices did begin to move in the same direction month after month. As a result, any time series analysis that begins well before 2006 and ends in either 2007 or 2008 misses some key episodes in the development of links between biofuel policies, corn (and oilseed) prices, and energy prices. (It should also be noted that ethanol prices can float above and away from gasoline [oil] prices when mandates become binding and temporarily de-link corn and oil prices.)

20.2.6 *The Corn Ethanol Price Transmission Coefficient*[17]

The global corn price increases approximately US$0.04/bushel (bu) for every US$0.01 increase in the ethanol price (Drabik 2011).[18] Since January 2007,

[17] For a summary of what the structure of biofuel policy predicts regarding food grain commodity prices, see de Gorter and Just (2010b); Drabik (2011); Cui et al. (2011); de Gorter and Drabik (2012b); and Lapan and Moschini (2012).

[18] Abbott, Hurt, and Tyner (2008) claim that the change in the corn price is two times the tax credit in US$/gal rather than approximately four times, as Drabik (2011) shows.

the ethanol price has exceeded the 'no policy' ethanol price, on average, by US$0.65/gal (Drabik 2011). As previously explained, this difference equals more than the value of the tax credit. The corn ethanol price transmission coefficient was estimated to be 3.85 in 2010 (Drabik 2011). Multiplying 3.85 by the US$0.65/gal ethanol price premium would imply a corn price increase of US$2.50/bu, on average. This is not expected, because part of the ethanol price premium is redundant: the intercept of the ethanol supply curve is above the free market ethanol price (for an explanation, see de Gorter and Just 2008). Nonetheless, for 2010, the corn price has been estimated to have been 45 per cent higher than it would have been had the various US ethanol policies not been enacted (Drabik 2011).[19] But even this figure is an underestimate, because the supply and demand curves that Drabik (2011) calibrated for corn ignore the effects of US biodiesel and biofuel policies on the rest of the world. These other biofuel policies continue to drive corn prices higher: US biodiesel policy, for example, causes farmland to be reallocated from corn to soybeans, increasing the 'no ethanol' corn price. Since other biofuel policies (including those in the rest of the world) have caused the counterfactual corn price (i.e., the price assuming no effect from US ethanol policy) to be higher than would otherwise have been the case, the Drabik estimate of a 45 per cent increase in corn prices for 2010 does not reflect all of the feedback loops.

20.2.7 *The Interactions of Global Ethanol Policies*

In 2010, the USA not only became a significant net exporter of ethanol but the world's largest ethanol exporter. World ethanol prices in 2010–12 were seemingly determined on the margin in the European Union and Brazil, where ethanol prices were significantly higher than they were in the USA.[20] Brazil had suspended its import tariff in 2009; meanwhile, the US managed to negotiate an agreement with at least five EU countries that allowed 2.1 per cent denatured ethanol to be classified as a blended fuel. This agreement meant that US exporters only had to pay one-third of the approximately 67 per cent EU import tariff on ethanol. In addition, the US tax credit on ethanol exports to the European Union and Brazil acted as a production subsidy for US ethanol producers, in the form of higher ethanol market prices (de Gorter, Drabik, and Just 2011; Kliauga, de Gorter, and Just 2011). Indeed, 80 per cent of US ethanol exports received the tax credit for as long as it existed (until well into 2011). However, in December 2011, two events altered this protection

[19] For an alternative structural explanation, focusing on stockholding behaviour, that generates similar results, see Carter, Rausser, and Smith (2012).

[20] After mid-2009, Brazilian ethanol prices surpassed US prices, and they remain higher to this day.

of US ethanol production and exports: the European Union closed the tariff loophole the USA had negotiated with some of the Union's members that had classified ethanol exports as fuel, [21] and the US ethanol tax credit on all exports expired. These two events combined to cause US ethanol prices to decline sharply.

In Brazil, market developments in the sugarcane and sugar ethanol markets since 2009 have been relatively dramatic (de Gorter, Drabik, and Kliauga 2012). Brazil's ethanol production has expanded threefold since 2003, and, as noted above, Brazilian ethanol market prices exceeded US prices from mid-2009 onwards. At the same time, Brazil's peak ethanol consumption of 22.8 billion litres in 2009 declined by 19 per cent in 2011, to about 18.5 billion litres. Meanwhile, gasoline consumption in Brazil has increased 24 per cent since 2008. Brazil's ethanol exports peaked at 2.4 billion litres in 2008 and have been around one billion litres in the last two years.

Ethanol prices in Brazil have been driven upward by a strong currency and a sugar export demand shock that took place when world sugar prices reached record levels. In addition, a domestic ethanol demand shock has occurred; demand for ethanol as a transportation fuel has increased as incomes have grown and more consumers buy cars, especially flex-fuel cars. Domestic ethanol supply shocks have also occurred: two years of bad weather, longer rotation in sugarcane crop, and some lingering effects of the financial crisis. The Brazilian ethanol mandate (currently, 20 per cent of the gasoline ethanol mixture is required to be anhydrous ethanol), and governmental control of the gasoline price below the world market price have also helped stimulate both gasoline and anhydrous ethanol consumption.

These developments in Brazil strongly affect US and world ethanol prices. Had it not been for these trends, for example, the US ethanol mandate (RFS) might have resulted in much lower US domestic ethanol prices. The key point is that since 2010, developments in grain markets directly affect the sugar market and vice versa. Some commodity markets have now become more closely linked now that US corn prices are linked, through energy markets, to sugar prices and vice versa.[22]

20.2.8 *The Effect of Biodiesel Policies on Commodity Markets*

Before the middle of 2010, when the US biodiesel mandate was finally enforced, the impact of the US biodiesel tax credit on commodity markets

[21] In late 2011, the EU's Customs Code Committee raised the import tariff on such ethanol blends. See http://www.biofuelsdigest.com/bdigest/2011/10/18/eu-boosts-tariffs-to-block-low-cost-us-ethanol/.

[22] Even though Mitchell (2008) correctly recognized that for earlier periods Brazilian sugarcane ethanol production did not have an impact on cereal prices that may no longer be the case.

was influenced by Canadian and EU biodiesel policies (de Gorter, Drabik, and Just 2011). US biodiesel production was essentially zero until 2004 and then increased sharply in 2005–08, when US biodiesel exporters became eligible to receive a US$1/gal tax credit for the biodiesel fuel they exported, even when they simply added small amounts of diesel fuel to much larger amounts of biodiesel ('splash and dash').[23] Some of the biodiesel was imported from other countries, such as palm oil from Malaysia.[24] This tax credit helped raise the US price of biodiesel by making exports to the EU more profitable. It therefore led to increased soybean prices, which, in turn, raised the price of corn, as land was taken out of corn production and put into soybean production.

However, US biodiesel production (and domestic prices) fell sharply in June 2008, when the European Union began to investigate the 'splash and dash' practice. US biodiesel prices and production plunged, because the US tax credit had acted as a biodiesel production subsidy (even though it was actually a consumption subsidy) when biodiesel prices were determined outside the USA (de Gorter, Drabik, and Just 2011). Although the US tax credit was still valid, it could no longer keep prices at historical levels. After the European Union instituted anti-dumping and countervailing duties in March 2009, US biodiesel prices stabilized at lower levels than those prior to mid-2008. The US–EU biodiesel price gap, which had widened sharply in 2008, persisted until mid-2010. At that point, however, the US biodiesel mandate was finally enforced. Since mid-2010, US biodiesel prices and production have increased sharply: current prices (April 2012) are just under US$5/gal, well above what prices would likely be if the only US biodiesel policy were the US$1/gal tax credit. In fact, the expiration of the biodiesel tax credit at the end of 2011 has had little effect on US biodiesel prices. Currently, domestic prices of US biofuel are not directly linked to world prices.[25]

20.2.9 *Interaction Effects between Mandates and Subsidies*

The literature on the economics of biofuel policies has generated the important insight that biofuel mandates interact with production, consumption, and input subsidies through mechanisms that sometimes create unexpected results (de Gorter and Just 2010a). For example, when a premium on the

[23] 'Splash and dash' refers to the practice of mixing a small amount of diesel (as little as 0.1 per cent—hence the term 'splash') into a boatload of biodiesel so that exporters could receive the blender's tax credit of US$1/gal and then export the mixture to Europe.

[24] In 2007 and 2008, all Canadian biodiesel production was exported, triple-dipping with domestic production subsidies, the US tax credit, and then selling in EU markets with high prices due to tax exemptions at the pump.

[25] Note that Brazil insulates its biodiesel sector from world markets.

ethanol price is greater than a tax credit, both measures are clearly not necessary. Moreover, the tax credit subsidizes fuel consumption, most of which is gasoline (de Gorter and Just 2009). The tax credit, therefore, is inherently inconsistent with the environmental and energy goals outlined earlier. The same reasoning applies to production subsidies for both biofuels and their feedstock inputs (e.g., corn production subsidies), although the exact economic mechanisms vary (for details, see Drabik 2011).

The literature has emphasized the superiority of mandates over subsidies from a welfare perspective (Lapan and Moschini 2012). Rajagopal and Zilberman (2007) express concern that enforcing mandates will amplify high commodity prices during periods of commodity shortages. They suggest that biofuel mandates should be temporarily suspended under such conditions. This recommendation has been incorporated into laws but not yet implemented. However, Babcock (2012) suggests that even if mandates are temporarily lifted, their impact on corn prices will be very small because oil refiners have already made substantial investments in the technology of using ethanol as an octane enhancer and face serious switching barriers.

20.2.10 *Biofuel Policies, Market Shocks, and Grain Price Volatility*

The volatility of corn prices, whether caused by corn supply or oil price shocks, depends on whether a tax credit or a mandate is binding (Yano, Blandford, and Surry 2010, 2011). When a fuel blender's tax credit is binding, the corn price is directly linked to the oil price. Under such a binding tax credit, exogenous shocks to corn supply or demand sourced with bad weather, exchange rate depreciation, increasing demand for corn in developing countries, and/or the initial levels of stocks in the supply-of-storage model have no effects on the corn price level or on corn price volatility (unless the change in ethanol production changes the oil price or there is a resulting regime switch to a mandate) (de Gorter and Drabik 2012a). The volatility in the oil price gets translated into corn price volatility when oil prices determine ethanol prices (through the binding tax credit), because under any biofuel policy, ethanol prices influence corn prices (Drabik 2011).

However, if a fuel blend mandate (rather than a tax credit) determines the ethanol market price, corn prices do respond to corn supply and demand shocks. This vulnerability occurs because the blend mandate significantly weakens the link between ethanol and oil prices (de Gorter and Just 2009). In fact, higher oil prices mean lower corn prices, because fuel consumption generally declines. Given a fixed ethanol blend requirement, ethanol production contracts as well when oil prices rise, with the result that both ethanol and corn prices decline. But a countervailing effect also exists: a higher oil price translates into higher energy costs in corn production and results in higher corn prices (Baffes and Haniotis 2010). The net change in corn prices due to an oil price increase is indeterminate a priori.

Any analysis of corn price volatility must recognize which biofuel policy is operative (e.g., a tax credit/tax exemption or a blend mandate). It must also analyse the volatility that results from switching between mandates and tax credits (an oil price shock could precipitate such a switch) or from interactions between policies across countries. Surely, in a 'but-for' world without tariffs, the USA would likely have been importing ethanol and so tempering any volatility resulting from corn ethanol linkages.[26]

20.2.11 *Evolutionary Assessment of Biofuel Policies and Grain Price Fluctuations*

It is important to recognize that the first two categories of biofuel policies, tax credits and mandates, do not, by themselves, discriminate against international trade. But other policies do, and the fact that many were in place for over thirty years in the USA explains, in part, why we have observed increasing corn ethanol production in the USA (rather than, for example, import of less expensive sugarcane ethanol from Brazil). Such anti-international trade policies also contributed to sharp increases in US ethanol production after 2005, so that world food grain commodity prices increased more sharply. Furthermore, the gap in distribution of welfare gains and losses between developed and developing countries widened.

Imported sugarcane ethanol from Brazil was unable to supply the ethanol market in the near term around 2005. Brazil needed time and significant investment in order to increase sugarcane production and expand infrastructure to move ethanol to ports. This obstacle led US corn ethanol production to increase sharply as farmers converted land from other uses in order to increase supply immediately. Here, long-term policies had large short-term implications. If no trade discriminatory biofuel policies had existed, more money would likely have been invested in foreign ethanol production. The sugarcane crop in Brazil, for example, would almost certainly have had a higher production base, and more ethanol infrastructure would have been built to supply world sugar and ethanol markets. Likewise, if US environmental policies had been implemented more gradually, US biofuels would not have had such a dramatic effect on commodity prices. In this respect, US biofuel policies constitute new episodes in the saga of distortionary agricultural policies that not only cause world price instability but also harm the welfare of consumers in food-importing developing countries.

[26] Developing country policy responses to higher commodity prices in 2008 (caused by US and EU biofuel policies) in the form of export taxes, for example, further exacerbated commodity price volatility (Carter, Rausser, and Smith 2011).

Thus, while US agricultural and macroeconomic policies have strongly affected food grain commodity prices and volatility, so have US environmental and energy policies. The roller-coaster ride in market volatility since the financial crisis of 2008, and the re-emergence of peaks in corn, wheat, and soybean prices in 2011, can be traced to all three forms of intervention: US renewable-energy, environmental, and agricultural policies. An open question remains as to their relative effect on the level and volatility of grain prices compared to crop supply/demand shocks. In 2009–10, however, corn prices would surely have fallen lower than US$3.21/bu if US renewable energy and biofuel policies had not supported the market.

US agricultural and biofuel policies have not been the sole influences on programme commodities (especially corn, soybeans, and wheat). Heavy-handed US governmental intervention in domestic and global sugar systems has also influenced world corn prices. US import quotas and internal insulated sugar price supports initially depressed world sugar production and prices. This price depression led Brazil to reallocate sugarcane production away from sugar to ethanol markets. Brazilian sugar ethanol production also responded to increases in crude oil prices that have occurred since the mid-1970s. Currently, however, US biofuel policies are helping to stabilize the ethanol market in Brazil that was earlier destabilized by US sugar policy.

20.3 The Political Economy of US Farm, Energy, and Environmental Policies

The major groups that have been promoting biofuel policies include certain growers' associations, fuel transporters, biofuel producers, automakers, some environmentalists, and the energy security community.[27] Many of these groups continue to support biofuel policies. Even some environmental groups that opposed tax credits and tariffs now seek to retain mandates. However, other groups are coalescing in opposition to mandates, tax credits, and subsidies. Because ethanol policies support feed grain markets through higher prices, other groups, such as livestock, dairy, and poultry producers, are beginning to form organized opposition to continued support for ethanol producers. So are food processors that no longer enjoy the low market prices that traditional agricultural policies supported. One example of these new interest groups is BalancedFoodandFuel.org, whose members include various meat, livestock, poultry, and dairy producer associations (Hahn 2008).

[27] Members of the energy security community include retired US Army General Wesley Clark, who is affiliated with Growth Energy. Along with the Renewable Fuels Association, Growth Energy lobbies aggressively for policies advantageous to ethanol producers.

20.3.1 *Implications for Future US Biofuel Policies*

Current biofuel policies confirm the *information and agency problems* of modern political theory. This term refers to the claim that politicians and lobby groups deceive voters (or withhold information from 'rationally ignorant voters') because such groups stand to benefit from doing so.[28] Obfuscation increases politicians' chances of re-election by making it more difficult for voters to accurately assess policies and programmes that may not serve voters' interests and by attracting support from those who benefit from such policies. Voters' ignorance of such policies' concealed costs (such as disguised transfers) enhances the political strength of proactive interest groups. Specifically, current US biofuel policies have yielded concentrated benefits for farmers and ethanol producers to the detriment of domestic and international consumers. The implication of these information and agency problems for biofuel policy is that the multitude of different policy goals and their complex interactions facilitates this obfuscation—and may even make it inevitable (Johnson and Libecap 2001; Lawrence 2010).

Even if less distortionary policies are instituted, the political theory of *enforcement and commitment problems* helps explain why such policies may not be fully implemented. Political economic trades between individuals and groups rely on contracts and promises that are not enforceable. Governments and political candidates may renege on their policy promises, and citizens may renege on their promised votes. Such enforcement and commitment problems explain why biofuel policies can be difficult to reform. These problems also undermine the possibility of reaching efficient cooperative outcomes.

20.4 Conclusion

US macroeconomic and agricultural policies have always played a significant role in grain price levels and volatility. Up until the period that has been the focus of our analysis (2006–12), even though US agricultural policies often fostered greater world price volatility, they did so largely by depressing world prices. In sharp contrast, more recent US biofuel policies have introduced new causal mechanisms that have elevated not only domestic but also world prices. For some policy regimes, a direct link has been established between grain prices and energy prices. These commodity prices initially rose in 2006–8, then plummeted in 2008–9 alongside lower oil prices, and finally rose again in 2011 almost to their 2008 peak levels.

[28] 'Rationally ignorant voters' prefer to remain ignorant of issues because they believe the cost of learning about them exceeds the potential benefits (Rausser, Swinnen, and Zusman 2011).

These effects partly explain why we emphasize the unique role of the US energy and environmental policies that have been enacted during the last six years. These policies, directed toward energy security, farm policy, and environmental goals, have fostered a more direct link between crude oil, ethanol, and grain prices (particularly corn and soybeans). The actual causal links among these policies did not emerge until September 2006, because prior to that date, tax credits were dormant and mandates had not yet been instituted. From October 2006 through August 2007, a period of disequilibrium adjustments unfolded, and finally, a direct link between corn and ethanol prices was established. Subsequent causal links to crude oil markets via the ethanol market have depended on the policy regime: the link to crude oil can be negative (mandates) or positive (tax credits). Accordingly, US policies that directly affect commodity prices have moved beyond the policy instruments emerging from US Farm Bills to include environmental and energy legislation.

Recognizing that the USA has been a dominant ('large country') player in the implementation of biofuel policies, we have also identified strong linkages between biofuel policies in the USA and in other countries. We have presented evidence that the interactions of biofuel policies instituted by the European Union and Brazil established a nexus for supporting price surges not only for corn, oilseeds, and other coarse grains, but also for wheat and rice. Moreover, the temporary agreement between the USA and five EU countries that allowed the US tax credit on ethanol exports to the European Union to take the form of a production subsidy for US ethanol producers had both short- and long-term effects, including some that failed to increase energy efficiency or to decrease global inequalities. Along similar lines, since the middle of 2010, when the US biodiesel mandate was finally enforced, interactions have taken place between US, Canadian, and EU biodiesel policies that have also increased prices and volatility. Finally, in contrast to some other countries that responded directly to commodity price spikes and volatility, the USA's responses to such phenomena have been largely inconsequential.[29]

In summary, the organized interest group landscape for US agricultural commodity policy has changed in recent years. It is now in the throes of a potential transformation. The 'iron triangle' that once influenced governmental intervention in programme commodity markets has expanded into an 'iron maze' of environmental, energy, and agricultural organized interest groups—not to mention at least three executive branch agencies (the Department of Energy, the United States Department of Agriculuture (USDA), and the Environmetal Protection Agency (EPA)). Despite—and because of—these developments, it remains to be to be seen whether such changes can lead to more enlightened policies.

[29] An exception was the negotiation by the USA of the release of Japanese rice stocks in 2008 (mentioned in the Introduction).

References

Abbott, P., C. Hurt, and W. E. Tyner (2008). 'What's Driving Food Prices?' *Farm Foundation Issue Report*. Oak Brook, IL: Farm Foundation.

Babcock, B. (2012). 'Updated Assessment of the Drought's Impacts on Crop Prices and Biofuel Production'. Policy Brief 12-PB 8. Ames, IA: Iowa State University, Center for Agricultural and Rural Development.

Babcock, B. N., and N. Paulson (2012). 'Potential Impact of Proposed 2012 Farm Bill Commodity Programmes on Developing Countries'. ICTSD Programme on Agricultural Trade and Sustainable Development, Issue Paper No. 45.

Baffes, J., and T. Haniotis (2010). 'Placing the 2006/08 Commodity Price Boom into Perspective'. Policy Research Working Paper No. 5371. Washington, DC: World Bank.

Carter, C., G. C. Rausser, and A. Smith (2011). 'Commodity Booms and Busts'. *Annual Review of Resource Economics* 3: 87–118.

Carter, C., G. C. Rausser, and A. Smith (2012). 'The Effect of the U.S. Ethanol Mandate on Corn Prices'. Unpublished Manuscript.

Congressional Budget Office (2008). Letter from Peter R. Orszag, Director, to Honorable Tom Harkin, Chairman, Committee on Agriculture, Nutrition and Forestry, US Senate (May 13). Available at: <http://www.cbo.gov/sites/default/files/cbofiles/ftpdocs/92xx/doc9230/hr2419conf.pdf>.

Cui, J., H. E. Lapan, G. C. Moschini, and J. C. Cooper (2011). 'Welfare Impacts of Alternative Biofuel and Energy Policies'. *American Journal of Agricultural Economics* 93(5): 1235–56.

Dawe, D., and T. Slayton (2010). 'The World Rice Market Crisis of 2007–2008'. In D. Dawe (ed.), *The Rice Crisis: Markets, Polices and Food Security*. London and Washington, DC: Food and Agriculture Organization Rome and Earthscan Publishing.

de Gorter, H., and D. Drabik (2012a). 'Biofuel Policies and Grain Crop Price Volatility'. *Biofuels* 3(2): 111–13.

de Gorter, H., and D. Drabik (2012b). 'The Effect of Biofuel Policies on Food Grain Commodity Prices'. *Biofuels* 3(1): 21–4.

de Gorter, H., and D. R. Just (2008). '"Water" in the US Ethanol Tax Credit and Mandate: Implications for Rectangular Deadweight Costs and the Corn-Oil Price Relationship'. *Review of Agricultural Economics* 30(3): 397–410.

de Gorter, H., and D. R. Just (2009). 'The Economics of a Blend Mandate for Biofuels'. *American Journal of Agricultural Economics* 91(3): 738–50.

de Gorter, H., and D. R. Just (2010a). 'The Social Costs and Benefits of Biofuels: The Intersection of Environmental, Energy and Agricultural Policy'. *Applied Economic Perspectives and Policy* 32(1): 4–32.

de Gorter, H., and D. R. Just (2010b). 'Ethanol and Corn Prices: The Role of US Tax Credits, Mandates and Import Tariffs'. In V. Eldon Ball, R. Fanfani and L. Gutierrez (eds), *The Economic Impact of Public Support to Agriculture: An International Perspective*. Studies in Productivity and Efficiency 7. NewYork/Dordrecht/Heidelberg/London: Springer.

de Gorter, H., D. Drabik, and D. R. Just (2011). 'The Economics of a Blender's Tax Credit versus a Tax Exemption: The Case of US "Splash and Dash" Biodiesel Exports to the European Union'. *Applied Economic Perspectives and Policy* 33(4): 510–27.

de Gorter, H., D. Drabik, and E. M. Kliauga (2012). 'Why Ethanol Prices Are So High in Brazil'. *Biofuels* 3(4): 371–73.

Drabik, D. (2011). 'The Theory of Biofuel Policy and Food Grain Prices'. Charles H. Dyson School of Applied Economics and Management Working Paper No. 2011-20. Cornell University.

Enders, W., and M. T. Holt (2012). 'Sharp Breaks or Smooth Shifts? An Investigation of the Evolution of Primary Commodity Prices'. *American Journal of Agricultural Economics* 94: 659–73.

Gardner, B. L. (1992). 'Changing Economic Perspectives on the Farm Problem'. *Journal of Economic Literature* 30: 62–101.

Hahn, R. W. (2008). 'Ethanol: Law, Economics, and Politics'. *Stanford Law and Policy Review* 19(3): 434–71.

Hochman, G., D. Rajagopal, G. Timilsina, and D. Zilberman (2011). 'The Role of Inventory Adjustments in Quantifying Factors Causing Food Price Inflation'. Policy Research Working Paper No. 5744. Washington, DC: World Bank.

Johnson, R. L., and G. D. Libecap (2001). 'Information Distortion and Competitive Remedies in Government Transfer Programmes: The Case of Ethanol'. *Economics of Governance* 2(2): 101–34.

Kliauga, E. M., H. de Gorter, and D. R. Just (2011). 'Measuring the Subsidy Component of Biofuel Tax Credits and Exemptions'. In A. Schmitz et al. (eds), *The Economics of Alternative Energy Sources and Globalization*. United Arab Emirates: Bentham Science Publishers.

Lapan, H. E., and G. Moschini (2012). 'Second-Best Biofuel Policies and the Welfare Effects of Quantity Mandates and Subsidies'. *Journal of Environmental Economics and Management* 63(2): 224–41.

Lawrence, R. Z. (2010). 'How Good Politics Results in Bad Policy: The Case of Biofuel Mandates'. Harvard Kennedy School of Government Faculty Research Working Paper Series No. RWP10-044. Cambridge, MA: Harvard University Press.

Mitchell, D. (2008). 'A Note on Rising Food Prices'. Policy Research Working Paper No. 4682. Washington, DC: World Bank.

Rajagopal, D., and D. Zilberman (2007). 'Review of Environmental, Economic and Policy Aspects of Biofuels'. World Bank Policy Research Working Paper No. WPS4341. Washington, DC: World Bank.

Rausser, G. C. (1992). 'Predatory Versus Productive Government: The Case of U.S. Agricultural Policy'. *Journal of Economic Perspectives* 6(3): 133–57.

Rausser, G. C., J. Swinnen, and P. Zusman (2011). *Political Power and Economic Policy: Theory, Analysis, and Empirical Applications*. Cambridge: Cambridge University Press.

Serra, T. (2012). 'Biofuel-Related Price Transmission Literature: A Review'. Castelldefels: Centre de Recerca en Economia i Desenvolupament Agroalimentari (CREDA). Unpublished manuscript.

Slayton, T. (2010). 'The "Diplomatic Crop", or How the US Provided Critical Leadership in Ending the Rice Crisis'. In D. Dawe (ed.), *The Rice Crisis: Markets, Polices and Food Security*. London and Washington, DC: Food and Agriculture Organization Rome and Earthscan Publishing.

Tyner, W. E. (2008). 'The US Ethanol and Biofuels Boom: Its Origins, Current Status, and Future Prospects'. *BioScience* 58(7): 646–53.

Wright, B. D. (2011). 'The Economics of Grain Price Volatility'. *Applied Economic Perspectives and Policy* 33(1): 32–58.

Yano, Y., D. Blandford, and Y. R. Surry (2010). 'The Impact of Feedstock Supply and Petroleum Price Variability on Domestic Biofuel and Feedstock Markets—The Case of the United States'. Working Paper No. 2010/3. Uppsala: Swedish University of Agricultural Sciences.

Yano, Y., D. Blandford, and Y. R. Surry (2011). 'Alternative Domestic and Trade Policies for Biofuels and Market Variability in the United States'. In Andrew Schmitz et al. (eds), *The Economics of Alternative Energy Sources and Globalization*. United Arab Emirates: Bentham Science Publishers.

Zilberman, D., G. Hochman, D. Rajagopal, S. Sexton, and G. Timilsina (2012). 'The Impact of Biofuels on Commodity Food Prices: Assessment of Findings'. *American Journal of Agricultural Economics* 1-7 (June 7).

Zulauf, C., and D. Orden (2012). 'US Farm Policy and Risk Assistance: The Competing Senate and House Agriculture Committee Bills of July 2012'. ICTSD Programme on Agricultural Trade and Sustainable Development, Issue Paper No. 44.

21

Food Price Volatility and EU Policies

Johan Swinnen, Louise Knops, and Kristine van Herck[*]

21.1 Introduction

The period 2007–11 was characterized by high volatility in global food prices. In many countries of the world this triggered important policy reactions with food exporters imposing export taxes or outright bans, and food importers lowering their import tariffs.

In this study we discuss the impact of the changes in world food prices on EU policies. We analyse how the changes in global prices have affected producers and consumers in the EU, and how this has resulted in policy reactions through the political process. We also discuss how EU policy changes, in turn, have influenced global food prices.

Traditional economic and political models of agriculture and food policies often focus on the impact of prices and policies on three types of agents: producers, consumers and taxpayers (see e.g., Gardner 1987; Swinnen 1994). Price changes directly affect producer and consumer welfare and may trigger demands by these groups for policy interventions. Because of expenditures on social policies and agricultural/food subsidies, taxpayers have always been an important actor in food policy discussions. In the EU their role in the policy debate has increased in recent years. With the shift from price and trade interventions to direct payments (in the 1990s), most of the support to farmers now comes through budget expenditures. In addition, the financial and economic crisis has had a major impact on member states' budgets and on their fiscal policy. This affects their willingness to allocate funds to EU policies (including the Common Agricultural Policy (CAP) and food aid) and to spend on domestic social policies.

[*] The authors thank Per Pinstrup-Andersen, participants at the Project Meeting 'The Political Economy of Food Price Policy', held at Cornell University, and two reviewers for useful comments.

Such a traditional political economy framework is useful when thinking about the economic and political relationship between food prices and EU policies. However, to get a more realistic perspective it is necessary to disaggregate the concept of 'producers' and 'consumers' and to include the impact on and influence of other types of agents—such as trading partners, landowners, environmental groups, the energy and financial sectors, etc. Landowners have lobbied intensively on EU farm policies in recent years as farm subsidies have been shifted from price and trade interventions to land-linked subsidies, directly affecting land prices (Swinnen and Vranken 2009; Ciaian, Kancs, and Swinnen 2010). Environmental groups have been increasingly vocal in agri-food policy debates and played a significant role in the 2003 reform (Swinnen 2008). As recent price spikes have been related to energy investments ('biofuels') and financial transactions ('speculation'), policy initiatives to regulate these have drawn energy and finance interest groups into the food policy debate as well. Further, the relationship between EU policies and global food prices is influenced by pressure from trading partners (Josling 2008).

Finally, decision-making in the EU is affected by various institutional factors. Some policies are set at the member state level (such as social policies), others at the EU level (such as agricultural policies). Some policies can be changed on a short-term basis (such as management of food policies within existing policy frameworks), others are fixed in multi-annual agreements (such as EU budget allocations and major CAP decisions). For some policies the EU Parliament has co-decision power, for others not, and some policies are constrained by international agreements, such as the General Agreement on Tariffs and Trade (GATT)/ World Trade Organisation (WTO) agreements.

Given the length constraints of this chapter it is impossible to integrate all these different policies, actors and institutional constraints into a single, integrated model. We will therefore take a rather pragmatic approach, referring to key agents and institutions, which influenced policy decisions on specific policies.

21.2 Impacts of Changes in Global Food Prices in the EU

The period 2007–11 was characterized by high volatility in global food prices. Figure 21.1 illustrates how average producer prices in the EU followed a similar trend to global food prices, although the scale of these changes was much smaller than those of the Food and Agriculture Organization (FAO) food price index. Compared to the 2005 prices, average prices for producers increased by less than 20 per cent in real terms in the first price spike and even less

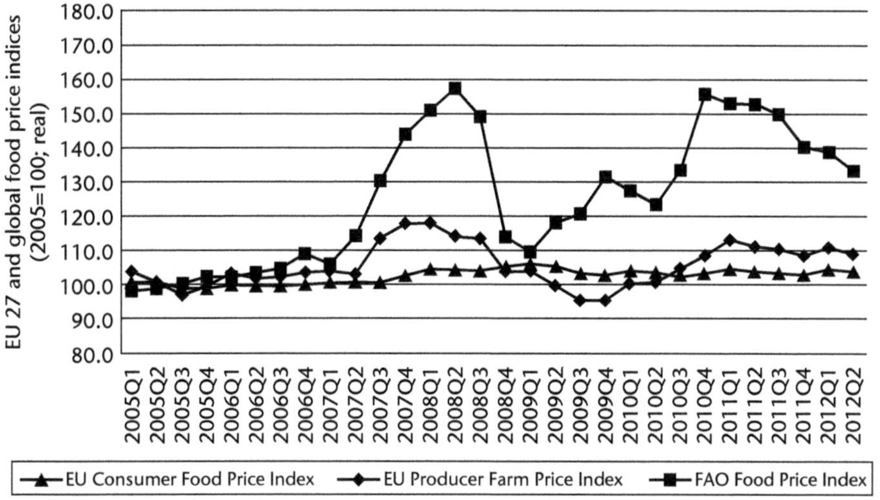

Figure 21.1 Evolution of EU 27 and global price indices (2005=100; real prices)
Source: FAO and EUROSTAT.

during the second price spike. Figure 21.2 shows that EU price volatility was lower than global price volatility indicators. There are important differences between agricultural commodities: EU cereal prices increased by 113 per cent, five times more than milk prices which increased by only 22 per cent between the first quarter of 2005 and the first quarter of 2008 (Figure 21.3). There are also large differences in price inflation between member states (see Swinnen, Knops, and Van Herck 2013).

These price changes are imperfect indicators of changes in producer welfare since they only capture part of the effects. Grain prices are output prices for grain producers, but input prices for livestock producers. In addition, there were significant changes in energy prices over the same period. The grain/fertilizer price ratio in the EU has been very volatile over the 2005–12 period, with a rapid increase in 2006 and 2007, a strong decline in 2008 and significant growth in 2010 (Figure 21.3). In contrast, the milk/animal feed price ratio has consistently declined since 2005. The 2012 ratio was 25 per cent lower than in 2005 as increases in dairy prices have been offset by increases in animal feed prices. Hence the impact of the global price changes on EU farmers was mixed.

There was little volatility in average consumer prices in the EU (Figure 21.1). The latter increased slightly over the 2005–12 period, with real food prices only 5 per cent higher in 2012 than in 2005.[1] An important reason is that

[1] There is also large heterogeneity between member states with respect to the change in consumer prices. In general, the figures on consumer price inflation were higher in the new member states than in the Western European countries (see Swinnen, Knops, and Van Herck 2013).

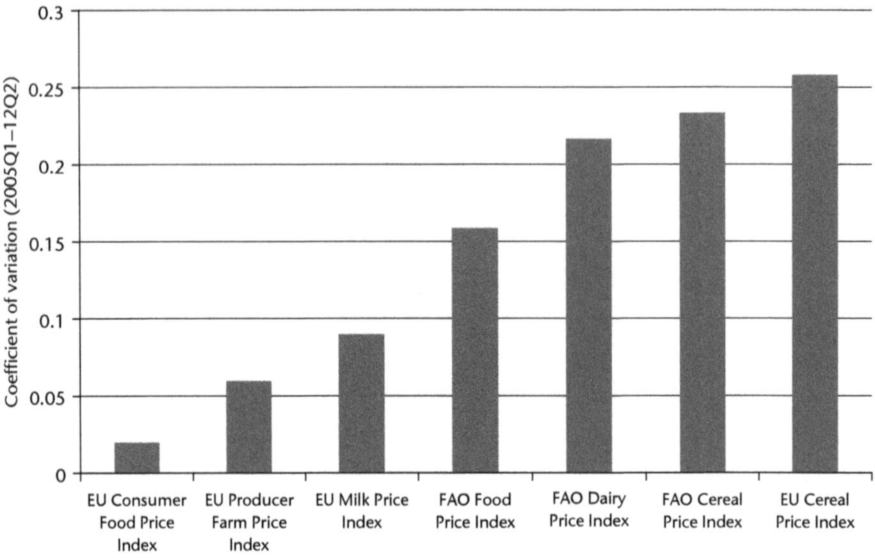

Figure 21.2 Coefficient of variation for global and EU food prices
Source: FAO and EUROSTAT (based on Swinnen et al. 2013).

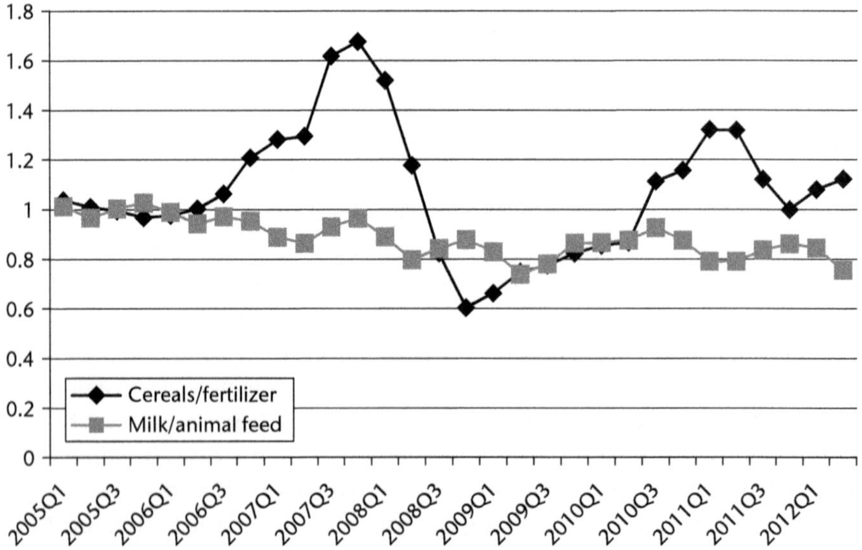

Figure 21.3 Evolution of the ratio of cereal over fertilizer prices and the ratio of milk over animal feed prices in the EU27
Source: FAO and EUROSTAT.

the cost of raw material is a small share of the price of the final food products in the EU. For example, the share of agricultural raw materials in the cost of bread is merely 5 per cent and on average 20 per cent for meat and livestock products (EC 2007).

The impact of these price changes on consumer welfare also depends on how much consumers spend on food. European consumers spend on average 15 per cent of their household budget on food. Changes of food prices therefore had a limited impact on the average EU household's welfare. However, there are significant differences between and within member states. Poorer families spend more on food. The share of the household budget spent on food varies from 10 per cent in the UK to more than 40 per cent in Romania.

Other factors had a significant effect on EU consumer incomes over the same period: the increase in energy prices, increasing costs for transport, heating, etc., and the economic and financial crisis causing falling employment and wages. There was zero growth on average in the EU27 and unemployment increased by more than 2 percentage points between 2007 and 2012 (see Figure 21.4). Macroeconomic changes also seem to have impacted food prices. Average food prices fell over the 2005–11 period in the countries hit the strongest by the economic crisis such as Portugal, Greece, Spain, and Ireland.

21.3 EU Policy Responses

The most important policy responses were: (i) policies to protect EU consumers; (ii) regulating 'speculation' on agricultural commodities; (iii) tightening sustainability requirements in the EU biofuel policy; (iv) international development and food aid; and (v) changes in the EU's CAP.

21.3.1 *Social Policy and Food Aid*

Social policies, such as unemployment benefits, pensions and disability payments, are still the responsibility of the member states. The increase in food prices induced pressures from consumers, in particular the poorest, to increase social spending. Increases in other prices, such as those for energy and transport, reinforced this pressure. While the financial and economic crisis constrained governments' budgets, social expenditures in the EU increased by approximately 7 per cent between 2005 and 2010 (Figure 21.5). Not surprisingly, there are large disparities among member states, but spending on social security benefits increased in almost all member states.

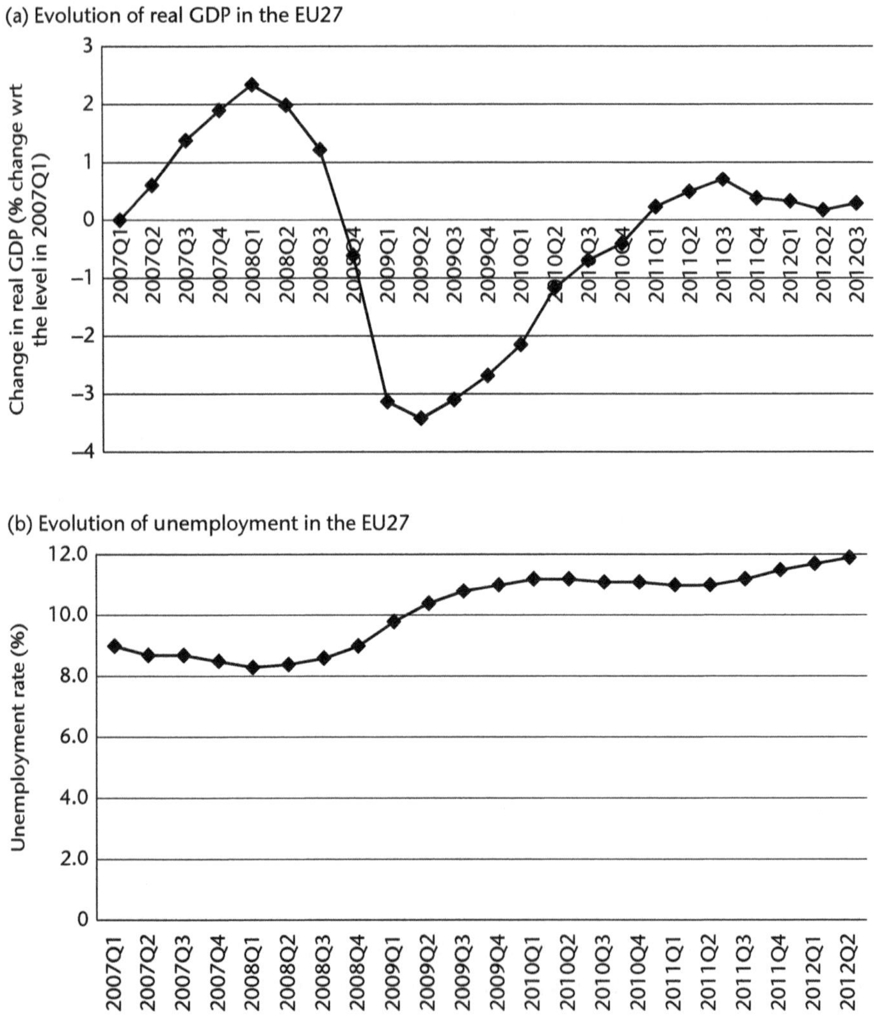

Figure 21.4 Evolution of real gross domestic product (GDP) and unemployment in the EU27

Source: EUROSTAT.

Since 1987, the EU has a food aid programme for the poor and the needy of Europe. First, this scheme consisted of the distribution of stocks of surplus food. However, reforms of the CAP towards a more market-oriented policy in the 1990s and 2000s reduced the amount of surpluses in the EU. As a consequence, the food aid scheme was revised in 2008 to buy products from the market. In 2010, the European Commission (EC) put a ceiling of €500 million/year on it and in 2011, under financial pressure, the EC proposed a drastic cut to €112 million. However, aid organizations argued that it was precisely

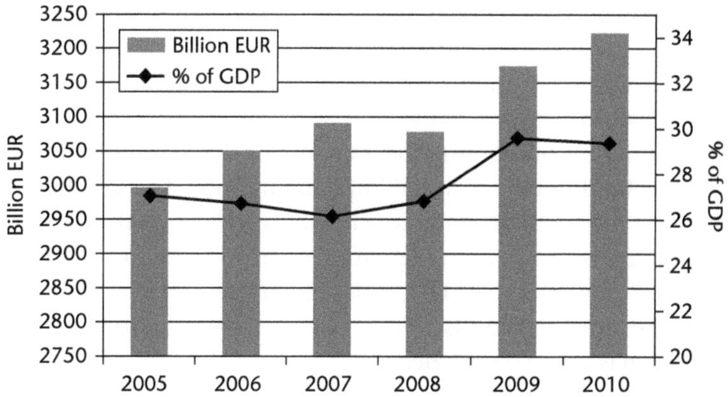

Figure 21.5 Evolution of social expenditures in the EU27 (in real terms)
Source: EUROSTAT.

in periods of rising food prices that such programmes were most needed. Negotiations took place on the amount of food aid and on (member states') co-financing requirements. Several member states argued that 'social policy' is a national competence. An agreement was finally reached to maintain the level of funding for the (€500 million) for 2013 only.

21.3.2 *Markets in Financial Instruments Directive (MiFID) 2: Fighting Speculation on Food Commodities*

The first version of the (MiFID 1) entered into force in 2007, just before the financial and food crises. MiFID 1 and its implementation were seen as successful but recent changes in trading techniques (e.g., computer-based high frequency trading), coupled with the financial crisis, induced the EC to review MiFID to evaluate whether more regulation was needed.

Whilst the commodity and commodity derivatives markets were 'exempted' from MiFID 1, they now represent a focus-area of MiFID 2, in response to claims of speculation on food commodities.[2] While there is increasing evidence that speculation did not play a major role in the food price developments of recent years (Irwin 2012), the EC launched a public consultation in 2010. This revealed a clear division between the stakeholders in the debate. Unsurprisingly, the financial actors made a plea for more 'flexibility' and argued that over-regulation of financial markets would be detrimental for

[2] After the first food price spike, many international observers (e.g., De Schutter 2010; UNCTAD 2011; World Development Movement 2012) argued that increasing volumes of financial investments in commodity derivatives since 2004 and the related increase in speculative behaviour was one of the main factors explaining the food price spikes (for the complete references, see Swinnen, Knops, and Van Herck 2013).

the entire EU economy, while a group of non-governmental organizations (NGOs) recommended that commodity markets should be further regulated to increase transparency and to discourage speculation.

It is unclear at this stage whether the outcome of MiFID 2 will effectively introduce regulation on commodity markets in the EU, as the EC proposal leaves latitude for different national implementations. This could allow strict regulation in some countries and more flexible regimes in others (with the UK clearly being in favour of a light regulation). The recent European Parliament (EP)'s response, amending the EC proposal, aims at removing loopholes and reinforcing the European regulatory oversight on commodity markets. A final agreement on has yet to be reached.

21.3.3 *Strengthening Sustainability Requirements for Biofuel Production*

The EC proposed what the press and industry have qualified as a policy U-turn on biofuels. From strongly encouraging this sector through binding targets and blending mandates (i.e., its target of 10 per cent of biofuel for transport by 2020), the EC is now backtracking and seeks to minimize the use of food crop-based biofuels. Biofuels have been an important driver of increasing food prices (de Gorter et al. 2013) and are claimed to be less environmentally-friendly than originally thought, because of indirect effects of land use change (Rausser and de Gorter, Chapter 20).

The 2009 EU biofuel sustainability scheme includes the following criteria: green house gas emissions (GHGE) savings from biofuels shall be at least 35 per cent; biofuels shall not be made from raw material obtained from land with high biodiversity or high carbon stock, or peat land; and EU agricultural raw materials used for biofuels shall satisfy the environmental requirements under the CAP. In 2012, the EC proposed limiting the use of food-crop-based biofuels at 5 per cent (EC 2012).

21.3.4 *International Food and Development Aid*

Somewhat paradoxically, despite high food prices the EU has not provided more (in-kind) food aid to poor countries. In fact Figure 21.6 illustrates that food aid declined from more than 3.5 million tons/year in the early 1990s, to close to zero. There are two reasons: studies showing that food aid could have detrimental effects on the local economies caused a shift from food aid towards development aid (OECD 2012a), and EU food aid was especially distributed when EU food stocks were high.

Instead, in 2008 the EU established a €1 billion 'food facility', including measures to improve access to agricultural inputs and services, and safety net

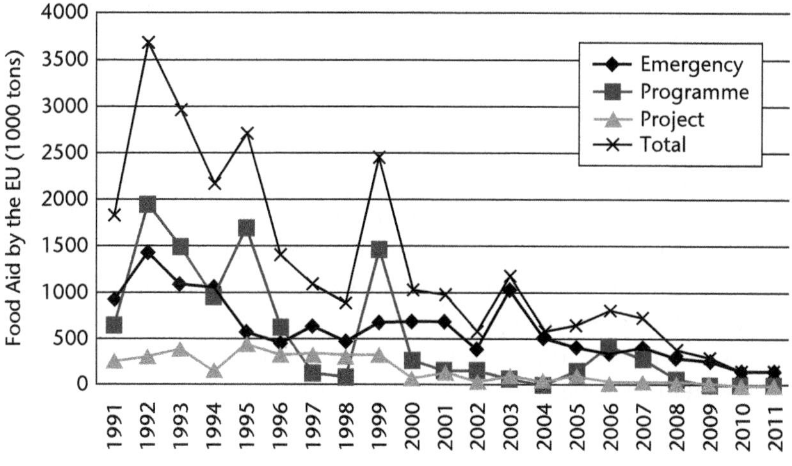

Figure 21.6 International food aid by the EU (thousand tons of wheat)
Source: World Food Programme FAIS database.

measures to increase the agricultural production capacity and help meet the food needs of the most vulnerable. Whilst the EC presented the Food Facility as its 'highest profile instrument' in development aid (EC 2010), the EP questioned the automatic extension of this instrument, as its ability to tackle food insecurity had been rather difficult to assess. The EP also emphasized the need to adopt a global and comprehensive response, to overcome the proliferation of separate actions since 2008 (EP 2011).

In 2008, French President Sarkozy proposed to make price volatility a Group of 20 (G20) priority. The G20 'Action Plan on Food Price Volatility and Agriculture' aimed, amongst other objectives, to improve and develop risk management tools for governments, firms and farmers in order to build capacity to manage and mitigate the risks associated with food price volatility, in particular in the poorest countries. In 2011, the G20 in Cannes—still under the French presidency—focused on improving the regulation and supervision of commodity derivatives markets, and in general on reinforcing transparency on agricultural markets (G20 2011).

21.4 The CAP and Global Food Prices

21.4.1 *A (Very) Brief Historical Perspective*

The relationship between food price volatility and the EU's CAP is arguably the most interesting from a (global) food policy perspective. For decades, surplus production resulted from a CAP system which provided strong protection to EU farmers through guaranteed prices, high import tariffs, and export subsidies.[3] While this created stability on the EU market it created instability on world markets, and distortions throughout the economy. High import tariffs and growing surpluses, exported with subsidies, caused already low prices on global food markets to decline even further. This system was particularly important for commodities such as cereals, beef, sugar, and dairy products.

In the 1980s, pressure increased to reduce the CAP distortions both from inside the EU and from outside—most importantly from the EU's trading partners and exporting nations and from developing countries and international organizations which argued that these policies were hurting the poor by contributing to low farm prices.

In response, the EU introduced a series of reforms to change the CAP into a policy system that maintains support to farmers, while creating less distortion on international markets (Josling 2008; Swinnen 2008). Reforms in the 1980s introduced supply constraints (quotas) in the sugar and dairy sectors. Reforms in the 1990s reduced price supports, tariffs and export subsidies and replaced these by payments for land and animals. These reforms were part of the Uruguay Round Agreement on Agriculture (URAA) of the GATT/WTO.

After 2000, partly in anticipation of a Doha Round agreement, the single farm payment (SFP)—a payment decoupled from production—was introduced (Swinbank and Daugbjerg 2006).[4] These reforms resulted in a decline in agricultural support in the EU, and in particular in a strong decline of the use of the most distortionary instruments (Figure 21.7). Agricultural support, measured by the Organisation for Economic Co-operation and Development (OECD)'s % Producer Support Estimate (PSE), declined from approximately 36 per cent in the period 1991–3 to approximately 20 per cent in 2009–11, and the %PSE for the coupled support fell below 10 per cent. Similarly, another measure of protection, the nominal rates of assistance (NRA) to agriculture estimates by Kym Anderson and the World Bank, show that the EU's NRA fell from 54 per cent in 1991–5 to 11 per cent in 2005–10.

21.4.2 *Reactions to Recent Price Changes*

Paradoxically, after the EU had gone through decades of reforms to reduce the CAP's (negative) impact on global food prices, the world became concerned with high food prices. After the price spikes of 2007–8, it was argued

[3] Political economists have explained this growth in protection by the decline in farm incomes compared to rapidly growing incomes in the rest of society as well as declining opposition of consumers and industry with less worker expenditures on food and increased organization of agribusinesses and food companies (Swinnen 2009).

[4] The political economy factors which made these radical reforms possible are discussed in Swinnen (2008). The impact of the GATT/ WTO on the shift towards less distorting policy instruments is shown in Swinnen, Olper, and Vandemoortele (2012).

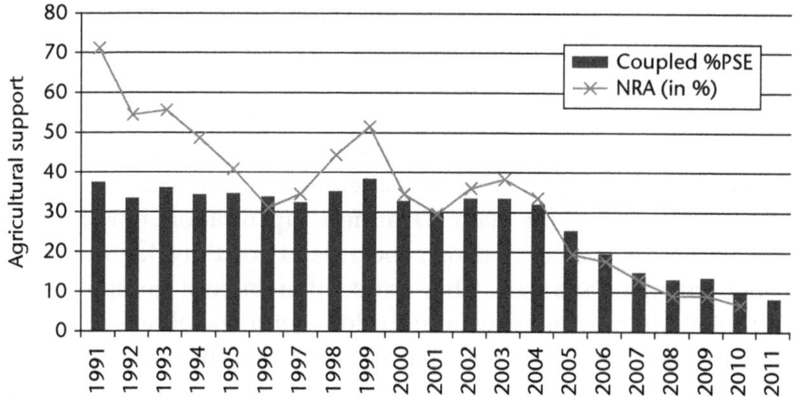

Figure 21.7 Agricultural support in the EU (%PSE and %NRA)
Source: OECD and World Bank.

that urban consumers were suffering from high food prices but also that rural households were suffering since there was imperfect price transmission of international prices and because many were net food buying households—arguments suspiciously absent from the pre-2008 discussions (Swinnen 2011).[5]

The timing of the recent food price changes coincided with important discussions in the EU on the future of the CAP. The first increase coincided with the conclusion of the so-called 'health check' reforms. The second price spike occurred when a new round of CAP reform discussions had been launched.

A series of policy adjustments were taken, mostly within the existing policy framework. The EC changed some market management measures to increase the supply of food in 2008: intervention stocks were sold, the 10 per cent obligatory set-aside for farmers was suspended, most import duties on cereals were lifted, and milk quotas were increased by 2 per cent.

At the same time the EC confirmed the agenda to stay on course to a more market-based CAP. Reforms further decoupled support and reduced intervention in markets for pig meat, cereals and dairy products. This, according to the EC, aimed to 'modernize, simplify and streamline the CAP and remove restrictions on farmers, thus helping them to respond better to signals from the market and to face new challenges' (EC 2008).

In response to the crisis in the dairy sector, where farmers saw their income decreasing with increasing costs (see above), a so-called 'milk package' was introduced in 2010. Despite considerable pressure of dairy organizations, the 'milk package' did not include measures to directly intervene in the markets.

[5] See Swinnen, Squicciarini, and Vandemoortele (2011) for a political economy explanation.

Instead the policy initiatives focused on strengthening the position of farmers in the supply chain (by improving contracts between farmers and dairies and strengthening farmers' collective bargaining power).

The price changes also affected discussions on the longer term CAP framework itself, and the discourse of interest groups and policy makers, however generally without fundamentally altering their proposals. For example, COPA-COGECA (2011), the main EU farmers' organization, now argues that, despite high prices, farmers are losers because of volatility, high input prices and 'food chain imbalances'. They—and other interest groups—asked for more regulations, moving away from the long-term liberalization strategy for the CAP. So far, however, the EU has (i) reaffirmed the engagement of the EU towards an open trade policy—also by underlining the harm done by the restrictive export policies implemented by some countries in response to price volatility; and (ii) stayed on course with its reform proposals in specific sectors such as dairy and sugar (phasing out the quota regime), despite a slight change in argumentation, i.e., by also linking the motivation to price volatility.

21.4.3 *Negotiations on the Future CAP: A Return to Intervention or Not?*

There is uncertainty whether this course will be continued in the future, as the EP, which now enjoys full legislative influence in the CAP reform process (Roederer-Rynning 2003), seems to be leaning towards a more interventionist approach, possibly because interest groups which favour more regulation, such as some of the farmers associations, appear to be more influential in the EP than in the EC.

The 2011 EC proposal on the future CAP proposed to introduce some minor changes in the form of payments but without a return to market interventions. The changes in the payments can be summarized in three key words: convergence, greening and capping: support is to be more equally distributed (convergence), better linked to environmental objectives (greening) and with a maximum ceiling (capping). The proposals use price volatility as a justification to maintain the CAP direct payments (as 'safety net') to protect farmers against price volatility: they give 'basic financial security to farmers, without distorting international markets' (EC 2011).

The proposal also includes a new 'crisis reserve fund' and a 'crisis management toolkit' (to respond rapidly to extreme events of price volatility), which include funds for crop and weather insurance, and income stabilization to compensate farmers if their income drops by 30 per cent (EC 2011). Bureau (2012) concludes that various conditionalities such as maximum quantities on intervention, limits on compensation and co-financing requirements make these measures consistent with WTO disciplines and limited in practice.

In addition, the EC proposes to allocate a €4.5 billion envelope for research and innovation on food security, the bio-economy and sustainable agriculture but the impact is likely modest since a large share is a reallocation within the EU Budget (Bureau 2012).

There are clear signals that the EP prefers a more interventionist approach and more market regulation. This was evident from the EP's reactions to the EC proposals on MiFID2, the EC communication on 'A Better Functioning Food Supply Chain in Europe', on competition rules in agriculture and in the debate on the end of sugar quotas. The EC has several times confirmed the ending of the sugar quota regime by 2015, arguing that, considering rising demand, maintaining sugar quotas would be completely counterproductive in the context of price volatility. However, key members of the EP have argued that the extension of the sugar quota regime is crucial to stabilize markets at a time of increasing price volatility, a position backed by the major sugar producing countries. Hence, both groups argue that their solution would reduce volatility and improve the competitiveness of the sugar sector (Matthews 2012).

In conclusion, the food price spikes have influenced the debate on the future CAP reform and its outcome is still uncertain. So far the effect has been minimal, mostly affecting arguments, much less the main policies, as the current CAP proposals do not fundamentally alter the trend followed by the EC before 2008. The EC has used price volatility as a justification to move towards more market liberalization in the agricultural sector and reduce intervention mechanisms, and as a justification to maintain existing CAP payments (as 'safety net') to protect farmers against price volatility. However, the outcome of the current CAP reform negotiations are still uncertain and the EP, which now has a much larger policy influence in this policy field, appears to favour a return to a more interventionist approach. The amendments on CAP reform, adopted by the EP in 2013, indicate that the EP is indeed trying to reinforce public intervention.

21.5 Political Economy Considerations

From a political economy perspective it is interesting to observe how EU policies have (not) responded to price volatility and the impact of the institutional organization of the decision-making. It is well-known that there are important political incentives for decision makers to adjust policies to changing market conditions. The so-called anti-cyclical policy pattern is well-documented as interest groups turn to governments to assist them when market conditions turn against them (Swinnen 1994; Olper 1998) and there is considerable empirical evidence on this in agri-food markets, both in Europe (e.g., Swinnen 2009) and elsewhere (Anderson and Hayami 1986; Anderson, Rausser, and Swinnen 2013). It is therefore logical to expect that policies in the EU, as elsewhere, may have been adjusted in response to the dramatic changes on the world food markets.

First, the lack of major interventions is consistent with the fact that incomes of EU farmers have increased on average over the 2005–11 period (Figure 21.8). They have benefited from higher prices while receiving constant levels of payments from the EU. However, as mentioned earlier, there were major differences among farmers. In particular the dairy sector has seen an income decline. The introduction of the milk package to assist the dairy sector is a response to this.

Second, compensation for higher food prices to consumers has occurred mostly through increased social spending, not through food market regulations. Several factors play a role here: social spending is a more efficient and more targeted instrument than limiting the price of food, in particular in a large and heterogeneous EU27. This heterogeneity is also reflected in large variations in the share of food in consumer expenditures in the EU27, which should have triggered very different consumer reactions. Social spending is also more efficient because farm prices make up a small share in consumer food prices.

Third, most policy discussions on the CAP in the past years have focused on how to reform the farm payments, as increased pressure from taxpayers and demands from environmental groups challenge the need to continue the type of payments as they currently exist. Farmers' organizations have concentrated more on lobbying to secure the payments rather than on a major

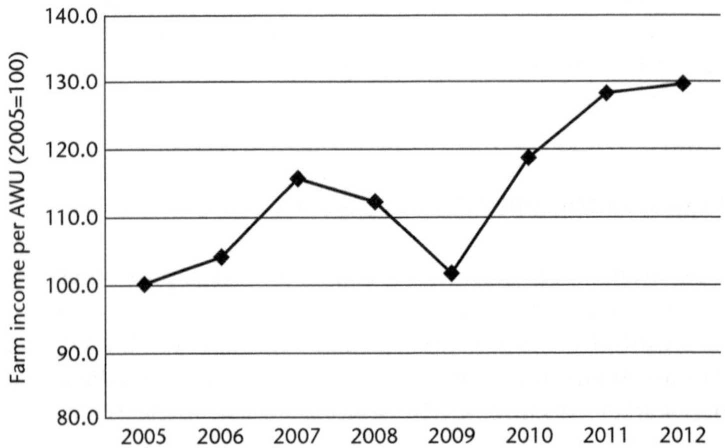

Figure 21.8 Index of real farm income per annual working unit (2005=100)
Source: EC-DG Agriculture and Rural Development.

shift towards more regulation. They have been supported by landowners who are benefiting from higher land prices with land-based payments (Ciaian, Kancs, and Swinnen 2010).

Fourth, an interesting issue is the different position of the EC and the EP, with the latter taking a more interventionist stance. It is difficult to draw strong conclusions on this since the policy is still debated and the issue has not been resolved yet. Still it appears that the differences can be related to (at least) two factors. The EC has played a leadership role in steering the CAP reforms in the 1990s and 2000s and, as a bureaucracy that had the right to table the policy proposals combined with strong leadership and a strong capacity in analysis and policy preparation, has been able to steer the reforms through the political process, carefully arranging a qualified majority of votes in the European Council, and largely ignoring the EP (Swinnen 2008). Another factor is that the EC is very well aware of the international dimensions, in particular the WTO constraints and ongoing negotiations, since they have been intensely involved in these negotiations where the agricultural commissioner has collaborated with the trade commissioner. It appears that the EC wants to stay on course in moving the CAP towards more market orientation, continuing its 20-year strategy, and legacy.

In contrast, the EP does not have such a legacy as it is just now being involved in the actual decision-making. Moreover, the Agricultural Committee of the EP, where the key positions are prepared, is filled with members who are linked to traditional agricultural interests, such as farmers' organizations, former ministers of agriculture, etc. (Crombez, Knops, and Swinnen 2013; Roederer-Rynning 2003). This contrasts with the EC's approach in the past decade to broaden the support base for the CAP by reaching out to environmental groups, consumers, etc. Farmers' organizations have started to target the EP's Agricultural Committee as their key area for lobbying activities. However, obviously, also here the WTO agreements do impose real constraints on policy reactions.

Finally, the limited response in important EU policies to price volatility has also to do with the fact that policies such as the CAP and any policy relying on EU budgetary expenditures is regulated within a multi-annual agreement, and can only be changed after long negotiations. Hence, policy reactions from 2007 to now have been constrained by the CAP and budget agreements covering the 2006–13 period.

21.6 Impact of EU Policies on Global Food Prices

As explained in the previous section, the impact of the current CAP on global prices is much smaller than in the past. Several studies show the large impact of EU policies on global food markets during the 1980s (Van Meijl and van

Tongeren 2002). Recent studies on the price volatility of major food commodities (Anderson and Nelgen 2012; Anderson, Ivanic, and Martin 2012) show that EU policies had little or no impact on volatility in the grain and oil seed market.

Unlike other countries, the EU has neither introduced export constraints for food nor caused a major use of agricultural products for biofuels so far. The new proposal to change the EU biofuel targets may have a significant impact in the future (compared to the situation if this would not be the case).

Increased social policies and development aid may have had some indirect effects by compensating consumers in the EU and in developing countries for higher food prices and thus stimulating more consumption and thus higher prices, but there are no estimates on the impact of these spending increases.

The CAP of the 1970s and 1980s would have had a much stronger effect in countering high food prices than the current CAP as the surplus production and the large food stocks in the EU could have been used to export food (including cereals) and thus to reduce prices when they were rising, both as commercial exports and as food aid. The policy reforms over the past two decades which have reduced the distortionary effects of EU policies on world food markets have also reduced its capacity to quickly increase food exports during price spikes.[6] This is illustrated by the fact that EU food aid to developing countries was at its lowest during the past five years, when food prices spiked (see Figure 21.6).

21.7 Conclusions

The period 2007–11 was characterized by high volatility in global food prices. EU producer prices followed a similar trend to global prices, but the size of the changes was much smaller with important differences between agricultural commodities. For example, cereal prices increased much more than dairy prices. Dairy farmers' income decreased with input feed prices increasing more than output prices.

Food prices for EU consumers have increased only slightly, with real food prices 5 per cent higher in 2012 than in 2005 and very little volatility. Changes of food prices therefore had a limited impact on the average EU households' welfare, but with significant heterogeneity within the EU. The EU and member states responded to the price volatility by a series of actions to mitigate short- and medium-term effects of the food price shock, to increase agricultural supply and to tackle the global effects of the price rises on the poor. In this study we focused on policies to protect EU consumers, attempts to regulate 'speculation' on agricultural commodities, revisions of

[6] Note that this should not be interpreted as an argument to reverse the CAP reforms.

sustainability requirements for biofuels, international development and food aid and changes in the EU's CAP.

Arguments that increasing volumes of financial investments in commodity derivatives led to speculative behaviour in food markets causing increased price volatility triggered EC initiatives to regulate this. The financial sector argued against 'over-regulation' of financial markets while other groups insisted on further regulation to increase transparency and to discourage speculation. A final agreement on a directive has yet to be reached.

The EC proposed large changes in its biofuel strategy when it became clear that biofuel production was an important factor in increased food prices and when arguments and evidence appeared on uncertain environmental benefits because of indirect effects of land use. From encouraging biofuels through binding targets and blending mandates, the EC now seeks to minimize the use of food crop-based biofuels.

Food aid declined over the past two decades due to a shift from food aid towards development aid and because of falling intervention food stocks due to CAP reforms. The EU established a €1 billion 'food facility' and supported G20 initiatives to reduce price volatility and to reinforce transparency on agricultural markets.

For decades the CAP depressed global food prices as the EU imposed high tariffs on imports and exported its subsidized food surplus production. A series of reforms led to a policy system that maintains large government support to farmers, while creating less distortion on international markets.

Global price volatility induced a series of relatively minor policy adjustments that could be taken within the existing policy framework. So far the EU has reaffirmed its engagement towards an open trade policy and stayed on course with its reform proposals in specific sectors, despite a change in argumentation, i.e., by linking the motivation to price volatility.

The lack of major interventions is consistent with the fact that incomes of EU farmers have increased on average over the 2005–11 period, except for sectors such as the dairy sector, where the EU has responded by supporting this sector through new initiatives. Farmers' organizations have concentrated more on lobbying to secure the existing CAP payments rather than on a major shift towards more regulation, as increased pressure from taxpayers and demands from environmental groups challenge the need to continue the type of payments as they currently exist. Farmers have been supported in these political pressures by landowners.

Compensation for consumers has occurred mostly through increased social spending, not through food market regulations. Despite (or because of) the financial and economic crisis, social expenditures by EU member states increased by approximately 7 per cent between 2005 and 2010. Social spending is a more efficient and more targeted instrument than limiting the price of food, in particular in a large and heterogeneous EU27 and because farm prices make up a small share in consumer food prices.

There is uncertainty whether this course will be continued in the future, as the EP, which now enjoys full legislative influence in the CAP reform process, seems to be leaning towards a more interventionist approach.

While the EC wants to continue its twenty-year strategy in moving the CAP towards more market orientation and broadening the support base for the CAP by reaching out to environmental groups, consumers, etc., the EP does not have such a legacy as it is just now being involved in the actual decision-making. The Agricultural Committee of the EP is controlled by members with links to more traditional agricultural interests. Discussions on the future of the CAP (for the 2013–20 period) have been on-going since 2009, but the decision-making process is slow because of the institutional framework and because of the simultaneous negotiations on the EU budget. Decisions are likely to be taken in 2013.

The limited response in important EU policies to price volatility has also to do with WTO agreements on agricultural policies which do impose real constraints on policy reactions and the fact that policies such as the CAP (and any policy relying on EU budgetary expenditures) are regulated within a multi-annual agreement. Policy reactions from 2007 to now have been constrained by the CAP and budget agreements covering the 2006–13 period.

Finally, the impact of the current CAP on global prices is much smaller than in the past. Recent studies show that EU policies had no or very little impact on volatility in key food markets. Increased social policies and development aid may have had some indirect effects by compensating consumers in the EU and in developing countries for higher food prices and thus stimulating more consumption and thus higher prices, but there are no estimates on the impact of these spending increases.

Paradoxically, the CAP of the 1970s and 1980s would have had a much stronger effect in countering high food prices than the current CAP. Policy reforms over the past which have reduced the distortionary effects on world food markets have also reduced the EU's capacity to quickly increase food exports, either as commercial exports or as food aid.

References[7]

Anderson, K., and Y. Hayami (1986). *The Political Economy of Agricultural Protection: East Asia in International Perspective*. London: Allen and Unwin.

[7] For a more complete list of relevant official documents of the European Institutions, see Swinnen, Knops, and Van Herck (2013).

Anderson, K., and S. Nelgen (2012). 'Agricultural Trade Distortions during the Global Financial Crisis'. *Oxford Review of Economic Policy* 28(1): 235–60.

Anderson, K., M. Ivanic, and W. Martin (2012). 'Food Price Spikes, Price Insulation and Poverty'. Paper presented at the NBER conference, 15–16 August. Seattle.

Anderson, K., G. Rausser, and J. Swinnen (2013). 'Political Economy of Public Policies: Insights from Distortions to Agricultural and Food Markets'. *Journal of Economic Literature* 51(2), 423–77.

Bureau, J. C. (2012). 'Where Is the Common Agricultural Policy Heading?' *Intereconomics* 47(6): 316–21.

Ciaian, P., D. Kancs, and J. Swinnen (2010). *EU Land Markets and the Common Agricultural Policy*. Brussels: Centre for European Policy Studies.

COPA COGECA (2011). 'The Future of the Common Agricultural Policy Post-2013: COPA COGECA's Reaction to the Commission's communication'. Brussels: COPA COGECA.

Crombez, C., L. Knops, and J. Swinnen (2012). 'Reform of the Common Agricultural Policy Under the Co-decision Procedure'. *Intereconomics* 47(6): 336–42.

de Gorter, H., D. Drabik, D. R. Just, and E. M. Kliauga (2013). 'The Impact of OECD Biofuels Policies on Developing Countries'. *Agricultural Economics* (forthcoming).

De Schutter, O. (2010). 'Food Commodities Speculation and Food Price Crises: Regulation to Reduce the Risks of Price Volatility'. Briefing Note 02. New York: United Nations.

European Commission (EC) (2007). 'The Impact of the Developments in Agricultural Producer Prices on Consumers'. Document CM/WM/PB 34703. Brussels: EU.

European Commission (2010). 'An EU Policy Framework to Assist Developing Countries in Addressing Food Security Challenges'. Document COM (2010) 127 (final). Brussels: EU.

European Commission (2011). 'A Budget for Europe 2020'. Document SEC (2011) 867 final, COM (2011) 500 (final). Brussels: EU.

European Commission (2012). 'Proposal for a Directive of the European Parliament and of the Council amending Directive 98/70/EC and amending Directive 2009/28/EC. Brussels: EU.

European Parliament (EP) (2011). 'Resolution on an EU Policy Framework to assist Developing Countries in Addressing Food Security Challenges'. Document (2010/2100(INI)). Brussels: EP.

G20 (2011). 'G20 Leaders Summit final Communiqué'. Agricultural Ministers Communiqué, 3–4 November. Cannes.

Gardner, B. L. (1987). *The Economics of Agricultural Policies*. New York: Macmillan.

Irwin, S. H. (2012). 'Does the Masters Hypothesis Explain Recent Food Price Spikes?' International Association of Agricultural Economists Conference, 18–24 August, Foz do Iguacu, Brazil.

Irwin, S. H. (2013). 'Does the Masters Hypothesis Explain Recent Food Price Spikes?' Unpublished Manuscript.

Josling, T. (2008). 'External Influences on CAP Reforms: An Historical Perspective'. In J. Swinnen (ed.), *The Perfect Storm: The Political Economy of the Fischler Reforms of the Common Agricultural Policy*. Brussels: Centre for European Policy Studies.

Matthews A. (2012). 'The Political Economy of Eliminating Sugar Quotas in 2015'. CAPreform.eu. Available at: <http://www.capreform.eu/the-political-economy-of-eliminating-sugar-quotas-in-2015>.

OECD (Organisation for Economic Co-operation and Development) (2012a). 'Creditor Reporting System'. Paris: OECD.

OECD (Organisation for Economic Co-operation and Development) (2012b). 'Producer and Consumer Support Estimates Database'. Paris: OECD.

Olper, A. (1998). 'Political Economy Determinants of Agricultural Protection Levels in the EU Member States: An Empirical Investigation'. *European Review of Agricultural Economics* 25(4): 463–87.

Roederer-Rynning, C. (2003). 'From "Talking Shop" to "Working Parliament"'? The European Parliament and Agricultural Change'. *Journal of Common Market Studies* 41(1): 13–35.

Swinbank, A., and C. Daugbjerg (2006). 'The 2003 CAP Reform: Accommodating WTO Pressures'. *Comparative European Politics* 4(1): 47–64.

Swinnen, J. (1994). 'A Positive Theory of Agricultural Protection'. *American Journal of Agricultural Economics* 76(1): 1–14.

Swinnen J. (2008). 'The Perfect Storm'. Brussels: Centre for European Policy Studies.

Swinnen J. (2009). 'The Growth of Agricultural Protection in Europe in the 19th and 20th Centuries'. *The World Economy* 32(11): 1499–537.

Swinnen, J. (2011). 'The Right Price of Food'. *Development Policy Review* 29(6): 667–88.

Swinnen, J., and L. Vranken (2009). 'Land & EU Accession'. Brussels: Centre for European Policy Studies.

Swinnen, J., A. Banerjee, and H. de Gorter (2001). 'Economic Development, Institutional Change and the Political Economy of Agricultural Protection: An Empirical Study of Belgium since the 19th Century'. *Agricultural Economics* 26(1): 25–43.

Swinnen, J., A. Olper, and T. Vandemoortele (2012). 'Impact of the WTO on Agricultural and Food Policies'. *The World Economy* 35(9): 1089–101.

Swinnen, J., P. Squicciarini, and T. Vandemoortele (2011). 'The Food Crisis, Mass Media and the Political Economy of Policy Analysis and Communication'. *European Review of Agricultural Economics* 38(3): 409–26.

Swinnen, J., L. Knops, and K. Van Herck (2013), 'Food Price Volatility and EU Policies', Working Paper No. 2013/032. Helsinki: UNU-WIDER.

UNCTAD (United Nations Conference on Trade and Develoment) (2011). 'Price Formation in Financialized Commodity Markets: The Role of Information'. New York and Geneva: UNCTAD.

Van Meijl, H., and F. van Tongeren (2002). 'The Agenda 2000 CAP Reform, World Prices and GATT–WTO Export Constraints'. *European Review of Agricultural Economics* 29(4): 445–70.

Part VIII
Conclusions and Recommendations

22

The Political Economy of Food Price Policy

Key Policy-related Lessons

Per Pinstrup-Andersen

22.1 Introduction

This brief concluding chapter addresses the most important general policy-related lessons learned from the research reported in the previous chapters. Many more lessons are reported in the syntheses shown in Chapters 2 to 5.[1] Recommendations for specific policy interventions that national policy makers may wish to follow are context specific and should be made within the relevant country context. They are found in Chapters 6 to 21.[2] Eight policy recommendations expected to be relevant for many countries are presented in this chapter.

The aim of this chapter is to highlight lessons that may assist governments in designing and implementing policies to deal with future increases in food price volatility. Contrary to a world in which policies are made exclusively on economic efficiency grounds, there is no unique definition of what is a better or worse policy in a political economy framework. What is good for one stakeholder group may be bad for another. In theory, policies could be guided by the goal of maximizing a social welfare function in which each of the stakeholder groups is assigned a relative weight. While such a goal may, in fact, be implicit in some policy-making, the assignment of relative weights—if

[1] See in particular Baltzer's four categories of countries and their price transmission based on a synthesis of trade status (Chapter 2); Bryan's classification of the study-countries into three categories on the basis of the extent of policy intervention (Chapter 3); Babu's 12 lessons drawn from an analysis of the policy processes (Chapter 4); and Watson's 11 political economy claims based on a synthesis of the country studies (Chapter 5).

[2] A list of potential national policy responses to food crises and likely effects is shown in Benson (2008).

attempted—tends to be subjective depending on who does the assignment and would be an obscure and non-transparent process. Furthermore, since as demonstrated in the country studies, most governments do not operate as unitary decision-making units, attempts to assign relative weight by different government agencies are likely to result in very different outcomes. Although as mentioned by Watson in Chapter 5, improved food security was the stated overall goal of several of the study-country governments, the choice of policy interventions points towards the protection of government legitimacy as the ultimate goal.

As mentioned in Chapter 1, rapid increases in the world market prices for rice, wheat, and maize beginning in 2007 and followed by large price fluctuations, attracted much attention in both high- and low-income countries. The news media and some international organizations and non-government organizations (NGOs) were particularly vocal. Doomsday-Sayers had a field day because they finally got support for their view that the world was rapidly moving towards a situation of not being able to feed itself. They were often supported by exaggerated reports and speculation by the news media. Some NGOs and national and international organizations called for more attention and—sometimes self-serving—financial support for agricultural development and other food-security-related activities. The Food and Agricultural Organization (FAO) reported that the food price increases in 2007–8 caused a large increase in the number of undernourished people, a claim it subsequently revised. The spill-over from the world market food price fluctuations to developing countries through the news media and other information sources made policy makers nervous and feel they should take action even if the 'crisis' was not visible in their domestic markets.

In fact the impact of the world market price increases and volatility was much less than expected in most developing countries, including the study-countries, because a relatively small fraction of the world market price change was transmitted to these countries (Chapter 2). While the price transmission varied among study-countries and food commodities, on average about one-third of the world market food price changes were transmitted to developing countries and the transmission may take place over an extended period of time.

The low price transmission from the world market and the much larger impact of national factors, such as extreme weather events, poorly functional domestic markets, and limited international food trade, on domestic prices in most developing countries, meant that the behaviour of food prices in the domestic markets of many developing countries during the period of the so-called 'food crisis' was not very different from the behaviour in prior periods with price volatility. Developing countries experience high food price volatility with great frequency. What was different in 2007–12 was that the price volatility occurred in the world market and therefore got much more international attention.

However, irrespective of whether price volatility in domestic markets is a result of food price volatility in the world market or caused by national and local factors, governments are faced with demands for policy interventions. Of course, the choice of specific interventions and their impact will depend on what brought the volatility about. There are no signs that the food crisis led to enduring shifts in food policy or significant policy reforms. In fact, most of the policy interventions were aimed at bandage solutions such as short-term price subsidies for food and fertilizers. This is understandable because it was a crisis response and most of the interventions were similar to those used in previous food price fluctuations. Lip service was paid to structural changes with expected long-term impact, such as structural changes in the agricultural sector, but as soon as the food prices came back down, few of the countries implemented them. There is reason to believe that the countries are in no better position to deal with future food price fluctuations than they were in 2007. Some of the countries considered policy interventions aimed at a higher degree of food self-sufficiency and reduced dependence on the world market but these interventions were primarily focused on higher prices to farmers, which were short-lived because of high fiscal costs and the accumulation of food surpluses in the hands of governments. However, price subsidies to farmers did result in production expansions in some countries.

It is important to differentiate between food price increase and food price volatility. An increasing food price trend is likely to require different policy interventions than fluctuations around the mean. As mentioned in Chapter 1, much of the literature concerning food price increases and increasing volatility since 2007 fail to make such a distinction and it is unclear whether policy recommendations and design were aimed at reducing food price increases, volatility, or both. What seems clear from the country studies reported in this volume is that, except for countries with politically powerful agricultural sectors such as Brazil, governments were much more likely to take action on the up-side of a food price spike than on the downside, reflecting a consumer-bias. However, some countries, including India and Zambia, introduced agricultural price support aimed at the dual purpose of increasing farmer incomes and expanding food supplies on the downside. Several other countries introduced fertilizer subsidies, presumably for the same reasons although some of those subsidies were initiated prior to the food crisis. However, both price and fertilizer subsidies quickly became an unacceptable fiscal burden. The rest of this chapter focuses on policies to deal with volatility although some of the interventions are likely to also serve to deal with longer term price trends. The extent to which these policies can be implemented in a particular country context will depend on the existing political economy, including the goals and relative power of the various stakeholder groups participating in the policy formation.

The choice of intervention will depend on political economy factors, e.g., perceived gains and losses by various stakeholder groups and the relative power of each of them. In its most simplistic version, we can conclude that policies to keep food prices from increasing would hurt farmers and benefit consumers while the impact of policies to reduce price volatility is tenuous. Attempts to keep food prices from increasing without reducing price volatility would send two signals to farmers not to increase production: lower prices and higher risks. This, in turn, would reduce supplies and increase prices to the consumer, thus countering the efforts to keep food prices low. At the same time, failure to reduce volatility would increase risks of transitory food insecurity and malnutrition among low-income consumers although the impact on chronic food insecurity is less clear. Thus, a single-minded policy focus on the price level while ignoring the negative effects of price volatility may not have a positive food security outcome unless it is accompanied by effective risk management tools for farmers and consumers.

A more complete political economy analysis needed to guide national policies would include several other stakeholder groups such as traders, millers, and other food processing agents and different groups of farmers and consumers, each of which would be affected by both price increases and volatility.

One of the overriding issues facing governments in a situation of either increasing food prices or increasing price volatility is whether to intervene in the prices or leave price formation to the market and redistribute gains and losses through taxes, subsidies, and transfers. Interfering with price signals may have perverse results, e.g., attempts to keep prices low are likely to reduce supply and increase demand thus putting more upward pressures on prices. Transfers to low-income population groups with high-income elasticity for food may expand demand which also adds to the upward pressures on food prices.

Leaving prices resulting from market fundamentals (changes in demand and supply) alone and compensating losers from price fluctuations instead of intervening in price formation is usually preferable because it permits the correct signals to be sent to producers and consumers to change production and consumption. However, price stabilization may be justified to deal with price spikes of a duration shorter than a growing season because farmers will not be able to adjust production. A much better information base will be needed to predict the length of a price increase with acceptable accuracy.

Notwithstanding the above suggestion that the choice of specific policies should be made within a context-specific framework, some recommendations, including those shown below, are likely to be relevant for most countries.

22.2 Strengthen the Policy-related Evidence Base

Although most of the countries had experienced periods of very significant food price volatility in the past, the response to the 2007–8 volatility appears not to have been well-organized. Many of the governments responded to the food price volatility in an ad hoc manner. Policy reversals were common and delayed policy action reduced the effectiveness of the interventions. Failure to coordinate action by various government agencies added to the problem. Repeating past policy interventions was common and very little policy innovation was observed. Policy makers in most of the countries did not have access to relevant, reliable, and timely information about policy options and expected impact of each of such options on the various stakeholder groups. There is an urgent need to enhance access to such information within each country. This would include an improved data base, timely monitoring, and projections of food prices and those variables most likely to influence them. Projections and policy advice should be made within a political economy framework.

Strengthening the capacity to provide and make available to policy makers timely market information including high-probability forecasts is key to prepare orderly policy interventions and to manage a situation in which the access to relevant information is likely to vary among stakeholder groups. Such strengthening should take place between crises as exemplified by South Africa's introduction of a price monitoring board. Furthermore, there is a need to enhance the exchange of such information across countries. Expectations about impact in one country may be more realistic if knowledge is available about the results from similar policy options pursued in other countries. International organizations such as the International Food Policy Research Institute (IFPRI) and the United Nations FAO could strengthen their role in this regard. The recently created Agricultural Market Information System (AMIS) is a step in the right direction.

22.2.1 *Appropriate Use of Trade Policy and Interference in Price Signals*

Trade policy was widely used by the study-countries to reduce price transmission from the world market and stabilize domestic prices. In response to increasing world market prices, traditional exporters introduced export bans and other trade restrictions and importers removed import tariffs. Reducing world market supplies and increasing demand contributed to continued price increase in the world market. Such 'beggar-thy-neighbour' policies are common to meet domestic policy goals at the expense of orderly trade. Before the next round of high food price volatility hits the world market, negotiations are needed within the World Trade Organization (WTO) to strengthen the rules for abrupt and large changes in exporting countries' trade policies. Such negotiations have been tried before with very limited success and it is unclear whether the food crisis and the contributions the introduction of export restrictions will make will render such negotiations more likely to succeed. Permitting the transmission of world market prices to domestic markets and maintaining unrestricted trade would greatly reduce the magnitudes of price fluctuations in the international market. It would also send the right signals to producers, consumers and traders to adjust supply and demand. Attempts to keep prices from increasing, whether through trade policy or price controls, would do the opposite. Farmers and consumers would not be enticed to produce more and consume less.

Since, as mentioned above, most of the food price volatility in developing countries is caused by national and local factors and not by the world market, maintaining open trade would reduce price volatility in the domestic market. The impact of fluctuations in domestic production on domestic supply and prices would be dampened by changes in import or export. Sharing national production fluctuations with the rest of the world would help in stabilizing domestic prices. Some stakeholders would lose and others would gain from such policies, depending on whether prices without stabilization would have been higher or lower. Compensating losers may be a more effective way to meet government goals than interfering in the price signals in countries where the institutional framework for transfers and subsidies is in place.

International coordination of domestic policies, particularly trade policies, with well-defined rules and binding commitments might be mutually beneficial to exporters and importers. Uncertainty about individual countries' next move may encourage other countries to make moves that in the end would make all participating countries worse off. Without such coordination, the beggar-thy-neighbours policies we saw during the food crisis are likely to be repeated.

22.2.2 *Reduce Fiscal Costs of Short-term Interventions*

Export bans and other restrictions as well as elimination of import tariffs and reductions or elimination of value added taxes (VAT) on food caused significant fiscal revenue losses in many of the countries. Furthermore, some countries incurred large costs from the introduction or expansion of food and fertilizer subsidies and transfer programmes. Strengthening international agreements about export bans and restrictions might provide the support needed by national governments to withstand pressures from stakeholder groups for interventions in exports. This would maintain the revenues from export taxes and together with taxing some of the windfall gains captured by producers and exporters would make funds available for transfer programmes for consumers to compensate for the higher prices.

To help keep costs down, subsidies and transfer programmes such as fertilizer and food subsidies and safety net programmes should be targeted to those stakeholder groups that the government wishes to compensate. Low-income people who spend a large share of their income on food and are at risk of food insecurity and malnutrition would be a logical target group for governments that claim that improved food security and nutrition is an important policy goal. Some countries did in fact target food transfers and safety nets on these groups, but many others focused on lower-middle-class urban consumers, presumably because they are more likely to threaten the government's legitimacy. Except for fertilizer subsidies, which most often were targeted on smallholder farmers, subsidies, and transfers were targeted on consumers, primarily but not exclusively urban consumers.

22.2.3 *Investments to Increase Food Supply Elasticity*

Policies to facilitate the transmission of food price changes to farmers will only result in appropriate supply changes if farmers are able to respond. Investments to increase the supply elasticity, i.e., making the supply more price sensitive, of single food commodities and the total farm output is critically important to keep domestic food price fluctuations within reasonable margins. The specific measures to make this happen are context specific but in most developing countries the most important government action would be to invest in the public goods needed to develop a rural infrastructure that supports well-functioning input and output markets, competitive supply chains, and private investment. That includes rural roads, particularly feeder roads, as well as irrigation infrastructure, contract enforcement, institutions of various kinds, and other public goods. Policies to promote a competitive supply chain are important to avoid barriers to price transmission between producers and consumers.

A large share of the poor in all the study-countries is smallholder farmers. Most are net buyers of some food. Food price changes would affect them the same way other consumers would be affected. That was used by some governments to justify policies to keep food prices from rising. After all, it would be good for poor farmers as well as urban consumers. However, pursuing a policy of low food prices is unlikely to be sound in the longer run. First, while smallholders may be net buyers of some foods they are likely to be net sellers of others. Second, the main reason why many smallholders are net buyers of food is that low and falling prices between the middle of the 1970s and the end of the century made investment in farming unproductive and forced the smallholders into off-farm employment. Higher prices and investments in rural infrastructure, domestic markets and unit-cost and risk-reducing agricultural research and technology may bring them back to become net sellers. Thus, governments wishing to strengthen the agricultural sector on the basis of smallholders should reassess policies to keep food prices lower than the export or import parity prices.

22.2.4 *Facilitating Effective Risk Management Tools*

More effective risk management tools are needed by farmers, traders, and consumers to cope with extreme weather events and market fluctuations. Governments can play an important role in facilitating the development and maintenance of such tools. Much of what has been mentioned above, such as better market forecasts, timely dissemination of weather-related information, and research to develop risk reducing technology such as drought-tolerant and pest-resistant crop varieties may help managing risks and uncertainties. Effective monitoring of the domestic and international food supply, demand, and prices, and related factors such as weather patterns, market development, and timely dissemination of the results is key to strengthen resilience to food price volatility.

22.2.5 *Improve the Management of Public Sector Grain Stocks*

Several authors of country studies found that poor management of government grain reserves contributed to food price volatility. Untimely release of grain on the domestic market aimed at slowing price increases failed to do so and government purchases during periods of price increases put further upward pressure on prices and resulted in accumulation of surplus stocks in excess of storage capacity. While faulty forecasts undoubtedly played a role, deliberations among stakeholders and difficulties in arriving at a timely decision appear to have delayed the release. Untimely government purchases may have been a result of faulty expectations about future prices.

To avoid these problems in the future, it would be useful to create an institutional arrangement that, independent of stakeholder interests, would manage government grain reserves including the timing and quantity to release and purchase. The political economy process would be used to set guidelines for such an institution but the release and purchase decisions would not be subject to political deliberations.

22.2.6 *Make Demand for Raw Materials for Biofuel Price-related*

As mentioned in Chapter 1, the rapid expansion of biofuel production based on food commodities or resources used for their production was an important contributor to food price fluctuations in 2007–8. Blending mandates that are unrelated to the price of maize and other raw materials for biofuel, such as those currently found in the USA and the European Union, contribute to food price volatility because the quantity needed to comply with the mandate is removed from the maize market irrespective of its price. If food commodities, such as maize and soybeans, are to be used for biofuel, the impact on food price fluctuations would be reduced by replacing the mandate to a market-based programme in which the quantity demanded would be influenced by the market price. As the appropriate technology becomes available, biofuel production should be based on resources and commodities that do not compete with food supplies.

22.2.7 Improve Collaboration between the Public and Private Sector

Mutual mistrust between the public and private sectors was identified by several authors of the country studies as contributing to food price volatility. Large, abrupt, and unexpected policy interventions in the food and agricultural markets make it difficult for the private sector—whether farmers, traders, or processors—to operate efficiently. A higher degree of predictability and transparency in the behaviour of governments and the private sector is called for. Corruption in the public sector and anti-competitive behaviour in the supply chain contribute to food price volatility. Preparation of policy interventions to be implemented in future periods of increased food price volatility should be made before such periods occur. The preparations should be undertaken in a public-private partnership with participation by all relevant stakeholder groups. While this may sound naive, steps in that direction might reduce the problems associated with delayed, ad hoc interventions taken in a crisis mode as illustrated by action in some of the study-countries.

Irrespective of food price volatility, sustainable food security for all will only be achieved with both the public and the private sectors doing their jobs. Creative tension between the two sectors may be useful but mistrust, conflict, and attempts to undermine one another will make food security for all an illusion.

Index

Index